HOW CAN YOU EXPECT TO STOP SMOKING IF YOU EAT TOMATOES?

The NHA Yellow Book of Smoking Cessation

ROBERT S BRYNIN

To Leoni, Duncan and Jordan

Copyright © by Robert Brynin 2001

The right of Robert Brynin to be identified as the Author of the Work has been asserted by him in accordance with the Copyright, Designs and Patents Act 1988. First published in Great Britain in 2001 by NHA Research (Phoenix) Ltd.

All rights reserved. No part of this publication may be reproduced, stored in a retrieval system, or transmitted, in any form or by any means without the prior written permission of the publisher, nor be otherwise circulated in any form of binding or cover other than that in which it is published and without similar condition being imposed on the subsequent purchaser.

ISBN 0-9526343-1-7
Printed by Aldrington Press Ltd, Brighton

NHA Research (Phoenix) Ltd
P O Box 365   Hove   BN3 2AU
nha.research@amserve.net

TOMATOES ?

Believe it or not, a major reason why so many people fail to stop smoking is because they are eating tomatoes.

The tomato plant is a member of the *solanaceae* family, along with potato, capsicum and aubergine (and deadly nightshade). These plants all contain very similar genetic information.

When your body is looking for the molecular data from tobacco, but you're not smoking, it may be able to find it in tomato (and to a lesser extent the other foods). This could re-trigger the addiction to tobacco.

For this reason, anyone who has a strong liking for tomato must avoid it altogether for four days before stopping smoking and four days after. This includes any food made from tomato, including ketchup and sauce, and the foods made with those ingredients, like baked beans or pizza.

This simple precaution could greatly increase the success of any attempt to stop smoking, and of any stop-smoking product or service.

If you have failed a previous attempt, this one factor could have caused your failure. Of course, it's only one of many possible issues. Our job at NHA is to research every issue, so if you want to really understand about stopping smoking, read on ....

CONTENTS

FOREWORD
Lord Ennals — - 3

PREFACE
Dr D L J Freed, MD — - 1

1 THE YELLOW BOOK
The Short Explanation — 1 1
The Long Explanation — 1 3

2 WHY PEOPLE SMOKE
The Only Explanation — 2 1

3 WHY PEOPLE DON'T WANT TO STOP
The Short Explanation — 3 1
The Long Explanation — 3 5

4 WHY IT'S HARD TO STOP SMOKING
The Short Explanation — 4 1
The Long Explanation — 4 5

5 CHANGING ATTITUDES
The Short Explanation — 5 1
The Long Explanation — 5 4

6 ADDICTION
The Short Explanation 6 1
The Long Explanation 6 5

7 PSYCHOLOGICAL DEPENDENCE
The Short Explanation 7 1
The Long Explanation 7 3

8 HABIT
The Short Explanation 8 1
The Long Explanation 8 5

9 ENJOYING SMOKING
The Short Explanation 9 1
The Long Explanation 9 4

10 FEAR
The Short Explanation 10 1
The Long Explanation 10 5

11 STRESS
The Short Explanation 11 1
The Long Explanation 11 3

12 HOW TO STOP SMOKING
The Short Explanation 12 1
The Long Explanation 12 4

13 AFTER STOPPING
The Short Explanation   13 | 1
The Long Explanation   13 | 3

14 STAYING STOPPED
The Short Explanation   14 | 1
The Long Explanation   14 | 2

15 STOP-SMOKING METHODS
The Short Explanation   15 | 1
The Long Explanation   15 | 4

16 THE MISTAKES PEOPLE MAKE
The Short Explanation   16 | 1
The Long Explanation   16 | 4

17 THE QUESTIONS PEOPLE ASK
    17 | 1

18 SUCCESS AND FAILURE
The Short Explanation   18 | 1
The Long Explanation   18 | 3

FOREWORD

Reproduced from the first edition of The NHA Yellow Book, titled *Stop Smoking for Good.*

I welcome Stop Smoking for Good and am pleased to write this Foreword. There are still about fourteen million cigarette addicts in Britain and we all need to work together to help those who are risking their own health - and that of their families - especially since most smokers today cannot afford their addiction. It is a hard addiction to kick - I know: I smoked for twenty-five years!

I write as President of QUIT. We advise thousands of smokers every year and we know that smokers cannot be bullied into stopping. Many smokers believe they are being targeted as anti-social, but the campaign should not be against smokers, because they are the victims. We should be targeting those who cause the effects of tobacco abuse, not those who suffer. The targets must include the tobacco companies and the government, which permits them to continue to advertise their killer products.

Given that the tobacco industry needs to find three hundred new customers to replace those who die each day, we must find a way of keeping the young away from the drug long enough to avoid the pressure they are under to use it. And let us not be in any doubt that what we are fighting is an addictive drug proven to cause disease and death on a massive scale. In the USA the tobacco industry is fighting desperately for the right to sell innocent people this drug. In the UK, despite a dismal record of official action to curb the activities of the industry, there is a growing momentum, from organisations like ASH, QUIT and now NHA Research, towards giving people the right to a smoke-free environment and to protect their children from the pushers.

Since 1990 NHA, through its research into nicotine addiction, its networks of clinics, and its work with employers, has been making a growing contribution to the health of the nation. Although lacking funding and support from official sources, it has fought for the right of smokers to be accepted as victims. Alcoholics and hard drug users are given treatment and sympathy, but smoking is still seen as a self-inflicted problem.

NHA's objective is for the British medical authorities to accept that we have 14 million people who smoke not because they want to but because they have to. It is time to follow NHA's example, and treat smokers not as pathetic or weak-willed, but as true drug addicts.

The work done by Dr Richard Mackarness on nicotine addiction back in the 1970s will one day be recognised as a major medical breakthrough. NHA Research has already understood its value and has worked hard to develop his techniques. We now have a national resource in these clinics which GPs should be urgently investigating.

Meanwhile we have this invaluable book. Whilst there is no substitute for treatment, everyone reading it will benefit - at the very least from increasing their understanding of their inability to stop smoking. And very many people will go on to stop and stay stopped. The NHA Helpline is also invaluable; no matter how comprehensive a book is, anyone who stops smoking is likely to want answers to their specific problems, or just support from someone who understands and cares.

This book provides the key to the end of your dependence on cigarettes. Forget your previous difficulties; within a few weeks you can join the ever-growing band of non-smokers, and you will feel both fitter and richer.

Rt Hon. Lord Ennals
Secretary of State for Health 1976-9

PREFACE
By Dr D L J Freed MD

The world of smoking cessation is characterised by companies chasing a market about which not enough is known, with poorly thought-out products, in the pursuit of profit.

The result for smokers is that they are bombarded with publicity for new products that are more often than not variations on old products. This has led to large numbers of people who still smoke and are traumatised by alternating hope and failure.

For us doctors, particularly for my colleagues in general practice, there is frequently despair that anyone will ever properly research tobacco abuse and find real answers, so that we can offer our patients something new and of real value.

Some years ago I spent some time working with smokers for NHA Research. Over ten years the organisation has put more effort into this subject that anyone else I know. I find it shocking, as I am sure the reader will, that in this country we have no government-funded research into smoking cessation. The powers that be seem content to let the pharmaceutical industry dominate this important field, with the inevitable result that smokers are never offered anything other than drug products for what is already a drug problem.

I know how difficult it is to stand alone against powerful influences for a cause you believe in. This book is the culmination of ten years of work by a small team of dedicated people, headed by Robert Brynin. I can think of no-one, whether smoker, doctor or therapist, who will not learn from it and benefit.

THE NHA YELLOW BOOK
The Short Explanation

NHA Research is, as our name suggests, a research company. I could have written a definitive book about stopping smoking, but we are learning - from our patients - all the time, so what would definitive mean?

True, after more than ten years of research we know most of what there is to know about tobacco abuse. But every patient is different, and every one teaches us something new, even if it is just perhaps a better way to express what was already a good idea.

For this reason, we have published this book ourselves, because short print runs are necessary to ensure than it gets regularly updated. This means the copy you have in your hands is based on the very latest understanding available in this complex field.

You will already have noticed that some of the pages of the Yellow Book are indeed yellow. You might even have looked through these yellow pages before reading this introduction. Because we know people do that (read things in the wrong order), I have made this book particularly easy to read. The white pages are the boring bits - you know, how addiction works and so on. The yellow pages give you a summary of each chapter, so if you have a short attention span, or you're pushed for time, OR YOU WANT TO FIND OUT IF THE BORING BITS ARE WORTH READING (they are, I'm only joking when I say they're boring), read the summary first.

Another idea is to read all the yellow pages, like a short book. This will give you a jolly good overview of the subject, and in case you never get the time to read the whole book, you'll know the basics.

Note for Medical Professionals

If you run stop-smoking programmes, the white pages go into a lot of detail, which you may want to use for your own patients. As a service to you, we permit the copying of individual pages, 'within reason', if this is helpful to your patients.

THE NHA YELLOW BOOK
THE LONG EXPLANATION

At NHA Research we research primarily just one thing - why people smoke and can't stop, or more precisely the relationship between the psychology and the physiology of tobacco abuse.

It might surprise the reader to learn that such research is not carried out, either by the Department of Health, or by any company with an interest in smoking cessation, such as the pharmaceutical companies who make nicotine replacement products. It is not the job of drug companies; their approach is to come up with a product, and conduct research into how that product can be used. There is nothing wrong with that approach - it may have its limitations but it is how companies generally work. The Health Department does not fund original research into tobacco abuse.

Where then did we start at NHA Research? First we tried to understand the problem, and the only way to do that is by talking with smokers. Not just smokers who are trying to stop, but also with smokers who don't want to. The first thing therefore we needed to understand was how anyone could not want to stop. From the objective view, it is hard to understand how a product can be sold that is known to be dangerous but, say, at least 90% of users would not want to come off it. So what hold does tobacco have over its users? Only by learning the answer to that question would we understand how to break that hold.

So we ran clinics to help people stop smoking. We could do this right from the beginning because we had inherited the research into Addiction Neutralisation Therapy. With A.N.T., we could stop anyone being addicted to nicotine, and we found that was a very good place to start. Take away the addiction, and study what is left.

Once we had people off the drug, we found something we had not expected. Everyone in smoking cessation had been talking about the psychology, but we discovered that if there is no physiology (the addiction is broken) the psychology falls apart. This blew apart most of the work that had been done before. Suddenly, words like habit, stress and social smoking ceased to have the same relevance. Apparently, it wasn't these things that were keeping people smoking; it was the drug itself. (You might think this is obvious, but if it is obvious, why is no-one doing anything about it?)

This was confirmed by our patients, who were coming to the clinic with a history of failure, and all the fears and lack of self-confidence that comes with failure, but they were leaving changed. Not always completely changed, but enough to put the psychology into perspective.

We discovered that if we broke the control the drug has over the brain, then we could undo the psychological conditioning that was keeping people smoking.

Therefore the answer to our first question - why don't so many people want to stop smoking - turned out to be simply that the nature of drug addiction is that people don't want to break it. The received wisdom was that a smoker must want to stop to succeed, but our research effectively destroyed this, because we no longer could define what want means. Smokers were coming to us claiming they wanted to stop, but surely if they wanted to enough, they would have done it, no matter how hard it was. This then raised the question about what people mean when they say they want to stop smoking, because it no longer seemed to mean what we thought.

In the final analysis, what we came up with was that very few people who use tobacco want to come off it, but most of them know they should. So they try to come off it, but because they don't really want to, they fail.

That raised a serious problem. No matter what stop-smoking products or services are available to smokers, until someone could switch on their motivation - meaningful motivation - the success of any given technique was going to be disappointing. The logical answer to this seemed to us to be to increase the immediate success of any technique, and this might increase the motivation to go through with it.

This theory was proved correct when we looked at why people failed with the products they bought. In too many cases, the user failed early on, or at least had some serious difficulty, and they simply accepted that they had failed.

The techniques they were using were not good enough to demonstrate to them that they could succeed. Therefore what we would need to provide in our own clinics was something that would change their attitude quickly enough to overcome the readiness to fail.

It was necessary to study every current stop-smoking method so we could see where its weak points were, and the results of this research are presented for those who are interested in Chapter 15.

Having understood how to get people motivated to stop, and having found a way of getting them stopped by overcoming the real reasons they have failed before, the obvious next question was how to keep them stopped. Again, a good researcher asks the right questions, and this time the right question was, why do ex-smokers start again?

And again, the conventional theories were not too helpful. When we asked smokers themselves why they had restarted in the past, they came up with a very small range of answers. Usually it was because of stress, or perhaps they started when they were the opposite - relaxed - and possibly drink was involved.

But stress was far and away the biggest reason given for restarting, so we looked hard at the subject and, again, the theories just didn't hold water. It is true that people smoke more when they are stressed, and it's true that some people start smoking again when they come under stress, but we had a huge problem with these ideas. The problem was that smoking does not in fact in any significant way relieve stress. So the next two questions were, why do people use tobacco for stress if it doesn't help, and why do they believe it helps?

And yet again, we found that the answer lay not in the psychology but in the physiology. In other words, it is addiction itself that creates the stress / stress relief cycle that you will read about in Chapter 11. Having understood that smoking does not relieve stress was one of the biggest single breakthroughs (after learning how to control nicotine addiction) we have ever made.

So if stress was cited as the reason for restarting in the majority of cases, but stress cannot be the real reason, just what is the real reason? The confusion arises because ex-smokers will often smoke a cigarette when under stress, thinking it will help. But because it doesn't help, they smoke another one, thinking it's **got** to help. And because they smoke another one, they recreate the addiction, and it is the addiction that supports the stress / stress relief cycle. Therefore what smokers are doing is living with a false memory of stress relief from tobacco.

The mistake they make then is to think that if they smoke a couple of cigarettes, because say they are stressed, that means they have restarted. They accept failure, even years after they have succeeded. This itself raised a whole raft of new questions (a researcher's job is never done). For example, why would anyone accept failure after not smoking for years? What is the continuing hold tobacco has over its ex-users long after they think they have escaped it?

One interesting fact we learned was that, if you don't smoke for four or more days, you lose the adaptation to the poisons in tobacco, which means when you do smoke a cigarette it will probably taste horrible. So why were people having the first cigarette, disliking it, but making an effort to relearn how to smoke? This seemed quite illogical, and it pointed us in the direction of a whole new area of study - how the human brain can be controlled for years by a drug it has not recently experienced, to the extent that it will try to become re-addicted when it knows that is not actually what it wants.

These last questions have answers that are physical, psychological and social. I have tried throughout the book to keep the answers simple in the yellow pages, but for the full story read on into the white pages as well.

Having got this far with our research, we then started to see smoking in a way we had never seen it before, even though we were all ex-users ourselves. With thousands of patients in our clinics, we were beginning to form a picture that was difficult to reconcile with what logic told us must be true.

Smokers believe things that are not true, that cannot be true. They believe, as we have seen, that tobacco helps manage stress. And they also believe that habit makes it hard to stop smoking, that they enjoy smoking, that they will not enjoy life if they stop. This actually raises two separate issues. The first is, if these things are true, why doesn't everyone smoke? The second is, even if these things were true, would they be important enough to take a lethal drug?

Briefly, there are two answers. The first is that society is so accepting of tobacco that it never stops to think about the truth. For example, tobacco, the most dangerous drug on Earth (in epidemiological terms) is sold in sweetshops. Clearly this is insane, and yet we do it, and no-one even queries it. What is important about this is that it inevitably colours the way smokers see tobacco. So no matter how much they accept the need to stop smoking, they are actually in conflict with what seems like normality. The importance of this conflict cannot be overstated.

And the second answer to these illogicalities is that smokers are addicted to nicotine. By definition, you cannot see the drug you are on in the same way as do people who are not on it. Nicotine controls smokers - we know that because otherwise why would anyone buy the stuff? And if it controls the smoker, obviously it controls the way the smoker thinks. The sad conclusion is that users cannot and do not see tobacco the same way as non-users. They cannot, in fact, make rational judgments about tobacco. Therefore they believe things that are simply not true - because the tobacco is making them believe those things.

Understanding this is the key to bringing people off it. In fact so important is it that time and time again we have seen with our patients that the most straightforward and effective way to destroy the psychological dependence on smoking (which is what I have been talking about in the last few paragraphs) is to explain the truth to them.

It continually astonishes us how simple it can be to open a smoker's eyes. All right, we cheat, because we use A.N.T. to bring them off the drug, and frankly all our work with smokers is based on the fact that if someone is not addicted - under pressure to obtain relief from withdrawal symptoms - they are in control, and can start to see the truth. With this new-found control, they can actually do what they like, including never smoke again.

That is how you stop people smoking. Each of the following chapters looks at each of the problems with stopping smoking. In each case the yellow pages summarise the issue and then the white pages go into more detail. Each issue is critically important, and there are no issues that have not been covered.

☐ Something to Say?

If you are a smoker using The Yellow Book to try stopping, or a smoking cessation professional, and you have comments, criticisms or suggestions to make, please do write to the address on the title page. We learn from others, and value the input of other people's experiences to our ongoing research.

WHY PEOPLE SMOKE
The Short (and only) Explanation

2

The government, and particularly the Department of Health, bless them, consistently fail to understand why their anti-smoking message fails to get through. They have said smoking is bad for people, but those people just go on doing it. They have warned children about the danger of starting, but those kids go like lambs to the slaughter. They've tried sarcasm ('it will make you smell like an old ashtray') but that message is like water off a duck's back.

Whether the government actually wants people to not smoke, or whether it is merely politically important to them to be seen to be putting the message out, we cannot know. What we do know is that the message fails.

Primarily it fails because the government has failed to stop, before trying to find the answer, and look for the question. The question is: why do people smoke?

People smoke because other people smoke. If smoking were invented today, no-one, knowing that tobacco contains lethal addictive substances, would ever do it. When smoking was discovered, no-one knew it was dangerous, and they certainly did not know it was addictive. A lethal substance that is addictive is the most dangerous combination you can imagine.

So, one day we realised that smoking was dangerous but, importantly, this was before we realised it was also addictive, so we told people not to do it. But those people ignored what we said, because they were addicted. They didn't know they were addicted - they just carried on doing it. Because they didn't know they were addicted, they found other explanations for carrying on. They said they enjoyed it too much, or it helped when they were stressed, and so on.

In fact, even now there are some people who say tobacco is not addictive. Well, they use the word addictive, but they don't mean it. Not like with heroin or cocaine, or even alcohol.

Of course, we know they must be missing the point, because for all the misery hard drugs and alcohol cause, compared with tobacco they are child's play. The sheer numbers involved in tobacco abuse make everything else look silly.

The people who do not use the word addictive at all are the tobacco pushers (the manufacturers, the retailers, the advertising agencies). And the people who use the word but don't mean it are government agencies, like the Health Department. We know they don't mean it; they couldn't mean it because if they meant it they would have to prohibit its sale.

Of course it is possible that the very reason they don't talk seriously about addiction is because they don't want to prohibit its sale, but who knows?

Back to the plot. I said that people smoke because other people smoke. No matter how much money you throw at health education, if children see other people smoking, you are wasting your money. More importantly, you are doing nothing effective to save those children. And if those children see tobacco advertised, and sold in sweetshops and supermarkets, hoping they are going to believe you when you tell them smoking is dangerous is frankly puerile.

That then is why people **start** smoking. The reason they continue is different. Having tried a cigarette, the average child is under social pressure to learn how to smoke because everyone else who is doing it is 'enjoying' it. If they aren't (and they aren't) they must be doing it wrong, so they keep doing it until they get the hang of it. What they are actually doing, without knowing it, is becoming adapted to the poisons in tobacco smoke. This adaptation is what we call addiction.

Having become addicted, the child then continues to smoke because they see no reason not to. After a while, they simply become habituated to smoking cigarettes. And if you are addicted, then habituated, over a period of years you will become psychologically dependent (which means you no longer believe you can live without tobacco). The process is now complete. Meanwhile, every day you have smoked, some child has seen you doing it and joined the cycle. Every smoker recruits new users.

So as long as people smoke, people (by which I mean children) will start to smoke. As long as society accepts tobacco as a legitimate substance, people will use it. Then they will become addicted, then habituated, then psychologically dependent on it. Not until these fundamental issues are addressed, at government level, will the problem of tobacco abuse start to be solved.

You're lucky this time. There are no white pages to follow, because I have said everything I want to say on this particular subject already. The next chapter develops this theme, and explains why, once people are using tobacco, they don't want to stop. Once that explanation is out of the way, we can go on to explore why people who do want to stop have such problems.

WHY SMOKERS DON'T WANT TO STOP

The Short Explanation

If smoking is really dangerous, why would anyone still do it? The obvious answers you would get if you asked people in the street would be:

- Because I enjoy it
- Because I can't stop
- Because I need it when I'm stressed
- Because I've never thought seriously about stopping
- Because all my friends do
- Because I'm too young for it to matter
- Because I'm too old for it to matter
- Because I've got to die somehow, so why not enjoy it?

All smokers say some or all of these things at some time. All of them are, of course, nonsense. The reason people still smoke, and don't want to stop, is very important to you if you are trying to stop. It will help you understand why you have had such difficulty in the past, even though you actually do want to stop. As you will be reading in due course, a major factor in failure to come off tobacco is that most people, even though they are trying to come off it, don't in fact want to succeed. And they don't want to succeed because all drug addiction alters the user's perception of the drug they use. An ex-user can be very pleased they came off it, but only being off the drug gives them this clarity of vision.

There is a simple answer and a complicated answer to my question. The simple answer is that 14 million people in Britain smoke - and how could 14 million people be doing something utterly stupid, that is making them poorer, is affecting their everyday health and is going to shorten their lives? After all, most of them are, presumably, law-abiding people with some intelligence. So, despite all the fuss made to the contrary, it must be all right. That is what a lot of smokers think, anyway.

Now for the complicated answer. If by some miracle the government instituted a real campaign to get people off tobacco, and 7 million people actually did it over the next year (this is entirely possible - not the bit about the government, which is unthinkable, but the bit about 7 million smokers stopping), you would probably be one of the 7 million. And if you were not you would probably be so impressed that you would be in the second 7 million. Put simply, people smoke because other people do. And those smokers who don't want to stop often don't want to because other smokers don't want to.

It's a bit like being on a sinking ship. The ship always felt safe before, and now, just because it's listing a little, the crew want you to jump over the side. Perhaps the ship will right itself. Perhaps another ship will come to the rescue. Failing these, you are going to have to abandon ship - to jump into the unknown without any idea how long it will take to be rescued, or whether you will be rescued at all.

The 14 million people who still use tobacco are sailing on the SS Smoking. So what if the ship is listing rather badly now? It's still afloat, and 14 million people are clinging to it with you. Some are jumping, but you can't see them - they might not have survived. So long as smokers cling to the ship, the nightmare of jumping might go away.

The reason people don't want to stop smoking is the same as the reason people don't want to lose weight, or stop drinking, or leave a violent partner, or improve their lives in any other way (yes, some do, but I'm talking about the ones who don't). These things are all supposed to be a Good Idea, but on the other hand they mean changing the status quo. It is natural to feel comfortable in your present situation, even when that situation is wrong for you, because it is the situation you know and understand. Knowing, for example, that not smoking would be better than smoking is all very well but how can you really appreciate that if you have never done it?

This is why, in our clinics, we take stopping in two stages. First, just do it to find out what it's like. Then, once you are free to make an objective judgment (because nicotine is not controlling what you do) decide whether you prefer smoking or not smoking.

Lots of people know they really should come off tobacco, but they have no actual experience of living without it. How, then, are they supposed to make the decision to come off it in real terms?

Now add to that problem the difficulty of stopping, with its complicated mixture of addiction and psychological dependence, and you are asking someone to do something they don't feel capable of doing, with no real understanding of the consequences of doing it. Now you start to understand why most people don't want to stop smoking.

Unfortunately, this is one problem you cannot walk away from. Every day you smoke you are in deeper water.

The One-Minute Motivation Test

Question: If your fairy godmother could wave a magic wand and turn you into someone who had never started smoking, would you want that?

Yes ...   No ...

If you answered No, forget all about ever stopping smoking.

If you answered Yes, you want to be someone who doesn't smoke. Your problem is not **being** a non-smoker, but **becoming** one. The expression 'stopping smoking' is used so much, we tend to think of the stopping part and forget the result.

From now on, never forget that you want to be a non-smoker. You are motivated to be a non-smoker, but not to go through the process of becoming one. The difficulty of becoming one should never fool you into doubting your motivation to **be** a non-smoker again.

WHY SMOKERS DON'T WANT TO STOP | 3
The Long Explanation

Now let's examine in more detail the reasons people give for not wanting to stop smoking. You might recognise some or all of them yourself.

☐ *Because I Enjoy It*

On one special day in March hundreds of thousands of smokers can be seen jumping over the side with their eyes shut because they heard the order to abandon ship - otherwise known as National No-Smoking Day. But if these people don't want to stop on 364 days of the year, why do they suddenly answer the call on the 365th?

The fact is they *do* want to stop. And here we have one of the many contradictions encountered in stopping smoking. Why does someone who, deep down, wants to stop, persist with the excuse: 'Because I enjoy it'? If we could answer this question, we could start to solve the riddle of the nation's smoking problem.

In fact we can.

Let's look at the excuses / reasons for not wanting to stop that were listed in the yellow pages. They won't all apply to you but they will all give you food for thought. And let's start with that idea of enjoyment.

I won't try to convince you that you don't enjoy smoking, even though it is not the enjoyment you think it is (Chapter 9 explains why). Let's look at it another way and ask: is enjoyment a reason for continuing to smoke? And do you enjoy all the cigarettes you smoke?

☐ Exercise

Calculate the financial cost of tobacco each year. Assuming you smoke twenty a day, that represents about £1400 a year of your (taxed) income. Consider what else you could get for £1400, like two holidays every year. Is the enjoyment of smoking **better** than two holidays a year?

This is not a trick question, because in reality many smokers would say, "No, I would rather smoke - much as I would like two holidays a year". The interesting point is *why* you make this choice, which is an irrational one.

☐ *Because I Can't Stop*

Why can't you stop? If you knew the answer to that, you would have done it long ago. But for the purpose of this argument let's dispute the fact.

You say you don't want to stop because you can't. This makes some sense, but not a lot. Perhaps what it means is that, since you could not stop anyway, there is no point in wanting to, just as there is no point in wanting anything you cannot have, an idea that we retain from childhood.

☐ Exercise

You have to understand why you don't want to stop. If you could overcome this problem - in other words if you could find a guaranteed way to stop smoking - would you definitely want to? Most mature users would almost certainly want to stop if it were guaranteed with any particular method. So if you can say for sure that you would want to stop if it were guaranteed, then all you have to do is find that method and your motivation will soar. Then, bingo! You will be a non-smoker. So far, so good.

☐ *Because I Need It When I'm Stressed*

If smoking helps with stress - and that is a big 'if' - wouldn't it be better to go on doing it? If you need tobacco to deal with the stresses in your life, isn't this a valid reason for continuing?

There are two issues here. First, why is it that both non-smokers and ex-smokers survive quite well without cigarettes? It is because, when you smoke, you *believe* you need to do so in order to handle stress. Any addict would. Second, is the harm that tobacco does an acceptable price to pay to deal with stress?

☐ Exercise

Ask yourself whether the price you pay to smoke is worth it. For example, if you are worried about money, and you smoke twenty a day, how is spending £1400 a year going to help? If you are worried about your health, how is doing something guaranteed to make it worse going to help? If you are worried about someone else's health, how is being £1400 a year poorer, and less healthy, going to help? Just how does smoking tobacco help with any of the specific problems you have to deal with?

There are in fact two ways in which it helps. First, it is a narcotic drug, so it dulls the brain, and thus appears to remove the problem. But it doesn't actually remove the problem, and you know it doesn't. Second, as long as you believe it helps, then it does. Addicts always believe their drug helps. As long as you believe it helps, that is a good reason for not wanting to stop. Once you have reasoned that you would actually be better off without cigarettes, you will have a reason for stopping.

☐ *Because I've Never Thought Seriously About Stopping*

Most mature smokers have thought about stopping. Younger smokers tend to live in a make-believe world where old-age, infirmity and death are a long way off. When you reach the age of thirty they are a little closer, and by forty you start to see them rather more clearly. By fifty these events have already happened to some of your friends and family; and you know that, come hell or high water, they are going to happen to you.

Maybe the reason you now want to stop is no more than that. Or maybe you did think about it before, but not seriously, for any of the reasons I have mentioned. For example, you might not have believed you would be able to stop, so the idea remained an idea and never developed into a definite want.

☐ Exercise

If you have not thought seriously about stopping before, why do you want to now? In fact, *do* you want to stop? Try writing down your reasons. Health might come first, particularly if you are getting on in years or if you have recently developed some smoking-related illness.

Now ask yourself the question again, but in a different way. If you have a particular reason for stopping now, why did that reason not exist before?

Health: As we have just seen, age has a great deal to do with the matter.

Money: This is a little strange, because age tends to bring greater financial resources. Teenagers want to smoke but cannot afford to; retired people can often afford to but want to stop. So is money really an issue for you? It might be if you are a single parent, say, or unemployed. This does not necessarily mean, though, that you want to stop smoking; it might only mean that you cannot afford to smoke, which is not the same thing. Whilst it might be important to you, we know from experience that financial hardship is a poor motivator where stopping smoking is concerned.

Social pressure: This is a surprisingly significant factor. Teenagers are under pressure to smoke from their peers. As they get older, this pressure decreases and the pressure to stop increases. Although almost all smokers quote health as their main reason for wanting to stop, they underestimate the effect of social pressure from friends, family, the media and the medical profession. So, as you get older, your need to stop increases. Of course, the reasons were there all the time - it just took time to see them. That is one of the terrible tragedies of tobacco.

☐ *Because All My Friends Do*

As we have just seen, peer pressure is the main reason why young people start to smoke. It also keeps them at it even if they find they hate it. After a very short while peer pressure is no longer needed, because addiction, and then psychological dependence, take over.

The reason your friends smoke might be that their friends do. And the reason their friends do is that their friends do. And they smoke because you do.

This is not a reason, it is an excuse. The reason is addiction and psychological dependence. Face that fact now.

☐ Exercise

Imagine this scenario. All your smoking friends are gathered in one room: a magician enters, waves his magic wand, and they all stop smoking there and then and never think about cigarettes again. Would you want to be in the room with them?

If the answer is Yes - and it almost certainly will be - the reason you smoke is not because all your friends do. You all smoke because you cannot stop. If the answer is No, either you are deceiving yourself or you really do not want to come off tobacco. (In which case, why are you reading this book?)

☐ *Because I'm Too Young For It To Matter*

In some ways, young smokers are right: the incidence of smoking-related disease under forty is low. And that's precisely how the tobacco companies stay in business. Tobacco smoking shortens your life, but most users feel little or no ill effect in their first thirty years of smoking. If there were high emphysema or lung cancer rates among smokers in their twenties, the tobacco companies would have gone bust long ago.

So, in a way, in your twenties you *are* too young for it to matter. For two reasons, though, that viewpoint is terribly and tragically wrong. First, all the time you are smoking you are developing smoking-related disease. It might take thirty years to matter, but as long as you are smoking that time is coming.

Second, you might think you can smoke for thirty years before it matters, but by then you are likely to be hopelessly addicted and dependent, so you will have difficulty stopping even if you want to. It may be too late.

☐ Exercise

Ask yourself whether you still feel you can get away with smoking because of your age. If you think you can, you are looking for an excuse. As you have just read, the excuse is a futile one. You are only getting into deeper water.

☐ Because I'm Too Old For It To Matter

The ages of patients in our clinics range from twenty-five, the youngest we will accept, to over eighty. The older ones sometimes ask us if there is any point in stopping at their age. What they mean is, will there be any benefit, or, to put it more strongly, will the benefit outweigh the disadvantages - by which they mean the effort.

Given that it takes some years to recover fully from the damage done by smoking, and that recovery is slower in older people, it might not be worth their while stopping. There are, in fact, two disadvantages to consider.

The first is the effort involved in stopping. If stopping is painful, perhaps it should not be attempted. Interestingly, patients who have smoked for over half a century seem to have no more difficulty stopping than anyone else. In fact we often note a certain quiet resolve in them which is lacking in younger people.

And, in any case, why *should* stopping be painful? An eighty-year-old is not necessarily going to be any more addicted than a twenty-year-old, and it is breaking the addiction (if it is done without medical help) that hurts. The difference is the habit; it is not quite so easy to change a sixty-year habit as a ten-year one.

The second disadvantage is the loss of 'enjoyment' of smoking. We shall be looking closely at this idea of 'enjoyment' later, but for now we have to concede that, if a smoker believes in the 'enjoyment', sixty years are going to reinforce that belief more than ten years are.

Now we need to weigh against these two disadvantages the

reasons why coming off tobacco is so important in old age. As you get older, your body's ability to heal itself deteriorates. When you were younger, you had the strength to fight the damage that smoking was inflicting on you, but in old age you have less and less chance of winning. In addition, each cigarette you smoke is harming you, but conversely each day you don't smoke you are not harming yourself. And consider whether, as you get older and more infirm, you really want to abuse your body. A fit and healthy old age is infinitely better than one in which you need constant medical attention.

☐ Exercise

Ask yourself whether you would prefer to face old age with a smoking-related disease or without it. You might already have such a condition, but the question is still important. Do you want to do the best for your body or not?

☐ *Because I've Got To Die Somehow*

This is the ultimate drug addict's nonsense. If it doesn't matter how you die, or even when, why do you look before crossing the road? Getting killed by a 38-tonne truck is usually easier than a slow, agonising death from lung cancer.

By the time you are in your thirties or forties, you have grown out of this sort of stuff. If only we could teach our children what rubbish it is.

☐ Exercise

Ask yourself how seriously you take the issues, particularly health. The only really valid reason for coming off tobacco is that it will shorten your life. (It might be, of course, that living is not of interest to you - in which case be aware that smoking is one of the slowest, most expensive and most anti-social ways to commit suicide.) Do you genuinely believe that tobacco will shorten your life, and will also damage your health during that life? If you do, stop deceiving yourself that you don't care. If you don't, stop deceiving yourself that you want to stop smoking.

The NHA Lie Detector Test

If you believe you want to stop smoking, do this simple test. I want you to imagine that the government, bless it, has been secretly researching how to genetically alter tobacco plants so that cigarettes can be made from them that are almost completely safe.

The new tobacco is about to be launched commercially, and the government, bless it, has announced it wants everyone to change to it so it will not be taxed. And what's more, these new cigarettes will actually smell quite pleasant, so people won't mind you smoking in their houses.

Now, you can smoke cigarettes without the health, financial or social worries. Would you

A Still stop smoking   **B** Try the new cigarettes for a while

If you would still want to stop, then you do want to stop. If, however, you would try the new cigarettes first, you don't. You just don't want to pay the price (in the fullest sense) of smoking, which is not the same thing at all. Many patients in our clinics, when asked this question, say they would put the programme on hold, and try the new cigarettes first.

This doesn't mean they don't want to be non-smokers - it means they wish they didn't have to stop, which is different.

The Real Reasons

There are three main reasons why people don't want to stop smoking.

They are addicted to nicotine, so it is unreasonable to expect addicts to *want* to give up their drug. Because they are addicted, they don't believe they *can* stop. This belief is confirmed for them by the medical profession, which largely has no idea how to help them, and blames them for their problem. And society not only condones tobacco products, but actively participates in their manufacture and sale.

There is of course no easy answer. At NHA Research we are concerned not just with individual users, but with social attitudes to tobacco and with government involvement in the trade. You, understandably, are concerned with your own problem.

The Social Reason

In the very near future we are unlikely to see any significant shift away from social acceptance of the tobacco industry. You are simply going to have to accept that you want to stop using a lethal drug that is on sale in every supermarket and corner shop; that, as hard as you have tried to come off the drug, the government takes a large cut of the trade's proceeds but then gives its GPs and NHS the power to decide to refuse treatment to patients who are suffering the consequences of tobacco abuse.

All around you people are buying and smoking the drug, but you have to convince yourself that your decision to come off it is right. The only help I can offer at this stage is to ask you to remember two things:

The government has no interest in helping you. If it did, why would it permit the sale of a drug that kills two hundred times as many people as AIDS?

Other smokers continue to use the drug, not because they want to, but because they are addicted. They, like you, are victims. You, unlike them, are doing something about it.

☐ The Hopelessness Reason

As we have seen, many people don't even want to attempt to stop smoking, simply because they are afraid of failure. This applies to men and women in different ways. Men are better able to stop than women are (see below) but often find it harder to take the loss of face that goes with failure. So they cover their fear with bravado - they say they don't want to stop. If this applies to you, now is the time to come to terms with it. Forget your pride - years of your life are too high a price to pay for pride.

Women tend to be afraid of failure for a more important reason. They find it harder to stop than men, and often tell us in their clinics that it is because they have to endure more stress. But this is not the real reason.

First, women more readily become addicted, on average, than men; this is because women's bodies adapt differently from those of men to the poisons in tobacco. And second, partly because of this addictiveness they have a greater psychological dependence.

Currently more men than women are stopping smoking - although interestingly, women outnumber men in NHA clinics (this probably reflects men's resistance to accepting medical help more than anything else). If you are a woman who is afraid of trying to come off tobacco, read right through this book before making a decision; it will make the whole thing look more attainable and less frightening.

☐ The Addiction Reason

If tobacco were not addictive, it is probable that only a few people would start to smoke. And those who did would get fed up trying to adapt to it. It is the addiction that keeps the tobacco industry afloat. It is the addiction that captures smokers, then makes them psychologically dependent.

Until recently, the medical profession has had no idea how to treat nicotine addiction. Doctors have toyed with tobacco substitutes but they are not a cure - which you might have discovered for yourself. For this reason, you might have come to believe that you will never overcome the addiction. Please think about two things:

If you have not smoked for about a week, you are no longer addicted to nicotine. You may think you are (which is psychological dependence), but in fact you are not. If you can get through this one week, you have beaten the addiction. But don't do it this way. Work on your psychological dependence first, by doing things like learning to control your smoking habits, changing your stress response and so on. If you really cannot handle the withdrawal symptoms, medical help is now available. Ask your GP in the first place. If he or she doesn't offer Addiction Neutralisation Therapy (A.N.T.), ask the doctor to contact us for information. We will help the surgery to set up a programme for its patients.

WHY IT'S HARD TO STOP SMOKING 4
The Short Explanation

If you are a smoker, and you cannot stop, you are presumably reading this book to find out how to do it. Well, there is only one way to stop smoking; you stop smoking. But **you** can't do that, so there has to be something you are missing. The point you have perhaps missed is that your problem is not that you can't stop smoking. Anyone can stop smoking. Tie them up, put something over their mouth, lock them in a room for a week, and I promise you they will stop smoking.

Whether they will have gone crazy, and whether the first thing they will do when you release them is to smoke twenty cigarettes one after the other, we cannot know. But the point is made, that anyone can stop smoking; everyone can stop smoking, including you.

How long they stop for is another matter. But keep someone locked up for ever, and they will stop smoking for ever. And so on. I have a problem with the definition of stopping. A nicotine replacement product, for example, might help you to stop smoking, but it has nothing to do with breaking your addiction to nicotine, so you may start smoking again when you come off the product. Clearly you are not smoking while you use the product, but can it be said that you have 'stopped smoking', that you have achieved your objective? And what if you really do stop, altogether, again what does stopped mean? You stop smoking every night when you go to sleep, but I doubt you would call that stopped. Perhaps you go on a very long flight without smoking, but can that be called stopped? If you have been in hospital for a week without smoking, have you stopped? You are not smoking, but can that be called stopped? Many people do this and simply start again when they come out of hospital, even though they are no longer addicted and would find it relatively easy to stay stopped.

The point is that anyone - everyone - can stop smoking. Stopping is not the problem. The problem is staying stopped. Stop-smoking products and services don't help you to stop smoking at all; they help you to stay stopped.

If stopping smoking was really really important to you, you would stop. Everything has a value, and a price. If the value to you of stopping smoking is high enough, you will pay the price. Conversely, if the price is low enough, the value will probably increase. In other words, stopping smoking is about balancing the need to do it with the difficulty of doing it. Anyone can do it; they just need to find a balance that results in success.

In this chapter I am going to look at making it easier. The only intelligent way to make something easier is to understand first why it is hard. Going and buying some stop-smoking product or service has nothing to do with discovering why you have difficulty stopping. Understand what your difficulties are; then you will be in a position to purchase the products or services that are most likely to resolve those problems.

For example, nicotine replacement products are intended to help you overcome the habit of smoking. If habit is your primary problem, you may stop with NRPs. If, however, stress is your primary problem, NRPs do not address that problem so you are less likely to succeed with them.

For another example, acupuncture is good for dealing with stress. If stress is your primary problem, you may succeed with acupuncture. If, however, social pressure is your primary problem, acupuncture does not address that problem so you are less likely to succeed with it.

For my last example, hypnotherapy is good for dealing with the fear of never smoking again. If fear of success is your primary problem, you may succeed with hypnotherapy. If, however, addiction is your primary problem, hypnotherapy does not address that problem so you are less likely to succeed with it.

You get the picture. Read on through the white pages and you will understand better what your problems are. Once you have learned that, you will be in a position to find the stop-smoking technique that addresses those problems.

The technique you need might be a product from the chemist, or it might be a therapy. If you are a hard case, it might even be A.N.T. Or, it might be simply that having understood what your real problems are, you will at last have the knowledge and confidence to solve them yourself. But what you will not be doing again is wasting time and money, and getting frustrated and depressed, doing it the wrong way.

For some people, stopping smoking is hard, for others less so. To be honest, if it is hard for you, to some extent that is your bad luck. But the most important reason why so many people have difficulty stopping smoking is not actually because it is difficult to stop smoking (you don't want me to repeat the lesson about locking you up, do you?). It is because they go about it the wrong way. Every day, thousands of people rush out and buy something that is supposed to stop them smoking. They do it without ever stopping and thinking through why they fail. We are constantly astonished when patients come to us and report that they failed with some method and then went and bought it again, in the vain hope that some miracle would have taken place meanwhile and it would work the second time round.

There is a way for each smoker to stop. A sensible way that addresses their problems and makes it possible, nay easy, for them to succeed. The reason it is so hard is because they don't look for that way. Stopping smoking is hard because people do it wrong.

WHY IT'S HARD TO STOP SMOKING   4
The Long Explanation

If you knew why you can't stop smoking, you would presumably be able to do something about it. This seems logical, but it is not that simple. It's rather like saying 'If we knew what was wrong with the nation's economy we could fix it', or even, 'If we knew how to cure cancer we would do so'. We know how to make car engines that are twice as economical as the present type, but we don't make them. We know how to cure Crohn's disease (one of the two inflammatory bowel diseases), but we don't use the cure. The reasons why we don't always do what we are able to are usually political and economic, because these considerations outweigh the benefits.

You could stop smoking now, but you don't because the difficulties outweigh what you consider to be the benefits of smoking. People who come to our clinics pay us because the cost of the treatment is less than the difficulty they would experience without our help. What they haven't done is analyse why they cannot come off tobacco and what they need to do about it. Given the dearth of worthwhile information and support, let alone actual medical treatment for what is, after all, a serious medical problem, they cannot be blamed.

And when I say stopping smoking is hard, do I mean stopping smoking is hard, or do I mean **staying** stopped is hard? For some people, it is the stopping. If they could stop, say for a few days at least, they could stay stopped. But for others it is not hard to stop. It is the staying stopped that they find hard, and there are quite different reasons for this, because stopping and staying stopped involve many different issues.

☐ Stopping

Over a number of years we have treated thousands of smokers in our clinics, and we have learned a lot. So first let's start uncovering why *you* can't stop smoking. Here is the truth:

You are addicted to nicotine
You use cigarettes to deal with stress
You enjoy smoking
You give in to the habit
You are afraid to stop

Any or all of these might be true in your case. There are no other reasons, even though you may believe there are others. What you are going to do now is learn to fit your perceived reasons into these five, because they inevitably do fit. All five reasons are dealt with in detail in later chapters, but for now let's just look at the basics.

You are not addicted to smoking; smoking is not an addiction. Nicotine is an addictive drug, and smoking is merely the delivery method. Smokers who use nicotine replacement products prove this - as long as they are taking the product, they can usually survive without a cigarette.

☐ Exercise 1

So now ask yourself the real question: am I addicted to nicotine? Most users say they are, but frankly they don't actually know. In fact most of them are, even though they don't know how to tell. The mere fact that you keep smoking does not prove that you are addicted. The only way to find out is to stop. If you suffer withdrawal symptoms, you are addicted. If you don't, you might still be addicted, partly because some people take a long time to withdraw, and partly because not all smokers can distinguish genuine withdrawal symptoms from ordinary bad temper. Typical symptoms could be involuntary shaking, headaches, and tight chest and sweating. Hypoglycaemia may also be a problem here.

However, it is safe to say that if you suffer withdrawal symptoms within hours of waking up and not lighting a cigarette, you are addicted.

This is the first reason you can't stop smoking. Read Chapter 6 to understand addiction.

☐ Exercise 2

Have you ever stopped smoking and then started again? Why did this happen? For most people stress is the cause.

Do you find yourself smoking more heavily in a stress situation? Do you find yourself desperate to smoke when you have had a shock? Do you notice a marked calming effect when you take the first drag?

If you answer Yes to any of these questions, you clearly use tobacco to deal with stress, albeit in vain.

This is the second reason you can't stop smoking. Read Chapter 11 for more information on stress.

☐ Exercise 3

Ask yourself if you enjoy smoking (ignore the enjoyment of the first cigarette in the morning, because that is addiction). Are there times of the day, for instance when you are socialising, when you particularly enjoy a cigarette? Have you ever thought that you would really like to stop smoking if only you didn't enjoy it so much?

Enjoyment is not difficult to explain, but it is the most insidious reason why people can't stop smoking. This is because there are two types of enjoyment - physical and mental. The physical enjoyment is real, because you are using a narcotic drug, and satisfying your addiction. The mental enjoyment is just what it says - it is all in the mind.

This is the third reason you can't stop smoking. Read Chapter 9 for more information on enjoyment.

☐ Exercise 4

As you will be reading later, habit is never a reason why people cannot stop smoking. It is always, without exception, an excuse. You are certainly in the habit of smoking, but that is not the same as being unable to stop *because* of the habit.

Ask yourself if you have ever said that you cannot stop because of the habit. Most smokers would have to admit to this. If you have, it is not the habit that is the reason, but your belief in the habit. In other words, you give in to the habit.

This is the fourth reason you can't stop smoking. Read Chapter 8 for more information on habit.

☐ Exercise 5

Have you ever been an adult non-smoker? If you have smoked all your adult life, you do not know what not smoking is like. Logically, you can understand what it is likely to be like, but you have not actually experienced it.

Most people would accept that going into a new way of life, one that you have never tried, is likely to be a bit scary. The reason most people have trouble accepting their own fear is that it's actually hard to admit that not smoking - something that seems so ordinary - could be scary. Take it from me, this fear is one of the biggest problems for smokers.

This fear is the fifth reason you can't stop smoking. Read Chapter 10 for more details on fear.

☐ Exercise 6

Ask yourself if there are any other reasons. As you think of each one, see if it fits into one of the five categories above. You will find that it does.

For example, you might say you fail when you go out with friends, because you need to smoke in company. This is habit; if you didn't go out with your friends for a month, the problem would disappear. Or you might say you *could* change this habit of smoking with your friends, but that you feel more comfortable with a cigarette in your hand and would not enjoy their company as much without. No matter how long you stopped socialising, you might say, you feel you would need a cigarette in your hand when you started again. In this case, you feel stressed when you are in company. and you need a cigarette to overcome this stress. In neither case is your social life the real reason - it is only the *perceived* reason.

We are going to look at every single issue you have to face when you stop smoking. We are going to make sure they all fit into our five categories, and then we are going to look at how you can overcome these five problems.

And there is not going to be anything else. If you think there is, go back over this chapter again and make sure you understand it fully before you read on.

This does not mean, however, that these five problems are going to be easy to overcome. What I *am* saying is that there are reasons for everything in life, including not being able to stop smoking. There is nothing mysterious about these reasons, but because the problem is caused by a complex mix of issues, each feeding off the others, they can seem too confusing to overcome. If we separate them out they will become manageable.

☐ Staying Stopped

If you can stop, whether easily or with difficulty, a new set of problems may present themselves to stop you staying stopped. The difficulties of staying stopped are best understood if we look at why people start smoking again, which is examined in detail in Chapter 14.

CHANGING ATTITUDES
The Short Explanation

The world has an attitude problem. It has lots of attitude problems, but I'm talking about its attitude to tobacco.

Let's keep to this country:

The government has a strange attitude, because it allows the advertising and sale of a drug which it readily acknowledges to be lethal and addictive, the most dangerous combination imaginable.

Industry has a strange attitude, because no-one seems to be commenting, in a meaningful way, on the fact that we have a tobacco industry that is killing its customers.

Retail business has a strange attitude, because it sells tobacco in sweetshops and supermarkets and doesn't notice the insanity of what it is doing.

The media have a strange attitude, because they talk about tobacco as if it's naughty but nice.

Doctors have a strange attitude, because they refuse to see tobacco as an addictive drug, and therefore a medical issue.

Now let's look at whether you have a strange attitude towards tobacco. You, of course, are conditioned by society's attitude, like it or not. But more importantly, you are currently on the drug, so your attitude is controlled by the drug. You do not have the freedom to make judgments about the drug, at least not in the way non-users do, and I think you would accept that idea.

If you are going to come off tobacco, you have to change your attitude. First, you have to look at other people's attitudes, because when your motivation is waning, the attitude of the government, of industry, of business, of the media and of doctors is going to undermine your determination. You have to accept that the only sensible attitude is that all of these people are wrong, and you are right.

Don't worry that you might be the only sane person in the world (I don't). In fact millions of people don't use tobacco, and many of them also cannot understand how the tobacco industry can even exist. But they don't make a noise about it because it doesn't concern them. If they did make a noise about it, perhaps you would now see tobacco differently. Instead of seeing it as something you like but need to come off, you might see it as something evil you have been unable to come off but must as soon as possible.

What all this means is that when you decide to stop smoking, you are going to be challenged by the seeming normality of smoking. People will be doing it all around you, and this might make you feel they are right and you are wrong. Well, to overcome this conflict, ask yourself if you would feel the same about someone taking heroin. Of course not. You would pity them. The only difference between heroin and tobacco is that tobacco, for historical reasons, is a legal drug, and therefore infinitely more successful commercially.

In fact there is an argument that heroin is no more dangerous than tobacco. If heroin were also made legal (which would also bring the price down) it would probably be just as successful an industry as tobacco. For those historical reasons heroin is illegal and kills about one person a day; tobacco is legal and kills 300.

CHANGING ATTITUDES

The Long Explanation

5

At the moment, assuming you are seriously contemplating trying to come off tobacco, you have a list of problems. For example:

How will you cope with stress without cigarettes?
How will you overcome the craving?
How will you avoid being bad tempered?
How will you cope with changing your habits?
How will you enjoy socialising if you can't smoke?
How will you control your weight?
How will you fill your more boring days?
What will you do with your hands?
What will you do if you fail?

You can probably think of some more yourself.

And while you are doing a spot of thinking, consider something else too. If you had never smoked in your life, would you now be faced with these problems? No. So the problems are not caused by not smoking, but by *stopping* smoking. And if they are problems that non-smokers don't have, it is clear that you won't have them either once you have stopped.

For all of these problems this book contains an answer. Stop believing that being a non-smoker is going to make life worse, or harder, or less enjoyable. It is only addicts who believe their drug actually improves their lives.

Having started to undo the myth of life being better for smokers, start to look at how life might be better for non-smokers.

They have better health
They will live longer
They don't smell of stale tobacco
Like credit cards, they are accepted everywhere
They are richer
They don't have stained hands
They don't have to worry about their drug supply
They don't feel guilty
And they are free

When we ask our patients what they feel is the greatest benefit once they have come off tobacco, the most frequent answer is that they are free - by which they mean free of the addiction and free of dependence. When they have stopped smoking, they come to realise that their fears were caused by their addiction, and that their belief in the pleasure was caused by the addiction as well. If you live in a country run by a totalitarian dictatorship it is easy to believe it is a benevolent one because it tells you so. In the case of smoking, the dictatorship of tobacco has convinced you of its benevolence.

☐ The Freedom to Smoke

Smokers believe they have to protect their freedom to smoke, often where and when they want. But this is a terrible, tragic joke.

Smokers are not free. If they were free, why would they fear stopping? If they were free, they would be able to do what they want - but they cannot. It is non-smokers who are free. A non-smoker is free to make a choice - to smoke or not, as he or she pleases. You, a smoker, do not have that choice because you have not been able to stop smoking (which is why you are reading this book). So stop telling yourself you are free to smoke. You have been had. The tobacco companies insist you have the right to smoke. What they mean is that they have the right to sell you a drug that is going to shorten your life. Whenever you are tempted to believe in the myth of freedom, remember that the freedom the tobacco companies are talking about is the freedom for them to profit from your addiction.

If you are addicted to anything you are a slave, and slaves are not free. Become a non-smoker, because non-smokers have a choice. *Then* you will be free.

☐ Problems, Problems

Not only do non-smokers not have the problems you do, they also have fewer health and money worries and less guilt. Despite this, you are the one who is worried. Smoking has given you these problems, and it is quite logical that stopping smoking will remove them (notwithstanding any temporary difficulty while you are in the process of becoming a non-smoker). But it is not usually these temporary problems that worry would-be ex-smokers.

For example, you may be genuinely worried what you will do with your hands when you no longer smoke. This problem is caused at first by low-level cravings for nicotine, and afterwards because people believe they are addicted - the psychological dependence. But you had no problem with your hands before you started smoking, so why should you afterwards? Only because the dependence takes some time to get over. The problem exists because you have smoked, not because you have stopped.

Perhaps you worry about how you are going to fill your days without cigarettes, particularly if you have an unexciting job. If this describes you, ask your non-smoking colleagues how they cope. It is unlikely that you cope any better than they do simply because you smoke, even though it is common for people in boring jobs to pace themselves with cigarettes. And you do have a choice; to help, if you really want to, you can use a drug that kills three hundred users a day.

Many would-be ex-smokers worry about putting on weight if they stop smoking. It takes a weight gain of about three and a half stone to give you the same health risk as smoking twenty cigarettes a day, so what are you worrying about? If you are worrying about the health risks of getting overweight, by all means use a drug that gives people heart disease to keep your weight down. If you are worried about your looks, how do you think you look walking around with a fag hanging out of your mouth and smelling like an old ashtray?

In reality non-smokers are no heavier than smokers. What causes you to put on weight is the act of stopping, which may cause you temporarily to overeat because you substitute food for cigarettes. In other words, if you had never smoked the problem would not exist. If the act of stopping smoking might cause you to put on weight, then do it in such a way that it does not - deal with the addiction properly. And if you do put weight on, you can lose it again. Losing weight is always going to be easier than stopping smoking, so do get your priorities right.

To summarise, you can see that the problems you are currently faced with exist not because you are going to be a non-smoker, but because you have been a smoker. Realise that these problems cannot last for ever, and that they will be gone once you are a happy non-smoker. At the moment you are causing your own problems, because of your fear. And why do you have this fear?

Because you are an addict, and all addicts are afraid of losing their drug. Once you have overcome the addiction you will gain control over your psychological dependence, and with that control your fear will disappear.

☐ Pressures from Outside

Some years ago, NHA Research was asked by an insurance company to help staff in their computer department to stop smoking. After the first batch went through the clinic we never heard from them again, although the programme involves ongoing telephone monitoring of patients. So when the second batch attended, we asked them what had happened to the first lot. Apparently the company's no-smoking policy had been handled so badly that all the staff had volunteered for treatment, but agreed among themselves that that they would not actually use the neutrogen and would not stop smoking. It seemed to them a good way of getting back at the company. How sad it is that they were prepared to shorten their lives to spite their employer. It is never worth using tobacco to spite others. It really is cutting off your nose to spite your face.

If your employer has imposed a ban on smoking in the workplace, it is probably not for your benefit. It is for the benefit of the non-smokers and ultimately of the employer who doesn't want to be faced with future lawsuits for illness caused by passive smoking.

You might resent this intrusion, although a number of smokers do say they wish smoking were outlawed because it is the only way they are ever going to stop. We agree: tobacco products should be sold in a much more controlled way, particularly to prohibit their sale to children. But successive governments have shown that economic issues outweigh the health of the nation, and as long as the country is being run as a business, instead of a place fit for people to live in, this will continue to be so.

Many smokers tell us they resent the government's attitude, and also that of doctors who preach but don't help. In the case of doctors, it is probably more a case of inability to help than unwillingness. Doctors can only give their patients what the system, and their training, gives them. NHA Research has tried hard to interest GPs in being trained to neutralise tobacco addiction, but without success. This is not their fault; without financial backing, we have not had the resources to get the message across.

Much of the pressure being put on smokers is well-meaning but inept. If you feel pressured by your employer, your family and friends, the media, your GP or society generally, try to ignore it. It is highly unlikely that these people understand your problems, but resist the temptation to assert your 'freedom' to smoke because of them. You are the only one who will suffer.

☐ Pity the Children

Many smokers say they want to stop for their children's sake. If this is the motivation you need, fine. You might well wish you had never started to smoke as a child; if you did, it was probably because you saw adults smoke. As a society we are still teaching children to smoke. The next time you are in a tobacconist's / sweetshop look how the sweets are arranged; it is impossible for children not to see the cigarettes displayed directly behind them. The message is clear; when you are small you buy sweets, and when you grow up you buy the things higher up - cigarettes. As long as cigarettes are sold in sweetshops and supermarkets we are wasting our time telling children they shouldn't smoke, because they simply won't believe us.

If you have teenage children, you may have experienced an interesting phenomenon. Schoolchildren are often violently opposed to smoking - until they come under peer pressure. In our studies we have seen an astonishing transformation when this happens; young people simply cannot resist the pressure. Nothing you can say is going to help, because *you* smoke. The only way you can contribute to their survival in this jungle is not to lecture them, but to make sure they see what a hell of a time you have trying to come off tobacco. Let them share in the misery, and let them be quite clear on your attitude - that you wish you had never started, that you hate the smell on your body, on your clothes and in your home, that you resent wasting all that money, that the tobacco companies are using you to make profit, and that you smoke not because you enjoy it but because you *have* to smoke.

Of course, you might not believe all these things. However, if you can convince your children you might convince yourself.

☐ Nothing Comes Easy

Every smoker who wants to stop knows that they will have to work at it. Why is it, then, that they are so often surprised when it turns out to be really hard work?

The answer is that most smokers live on platitudes. 'Smoking is bad for me', 'You have to want to stop if you're going to succeed', and so on. But recognising that it is going to require an effort is not usually enough. Just take a little time to think through the changes you are going to be making:

You are on a drug as addictive as heroin
You are habituated to an activity you have done more than anything else in your life (see Chapter 8).
You have probably failed to stop before and are afraid of failing again.
You are afraid of a life without cigarettes.

All of this is going to have to be changed. It can certainly be done, because hundreds, if not thousands, of people come off tobacco every day. You need knowledge, which you are getting from this book; you need support, which is also available; you need determination, and only time will tell if you have enough. What you also need, as with any job this important, is a commitment to make the effort and find the time.

Do start thinking of coming off tobacco as a positive rather than a negative activity. Not smoking is negative - you are trying *not* to do something. But becoming a non-smoker is positive - you are trying to *be* something. Stopping smoking means losing something. Becoming a non-smoker means gaining something.

Your stop-smoking programme is a major event in your life. Devote to it the time and thought you would give to any other big project. View it in the same light as finding a new job, moving house or starting a new relationship - all things you would expect to occupy a great deal of your time, thoughts and energy. This book, like all the help we give to patients, involves *self*-help; our success is due to our policy of giving people the knowledge and support to enable them to help themselves.

Your Attitude to Tobacco

As long as you think of the object of your desire as a cigarette, you have an attitude that will make it harder to stop smoking. The object of your desire is actually the drug contained in that cigarette. The cigarette is merely the delivery method. It is not what smoking is about.

If you can persuade yourself to do it, it is helpful to change all thoughts of cigarettes to thoughts of nicotine, your drug. Even if it sounds strange, tell yourself you're going out to buy some nicotine, not some cigarettes. Tell yourself you need a fix, not a fag. By concentrating on the reason you smoke - to get the drug - you will gradually change your attitude to smoking. It will no longer be just smoking but drug taking. Once it is drug taking, it is no longer something you enjoy, it is something you want to be free of.

ADDICTION
The Short Explanation

There are many myths about addiction. Obviously, addiction is not well understood because if it were, someone would have come up with a cure, wouldn't they? (There is a cure, but because it is not a pharmaceutical cure, and only pharmaceutical cures get research funding because medical research in this country is funded not by the government but largely by pharmaceutical companies, and the cure, which was discovered in the 1970s, cannot be patented, so no-one can make a profit from it, doctors don't get told about it, and neither do the public.)

Well, now you are going to learn, in layman's terms, how addiction works. You will then know more than most people do about addiction; then you will be in a position to do something about it.

First let's look at the myths and destroy them, because they are no good to you. Once that has been done, and you no longer believe the silly things people say about it, you can learn the truth.

■ *Addiction happens because you like the substance so much you can't stop using it.*

How can this possibly be true? Look at typical addictive substances - tobacco, coffee and alcohol for example. Take a child who has never had any of these and give them some. If the theory of lethal attraction is right, the child will want more straight away. In fact, the first dose of any of these substances is unpleasant, even repellent. The child has to learn to like them. So the reason you are addicted to tobacco cannot be because it is so good you don't want to stop using it.

Just to be sure about this, let's consider whether any substance could be so good you would die for it. 14 million Britons use tobacco. The pack has a death threat on it (you might ignore this, but you haven't forgotten it). So 14 million people like tobacco so much they are prepared to die for it? Pull the other one.

■ *Some people are more addicted than others.*

This might be possible if the fatal attraction theory were valid - some people might be more fatally attracted than others. But it's not, so it isn't. Perhaps a heavy smoker is more addicted than a light smoker? Wrong again. Some people are light smokers during the working week and heavy smokers at the weekend. Does that mean they are more addicted at the weekend? That is just silly.

■ *Some people have an addictive personality.*

As you will read in the white pages, addiction is a purely physical phenomenon. It affects your personality, because you become psychologically dependent on it, but it can't happen the other way round - you can't have a personality that makes you addicted. You can have a dependent personality, and you might think, so what, this is just semantics. Well, excuse me, if we don't get the words right we're talking about the wrong thing, and how far are we likely to get doing that?

■ *Addiction doesn't matter when you're stopping smoking.*

OK, so if addiction doesn't matter, why do you smoke? What is the fatal flaw in your character that makes you use a drug that kills 300 Britons a day because you 'enjoy' it, or because it's just a 'habit', or because you like to smoke when you drink? This is a bit early to be claiming insanity.

In any case, how much of your problem is addiction, and how much psychological, is not what this chapter is about, so stop changing the subject.

■ OK, Now You Know What Addiction Isn't, What Is It?

Addiction occurs as a stage of adaptation to a poison. If you take a poison, it will harm you, possibly kill you. If you take that same poison in a sub-lethal dose, you can learn to take it, as long as you keep repeating the dose often enough for your body to build its adaptation. Once you have achieved adaptation, you will be able to tolerate larger and larger doses (or more frequent doses).

It is no coincidence that everything people become addicted to is poisonous (think about it). That is why even an addict can overdose. You know that's true if you have ever gone on a real smoking binge - your body struggles to absorb that much poison and you feel quite ill.

When you first smoked, it tasted bad (unless you were adapted through passive smoking - it's complicated). That's because your body recognised that the tobacco smoke was poisonous. You needed to learn to smoke, for social reasons, so you forced your body to adapt - to accept the poisons without reacting to them. You succeeded in doing this, and quickly became adapted. So far so good - you had learned to poison yourself.

Years later you decided to come off tobacco. But hold on, your body had learned to accept the poisons in tobacco smoke, because you insisted that it did, and now you want to switch it off, just like that. Well, that's not how adaptation works. Just as you became adapted, you have to become unadapted.

Breaking that adaptation will produce withdrawal symptoms, because your body will be fighting to maintain its adaptation (you told it to, remember?).

That is actually what addiction means. If this has whetted your appetite for understanding how a drug can control you physically, and why this is so important, read on.

ADDICTION

The Long Explanation

☐ How Addiction Works

When you smoked your first cigarette, unless you had been passive smoking it tasted awful. It might have made you feel dizzy and nauseous. Why was this? And why doesn't it do that now? The answer to these two questions is the explanation of how addiction works.

Your body has an inbuilt defence mechanism. If you take something poisonous (and tobacco is as poisonous as it gets) your body will try to protect you by giving you symptoms that warn you to stop. If you persist (because of the social pressure to learn to smoke), your body will learn to absorb the poisons. The only way it can do this is to learn the chemical structure of each one so that the next time you smoke it will recognise what you are doing.

To be able to absorb the poisons each time you smoke, those poisons must exist in your body to provide a database against which they can be compared chemically. To make sure that you keep the file updated, your body gives you symptoms (of withdrawal) to ask you to smoke, which is the delivery method for the chemicals. These symptoms are the same as hunger symptoms; your body needs food, so it gives you an unpleasant feeling to make you give it what it needs.

How your body compares the incoming poisons with what you are smoking is of the utmost importance. Each of the 4865 chemicals in tobacco smoke is itself made up of thousands of bits of molecular information. To speed up the process of learning to interpret the poisons, your body reads just one molecule, which it uses as a label. Providing that label molecule is present, your body can interpret the incoming poisons as tobacco smoke, and let them pass, as requested by your brain.

When you have a craving for tobacco, what your body is looking for is not tobacco, or even nicotine, but that chemical label. It is the only information you use to confirm that you are smoking and switch off the craving.

☐ The Difference Between Addiction and Dependence

Most people, including some doctors, fondly imagine that addiction and dependence are the same thing. The word *dependence* tends to get used to cover both sides of the problem, but we prefer to differentiate clearly between addiction, which has a physical cause, and dependence, which is psychological. So from now on I am going to refer to dependence as psychological dependence, and it is covered in the next chapter.

Similarly, many people, and this still includes a lot of doctors, refer to something called psychological addiction. This is a mistake. Addiction should only ever refer to the physical need for the drug. For example, you might say you are addicted to Mozart, but this would not be correct, because you cannot have a physical need to hear Mozart.

☐ Addiction is Physical

Once you start smoking, you are almost guaranteed to become addicted.

• When you wake up, do you quickly have a strong need to

smoke?
- When you smoke after a while without a cigarette, do you get a strong feeling of relief?
- Do you use more cigarettes in the first hour of the day than at any other time?
- When you are in a non-smoking environment, do you look forward to getting out so you can smoke?
- Do you stand outside, regardless of the weather, because you are not allowed to smoke at home or at work?
- Do you make sure you won't run out of cigarettes?
- When you try to stop smoking, do you get withdrawal symptoms such as mood changes, irritability, sweating palms, headaches, stomach cramps or any other abnormal physical symptoms?

If you can answer Yes to any of these questions, you are addicted to nicotine. In fact the effect of nicotine is so powerful that your adaptation mechanism reacts extremely quickly, making you physically addicted within weeks - providing you smoke enough to trigger the mechanism. Some people only smoke one or two cigarettes a day, and could easily stop. They don't, because they don't feel it is worth bothering. Why don't they get addicted? Well, they do. Even one cigarette each day is enough to become and remain addicted. They may not look like junkies, but they are technically addicted, and could experience withdrawal symptoms if they stop.

Many smokers find they can exercise enough willpower to cut down to about five or six cigarettes a day, but no further. They simply cannot understand why this is. There is a good reason. This amount of tobacco gives you enough doses of nicotine to comfortably maintain your addiction, and is called the Addiction Threshold. As long as you smoke that many you will remain addicted, because your adaptation mechanism is still working. Try to cut down even more, and you immediately challenge your addiction. (The person who smokes one or two a day just has an abnormally low Addiction Threshold.)

So your body is fighting to maintain its addiction, regardless of what *you* want. This proves a very important point: no matter how much you want to stop smoking, you will have to overcome the addiction - you will withdraw from nicotine, and the resulting symptoms will be outside your control.

The degree to which you experience these symptoms ranges enormously. Some people have very strong symptoms, while for others others they are so slight as to be unnoticeable - though this is not as common as some 'experts' would have you believe. For the thousands of patients whom we see in our medical centres, the withdrawal symptoms have been enough to stop their previous attempts to stop smoking.

So at this point let us destroy another myth. Willpower does not overcome addiction; it overcomes the *effects of withdrawal.* If you are addicted to nicotine, withdrawal symptoms of some kind are inevitable. Whether you overcome them depends on how bad they are and how much willpower you have.

And now, while we are exploding myths, let us take a look at another one. It is commonly believed that heavy smokers are more addicted than light smokers. This is absolutely not true.

The reason is simple. As explained above, you need about five or six cigarettes a day - and no more - to satisfy your addiction. But the average user gets through about twenty a day. So clearly you do not smoke twenty, thirty or whatever because of any physical craving - it must be for other reasons. You are addicted because your body has to maintain its adaptation to the poison; your body has no interest in nicotine, tobacco or cigarettes beyond that point.

☐ The Addiction Threshold and Your Addiction Level

Although most smokers have a similar Addiction Threshold,

each smoker has a specific Addiction Level. Despite this, smoking at the Addiction Threshold will satisfy the addictive craving. How is this apparent contradiction explained?

The challenge to your addiction happens at a particular level - the Addiction Threshold - but the way your body maintains its adaptation is specific to you. Cars offer a simple analogy. A 7-series BMW has a huge petrol tank but a Mini has a very small one; both cars, though, need only a trickle of petrol to start their engines. The BMW's tank is so big because of the consumption of the engine, but most of the 100 litres the tank contains is irrelevant to the trip to the supermarket. BMW drivers only challenge their car's fuel tank by driving hundreds of miles.

Like the BMW, your body is equipped in a way that satisfies your needs (to remain adapted to the poison). On a day-to-day basis, however, that complex machinery will not be needed. You only challenge your adaptation mechanism when your tobacco consumption drops below the Addiction Threshold. Once it does, the Addiction Level becomes important, because it is this which determines your ability to remain adapted to the poison.

Over the years you have smoked tobacco, your body has been using its adaptation mechanism to enable it to absorb a highly poisonous substance, nicotine, taken in by an extremely unpleasant delivery method, burning gases. It only does this because of the effect of nicotine and, once you got on the merry-go-round of smoking, because of the psychological pressure to continue smoking. But how did you adapt to the poison on the first place?

Whilst the mechanism of adaptation is the same for everyone, each person's ability to deal with any challenge to their health is different. This is one of the major failings of high-technology medicine; it treats everyone as a standard model. A fifteen-year-old girl who has only ever smoked the occasional cigarette, a fifty-year-old man who smokes eighty a day, and a seventy-year-old woman with emphysema all have the same adaptation mechanism, but clearly they each have a unique response to the challenge of smoking.

Similarly, everyone has a unique response to all the challenges life throws at them, a response which depends on a huge range of factors including age, sex, weight, physical health, mental health and current medication. The same flu virus does not affect everyone in the same way - some suffer more than others, and some people who have been exposed to the virus do not react at all.

When you started smoking, your body was faced with an extremely serious challenge. You had the same adaptation mechanism as other people, but the result of the adaptation process will have depended on a wide range of factors like those listed above. At some point, your adaptation mechanism succeeded in meeting the challenge. How far it had to go was individual to you, and it is what is called in this book your Addiction Level. (NHA doctors call it the Endpoint of the addiction, and they use it to prescribe the neutralising neutrogen in the correct concentration for patients.)

The Addiction Level is your body's own response to the challenge imposed by absorbing toxic substances, including nicotine. Once it has met that challenge (once it has worked out a means of absorbing the poison), how many cigarettes you go on to smoke is irrelevant. The Endpoint has been established - you have adapted to the poison. This is the adaptation your body will fight to maintain for as long as you are a user. Whether you smoke five or fifty a day will not change it. And when I refer to how addicted you are, this is what I am saying.

☐ Addicted or Dependent?

You are both. In the same way that many smokers think the

number of cigarettes they smoke determines how addicted they are, a lot of smokers think that the number of years they have smoked influences it. This is not true. Once you are addicted, that's it - the Addiction Level depends on your immune system's response to the poison. If you go on to smoke for fifty years you won't get any more addicted, but you *will* become more psychologically dependent.

Now we have seen what the difference is between addiction and dependence, let's take a look at how dependence works to keep you smoking and, ironically, how it keeps you addicted. Once you understand how the two conspire to keep you smoking, you will be able to separate them and deal with them individually, so that they lose their combined power.

Maintaining An Addiction

Although your body requires about five doses of tobacco each day to avoid going into withdrawal (the Addiction Threshold), it needs far less to maintain its adaptation. Nicotine remains in the body for about four days - now because you cannot maintain the adaptation unless your body still contains some nicotine, inevitably after four days the adaptation is lost.

Therefore the minimum requirement to maintain the adaptation is one dose every four days. If you smoke one cigarette every four days you will maintain your addiction. This explains why some people are 'social smokers' - even though they don't seem to be addicted, they are.

Withdrawal Symptoms Are Natural

You probably associate the word withdrawal with addiction, and perhaps believe that this is something to do with other people, but not you.

Withdrawal symptoms are a completely natural human function. If you didn't have them, you would die. Everyone has withdrawal symptoms every day, from two substances.

How do you know your body needs fluids? You get thirsty. How do you know when your body needs nutrition? You get hungry, usually manifested as a rumbling tummy, getting worse if you don't eat. Eventually, if you don't eat, you get symptoms like weakness, faintness and confusion.

All of these are symptoms your body uses to make your brain respond to a physical need. When your brain recognises the symptoms of hunger, it institutes the process of eating. When you have eaten, you feel satisfied and the withdrawal symptoms stop - until you need more food.

If all of this sounds much like smoking, it is. When you become addicted - to any drug - you use this existing withdrawal mechanism as the way you know you need feeding. The existence of this natural mechanism is one of the reasons why it is so easy to become addicted to nicotine.

And finally, how does this mechanism create psychological dependence? It's not hard to see that the physical need for food and water makes us fear being without them. Similarly, the physical need for nicotine, over many years, creates the dependence you feel on smoking, the delivery method for nicotine.

method for nicotine. Your body needs nicotine, your brain has learned to deliver it by smoking a cigarette. After the first hundred thousand cigarettes it is unsurprising that you think an awful lot about lighting cigarettes - perhaps enough to find it hard to imagine not lighting cigarettes.

First you adapt to the poisons in tobacco (including but not exclusively nicotine), then your adaptation develops into addiction, then you become so used to needing to smoke and relieving that need that you simply don't know how to live your life without doing it.

Now you have a problem, because you have what even you, the addict, must recognise is a completely irrational situation. You know tobacco is going to kill you, but you 'know' you need it. Tobacco is now controlling not only your body but your mind, because you want to live - you know you should come off tobacco - but you can't bring yourself to do it.

Psychological dependence in this case is defined as an irrational need that conflicts with your own self interests. Psychological dependence means doing something that you actually don't want to do. And because you have this terrible conflict, you try to rationalise it by claiming it's just a habit, or you enjoy it.

None of the reasons people give for smoking, other than addiction, actually means anything. They are only ever an attempt to explain the inexplicable. Why would anyone be scared of coming off a substance that is dragging them down towards a miserable end? So scared that they won't even admit they are scared? So scared that they will claim to be enjoying the very substance that is screwing up their life?

You will find the answers in the following chapters. You will start to see how the different elements of this dependence work and how, by analysing them rationally, you can destroy them.

PSYCHOLOGICAL DEPENDENCE

The Long Explanation

☐ Dependence Is In the Mind

One can enjoy the music of Mozart so much that to be without it is no fun. My teenage children might appear to be addicted to pop music, but what that means is that they like it an awful lot. And since we live in a society in which most of us can, within reason, have what we want, we feel deprived if we are prevented from having it. I should feel deprived if Mozart were banned, and my children would feel deprived if pop music were banned.

At a higher level, some people become obsessed. Football, for instance, seems to dominate the lives of its fans, although it leaves others quite cold. Take a football fan's TV set away from him and you would be in serious trouble. He might become depressed, even aggressive, and would suffer something like withdrawal symptoms; but he could not be called addicted.

He could, however, reasonably be called psychologically dependent. This is because his mental state depends, to some extent, on football. With it he is happy, without it he is unhappy. And this, as explained above, is caused at least in part by his expectations.

No matter what someone is psychologically dependent on, they can be weaned off it. Given the right support - perhaps some replacement for their dependence - and a good reason for doing it, most people can overcome such dependence.

An element of the psychology is that some people are more likely than others to become psychologically dependent. They have a poorer internal resource to cope with life, and are more susceptible to whatever makes life appear easier. Some children, for instance, are easily led, whilst others are relatively self-sufficient. The ones who are easily led are more likely to succumb to peer pressure. They will, for example, start smoking under such pressure, whilst other children will find it easier to say no.

Given the narcotic effect of nicotine, anyone who finds life stressful is going to respond positively to smoking. And if life seems easier when you smoke, you have the beginning of psychological dependence. So is it fair, if we admit that nicotine helps a little with life's difficulties (and who has an easy life?), to expect people to overcome their dependence on it? I can only hope that you are not in a situation where you feel you are actually better off if you continue to smoke.

Although dependence and addiction are separate entities, what keeps you on tobacco is the way they work together. Split them, tackle each of them in the appropriate way for the particular problem, and you will be in control. And with complete control you will be in a position to stop smoking.

☐ Dependence Makes You Believe in Habit

Smoking is a habit, but the habit does not have the power to make you smoke. Your *belief* that habit can make you smoke is proof that you are psychologically dependent. Habit, by definition, can be changed at will. If you really wanted to stop smoking, you would accept that you can change any habit.

So the effect of psychological dependence is that it makes you believe you cannot change your habits. Habit is dealt with in Chapter 8.

☐ Dependence Makes You Afraid of Failing

There are very few things you attempt in your life that are critically important. Many things seem so at the time, like your driving test, or someone you have just fallen in love with, or a house you desperately want to buy. With hindsight, almost nothing is critically important.

Many people attach an inordinate importance to succeeding when they attempt to come off tobacco. If you have smoked for thirty years, whether it takes one day or one month to stop is completely unimportant.

Because you are so dependent on smoking, you believe in failure, and you fear it. The fear of failing is dealt with in Chapter 10.

☐ Dependence Makes You Afraid of Succeeding

If you are dependent on tobacco, clearly you will be afraid of stopping, as much as you want to in your more rational moments. Fear of succeeding is an excellent way to fail. The slightest problem that crops up is enough to stop you trying any longer.

In our clinics we sometimes see patients who obviously do not want the neutrogen to work for them. What they are doing is coming along to the clinic, not using the neutrogen as prescribed, and continuing to smoke. 'Failing' with the neutrogen is all the excuse they need to smoke for the rest of their lives. They say to themselves, 'I tried, but obviously I am an impossible case'. There is no such thing.

Fear of success is dealt with in Chapter 10.

☐ Dependence Makes You Smoke When You Are Stressed

Although nicotine does have a narcotic effect, we know that on balance tobacco makes life more, not less, stressful. Because you are addicted, you believe in the ability of smoking to help you deal with life's stressors. In your more rational moments you might accept that the stress imposed by tobacco outweighs the narcotic and addictive effect, but you are rarely that rational when you have not smoked for three days.

Since the benefit of smoking is imaginary, we can reasonably say that this is an aspect of psychological dependence. This can cause you to fear life without the support of cigarettes.

The relationship between smoking and stress is covered in Chapter 11.

☐ Dependence Makes You Fear The Loss of Enjoyment

There is an element of enjoyment in smoking, but it is illusory. If you did not enjoy the first cigarette you ever smoked, you also won't enjoy a cigarette after not smoking for a week. Therefore smoking is not enjoyable - but you *believe* it is, and that belief is enough for the enjoyment to become real.

If you really wanted to come off tobacco, why would the enjoyment of smoking make you continue? Isn't that a complete contradiction? Yet we see a large number of patients who simply cannot explain this contradiction. The answer is not difficult. If the enjoyment of smoking is greater than the desire to stop, then you won't stop.

Unless you destroy the myth. If, after a week's abstinence, your next cigarette is not enjoyable, this is all the proof you could want that that you really don't enjoy smoking. You *think* you do, and this belief is called psychological dependence.

The myth of the enjoyment is smoking is dealt with in Chapter 9.

☐ **Dependence Makes You Believe That Smoking Gives Your Life Meaning**

Many users simply cannot imagine never smoking again - not necessarily because they are afraid of this situation, but because smoking has become such a major part of their daily routine. Smokers commonly use lighting up as a reward, or to punctuate a boring job. You have perhaps come to depend on smoking in these situations, but it almost goes without saying that the dependence is all in the mind.

The belief that your life needs cigarettes is dealt with in Chapter 9.

☐ **So Why Are You Dependent?**

This is a big question. If the reason you cannot come off tobacco is addiction and dependence, and if dependence means it is all in the mind, why can't you change your mind? Wouldn't this solve half the problem? The answer is that the addiction won't let you.

☐ **Exercise**

Imagine you have some habit that fits very roughly with smoking. Let's take chewing gum. You might say:

I enjoy gum
I like to hand gum round in company
I chew gum when I'm bored
I allow myself gum as a reward
I like to chew gum after a meal
Chewing gum can help me relax

Some years ago, it became known that a substance which people were in the habit of using every day was the cause of a massive amount of sickness and death. Just imagine that that substance was gum, and it was killing three hundred people a day, a lot of them children.

Is it conceivable that for most users the benefits of chewing gum would outweigh the danger? Would gum chewers say, 'I really want to stop but I can't, because I always chew gum after a meal. Don't remind me that it's going to shorten my life.'?

Naturally, in these circumstances chewing gum would be banned by the government, because there would be no profit for them in it. Either that or they would tax it, and if they taxed it so that it cost £1400 a year to chew gum most people would stop buying it anyway because, frankly, no-one needs to chew gum *that* much.

And that is the point. No-one *needs* to chew gum. They can have all the same habits with gum as with tobacco, and all the same associations with pleasure. What they do not have is the *need*. And there is only one thing that makes people need tobacco. Addiction.

☐ In That Case Why Does Dependence Keep You Smoking?

On its own it would seem that no matter how psychologically dependent you were on smoking, you would be able to overcome it. This raises two questions to which we must find answers:

- Why can't you overcome psychological dependence on smoking?
- Why don't you become psychologically dependent on other things?

The reason these two questions go together is that the answer to the second gives us the answer to the first.

I said earlier that some people become dependent to the point of obsession on watching football. But even this dependence is nothing like dependence on smoking. No other dependence, even dependence on gambling, is like dependence on smoking. The reason is one of stunning importance; there is nothing else you do which involves an addictive substance that makes you psychologically dependent.

(The exception (apart from illegal drugs) is alcohol, which is an addictive substance that makes its users psychologically dependent in the same way, but I don't want to discuss tobacco and alcohol together because there are important differences.)

That is why you cannot overcome the psychological dependence on smoking - or, more accurately, that is why you become dependent on smoking in the first place.

This leaves one more question:

- Why does an addictive substance make users psychologically dependent, if the two are not connected?

Well, they are not exactly connected, because they have different roots, but they do influence each other. They form a defensive circle, but also a vicious circle: a defensive circle because they protect each other, and a vicious circle because they can only satisfactorily be beaten if they are separated, and this is not easy.

Within a week of starting to smoke seriously, you are addicted - your brain is then prepared to fight to maintain your adaptation to the poison. It is perfectly natural that your perception of the addiction will be that you need the addictive substance (which you really do). Where this becomes a problem is when you are no longer addicted - but you still believe you are. The addiction will have gone, even without medical treatment, within a week, but it is quite unrealistic to expect the mind (as opposed to the brain) to recognise this fact in such a short time.

The psychological dependence on smoking takes a lot longer to get over than dependence on anything else, because of the addiction. The addiction plants in your mind a very powerful message that you must smoke. Even when that message is no longer valid, the memory of the message remains, and it is a message of fear.

☐ Addiction, Dependence - and Motivation

Now we have come full circle, because we have said that anyone who wants to stop smoking enough will do so. They will overcome the withdrawal symptoms until the addiction is dead. They will work through the dependence until they are in control. But they will only do these things if they want to do so *enough*.

But what does 'enough' mean? What is enough for one person will not be enough for another. You have your own specific Addiction Level, your own dependence issues, each with its own degree of severity, and your own motivation level. So what you actually have is a three-sided problem:

If you had enough motivation, the addiction and dependence would not matter so much. If you were less dependent, you would need less motivation. If you were not addicted, you would not be dependent. And so on.

It is very difficult to assess motivation. You should already have done The One-Minute Motivation Test on page 3 / 3, so you can see that motivation is profoundly affected by ability.

Once you have read this book with all the enthusiasm with which I have written it, you will be in a very strong position to tackle your psychological dependence. Once you have done that, at least enough to put yourself in control, you can tackle the addiction. At that point you can see you would have little difficulty stopping smoking; but you have got to get to that point.

In our clinics we cheat. We control the addiction clinically, and this has the most remarkable effect; it motivates people to stop smoking. Those who come to us for the right reasons seriously want to stop but cannot because they are addicted, and because the psychological dependence is too great. They have failed to stop before, and they are fed up, resentful, angry and hostile. They have enough motivation to come to us for help, but they are almost daring us to fail them (which we don't, because we don't know the meaning of the word).

So our patients are in control of the addiction from the first day of their programme. The next morning they can wake up and not need to smoke, and starting the day without a cigarette is a marvellous incentive to go on. You almost certainly smoked first thing this morning, so you do not have this advantage. That is why, if you try to stop smoking on your own, you should always address the psychological issues first, and resolve them to the best of your ability, before facing the challenge of withdrawal.

HABIT
The Short Explanation

8

Drug taking is always referred to as habit. But the word habit is also used to refer to the things you do that are frankly not very significant or important. So people use the word to talk about unimportant little things that they do, and drug taking as well.

With hard drugs, like heroin, people use the word habit and do **not** think it means something insignificant. Heroin is serious. But people also use the word habit in association with tobacco.

So we have a single word used for hard drugs, soft drugs, and unimportant little things we do without thinking. Using one word for three very different things is odd, and it also has an effect on the way we see the things we use the word habit to describe.

You might think that if people use the word habit for heroin, they would take tobacco to be just as serious. You might, on the other hand, think that if people use habit in association with unimportant little things they do, they would attach the label 'unimportant' and 'little' to tobacco smoking.

Clearly, the latter is true. Strangely, smoking tobacco is seen as a small matter. We can demonstrate this quite easily. Smokers will say it is 'just' a habit. Can you imagine a heroin user saying injecting heroin is 'just' a habit? That little word, 'just', is the key to society's view of this drug that you are on.

If heroin is a habit, and tobacco is 'just' a habit, clearly tobacco is not to be taken seriously. Do think about this, because this little word colours the way you look at smoking.

And if you look at smoking as 'just' a habit, you have misunderstood it.

You might think that I am going to say that smoking is not 'just' a habit. Wrong. I am going to say that habit has nothing whatever to do with smoking. Surprised? People are in the habit of doing lots of things. Some of them are quite insignificant, some (like biting their nails) are more important and some (like drug use) are life issues.

What this says is that the word 'habit' does not actually describe what the person does in any useful way. What using the word 'habit' does then is to attach insignificance to the word it is trying to describe. So it is the wrong word to describe drug taking. As long as you go along thinking that smoking tobacco is 'just a habit' you are completely misunderstanding your problem.

You can prove this to yourself. If you are really serious about stopping smoking, perhaps because you have a major health problem, or money or social issues are very important, and yet you can't understand why you can't stop, because after all, it's just a habit, how can the words 'just' or 'habit' possibly be relevant to your problem? No-one dies of lung cancer because they 'just' anything. There is no 'habit' in the world lethal enough.

And here are two practical tests you can do to find out whether habit is the reason you can't stop smoking.

First, write down a list of your habits. (If some of them aren't very nice, do this privately.) Now tick any of those habits that you would have difficulty breaking if, say your GP told you it was life-threatening. My guess is that you won't be ticking anything. Which leaves you wondering why smoking is a 'habit' like no other. Here is the answer. Go back to your list of habits, and now tick any that involve an addictive drug. If you are unable to do this for any habit other than smoking, the answer would seem to be that it is the addictive nature of the drug, not the habit of smoking it, that is your problem.

Now here is the second, and definitive test. How do you define habit? It is something you do automatically. You know what this means - you light a cigarette when you've finished a job, or when you make a phone call, or when you sit down and put the TV on. You're not lighting it because you need to, but because, well, you always do - it's just a habit.

If your contention is that habit makes you keep smoking, let's test that contention. To smoke out of habit, cigarettes have to be readily available, i.e. you must have some at home.

Well, don't. Throw them away. Clear the house, even the car, of cigarettes completely. Now you have made it impossible to smoke out of habit. Your habit problem is resolved. You can now stop smoking.

As you sit their with your mouth open, I know what you're thinking. You're thinking you would go down to the corner shop, or the all-night garage if necessary, and get some. So I'm wrong and you are right. Come on, how likely is that? Who gets paid for writing books on this subject?

If you go out and buy some, particularly if it's late at night, this is not habit, not in a million years. It is need. Habit, remember, means picking one up without thinking. Getting the car out on a rainy night, when normal people are watching the National Lottery results, requires a lot of thinking. It's not habit, is it?

You buy cigarettes because you need them. And because you've got them, you smoke them, out of habit. So you can solve your habit problem quite easily, but that will not solve your smoking problem. Because habit is not the reason you smoke. That reason is need. And we have a word for need. It is addiction.

So what we can be quite sure about is that you are using the wrong word to describe the reason you can't stop smoking. And if you are using the wrong word, you are trying to solve the wrong problem. If you are trying to solve the wrong problem, you are missing the real problem. If you are missing the real problem, you are not going to succeed. Are you?

HABIT
The Long Explanation

8

☐ The Biggest Habit of All

A lot gets said about smoking as a habit: 'That filthy habit', 'Break the habit', and so on. Doesn't that strike you as odd? Obviously, any habit can be changed if there is a good reason. And most people accept that smoking kills. So if smoking is just a habit, why don't more people just stop doing it?

But smoking is not 'just' a habit. It involves a habit and an addiction. And it is a habit like no other human activity. The more you do something, the more likely it is to become habitual. You go to work, eat meals, clean your teeth, drink cups of tea or coffee and so on. You are in the habit of doing these things.

How does smoking compare as a habit-forming activity? The box overleaf compares smoking thirty cigarettes a day for twenty-five years with a number of other everyday activities.

No matter what activities you include, it is very hard to get them all to add up to the number of times you light a cigarette in the same timespan. That one habitual activity has been registered in your memory more times than every other habitual activity added together. It looks like a formidable habit to change. In fact, for smokers it is simply irrelevant.

Habit is defined as 'a behavioural pattern that has a degree of automatism', and what is fascinating about it is that it is exactly as hard or as easy to change as we make it. A machine can be programmed to repeat a function again and again, indefinitely, but it can also be switched off. Unlike you, a machine cannot become addicted. Some patients in our clinics think they will never change the habit; it is amazing to watch them discover that the habit is a pushover without the addiction.

30 x 365 x 25 = 273,750 cigarettes	cups of tea / coffee	54,750
	meals	27,375
	go to bed	9,125
If you add up every habitual activity of the past 25 years, they don't come to the same number as the cigarettes you've smoked. So you'd think cigarettes are a formidable habit to break - but they're not.	get up	9,125
	go to work	5,000
	feed the cat	18,250
	brush your teeth	18,250
	blow your nose	36,500
	wash the car	1,300
	Total	179,675

☐ Habit or Addiction?

There are two keys to changing a habit. The first is deciding to do it - really deciding to do it, not wishful thinking. Habits don't change themselves. Something you have done more than a quarter of a million times is going to be the simplest thing in the world to keep doing. The second key is addiction. And frankly you are up against it if you try to change a habit of doing something you are addicted to.

This is a major reason why so many people make a complete hash of their attempts to stop smoking. It is sad to see smokers making all that effort to change their routine so as to avoid the habit, only to wake up in the morning and simply have to smoke before they can get moving. And as long as you smoke because of the habit, you will also trigger the addiction, because each cigarette demands the next one.

So the addiction won't let you change the habit, and the habit won't give you a chance to overcome the addiction. You're in a bit of a mess.

There is only one way to change a habit - you just change it (sorry, no miracle here). However, there are two ways to break an addiction. You can neutralise it (which takes medical treatment), or you can ignore it, which is usually called cold-turkey (although where turkeys come into this is a mystery).

To come off tobacco successfully, you are going to have to tackle habit and addiction together. They are mutually supporting, but this does not mean they are the same thing. Addiction is a chemical response in the body, over which you have no control; habit is 'all in the mind'.

Don't let anyone try to fool you that addiction is 'all in the mind'. Addiction is in the central nervous system (for our purposes, the brain), a physical organ subject to the same influences as all the other organs in the body. It has to be fed, just like your stomach, and it can be physically damaged, just like your heart or lungs. This 'all in the mind' stuff is something made up by psychologists. You cannot change your addictive response by mind over matter.

Nicotine is a chemical. It has a chemical effect on your brain, and the human brain has no control over its own chemical status. The control you do have is in the mind, which is the data processing function of the physical organ called the brain. The brain is computer hardware, the mind is the software. They are separate but inter-dependent.

The effect of nicotine on the brain is like the effect of electricity on computer hardware. The program loaded into memory has no control over it, but is affected by it. Come what may, nicotine will affect your brain, and lack of nicotine will produce a withdrawal response. How you respond to that withdrawal will depend not on the hardware but on the software - your psychological conditioning, your emotional dependence and your willpower. All these things are in the mind; they are, ultimately, under your control.

But isn't it interesting that, when you look at the list of habits above (or a specific list of your own habits) none of them would be difficult to change? Is this because of the smaller number of times you do these things compared to the number of cigarettes you light? Certainly that is a major factor; but equally important at least is the fact that no-one ever became addicted to feeding the cat or washing the car.

That is because none of these activities has a chemical effect on the brain - they are non-addictive. You might think that eating is addictive for some people. This is not true; some people become psychologically dependent on eating, but that is quite different from addiction. And some people become addicted to certain foods (you might be surprised at how many foods are addictive) but they are not addicted to eating.

It is commonly believed that some people can get addicted to jogging. This is not strictly true. What they are doing is becoming addicted to the endorphins (a type of hormone) produced when jogging. These endorphins are first interpreted by the brain as a reward, and then addiction sets in, so the runner keeps running, not because running itself is addictive. It is the result of running, not running itself, that addicts.

Similarly, we could say that it is the result of smoking, not smoking itself, that is addictive. The lighting and smoking of cigarettes is a habit; the effect is addictive. You can become psychologically dependent on the activity, but the addiction is to the chemical effect on your brain.

In short, you are in the habit of smoking - but habit cannot be the reason you are unable to stop.

☐ Don't 'Break The Habit'

You might have noticed that I don't talk about 'breaking the habit'; I talk about 'changing habits'. Why is this?

If we say 'the habit', we are saying that smoking is the habit that makes you continue smoking. This is clearly nonsense. It is *a* habit, not *the* habit, no matter how deeply entrenched. It is one of the habits you have but (I hope) it is the only one that involves an addictive drug. Always refer to it as *a* habit, and you will keep it in its proper place.

More importantly, this is not about breaking a habit. It is about changing your habits. If you can change your smoking habits - without even stopping smoking - you will learn to take control. Coming off tobacco is entirely about taking control. If you can control *when* you smoke, you are well on the way to controlling *if* you smoke. If you can say, 'I am in the habit of smoking, now, after lunch, but I decide when I smoke - and today I decide not to, and I choose to leave it for another hour', you can control your desire to smoke. You will not use that control fully until you have dealt with the addiction and the other issues. But when you do use it, you will succeed.

SMOKING AND PLEASURE

The Short Explanation

Almost all smokers, when they are thinking of stopping, have at least a moment of regret - will life be as enjoyable without the pleasure of a cigarette? Some smokers worry so much about this that they simply cannot face going ahead. And of course, ask anyone who has no intention of coming off tobacco why not and they will probably say because they enjoy it too much.

There are two issues you need to think about. Is smoking as good as you think? And if it is, is it good enough to die for?

First, let us assume it really is as good as you think, in which case how good does a substance have to be to use it in the full knowledge that it will destroy your health? Either you are certifiably insane to even suggest that anything on Earth could be so good you would die for it, or you don't accept that it is really as bad as people make out, or you have no choice.

Let us assume for the moment that your mental health is in the normal range. Do you believe that tobacco smoking is harming you? If not, you would be unlikely to be reading this book, so I shall assume you accept the destructive nature of the substance. So what is left?

What is left is that you accept the damage it is doing in return for the pleasure it brings. In other words, yes you do believe it is worth dying for. But hold on. Put like that it doesn't make any sense does it? This still raises questions. Why would you think that smoking brings so much pleasure you are prepared to give up ten years of your life for it? And we still need to find out if it is as good as you think. (Yes, I will be coming to that.)

First, why does smoking a cigarette seem so great? In this short explanation, suffice it to say that this is a trick, and briefly this is how the trick works.

When you light a cigarette for the very first time, it tastes awful (unless you are adapted by passive smoking). It tastes awful because it is awful. That's quite reasonable. You force yourself to adapt to it, as we have seen in the chapter on addiction. Then you become addicted, which means you need to smoke to get the drug to stop yourself feeling the unpleasant symptoms of withdrawal.

It is hardly surprising that if you relieve the unpleasant symptoms of withdrawal, or even if you prevent them occurring, you are going to learn, after the first hundred thousand cigarettes, that smoking a cigarette is enjoyable. In fact, it is nothing more than the relief of displeasure (or the prevention of expected displeasure). That, in one sentence is why smoking seems to be enjoyable. Don't be surprised by this. Ask a heroin addict which is the worst moment in their day and which the best. The worst is immediately before they get a fix, and the best is immediately after.

It looks like smoking is in fact not as good as you think. It looks like you have sacrificed part of your life for a confidence trick. You have been taken for a ride. It's not your fault, because no-one explained it to you. But now you know, if you continue to tell yourself tobacco is worth dying for, you must take responsibility for the inevitable consequences.

So never again can you say the reason you can't stop smoking is because you enjoy it too much. Imagine you have decided to stop, say on January 1st. By January 2nd you are desperate. You would kill for a fag. You miss it so much, your resolutions are now in shreds.

But hold on. We have just learned (what am I talking about - you have just learned - I knew it already) that you didn't enjoy smoking when you were doing it. You were just drug taking, feeling unhappy if you didn't get your drug, and happy when you did. That must mean what you are feeling now is very unhappy because it has been a day or more since you had it. Be quite clear here. What you want is not the pleasure of smoking. It is an end to the displeasure of not smoking. The difference could save your life.

OK, so the displeasure is nasty, but that would be to ignore the important point, which is that the reason you want to smoke is not because you miss the pleasure. Now if that is the case, and it is, trust me, where do you go from here? You could go down to the shops and buy some cigarettes. Or you could face the truth. Whenever you come off tobacco you are going to miss it. You are supposed to; that is what the tobacco companies expect you to do.

If you satisfy the urge to smoke, it will be a relief. But it will also create the next urge to smoke. So what have you gained? Whereas, if you do not satisfy the urge, eventually it will go away. Don't take my word or it, ask anyone who has stopped smoking. Ask them, when they had an urge, but they ignored it, whether it stayed with them, perhaps for years. Ask them if they wake up each morning wanting to smoke. No, of course they don't, which means the best way to beat an urge is to ignore it, for the simple reason that it disappears.

I fully accept that this might not be easy or nice. But then lung cancer is not easy and it is not nice, so it's time to decide which you prefer.

SMOKING AND PLEASURE
The Long Explanation

Most smokers who want to stop admit they enjoy smoking. This is a terrible conflict; it would be bad enough trying to overcome an addiction to something unpleasant, but smoking is not unpleasant. Or is it?

Think back to the first time you ever smoked - probably an illicit cigarette when you were a teenager. The chances are, even now, that you remember thinking it was foul. It might have made you feel sick or dizzy; you will have coughed - the human throat was not designed to swallow the smoke from burning tar. However, you persevered, because you had a good reason for wanting to smoke. What started as an ordeal became bearable, and then it became pleasant (it didn't become necessary until somewhat later).

And now you enjoy smoking. What happened between the coughing and spluttering stage and the 'I enjoy smoking and I don't care if I do die of lung cancer, I've got to go sometime' stage? It is not habit. Habit is the *result* of continual smoking. It is addiction that is the *cause* of continual smoking. Habit will not lead you to believe in the enjoyment, but addiction does.

That is not to say that the enjoyment is a figment of your imagination produced by your addiction. Once learned, smoking really is enjoyable - or rather, the immediate result of smoking is enjoyable. The physical act of smoking in the sense of drawing poisonous gases through your throat into your lungs is not enjoyable - it is simply the mechanism by which the effect of nicotine can be enjoyed. But do it a quarter of a million times and the poor old brain is deluded into thinking it is the cigarette you are enjoying.

So what? You might well ask. Enjoyment is enjoyment. The point is this. You have learned to believe that the enjoyment you get from smoking comes from smoking itself. It does not; it comes from the drug contained in the cigarette. If you can get used to the idea of separating the activity from the result, you are on the the way to understanding how you stop enjoying smoking. And that is precisely what you are going to have to do.

We all know the old chestnut about enjoying not banging your head against a wall; as a statement it is obviously silly, but then the opposite is even sillier. What it means is that not until you stop banging your head against a wall do you appreciate how comfortable *not* banging you head against a wall can be. Similarly, while you are a smoker you have no idea how good being a non-smoker can be. It is just possible that if you stopped you would suddenly realise that, whilst you thought you enjoyed it, not doing it is actually ten times better.

☐ Some Cigarettes Are Better Than Others

Think about the cigarettes you smoke through the day. Do you enjoy *all* of them? Probably not. As you go through a day's smoking make a list of those you particularly enjoy, those you quite enjoy, and those you just smoke but don't know why.

And now answer this question. Do you enjoy smoking, or do you enjoy smoking sometimes? The chances are that you really enjoy smoking sometimes, and those times are likely to include:

- First thing in the morning
- With a drink

- In a social setting
- After a meal
- Relaxing after a hard day

Now if you enjoy smoking, say, after a meal, it is not actually smoking that you are enjoying but smoking after a meal. In other words, the meal is an important element on the enjoyment of that particular cigarette. Take the meal away, and it is not your after-dinner cigarette but just any old cigarette.

The idea is to split the enjoyment into its real causes. To do so, you need to understand exactly what it is you are enjoying.

Look at it like this. You might currently say you enjoy smoking after a meal. Imagine that your meals consisted of no more than dried pellets taken in a space capsule whizzing round the Earth. Do you think such a meal would trigger the desire to smoke? Almost certainly not (of course space capsules are no-smoking areas, but you take the point).

So now you have to face up to the fact that it is not actually smoking you enjoy, but that something triggers you to smoke, and your response - smoking - is enjoyed. That trigger could be any of the events we just mentioned, like a meal. Let's look now at each of them, try to understand why they are triggers, and why enjoyment is the result of your response to the trigger.

☐ First Thing in The Morning

In our clinics we often ask people which part of their smoking 'habit' they are going to find hardest to break. Typically they say it is the first one in the morning.

There is a lot of misunderstanding about this first cigarette of the day. The reason you enjoy it so much is not habit (habit, almost by definition, does not actually produce pleasure because it is something you do automatically). Neither do you wake up and think, 'You know, what I would really enjoy now is a cigarette'. You smoke that first one because the level of nicotine in your body has dropped so drastically that you need to top it up, and quickly. So that first one of the day can be crossed off our list of enjoyment cigarettes.

☐ With a Drink

Most smokers agree that when they have glass in one hand, they have a strong need for a cigarette in the other. Perhaps this cigarette really is enjoyed. But then perhaps not.

Question - does the cigarette make the drink more enjoyable, or does the drink make the cigarette more enjoyable? Do the drink and the cigarette make the company more enjoyable, or does the company make the drink and the cigarette more enjoyable?

It's very unlikely that you can answer this question. But it will help if, next time you are in a social setting and people are standing around drinking, you take a look at those who are smoking, and then at those who are not. (If you are caught out staring at an attractive member of the opposite sex, just say you are conducting important research.)

Are the drinkers who are smoking enjoying themselves more than the drinkers who are not? Conversely, are those who are not smoking enjoying themselves less than those who are? It is highly unlikely that you will be able to detect the slightest difference.

The reason you enjoy a cigarette with a drink is that you associate the two. And the reason you associate the two is habit. People in pubs smoke. You smoke in the pub. Therefore you enjoy yourself more when you smoke in the pub. And now you are in the habit of smoking in the pub, and you enjoy yourself in the pub, so you must enjoy a cigarette when you're having a drink.

It's somehow logical, but this doesn't make it any more sensible. The fact is, a cigarette is no more enjoyable with a drink than at any other time. It seems as though it is - but that is just the effect of brainwashing. Now that you know it isn't really true, you can start to work on breaking the association. You have got to convince yourself that you can enjoy a drink without a cigarette.

There is no special trick; the important thing is to keep reminding yourself that it is only a habitual association - not an association you are forced to keep making. There is no real connection between drinking and smoking, other than that you remember you have always done it. So this is a habit, not a real need, and habits can be changed.

The main reason people fail to change their habits is that they believe the habit controls them - they refuse to accept responsibility for changing the habit, because it isn't easy. Ask yourself if you accept responsibility for changing the habit. Or are you letting the habit control you because it is easier than taking control? If you are really honest with yourself, you will probably have to admit that you have tended to take the easy option. Now you have to take control. After all, you want to be a non-smoker, don't you? So why would you want to smoke?

☐ In a Social Setting

A large part of the enjoyment of smoking in a social setting comes from the association between smoking and drinking, which we have just demolished.

Another part is the fact that other people are smoking. Of

course, a lot of them will not be smoking, because social settings are increasingly less smoky than they used to be.

But there will probably still be enough people smoking to remind you that you would enjoy a cigarette.

Why do you enjoy a cigarette more when other people are smoking? Probably for two reasons. The first is that we are herd animals; we like to do what other people are doing. You could argue that, since the majority are *not* smoking, the herd instinct should make us copy them instead. But not doing something is never going to inspire as much imitation as doing something. So seeing people around you smoking is naturally going to encourage you to smoke.

The second reason is more interesting. You are a smoker, and you need to smoke at regular intervals because you are addicted to nicotine. It takes very little indeed to trigger the desire for a cigarette, because there is an underlying desire all the time. The slightest thing will make you light up, and being with other smokers is ample.

I started by saying that you enjoy smoking in company, but perhaps what I am saying is that this is not actually the reason you smoke in company. You need nicotine, you receive a trigger (other users), you respond to the trigger. There are two stages in overcoming this trigger, or enjoyment as you have been calling it. In the short term you stop exposing yourself to the trigger - for as long as possible you stop socialising with smokers. (You might feel this is too high a price to pay - in which case you are wasting your time trying to stop smoking, and you might as well give this book to someone who will make better use of it.)

Having removed the immediate trigger and given yourself some breathing space, the next task is to undo the brainwashing. Read this section again, and really understand this issue. You used to think you enjoyed smoking in company, and this turned out to be a myth, didn't it? You could continue to 'enjoy' smoking, but why would you?

After all, you want to be a non-smoker, don't you? So why would you want to smoke?

☐ After a Meal

The reason you want to smoke after a meal is mostly the same as the reason you want to smoke with a drink. It has become a habit.

But for many smokers there is another reason, too. Apart from those people who have to smoke during a meal itself, most smokers are going without nicotine for perhaps half an hour, an hour or even longer. The nicotine level in the body drops considerably in an hour. If you smoke twenty a day, your body is used to getting a fix roughly once or twice an hour. If you don't smoke - whether it is because you are in a non-smoking environment or because you are eating - you will certainly be ready for one as soon as possible.

What we have here, therefore, is both habit and need. You will have to work backwards on this, because you had a need first (lack of nicotine), so you smoked after meals; and you developed a habit as a result. The habit will need to be undone first, in the same way as your association between drinking and smoking. You have to learn to take control, because habit is always within your control, and that is one of the most important lessons you are going to have to learn.

An easy way to control this particular habit is simply to extend the time between finishing your meal and smoking. Leave it just half an hour. What you find is a strong urge to smoke, because of the habit, but satisfaction when you finally light up.

Habits are never really *broken*. You could say they are always replaced, because if you change your habits you are actually creating new ones. For example, *not* smoking after a meal is a habit.

So replace your habit with a new habit. If nothing else, this demonstrates that you can do whatever you want, because habit is always under your control. This will leave you with the original problem - if you don't smoke for an hour, your body is going to start asking you to.

This is addiction, which is dealt with in Chapter 6. All I want to say here is that this is the time to stop believing the myth about having to smoke after a meal. You could, of course, give in to the habit, and let it control you. You could have just one at that time, because that is the one you really enjoy. Or you could take control.

After all, you want to be a non-smoker, don't you? So why would you want to smoke?

☐ Relaxing After a Hard Day

Have you ever experienced that special pleasure of smoking a cigarette after a long day at work, or after finishing a particularly difficult task, or simply after struggling home from the supermarket? Probably thousands of times.

This is the pleasure of reward, and it is quite normal to reward ourselves in these circumstances. Tobacco, however, gives us a unique kind or reward, although alcohol is similar. The main difference is that for most people intake of alcohol is restricted by time of day and frequency. But there is no limit to when or how often you can reward yourself with a cigarette.

Yet again we have to break down this particular use, as we did with after-dinner smoking and smoking with a drink. And as with this, not only do you have a reason for smoking in this way, but you have become used to doing it. You needed or wanted to smoke as a reward, you got used to getting the reward - in other words, you created the habit.

So, yet again, the way out of this situation is gradually to change your habit. You are in the habit of rewarding yourself with a cigarette when you finish a job, so the first step is a small change - leave the cigarette half an hour, so you are still getting your fix, but you are breaking the close association between effort and reward.

Surprising as it may seem, this association is not entirely psychological. There are two potential physical reasons why smoking is used as a reward.

The first is that nicotine is a psychoactive drug - a narcotic; you could almost call it a 'recreational' drug. Particularly after expending mental energy, nicotine can give you a lift. Curiously, if the expenditure of energy has left you mentally stressed, nicotine can do the opposite by tranquillising you, depending on how you use it.

Whichever of these two uses applies to you, you will get a direct and rapid chemical effect from a cigarette, and this 'pleasure' is a very obvious reward. You will be conditioned to expect that 'pleasure' when you feel you need a reward, rather like a laboratory animal is conditioned to get a reward for performing the task desired by an experimenter.

The second kind of physical reward comes because, if you have been engaged in some task during which you cannot smoke, you will have started to withdraw from nicotine. Remember, your body is used to getting its fix at least once an hour if you smoke twenty a day, so when a job is finished it will be looking for nicotine. This is not the sort of withdrawal experienced when you actually try to stop smoking; it is very low-level withdrawal which you do not notice consciously, but which keeps you smoking all day, every day.

Getting that fix is simply going to be interpreted in your brain as reward. In crude terms, abstention equals craving, unsatisfied craving equals withdrawal, withdrawal demands fix, fix stops withdrawal, and the brain interprets the end of withdrawal as pleasure.

☐ What All This Means

What we have been doing so far in this chapter is to look at what you yourself describe as the enjoyment of smoking. You might say that you enjoy smoking generally but this is true of very few smokers. Most would have to admit that they enjoy smoking more at some times than at others. As soon as they say this, they have to realise that their enjoyment depends on the situation, not just the cigarette. Those situations fall into just two categories.

The first category consists of the situations we have been looking at so far, which are typically first thing in the morning, with a drink, in a social setting, after a meal, and relaxing after a hard day. In each of these cases it is the situation which partly creates the enjoyment. Remove the situation and, by your own admission, you remove the enjoyment.

To stop smoking you need to undo the concept of enjoyment. To achieve this, you must recognise the 'enjoyment' situations and do something constructive about altering them.

In the second category there are times when you enjoy a cigarette, and yet you could not say the enjoyment is situation-dependent. The best example is of course the first one in the morning. As we have just seen, this is not enjoyment in the same sense at all. It is need. You need to smoke, and you enjoy the satisfaction of that need.

At other times during the day you just enjoy a smoke. In each of these cases, if you really analyse it, you will find that what you are doing is satisfying a need. By doing so you are, in a way, creating enjoyment. However, it is not enjoyment in the sense of hearing a beautiful piece of music, spending a weekend in Paris, or even consuming a hot salt-beef sandwich. Remember, the delivery method of this enjoyment is burning tar smoke down your throat - something you found awful the first time you tried it. So it is, by definition, not enjoyable. The enjoyment is something you have come to believe in for a number of reasons, none of them connected with burning tar smoke down your throat.

So what are these needs that smoking satisfies, and then makes you believe it is enjoyable?

The first is obviously addiction to nicotine. And while you are addicted to any substance you will always interpret the satisfaction of your addiction as pleasure, regardless of the reality of the delivery method.

Then there is stress. Smoking is used universally to alleviate stress. Within seconds of getting a shot of nicotine, you are more relaxed. So potent is this effect that the interpretation of it as enjoyment is inevitable. The nicotine tranquillises, and tranquillity has to be felt as enjoyment.

There are other needs that smoking satisfies which might be specific to you, but these two, addiction and stress, cover most of them. The important question for you now is this: are these real needs which smoking satisfies, or have you created them yourself? Or even worse, has smoking itself created the needs? The short answer is that non-smokers don't have the needs - at least they don't have needs that only smoking can satisfy - so we have to come to the unfortunate but inevitable conclusion that these needs are created because you smoke. You thought that smoking was fulfilling your needs, instead of which it turns out that smoking is creating the needs and then fulfilling them. And what's more, they are needs that non-smokers don't have, and so don't have to bother fulfilling. Crafty, isn't it?

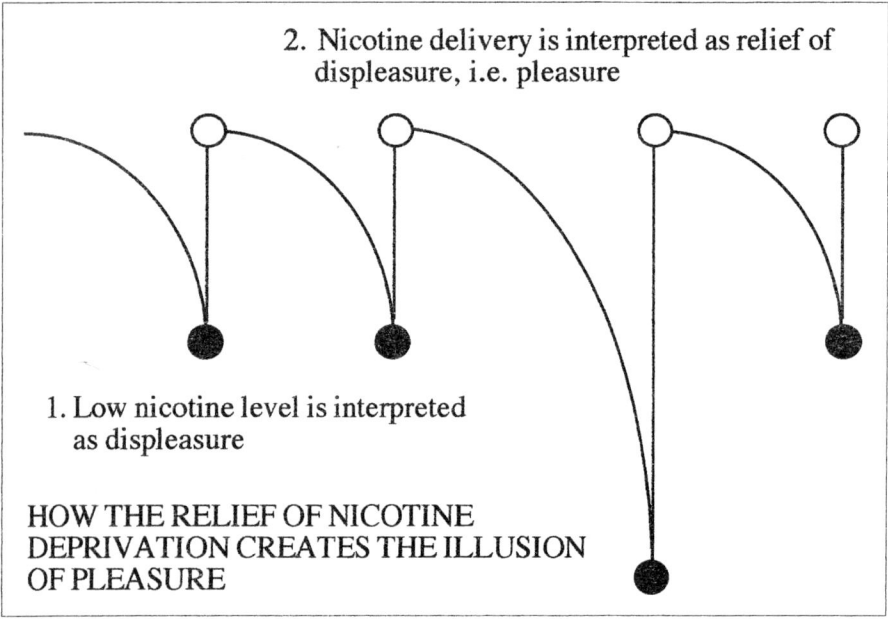

And to go back to our earlier point, by satisfying these needs you are interpreting smoking as enjoyable. So you started smoking, then you developed needs which only smoking could satisfy, then you came to believe that the enjoyment which resulted from satisfying these needs stops you stopping smoking.

Most users say they enjoy smoking, and we have seen that, whatever the reasons, this is true. But what we have also seen is that it is smoking which creates the situation where you don't want to give up the enjoyment.

At this stage ask yourself a very important and rather interesting question. Do non-smokers enjoy themselves? Of course they do. To say that all smokers enjoy their lives more than non-smokers do would be nonsense. And yet there are millions of smokers saying they cannot stop because they enjoy it. That is not the reason at all.

If users admit that they know smoking is likely to make them ill and shorten their lives, they need a much stronger reason for continuing than enjoyment. Yes, they enjoy it in a way, but the 'enjoyment' is not the reason they cannot stop. They think it is, but they are mistaken. If life is as enjoyable for non-smokers as for smokers - and it is almost certainly *more* enjoyable because they are healthier and wealthier - the reason 'enjoyment' stops smokers stopping is that what is interpreted as enjoyment is not actually an obstacle but an excuse. Genuine though the enjoyment might be for you, why do you need to use it as a reason for not being able to stop smoking?

Because you have to continue smoking. Because you are addicted. Because you have no other means for dealing with stress. And because you are therefore psychologically dependent. What you are not, however, is dependent on the enjoyment, so stop using it as an excuse right now.

Two-Minute Enjoyment Test

To find out whether you enjoy smoking, buy a brand you never normally smoke, with a similar tar / nicotine content. If you don't enjoy it, it is not *smoking* you enjoy. Your enjoyment is drug-specific - even brand specific.

FEAR

The Short Explanation

Smokers have three fears that non-smokers don't have. They are afraid of what smoking is doing to them, they are afraid of stopping, and they are afraid of failing to stop.

Remember that non-smokers don't have any of these fears. So, before we even start to look at these fears and what you might do about them, you must accept that people who don't use tobacco simply don't have them. You, the user, are carrying a psychological burden that non-users don't have.

But back to the fear. The first one - what smoking is doing to you, will not stop you stopping, so I am going to ignore it. If anything, it should motivate you to stop.

■ The Fear of Success

This means being anxious about living the rest of your life without ever smoking again. Some people, when they stop, don't have this fear - they just look forward to not needing tobacco. But I am going to assume that you, the reader, do feel some anxiety about a life without cigarettes. (If you don't, you're excused this section.)

First, let's look at the rationality of worrying about never smoking again. Ask someone who has never smoked, whether they worry about never smoking. They will say no, why would they? So clearly, this fear can only occur in smokers. But check that by asking an ex-smoker if they worry about never smoking again. They will almost certainly say no, so now you have a problem.

Apparently, once you have come off tobacco, the rest of your life without it looks OK. So it's only people currently on it who worry about coming off it. What does this tell you? That if you come off it, you will stop worrying about not using it. It's brutal, but it's logical.

The fear of living without tobacco is in fact the most dangerous thing tobacco does to its users. This is true psychological dependence. It is a major reason why people do not even want to come off tobacco, and it causes very many people to fail to stop smoking. This fear is caused directly by the addiction to nicotine, and it is the relationship between the addiction and the dependence it causes that we at NHA Research spend so much of our time studying, because it is the key to stopping people smoking (once you have control over their addiction). Sadly, this relationship receives no research funding whatever from the British government or the European Commission.

■ The Fear of Failure

One of the major reasons people do not want to stop smoking is not because they want to smoke, but because they don't think they can stop. We know this is true from our own research, because we have asked people who say they don't want to stop, if they have ever tried, and very many of them have. So they have wanted to stop before, and they have failed. They might have just changed their minds but this seems unlikely. Therefore it is the belief that they cannot succeed that determines whether they want to do it again. In other words, they want to be non-smokers, but they don't want to go through the process of stopping. Not because it's hard (after all, we're only talking about a short while) but because they don't believe in their ability to succeed.

It can be supposed that most people therefore approach stopping with a fear that they are going to fail. And what happens is they experience some difficulty, a day or a week after the last cigarette, and they think, "I knew I couldn't do it, I'm failing" and that is precisely what they do - they fail. Second attempts at stopping smoking are a bit like second marriages, they are easier to fail than the first one.

What we have so far is that an awful lot of people fail to stop smoking because they believe in failure. They are afraid of it, so it happens. But hold on. What would happen if they didn't believe in it? Aha, you say, that's a good psychological trick if you can manage it. Well this is how you do it. Every day you don't smoke a cigarette, you are succeeding. Now for the first four days you might suffer horrible withdrawal symptoms (unless you are on A.N.T.), but they can only last for four days (medical fact) so would it be worth four days of misery for a chance to break the addiction to nicotine? If it would, good. Having lasted four days, you are clearly succeeding, not failing. And you have proved something very important. You have proved that you can come off the most addictive drug on Earth. All right, you might start smoking again, but that can never alter the fact that you beat a drug that is so addictive that 120,000 people in this country die for it each year.

Now you have proved you can succeed. Not necessarily that you can succeed in stopping smoking altogether, but that you are a person who can take on a difficult job and succeed. Now we know what sort of person you are, we can see that you can succeed at anything, providing it's reasonable. And for someone who has not smoked for four days, and is therefore not addicted to nicotine, to carry on not smoking is actually entirely reasonable.

Look, of course I accept that you might not be able to stop

for the four days. Perhaps the withdrawal symptoms will beat you. But that doesn't mean you are a failure, it just means you don't have the means to solve the problem, which is something different. But do me a favour, and at least try. (What am I talking about, do me a favour - do yourself a favour!)

FEAR

The Long Explanation

☐ The Fear of Success

Imagine you are visiting a strange and remote country. One day you are in the city's main square and you witness a demonstration against the government. Unwittingly you get swept along and, when the paramilitary police intervene, you find yourself slung unceremoniously into a van with the arrested demonstrators.

You are taken to an ominous castle where you are thrown, on your own, into a damp dark stone cell. There is no window and no light. You are in a state of complete shock and fear. You don't know where you are and, what is worse, neither does anyone who might rescue you. You don't feel optimistic.

After some time (you can't see your watch) a small hatch opens and a food tray is passed through. You eat in the dark, which is just as well. And you wait.

After another indeterminate interval there is suddenly a bright light (the cell door has opened) and framed by the light is the large figure of a man. He promptly beats the living daylights out of you. The light goes off (the door closes) and you are left in a sodden terrified heap on the floor.

To cut a long story short, at some later time the door opens again, the man comes in and beats you up again. And this happens with horrible regularity. Your body clock tells you it's happening once every day. And it goes on for weeks, then months. You have by now lost all hope of ever being rescued or released. You cannot imagine anything but this.

But one day (or so you assume - there's no window, remember) he doesn't come. Perhaps he's just delayed, but no, he really doesn't come. Unbeknown to you, his grandmother has died and he's gone to the funeral.

How do you think you would feel when you realise he's not coming? Relieved, or scared? Perhaps this time it's a firing squad. What is worse, the certainty of being beaten up, or the uncertainty?

The next day, there you are, scared, and suddenly the door is flung open, the bright light blinds you, and your old friend (?) is there. Are you scared, or relieved? I think when he didn't turn up you were scared, and when he does you are relieved. When you are being beaten up, at least you know where you are.

What has all this to do with smoking? Everything. When you try your first cigarette, it's a bit like being beaten up. By the time an opportunity comes to escape from the prison (of tobacco abuse) you are scared of not being beaten up.

Let's take another analogy, less painful but still involving prison (I like talking about prisons in association with smoking). One sunny day you are walking along, and you happen to come to the local prison. Standing in the doorway there is a man (or woman, as appropriate), with a tattered suitcase. He has obviously just been released.

Being in one of those strange moods, you approach him and strike up a conversation. He tells you his story; "I've been locked up for seven years. First I counted the years, then the months and weeks, then the days and today I've counted the hours. All I could think about was getting out. I even tried escaping, but they caught me and added a year to my sentence."

So, you wonder, what is the problem now? Why the hesitation? After seven years in prison he would be completely institutionalised. As much as he wanted to get out, he has no experience of life outside that he can remember. He wants to get out there, but he doesn't know what out there is like. Can you blame him for being afraid of the very thing he has wanted for so long? You know what the answer is - to go out there and learn what it is like. By experiencing it, he will stop being afraid of it.

That is why so many smokers are afraid of never smoking again. The average long-term user has no experience of adult life without tobacco. Think about that and it is quite unsurprising that so many users, despite wanting to stop, and despite repeated attempts to escape, are afraid of the very thing they seek.

And here's another little story, this time a true one. I am very short sighted. Without my glasses, I can't see far in front of my face. Years ago, I used to go swimming every week with colleagues. I love swimming, and am never happier than in water. So I went to the pool, but I couldn't dive. Why couldn't I dive? If you are also short-sighted, you will know the answer to this - I couldn't see the water. True, I could see an expanse of blue in front of me, but I could not judge exactly where it was.

Now this is silly, because of course logic told me where it was. But without my specs the water was just a blue haze. I knew where it was, and it wasn't far. I knew I wouldn't come to any harm if I dived into it. But being unable to judge exactly when I would hit the water, I couldn't make that leap of faith. I was afraid of the unknown, even though on the intellectual level I knew all there was to know about it.

But one day I just got angry about this. I told myself, "Brynin, you know it's there, just do it". Now you couldn't stop me. All those wasted years, not doing something because I was afraid of it, when there was nothing to be afraid of.

Ask anyone who is trying to stop smoking, if they are a little afraid of a life without cigarettes, and they will probably say yes. Ask anyone who has not smoked for the last six months if they are afraid of never smoking again, and they will say no. What is the difference? Simply that once you have done it you will realise there was nothing to be afraid of. You will wish you had done it sooner.

In our clinics we ask all our patients to do a deal with themselves. Because of the treatment our doctors provide, there will be no pain when they stop. The deal is to stop, not because they want to stop necessarily, but because they need experience of not smoking. I would ask you to do the same deal. Don't be afraid of something just because you have no experience of it, even though you know there are millions of people who have stopped smoking and who are perfectly happy not smoking. Stop first, then decide if not smoking is scary. You are only anxious about never smoking again because you currently smoke. So stop and find out what joining the rest of the human race is like.

Many people flick through a book and look at short passages enclosed in a box, just as you are reading this one perhaps. This box is here because I want to emphasise the single most important reason why people fail to stop smoking.

Many people say the worst part of stopping smoking is the psychological dependence (although they may not know precisely what this means). And many others say it is the addiction that's the real problem. In fact neither is true. The addiction on its own would not be enough to keep people smoking, because they would know that after a few days it would be over, so they would go through the pain willingly. And psychological dependence cannot occur until you are addicted. So the problem is in fact the relationship between addiction and dependence.

And the most significant element of the psychological dependence is without question the fear of living without tobacco. If you make someone physically dependent of anything, they will learn to be afraid of not having it. You are physically dependent on your mother as a baby, and she quickly becomes the person you love the most; and of course she then becomes the person you most fear losing. Anyone who has lived through a war with food rationing is likely to worry about having enough food in the house, even years later. If your body demands nicotine twenty or thirty times each day, your brain is going to become thoroughly conditioned to living with that need. Even the thought of not needing tobacco worries smokers.

Many, if not most, tobacco users do not know this has happened to them, but I promise you it is of the utmost importance. We see it in our clinics every day. We take people off the drug with a neutrogen, and some of them still cannot cope with the idea of not needing it. Time and time again a patient calls us the day after the clinic appointment and says they have no desire to smoke, and no withdrawal symptoms, but they show all the symptoms of fear.

That fear will sometimes overcome all rational thought, even though the patient does not know they are afraid. In these cases, a great deal of gentle support is necessary, but the first thing we have to do is show the patient that it is this fear that is causing the problem.

☐ The Fear of Failure

Our own patients can't fail our programme, because it's not a test. Similarly, why would you challenge yourself? That is what fear of failure is about, so don't.

Failing because you are afraid of failing is frankly silly. You will find all the answers to this issue later, in Chapter 18.

SMOKING AND STRESS

The Short Explanation

Stress is always quoted as the biggest single reason people return to smoking. Smoking is quoted by youngsters as necessary to get them through the stress of exams. It is quoted by people in high stress jobs as the way they cope. Poor people spend money on cigarettes because they say it is all they have.

Smoking does not, and cannot, make you less stressed. It makes you **more** stressed. Don't forget that with tobacco we are talking about the biggest confidence trick ever played on an innocent population; it is not hard to imagine therefore that the relationship between smoking and stress is entirely mythical.

You might at this point be thinking I don't know what I am talking about, because you have personal experience of smoking making you feel less stressed. Well, you could be right, I might not know what I am talking about, but that is frankly unlikely, because I am committing my reputation on these pages, so I probably have a good case, and I do.

If you really believe smoking makes you feel less stressed, do this little test. At this point you believe you are right, you know what you're talking about. You have years of experience with smoking and you know what you feel when you do it. You are a rational person, and you can tell right from wrong.

You also pay good money for a product known to kill 120,000 people a year. It says so on the pack. There is no question about it - it's true, and you still buy it. So at this point ask yourself whether there is just a chance that whatever you believe about tobacco might not be completely rational, that tobacco might actually be controlling the way you think.

Destroying the myth that smoking will help with stress is the most important thing you can do if you are going to remain a non-smoker once you have stopped. That is because, as I said above, stress is the main reason people start smoking again. If you thoroughly destroy the relationship in your mind, because for the first time you are completely clear on the fact that the relationship is a lie, you will never use stress as an excuse to smoke.

There are many many ways to relieve stress. Some involve drugs, and some don't. But a drug that kills 300 people a day has got to be the very worst way imaginable to do it. And given that it doesn't even work, you wonder how you could ever again do such a bizarre thing.

SMOKING AND STRESS
The Long Explanation

If stress makes you smoke, you are going to have to deal with it. So do it now.

There are two distinct ways to approach this subject.

The first is for you to get to work on stress. This is going to help you stay off cigarettes, and it is also going to help you live the rest of your life.

The second is for you to accept that no amount of smoking is going to make your life less stressful. Smoking simply does not help you deal with stress. On the other hand, it would be wrong to say that the help you believe you get from smoking is entirely an illusion. The help you have got over your smoking career has convinced you that you need to smoke to cope with life. This is psychological dependence.

When you were a small child you could not have imagined coping in the big wide world without your parents; unsurprisingly, you do. Don't allow yourself to believe that anything is essential for your survival, because nature made you perfectly capable of surviving with what you have.

When *homo sapiens* evolved it had all the biological means to survive in the world, and did so for tens of thousands of years without tobacco. You were not born a smoker, and it is fairly unlikely that you started smoking because of stress. So stress does not make you smoke - rather, you smoke because, if you did not, you would be stressed. This is entirely different and is, you will agree, a kind of dependence; you did not need to smoke for stress when you were a non-smoker, but you do now you are a smoker. Don't you find that rather suspicious? And a little sad?

☐ How You Develop Stress-Related Dependence

☐Stage 1

You are not stressed. You are smoking your usual amount, say one cigarette every fifty minutes. This is a natural rhythm which you have subconsciously established to keep you free of nicotine craving - every drug addict has a craving / relief cycle, even if they are not conscious of it. When your nicotine level drops, it triggers a signal to the brain to find more, and this is what you feel as a desire to smoke. That trigger is a stressor. It's not a major stressor, but what is important is that it is a frequent one. If you smoke twenty a day, that is twenty times each day you put your body under the same stress, and twenty times a day that you relieve it. The result is that you learn to relieve the stress of not smoking by smoking, but of course the only stress smoking can relieve is the stress of **not** smoking.

☐Stage 2

A stressor occurs. Assuming it is at least thirty minutes since your last shot of nicotine, a cigarette at this point makes you feel better, partly because your inhalation method is long (see page 11 / 7), which provides enough nicotine to have a narcotic effect, but also by relieving unrecognised craving. Your brain interprets this feeling better as stress relief - the stress would be even worse if you were also craving your drug.

Smoking also replaces up to fifteen percent of the oxygen in your brain with carbon monoxide, which will increase the deadening effect.

☐ Stage 3

If this process occurs frequently enough, you subconsciously learn to relieve stress by going through this craving / relief process. The more you do it, the more often you feel the benefit.

☐ Stage 4

Because you are now dependent on the process of relieving low-level craving to relieve stress, combined with the effect of the drug itself, you experience anxiety if the drug is not available when a stressor occurs. The only way out of this predicament is to adopt a new mechanism to replace nicotine.

No matter how old you are, you retain from childhood the need for someone or something to comfort you in times of stress. As a child it was your mother or a teddy bear. Now it is cigarettes. You grew up and no longer needed your mother. You can stop needing tobacco.

☐ Understanding Stress and Stressors

Stress is your response to stressors. Stressors are, in themselves, not harmful - at least not in the way you think of. When you learn to drive, you are stressed; this is the fear that you will do something wrong and crash. The fear itself is not harmful, but the crash would be; so, assuming you don't actually crash, the fear is worse than the actuality.

In this case stress is unnecessary. No-one has been hurt, but worrying about the possibility has caused stress. Of course there are times when stress is necessary, like perhaps when a close relative is seriously ill. Or perhaps not.

There is an old adage that worrying never solved anything, and it is true. You will naturally worry greatly in this situation, but will it help? In fact, not only will it not help but it will make matters worse, because the effects of stress on you will reduce your coping ability.

If by stress we mean *distress*, it can be seen that stress is always unhelpful and unnecessary. It doesn't help you to cope, and coping is what you need in the face of stressors. So, if stress is always a bad thing, why do we have a stress response at all? The answer goes back a hundred thousand years, when *Homo sapiens* lived in an entirely different world.

Sabre-tooth tigers and mammoths roamed the planet, and man had to compete for food; food was in fact man's greatest priority, and it still is in very primitive tribes who have a similar lifestyle to our prehistoric ancestors. Faced with a sudden threat of imminent death from something large and hairy, the only response was either to attack it or to run like hell. It is what is called the 'fight or flight response'. The body suddenly produces adrenalin, which stimulates the heart and raises blood pressure. The whole body, brain and all, works better and faster, ready to fight to the death or escape. When faced with a huge and hairy beast, it is an entirely appropriate response.

But when faced with a recalcitrant child, a gas bill or a car that doesn't start it is an entirely inappropriate response. Unfortunately our bodies don't know that we are living in the twenty-first century, because they haven't evolved fast enough. Evolution takes place over hundreds of thousands, or even millions, of years - much more slowly than lifestyle, which in the western world has developed immeasurably since the industrial revolution and again since the Second World War.

So far as our bodies are concerned, we are living in an alien world. People respond to twentieth-century situations as if they were cavemen because their adrenal glands have not developed since then. Most of our work in NHA Research is about the health implications of adaptation to modern life, from maladaptation to the poor quality of our food to the structural damage caused by asking our bodies to adapt to sitting in chairs, which we were not designed to do. Producing adrenalin all day to cope with frequent challenges of a minor nature is something we are not adapted to, because our adrenal glands were meant to cope with infrequent challenges of a life-threatening nature.

☐ Nicotine - Stressor or Sedative?

What is the relevance of all this to smoking? First, smoking has an effect on this stress mechanism. It raises blood sugar levels and promotes the production of adrenalin. In other words, it stimulates your stress response. But paradoxically it is also a narcotic - it slows brain activity. So it can both relax you and stimulate you. You can use nicotine in two opposite ways; a short puff on a cigarette will supply enough nicotine to the brain to stimulate it, but a long drag will have the desired narcotic effect. When you are tired, you will take short puffs, and when you are stressed you will take long drags, and you do this instinctively, without knowing you are doing it.

So you use your smoking, or more accurately your access to nicotine, to regulate your stress response. But you use it badly, because of the paradoxical nature of the drug; and because of the addictive nature of the drug you are now stuck with a dependence on it to control that very stress response. Because of this dependence, stopping smoking will actually reduce your ability to cope with stress in the short term. The critical point is that non-users cope with stress just as well as users, so you can be sure that, once that dependence is overcome, you will handle stress just as well as before.

In fact, without the additional stressors imposed by smoking when you are trying not to, you will be less stressed.

☐ Is Smoking The Best Way to Manage Stress?

As long ago as 1963, an internal memorandum from a tobacco company lawyer read, "We are, then, in the business of selling nicotine, an addictive drug effective in the release of stress". One of NHA Research's doctors is fond of telling patients that nicotine is such a good sedative that it would be prescribed were it not for the fact that it kills three hundred people a day.

Both of these statements are exaggerated but clearly, even if it has a therapeutic effect in some ways, nicotine is completely inappropriate as a tranquiliser. So you have to make a choice. If you want to stop smoking, you have to do two things:

Accept that no matter how good nicotine seems to have been for tranquilising you in the past, the cost grossly outweighs the benefits.

Find something better.

☐ Is There Something Better than Nicotine?

On the basis that nicotine comes packaged in tobacco, and tobacco is going to shorten your life, the answer has to be Yes. But let's forget that point for now, and look at the question in another way. Is there anything you could use that would help you to deal with with stress in the place of cigarettes?

First you must come to terms with a fundamental truth. You are habituated to using the drug you are addicted to for helping with stress. Nothing else is going to have the same appeal at this stage, and nothing else is going to work as well as long as your memory is searching for your drug. Nevertheless, if you really want to stop smoking, and stress makes you smoke, what choice do you have?

There are many drugs which will help you to cope with your life just as well as nicotine, if not better. Heroin will take your problems away, for example. You don't use heroin because it is a dangerous addictive drug. You use nicotine *despite* it being a dangerous addictive drug; the difference is that you are already addicted to nicotine, so it is your drug of choice, but it could just as easily have been heroin.

So somewhere out there there must be something (let's assume for the moment a drug) which will help you to cope with life. In all seriousness, look for something you can use instead of nicotine which will help. Put it this way; imagine you had never heard of tobacco, and you went to your GP for a tranquiliser. She offered you a prescription for a new drug called tobacco. You happened to ask if there were any side-effects, to which she replied:

'Some'.
'What do you mean, "Some"? Has anyone been made ill by it?'
'Yes, quite'.
'Quite ill, or quite a lot of people?'
'Both actually'.
'Well how ill? And how many people?'
'Very ill, I'm afraid'
'Don't tell me someone has died.'
'I'm afraid so, quite a few.'
'You mean you want me to use a drug that has killed people? How many people?'
'Well, in this country, about three hundred a day.'
'I beg your pardon?'

Bizarre, isn't it? The reason you use tobacco is not because it is an appropriate drug, but purely and simply because you are addicted to it. Even when the addiction is broken, you will remain psychologically dependent on it for stress management for years. There you have it. You actually believe that a drug that is going to shorten your life by ten or more years is a good way to handle stress. Almost any other drug would be better, although I assume you would choose one that is legal.

☐ Is There a Drug-Free Way to Handle Stress?

Of course there is, but everyone wants a quick fix. Narcotic drugs were used in the most primitive societies, and why not? There is still a general belief that tobacco is a reasonable way to handle stress, and given that you are dependent on it this makes it difficult for you to consider the alternatives.

If you accept that your aim is to be a non-smoker, you have no choice but to look for some other means to control your stress response. In our clinics we use two techniques, shiatsu and correct breathing.

☐ A Fatal Mistake

Stress is the most common reason for going back to tobacco. And yet built into this simple statement is a terrible error on the part of users. When under extreme stress you might smoke, despite everything you have learned from this book, but please read this next part very carefully, and keep it in mind always.

Because smoking a cigarette when you are not addicted will not relieve stress, the temptation will be to smoke another, because you remember it did used to help, and you have forgotten that you have to be addicted to nicotine to get stress relief from it. This is how stress gets people started again - read about it in detail in Chapter 14, so you will never fall for it again.

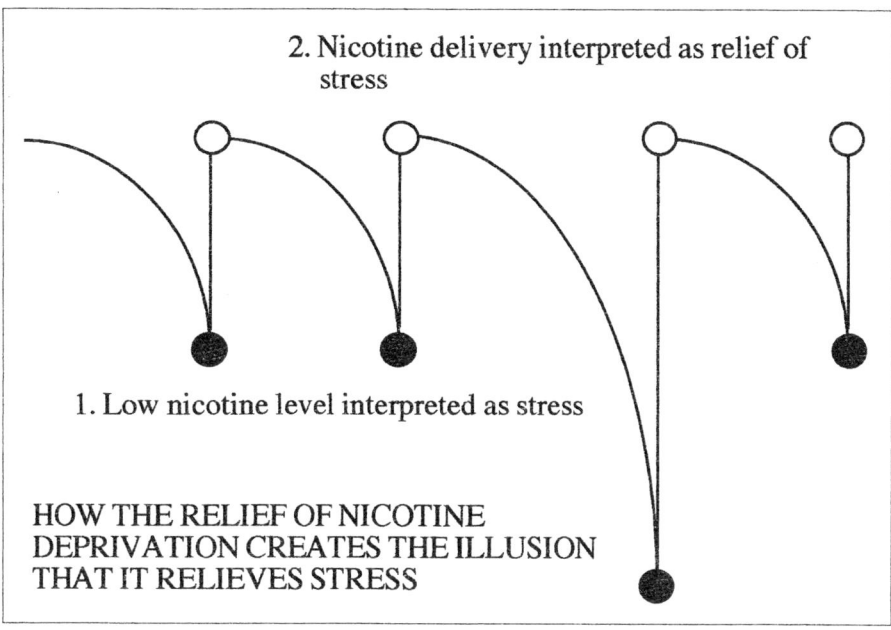

HOW THE RELIEF OF NICOTINE DEPRIVATION CREATES THE ILLUSION THAT IT RELIEVES STRESS

How Smoking Causes Stress

• Nicotine is a stimulant - it stimulates the production of adrenalin, putting the body under unnatural stress with every cigarette smoked.

• Tobacco is extremely poisonous, which is a major physical stressor. Every cigarette that is lit is a serious toxic assault on the body, which takes a toll over the years.

• Because the user has an addictive need for nicotine, putting out each cigarette puts the body under stress, until this is relieved by the next cigarette.

• Most users worry about smoking.

HOW TO STOP SMOKING
The Short Explanation

This chapter is not going to be what you expect. If you have read any other stop-smoking book, you are expecting The Robert Brynin Patent Method Of Stopping Smoking. There isn't one. In our clinics we do provide a programme, but it is a clinical programme, and you can't get medical treatment from a book.

There is no miracle way to stop smoking. But by the same token there is a way for everyone to do it. Which means that the way for you to stop is already out there; you just haven't found it yet. And probably it will involve more than one technique. The dumb way to try stopping is just to buy whatever is advertised. The clever way is to look at what your problems are, look at what the market is offering, and fit the two together.

Most people fail at least once, usually because they didn't do it right. Read this chapter and decide which approach is best for you. If you have any questions, call the NHA Helpline (01273 205196) or visit your nearest NHA StopShop for free advice.

You're not going to like the next bit. Before you decide which approach to take, you have to understand what your problems are. This will involve some work, and honest self-analysis. You could go to the chemist and pay for something that might or might not work, but isn't that an abdication of responsibility?

Isn't that using money to solve a problem, something it is notoriously bad at? Your first objective is to succeed. Your second objective is to succeed as cheaply as possible. So do the work.

■ A Real Stop-Smoking Programme

Everyone who tries to stop smoking, let's say with a particular method, uses just that method on its own. Well, this doesn't make a lot of sense. Why not put together your own stop-smoking programme, taking the best of a number of methods and combining them? For example, if your main issues are stress and habit, you could join a yoga class, and Chapter 8 of this book will explain to you how to deal with the habit issue. What is the point, if your problems are habit and stress, going to the chemist and buying a product that is supposed to wean you off nicotine (whether that is likely to happen or not), but has no bearing on habit and stress?

Or perhaps your main issue is social smoking. Acupuncture might help you control the urge to smoke when you're in the pub, but why not design yourself a programme of avoiding the pub and gradually reintroducing it when you are over the worst, combined with the acupuncture?

In our clinics we see lots of people who have used acupuncture, and lots of people who have used hypnotherapy. What we have never seen is someone who used acupuncture and hypnotherapy together. Well, why not? You might say, because it would cost too much. Is this true? Say you spent £100 on acupuncture, and it didn't work. Then you spent £100 on hypnotherapy, and that didn't work. So you spent £200 and got nowhere. But a serious analysis of your problems might reveal that you have a need for the psychological help provided by hypnotherapy and the stress relief provided by acupuncture, but they must be done at the same time. In this case, you would spend £200 and succeed. And if £200 is what you spend on smoking in 10 weeks, that is a small price to pay to save £1000 a year, let alone the cost to your health.

So spending money on help is not really the issue. The issue is spending it wisely.

For example, if you know from experience that you have dreadful withdrawal symptoms that seem to go on for weeks, you will learn from this book that that cannot be true. The withdrawal symptoms will last no more than four days. After that the symptoms are caused either psychologically, or by the detoxification process. So why not go away for the four days (or just lock yourself away at home, which is cheaper) in the certain knowledge that it is for four days only? Then you could put yourself on a serious detox regime of supplementation (see your local health food shop for advice), plus some serious exercise to sweat out the toxins. The exercise will make you feel tons better anyway.

So you can see how first analysing the issues you need to deal with, then putting together your own programme using the products and services available to you, is so much better than the simplistic approach of going and paying for something that is 'supposed to stop people smoking'.

But before you get too excited, the first stage is to do that analysis, with the help of the questionnaire in the white pages. Having done that, and read through the detailed answers that apply to you, the next stage is to look in detail at the different techniques explained in Chapter 15. Once you understand what your problems are, and also what each technique can and can't do, you select any one or more techniques, to construct a programme that is tailor-made and more likely to succeed than anything you've done yet.

HOW TO STOP SMOKING
The Long Explanation

Why Do Stop-Smoking Methods Fail?

They don't. They all work. If the method or methods you have tried did not work, it does not mean they don't work - didn't and don't are not the same thing. Use this chapter to learn more about your previous attempts and why they failed. But don't be put off trying to stop smoking just because the method you used was not right for you. It's not you who failed to stop smoking; it's the method that failed to help you.

WARNING: don't just buy stop-smoking products and services because they are on the market and are supposed to 'work'. That is why so many people fail, and it makes them jolly miserable and it makes the people who sell them a nice living. It's not immoral - because the things they sell work for some people. The mistake is on the part of the smoker. Look first at your problems - the problems you are trying to solve - then find out which techniques, or combination of techniques, is likely to help.

Now go through the following questions to find out why you have failed so far, and whether any given technique could be used better. And remember, think about designing your own programme with a combination of techniques. You will increase your chance of success enormously.

Question 1
Have you ever tried to stop smoking?
☐ No   Go to Question 2
☐ And failed   Go to Question 3
☐ And succeeded   Go to Question 6

Question 2
Why not?
☐ Never thought of it   Go to Box 1
☐ Never thought you could   Go to Box 1
☐ Kept putting it off   Go to Box 1

Question 3
What do you mean by failed?
☐ Did not stop at all (less than 1 day)   Go to Box 2
☐ Stopped for less than 4 days   Go to Box 3
☐ Stopped for 4 days or more   Go to Box 4

Question 4
Why do you fail (on your own)
☐ Irritability
☐ Physical symptoms
☐ Desperate craving
☐ Habit
☐ Stress (but not the stress of stopping smoking)
☐ Alcohol / relaxation
☐ Don't know

Each of these causes is addressed elsewhere in this book, so you should turn to the relevant chapters for the answers.

Question 5
Which of these products or services have you tried?
☐ Hypnotherapy   Go to Box 5
☐ Acupuncture   Go to Box 6
☐ NRPs (gum / patch / inhaler / spray)   Go to Box 7
☐ Group therapy (inc Allen Carr)   Go to Box 8

☐ Zyban   Go to Box 9

Question 6
Why did you start again?
☐ Stress
☐ Relaxation / alcohol
☐ Social pressure
☐ No particular reason

Each of these causes is addressed in Chapter 14.

BOX 1 WHY HAVEN'T YOU TRIED STOPPING?

The answer is almost certainly that you have. But you have not thought about it seriously. Why not? Probably because you didn't think you could, so you didn't address it seriously. Presumably you are reading this book because you now think you can stop, even if you are not sure how, so there is a change. Or perhaps this really is the first time you have thought seriously about stopping. Why? How can anyone use a drug with a death threat on the pack and not even think about coming off it?

This is not sarcasm; it's a real question. The answer is because the drug has such complete control over the user's mind that it takes a long time before they start to think objectively about it. So if ever you doubt your motivation to stop (or to stay stopped) remember the control the drug has, because in fact everyone who uses it does want to come off it; it just takes years for most people before they can break free enough to realise what tobacco has done to them.

BOX 2   YOU DIDN'T STOP AT ALL

Not only did the withdrawal symptoms probably defeat you, it looks like you panicked as soon as they started. Frankly, you have a lot of work to do, and I have to say the chance of you stopping smoking on your own is limited. Realistically, you should be looking for professional help. What form that help will take will depend on the result of your self-analysis. Now go to Question 4.

BOX 3   YOU STOPPED FOR LESS THAN FOUR DAYS

When you started smoking again you were still addicted, so you didn't get as far as dealing with your psychological issues, because you were still under physical pressure from the drug itself. You need to concentrate on methods of dealing with your withdrawal symptoms first, so read Chapter 6. Once you get past the first four days, you will know for sure that you are not addicted to nicotine, which is very important, because you realise at that point that you, not the drug, have control over your actions. Check this with Question 4.

BOX 4   YOU STOPPED FOR FOUR DAYS OR MORE

If you did not smoke for more than four days, you had overcome the addiction. You might not have thought you had, because perhaps you still wanted to smoke, but that is not the same thing. At that point your problem was psychological. If this is your problem - that you can stop for a few days but can't stay stopped - you can forget about the addiction part of this book and concentrate on the chapters that address your psychological problems. Now go to Question 4.

BOX 5   HYPNOTHERAPY

There are 4 possible reasons why you failed with hypnotherapy:

1. Did the therapist fail to gain your trust?

Finding another hypnotherapist might be worth trying. The NHA Helpline can help you to find one who is qualified.

2. Was the treatment therapeutic?

If the hypnotherapy session itself was satisfactory, but still made no difference to your desire to smoke, another therapist might be better, but the chance is limited, because you were probably using the wrong therapy.

3. Did it work for a while but wear off? If you went back, did it fail to work a second time?

It is unlikely hypnotherapy would work for you again, because it is very difficult for a therapist to create the same effect twice. Try something else.

4. Did it work every time you went, but fail to last?

Hypnotherapy is good at getting you stopped, but not at keeping you stopped, because the reasons you re-start are not amenable to hypnotherapy. Read Chapter 14 before trying again.

In this case you should continue hypnotherapy, with a support programme. The NHA Helpline can give you details.

BOX 6 ACUPUNCTURE

There are 3 possible reasons why you failed with acupuncture:

1. Could you use it?

Assuming the acupuncturist left a needle or bead in your ear, if this came out, which it often does, you couldn't use it. Ask yourself if it was helping when it was in. If it was, try it again but explain the problem to the therapist, so it doesn't happen again.

2. If you could use it, did it fail to relieve your stress?

In this case acupuncture is not doing the one job it is supposed to do, so forget it.

3. Could you use it, and get stress relief with it, but still want to smoke?

You could still have acupuncture, but you should join a support programme to help with the psychological issues.

BOX 7 NICOTINE REPLACEMENT PRODUCTS (NRPs)

NICOTINE GUM
1. Did you have difficulty using it (sore mouth, stomach ache, just didn't like it)?

Not everyone can use it, and apparently you can't. Would a

different NRP be better?

2. Did it satisfy your need to smoke?

If not, for complicated reasons you don't want to bother about at this stage, it is unlikely it ever would. Read about how addiction works in Chapter 6 for the full details.

3. Did you complete the course, then go back to smoking?

Because the gum satisfied your addiction, as long as you use it you can refrain from smoking. This is not the same thing as success, because then you have to come off nicotine. This demonstrates that your problem is addiction, in which case using gum again, or any other NRP, would be pointless.

NICOTINE PATCH
1. Did you have difficulty using it (sore skin, sleep disturbance)?

If you can't use the product, it is never going to stop you smoking.

2. Did it satisfy your need to smoke?

If not, don't get despondent. About 50% of NHA patients report this with patches. It just means that the nicotine in the patch was not what your body was looking for. Read Chapter 15 for more details.

3. Did you complete the course, then go back to smoking?

Your problem is clearly addiction, in which case NRPs, of any kind, are not appropriate for you.

NICOTINE INHALER

1. Did you have difficulty using it (problems with sucking the tube)

You can't know if it was ever going to work, if you couldn't use it properly.

2. Did it satisfy your need to smoke?

If not, it demonstrates that having something in your hand is not the issue. It's an NRP, which means, if you still wanted to smoke, it wasn't delivering the nicotine you need, in the way you need it.

3. Did you complete the course, then go back to smoking?

Addiction is the problem you must address, and taking nicotine, in any form, is not in your case addressing the problem.

BOX 8 GROUP THERAPY

Group therapy has lost its popularity, which is sad because it really does suit some people. Because the provision of medical services in this country is controlled by the pharmaceutical industry, nurses in general practice only have nicotine replacement products available to them now.

Group therapy can provide both expert guidance and support. At NHA Research we will consider setting up groups in any part of the country where we have staff, so it is worth calling us to discuss this.

Box 9 BUPROPION HYDROCHLORIDE (Zyban)

The theory behind Zyban was a reasonable one, but the use of such a powerful drug in smoking cessation was less successful than the manufacturers had hoped for. At the time of writing, this product is used as a drug of last resort only.

☐ Constructing Your Personal Stop-Smoking Programme

By now, you should have a fairly good idea why you fail to stop smoking. There are a number of aids available, each of which is sold to stop people smoking, but is only able to do one thing. This is why they are called single discipline therapies / products. A successful programme looks at the range of problems and combines a range of methods to solve each one.

From long experience, I would say the following cases are typical. If you find a case that approximates to you, read how to construct a programme for your circumstances. You might need to combine cases to suit your particular issues.

☐ CASE 1

Has smoked for many years, has tried many times to stop, with no success at all because of short-term withdrawal symptoms. Cannot imagine living without cigarettes.

- Acupuncture might alleviate the withdrawal symptoms, otherwise A.N.T. will be needed.
- A good support programme will provide long-term counselling and advice.

☐ CASE 2

Has smoked for many years, never tried seriously to stop, other than patches, which did nothing.

- This person should try stopping on their own before spending money on a product or service they might not need.
- They should not bother with another NRP, because if one doesn't help, the others are unlikely to.
- Group therapy might provide the encouragement and support needed.
- A good book is invaluable to explain how stopping smoking works. Luckily, you have one in your hands.

☐ CASE 3

Has smoked for many years, tried several times to stop on their own, each time with short-term success. Starts again when stressed, but also when on holiday.

- This person can stop but can't stay stopped. A change of attitude is needed, to stop seeing tobacco as desirable.
- A stress management programme, or relaxation classes such as yoga, might be beneficial.
- Acupuncture might alleviate the stress.
- A pack of herbal cigarettes should be kept handy in case of emergencies.

☐ CASE 4

Stopped smoking after several years, on their own. Stayed stopped for two years, and started again without reason. Has tried acupuncture since with only two days success. Suffers withdrawal symptoms, but struggles through them.

- This is not a stress issue, so acupuncture is unlikely to help.
- A.N.T. would deal with the withdrawal symptoms.
- A support programme should be used, for those moments of temptation.

☐ CASE 5

Stopped smoking with group therapy, but only as long as the group lasted. Tried hypnotherapy, but again success only lasted while they had the therapy.

- The right hypnotherapist might be able to produce more permanent results.
- A support programme would be helpful.
- A.N.T. might be appropriate because it provides long-term support.

☐ CASE 6

Never tried to stop, but needs to now for serious health reasons. Considering NRPs but worried about their heart condition.

- It is unlikely NRPs could be used because of the health implications.
- Anyone who has not tried to stop should do so on their own first.
- Hypnotherapy could help, but should be combined with a support programme.

AFTER STOPPING
The Short Explanation

If you have never been an adult non-smoker, when you are thinking of stopping one of the issues you will be facing will be trying to imagine what it will be like not smoking. You know it's what you want, but you have no experience of it, so it is natural to feel anxious.

Forget for the moment any trauma associated with the stopping process. What will it feel like after the first few days? What will happen to your body? How will you feel emotionally?

The first thing will be detoxification, plus post-cessation shock. These two are indistinguishable; they mean your body will need time to adjust both to not being poisoned any longer, and to getting rid of the poisons stored up over the years. So this stage can be unpleasant, or worse. You might come down with opportunistic infections while your immune system is being challenged. You might feel tired and run-down while your body fights to re-balance itself. Or you might feel absolutely fine.

Then your body will need time to heal itself. If you have been abusing it for perhaps thirty years, allow a few months before you really feel the physical benefit. On the other hand, you might feel fitter straight away.

The way you get through all these processes is; correct supplementation, particularly high-dose vitamin C and B complex, plus anything recommended for strengthening the immune system by your health food shop; high fluid intake, particularly water, to flush out the toxins; and finally exercise, preferably outdoors.

A word of warning. All of the above problems can feel like withdrawal symptoms to smokers who don't know any better. Once you have passed the four day mark, they are not withdrawal symptoms. They are the inevitable healing process, in fact they are the reason you stopped smoking - because you want to get better.

So how are you going to feel emotionally? The most serious danger is that you will regret stopping. This again is natural; within the first few weeks you will be letting go of cigarettes, and this might hurt. It is natural to resent stopping, to miss smoking and to think about smoking again, despite all the effort you have just been through to stop. The point here is that if you give in to this self-pity, you will only have to go through it all again the next time you try. Given that this stage is self-limiting, you might as well go through it now and put it behind you.

Having done that, one emotion commonly felt is elation. At this point many ex-smokers feel very pleased with themselves. There is a great sense of achievement but more importantly many of our patients report feeling they have regained control of their lives. Only when they get that control back do they fully appreciate just how much tobacco had been running their lives.

You will always be someone who used to smoke; therefore there will be times when you miss it. That is unfortunate but there is nothing that can be done about it. Except perhaps to get angry that you have been conditioned to miss a killer drug. We encourage our patients to look at tobacco as bizarre, at all those people still smoking as abused. You can change how you see smoking, but only once you have stopped, so the main psychological effect of coming off tobacco is that you rejoin the rest of the human race.

AFTER STOPPING
The Long Explanation   13

☐ How You Will Feel After Stopping - Physically

Just imagine you have been ill for thirty years, and no-one could find a cure for your disease. Then suddenly a cure is found, and you go into hospital for the treatment. Afterwards the doctor comes to your bed and tells you the treatment has been completely successful and you can go home. Naturally, they say, you will need to spend some time convalescing; you will be tired for a few weeks, and there will be aches and pains as your body recovers from thirty years of illness. That's what you would expect, isn't it?

Why is it then that patients who come to our clinics after smoking for thirty years are so surprised when they don't feel as fit as a flea the day after they stop?

☐ The Chemical Punishment

Each time you smoke a cigarette, these are some of the biologically-active agents you are consuming:

Carbon monoxide, nicotine, acetaldehyde, acetone, NOx, formic acid, hydrogen cyanide, catechol, ammonia, benzene, acrolein, acrylonitrile, phenol, formaldehyde, carbazole, 2-nitropropane, N'-nitrosonornicotine, 4-(methylnitrosamino)-1-(3-pyridil)-1-butanone, N-nitrosoanabasine, N-nitrosodiethanolomine, N-nitrosopyrrolidine, N-nitrosodimethylamine, N-nitrosomethylethylamine, N-nitrosodiethylamine, N-nitrosodi-n-propylamine, N-nitrosodi-n-butylamine, N-nitrosopiperidine, hydrazine, urethane, vinyl chloride, benzanthracine, benzopyrene, 5-methylcrysene, dibenzacridine, 2-napthylamine, 4-aminobiphenyl, 2-toluidine, polonium-210.

Frightening, isn't it? And hardly surprising that it is going to take some time to recover. To put these ingredients into perspective, here is a list of the compounds you have been consuming, under their major groupings, with the number of individual compounds in brackets:

Amines, imides, lactones (240), carboxylic acids anhydrides (240), lactones (150), esters (475), aldehydes (110), ketones (520), alcohols (380), phenols (285), amines (200), N-nitrosamines (922), N-heterocyclics (920), hydrocarbons (755), nitriles (105), carbohydrates (45), ethers (310).

This brings the total number of compounds you have been consuming to 4865. Multiply that by the number of times you have smoked, and you get some idea of your daily consumption of substances too awful even for E-numbers. Are you sure you enjoy tobacco?

☐ The Effect on Your Body

If you have smoked for any length of time you will have damaged your body, particularly your lungs. It is not possible for the human body to inhale thousands of chemicals in a base of burning tar and not suffer. We are capable of taking a lot of punishment, but that is too much.

So the first thing to assume is that you have damaged your body by smoking tobacco. This applies even if you are unaware of it, on account of the body's wonderful ability to overcome much of the abuse to which we subject it. The amount of damage will depend not just on the type of tobacco you have smoked, how many cigarettes you have smoked each day and for how many years, but also on your own strength - your body's ability to protect itself from what you do to it.

Diet is a good example of use and abuse. Much of the food consumed in the West does more harm than good, and yet many people seem to do quite well on it. This raises doubts in some people's minds about the importance of good diet - perhaps we really can eat any old junk. The human body does indeed possess the ability to survive on far less than the optimum diet but your health would be very different if you ate a better diet. You might seem fine, but that doesn't mean you would not be better on better food.

We in the West have become accustomed to compromising on our health. Time and time again we hear patients and even doctors treat ill-health as an inevitable consequence of living. It is not. Almost everyone could enjoy better health and greater vigour than they currently do. We have lost the ability to distinguish between good health and indifferent health.

So, if you don't actually suffer from a smoking-related disease, such as emphysema, bronchitis or heart trouble, you might believe you have escaped completely. You haven't. You might not be aware of it while you are smoking but you might very well become aware of it once you have stopped. We have seen that withdrawal symptoms are short-lived - a few days perhaps. And we have also seen that psychological withdrawal is long-term, sometimes lasting for years, but gradually diminishing. There is a third kind of withdrawal, though, that has nothing to do with addiction or dependence.

If you have smoked, say, for thirty years, your body is going to take time to adjust, as explained above. Just imagine its reaction to no longer getting its intake of twenty or thirty cigarettes a day, which previously represented a significant proportion of your diet. Indeed, many heavy smokers will, over the years, have replaced with tobacco a large amount of the food they used to eat. Imagine you had emigrated to another part of the world, where the food was nothing whatever like the food you are used to. You might have an upset stomach for a while until you adjusted. When you come off tobacco that too represents a major change in your diet, so you might expect to feel unwell.

Another major change will take place in your lungs. If you fill them up with poisonous gases twenty or thirty times a day for say thirty years, it is hardly surprising if they notice the difference when they stop doing so. The shock, however, is short-lived; within days your lungs will start to function normally.

While you have been smoking you have been laying down tar in your lungs which stayed there because it is sticky, and you kept putting more on top of it. Your lungs have never had the chance to fight back. But as soon as you stop smoking they can do just that. The result for many ex-smokers is coughs, colds, sore throats and a host of other infections which they never used to get. These infections are often interpreted by the new non-smoker as a problem. They might be problematic in that they are undesirable, but that doesn't mean they are going to cause a problem to your stop-smoking programme. People going through this process can feel a temptation to start smoking again, reasoning that smoking will stop them feeling ill - and they are probably right.

If a few weeks of convalescence is too high a price to pay for coming off tobacco, don't bother. This convalescence period is inevitable, whether you stop smoking now or in five or ten years' time. No-one has yet conducted any research to discover the number of people who go back to smoking because they mistake this convalescence for withdrawal symptoms, but we believe it is likely to be high. Unfortunately, many new non-smokers go to their GP at this stage and complain about feeling unwell, and because GPs are not normally trained in addiction management or smoking cessation they are often unable to help and sometimes give the wrong advice. This is a major factor in making people go back to tobacco. If more GPs understood this mechanism, they would be able to help people at this critical stage. It is particularly sad that these people will already have overcome the worst part - the addiction - and go back to smoking tobacco for what is really such a minor reason.

☐ Withdrawal Symptoms or Convalescence?

So do expect to feel unwell after the first two or three days as an ex-smoker, and don't misidentify the way you feel as withdrawal symptoms. There is a simple test you can use to differentiate the two.

Withdrawal, for most smokers, will usually take place within hours of the last cigarette, or within a day or two in exceptional cases. People who come to our clinics don't go through this phase because we give them the neutrogen, so our helpline staff know for certain at what point convalescence starts since there are no withdrawal symptoms to start with. But you will be dealing with the addiction phase on your own, so it is important that you make a written record of your withdrawal symptoms (for example, mood changes, sleeplessness and headaches).

If after two to four days these symptoms change, make another note. This change will probably represent the progression from withdrawal to convalescence. This is real progress. Whatever the new symptoms, they will inevitably diminish in time, possibly over a week or two.

Conversely, you will know when convalescence starts because it will be quite different from your withdrawal symptoms. Withdrawal lasts a maximum of five days. There is a way you can be sure that this phase is not withdrawal. Always remember what withdrawal means - it is the symptoms you get when you are unable to satisfy a physical craving for your drug. If you are feeling rough, but you can honestly say you don't have a strong craving to smoke, then this is not withdrawal but convalescence, and you are on the way to succeeding. Convalescence is often experienced as a problem, but it is actually a sign that you are coming through.

Many smokers get a very nasty taste in the mouth when they stop, and often interpret this as a withdrawal symptom. It is not. The mouth is a primary escape route for the toxin-impregnated tar from your lungs, and this, unsurprisingly, doesn't taste nice. Better out than in.

Tar consumed over 20 years smoking

		1	4	6	8	9	12
	60	438g	1.75kg	2.63kg	3.50kg	3.94kg	5.26kg
	50	365g	1.46kg	2.19kg	2.92kg	3.29kg	4.38kg
cigs per day	40	292g	1.17kg	1.75kg	2.34kg	2.63kg	3.50kg
	30	219g	876g	1.31kg	1.75kg	1.97kg	2.63kg
	20	146g	584g	876g	1.17kg	1.31kg	1.75kg
	10	73g	292g	438g	584g	657g	876g

mg tar in each cigarette

Smoking and Asthma

Cigarette smoking has two opposing effects on the bronchi (air tubes) of the lungs. On the one hand, the complex mixture of tars and combustion products includes many allergens (substances which allergy-prone individuals are likely to react to), and therefore certain people tend to become allergic to cigarette smoke. Since allergy in the lungs leads to asthma, smoking tends to make allergic smokers worse.

On the other hand, the smoke also contains nicotine and other drug-like constituents which relax the bronchi and loosen the mucus so it can be coughed up. Many asthmatics find that a deep draw on a cigarette helps them cough up their phlegm and breathe more easily. Fifty years ago doctors used to recommend smoking to asthmatics for this reason.

Thus smoking is doing two things at once, one good and one bad, for asthmatics. The 'good' reaction - relieving the breathing - is fast and easily noticed. The 'bad' effect - aggravating the allergy - is slow and not easily recognised by the sufferer; it takes many years to cause a gradual and insidious deterioration of lung function.

Asthmatics who stop smoking may find their asthma aggravated. Smokers who never had asthma may develop it - for the first time in their lives - after stopping. This is because they no longer enjoy the short-term relief afforded by the smoke. We therefore consider it essential that allergy to smoke (when it exists) is treated at the same time as stopping.

In practice this is easily brought about by Addiction Neutralisation Therapy. As well as abolishing or reducing the addiction, it abolishes or reduces the allergy. Experience so far shows that patients who are effectively neutralised for tobacco smoke do not develop asthma when they stop smoking, and those who were already asthmatic get better, not worse. As with non-allergic ex-smokers the patient's need for the neutrogen diminishes with time, although asthmatics are likely to need the drops for somewhat longer, especially when subjected to passive smoking.

☐ How You Will Feel After Stopping - Emotionally

We find that our patients go through quite a clear pattern of emotions, the negative ones being:

Before the treatment Doubt about their motivation
 Doubt about our ability to help them
 Fear of failure
After the treatment Doubt about their motivation
 Fear of success
Longer term Doubt about their motivation
 Anger at us for stopping them smoking
 Resentment at the loss of pleasure

If you will be stopping smoking on your own, you are likely to go through a similar pattern. You will notice that the underlying emotion is always doubt about motivation. This is because so many people try to stop smoking for the wrong reason - because the world is telling them that they should not or must not smoke. Even if the main reason is health, they don't stop because they really want to stop (which, given their addiction, is exactly what we would expect).

As you go through the withdrawal phase, the addiction will be challenging your motivation. As you go through the dependence phase, your dependence will be challenging your motivation. At all times, your motivation will be in doubt. You will be vulnerable. No matter what difficulties there are with stopping smoking, if people were totally motivated, they would be able to overcome them. That you have not been able to overcome them proves that your motivation was insufficient.

Those in positions of authority over the nation's health try to convince us that smokers will stop if they are motivated enough. What does enough mean? Enough to overcome the withdrawal symptoms some smokers have? Enough to overcome the fear of never smoking again? Enough to overcome perhaps forty years of learned behaviour (habit)? In our clinics we consistently find there is only one real way to give smokers good motivation - by making it easy for them to stop.

When you tried to stop smoking before, you presumably were not sufficiently motivated (or you would have succeeded). If you succeeded before, but started again, you had enough motivation to stop but not to stay stopped. We often find a backlash against stopping after two to four weeks of success; some patients suddenly wonder why they bothered in the first place. All of this raises questions about people's real reasons for wanting to stop. Before they stop, they are comfortably addicted to a drug that they believe gives them pleasure, that helps them to stay calm in times of stress, that they can enjoy with their friends. During the backlash phase they might well remember these things, and the memory seriously challenges their motivation. This, as you will realise, is what I have been calling psychological dependence. Understanding it will help you to overcome it, and in time it will get easier.

This backlash causes a lot of people to go back to smoking who otherwise were doing very well. Recognise that this is your dependence challenging you, and that the dependence is simply a function of long-term drug addiction. Give yourself time.

☐ No Regrets?

After you have come off tobacco, you might look at people smoking and envy them. They can do what you aren't allowed to do. Well, you *are* allowed to do it. No-one has stopped you except yourself. You decided to stop, for your own reasons, so why would you be jealous of people who are still smoking? Or, to put it another way, why would you regret what you have done? That you might regret it is not actually surprising, because you were not totally convinced in the first place.

Addicts don't want to lose their addiction - that is what addiction means. If you are pushed into coming off tobacco (through health worries and so on) you are going to be in conflict before you even start. To see this conflict demonstrated, look at any woman who stops smoking as soon as she gets pregnant; then as soon as the baby is born she starts smoking again. Why start again, when she's beaten it? Because she didn't want to stop in the first place.

So you need to stop, but you would prefer to continue. Always remember that wanting to continue is not quite 'real' though. After all, non-smokers don't want to start, so why would you want to continue? It is unlikely that, among the millions of people in the country who have never smoked, you would find even one who wants to smoke and regrets not being able to. Why should this be? It's because there is no reason to smoke. Unless, of course, you are addicted, in which case you have no choice.

So what you regret is not being a non-smoker, but being an ex-smoker. People who have never smoked simply do not regret being non-smokers (which you must admit would be ridiculous). People who used to smoke often regret, at least for a while, being ex-smokers. It is possible that non-smokers don't know what they are missing, but it is more likely that ex-smokers are missing something. Let's look at what you might miss once you have stopped.

☐ Your Pleasure

We looked at this idea in Chapter 9. The enjoyment you used to get was the result of continually satisfying low-level cravings for nicotine, even if you were not conscious of them. However, most ex-smokers miss what they think of as the pleasure of smoking, and you might not want to be told that the pleasure was all in your mind. After all, that is where you feel all pleasure, isn't it?

In a way, yes. But if the pleasure is actually relief from 'displeasure' (low-level craving), because it is really only a fix of your drug, then the pleasure is not a real one, and sooner or later you will have to come to terms with this fact. The pleasure of smoking is largely the pleasure of drug addiction, which is always false.

So what you have to do every time you find yourself pining for the lost enjoyment is keep reading this section until you believe it.

☐ Your Friend

Many patients, when they first come to our clinics, talk of cigarettes as being some kind of friend they are going to miss. I could state the obvious - with a friend that is going to shorten your life, who needs enemies? - but I shan't. Again, this is the addiction talking. Tobacco is only a friend in as much as you are dependent on it, like you might be with a true friend. The dependence is real, but that does not make tobacco a true friend.

Nevertheless, it is going to take time for you to accept all this. Meanwhile, it is quite all right to mourn the loss of your 'friend'. It is difficult to know how to advise patients in this respect, because everyone is different. Whilst we find it is generally helpful for patients to go through a period of mourning, some are psychologically so dependent that they cannot cope with anything but complete rejection at the point of stopping smoking. The best advice is; don't be afraid to feel sorry for yourself, and sorry for the loss. This might be healthier than pretending to be glad you have stopped, when really you are feeling bereft.

☐ Your Crutch

When you smoke your last cigarette, your overwhelming feeling is likely to be fear - of the unknown. How are you going to manage without cigarettes?

Probably just like everyone else. At this point, you are highly dependent on tobacco, and this dependence takes time to overcome. But no-one remains dependent on a drug they haven't had for years. So you can be quite sure that the time will come when you will be managing very well without tobacco. The only question is, not how will you manage, but how long will it be before you can manage?

Some ex-users say they will always feel a little sad about the fact that they stopped. This doesn't mean they are still dependent. It means they used to be dependent. and addicted, and they will pay a small price for that for the rest of their lives. It doesn't matter, and it is certainly no reason to start smoking again.

You Still Want to Smoke

It comes as a surprise to people who have just stopped, even people on A.N.T., that they sometimes want to smoke.

And yet anyone who has smoked for years, has been addicted to nicotine, and has been psychologically dependent on cigarettes, is surely going to want to smoke sometimes. Even though this completely conflicts with their desire to stop smoking.

What catches people out is this very fact - that they 'want' to smoke. They don't want to become smokers again - they just 'want' to smoke. This actually means they want to smoke a cigarette - perhaps just one cigarette. This is a very understandable desire after years of addiction but just days of freedom. What is less understandable is that they would be surprised that they want to smoke.

The secret is in not being surprised - not being caught out. Wanting a cigarette does NOT mean you are failing. It means you want a cigarette - an understandable, and manageable, reaction to stopping.

STAYING STOPPED

The Short Explanation

14

If all we ever did in our clinics was to help people stop smoking, but we did nothing to help them stay stopped, our long-term success might be little better than any other method. After all, everyone can stop, and they do so every night when they go to bed. So, first what do we mean by stopping?

Because our approach is to control the addiction to nicotine medically, one logical measure of stopping is whether the patient goes more than four days without smoking, because after this time they are no longer being controlled by the physical need for the drug. So we could say that after more than four days, the person has stopped smoking, and the job now is to keep them stopped.

At this point, every issue around staying stopped is psychological, so clearly staying stopped is entirely a psychological issue and addiction has nothing to do with it. At this point the person has no use for nicotine, but thinks they do. Therefore, staying stopped is about changing the way you think about smoking. Now that nicotine has released its control over your body, staying stopped is about exercising control over your mind.

The next step then must be to analyse why you might start smoking again. However, even this is not that simple, because what we in NHA Research mean by starting again is not always what ex-smokers mean. We do not mean smoking a cigarette. We do mean giving up all pretence of not smoking.

STAYING STOPPED

The Smoker Explanation

What we never did in our classes was convince people to stop smoking, but we do our best to help them stop. Stopped, our long-term success seems so little to my thinking either medical. After all, we know how we do not mean we have stopped smoking? So first what do we mean by stopping?

Because our approach is to look at the addiction to a conflict medically and logical measure of stopping is whether the patient goes twenty-four hours one day without smoking. A pause after this time, they are no longer being controlled by the physical demand for the drug, so we could say that after one day or two days, the person has stopped smoking, and the problem is to keep them stopped.

Of this point, every issue around staying stopped is psychological, not clearly. Staying stopped is something all psychologists, users and addiction are having to deal with. At this point, the person has no use for the drug, but thinks they do. Therefore, staying stopped is about changing the way you think about smoking. You have decided you do not want to continue smoking. Staying stopped is about regaining control over your mind.

The next step then must be to analyze why you might start smoking again. However, these little essays are simplified because what we mean is. Remember we are starting again — one at a time what ex-smokers mean. We do not mean smoking a cigarette. We do mean giving up all pretence of not smoking.

STAYING STOPPED
The Long Explanation

14

Just as we have to study why people can't stop smoking, before we can help them do so, we have to study how to keep people stopped, and to do this we have to ask just one question - why do ex-smokers start again?

Why would anyone who has achieved what they set out to do - stop smoking - start again?

First we have the fact that most people who stop smoking don't actually want to. They know they should. They might think they want to. But they don't want to. They may very well want to be non-smokers, but what they don't want is to stop smoking. It's really not that complicated. You are on a drug but wish you weren't. Most drug users wish they weren't.

Now let's move forward in time. The smoker has stopped, successfully. And they are probably pleased, most if not all the time, that they succeeded. But it doesn't change the fact that they didn't want to stop smoking. They stopped because it was the right thing to do, but that is not the same as wanting to stop. In which case what do I mean by wanting to stop? They wanted to be a non-smoker, but they didn't want to go through the process of stopping. But surely, if someone has got through the pain, and is now a non-smoker, they wouldn't want to waste the pain, and start again? It sounds logical, but it is only when you understand the immensely powerful hold tobacco has over its users that you start to see why that is not actually true.

The would-be ex-smoker is almost always afraid of stopping, as you read about in Chapter 10. So you would think that if they have succeeded, they would be over the fear. However, you cannot smoke tobacco for, say, thirty years, and lose the fear just because you suddenly don't smoke it any more. Even when you have stopped using it, the fear lives on. That is how powerful it is. Believe it or not, some people who no longer smoke are actually afraid of not smoking, even though they are experiencing it and it's OK.

That fear takes a long time to die, and it is during this period that ex-smokers are highly vulnerable. They will smoke a cigarette given any excuse - stress, relaxation or just sheer bloody-mindedness.

And smoking again will make them feel safe again. They will regret it, but at the same time they will feel better, because they can smoke again.

So how do we deal with this problem, as impossible as it looks? The key is in the word can. Anyone can smoke. Thinking you can't is a major incentive to have one, to prove you can. But you can, without actually having to do it. In our own programme, we occasionally get a patient phoning the helpline, saying, "Help, I'm suddenly desperate to smoke", perhaps weeks after they stopped successfully. We call this a psychological backlash. It's the fear coming back, not this time fear of what *might* happen but fear of what has happened. They are thinking, "Oh my god, I've really done it this time. I'll never be able to smoke again". And that fear can make them smoke.

So what do we do? We tell them to smoke. They actually light a cigarette while they are on the phone. It tastes horrible, which proves to them that their body does not want to smoke. It's their brain that's demanding one, because of the fear of never smoking again. So they light one, it tastes dreadful, and they are taught that they can smoke, but they actually don't need to. No-one has taken cigarettes away from them, but at the same time smoking one turned out to be pointless. They wanted one not because they wanted one, but because they needed the reassurance that they could have one. Now they know they can, so there is no point having any more.

At this point many people, who are not getting this kind of support, will simply carry on smoking, because they don't understand what is going on. All they know is it feels better not to have to make the effort. It's always easier to wallow in self-pity than try.

Most people who work in smoking cessation tell their clients never to have even one, because that will be a disaster. It is that very attitude that makes people fail, because they have one and believe the myth that one means failure, so they think, to hell with it, I've failed, and off they go. What we have shown is that having that one is an important safety valve, because our patient now knows that it's no big deal (although we always do this under supervision, so we are in control of the situation).

They can now go on not smoking, not because they can't but because they choose not to.

☐ Jealousy

A new ex-smoker is a pathetic creature. They look at people smoking and feel jealous. Jealous of someone still on the treadmill they just came off! Why can they smoke when you can't? As we have just seen, you can but you choose not to, which is quite different.

Sadly, when you come off tobacco you will never be able to walk away from it, because a quarter of the adult population in this country is still on tobacco. You will see it being smoked in the street, you will see it in the shops, you will see advertisements. All of this sends you a very significant message.

It says that smoking is normal. You decided to stop but you might in fact have been wrong.

Other people are doing it and they're not dropping dead in the street. It's sold in sweetshops and it's advertised, so clearly it can't be as dangerous as you thought. The overwhelming message is that tobacco, and smoking it, is normal. You then must be abnormal, because you're not smoking it.

Don't underestimate the power of this message. No-one who has successfully come off tobacco can ever escape it. For the rest of your life society will be telling you that smoking is OK and you are missing something.

Well let's see if that's true. First of all, is it normal? Yes, in as much as millions of people do it. But I have a problem with the idea that millions of people doing it makes it normal. I guess it depends on what we mean by normal. If we mean commonly done, then yes. But if we mean sensible, then no. I, as an ex-user, and who do this professionally, can see that millions of people are doing something that doesn't make any sense. You may not be able to see that, particularly when you are going through the stage of letting go of tobacco.

The control tobacco exerts is so powerful that someone who no longer needs it can look at people who still do and be jealous. The answer is that you have to change the way you see tobacco, and its users. First, you will have noticed by now that I tend not to say smokers but users. That is because I see people who smoke tobacco as drug users. You may not, because you might not like to think of yourself in this way. But once you are no longer on the treadmill, see if calling people users rather than smokers helps you to stop being jealous.

And when you look at someone, say in the pub, apparently enjoying a cigarette when you're having a drink without one, don't assume they have the better deal. How do you know they don't have lung cancer, but just can't stop smoking? How do you know they haven't just come from the hospital where their mother has died of emphysema, and have gone to the pub to drown their sorrows? How do you know they are not looking at you thinking, "How can they enjoy a drink without smoking, when I can't?". How do you know they are not trying desperately to come off tobacco and are in fact jealous of you?

Now let's look at not just why people start again, but how.

☐ How People Start Smoking Again

The mechanisms involved in restarting are actually rather interesting. We find with our own patients that understanding these mechanisms goes a long way to undoing them. You might be surprised how many people start smoking again for no better reason than they cannot see the mistakes they are making.

Let's look at a pretty common re-start situation. You are in a pub, say a few weeks after stopping smoking. You are pleased you stopped, and you have no intention of smoking tonight. The evening wears on, and you've had a few drinks, but you are in control. The group around you is mostly smokers; early in the evening it didn't bother you, but now you look at them and wonder if you could have just one.

Even now, you are being strong, and not asking for one, but then a friend of a friend joins the group, and offers you a cigarette. To this day you can't remember why you took it, but before you could say, no thanks I don't smoke, it was between your lips and you were drawing on it.

You made a big mistake, but at this stage you could rectify that mistake. You draw on the cigarette but lo and behold, all these weeks you've been missing the taste and now you're smoking and it doesn't taste right. I just said you could rectify your mistake, but you don't. Instead of asking yourself why it doesn't taste good (there is an excellent reason, which by now you should have learned from this book), you keep smoking it and, when it still doesn't taste good, you accept another one. By the end of this one you are starting to get the taste back. You can't think why it took a couple to get the hang of it again, but there you go, now it's OK. And the third one is not just OK, it's pretty good.

By the end of the evening you have accepted five cigarettes, and what do you do? You make the next mistake; you buy a pack of twenty. You give five back to the people you cadged them from, smoke one more on the way home, and go to bed.

The next morning you wake up with a thick head and, as you open your eyes, there on the bedside table there's a packet with fourteen cigarettes in it. What have you done? More importantly, what do you do now? Well, to tell the truth, you make the next mistake - you think, to hell with it, I've smoked now, I've paid for these, I might as well finish the pack.

So you do. And because now it's Saturday, and you're out with friends again tonight, you buy another pack - the next mistake. You'll stop again tomorrow. You've done it before, you can do it again. That night, you run out of cigarettes before the evening's over, so you buy another pack. On Sunday morning, you've got a pack of 18, so you make the next mistake and smoke them. You'll stop tomorrow - you'll be at work and that's the best way to stop.

But you've only got one week to go to your holiday, so what do you do on Monday morning? That's right, you make another mistake. You decide to carry on for now because you'll be able to get cheap fags on holiday.

By the time you get home from Spain, you admit to yourself that you have 'started smoking again'. But why? Surely you wanted to stop? Surely you enjoyed your success? Surely you liked being a non-smoker? So why was it so easy to start again? The answer is that you made one mistake, and because sadly you didn't know what was going on, you made the next and the next. At any stage, with the right advice and support, you could have avoided starting again. So let's look at that same scenario, and see how not to make the mistakes.

You are in the pub and a friend of a friend offers you one. The first tip we teach our patients is never to say, when offered a cigarette, "No thanks I've just stopped" or, "No thanks I'm trying to give up". Many users, sadly, need others to keep smoking, because it supports what they are doing, and as insane as it seems, they will try to trip you up. Well, that's drug addiction for you. Always say, "No thanks, I don't smoke".

Let's say you fail this first test, and you accept one. That one tastes bad - not what you have been hankering for all evening. This is because you have lost the adaptation to the poisons in tobacco. In other words, a regular user has deliberately switched off the ability to detect the poisons but you have regained that ability. You can now save your life by, for perhaps the first time, listening to the life-saving information your body is giving you. It is saying, this is poisonous, please don't use it. This is the most wonderful opportunity for you. Don't throw it away; you might regret it for the rest of your life.

However, let's assume you make the same old mistake, and smoke another one, and you re-adapt yourself that evening. That is not a reason to buy another pack. And if you do buy another pack, that is not a reason to take them home. And if you do take them home? That is not a reason to buy another pack the next morning. And if you do that? That is not a reason to say, to hell with it, I'd rather smoke on holiday and stop when I get back.

Why is it not a reason to do that? Because if you do that you are admitting something you may never have thought about. You didn't actually want to stop smoking at all. You can't have, otherwise you would not be making plans to enjoy two weeks of smoking in Spain.

But I have a big problem with all this. When I say you didn't want to stop in the first place, you will recognise, if you have been paying attention, that this word is almost undefinable. I believe every tobacco user wants to come off it. The problem is, the tobacco companies don't want users to come off it, and they have a very powerful way to make that happen. Their product.

STOP-SMOKING METHODS
The Short Explanation

If everyone who smokes can stop, which must be true, but most attempts fail, it seems only logical that they are doing it the wrong way. There is a right way, but they apparently have not yet found it.

In a survey of our patients, we asked how many had analysed why they fail, and therefore what help they needed, before buying any of the methods they had failed with. The answer was none.

We also surveyed General Practitioners and chemists to find out how many went through this kind of analysis before recommending a course of action, and again the answer was none.

So the fact that so many people try to stop smoking and fail is unsurprising. It is not even indicative of the efficacy of the stop-smoking methods available. If anything, it is an indictment of the government, which offers no help whatever, either through family doctors, chemists or health promotion departments, to ensure smokers are getting the help that is appropriate to their needs.

Even with our own programme, smokers don't come to us because they have analysed every method and judged ours to be the most appropriate. They come because they have failed with everything else and then found us by chance. And the programme is not always the answer; we vet smokers who call us before even sending them details of it, to make sure it really is what they need.

Each smoker has one or more problems with stopping. Each stop-smoking product or service is different, and it does a different job. It addresses some, all or perhaps none of the problems of any one smoker. Success comes when the problems are matched up with the method that is designed to solve those problems. That some methods might be better than others is not the point. Some are better than others for any given smoker.

First let's look at the problems likely to be experienced when trying to 'stop smoking', so if you are currently trying you can start to find out which direction is most likely to be successful. Then, in the white pages, I have analysed each method in detail, so you can see clearly what it can and cannot do for you.

■ Withdrawal Symptoms
(Desperate craving during first four days, irritability and other mood swings, headaches, sweating, stomach cramps.)

Other than Addiction Neutralisation Therapy (available only from NHA), there is no sure-fired method of overcoming the effects of withdrawal (although acupuncture will help). However, since the symptoms of withdrawal cannot persist for longer than four days, every smoker should consider whether four days, even if it is absolute hell, are not too high a price to pay for success, before looking for help.

Because of the short-term nature of this problem, many people feel, rightly or wrongly, that 'stopping' means stopping for more than these four days, so that the addiction is overcome.

■ Fear of Success (of never smoking again)

We find this is a problem in at least three quarters of our patients, and intensive counselling and support is needed to overcome it. Any programme that provides this kind of support will help, and hypnotherapy can sometimes help as well.

This fear can make people unable to contemplate stopping, but it can also kick in after the first stage of stopping. Intensive support is essential to overcome a long-term problem.

■ Fear of Failing to Stop

This is surprisingly common, particularly in our clinics where we see patients with a long history of failure. There is no cure for it, other than experiencing success (and possibly hypnotherapy).

■ Stress

It depends whether by this one means the stress of stopping smoking (see Withdrawal Symptoms, above) or stress generally. There are two solutions. The first is to get help with the stress - stop-smoking products and services are unlikely to help here (with the exception of acupuncture). The second is to learn that smoking does not relieve stress anyway (see Chapter 11).

Which method works?

We often hear people asking if a particular method works. They all work. But they do not make you stop smoking - *you* make you stop smoking. A smoking cessation method is a tool. It might be the right or wrong tool. You might or might not know how to use it. It might be a well-designed tool but badly made. It might or might not come with after-sales service. NRPs, hypnotherapy and acupuncture are all tools, with all these conditions attached to them. If you use them and fail, it does not mean the tool does not work, but that it did not work for you.

STOP-SMOKING METHODS
The Long Explanation

☐ On Your Own

There is only one way to find out if you need to buy anything to help you stop - try it on your own first. There is a lot of mythology about stopping, and one of the myths is that everyone finds it hard. Many people find it hard, but some don't, so always try on your own first.

This is not just to save you money. If, say, you have not really tried, and you go to the chemist and buy some newly-advertised product, how do you know whether that product is designed to solve your problems? If you haven't seriously tried, and failed, how do you know why you fail, and therefore what you need to succeed?

Even if you have tried before and failed, I suggest you give it another go, not necessarily because you might succeed, but as a diagnostic tool to find out *why* you fail. Set yourself a target, say one week, and be as determined as you can to succeed. Each day, write down how you feel, what symptoms you experience and so on. If you do smoke, write down why. It's very easy to say you don't know why, but please think about it. That question has an answer that is the key to your eventual success.

If indeed you fail, there is one particular question that is crucial at this stage:

Did you fail to stop at all, say for more than a few days, or did you stop for more than four days and then fail?

Why is this question so important? Because if you stopped for a few days, you can stop. Your problem is not stopping, it is staying stopped. If, on the other hand, you could not stop at all, that is quite different. What method you use to get stopped might be quite different from a method of staying stopped. So what you have done at this early stage is start to analyse where you begin to solve your problems.

☐ NICOTINE REPLACEMENT PRODUCTS

NRPs are for people who can't stop. They have no influence on staying stopped.

Their function is to maintain your addiction so you can get a fix without the need to light a cigarette. The effect of this is to break your psychological dependence on cigarettes, particularly the habit of lighting up. Therefore NRPs are a psychological method, and are aimed particularly at breaking habit.

If you have no difficulty breaking the addiction, but do have a problem with habit, NRPs are indicated. Some people complain about the cost of NRPs, but the cost of each product is always about the same as smoking 20 cigarettes a day, so that should not be an issue. Once you have established you need NRPs, the next decision is which one. For each product there are three issues that will affect your choice, and you really have to try each one before you can be sure.

☐ NICOTINE GUM

☐ Can you use it?

Some people like to chew, others don't. If you don't, it's probably not even worth trying. The gum can be unpleasant to chew, although there is a mint-flavoured gum which some users will prefer.

Some users suffer side-effects, such as a sore mouth, stomach aches and overdose symptoms like palpitations. In this case it might be worth trying a different NRP.

☐ Does it Do its Job?

By this I mean does it satisfy your craving? If it does, then at least you have established that your stop-smoking problem is addiction, because satisfying the addiction is enough. If it doesn't satisfy the craving, it is not doing its job, so there is no point persisting. It is also unlikely that a different NRP would satisfy your craving either. See the box at the end of this section to understand why NRPs don't satisfy the craving for some people.

☐ Is There Any Point?

By this I mean, if you can use the product, and if you get relief from craving and withdrawal symptoms with it, can you stop using it and not go back to smoking? In other words, does using this product help you to stop smoking, not just while you are using it, but afterwards? Stopping chewing nicotine gum is the only way to find out. If you can stop the gum, then it can help you to stop smoking. As I just said, the next issue is how you stay stopped, without continuing to chew the gum.

☐ NICOTINE PATCHES

☐ Can You Use Them?

Some users report skin reactions, either to the plaster or to the nicotine itself, or both. A smaller number report sleep disturbance on the 24-hour patch, including nightmares. We have also seen what look like overdose reactions, like overstimulation of the brain, resulting in nervous overactivity.

☐ Do they do their job?

If you still need to smoke, then no, they don't. And if you do need to smoke, for heaven's sake take the patch off first. If you are still craving, you will never find out whether you would have stopped smoking, because stopping the craving is the only thing the patches need to do at this stage, but they must do that.

☐ Is there any point?

You know if the patches have 'worked' when you take the last one off. You'll know at that point whether you have stopped smoking, or otherwise.

☐ NICOTINE INHALER

To save boring you, this is the same as the other two methods.

Why NRPs Don't Satisfy the Addiction for Some Users

This explanation will not make a lot of sense unless you understand the basics of how addiction works, so do read Chapter 6 first.

When you learn to smoke (when you teach your body to accept the poisons in tobacco) your receptors learn to read a particular chemical molecule which they find in the tobacco smoke to satisfy the need for the drug. It is this information that the receptors use to switch off the craving. However, this molecular information is extracted from tobacco **smoke**, and if you think about it you cannot smoke a nicotine patch. The nicotine from an NRP is absorbed through the lining of the mouth, or the skin, or even inhaled, but none of it is the same chemical form as burning tobacco.

Your body is adapted to burning tobacco. Therefore it might not be able to read the molecular information present in the NRP. If it can, the product might satisfy your craving. If it can't it won't, and you will still want to smoke.

But what happens for many users is that it **partially** recognises it; the NRP sort of satisfies the craving, but not completely. The result is that you never get satisfaction, but neither do you actually have to smoke. Instead, you go through never-ending low-level withdrawal. Your addiction is constantly being challenged, and this can be very wearing. So now you know; it is not the quantity of nicotine that satisfies the craving but the way it is presented. If you cannot get satisfaction from the product, it is simply because your body cannot read that product.

NOTE. Our legal advisors have instructed us to add that none of this is scientifically proven and is the result of our own, uncorroborated, research.

☐HYPNOTHERAPY

☐ Can You Use It?

The main problem reported with hypnotherapy is not so much the treatment itself but the therapist who does it. The theory is perfectly valid, but some therapists, shall we say, are less effective than others.

The first problem is that the hypnotherapist is well meaning but ineffectual. The second is the therapist is not well meaning. Sadly, there are some quasi-qualified people making all sorts of claims and frankly you would not want to be unconscious in their front room.

The rules are: only go to someone who has qualifications you can verify (preferably a member of the National Register of Practitioners in Smoking Cessation), and preferably go to someone on a personal recommendation. And don't be shy about speaking with them on the telephone and asking lots of questions before you make an appointment.

☐ Does It Do Its Job?

The function of hypnotherapy for smoking cessation is to convince you through the back door (your subconscious mind) that you don't want to smoke. Its job is not to solve your life's problems, and don't listen to a therapist who says it is. If the first session leaves you gasping for a cigarette there is little point spending money on a second session. If, however, you come out feeling good about not smoking, don't judge the therapy on the basis of stopping forever after just one session. See how long you can stay stopped for, but do use the therapist again to take you further.

☐ Is There Any Point?

With any therapy, this question means is it a viable way to stop smoking. Well, yes hypnotherapy is viable, but only if your stop-smoking problems are amenable to what hypnotherapy does.

For example, if your problem is clearly addiction, hypnotherapy might or might not help. If your problem is stress, it might. If your problem is the fear of living without smoking, it probably will.

Hypnotherapy is a perfectly valid way to overcome the psychological dependence on smoking. And for some people, approaching the addiction through the mind with hypnotherapy is a good idea.

☐ ACUPUNCTURE

☐ Can You Use It?

Acupuncturists, being part of the medical world, are well regulated, so you can be pretty sure that if you go to someone with a recognised qualification they are going to know their job. Look for one who is a member of either the British Acupuncture Council (MBAcC) or the British Medical Acupuncture Society. And membership of the NRPSC (see above) is invaluable.

So any problems are likely to revolve around the treatment itself. Commonly, the practitioner will put either a seed or a small needle in your earlobe for you to press each time you want to smoke. This tends to be the cause of problems, because the device can fall out (it's usually held by a plaster) or be uncomfortable to sleep with.

☐ Does It Do Its Job?

The function of acupuncture is to help you relax whenever you feel stressed about not smoking. It does this by stimulating the production of endorphins, your body's inbuilt tranquiliser. It will almost always succeed in doing this.

☐ Is There Any Point?

This is harder to answer. Yes, if your problem is mainly stress, relieving stress with acupuncture is likely to be helpful. But of course if your smoking problem is not stress, then you are not going to be addressing your problem with acupuncture. In our own programme we recognise the benefit of stress management in smoking cessation, and we incorporate shiatsu (acupressure) into the programme for this reason.

☐ ADDICTION NEUTRALISATION THERAPY

A.N.T. is the best kept secret in smoking cessation. It was brought from America by Dr Richard Mackarness in the 1970s, and he used it within the National Health Service at Basingstoke District General Hospital where he was a consultant.

The technique had already been in use for many years as a method of neutralising allergic reactions, and is commonly used in countries with advanced medical services like Germany and the U.S.A. An example of the benefit of neutralisation is with hayfever, which is quite curable, and other autoimmune diseases such as Crohn's disease, rheumatoid arthritis and migraine. (The fact that the cures for these diseases are not available to the public is not because they don't work, but because they don't involve drugs or surgery, the only branches of medicine with research budgets.)

Because allergy and addiction are basically the same thing, Dr Mackarness hypothesised that what would control one would control the other. So he made a vaccine from tobacco, and gave it to 300 smokers at the hospital. In every case, without exception, the vaccine controlled the craving for tobacco and the consequent withdrawal symptoms. He had found a simple, inexpensive, foolproof, safe way to control drug addiction. With the technique he could, and did, bring users off a range of drugs, including heroin. He replicated his success at a clinic set up for him in Melbourne, Australia by the Alcohol and Drug Dependency Service of the State of Victoria Health Commission.

In fact so successful is A.N.T. that the British Government has become worried the public will start demanding it on the NHS, so they have withheld research funding for it in the hope it will go away. That is purely a function of the political and commercial pressures on both tobacco consumption and healthcare in Britain and Europe, which are not the subject of this book, so I shall not go into it further here.

Nevertheless, A.N.T. is obviously a lifesaver, so at NHA Research we made a decision in 1991 that we would further develop it and make it available to the public as widely as possible. We started running clinics using the treatment, but it quickly became apparent that stopping the addiction is not the whole story, and it took years of research, with thousands of smokers, to develop a sophisticated programme that would combine A.N.T. with the best techniques for overcoming the psychological dependence caused by the addiction. To date, A.N.T. is available in the UK only as part of that programme.

☐ Can You Use It?

To date we have been unable to find any difficulty in using the treatment. However, we limit our programme to smokers over the age of 25, with a history of failure, but there is no reason why, for example, GPs should not provide it on the NHS under different criteria.

Safety is always a consideration. To date there has been no recorded incident of unwelcome side-effects with A.N.T.

☐ Does It Do Its Job?

The obvious, and only, function of A.N.T. is to control craving and withdrawal symptoms. Its job is not to stop people smoking, which is the function of any programme into which it is incorporated (such as ours). The number of patients given the treatment at the time of writing is almost 5000, and there has been no recorded failure.

☐ Is There Any Point?

This question means, in this case, does control over craving and withdrawal symptoms serve a purpose in helping people come off tobacco? The answer is self-evident. No-one is claiming it is the only factor, but the difference between NHA Research and almost everyone else in this field is that everyone else is saying smoking is a psychological issue but we are saying it is **always** an addiction issue as well, given the relationship we now understand between addiction and psychological dependence.

Obviously there are other ways to approach the problem. Acupuncture, for example, helps directly with withdrawal symptoms, and hypnotherapy can help overcome the psychological dependence created by the addiction, so there is more than one way to skin this particular cat.

☐ Herbal Cigarettes

Herbal cigarettes are a very useful aid to stopping smoking. The secret is in understanding, a) Exactly what they are for and b) How to use them.

First, be clear on what they are not. They are not a safe way to smoke. They were not designed to be and they don't pretend to be. Anything you burn and put in your mouth is going to put the products of combustion into your body.

Their actual purpose is to allow you to continue 'smoking', without taking nicotine. They are, then, nicotine-free cigarettes. The benefit is in allowing you to tackle one problem at a time. If, while going through withdrawal from nicotine, you don't have to go through the 'loss' of smoking, this can be a big help. Having come off nicotine, stopping the herbal cigarettes is quite easy.

☐ Can You Use Them?

Some people get on with them, some don't. They do taste and smell a bit odd, but then so does burning tobacco if you're not a user. If you've found them unpalatable before, try a different one. There are two brands, Honeyrose and NTB. Honeyrose make a wide range, including menthol which, even if you don't normally smoke menthol, can be quite smokable.

☐ Does It Do Its Job?

Given that its function is to satisfy the desire to smoke, then since you will be smoking, yes, it tends to do just that.

☐ Is There Any Point?

Yes, but only if used as part of a structured plan to stop smoking. There is considerable benefit in reducing the fear of success whilst dealing with the addiction. There is no reason, if you are using another therapy, such as acupuncture or hypnotherapy, why herbal cigarettes should not be used as a short-term prop, but do take advice from your therapist first.

Cannabis

If you smoke cannabis and want to stop using tobacco to roll a joint, Honeyrose makes a hand-rolling mixture, which works fairly well in joints. It's available from most health-food shop and some chemists.

☐ Other Methods

There will always be new methods to stop smoking. Some that come along are clearly either hair-brained or quackery. Others are good, but in a world dominated by the advertising muscle of the drug companies, the public simply don't get to hear about them. If you are considering something new, call us for advice; we might know something about it.

CASE HISTORY

Carolyn from Manchester was clearly distressed about stopping smoking. So much so that she was advised not to try stopping immediately, but to go home from the clinic and do some preparatory work first.

She called on day two of the programme to say she was in fact trying to stop, so we felt we should give her something in addition to the neutrogen to support her while she did it. The doctor prescribed a homeopathic remedy (Arg Nit 200 for those with an interest). This had an immediate effect and Carolyn completed the programme.

What this demonstrated was that every issue has to be tackled. The neutrogen suppressed her addiction, the counselling in the clinic changed the way she saw smoking, but the homeopathic remedy was also needed to control the fear.

A multi-discipline approach is often called for. At NHA we use such an approach, and many acupuncturists and hypnotherapists do so as well.

THE MISTAKES PEOPLE MAKE

The Short Explanation

If it is true that everyone who smokes can stop, and it must be true, why do they fail? Well, we have already looked at that in some detail, but there is another way of looking at failure. What mistakes do people make when they try to come off tobacco - mistakes they might not make if they knew differently? For these yellow pages, this is a summary of them:

■ *Belief: Craving weeks after stopping is caused by addiction.*

☐ **Truth**: Addiction cannot last more than four days without being fed - medical fact - but craving and withdrawal are not the same thing, so read the full explanation in the white pages.

■ *Belief: It's not addiction - it's all in the mind.*

☐ **Truth**: If you smoke more than one cigarette every four days, you are addicted. Again, there is more to it than that though.

■ *Belief: When stressed, a cigarette will help.*

☐ **Truth**: Smoking tobacco creates far more stress than it could ever relieve; and it doesn't relieve stress anyway.

■ *Belief: One won't matter.*

☐ **Truth**: It's true that one will probably not re-addict you, or give you lung cancer, but the psychological effect can be critical to whether you start smoking again.

■ *Belief: One cigarette means failure.*

☐ **Truth**: It might mean failure if that's what you want to believe, but it never needs to. This mistaken belief is the biggest single cause of ex-smokers starting again.

■ *Belief: The feeling of deprivation will never end.*

☐ **Truth**: It feels like that, but no-one actually believes it. However, at the time it's enough to make you smoke again, which is what addiction is supposed to do.

■ *Belief: It's impossible to overcome the habit.*

☐ **Truth**: Contrary to popular belief, habit can't make you smoke.

■ *Belief: It is possible to wean yourself off nicotine.*

☐ **Truth**: You are either addicted, or you are not. You cannot get less addicted, or more addicted, therefore it is not possible to wean yourself off any addictive drug. But remember what addiction means - it's not the same as dependence.

■ *Belief: A low-nicotine cigarette is less addictive.*

☐ **Truth**: There is no such thing as less addictive.

■ *Belief: Once a smoker, always a smoker.*

☐ **Truth**: Once a smoker, always an ex-smoker, which is not the same thing at all, as will be explained in the white pages.

■ *Belief: There is no point cutting down.*

☐ **Truth**: If this were true, there would be no problem smoking more.

■ *Belief: Some people have an addictive personality.*

☐ **Truth**: This is a contradiction in terms, but believing it is a good reason to fail.

■ *Belief: You have to want to stop to succeed.*

☐ **Truth**: Very few people who try to stop want to stop. They need to stop, but that's not the same thing. If you wait until you really want to stop, you could die waiting.

■ **Truth:** If this were true, there would be no problem smoking more...

■ **Belief:** Some people think an addiction is no conflict.

■ **Truth:** This is a common lie worth leaving; rationalizing it is a good reason to quit.

■ **Belief:** You have to want to stop to do so.

■ **Truth:** Very few people who have to stop want to stop. They need to stop, but that's not the same thing. If you can't quit, you really want to stop, you could try writing.

THE MISTAKES PEOPLE MAKE
The Long Explanation

☐ *Craving Weeks After Stopping is Caused by Addiction*

Many people still crave a cigarette long after stopping, and they will often instinctively call it withdrawal, because withdrawal is what you feel when you stop smoking, isn't it?

But what you call any given problem is actually very important, because if you give a problem the wrong name, you will be trying to resolve the wrong thing, in which case you are unlikely to succeed. Knowing it is impossible to be experiencing withdrawal symptoms more than a few days after your last cigarette will help to address the real problems, thereby increasing your chance of success.

We do need to be careful though when saying you cannot experience withdrawal symptoms after the first few days, because what do we mean by not smoking? You might think you are not smoking, but if you are passive smoking, you are smoking, because passive smoking is enough to keep you addicted. By passive smoking we mean regularly breathing other people's cigarette smoke, for example sitting at a table with someone smoking, or going into the smoking room at work.

If you are genuinely not smoking, and therefore not addicted, why would you still want to smoke? That is rather like me saying why would I still hanker after a smoked salmon sandwich when I haven't had one for months. I haven't forgotten what smoked salmon tasted like. And you haven't forgotten how tobacco relieves the physical craving for nicotine - long after you no longer have the craving or need to relieve it.

☐ It's Not Addiction - It's All in The Mind

That's possible, I suppose, so let's investigate how likely it is. Take a substance, say tobacco, which for the sake of this argument, no-one has ever used. Dream up some marketing campaign to get people not only to try it, but to convince them that, although it tastes revolting, they should keep using it until they can overcome their distaste. Despite massive punitive taxation, persuade every user that their life would not be worth living without it, even if they are on benefit and have to go without food to get it. Then put a death threat on the pack, backed up by statistics that it kills one user every six minutes.

The person who could do all this does not exist. Either millions of people are certifiably insane, or there is something in tobacco that forces them to continue using it.

☐ When Stressed a Cigarette Will Help

This is covered thoroughly in Chapter 11.

☐ One Won't Matter

It depends on what is meant by matter. Will it kill you? No. Will it re-addict you? Probably not. Will it make you believe you have started smoking again, thereby destroying all the good work you have done? Quite likely, which is why it will matter. Now ask yourself why anyone would say one won't matter. If it really wouldn't matter, what is the point of smoking it? If you are planning to spend the rest of your life without smoking, what conceivable point could there be in smoking just one? To find out if you can? Well of course you can. To find out what they taste like? You know what they taste like.

The point of smoking just one is that you have been programmed by the tobacco companies to think like that. That 'just one' has tripped thousands of people up at the last minute, just as they they thought they were becoming free. The sole purpose of having just one is to get you back on the product.

☐ *One Cigarette Means Failure*

And having had just one, the next thing you think is that it means you have failed - even if you didn't smoke the previous thousand! That is why you were supposed to think one wouldn't hurt, because the next step is usually to smoke more. If you do smoke one cigarette, it does not mean you have failed. It means you have smoked one cigarette.

If one means failure, how come not smoking a thousand, or a hundred, or even ten, doesn't mean success? And if you didn't smoke the last ten, or you didn't smoke for the last twenty-four hours, you have succeeded. If then you smoke one, I really don't see how you can call that failure. Put it out and get on with the rest of your life.

☐ *The Feeling of Deprivation Will Never End*

How likely is this to be true? Ask someone who has not smoked for six months if they still feel that way, and they will say no. What about three months?

If you feel deprived, what are you depriving yourself of? Smoke again, and satisfy that feeling - then start the whole process again, because you have got to go through it some time and you might as well do it now.

☐ *It's Impossible to Overcome the Habit*

This is covered in detail in Chapter 8

☐ *It is Possible to Wean Yourself off Nicotine*

Many people buy a nicotine replacement product in the mistaken belief that it will help to wean them off nicotine. This is not what NRPs are for, as you read in Chapter 15.

If you consume nicotine, your body knows, and it switches off the craving for it. Your body is extremely good at this, and it will find nicotine in the tiniest dose. Clearly, every dose of an NRP contains nicotine; it is supposed to. Therefore, when you use the product, your body, as it is supposed to, detects nicotine. How do you imagine it suddenly decides "Oh, that wasn't much, so I won't treat it as nicotine"? What mechanism could possibly exist in your body to stop seeing nicotine as nicotine? If you take a drug, your body will use that drug. If it uses the drug, you are still addicted. When you stop using the drug, you go through withdrawal from that drug.

This does not mean that NRPs don't work; it means they don't wean you off nicotine, because they are not intended for that purpose. Only when you understand what their true purpose is will you have a chance of using them correctly and perhaps succeeding.

If you really want to wean yourself off nicotine, try weaning yourself off cigarettes, perhaps by smoking fewer, and smoking less of each one. At some point (probably at the Addiction Threshold) you will go into withdrawal. That is the point at which you stop smoking altogether, because, as you will have read before, you have four days of withdrawal, so go for it.

There is an argument that by using an NRP you will be taking less tar into your body, but that has nothing to do with stopping smoking. If you are using an NRP to wean yourself off nicotine you are doing it wrong.

☐ A Low-Nicotine Cigarette is Less Addictive

Because you are either addicted or you are not, the quantity of nicotine you take at any one time has no bearing on that addiction. You get satisfaction from a cigarette or you don't. If you do, that cigarette has provided you with the amount of nicotine you need. In fact your body only uses a minute amount of chemical data from the nicotine to fulfil its needs - more than 99% of even the weakest cigarette is not used by your body.

However, a low-nicotine cigarette is also a low-tar cigarette, and that, although it has nothing to do with your addiction, must be less harmful to your health.

☐ Some People Have an Addictive Personality

As you have already read in Chapter 6, addiction is not in the mind, and therefore what kind of personality you have does not affect whether or not you become addicted. Your personality will affect what happens *after* you become addicted, which means how likely you are to become deeply psychologically dependent, and we would call that a dependent personality. Such a personality might make someone afraid to stop smoking because they think they need it. Understanding the difference may be important.

☐ Once a Smoker Always a Smoker

I'm going to be picky here, because to some extent this is true, but it really means once you have smoked, you will always be someone who has smoked. Tobacco dependence changes the way the brain works, for ever. Once your brain has been altered by continued use of tobacco, you cannot change it back again. That is something you will have to learn to live with. It's not particularly hard - ask any ex-smoker.

But living the life of someone who used to smoke does not mean you are going to be fighting it for ever. I used to smoke, and I look at people doing it and feel no desire whatever; what I do feel is recognition, which frankly is not a problem.

If you have a friend who tells you they still want to smoke, years after stopping, ask them why they don't. What they actually mean is that they recognise smoking, and remember what it used to be like. That is not the same thing as fighting off the desire to do it again. And to some extent ex-smokers enjoy feeling a bit deprived, perhaps because it makes them feel a bit virtuous.

☐ *There Is No Point Cutting Down*

This is covered in Chapter 18

☐ *You Have to Want to Stop to Succeed*

You don't want to stop. You want to be a non-smoker, but don't confuse that with wanting to stop, because they are quite different. To succeed, the thing you need more than anything else is to accept one fact - that you want to be a non-smoker. How do you know you want to be a non-smoker? Ask yourself this question: Do you wish you had never started smoking? If the answer is yes, then you want to be a non-smoker. That is all you need to know. Forget about whether you want to stop - from now on never forget you want to be a non-smoker.

THE QUESTIONS PEOPLE ASK

(The number in brackets denotes the chapter that covers the subject fully.)

■ *If smoking is as dangerous as we are told, why are 14 million people still doing it?* (3)

☐ It's a strange quirk of history. Those people are addicted, so they don't look at smoking the way non-users do. They know it's wrong, but they can't feel it's wrong, because the drug won't let them.

■ *What is the point of stopping if I'm under thirty?*

☐ As you get older, you become psychologically more dependent (but not more addicted). People don't stop when they are young, which is when they could do it, then they want to when they are older, when they can't. So give it a try, and decide once you have succeeded if you really want to go back to tobacco.

■ *What is the point of stopping if I'm over sixty?* (3)

☐ Smoking makes you unhealthy. When you are young and strong, poor health can be overcome, but not so well when you are old.

■ *How can I be expected to stop while society and the government condone smoking?* (3)

☐ The only sensible answer is that you have to accept responsibility yourself. If you wait for the government to ban a drug that kills 120,000 people a year, you will be long dead.

■ *Isn't smoking just a habit?* (8)

☐ No. No habit is powerful enough to get 14 million people spending good money on a product known to kill 300 users a day.

■ *Am I addicted to smoking?* (4)

☐ No. No-one is addicted to smoking. You are addicted to nicotine, and you smoke because cigarettes are the delivery method for the drug - and this makes you psychologically dependent on cigarettes.

■ *Does habit stop me giving up?* (4)

☐ No. As long as you are addicted you will remain psychologically dependent, and as long as you are dependent you will believe that habit makes you smoke, but it's not true.

■ *How can I tell if it's habit or addiction that makes me smoke?* (8)

☐ Easily. Habit can't make you smoke, so it must be addiction.

■ *How can some people just be social smokers?* (6)

Although the Addiction Threshold is about 5 a day, one cigarette every four days is enough to keep you addicted. Even passive smoking is enough to keep you addicted. Most social smokers in fact use tobacco once or twice a week, and passive smoke as well.

■ *Why is smoking the only habit I can't change?* (8)

☐ Because it is the only habit you have that involves an addictive drug.

■ *How do I stop using cigarettes as rewards?* (8)

☐ A cigarette is a reward for not smoking. It is not a reward for finishing the ironing. Check it out by smoking just before you finish the ironing.

■ *Why can I cut down to five or six a day but no further?* (6)

☐ This is how many it takes, on average, to maintain the addiction comfortably (the Addiction Threshold). When you cut down, say from 20 a day, you change your habits and do other things which you can control. If you go below your threshold, you will experience withdrawal symptoms to make you increase the fix rate.

■ *What is the difference between the Addiction Threshold and the Addiction Level?* (6)

☐ Your Addiction Threshold is the number of fixes you need each day to keep withdrawal symptoms at bay. It's typically five or six. Your Addiction Level is the chemical information your body uses to interpret the poisons in tobacco smoke. It is a clinical measure taken when assessing the endpoint for tobacco neutralisation, and concerns you only if you are undergoing A.N.T.

■ *How does dependence reduce my motivation to stop smoking?* (7)

☐ When you are addicted to a drug, this produces fear of coming off that drug. This fear is the main element of psychological dependence, and it is probably the most important psychological hold that tobacco has over its users.

■ *How do I control my addiction?* (6)

☐ Unless you are on A.N.T., you just come off it. What is important to remember is that this process takes only four days, so do not confuse addiction with what is left - your psychological dependence.

■ *Why don't I enjoy all the cigarettes I smoke?* (9)

☐ Because enjoyment stems from the satisfaction of low-level craving, you will enjoy those cigarettes more which satisfy the greatest need. Many of your cigarettes are smoked simply out of habit, and this brings little or no 'enjoyment' because the need is missing. This proves that you don't actually enjoy smoking, otherwise you would enjoy all the cigarettes you smoke.

■ *Will I enjoy going to the pub again if I don't smoke?* (9)

☐ Yes.

■ *What will I do after meals when I no longer smoke?* (9)

☐ The washing up.

■ *Why do I enjoy smoking even though I want to stop?* (9)

☐ As long as you are addicted, you will 'enjoy' the relief from subliminal withdrawal that a cigarette always gives you, particularly if you have not had one for a while. Wanting to stop does not change this. What is important to remember is that after you have come off tobacco, you will stop enjoying it, because only an addict can get that enjoyment. So you are not giving anything up.

■ *Why is it I hated smoking at first but now enjoy it?* (9)

☐ Smoking is unpleasant. It only becomes pleasant once you are addicted to the nicotine it delivers. You do not enjoy smoking, but you do enjoy the result - the relief of the need to smoke.

■ *Will I ever stop enjoying smoking?* (9)

☐ Yes, within five days of stopping. After that you might think you would enjoy one, and if you want to find out, smoke one, because you cannot enjoy a cigarette if you are not addicted to nicotine.

■ *Is smoking my own fault?* (18)

☐ No. It is the fault of the manufacturers, the pushers, the government, the medical profession, and a society that is too blind to see the insanity.

■ *How do I know when I've failed to stop?* (18)

☐ You can't, ever.

■ *How do I know when I've succeeded?* (18)

☐ If you don't smoke for one day, you have succeeded - at stopping smoking for one day. All you have to do now is do it again. And again.

■ *What is the point of cutting down?* (18)

☐ Smoking is bad for you. The less you do it, the less bad it is.

■ *Why can't I stop thinking about smoking when I stop?* (18)

☐ You cannot walk away from tobacco abuse. You can stop doing it, but you can never become someone who never smoked. The psychological dependence will never go away, it can only diminish (eventually to the point where it no longer matters). Think about it all you like, just don't do it.

■ *Does stress make me smoke?* (11)

☐ No. It might make you smoke more if you are currently a user, but it can't make you smoke if you're not.

■ *If the addiction is over in a few days, why do I still feel ill weeks later?* (13)

☐ Withdrawal symptoms can make you feel ill, but so can detoxification, as can the recovery process. Whatever is causing it, it will stop.

■ *If the addiction is over in a few days, why do I still want to smoke weeks later?* (7)

☐ There are many reasons for wanting to smoke, one of which is the mistaken belief that you can't. You can, so it is a mistake to go around thinking you are being deprived. You can - but you don't need to.

SUCCESS AND FAILURE

The Short Explanation

This is probably the only book on stopping smoking that actually explains the difference between success and failure. You wouldn't think I would need to, but you would be wrong. How many times have smokers rung us and said they had succeeded, only to reveal that they were still on nicotine patches, so they didn't in fact know whether they were succeeding or not, because they were only dealing with the one small part of their smoking problem, the habit of lighting cigarettes.

And in our clinics we always ask patients about their history of trying to stop. They will often say they stopped with a nicotine replacement product, but what do they mean by stopped? What they mean is they weren't smoking, but they started smoking again when they stopped using the NRP, so what do they mean when they say they were successful?

Conversely, we get people saying they failed some previous attempt, perhaps because they stopped for just a few weeks (without substitutes) and then started again. I don't believe they failed. I believe they succeeded, and then started smoking again. At the time they were not smoking, they had succeeded.

Some years ago we had an elderly patient who was of a nervous disposition. To her surprise, she succeeded, but she had a lot of stress issues in her life, and we referred her to her GP. She told him she had stopped smoking, to which he replied, "Oh yes, how long for?" She told him it had been five weeks so far, and his answer was, "Come off it, five weeks is nothing. Let me know when you haven't smoked for a year, then I'll believe you've succeeded".

Were I in authority, that doctor would at that moment have lost his licence. The patient was so distressed at being told she was not succeeding, she failed. Apart from the fact that the doctor was a disgrace to his profession for using a patient to show off his power, he was commenting on a subject about which his sum total of knowledge would fit on a postage stamp and leave room to spare.

This story is a very good illustration of one of the main reasons people fail to stop smoking. They judge whether they are succeeding, and if they feel they might not be, they give up.

So my advice is always this - do whatever you have to do to come off tobacco. Do not attempt to decide whether you are doing well or not, because it doesn't matter. Whatever you are doing is better than sitting on your backside. Do not listen to other people, doctors, smokers or ex-smokers, because between them they know nothing. Only you know what is happening to you, and if you are not smoking, you are succeeding. If you are smoking less than normal, you are succeeding. Every day you are trying to stop, you are succeeding. By reading this book, you are trying, so you are succeeding. Well done.

SUCCESS AND FAILURE   18
The Long Explanation

Almost everyone who tries to come off tobacco underestimates the task. They expect to succeed, and to succeed immediately. The conventional wisdom is that you have to choose your moment, then stop dead and just forget you were ever a smoker. This is naive nonsense.

Typically this sort of misinformation is put about by those who would like to believe it is true because they have no other answer. Time and time again we see patients who say they have been told to stop, as if such advice were some sort of miracle cure. If anything it is arrogant and patronising, and smokers resent it.

One group of people who tell you simply to stop is ex-smokers. "You don't need any patches or other gimmicks, I just woke up one morning and decided I'd had enough, so I stopped, there and then, mind you wouldn't it be nice if I could be a social smoker but I can't, I know I couldn't trust myself, it's been ten years now and not a week goes by when I don't feel tempted, you ask my wife, mind you she's been trying for years, got no willpower, spends a fortune trying to stop, you should hear her coughing of a morning, blather, blather, blather......."

If you are being troubled by a smug ex-smoker show them this book. Even if they don't actually read it, its very thickness should make them see there's more to it than they realise. The fact is that some smokers can stop easily, and some can't. And since you are reading this book the chances are you have difficulty stopping, so you are not one of the lucky ones.

The result of all the well-meant if clumsy advice is that when you finally have a real go at stopping, anything less than immediate and absolute success is seen as failure. But forget that idea and just put the whole thing into perspective.

- You are currently dependent on a drug as addictive as heroin. Would you expect a heroin addict to stop 'just like that"?

- You have smoked for a long time. How many years is it? Do you seriously expect to be instantly able to stop something you have been doing for that length of time?

- You have been using nicotine as a tranquiliser and probably as a stimulant as well. Are you suddenly going to be able to do without that tranquiliser, and the stimulant, just because you decided to stop smoking?

☐ Stop Blaming Yourself

With all the pressure to stop, you are left with the belief not only that you should do it, but also that it is your fault if you can't. Let's look at this idea because you almost certainly do believe it is your fault.

In our research clinics we ask the following question:

Who do you blame most for your inability to stop smoking?

A. The tobacco industry, government, doctors
B. Yourself

Which would you tick? If you are like 99% of patients, you would blame yourself. Now let's see if this is reasonable. Try to think back to when you first smoked. The reason you started was almost certainly that someone either gave you a cigarette, or at least put the idea into your mind. Most young people start smoking because of peer pressure.

The reason you persevered, despite your strong distaste for tobacco, was the pressure not to give up, because if other people enjoy it it must be good. (This is a fascinating contradiction - your own intelligence was telling you it was awful, but you were determined to enjoy it because other people did!)

It takes as little as a week to become addicted to nicotine, so while you were still desperately trying to get used to being a smoker, you were already addicted. So now you were smoking, not because you wanted to, but because you had to.

You were not to blame for trying cigarettes. You were under pressure to do so. You were foolish to give in to the pressure, but foolishness is a part of the human condition. You were not to blame for being determined to overcome the difficulty of smoking, for the same reason. And you were not to blame for becoming addicted. That was the fault of the drug, and the pushers - the tobacco companies.

No-one told you, all those years ago, in a meaningful way, that smoking would shorten your life, would drastically reduce your spending power, and would one day make you a social outcast, did they? You are not the culprit in your smoking problem. You are the victim.

And if you are the victim, just who *is* to blame? Think about it. Who makes the cigarettes? Who sells them? Who taxes them? Who tells you to stop smoking but has no way of helping you? Now do you know who is to blame?

So for goodness' sake, stop blaming yourself. Start to think of yourself as a victim. You have been had. You are spending a great chunk of your income on something you don't want, you know is going to shorten your life, and you feel guilty about.

You think you are stupid for doing it, don't you? If the answer is Yes, then read the last few paragraphs again, because you aren't. At all times, while you are trying to come off tobacco, say to yourself, "It is not my fault, I am not stupid, I have been fooled into becoming a drug addict and I am trying to do something about it". You might want to add, "With a fat lot of help from anyone else".

As long as you blame yourself, you aren't going to have a lot of patience with yourself. And you are going to need a great deal of patience.

☐ Stop Believing You Are a Failure.

None of this is intended to put you off trying. In our long experience in clinics, smokers have shown repeatedly that they have failed not because they can't stop smoking, but because they were expecting too much, too quickly.

I could, with some justification, say that stopping smoking is easy. After all, if you were locked in a cell you couldn't smoke. If you had no money at all, and no friends to cadge from, you couldn't smoke. If your hands were tied behind your back you couldn't smoke. And if you had some serious disease of the mouth you couldn't smoke.

What this means is that if the ability to smoke were outside your control, you would not be able to do it. The reason you *can* do it is precisely because it *is* in your control. Given that you are a rational human being, you should be able to exercise enough control to stop smoking. That you cannot do so is testament not to the impossibility of stopping smoking but to your own lack of control.

I have spent some time explaining it because you have got to stop thinking in terms of success and failure. Anyone can stop smoking - *everyone* can stop smoking. Recognise that success is available to you, but that it is going to take time, effort and understanding. If you have difficulty stopping smoking, don't give up trying.

So many people fall into the trap of thinking that unless they are immediately successful they have failed. They haven't failed - they just haven't succeeded *yet*. The task is simply going to take longer than they thought.

Just imagine that you are trying to stop smoking right now. Let's say you normally smoke twenty a day. In the last twenty four hours you have struggled with a desperate craving but you haven't given in to it, and you finally go to bed praying that tomorrow will be better. But tomorrow is worse, much worse. You wake up wishing you were dead. You cannot possibly face the day without a cigarette. Finally you cave in - you dash to the corner shop and smoke like there is no tomorrow. Before you know it you have smoked three. You are sitting at the kitchen table with a cup of tea and seventeen cigarettes in the pack. You light another.

It's not that you would normally have four in half an hour, but you need to make up for lost time. Sixteen left in the pack and the whole day ahead of you. You might as well smoke that day, and try again tomorrow. At this point you are a hundred percent failure.

☐ Start Believing in Cutting Down

Now let's look at another scenario. Alright, so you go and buy a pack. But cigarettes come in tens as well as twenties. Why would you buy twenty? Ten is more than enough to avoid disaster. You get home having smoked two. Now *wait*. You wait because you must give your body time to get the 'benefit' of the two cigarettes. Sure, you have a cup of tea, but now you are exercising some self-control, so you don't light up the third one.

Of course, you don't have to exercise self-control. You can smoke instead, that's entirely up to you. You are the one who wants to stop smoking. And if you really do want to stop, why would you light the third one? Light it, and you've given up trying. Don't light it, and you're in control.

If you don't light it, you have passed the test. Now let's imagine the rest of the day. You don't smoke any more that morning, but you have one with your afternoon cup of tea, and one that evening. Is this failure? If you have smoked a pack of twenty, you would have been a hundred percent failure, but you only smoked four. You reduced your smoking by eighty percent, so you are only a twenty percent failure. Well done.

Now a spoilsport will tell you that what you have managed is no good - either you stop smoking or you don't. That if you smoke at all you are a failure. This is rubbish. We are talking about one day, not the rest of your life. Cutting your smoking by eighty percent cannot conceivably be regarded as failure.

Would you expect a child to walk as soon as it learns to stand, to run as soon as it can walk? So why do so many people insist that smoking four cigarettes means failure? Frankly, even a twenty percent reduction is better than nothing, but almost any smoker could reduce their consumption by fifty percent at a stroke, if they were serious about it. You need only five or six cigarettes a day to maintain your addiction, so to cut down from twenty to ten is not as difficult as you think. To cut down from forty to twenty is even easier. Twenty is the average usage per day, so how can smoking twenty be difficult? Cutting down doesn't take a lot of effort, just thought. And the thought is this: stop trying to succeed instantly.

☐ Start Exercising Self-Control

Imagine you are a forty-a-day smoker. Wouldn't it be nice to be a twenty-a-day smoker instead? You would probably agree that it is easier to stop smoking if you are a twenty-a-day person than if you are a forty-a-day person, so there is definitely some point in cutting down like this. And by the same token there is some point in cutting down, if you currently smoke twenty, to ten. It isn't the end of smoking, but it *is* the beginning of the end. It means you are taking control, instead of tobacco controlling you. With control you are in a position of power.

If you can demonstrate to yourself that you can control your smoking, you will believe in your eventual success. But by saying to yourself, "If I've smoked one I might as well continue", you are just demonstrating that you have no serious intention of stopping.

Now imagine that you have shown this self-control and halved your smoking. And imagine that you can keep at the same level for several months. You are on the way to becoming a non-smoker, but instead of being one of those people who are forever stopping and starting you are in control, you are halving the damage to your health and you are saving a lot of money. Well done.

What you may be thinking at this stage is that it is not possible to cut down your smoking like this because it will simply go back up again. Let's examine this idea. Is it true, or is it a myth?

If you tried cutting down before, and found that you did indeed gradually increase again, think now why this happened. There were probably two reasons. The first would have been that you were stressed, and you believed you needed to smoke to deal with the stress. The second would have been that you couldn't see the point of keeping your smoking down anyway.

This was because you had been brainwashed into believing that you should either stop completely or not at all.

From now on, even if the same thing happens, remember that there is always a point in reducing the amount you smoke. Because if you can't control **how many** you smoke, how are you ever going to control **whether** you smoke?

☐ Stop Allowing Yourself The Luxury of Failure

If you stop smoking for six months you will feel great. You are a winner. And if you then give in momentarily you are suddenly a failure. This is what some experts try to make you believe anyway. They say you are only a success if you stop smoking for a year or more. How silly this is - a heavy smoker would be delighted to stop smoking for six months. If you stop smoking for six months, you are at that point a success. One day's smoking, or even one week's smoking, does not make you a failure.

If you have a temporary lapse, you are only a *temporary* failure. The critical thing is to come to terms with what has happened and to accept that the failure is temporary. You could even say it is not a failure at all, because as long as you really want to stop smoking (but see Chapter 3), and are prepared to continue working at it, how can you be a failure? You just haven't succeeded *yet*.

This belief that temporary failure equals total failure is one of the most depressing myths in the whole business of stopping smoking. Don't ever be fooled into believing it.

Why do so many people believe in failure at this point? Remember that all the time you are trying to stop smoking there is a little devil inside your head trying to persuade you to start again. You are constantly in conflict with yourself - you want to stop but you are psychologically dependent, so you always harbour a small hope that you will fail.

Most smokers subconsciously hope for failure because they can then say, "I've really tried. I really did want to stop smoking, but I failed. It's obviously impossible for me to stop, so I'm just making life harder by trying." Have you ever felt this way?

If you have, you can see how easy it is to believe in failure. And one cigarette, or even a whole day's cigarettes, can be enough to make you believe you have failed. Giving in to failure is easy. Anyone can do it. The point is though, that you have not failed. You may not have succeeded but you have not failed either. You have not failed until the day you die, and if you stop smoking the day before you die, you succeeded.

And this brings me very conveniently to the question of what exactly success means.

☐ How Do You Know When You Have Succeeded?

At the moment you have a desire - to stop smoking. But what does this mean? How do you define your target? Stop smoking for ever, or just for the next twenty years? If it is indeed only twenty years (and you really wanted to stop for ever) will you have failed? Obviously, twenty years as a non-smoker cannot be called failure. But what about ten years, or five? It is common for people to stop for five years and then start again, but few of them would say after four years and eleven months that they had failed to stop smoking. Even after they started again, they would probably say they had stopped successfully for five years but then started again.

Your target is to come off tobacco for ever, but there will be a point at which you would accept that you have succeeded. When do you think that will be? After one year, two, three? If you are a heavy smoker (forty-a-day or more) six months might look like a long time (let's face it, one week might look like a long time).

Similarly how do you define failure? Logically you have failed if you haven't achieved your target, but we have a problem here. Your target is to stop smoking for ever, and yet we have just agreed that twenty years, even though it is not for ever, would be considered success. And so would ten years, or five, or perhaps even one.

So now you need to ask yourself an interesting question. How do you know when you have failed? Confusing, isn't it?

The point is that you cannot actually define failure, so stop believing in it. You have only failed when you give up trying to succeed. And you stopped trying to succeed in the past because you thought you might as well.

Apart from the obvious practical reasons, the reasons people fail when trying to stop smoking are:

- They don't know how to stop, because no-one tells them.
- They set impossible targets, because our national culture is built on reward for success, instead of support.

In our clinics our culture is one of support, rather than targets. Our patients know they will be supported indefinitely, so worrying about success and failure is pointless. Even if they start smoking again, they haven't failed; there is just more work to do. Despite all this, we get depressed at the number of times we encounter smokers who cannot make this cultural change.

☐ Learning From Your Attempts

The chances are that you've tried to stop smoking before and failed. What lessons do you feel you learned from that failure? Probably that you yourself were to blame for your failure, you are a failure yourself, you are no good, you have no willpower, you are stupid and everything is your fault - none of which is likely to be true, and you probably know it in your more rational moments.

It is just possible that it wasn't your fault. And, in any case, where does fault come into it? Since you almost certainly underestimated the difficulty of overcoming the addiction, and were given no expert help with handling stress, and quite possibly got little or no support from those who should have helped you, you would seem to have learned entirely the wrong lessons.

☐ Exercise

Take a sheet of paper for each attempt you have made to stop smoking. Write down the reasons you have failed in each case - or for going back to smoking after you had succeeded, to put it correctly - whether it was very short-term success (days or weeks, or for quite a while (months or years). I'm going to guess what your reasons were, and suggest the lessons you might learn from them.

☐ Bad Temper / Irritability / Inability to Concentrate

Reason: These are withdrawal symptoms, over which you had no control.

You thought: you were weak-willed, because you believed you should have been able to control them.

Lesson: Recognise the symptoms (see Chapter 6), and accept that they are inevitable (unless you are on A.N.T.). Decide before you try to stop smoking what you are going to do about withdrawal symptoms, but don't be surprised by them.

☐ You Couldn't Get Cigarettes off Your Mind

Reason: When you stop smoking after many years you don't suddenly forget about it, much as you would like to. You are practising what is known as the wishful thinking method of stopping smoking.

You thought: you were never going to forget about smoking, and that you were quite likely to to be taken away by men in white coats.

Lesson: You were expecting too much, too quickly. You were probably in conflict because you were afraid of success and / or failure. Stop putting yourself under pressure. If it helps to have a pack of cigarettes handy, allow yourself to. Don't believe the myth (which you might have created yourself) that this will make you smoke.

☐ You Couldn't Get Over The Habit

Reason: Habit is a reason for continuing to smoke - it is not a reason for not being able to stop. Since you didn't understand that the habit was under your own control, you made no serious attempt to do so. You might have convinced yourself that you could not change your habits, but you were wrong.

You thought: that the habit was keeping you addicted. Naturally, you were wrong. What was keeping you addicted was the drug.

Lesson: First, come to terms with being responsible for your habits. Second, stop confusing habit and addiction. You can change your habits without help, but addiction might take more.

Third, having accepted responsibility for your habits, do something about them (see Chapter 8).

☐ You Needed to Smoke in a Social Setting

Reason: You have naturally always associated socialising with smoking. This might be no more than an habitual association or you might consciously feel that smoking is a prop in a social setting.

You thought: that this was a habit you would never break. If you were using a cigarette as a prop, you might also have believed you would not be able to cope in company without one.

Lesson: There are two separate lessons, because there are two possible problems. If it is an association problem you really do believe a glass in one hand means a cigarette in the other. But take a look at drinking, socialising non-smokers - do they have a cigarette in the other hand? No, so the association is not a fact of life but is personal to you. Logically then, you could become one of those non-smokers who do not make the association. This lies within your control.

The second potential problem is that you cannot manage in company without a cigarette. This may be true. However, the problem won't be removed by any stop-smoking therapy, so you are going to have to face up to it. Recognise that your problem is not that you cannot stop smoking but that you lack self-confidence. At this point ask yourself a question. You want to stop smoking, but you need cigarettes to cope with being in company. Are you going to tackle the issue of self-confidence, or are you going to hide behind smoking? Always deal with the real problem - in this case cigarettes are not the issue, stress is.

And now a thought to destroy the myth of needing to smoke in company. When you go out, say to the pub, who are you socialising with? The chances are that most of the company consists of old friends. And you can't have a drink and a chat with with friends you have known for years unless you have a cigarette in your hand? You've been kidding yourself. It is an excuse.

☐ You Were Fine Until You Came Under Stress

Reason: Stress did not make you smoke. It can't have done, because stress doesn't make non-smokers smoke. What made you smoke was the *belief* that you needed to smoke to cope with stress.

You thought: that smoking even a single cigarette would help. You were wrong.

Lesson: The first lesson is that smoking doesn't reduce stress. When are you going to learn this? Why is it so hard to learn? Because, for as long as you are addicted to nicotine, you will believe in the power of the drug. Even when you have overcome the addiction you will have years of conditioning to undo - but believe me when I say that you will, one day, realise that smoking was increasing your stress, not decreasing it.

The second lesson is what just one cigarette does. It gives you perhaps a 50-50 chance of becoming a smoker again. The reason is that all the time you were trying not to smoke you were in conflict with yourself. Wouldn't it be nice if you could have just one? As soon as you smoke just one, the memory of perhaps a quarter of a million cigarettes comes flooding back - and the overwhelming memory is of pleasure (because addicts 'enjoy' their drug). If you smoke just a few more, you will regain the adaptation you fought so hard to lose, by which I mean you will become addicted again.

☐ You Were Afraid of Your Success

Reason: Many would-be ex-smokers are afraid of succeeding, but this fear doesn't just go away once you have succeeded (if we count success as short term). In fact, immediate success can have an unfortunate effect: it sometimes makes people realise just how much they were secretly hoping to fail - they have succeeded almost against their will. We see this in our clinics, because the neutrogen stops the addiction so quickly. This removes the normal excuse of the addiction, which can raise the paradoxical problem of unwanted success. The patient is then faced with issues he or she was perhaps unprepared for.

You thought: that you might have made a mistake - perhaps you were wrong about wanting to come off tobacco? Perhaps you were not ready? Perhaps it was a bad time to try? Perhaps nothing.

Lesson: Recognise that addiction and dependence are self-sustaining; by definition they fight for their own survival. Remember that dependence means you *think* you are still addicted, even when you no longer are. Think of dependence as your addiction's last line of defence.

At this stage you are primarily worried about the thought that you will never smoke again. Just a moment though - isn't this what you wanted? Why is there a conflict? The conflict arises because you only *thought* you wanted to stop; the desire to stop was in conflict with the addiction. No-one's desire to stop is 100 percent. What you are fighting is not your doubts about stopping, but nicotine and the dependence it has caused. Don't fight yourself, because you are not the enemy. The drug is the enemy. Think of it as a parasite that you have finally managed to expel but that is trying to re-invade you. If you allow it to do so, you have lost. Don't allow the enemy in, because once it has breached your defences not only will it be killing you but it will convince you that it is doing so for your own good.

CASE HISTORY

Mrs M. from Essex came into our London clinic, and was shocked when the neutrogen actually stopped her craving - within half an hour of the treatment she was bubbling with excitement because her addiction was suddenly under her own control. Two days later she smoked seven cigarettes, and she smoked between five and ten a day after that. Why?

She became afraid of her success, so she smoked a cigarette, and then she gave in to failure. She did not want to smoke that many - three or four a day would have been enough - but she gave in to the luxury of failing. It was easier to wallow in self-pity than make that one final effort to break out of her past.

On the other hand, even ten a day is a 75% reduction from forty. It took extended telephone counselling to persuade Mrs M that she had not failed. She kept saying, "Oh well, I'll try again". That was nonsense; she didn't need to try again, because she was succeeding. Other people had let her down before, and she expected us to do so now. It takes some patients a long time to accept that we aren't going to do that.

After thirty-six years as a heavy smoker, it was going to take Mrs M more than three weeks to become a non-smoker.

With the control over her addiction achieved by the neutrogen, and with a new attitude, she did indeed go on to become a non-smoker. But it took four months of learning to look for success, not out of a bottle or a packet, but within herself. Mrs M thinks we performed a miracle, but we didn't; we just helped her to achieve what had always been possible.

RESOURCES

For help and advice, you can contact the following:

■ Nicotine Replacement Products

    Quitline   0800 002200
    NHS Helpline   0800 1690169

    Both are run by Quit, which receives sponsorship from the drug companies, so both lines are restricted to advice on drug products, like NRPs and even Zyban.

■ Hypnotherapy and acupuncture

    NRPSC   www.nrpsc.org

    The National Register of Practitioners in Smoking Cessation advises on the use of acupuncture and hypnotherapy, and can direct you to a member in your area who is qualified and has experience in smoking cessation.

■ Addiction Neutralisation Therapy (A.N.T.)

    NHA   01273 205196
                    www.stop-smokingcentres.co.uk

    NHA National Stop-Smoking Centres are the only providers of A.N.T. in Britain, through The Phoenix Programme in our network of clinics.

■ Herbal cigarettes

   Honeyrose Customer Helpline   01449 612137

   Stocked by most health food shops (particularly Holland & Barrett) and some chemists.

■ Allen Carr's Easyway

   020 8944 7761

   A network of centres providing a form of cognitive therapy / hypnotherapy.

CHARLES JOHN PHIPPS F.S.A.
ARCHITECT TO THE VICTORIAN THEATRE

Görel Garlick

Entertainment Technology Press

Charles John Phipps F.S.A
Architect to the Victorian Theatre

© Görel Garlick

First published September 2016
Entertainment Technology Press Ltd
The Studio, High Green, Great Shelford, Cambridge CB22 5EG
Internet: www.etnow.com

ISBN 978 1 904031 89 5

A title within the
Entertainment Technology Press Historical Series
Series editor: John Offord

All rights reserved. No part of this publication may be reproduced in any material form (including photocopying or storing in any medium by electronic means and whether or not transiently or incidentally to some other use of this publication) without the written permission of the copyright holder except in accordance with the provisions of the Copyright, Designs and Patents Act 1988. Applications for the copyright holder's written permission to reproduce any part of this publication should be addressed to the publishers.

CODE / CJP-002 12-17

ACKNOWLEDGEMENTS

I would like to acknowledge my debt to earlier studies of this multifaceted architect, particularly to Dr Hugh Maguire's Ph. D. thesis 'C. J. Phipps (1835-1897) and Nineteenth Century Theatre Architecture', as well as to David Anderson's The Exeter Theatre Fire and to Mark Jones's and John Pick's Mr Phipps' Theatre – The Sensational Story of Eastbourne's Royal Hippodrome. I would also like to thank Mike Sell for suggesting new avenues of research when I stalled and Terry Sawyer for his information on the scene-painter and decorator George Gordon.

As always with a work of this kind, the invariably courteous assistance given to me over the years by archivists and librarians around the country has been invaluable. In particular I would like to thank the staff at the RIBA Institutional Archives, the British Architectural Library, the City of Bath Record Office, the Bath Central Library, the Victoria Art Gallery, Bath, the University of Bristol Theatre Collection, the Devon Heritage Centre, the Edinburgh City Archives, the Glasgow Life Archives, the Aberdeen City Archives and Library, the Leamington Spa Local History Society, the Leicestershire Record Office, the Sheffield City Archives and Central Library, the National Archives, and the London Metropolitan Archives.

I would also like to lavish thanks on my friend John Earl, who has patiently acted as my unofficial editor over all these years and generously provided many of the images for this book.

I also owe my husband a great debt for putting up with living in a ménage à trois with Mr Phipps for so long and for cheerfully accompanying me on countless journeys in search of Phipps's theatres.

Finally, I would like to express my gratitude to my publisher John Offord for taking on the book and to Jackie Staines, my technical editor, for her invaluable expertise and patience.

Görel Garlick

CONTENTS

INTRODUCTION 11

LIST OF ILLUSTRATIONS 13

1 ASPIRATION 19

2 COMPETITION 1862-63 33

3 OPPORTUNITY AND COMPROMISE 1864-68 49

4 NAVIGATING THE THEATRICAL FREE TRADE 69
    The London Gaiety and Mecklenburgh Square 69
    The London Vaudeville, the Dublin Gaiety
    and the Aberdeen Tivoli 78

5 FIGHTING SPIRIT 1875-77 93

6 PERPETUUM MOBILE 1877 - MAY 1880 105
    Three opera houses, two fires and
    Sadler's Wells 105
    The Haymarket Theatre Royal 116
    Torquay Theatre Royal 121

7 ENMESHED IN RED TAPE
   JUNE 1880- DECEMBER 1881 129
    The Savoy Theatre 135
    Belfast and Bristol 143

8 A MAN OF PROPERTY 1882 - 83 149
    The 'Gentlemen Upstairs', Captain Shaw and
    Drury Lane 149
    The Royal Strand Theatre, Hastings and
    Leamington Spa 155

	Eastbourne Theatre Royal 159
9	THE MASTER BUILDER 1883 - 1885 165
	The Edinburgh Lyceum 165
	The Prince's Theatre 169
	Trouble at Eastbourne 174
	Northampton and Portsmouth 176
	More trouble at Eastbourne 180
10	HUBRIS JUNE 1884 - NOVEMBER 1886 185
	Edinburgh Theatre Royal, Hengler's Grande Cirque and the Savoy Turkish Baths 185
	Exeter Theatre Royal, the London Lyceum and Dublin's Leinster Hall 188
11	BETRAYAL SEPTEMBER 1887 199
	The Fire 199
	The Interview 204
	The Home Office 211
12	THE INQUEST 217
	The Coroner 217
	The Justices' Clerk, Horace Lloyd J.P. and the City Surveyor 219
	The Architect 228
13	THE VERDICT 237
14	THE REPORT 249
15	ATONEMENT 259

16	THE SPECTRE OF CORRUPTION DECEMBER 1887 – OCTOBER 1888	273
	The Deputation	273
	The Royal Commission of Inquiry into the Metropolitan Board of Works	278
17	THE RE-LAUNCH	288
	The Shaftesbury Theatre	288
	The Lyric Club and the Lyric Theatre	294
18	LONG SHADOWS JUNE 1890 - DECEMBER 1893	307
19	THINKING DIFFERENTLY 1894-95	325
	Glasgow Theatre Royal and the National Skating Palace	330
20	RESOLUTION 1896 - 97	339
21	EPILOGUE	351

APPENDIX 1 THE STAGE AT THE THEATRE ROYAL, BATH IN 1863 ... 357

APPENDIX 2 THEATRE ROYAL HAYMARKET ... 359

APPENDIX 3 LIST OF THEATRES DESIGNED OR ALTERED BY C.J. PHIPPS ... 363

APPENDIX 4 ARCHITECTURAL DRAWINGS EXHIBITED AT THE ROYAL WEST OF ENGLAND ACADEMY BY C. J. PHIPPS ... 367

APPENDIX 5 LIST OF ARCHITECTURAL DESIGNS EXHIBITED BY C. J. PHIPPS AT THE ROYAL ACADEMY ... 368

APPENDIX 6 NON-THEATRE WORK BY C.J. PHIPPS 371

APPENDIX 7 PHIPPS FAMILY TREE 373

APPENDIX 8 THE LORD CHAMBERLAIN'S RULES AND REGULATIONS FOR THEATRES WITHIN HIS JURISDICTION 375

BIBLIOGRAPHY 379

INTRODUCTION

In the early eighteen-sixties, theatre design was no longer a field where serious-minded architects ventured if they could avoid it. They had every reason to stay clear. Theatre proprietors and managers, both in London and in the provinces, had a reputation for being the worst of clients, resistant to new-fangled ideas of more comfortable seating, spacious circulation areas and modern stage machinery. They clung to their old, worn down Georgian playhouses and when necessary replaced them with new Georgian-style buildings loaded with 'gingerbread-style' decoration intended to give a festive air to what was all too often no more than a draughty hall with tightly packed seating. That this insistence on a conservative design might be one reason why the upper and middle classes now rarely visited their theatres, was a notion that cash-strapped theatre owners were reluctant to consider.

It fell to a young architect in city of Bath, Charles John Phipps (1835-1897), to inject a new vitality and modernity into English theatre design when he won the competition to rebuild the Bath Theatre Royal after major fire in 1862. The design was widely publicised in the architectural press and Phipps, who had planned to specialise in church architecture, bravely switched to theatres and before long became the leading theatre architect of his generation.

When Phipps died in 1897, he had built and refurbished around 50 theatres, many of which are still in use, though altered in tune with modern requirements. They include: The Bath Theatre Royal; The Nottingham Theatre Royal; The Vaudeville, London; The Tivoli Theatre, Aberdeen; The Dublin Gaiety; The Glasgow Theatre Royal; The Lyceum, Edinburgh; The Royal Hippodrome, Eastbourne; Northampton Theatre Royal; Portsmouth Theatre Royal; The Lyric Theatre, London; The Grand Theatre, Wolverhampton; and Her Majesty's Theatre, London.

The design and construction process of nineteenth-century theatres seldom ran smoothly. The Victorian proscenium playhouse, with its intricate structural configurations both in front and behind the curtain, presented infinitely more pitfalls than a town hall or country house. The client's vision of his theatre was pivotal and Phipps produced his best buildings when he and his client were at ease with each other in a mutual understanding of how the final building should look internally and externally.

Yet, Phipps's glowing career also harbours a mystery: a careless and deeply flawed design for the Exeter Theatre Royal (1886) dashed off at the height of his fame. But for the disastrous fire in 1887, when around 180 people perished, the glaring shortcomings of the design, which undoubtedly contributed to the high death toll, would never have been exposed. The fire sent shockwaves through the nation from the Home Office and the London theatre establishment to the provincial magistracy and local theatre managers, all of whom scrambled to rectify a country-wide lack of enforcement of existing safety regulations.

Phipps, condemned in the architectural press as a disgrace to the profession, did all he could to reclaim his professional integrity. It took some time, during which Frank Matcham replaced him as Britain's leading theatre architect, but in the last three years of his life he returned with renewed vigour and produced innovative designs for three major theatres: the Grand Theatre, Wolverhampton, the Theatre Royal, Glasgow and his swansong, Her Majesty's Theatre in London.

LIST OF ILLUSTRATIONS

Chapter 1: ASPIRATION (1835-1862)
No. 1. Spencer's Belle Vue, Bath. Author's Collection.
No. 2. The Beaufort Square exterior of the Theatre Royal, Bath, designed by George Dance, 1805. Author's Collection.
No. 3. Number 5, Paragon Buildings, Bath. Author's Collection.

Chapter 2: COMPETITION (1862-1863)
No. 4. The Theatre Royal, Bath. Plan at Dress Circle level 1863, signed by Phipps. Photocopied drawing – original now lost. Bath Record Office.
No. 5. 'Le theatre au Bath', c. 1863. Watercolour of the auditorium of Bath theatre Royal by C.J. Phipps. Victoria Art Gallery, Bath and North East Somerset Council.
No. 6. Sawclose exterior of the Theatre Royal, Bath designed by C.J. Phipps. Author's Collection.
No. 7. Detail of carved capital from Sawclose exterior. Author's Collection.

Chapter 3: OPPORTUNITY AND COMPROMISE (1864-1867)
No. 8. Portrait of C.J. Phipps, late 1860s. Seated surrounded by books. Author's Collection.
No. 9. The Theatre Royal, Nottingham. Façade. Author's Collection.
No. 10. The Theatre Royal, Nottingham. Plan at Dress Circle level. Author's Collection.
No. 11. The Prince's Theatre, Park Row, Bristol. Main frontage. © Bristol Record Office.
No. 12. The Prince's Theatre, Park Row, Bristol. Site plan. © Bristol Record Office.
No. 13. The Queen's Theatre, 1867. View of auditorium. © Victoria and Albert Museum.

Chapter 4: NAVIGATING THE THEATRICAL FREE TRADE (1867-1874)
No. 14. The Gaiety Theatre, London. Plan 1867. John Earl Collection.

No. 15. The Gaiety Theatre, London. View of auditorium. John Earl Collection.
No. 16. Mecklenburgh Square, London. Exterior view. Author's Collection.
No. 17. The Hoxton Variety Theatre, London. John Earl Collection.
No. 18. The Vaudeville Theatre, London. View of auditorium 1879. John Earl Collection.
No. 19. The Gaiety Theatre, Dublin. View of the auditorium. Coloured lithograph, n.d. John Earl Collection.
No. 20. The Tivoli Theatre, Aberdeen. Balcony plan. 1872. © Aberdeen City Archives.
No. 21. The Tivoli Theatre, Aberdeen. Main frontage. Courtesy of Aberdeen Central Library.

Chapter 5: FIGHTING SPIRIT (1875-1877)
No illustrations.

Chapter 6: PERPETUUM MOBILE (August 1877-May 1880)
No. 22. The Theatre Royal, Plymouth., designed by John Foulston, 1810. Main Frontage. Author's Collection.
No. 23. The Theatre Royal Plymouth, designed by John Foulston. Ground plan. Author's Collection.
No. 24. The Royal Opera House, Leicester. Ground and Pit Plan signed by C.J. Phipps. © Leicester Record Office.
No. 25. The Theatre Royal, Haymarket, London, designed by John Nash. Author's Collection.
No. 26. The Theatre Royal, Haymarket, London. Plan at Balcony Level, 1879 by C.J. Phipps. Coloured drawing. Crown Copyright, National Archives.
No. 27. The Theatre Royal, Haymarket, London. Composite view of interior, 1880. Author's Collection.
No. 28. The Theatre Royal, Torquay. Main frontage. Author's Collection.

Chapter 7: ENMESHED IN RED TAPE (June 1880-December 1881).
No. 29. The Princess's Theatre, London. Composite view of interior, 1880. Author's Collection.

No. 30. The Savoy Theatre, London, c. 1880. The Embankment frontage. Author's Collection.
No. 31. The Savoy Theatre, London. Plan at Balcony Level by C.J. Phipps, 1880. Coloured drawing. Crown Copyright, National Archives.
No. 32. View of the auditorium of the Savoy Theatre, London, 1881. John Earl Collection.

Chapter 8: MAN OF PROPERTY (1882-1883)
No. 33. The Theatre Royal, Leamington Spa. Main frontage. Courtesy of Leamington Spa History Group.
No. 34. The Theatre Royal, Leamington Spa. View of Auditorium from stage. Courtesy of Leamington Spa History Group.

Chapter 9: THE MASTER BUILDER (1883-1884)
No. 35. The Royal Lyceum Theatre, Edinburgh. Main frontage. © Historic Environment Scotland (Scottish Colorfoto Collection).
No. 36. The Royal Lyceum Theatre, Edinburgh. Balcony Plan signed by C.J. Phipps. Coloured drawing. Courtesy of Edinburgh City Archives.
No. 37. The Prince's Theatre, London. Composite views of exterior and interior, 1884. John Earl Collection.
No. 38. The Theatre Royal, Portsmouth, 1884. Ground plan from Deeds, n.d. Ref. 1297A (6). Reproduced by kind permission of Portsmouth Libraries & Archives Service, Portsmouth City Council. All rights reserved.

Chapter 10: HUBRIS (June 1884-December 1886)
No. 39. The Theatre Royal, Edinburgh on fire, 1884. John Earl Collection.
No. 40. The Theatre Royal, Exeter. Ground plan, based on the architect's original plan, 1887. John Earl collection.
No. 41. The Theatre Royal, Exeter, 1886. Main frontage. John Earl Collection.

Chapter 11: BETRAYAL (September 1887)
No. 42. The Theatre Royal, Exeter on fire. 'The bulging of the curtain', 1887. John Earl Collection.
No. 43. The Theatre Royal, Exeter. The fire as seen from the street,1887. John Earl Collection.
No. 44. The Theatre Royal, Exeter. The auditorium after the fire, 1887. John Earl Collection.
No. 45. The Theatre Royal, Exeter. The third flight of the gallery stairs with pay box after the fire, 1887. John Earl Collection.
No. 46. 'Bodies awaiting identification at the London Inn', 1887. John Earl Collection.

Chapter 12: THE INQUEST (September 1887)
No. 47. Captain E. M. Shaw. Author's Collection.

Chapter 13: THE VERDICT (September 1887)
No illustrations.

Chapter 14: THE REPORT (October 1887)
No illustrations.

Chapter 15: ATONEMENT (October- December 1887)
No illustrations.

Chapter 16: THE SPECTRE OF CORRUPTION (December 1887-October 1888).
No illustrations.

Chapter 17: THE RE-LAUNCH (1888-1890)
No. 48. New Theatre Royal, Exeter. Plan by A. Darbyshire and E. Bennett Smith. Reproduced with the kind permission of the Devon Archives and Local Studies Service.
No. 49. The Shaftesbury Theatre, London. Main frontage. Author's Collection.
No. 50. The Shaftesbury Theatre, London. Plan at Balcony level, 1887. John Earl Collection.

No. 51. The Lyric Theatre, London. Main frontage. Theatres Trust. Knight Brothers' British Mirror Series.
No. 52. The Lyric Theatre, 1888. View of the auditorium. Author's Collection.
No. 53. Portrait of C. J. Phipps 1890, published in Building News. Author's Collection.

Chapter 18: LONG SHADOWS (June 1890- December 1893)
No illustrations.

Chapter 19: THINKING DIFFERENTLY (1894-1896)
No. 54. The Grand Theatre, Wolverhampton. Main frontage, Lichfield Street. From the Collections of Wolverhampton Archives and Local Studies.
No. 55. The Grand Theatre, Wolverhampton. View of proscenium with ornamented iron curtain. From the Collections of Wolverhampton Archives and Local Studies.
No. 56. The Theatre Royal, Glasgow. Dress circle plan, 1895, by C.J. Phipps. Coloured drawing. © Glasgow City Archives.
No. 57. The Theatre Royal, Glasgow. Longitudinal section, 1895. Author's Collection.

Chapter 20. RESOLUTION (1896-1897)
No. 58. Her Majesty's Theatre, London. Composite view of exterior and interior. Author's Collection.
No. 59. Her Majesty's Theatre, London. Plan at Balcony level. John Earl Collection.
No. 60. Her Majesty's Theatre, London. Longitudinal section, 1896. John Earl Collection.

Chapter 21. EPILOGUE
No illustrations.

1 ASPIRATION

Charles John Phipps was born into a family of up-market shoemakers with a sideline in property investments. The date was 23 March 1835, the place was Charlcombe,[1] a small village on the northern outskirts of Bath. His father, Mr John Rashleigh Phipps, owned a "Ladies Boot and Shoemaker's" shop in Bath, at no. 4 Saville Row, a narrow street situated in a fashionable part of town directly behind the Assembly Rooms, while his paternal grandfather, James Phipps, had his home and business as 'Ladies shoemaker' in Gay Street, a spacious shopping and residential street linking the elegant Circus with the equally stylish Queen Square. At the time of Charles's birth, James Phipps ran the business in partnership with a William Phipps, another shoemaker who was also a currier and probably supplied some of the leather for the shoes. William Phipps was eighteen years younger than James, but how they were related, if at all, has not been possible to establish.[2]

Charles Phipps's mother, Elizabeth Phipps, née Neate, was an independent-spirited governess from Wiltshire, with aspirations to establish her own school for young ladies regardless of marriage and children. At the time of the marriage in 1834, Elizabeth was twenty-four years old while her husband, a widower, was thirty-four.[3]

With a family firmly ensconced at the top-end of the retail market in ladies' shoes, Charles could reasonably have been expected to carry on the trade. Not so; his parents were clearly determined to give their son every opportunity to carve out a professional career, though it is highly unlikely that they ever envisaged a future in theatre architecture for their son. By the mid-1830s, the golden age of the English provincial theatre, which had begun in the 1770s, was on the wane.[4] The playhouse had lost its status as an exemplar of 'rational amusement' and, had instead, become a place of iniquity in the eyes of provincial middle class families striving for unimpeachable respectability. This suspicion of the theatre was particularly strong among non-conformists and both Charles's father and his paternal grand-father were members of the Wesleyan Methodist Church,[5] which did not look kindly on the playhouse. Elizabeth Phipps would appear to have been of a similar persuasion, judging by Charles Phipps's later recollection that his parents, stayed away from the theatre 'on religious grounds'.[6]

Mr and Mrs Phipps wasted no time in implementing their aspirations. Soon after the birth of Charles, they established themselves at no. 3 Spencer's Belle Vue, a substantial four-storey late eighteenth-century terraced house in Lansdown Road on the north side of the city.

Spencer's Belle Vue, Bath. Author's Collection.

The house enjoyed fine views of the surrounding countryside from the upper windows to the north-east and of the elegant crescents of Georgian townhouses to the south-west. It was a safe and healthy environment, away from the working class area in the centre, yet within walking distance of the city's fashionable parts and the shoe shop in Saville Row. It was perfect for a small boarding school for young ladies and in the *Bath Annual Directory* of 1835 Mrs Elizabeth Phipps is listed as 'School Mistress' at no. 3 Spencer's Belle Vue'.

Thus, Charles Phipps grew up in an unusually healthy city situated in a river valley and surrounded by green hills, as yet free from any industrial pollution, a city which also displayed a remarkably orderly architectural setting based on a restrained classical style coupled with judicious planning. This stylistic coherence owed its origins to a local architect John Wood the elder (1704-54) and his son, John Wood the younger (1728-81), who realised that the numerous hot sulphurous springs within the city which the Romans had once enjoyed, were bound to attract the English upper classes looking for a miracle cure to for the debilitating gout that increasingly plagued them. Drinking the foul-tasting water as well as bathing in it was highly recommended and wealthy visitors flocked to the city where enterprising local householders were not slow to take advantage of this lucrative invasion.

John Wood embarked on a speculative building spree leasing large areas of land on which he and his son built terraces of handsome three- and four storey town houses in the local stone in a sober classical style along a carefully planned townscape incorporating restorative parks and walks and shopping arcades. The city's first theatre, however, predates the Woods; it was erected in 1705 and replaced by a larger one in Orchard Street in 1750. By the early nineteenth century, when Bath's reputation as the place to be seen was at its height, a new purpose-built theatre was erected (1805) in Beaufort Square to the designs of the London-based architect George Dance (1741-1825) and under the supervision of the Bath city architect John Palmer.[7]

The Beaufort Square exterior of the Theatre Royal, Bath, designed by George Dance, 1805. Author's Collection.

At the end of the Napoleonic wars when continental travel became possible again and the royals decided that sea-bathing in Brighton was a more fulfilling experience than partaking of the Bath mineral water, Bath's popularity declined. The city was left with its healthy natural environment, and a surplus of large, solidly built houses, two attractions which made it a suitable place for schools but also for a growing middle class of fund holders, officers and clergymen in search of a quiet but stylish retirement.[8] There was no shortage of tradesmen and servants left over from the city's heyday as a tourist resort and during the 1830s and 1840s Bath slowly become a centre for education and retirement. The dominant presence of school pupils and pensioners did not foster a vibrant economy, but it generated respectability and kept many of the tradesmen, not least dressmakers, tailors and shoemakers in business, and offered employment to female servants for meagre wages.

In December 1836 Charles's grandfather, James Phipps, died and his father, John Rashleigh moved his business premises to 32 Gay Street.[9]

Thus, from 1837 the shop was listed under J. R. Phipps and William Phipps in the Bath directories. In 1841 the two men formalised their business relationship by a 'Bond of partnership'.[10] In the census of the same year, John Rashleigh described his occupation as 'leather sales'[11] suggesting that he was mainly concerned with the leather wholesale business perhaps, or, it might possibly have been a euphemism for shoemaker, which is how John R. Phipps later described himself in his will of 1849. Interestingly, in the Bath Poll Book of 1847, Charles's father described himself as 'Gentleman', implying that he was not just a tradesman.[12] He is likely to have some grounds for this as the Poll Book was a public document and as the husband of a headmistress he needed to present himself in the most respectable light possible. No. 3 Spencer's Belle Vue had become both home and business where the question of profit making, whether in footwear/leather sales or education, coupled with the thorny issues of social status and respectability, were ever present as was the sound of swishing skirts and giggling girls.

By 1841 Charles had a three-year-old brother, Henry James, and a three-month-old sister, Mary. In addition to Mr and Mrs Phipps, the 1841 census reveals the presence of 7 boarders aged from 10 to 15, Mrs Phipps's sister Naomi Neate, her sister-in-law Jane Wood, who might both have been helping out with the teaching and/or the children, plus three domestic servants.

Elizabeth Phipps must have been more than fully occupied with both school and family. She could not afford to let the duties of motherhood interrupt the smooth running of her school as there was stiff competition in Bath's education market. The Bath Post Office Directory of 1846 lists 115 private schools, an impressive figure for a city which in 1841 had a population of just over 38,000. There were also numerous private tutors in a range of subjects from classics to music, indeed the city was brimful with educational expertise, an unexpected development, perhaps, for a place that forty years earlier had been the most fashionable leisure-city in Britain.

Among this surfeit of schools and academies, the young Charles Phipps was educated at St Catherine's Hermitage run by a Mr Horner,[13] according to an interview for the *Biograph* in 1880. During the 1840s the only Mr Horner listed in the Bath Post Office Directories in connection with educational establishments was a William Horner who ran a "Classical and Mathematical School" at 33 Grosvenor Place on the London Road, within walking distance of Spencer's Belle Vue. Grosvenor Place exuded middle-class decorum: it consisted of two substantial terraces where retired residents were hemmed in by boarding schools of varying sizes. Mr Horner had 18 boarders between the ages of nine and 15 in 1841, and would, undoubtedly, have provided the right kind of education and social environment for the eldest son of ambitious middle class parents.[14] The school's curriculum with emphasis on Latin, Greek and mathematics was designed to prepare boys for university entry, for the law as well as for commerce and, possibly unintentionally, for an architectural career.

At some point between 1846/7 and 1851 Mr Horner moved his school to Somerset Lane and the nearby St Catherine's Hermitage where he had expanded to 25 boarders, while apparently narrowing the curriculum as his establishment was now described as a 'Classical School'.[15]

By the spring of 1851 Phipps had left school and was working as a 'Coroner's and Solicitor's Clerk' in Bath. This was a prestigious position for a 16-year-old,[16] which opened doors to respectability and social standing as well as a reliable income that would not be subject to the whims of middle class fashion. Instead he could look forward to a steady stream of convoluted property contracts, contested wills and general litigation with greater power to exact payment from his clients than his parents had ever had.

In 1851 his parents' business ventures seemed to be going well. The school had 12 boarders and Charles's father described himself as "Proprietor of Houses etc" in the census, thus avoiding any direct reference to the shoemaking firm. In the 1852 Electoral Register for Bath, Walcot Parish, he is listed as owning a freehold property 'Belle Vue' on the Upper Bristol Road, near Weston. His business partner, William Phipps, then living at 13 Walcot Parade, a row of terraced houses on the London Road, described himself as a 'Shoemaker and Employer employing 18 men', which suggests that the trade in ladies shoes was remarkably buoyant. William Phipps also employed two men and an apprentice in a currier business safely tucked away at no 3 Bath Street in the working class area. Whether these properties were owned jointly by the two men is unclear.

In 1853 two events took place, which were to affect Phipps's future profoundly: firstly, the death of his father on 19 May 1853,[17] and secondly, the arrival of the highly experienced and eminently respectable theatre manager James Henry Chute. Adjusting to the loss of his father, Phipps probably took little notice of Chute's entrance on the Bath scene; he could not possibly have foreseen that ten years later James Chute would become his mentor, friend and powerful ally.

In his will John Rashleigh Phipps left interest, proceeds and profits of his property, subject to the Bond of his partnership agreement of 1841, to his wife for "as long as she remained a widow" as well as to his three children, to be held in trust by his three executors until his daughter was 23 and the sons 25 years old. One of the executors was his 'dear wife'; the other two were well established tradesmen, like himself serving the upper and middle classes: William Withers, a hatter, hosier and glover, and John Gould, a tailor and clerical robe maker.[18] Not long after her husband's death, Elizabeth Phipps gave up her school, and moved out of Spencer's Belle Vue to 13 Walcot Parade,[19] the home of her husband's partner William Phipps. She was still there in 1856 and Charles is registered under that address in the 1857 poll book.

It is unclear whether Phipps was still working as a solicitor's clerk at the time of his father's death, but at this juncture, either just before or, perhaps more likely, just after his father died, he abandoned the study of legal documents and court rituals and entered instead into an apprenticeship at the architectural practice of James Wilson and Thomas Fuller at 1 Belmont, situated just east of the Assembly Rooms. This was a remarkable change of direction and it suggests that Charles might have had architectural leanings for some time but that his father had thought an architectural career too risky in uncertain economic times. The Bath architectural scene was fairly crowded in the early 1850s with ten practices in fierce competition over a small number of public buildings and relying heavily on 'bread-and-butter' work such as the refurbishment of old villas or, with luck, the building of new ones.

James Wilson (1816 -1900) was one of Bath's leading architects who had designed St Stephen's Church in Lansdown Road situated about 400 metres up a steep hill from Spencer's Belle Vue. The church was an impressive example of the burgeoning Gothic Revival with a spectacular square-based, octagonal tower culminating in corner pinnacles held down by elegant flying buttresses. It became the Lansdown parish church in 1845. The building, if not its services, must have been familiar to her eldest son and might possibly have triggered thoughts of an architectural career in early years.

Wilson's enthusiasm for the Gothic style seems to have encouraged a similar fascination with mediaeval architecture in Phipps who embraced his studies with an eagerness bordering on devotion spending, according to *The Biograph*, 'all his spare time sketching and drawing mediaeval churches and antiquities in Somerset and surrounding counties'.[20]

Wilson and Fuller also showed him that the Gothic style could equally be applied to secular buildings such as villas, town halls and schools, among the latter was The Proprietary College in Lansdown Road (now part of the Bath Royal High School) designed by Wilson in an exuberant Gothic idiom with a reckless disregard for symmetry and a generous application of elegant and wilful tracery. It was an exciting time to embark on an architectural career; anything seemed possible as the authority of a somewhat careworn Classicism was challenged by a rejuvenated Gothic in the 'Battle of the Styles'.

Not that the Gothic revivalists were merely concerned with new principles of beauty; the most ardent among them were equally, if not more so, motivated by the Christian roots of Gothic architecture. To them the Gothic Revival had a moral dimension, it proclaimed the true English Catholic values on which Britain had been founded and which had made the country a great power, but which had been pushed aside for too long under a welter of aggressive Protestantism. In order to proclaim these values more clearly through architecture, it followed that the design of churches from the shape of the ground plan to the height of the opening in the chancel arch (through which the elevation of the host might be seen), must be clearly rooted in Catholic tenets and ritual. It was a new functionalism which required architects to immerse themselves in the minutiae of High Church ritual, without straying too close to Rome, a task which would almost have been impossible without a certain sympathy with the Anglo Catholic world view. For Phipps, brought up in a Methodist household, the Anglo Catholic view of Christianity proved attractive, and he remained an Anglo Catholic all his life.

There is no evidence to suggest that his training under Wilson and Fuller gave much or, indeed, any consideration, to theatre design. Judging by the list of commissions, in the RIBA Drawings Collection, carried out by Wilson, the bulk of the work in the practice consisted of churches and chapels, with or without schools attached, town halls, police stations, villas and alterations to country houses, all in a variety of styles including classical, Romanesque, Gothic and Italian renaissance. There is no mention of theatres.

Even the architectural student's bible, Joseph Gwilt's *Encyclopaedia of Architecture*, 1842, has only a relatively short chapter on theatres which draws heavily on B.D. Wyatt's *Observations on the Design for the Theatre Royal Drury Lane,* 1813, which by the time of Gwilt's publication was a little out of date. Gwilt's lack of interest in theatres is a reflection of the time, by 1840 the drama on stage had lost its hold on the upper and middle classes both in London and outside the capital for a variety of reasons to do with a rising tide of evangelism, economic stagnation, fear of unruly behaviour among the 'gods' and the ever present prostitutes, and, not least, of the foul air that enveloped the auditorium. London stars in combination with Shakespeare could still draw the crowds, but from the architectural point of view, theatre buildings had lost their late eighteenth-century status as a popular public monument and sunk to the level of a low-grade commercial structure unlikely to bring fame or fortune to its designer.

In June eighteen fifty-seven, Phipps left Wilson and Fuller, and set off on the customary European tour to broaden his architectural horizons. He journeyed through Belgium, Bavaria and Lombardy to Rome where he made drawings of the Marcellus Theatre 'based on personal inspection'.[21] His attention to this masterpiece of Roman theatre architecture does not necessarily imply a serious interest in theatre design, the then ruinous building was one of the 'must see' works on any young architect's itinerary chiefly because of its magnificent scale and elegant structure. However, his stay in Rome was cut short by a 'fever', which forced him to return home earlier than he had originally intended. Phipps did not reveal the nature of the fever, but his early return suggests it had been serious enough to make too fatigued for any further travel.

Once back in Bath in early 1858, Phipps wasted no time in setting up his first practice at 2, Widcombe Crescent, just south of the river. Widcombe Crescent consisted of a curved terrace of substantial houses, a little grand for a young architect, perhaps, but he was joined here by his mother[22] and possibly also by his brother Henry, now 20, and sister, Mary aged 17. His mother might have been attracted by a potential teaching opportunity

Number 5, Paragon Buildings, Bath.
Author's Collection

offered by the presence of a girl's boarding school in no 5. The same year, Phipps was invited to join the Freemasons and was initiated into the Royal Cumberland Lodge,[23] thus laying the foundation for a network of useful connections.

Phipps and his mother did not stay in Widcombe Crescent for long; in 1859 they moved back north of the river to 5, Paragon Buildings.[24] Paragon Buildings was a grand name for the middle section of an extensive 18th-century terrace of four-storey houses with small gardens backing on to the busy Walcot Street in the commercial centre of Bath. It had the advantage of being more easily reached by prospective clients than Widcombe Crescent, and, judging by Phipps's neighbours, on one side a 25 year-old general practitioner, on the other a lodging house keeper, the leases were probably fairly reasonable.

At this stage, Phipps was doing his utmost to get his career off the ground and establish his credentials. In December 1859 he applied for associate membership of the Royal Institute of British Architects and was elected the following January. His nomination papers were signed by George Gilbert Scott, the nations' leading champion of the Gothic Revival, soon to begin a restoration project at Bath Abbey, and two lesser known RIBA fellows, Edward Hanson and John Whickham whose work is now largely unknown.[25] Having secured his entry into the most prestigious architectural association in the country he was then elected to membership of the Ecclesiological Society on 1st March, which suggests not only that he fully embraced the new functional church design which the society championed,[26] but also that he hoped and was ready to pursue a career in this particular branch of architecture.

This launching of his career on paper was, at least a start, while waiting for something more concrete to appear. Phipps probably also hoped that his recognition by professional bodies would impress his future father-in-law Eugene Hicks, a fund-holder and landed proprietor from Berkshire, whose daughter, Honnor Hicks, Phipps was most anxious to marry sooner rather than later. The couple waited until Phipps had received his share of whatever remained of the money left in trust by his father, which he was due on his 25th birthday, before marrying on 10 April 1860, in Bath at Lyncombe Parish Church.[27] There was some urgency with the marriage as Honnor seems to have already been pregnant. Their first child was born six months later, on 16 October 1860.[28] That money was tight, is clear from the 1861 census. The Phipps family had only one resident servant, a young girl of 17. Phipps's mother had then left the young family and moved back south of the river to no.1 Elm Place on the Wells Road.

The marriage to the daughter of a landed proprietor confirmed Phipps's rise up the social ladder from tradesman's son to professional man, however his new social status also put additional pressure on him to acquire public, preferably major commissions. The standard route for such work was mainly through architectural competitions and in 1861 Phipps tried his utmost with smaller projects, including a drinking fountain in Boston, Lincolnshire and a Corn Exchange in Newbury, neither of which resulted in a commission.[29] These disappointments were, to some extent, mitigated by a commission from the Bath Hanoverian Band Committee for a spacious bandstand for 60 players in Sydney Gardens, the city's main pleasure grounds.[30] A delightful watercolour by Phipps, reveals an open structure with a curved and upward-sloping sounding board supported on slim iron columns with the band in their red uniforms in action.[31] And his situation began to improve. He entered a competition for a mortuary chapel and cemetery in Pewsey, Wiltshire, where his interpretation of the Gothic Revival appealed to the judges who awarded him the commission in early 1862.[32] It could not have been more timely; his second child, Charles Eugene was born on 25 January 1862.[33]

To raise Phipps's profile with other potential diocesan patrons his old mentor, James Wilson together with George Gilbert Scott, both fellows of the Society of Antiquaries, offered their personal support by recommending him for election to the Society, a move which was also promoted by a distinguished Bath resident and former Director of the Society, James Heywood Markland[34] and by Joseph Clarke, the architect to the dioceses of Canterbury, Rochester and St Albans.

Phipps's election as a fellow was a remarkable honour for a young architect with limited professional experience and an indication of the confidence his eminent supporters professed not only in his antiquarian knowledge, but also in his future architectural career. It is hardly surprising that Phipps proudly added the letters FSA after his name immediately after his election on 19 June 1862, even though it took another 15 years before he was formally admitted to the Society in 1877.[35]

The mortuary chapel in Pewsey was an honourable and appropriate work for someone aiming for a career in church architecture but not terribly lucrative. Nor would a 'new picturesque front' and internal alterations to the Greyhound Hotel, a small commercial hostelry in central Bath, do much to forward his career or strengthen his bank balance.[36] Phipps needed a major public commission, if not a church perhaps a town hall; his other mentor Thomas Fuller had, after all, won a competition for a new town hall in Ottawa, Canada in 1856, while Phipps was still training. Fuller's success was an inspiring example.

Salvation would come from an unexpected quarter. On the morning of Good Friday 18 April 1862, a fierce and spectacular fire started at the Bath Theatre Royal which soon threatened to engulf the centre of the city. The leaping sheets of flame and shooting sparks would have been seen from the upper floors of the Paragon Buildings as the fire brigade struggled manfully, but ineffectually, to control the conflagration. As the centre seemed doomed to wholesale destruction, a miracle happened. The wind changed and instead of driving the fire out of the theatre forced it back into the empty shell where the flames expired inside the still relatively intact outer walls.

Dance's theatre had been part of the city's identity, a symbol of its cultural and civic aspirations, if not always loyally supported by its residents. However, the manager, James Henry Chute, who had run the Bath theatre jointly with the Bristol Theatre Royal since 1853, had succeeded in making both playhouses profitable as well as respectable by mounting his production with the utmost care to choice of play, the standard of acting, scenery and costumes. He shared the conservative and moral world view of the local business and professional communities in both cities and had over the years become recognised as one of their number. At a public meeting in the Guildhall on 7 May 1862, a provisional committee including Chute, and under the chairmanship of the mayor, was quickly formed to consider the practicalities of rebuilding the playhouse. It would be financed through a limited liability company with a proposed capital of £12,000 in £5 shares. Fundraising began with a flourish, but soon began to stall and not until two months later, on 3 July did a new executive committee, with Chute still on board, feel they had enough funds to be able to announce a competition for a new theatre on the old site with costs not to exceed £5000. Potential competitors had no time to loose. Plans had to be submitted within six weeks.

The mortuary chapel in Pewsey not withstanding, Phipps could not afford to ignore this opportunity. Whatever his private views on the theatre's role in society, the spectre of professional oblivion, or, at least, side-lining, coupled with embarrassing financial difficulties, hovered in the wings. There were, however, two major obstacles in his way to winning this competition and win he must: firstly, his own ignorance of theatre design – the Sydney Gardens bandstand had been a mere fleeting brush with entertainment structures – and secondly, Major Charles Davis, the city architect.

Endnotes

1. Somerset Heritage Service, Somerset Parish Records,1538-1913, Ref. no. D\P\chc/2/1/9. Entry for Charlcombe Parish Church.
2. Bath Post Office Directories, 1829-36. William Phipps was born in Cork, Ireland in 1791. Bath Census 1851.
3. Married by licence. Charlcombe Parish Records, Marriages. Somerset Heritage Centre. *Bath Chronicle and Weekly Gazette,* 26 June 1834.
4. See G. Garlick, 'Theatre Outside London, 1660-1775', *The Cambridge History of British Theatre, Volume 2, 1660-1895.* Cambridge University Press, 2004.
5. BDM, Non-conformist records of births, baptisms, marriages and burials, list the baptism of John Rashleigh Phipps's two children by his first marriage, but not those of his second marriage. For James Phipps see England and Wales Non-conformist burials, Somerset: Bath, Ref. TNA/RG/4/3252.
6. *The Biograph,* Nov. 1880, pp. 399-401.
7. D. Stroud, *George Dance Architect 1741-1825.* Faber and Faber, 1971, p. 205. See also G. Garlick, *Neoclassicism and English theatre Architecture 1775-1843,* Ph. D. Thesis, Exeter University 1996, pp. 218-21.
8. The census returns from 1841 and 1851 for the more salubrious areas of Bath, including the parish of Walcot where the Phipps family lived, reveal a number of small boarding schools interspersed with retired officers, clergy and female annuitants.
9. He was buried on 1 January 1837. England and Wales Non-conformist burials, Somerset: Bath, Wesleyan burials, REF.TNA/RG/4/32/52.
10. See J. R. Phipps's will of 1849. NA, ref. prob. 11/2177.
11. 1841 Census, Bath, Walcot parish.
12. Bath Record Office.
13. *The Biograph,* Nov. 1880, p. 399.
14. Bath, 1841 Census. *Post Office Directory for Bath* 1846.
15. Bath, 1851 Census.
16. Bath, 1851 Census.
17. Somerset Monumental Inscriptions transcription, ref.8. Somerset and Dorset Family History Society.
18. Will of John Rashleigh Phipps, 1849 and Bath Annual Directory 1852.
19. *Bath Post Office Directory* 1854 and 1856 lists Mrs John Phipps at 13 Walcot Parade.
20. *Biograph,* November 1880, p. 401.
21. *Biograph,* November 1880, p. 401. *Building News,* 24 April, 1863, p. 319.
22. *Bath Post Office Directory* 1858.
23. Information kindly supplied by Mike Sell.

24 *Bath Post Office Directory* 1859-60, lists both C.J. Phipps and Mrs John Phipps at 5 Paragon Buildings.
25 RIBA, Biography file on C.J. Phipps. The RIBA has a meagre biography file on Hanson but no records of Whickham.
26 *Ecclesiologist*, vol. cxxxvii, April 1860, p. 90. He was elected on 1 March 1860.
27 Marriage certificate, 1860, Bath, April-June, v. 5c, p. 1246.
28 Birth certificate, 1860, Oct.-Dec., Bath, v. 5c, p. 630.
29 R.H. Harper, *Victorian Architectural Competitions: An Index to British and Irish Architectural Competitions,* 1983, pp. xiii-xvii. The Victoria Art Gallery, Bath, has a water colour by Phipps of the exterior of the Newbury Corn Exchange, BATVG:P:1991.195, and one of a 'Drinking Fountain', BATVG:P:1991.196.
30 *Bath Journal*, 6 March 1961.
31 The Victoria Art Gallery, Bath, BATVG:P:1932.11.
32 The Victoria Art Gallery, Bath, BATVG:P:191.199.
33 Birth certificate, Bath Jan-Mar., v. 5c, p. 729.
34 James Markland, Doctor of Civil Law, FSA and Private Gentleman resided at 1 Lansdown Crescent with his wife and a cohort of servants. 1861 Bath Census.
35 H. Maguire, 'C.J. Phipps and Nineteenth-Century Theatre Architecture', Ph.D. Thesis, University of London, 1988, pp. 53- 54.
36 Bath Central Library, Hunt Vol.P.96. Newspaper cutting, July 1862.

2 COMPETITION 1862-63

Defeating Major Davis required careful strategic planning. Davis, as befits a major, was a man of action. Barely a week into his post as city architect before the theatre went up in flames, he had lost no time in rushing out a radical and ambitious proposal recommending replacing the smouldering ruin with a multi-purpose hall, holding 2000, suitable for lectures, concerts and dramatic performances, all for £10,000.[1] The citizens were not impressed; they demanded a purpose-built theatre and Davis found himself having to draw up specifications for an unwelcome public competition for the new theatre.

There is no evidence that Davis was particularly versed in theatre design, the multi-purpose hall project suggests that he was not, but, in addition to his official post, he ran a large private practice with draughtsmen and apprentices who could produce impressive drawings quickly and had, no doubt, done so for the multi-purpose hall. Although thwarted in this initial attempt to scoop the prize, his proposal sent a warning signal to other local architects that he regarded the proposed theatre as his almost as of right. And he took care to associate his name with the project in other ways too. He was an energetic fundraiser for the new theatre persuading his many friends among the local councillors to sign the subscription lists. On the face of it, victory was his.

However, Davis was not universally popular. His decision to use his practice through which to enter the theatre competition as a private individual, a competition for which he had laid down the rules, caused considerable unease among many Bath residents who regarded this as dubious professional conduct. His stubborn refusal to concede their point had brought him as many enemies on the council as friends, but as no one wished to derail the fundraising efforts by alienating either the pro-Davis or the anti-Davis faction, the competition committee decided that in the interests of fair play the entries were to be anonymous and identified only by a motto.

Phipps was very well aware of Davis's power and ruthlessness and his tendency to flatten any potential rival projects before they got off the drawing board. If he were to outwit the Major he would need to some supporters of his own. He could, of course, not discount the possibility of an outsider gaining the commission but, Phipps, conversant with provincial society's tendency to look inwards rather than outwards, could be fairly confident that the committee members would most likely opt for a local man and that a number of them would look favourably on a challenger of Major Davis.

All these calculations were based on the assumption that Phipps would be able to master the intricacies of theatre design in time; he needed expert advice and fast and, unlike Davis, he was prepared to seek it out. He picked his advisors with care: James Henry Chute (1810/1-78) the manager of the Bristol and Bath theatres and, crucially, a member of the competition committee, and Edward Godwin (1833-86), a Bristol-based architect and theatre critic, who had recently restarted the moribund Bristol Society of Architects of which Phipps had become a member.[2] Godwin and Chute knew each other well, and despite Godwin's occasionally acerbic comments on Chute's productions, they shared a common view of the theatre as an instrument for education as well as entertainment.

To an inexperienced theatre architect the advice of an experienced theatre manager such as Chute must have been invaluable. Chute knew exactly what made a theatre work, or not as the case might be, and would have impressed upon Phipps the absolute necessity of creating a spatial relationship between auditorium and stage that made it possible for the actors to reach out to the spectators and draw them into the performance while paying careful attention to acoustics and sightlines from all parts of the house. He would also have furnished Phipps with the best dimensions for a stage capable of handling the sophisticated scenery that audiences now demanded and stressed the importance of an adequate number of heated dressing rooms and greenrooms, not to mention the best siting of the manager's room. The latter should be as 'inaccessible and mysterious as possible, for no one is so besieged with talkers and importunate persons as a manager'.[3] Chute was the person who knew better than anyone else the shortcomings of the old theatre and how these could and must be rectified to continue to attract a growing audience. With Phipps he had, at last, the opportunity to create a theatre in accordance with his own ideas honed over many years of labouring in less than perfect playhouses. What is more, he had a good chance of seeing it built.

In common with Chute, Godwin would have emphasised to Phipps the importance of bringing something new and fresh to the design, but while Chute was primarily concerned with the nuts and bolts of the building, Godwin's chief concern lay with the decoration of the auditorium. He despaired of English theatre architecture in its current state: the design was dismal, the interior decorations paltry and uninspired, a state of affairs he blamed on theatre proprietors and managers 'the most tyrannical of clients'. He defied anyone in England to build a theatre 'without the handcuffs of tradition being put upon him, and the shackle of a great-grandmother kind of antiquity rivetted on him by an ignoble conservatism'.[4]

Phipps was, literally, hand-cuffed from the start by the existing outer walls not to mention the cost limit of £5000. He was also shackled by a deep-rooted conservatism, exemplified by the argument that 'the pit must be large for it is the pit and the popular shilling that pay'.[5] Phipps, who had a sharp commercial nose, challenged this assertion in a lecture on theatre architecture to the Bristol Society of Architects on 9 April 1863, arguing instead that as the 'pit is the best part [it] should be throughout at the highest price, forming a continuation of the first circle'.[6] In other words, the pit should no longer be left to those on lower incomes whose alleged perspicacity in dramatic matters had, through the centuries, helped mould the English drama.

That Phipps had a valid point is borne out by the extant account books of the Bath Theatre Royal from 1839, which reveal that it was the boxes, at 5 shillings a ticket, that brought in the money, even when only half full, and that the 'popular' shilling-gallery was rarely full and mostly populated by 'half-pricers'. The pit audience was more loyal, but at 2 s.6d. a ticket, not really a money spinner.[7] However, Phipps's modern, commercially-driven thinking, did not find any takers among the traditionally-minded theatre proprietors of the Bath Theatre Royal.

Both Godwin and Chute seem to have envisaged the theatre experience as an integrated whole which encompassed the building, the decoration and the performance, and where the two main spatial units, auditorium and stage, that made up the theatre's structural core, were united and brought alive through the both design as well as the actors engagement with the spectators. It was a view which was not dissimilar to the design approach recommended in the first English book on theatre architecture,

George Saunders's *A Treatise on Theatre*, 1790, a work which Phipps appears to have consulted extensively and which underpinned his Bristol lecture on theatre architecture in 1863.

Saunders argued that the architect should take the actor and his voice as the starting point for the design, not abstract notions of architectural beauty. Through his own experiments with the carrying-distance of the human voice indoors and outdoors, he arrived at, as he saw it, a scientifically grounded design consisting of a circular-shaped auditorium. That this had also been the preferred shape in antiquity merely proved its perfection. This design approach, based on a judicious blend of science and antiquity, was similar to that promulgated by the Ecclesiological Society in respect of church architecture, where religious ritual formed the starting point. Determining the height and width of a proscenium arch was not so very different from calculating the dimensions of a chancel arch; it was a matter of substituting one set of rituals for another.

Phipps was at ease with ritual, the society in which he had grown up was imbued with it, in the home, at work, at worship, at leisure – and he knew its worth. He instinctively understood the rituals embedded in theatre-going among the wealthier classes, the arrival, the departure, the socialising in the interval and the importance of providing the right kind of ingress and egress and saloons for the different social strata. The classes must not mingle, they must each have their separate spaces as Phipps pointed out in his lecture. The upper and middle classes must have their comfort and security, while the lower classes, that flowing unpredictable mass, must be suitably contained within and without the auditorium. In this he was at one with theatre proprietors and managers; the English theatre's most renowned actor David Garrick might have bowed to the 'gods' a hundred years earlier, and early nineteenth-century critics, such as William Hazlitt and Leigh Hunt, might have defended the right of the lower classes to the drama and exalted the social inclusiveness of the theatre experience, but unsuccessful attempts by theatre proprietors since the end of the eighteenth century to dispose of the one-shilling gallery altogether, demonstrate a less generous view of their presence.[8] Their inclusion, especially in large numbers, impacted on the harmonious design of the audience space and raised building costs, as the architect must ensure that they could both see and hear from their confined space at the back and uppermost regions of the auditorium lest unsavoury missiles, wet or dry, landed on the hapless pittites. To keep 'the gods' at bay the actors needed strong lungs and well-trained vocal chords plus a powerful personal presence, with which to seduce the 'great unwashed'. For the class-conscious Phipps, anxious to keep social inclusiveness at bay, the large gallery must have seemed like another shackle riveted onto his design.

Phipps entitled his design proposal 'A Midsummer Night's Dream', a clever motto suggesting a theatre that would be both elegant and exciting but with an undertone of seriousness and emphasis on moral virtue. It was a title to lift the spirit, unlike Major Davis's 'Much Ado About Nothing', which smelt slightly of sour grapes with its underlying implication that the proposed theatre was hardly deserving of all this kerfuffle and that the whole matter could have been settled more simply by the city architect. Whether Phipps's choice of motto was entirely his own idea is a moot point. It so happened that *A Midsummer Night's Dream* was to be the opening production of the new theatre and it is quite possible, indeed likely, that the choice of play for the opening night would have come up at some point in the discussions between Chute, Phipps and Godwin.

In the supporting letter which accompanied his entry, and which was later printed in the *Bath Chronicle*, Phipps, mindful of his inexperience of theatre design, assured the competition jury that he was actually very well qualified for the task:

– 'Having visited the principal theatres in France, Germany and Italy specially for the purpose of this competition and all the principal theatres of London, I have come to the conclusion that the model of the old house, with very slight alterations, is the correct one both as regards beauty of form and evidence of arrangement, there being, however, many defects which I have endeavoured in my design to remedy.'[9]

How long Phipps spent examining European theatres, given the limited time available to him remains an open question. The competition was not formally announced until 3 July 1862, and then with a 6-week deadline though Phipps might well have started his theatre research when the proposal for a rebuild was first mooted in May. However, in his lecture to the Bristol Architect's Society a year later, he admitted that 'he had not been able yet to visit the new theatres that have lately been built [in Paris].[10] The lecture, as reported in the *Building News*, implies that

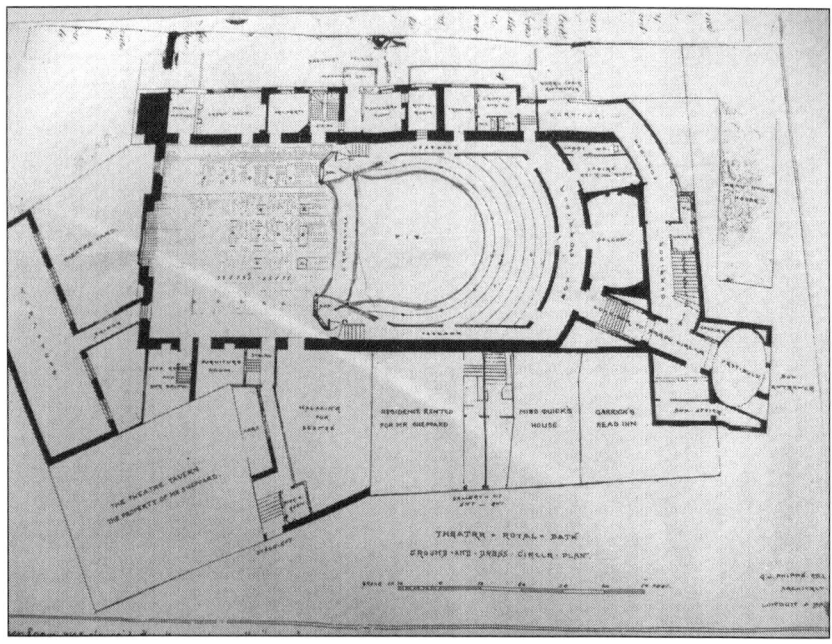

Site Plan of Bath Theatre Royal, 1863 © Friends of Bath Theatre Royal.

he had visited Bordeaux, but does not include any references to Phipps having examined any 'lately built' theatres elsewhere in Europe.

As for the principal London theatres, Phipps was downright dismissive:

– 'There was none, with the exception of the new Adelphi, which called for special comment'. The latter, at least, was 'an advance in the right direction'.[11]

Phipps's letter and the subsequent lecture suggest a readiness to exaggerate his own professional expertise, a necessary attribute in the competitive architectural profession, but in the last paragraph of his supporting letter the tone is far less hubristic, almost veering on the pleading:

– 'I have entered upon the competition with great zeal and an earnest desire to produce a design, which should be generally acceptable and rival even the theatres of the metropolis, and while I am anxious that success should attend my efforts I should wish that success to be attained by merit only; though should my design be considered equal to any other that may be submitted and the choice doubtful, I should have no objection to be associated with the author of such design in carrying out the works.'

This sudden lurch into humility suggests a man who was desperate to obtain the commission. Even half a commission would do if necessary. He needed the work.

While Phipps was at pains, in his letter, to reassure the committee that 'the plan of the auditory was only slightly varied' from the old one even the less visually literate members of the competition committee should have noticed the substitution of the old U-shaped auditorium with one of a circular shape with the box fronts approaching the proscenium along 'a slight contrary flexure' which echoes T. H. Wyatt's Adelphi. There was also a the projecting new entrance to the dress and upper boxes in the Sawclose with a graceful elliptical vestibule complete with box office and, finally, the enlarged gallery extending all the way across the building but set well back. They would also have been relieved by Phipps's promise that 'No elaborate plan for decoration is proposed'. This laconic and seemingly dismissive attitude to the decorative treatment of the auditorium beyond a traditional 'motif' of white and gold with the Bath arms in the centre of the proscenium arch and the names of English dramatists on the box fronts was not likely to further Phipps's professional standing, but it would almost certainly play well with the cash-strapped proprietors. There was also the question of time; it is doubtful if Phipps would have been able to devote sufficient hours for a sophisticated decorative programme by the given deadline.

As for the stage, Phipps, rather than blinding the committee with technical details which they might have had some difficulty in grasping fully, confidently asserted:

'The Stage Arrangements are considered to be very satisfactorily set forth'.

He does not reveal who had passed this favourable judgement on his efforts, but the most likely person would seem to be Chute.

Phipps had done everything in his power to ensure he was well placed to out-manoeuvre Major Davis, as well as Finch Hill and Paraire from London and a Mr Green from Bristol, who, together with Phipps, made it to the final stage. He was offering an elegant, but not extravagant theatre holding an estimated 1,995 spectators for the specified cost of £5000. It was a bargain, by any standards. The competition committee was impressed but wavered; Davis's supporters argued strongly for his 'Much Ado' design but in the end his proposal was outgunned by the 'Midsummer Night's' advocates. Chute is likely to have played a pivotal part in the final decision; he would not let a design, partly moulded according to his own ideas, be overtaken by a proposal by an architect who would brook no interference let alone listen to advice. The proprietors were anxious to retain Chute as a manager, but he had not yet signed an agreement with them to that effect. In the circumstances his preference would surely have carried considerable weight.

Construction work got under way at the beginning of October and not long after Phipps audaciously presented a new, more elaborate decorative scheme for the auditorium.[12] This was a calculated risk, not least because it would increase costs, but also because it might also delay the opening night scheduled for 4 March 1863. No doubt both Chute and Godwin had impressed upon Phipps that if the theatre were to make the necessary positive impact on the expectant audience as well as on the architectural press and prospective clients, he had to provide a novel and aspiring decorative scheme which reinforced the theatre's dual role as entertainer and educator and, at the same time, created a sense of excitement and raised expectations among the audience. It must, on no account, turn a potentially positive mood among the spectators towards the evening's offerings into the opposite and leave the performers struggling with an unresponsive audience. Sticking to his original minimalist scheme was not really an option; the Bath auditorium must signal a new departure in theatre decoration.

An undated watercolour entitled 'Le theatre au Bath',[13] gives a stunning impression of Phipps's redesigned decorative scheme and corresponds very closely with the description of the completed theatre by Edward Godwin.[14] The most striking features in the watercolour are the deep blue proscenium arch with its row of grey figures and the contrasting profusion of delicately painted gothic-style ornament in blue, gold and white on the arches above the slips and on the circular ceiling where it is interspersed with carefully delineated figures. This kind of auditorium decoration where the classical and the gothic intermingle to startling effect certainly marked a break with the moribund traditions of the mid-Victorian theatre. It is a design that suggests newness, but not too loudly, and, most importantly, lifts the spirit.

Le theatre au Bath', c. 1863. Watercolour of the auditorium of Bath Theatre Royal by C.J. Phipps. Copyright Victoria Art Gallery, Bath and Bath and North East Somerset Council.

Many of the ideas behind the new scheme came from Godwin and his friend Charles Kean, a fact that Phipps was only too happy to acknowledge at the end of his description of the finished theatre published in the *Bath Chronicle*:

> 'The whole has been erected under the superintendence of Mr Charles J. Phipps, who has received valuable assistance from the Bristol Society of Architects and particularly its indefatigable hon. Secretary E.W. Godwin, Esq., FSA, who has arranged the various subjects for the plays of Shakespeare that are painted on the box fronts, in conjunction with Charles Kean, Esq., FSA.'[15]

The watercolour is not dated though the most likely purpose of the painting would seem to be, on the one hand, to act as a means of persuasion, to sell the new scheme to the manager and the proprietors and, on the other, to act as a guide for the chief decorator from which to draw up his own sketches.

Godwin and Phipps shared a love of Gothic architecture but Godwin, apart from organising lectures on design and archaeological issues for like-minded architects, also held regular Shakespeare readings at his home – he was also the secretary of the Bristol Shakespeare Society – where his architectural friends could meet the resident performers from Chute's company.[16] These meetings, where architects and actors had the opportunity to discover each other's ways of thinking under Godwin's tutelage, must have had a profound impact on both groups. Whatever misgivings Phipps might have inherited from his parents regarding the absence of educational standards and moral fibre in the acting profession, he would have realised that these social gatherings were a unique opportunity to explore ideas about what constituted an inspirational, or, at least, a workable, theatre, and it appears he attended some of the readings. The experience would have been invaluable not just for the successful completion of the Bath design, but for any future excursions into theatre architecture.

Apart from the auditorium decoration, the finished building appears to have stuck more or less to the original proposal.[17] The stage and auditorium cover an area 117 ft. long by 55 ft. wide, which is surrounded by box corridors, staircases, scene-rooms, workshops and dressing-rooms forming a separate block of 190 ft by 128 ft.[18] The box entrance and *porte cochère* is at the south end of the theatre in the Sawclose where the limited available space was (and still is) sandwiched between, on the right the handsome house o f Beau Nash – originally the home of Bath's most venerated eighteenth-century Master of Ceremonies and therefore sacrosanct – and, on the left, by the equally valued Garrick's Head pub.

The previous box entrance and attendant pay office, a plain one-storey rectangular projection with a single door in the centre,[19] had been all too easy to ignore and Phipps, determined to make an architectural statement, designed a new rectangular one-storey extension – anything higher would have blocked the windows in the dress circle saloon on the first floor – and filled it with three entrance doors set into severe round-arches supported by medieval-style squat columns with capitals sporting intricate carvings of mischievous dragons and lions chasing each other's tails among dense foliage. Above the columns, he placed a discrete balcony with the Theatre Royal Arms proudly displayed in the centre of the balustrade. It is a reassuringly solid-looking entrance exuding bourgeois respectability but with a hint of playfulness as befits a theatre.

Sawclose exterior of the Theatre Royal, Bath designed by C.J. Phipps. Author's Collection.

The doors led into an elliptically shaped vestibule (with the box office on one side) followed by a straight corridor through to the dress circle with the stairs to the upper boxes branching off to the right. 'At the foot of this staircase was another corridor, 8ft. wide, leading to another entrance in Beaufort Square for 'wheelchairs'.[20] The pit entrance was also in Beaufort Square about three feet below the level of the street 'with an inclined way'.

Detail of carved capital from Sawclose exterior. Author's Collection.

Having originally assured the proprietors that his plan was not so very different from the old theatre, Phipps is now at pains to emphasise the innovative nature of his design:

'The plan of the house is totally different to that of the old theatre', before going on to explain how he had arrived at what was to become his hall-mark design feature, namely the circular auditorium with a 'contrary flexure'.

The diameter of the circle was 36 ft. with a depth of 46 ft. from the proscenium wall to the back of the pit or front of the box tiers; in other words the pit did not extend under the dress circle. The diameter contracted to 33 ft. in a straight line to the proscenium pillars (28 ft. wide) opening by a convex curve to 35 ft. in a line parallel to the diameter. The stage projected around 6 ft. beyond the curtain line and the orchestra pit was 4 ft. 4 in. below the front of the stage. The floor of the pit rose 9 in. above this and inclined seven-eighths to a foot to the front of the dress circle. The pit held 350 on padded seats 'sloping towards the back', supported by raking backs – a thoughtful touch which would prevent any pittites accidentally falling backwards when craning their necks.

The dress circle, seating 230, was 18 ft. deep in the centre with seven rows, gradually diminishing to two at the sides. The front of the dress circle was 6 ft. 6 in. high and so within reach of tall pittites and creating a close relationship between the two sections reminiscent of the one in the old theatre.

The upper circle was raised 9 ft. above the dress circle and supported by eight iron columns placed behind the second row of the dress circle seats. It held 220. Both tiers were furnished with separate, hinged seats with stuffed seats and arm, the backs inclining by 4 inches. They were all covered in crimson cloth.

The gallery was situated 9 ft. above the upper tier with 12 ft. from the front of the gallery floor to the soffit round the cove of the ceiling. Phipps does not reveal the height at the back of the gallery, which would have been rather less. He claimed that he had gone to considerable lengths to make the stage visible to the majority of the galleryites by pushing the seating back 'to a depth on the incline of 51 ft. from the front' and spreading it across the whole width of the building.[21] This vast space provided seating, albeit cramped, for 600 spectators, well over a third of the theatre's total estimated capacity of 1,650 (down by 300 from the original estimate). The sides of the gallery were formed by arches 'at the same springing as the proscenium' and took in the first three rows and thus became an amphitheatre that 'could be filled at either pit or upper box prices'. They had space for 200.

This maximising of gallery seating left no room for gallery stairs, let alone any other conveniences, but Phipps solved the entry and exit problem by simply tacking on an external staircase in St. John's Court.[22] His hitherto successful attempts to break away from the 'ignoble conservatism' of earlier theatre designs and put safety and comfort first, fell back in the face of the gallery multitude.

Godwin, in his critique of the finished Bath theatre, expressed, to his almost palpable relief, that Phipps had had the courage to dispense with his original conservative notions and steered clear of the traditional tangles of ribbons, cornucopias, 'struggling cupids', birds and scrolls, which hitherto had dominated the English auditorium. Instead Phipps had introduced 'Early Gothic scrolls with entwining dragons in proper subserviency ... [and] delicate Grecian flower ornaments and Italian fretwork', which formed a harmonious background to an elaborate dress circle front. The latter was now divided into alternating circular, diamond-shaped, and rectangular recessed panels, the circles depicting the kings of England immortalized by Shakespeare, the diamonds the royal arms from different periods of history, and the rectangles scenes from 'the more important' of Shakespeare's plays. The scenes were painted in strong lines and flat tints against a gilded background, with 'evidence of decided antiquarian knowledge' in the costumes and a 'critical appreciation of Shakespeare' in the selection of scenes. It was a visual lecture in English history and drama, and, as Godwin pointed out, 'quite a new feature, both in idea and treatment'. It is a sign of Godwin's spirit of generosity that he does not mention his own involvement, or that of Kean's, in this revolutionary break with the past.

The decorations were executed by the well-established London firm Messrs. Green and King and their chief artist, Mr Devilder, who must have been under pressure to complete the work in time. Godwin, who was a fine draughtsman, was distinctly unimpressed by the quality of the drawing of the figures which 'seemed to have been executed hurriedly'. However, he commended Devilder for the figures in the flat-domed octagonal ceiling where representations of Tragedy, Comedy, Opera,

Burlesque, Pantomime, etc. promised a variety of delights to future audiences. The ceiling was a flat dome, 36 ft in diameter rising around 3 ft. in the centre and both it and the proscenium arch had been painted in flat oils on canvas which had been pasted on.

The 30 ft. high proscenium arch was more sobering with black and white life-size figures of the Seven Ages of Man, 'the last Age shown tottering towards his grave ... painted in outline with strong black lines and slight shadow on pale blue ground'. They were later replaced by more festive-looking diamond-shaped panels.

Phipps's figurative motifs struck just the right moral tone for the increasingly prosperous elite of mid-Victorian Britain in whose hands lay the survival and, with luck, the future success of the provincial theatre. The panels underlined the theatre's role as educator, entertainer and, not least, as a buttress of national identity. The background of judiciously placed fretwork with stylistically correct Gothic dragons and Grecian flowers added a lighter, more festive touch, a fitting backdrop to *A Midsummer Night's Dream*, alluding to the antiquarian spirit of the time. The antiquarian Phipps, with assistance from Godwin and Charles Kean, had thus managed to transform his research, originally undertaken in pursuit of a new church architecture, into a novel and elegant feature in this the most secular of building types.

The audience on the opening night 4 March 1863 was delighted and willing to be seduced by it all: the new building, its decoration and the sparkling performance of *A Midsummer Night's Dream* with the young Ellen Terry as Titania in a costume designed by Godwin.[23] The fact that the theatre opened on the pre-announced date, was, according to the local paper, nothing short of a miracle:

'As the audience came in one door the workmen had barely time to vanish at another door.'[24]

There was, however, one minor defect:

'Some better mode of lighting the back of the two tiers of boxes and of the gallery will have to be adopted, the sunlight not being sufficient for the purpose.'

As the curtain went up for the prologue the audience cheered and clapped and called for Mr Chute who 'stepped forward leading on Mr Phipps'.[25] The two were cheered for several minutes, their partnership visible for all to see, the one relying on the other.

The performance took full advantage of the well equipped stage which had been constructed in consultation with Mr D. Sloman, the chief machinist at Her Majesty's Theatre in London. A width of 55 ft. and an uninterrupted length of 46 ft. (from behind the proscenium wall) ensured enough space for the changing of flats and wings without unwelcome collisions between stage-hands and actors or pile-ups of scenery on or off stage. This was essential; *A Midsummer Night's Dream* demanded frequent and complex scene changes and the depth below the working stage was not sufficient for flats and wings to be dropped in their entirety. (See Appendix 1 for details of stage construction).

Phipps's efforts had paid off handsomely for all concerned, though the proprietors had to find another £2000 to cover additional costs. Professionally Phipps had at last made his mark, inspired and supported by Chute and Godwin, he had ushered in a new beginning for English theatre architecture, and returned the provincial playhouse to the status of a desirable public building. Laudatory write-ups in the architectural and national press ensured that news of Phipps's achievement spread beyond Bath to other ambitious theatre proprietors.

A few weeks after the Bath theatre's triumphant opening, Phipps, determined to secure his foothold in the budding world of theatre architecture, delivered his lecture in Bristol on the nature of theatre design, thus staking his claim, among his professional colleagues, to this slippery domain. He also exhibited his design at the Royal Academy and the Royal West of England Academy. Only a year after the burning down of Bath's old Theatre Royal, Phipps had banished the spectre of professional failure and could set his sights on an office in London. Thoughts of ecclesiastical design became less tempting, the theatre had invaded his architectural soul and tickled his vanity – no other building generated public applause for its architect on its completion – and he could sense a promising business potential. As for Godwin's warning of 'tyrannical clients', Phipps knew, from his parents, the art and value of adapting to the patron's needs; the wives and daughters of the gentry, in search of shoes and schools, took readily to tyranny. It would be a gamble, but there was Chute's projected theatre in Bristol to look forward to and there would surely be more fires?

Endnotes

1. B. S. Penley, *The Bath Stage*, London: Lewis, 1892, p. 162.
2. L. Wright, "The Bristol Society of architects, 1850-1950" *RIBA Journal*, April 1950, 225-29, p2.25
3. Phipps citing a 'friend' in his lecture on theatre architecture. *The Builder*, 23 April 1863, p. 292.
4. *Building News*, 6 March 1863, p. 174.
5. *Builder*, 25 April 1863, p. 292.
6. *Building News*, 24 April, 1863, p. 319.
7. Bath Record Office. Acc. 310, Box 5. Most of the theatre's account books were destroyed in the fire.
8. W. Hazlitt, *Complete Works*, xvii, 1930-34, p. 237; L. Hunt, *Dramatic Criticism 1808-31*, 1949, p. 745.
9. *Bath Chronicle*, 21 August 1862, p. 3.
10. *Building News,* 24 April 1864, p. 319.
11. *Building News*, 24 April 1864, p. 319.
12. Report in the *Builder*, 24 January 1863, p. 68, by which time the new scheme was well under way.
13. It was presented to the Victoria Art Gallery, Bath, by Arthur Blomfield Jackson, Phipps's son-in-law and partner.
14. *Building News,* 6 March 1863, pp. 174-5.
15. *Bath Chronicle,* 5 March 1863, p. 7.
16. K. Barker, "The Terrys and Godwin in Bristol", *Theatre Notebook*, xxii, pp. 27-43.
17. Photocopy of Deed Plan of the Bath Theatre Royal by C. Phipps, Accession 0310/2/2/2/1, Bath Record Office. The Block Plan is also at Bath Record Office in a bundle of architectural drawings of Bath Theatre Royal from 1915.
18. *Builder* 7 March 1863, ppp164.
19. Engraving of 'Theatre and Beau Nash's House, Bath', 1861. Bath Central Library, Coll. Ref. Hunt Vol. IV, p. 141 IOB 722.
20. *Builder,* 7 March 1863, p. 165.
21. *Builder*, 7 March 1863, p. 165.
22. *Builder*, 7 March 1863, p. 165.
23. D. Harbron, "Edward Godwin", *Edwardian Architecture and Its Origins,* ed. by A. Service, Architectural Press, 1975, pp. 57-67, p. 58.
24. *Bath Chronicle*, 5 March 1863, p. 5.
25. Penley, B., *The Bath Stage,* London, 1892, p. 167.

3 OPPORTUNITY AND COMPROMISE 1864-68

Phipps knew that his hopes for a career as a theatre architect were unlikely to be realised if he remained in his home city; he could not expect metropolitan and provincial theatre proprietors to take the train to Bath to seek him out. He needed an office in central London readily accessible to everybody connected with the running of theatres everywhere. By the end of 1863 he had found suitable premises at 48 Cornhill in the City of London,[1] though he still retained his office and home at no. 5 Paragon Buildings for the time being. In Bath he was busy with a large Militia Barracks, situated just west of Bath's city centre. It had been commissioned for the Second Militia Regiment of Somerset and was complete in 1864. Part of the main block is now incorporated into Hayesfield Girls School.[2]

He did not have to wait too long before the detailed descriptions in the architectural press on the Bath Theatre Royal bore fruit. Two wealthy lace manufacturers from Nottingham, John and William Lambert, called on him in London sometime in the autumn of 1864. This was timely as Phipps now had three young children to provide for, a second daughter, Ida, had arrived earlier in the year.

The Lambert brothers were, on the face of it, the ideal client for a young theatre architect anxious to show his prowess. They had ambitious plans for an entirely new Theatre Royal – not a rebuild – in their home town, and as seasoned industrialists and local politicians they were used to getting their own way. But first Phipps needed to impress them; he did not wish the Lamberts to call on the more renowned theatre and music hall architects Finch Hill and Paraire in Oxford Street, who had been a serious rival for the Bath Theatre Royal and whose design for the Britannia Theatre in Hoxton Road (1858) – now Hoxton Street – with a capacity of nearly 4000, was legendary.

A formal undated photograph of Phipps in the early stages of his career gives some idea of the appearance of the rising young architect who greeted the Lamberts in London. We see a bearded young man dressed in a wholesome and well cut tweed suit with polished but slightly worn

Portrait of C.J. Phipps, late 1860s. Author's Collection.

boots, leaning against the corner of a table deeply engrossed in what would appear to be a technical or antiquarian book, with additional tomes artfully dispersed on the table. The pose is casual, slightly twisted, as if he has just come in from inspecting a building site or perhaps some antiquarian remains and is checking an interesting discovery in his well-stocked library. It is a portrait of the educated man of action, confident, reliable and dependable – perhaps more the antiquarian than the architect. There is no sign of architectural drawings or drawing instruments. It is a man who would be at one with the Lambert's faith in the theatre as an instrument of education and who would strive to meet their expectations of a theatre where a "well-conducted ... company [would be] fulfilling its great mission, viz. a teacher of the highest morality ...".[3]

The Nottingham theatre was a more complex proposition than Finch Hill's and Paraire's usual commissions; it required someone with a good understanding of the social pyramid of provincial towns and someone steeped in antiquarian knowledge as the Lamberts, it seems, had already decided on a full-blown neoclassical frontage in the continental tradition. As Phipps later explained to the local press: "The style of the façade was fixed by his clients and not suggested by him; consequently whatever merit attaches to it must be awarded to them."[4] This slightly cryptic statement leaves open the question whether Phipps had suggested a rather different design, or whether he had actually been given the opportunity to present one at all.

The Lamberts had a acquired a substantial site on the north side of the city on the corner of Upper Parliament Street, a main thoroughfare in need of an imposing frontage, and the narrower Sherwood Street, where entrances to gallery, pit and stage could be safely placed. The Parliament Street frontage is, indeed, imposing, not to say majestic. Six giant Corinthian columns of Ancaster Stone set on high pedestals carry an elegant entablature surmounted by a tall attic story, probably originally intended to act as a backdrop for appropriate statuary but which, in the end had to content itself with a row of gracious urns. Behind the portico rose a two-storey façade, the round-arched doors and windows flanked by giant Corinthian pilasters, creating a suitable context for the dress- and upper-circle spectators.

Given the Lambert's firm views on the façade one suspects that they had equally strong views on the auditorium design. They had visited the Bath theatre[5] and seem to have liked the circular shape with its curves of contrary flexure, because this is what Phipps provided for Nottingham though here, having a wider site to play with, he was able to carry the circular shape into the back wall of the auditorium. In this way he created a very capacious pit holding 850 people, which extended underneath the dress circle – a practice he condemned in his Bristol lecture. The air at the back of the pit was probably even more pestiferous than in the uppermost part of the gallery, which was set well back and spread over the box corridors and held around 800. For those who could afford to pay for more comfortable seats and better ventilation, the dress circle – with seats based on Phipps's own design – and in the upper circle each offered 250 places. The ultimate luxury, the private proscenium boxes, their superior separateness ensured by pairs of Corinthian columns, accommodated 50. The columns nearest the stage flanked the 30 ft. wide stage opening and a flat arch above which was a large panel painting by Henry Holiday depicting Shakespeare seated on a throne and surrounded by his principal characters flanked by figures representing Comedy and Tragedy.

The classical theme was continued in the decoration, executed by Green and King. Thus, Phipps designed, possibly at the Lamberts' request, a circular ceiling painted with radiating coloured arabesques between blue panels "powdered with gold stars ... like a *velarium*". He also slipped in a sprinkling of grotesque dragons running around the circumference, between the heads of Elizabethan dramatists. The pittites crowding in underneath the dress circle would hardly have noticed the finer points of the ceiling decoration, but they might have caught a glimpse of the painting above the proscenium.

Unlike many provincial theatre proprietors the Lamberts insisted on a generous stage which measured 64 ft wide by 50 ft. deep (including the scene dock) and with a floor composed of sliders and thus entirely flexible as at Bath. Gone were the days when provincial audiences would tolerate the all too familiar multi-purpose stock scenery of miscellaneous woods, interiors and street scenes; in the 1860s only spectacular flying and sinking scenery commensurate with London theatres would do and Phipps provided a depth under the stage of 18 ft. and fly floors 22 ft. above the stage floor. As for the actors who usually had to make do with grubby, cramped and unsanitary dressing rooms, here they were presented with 10 dressing rooms spread over four floors in a block beside the stage with separate water closets on all floors. The building was truly a fine example of a modern provincial theatre, a clever combination of modern technology with classical antiquity. Phipps put in a bill for £371 which was the customary 5% of the cost of works which in this case amounted to £7,425, a figure which included designs, obtaining specifications, superintendence of construction and 5% commission on subcontracts to decorators and furnishers.[6] The site had cost slightly more, around £8000.

The work of excavating and clearing the ground had begun on 27 March 1865 and six months later the theatre was ready to open on 25 September. This speedy completion Phipps generously attributed to this resident clerk of works, George Tasker, who had assisted him in Bath. Tasker "had acted throughout ... with a firmness of bearing and a determination of purpose highly commendable and to his exertions mainly are due the speedy completion of the undertaking".[7] Theatre architects depended heavily on their clerk of works, most provincial contractors were not familiar with the complexity of such buildings and they needed constant supervision to ensure the work was completed on time, according to plan and on budget. Tasker's expertise was invaluable and not easily replaced.

With the Nottingham Theatre Royal completed, Phipps wasted no time drawing attention to his work as an up-and-coming theatre architect of note in the architectural press providing a detailed description of the new playhouse.

News that Phipps had won the competition for the proposed South Shields Theatre Royal reached him just as the construction of the Nottingham theatre got under way in April 1865. However, it was only a partial victory; the directors of the new theatre company had rejected his

The Theatre Royal, Nottingham. Façade. Author's Collection.

façade in favour of that proposed by the South Shields Borough Surveyor (and theatre company shareholder) T. H. Clemence,[8] who seems to have wielded similar power to that of Major Davis in Bath. It is quite possible that Clemence's confident classical three-storey frontage with Giant Corinthian pilasters was stylistically more satisfactory than whatever Phipps had planned, but his failure to win the competition outright must have irked him.

South Shields, a port with a profitable export trade in coal from the north-east coalfields, was socially and architecturally very different from Nottingham, but like the latter, in need of a new theatre, here to be funded by a joint stock company. Its civic leaders had hitherto given little thought to the architectural appearance of their town and it is understandable that the borough surveyor would want to make his mark in association with a prominent building now that the opportunity had finally arisen. As for the auditorium, there was no need for an upper circle in the theatre; a dress circle for 230, private boxes for 30, a pit for 500 and a gallery of 800 was all that was required. Phipps applied his circular formula and repeated much of the decorative scheme for Nottingham, including the stars on 'azure ground' together with dragons and arabesques, but he omitted any references to Shakespeare. George Gordon was responsible for the act drop.

Building work started sometime in late autumn 1865, but did not get off to a good start. A local man, probably chosen by Clemence, was appointed clerk of works. He was not used to theatres and in January 1866 he was replaced by George Tasker, quite possibly at Phipps's insistence. By this time Phipps's professional confidence had been boosted by his election as a Fellow of the RIBA, on the recommendation of the leading Gothic Revivalists, George Gilbert Scott, William Burgess and his old friend Edward Godwin.[9] He could afford to stand his ground.

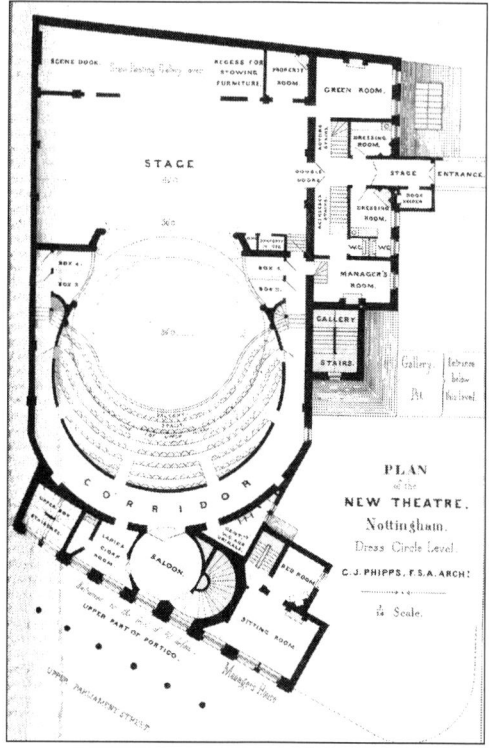

The Theatre Royal, Nottingham. Plan at Dress Circle level. Author's Collection.

Tasker had four months to force the pace of the South Shields building workers as well as to design the stage and its machinery so that the theatre could open as planned on 21 May 1866, an altogether impossible mission in the eyes of the locals.[10] Tasker, however, was as determined as his master and completed the theatre on time, and in the circumstances the opening night's main feature, the comedy *Extremes or Men of the Day,* seemed rather apt. Fittingly, both Phipps and Clemence wished that "the energy and perseverance he [Tasker] has shown in the conduct of a work involving much mechanical skill and complicated detail should be especially recognized".[11]

There was no time to rest on laurels. With work in South Shields completed Phipps turned his attention to the Theatre Royal Brighton. Here, his task was to enlarge the old 1807-playhouse in New Road, primarily the auditorium and stage, while keeping within the existing outer walls and leaving the main frontage with its Doric portico intact. While less exciting than a virgin site, the surveying work entailed in the refurbishing of old theatres before any plans could be drawn up, provided useful training for his pupils, though how many he had at this point is not known. However, in 1866 he took on 15-year-old, Arthur Garner, who had been educated at the same school as Phipps.[12]

The Brighton project revealed Phipps's ingenuity when it came to conjuring up space where none seemed to be available. By the end of June 1866 the theatre was gutted and roofless and Phipps, clearly determined to increase the width of the audience space in order to install a semicircular dress circle (28 ft. in diameter) 'opening by curves of contrary flexure to a width of 40 ft. at the first column of the proscenium', pierced the side walls and incorporated the passages on either side, previously used as entrances to pit, gallery and stage.[13] The width of the stage opening was 30 ft. and the height 28 ft. 9 in., the latter made possible by the construction of an additional storey. The extra height enabled Phipps to include a gallery seating 700, and to raise the slightly domed auditorium ceiling to 44 ft. above the pit floor, 'a height which allows the audience at the extreme back of the gallery to see the top of the scene on the stage'.[14] The enlarged pit held 610, with 50 orchestra stalls in front, while the dress circle accommodated 175, the upper circle 200 and the amphitheatre 100.

The proscenium design, with its pairs of coupled columns flanking a private box level with each of the three tiers, echoed Nottingham Theatre Royal, as did 'the 9 ft. deep cornice [entablature] ... from the top of the proscenium to the ceiling, the frieze of which is decorated with figures'. A solid 18 in. thick brick wall separated the stage from the auditorium and was carried by an arch over the proscenium opening through to the main roof.

As for the decoration, Phipps stuck to Godwin's past advice and eschewed all plaster ornament in favour of painting, which was carried out by Messrs. Green & King of London. Warm purple arabesques on buff ground with occasional masses of red or blue and sparsely place gold ornamentation graced the tier fronts and the ceiling, designed to look like a *velarium*, was sprinkled with gold stars on buff ground.

After four months, with George Tasker acting as the clerk of works, the Brighton Theatre Royal re-opened on 15 October 1866. Phipps 'so clever and affable' was publicly thanked by the manager for his efforts, as were Tasker and the builder, David Bland of London.[15]

Although the Brighton remodelling was a relatively minor project in comparison with his previous commissions, Phipps nevertheless provided the architectural press with a detailed description, which both underlined the importance of a thick proscenium wall as an aid to fire prevention and emphasised the lack of plaster ornamentation in favour of a painted décor thereby presenting himself squarely as an architect ready and able to bring new thinking into theatre design. These 'official particulars', peppered with carefully selected references to size of stage openings, distance from curtain line to centre front of dress circle, height from pit floor to ceiling and seat distribution etc., presented Phipps as an architect well versed in the complexities of theatre design, a man that would deliver a sound building fit for purpose to any serious-minded theatre proprietor, though how many theatre proprietors or speculators read the *Builder* and *Building News* is debatable.

Given what we know of Phipps's training, interests and temperament, these descriptions, almost certainly, had an additional aim, namely to raise the profile of theatre architecture in general among his architectural colleagues and to make it a legitimate subject for serious debate at an intellectual level which the British had hitherto avoided. Phipps, who had had the support of some of the nation's foremost architects supporting his RIBA membership, needed to show the architectural establishment that he was devoting his energies to worthwhile buildings. He was not going to let the fact that he had been catapulted into theatre design by the combination of dire necessity and a propitious fire cast him in the role of a mere constructor of insubstantial entertainment buildings. On the contrary, he would hold his ground as a serious architect with a serious purpose: returning theatre design to the status of that of a public building.

In September 1866, as the Brighton Theatre was nearing completion, Phipps's old friend and mentor, James Chute, who had been toying with the idea of building a new theatre in the fashionable Clifton area of Bristol for some years, finally began negotiation for a large site in Park Row.[16] The road was a major thoroughfare between Bristol and Clifton and thus easily accessible, and the site, an old house with generous gardens, was ideal for a large theatre. Park Row was also a more salubrious area than King Street in the centre of Bristol, where the old Theatre Royal had opened in 1766 and Chute's aim was to attract the fickle Bristol box audience, who found the 18th century playhouse too small and singularly lacking in 19th-century comforts. From Phipps's point of view the commission was a golden opportunity to design a prominent façade entirely of his own making. It was a challenge; the site was 105 ft. wide and 130 ft. deep with an additional 50 ft. by 50 ft. frontage in Park Row.[17]

The purchase negotiations took some time, but by Christmas 1866, they were concluded and the spectators to the Pantomime were treated to a view – probably a back cloth – of Phipps's design for the main frontage 'with the announcement: Opening Night October 14, 1867'.[18] It was, as Chute admitted 'a long shot', as he had not actually got possession of the site.

The frontage incorporated the box entrances in the centre flanked by shops with the stage entrance at the west end and the pit and gallery entrances at the east end. Phipps adopted a classically inspired solution, possibly at Chute's behest, and turned the whole of the ground floor into a round-arched arcade of 14 bays, the arches resting on solid rather squat square pillars with Corinthian-like capitals into which entrances and shops could easily be fitted. Above rose a plain first floor with tall rectangular windows followed by a lower, equally plain second floor.

No. 12. The Prince's Theatre, Park Row, Bristol. Main frontage. Copyright Bristol Record Office.

Only a modestly projecting portico of six Doric columns in the centre announced that his was a building with aspirations, not a mere shopping arcade with classical overtones. It was not an extravagant façade, it was respectable, a little bland, designed not to cause offence and to be functional. Chute, would probably not have countenanced anything else even if Phipps hade suggested it; the former was paying for the theatre from his own resources and from short-term loans; he had had enough of proprietors' committees and ultimately raised £18,000 for the theatre.[19]

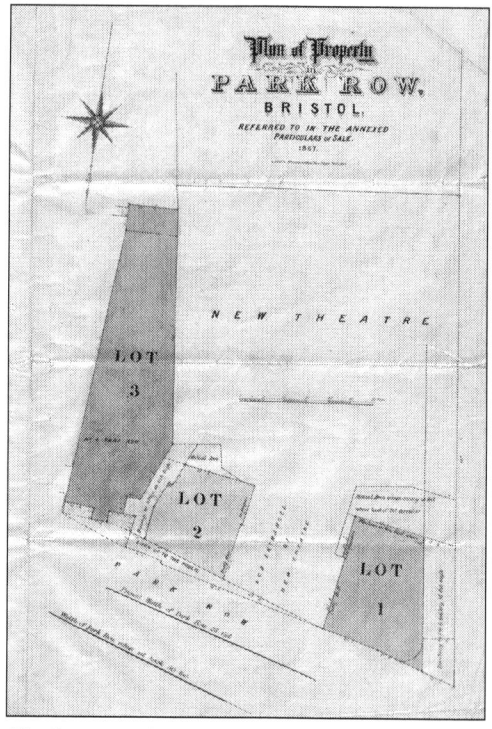

The Prince's Theatre, Park Row, Bristol. Site plan. Copyright Bristol Record Office.

Towards the end of February 1867, with Chute still not in possession of his new property, the press was invited to inspect the plans, which 'evince an amount of thought and study ... with no part of the building not above ground'.[20] As part of fire-prevention measures, the carpenter's, the machinist's and other workshops were placed outside the main building and there would be extra exit doors for the pit and gallery. To ensure good sightlines for everyone the 'sweep of the gallery and boxes will only be carried partially round the building ... and the work of preparatory demolition will begin almost immediately'.[21] It did not begin until Ash Wednesday, 6 March.

A delicately painted, unsigned watercolour of the auditorium looking towards the stage from the front of the dress circle and identified by Hugh Maguire as depicting the Park Row New Theatre Royal, reveals that the Phipps had largely repeated his circular Nottingham design but omitted the proscenium boxes.[22] Instead the slightly splayed proscenium is marked by ornamented square Corinthian columns supporting a curved entablature with a 30 ft. long painted frieze. The water colour might be by Phipps, or possibly by George Gordon to whom Phipps had entrusted both the design and execution of the auditorium decoration.[23]

The proscenium opening was 30 ft. wide and 27 ft. high and the stage 64 ft. wide, the same width as the pit, and 60 ft. deep with sinks at 21 ft.[24] 24 miles of rope were used in connection with the machinery.[25] Both the dress and upper circle terminated in three private boxes on either side, and a single small, square box was tucked in underneath the dress circle by the proscenium. The impression in the watercolour is of an upper-class drawing room whose owner had a penchant for classical arabesques and who wished to show off a large figure painting of Apollo and the Muses, strategically placed along the curved wall above the proscenium for all to see. The painting was by Henry Holiday while George Gordon had painted the act drop depicting a classical villa.

The tiers were set back from each other in the fashionable 'balcon-style' with the front of the dress circle 44 ft. 6 in. from the curtain line and the gallery 50 ft. away. The total capacity was 2,154 distributed as follows: stalls, 40; dress circle, 250; private boxes, 64; upper boxes and amphitheatre, 300; pit, 800; gallery, 700. The last two figures were probably overestimated, but even so the need for a generous provision of exits for such large numbers was another challenge for Phipps, which he did not quite manage. He confined the entrances to pit and gallery (one each) to the back of the theatre, a solution born of architectural convenience, widely used in the 18th century. However, in this case the doors did not open onto a separate street but were reached via a 20 ft. wide downward sloping passage from Park Row with a sharp left turn at the end. This was not a satisfactory entry route for 1500 people, even when separated by a barrier, and as an exit passage it was a short-cut to disaster, which Phipps had either not realised or chose to ignore.

Bristol's New Theatre Royal (later known as the Prince's) opened, as planned, on 14 October 1867, with a performance of *The Tempest*. Before the performance began, Chute invited Phipps on stage with the words: 'Let me introduce you to my friend, Mr Phipps'. The latter was greeted by tremendous cheering, as Chute continued:

'This is the man that designed the House that Jack built; this is the architect. I remember reading in the vaults of the Pantheon at Paris an inscription: "If you desire to see the monument of the architect, look around you". If my friend, Mr Phipps, should be called upon for a reference, or to produce a certificate of fitness, we might very fairly and proudly point to this building and say "Look around you".'[26]

To have his theatre design compared, albeit indirectly, to Jacques Soufflot's Pantheon (originally Ste. Geneviève), an eighteenth-century neoclassical masterpiece – albeit beset by structural problems – must have been immensely satisfying for Phipps. He had managed to achieve, at least in Bristol, what he had set out to do, namely to be accepted and respected as an architect of monumental public buildings. He would have known, even if the audience did not, that Soufflot had begun his career by designing a provincial theatre, the Theatre of Lyons, commissioned by the local council in 1754. The Lyons theatre was a landmark building much admired for its innovative planning and attention to fire prevention and regularly featured in the 18th and 19th century literature on theatre design.[27]

The completion of the Bristol theatre on time was all the more remarkable as Phipps and his clerk of works, George Tasker, were both engaged, at the same time, on the refurbishing of the Theatre Royal in Swansea and the more taxing conversion of St Martin's Hall in London into a theatre suitable for a comfort-loving West-end audience. Presumably the two men commuted back and forth as Phipps was still living at 5 Paragon Buildings and Tasker in Bristol.

In Swansea, which in the early 19th century had tried to market itself as the 'Brighton of Wales', Phipps's brief was to enlarge a rather small theatre originally erected in 1806 in Temple Street.[28] By pushing back the original proscenium he managed to create room for 350, as opposed to 100, in the pit, and to install a new stage ready for opening in June 1867.[29] As Tasker was his chief stage constructor he is likely to have been involved here too.

The conversion of St. Martin's Hall was the brainchild of Lionel Lawson, a wealthy manufacturer of printing ink and part proprietor of the *Daily Telegraph*. Lawson had his eye on the St Martin's Concert Hall in Long Acre, erected in 1850 and rebuilt after a fire in 1862, which he proposed gutting and converting into a theatre within the existing walls and roof. The work was Phipps's first opportunity to make his mark in London and, according to his pupil Arthur Garner, he wasted no time but promptly departed for London together with two senior articled pupils [unnamed] leaving the 16-year-old Garner in temporary charge of the Bath Office.[30]

Phipps needed to act fast. Lawson also wanted his New Queen's Theatre to open in October 1867, so there was no time to mull over an entirely new design; it was a matter of adapting the Bristol plans to fit into the large space that Lawson had offered him. By the middle of May, Phipps's 'admirable plans' had been completed, approved and adopted and 'operations will begin immediately'.[31] By early October, the rebuilding was nearing completion and the newly appointed manager, Alfred Wigan, issued a prospectus largely based on information supplied by Phipps.[32]

The plan of the auditorium was described as 'original', with 'the front of the dress circle forming three parts of an egg; the upper box tier similar but larger in radius; while the gallery resolves itself into a complete circle carried round over the proscenium and forming, as it were, a cornice', exactly like in Bristol. The audience in the amphitheatre, at the front of the gallery, only occupied half of the circle, 'the remaining part consisting of a handsome circular frieze'. With a good height to the tiers together with 'a thorough system of extracting flues the theatre will be kept clear of the vitiated air and effluvium from the gas usually so unpleasant'. In addition Phipps's 'luxurious seats in the stalls and dress circle', and the presence of ample refreshment and retiring rooms would add to the comfort and convenience of a still reluctant middle-class London audience, who, as the drama critic Henry Morley patiently explained, expected that:

'The payment for a seat should be made to secure, within the theatre, every service necessary to the enjoyment of it. Not only the seats, but approaches to them should be easy. Seats in the pit should be cushioned, backed and not overcrowded; in the boxes and stalls always comfortable chairs. Desire to reap quickly the fruit of every success still tempts nearly all managers to crowd their seats together, and grudge lines of open space to and fro.'[33]

These were sentiments that Phipps fully understood and while his design of tip-up armchairs would prove to be a successful means to this end, the problem of how best to dispose of 'vitiated air and effluvium' without creating a chilling draught, would dog him throughout his career.

The prospectus included detailed information about the width of seats and the distance between them in the form of a table:[34]

Place	No. of rows	Distance		Width of seat	No. front to back
		ft.	in.	in.	
Stalls	5	3	0	22½	110
Dress Circle	7	2	9	21	230
18 Private Boxes	-	-	-	-	64
Upper Boxes	6	2	8	21	230
Amphitheatre	2	2	2	20	100
Pit	19	2	0	18	640
Gallery	14	1	10½	16	610
				Seating	1284
				Standing	236
				Total	2220

There would have been little point in publishing these figures if they were not more generous than, or, at least, comparable with the best London theatres and their inclusion suggest that Phipps and his client believed the wealthier part of their potential audience measured their comfort in terms of allotted inches. He was probably right.

The distance from the curtain line to the front of the dress circle was 44 ft. 6 in. and the proscenium opening was almost square, 30 ft. wide and 29 ft. high in line with previous designs.[35] However, here the width of the stage between the walls was only 55 ft., thus making it difficult to arrange, as the prospectus noted, 'for the multifarious requirements behind the scenes'. Phipps's solution was to use the exceptional height of the building which allowed for a 30 ft. scene to be taken up out of sight, to compensate for the lack of width.

It seems that the stage and its machinery was entirely the work of

The Queen's Theatre, 1867. View of auditorium. © *Victoria and Albert Museum.*

Phipps and Tasker, no other name is mentioned in connection with it. Instead the prospectus proudly notes that 'the stage and machinery have been constructed under the immediate direction of the architect, by his chief clerk of works, Mr G. R. Tasker.

'The whole of the stage is "scruto" or made to slide away like a shutter. The transverse joists are laid in iron stirrups, fitting like saddles upon the longitudinal beams, and by a simple and expeditious contrivance the joists can all be pushed back, thus forming an enormous opening in the stage for the rise of castles bridges or other mechanical effects'.[36]

With George Gordon busy planning and executing the decorations in Bristol Phipps, perhaps unsure of the type of decorative scheme with which to impress the London audience, turned to his old friend Edward Godwin for advice. Godwin suggested engaging the painter Albert Moore, whose frieze-like paintings in subdued colouring had recently enthralled the Royal Academy visitors. Moore would be the ideal man to create a stunning and modern frieze above the proscenium and to advise on the colour and decoration throughout the house so that it would all be in harmony with the chief artwork.[37]

Delicate outlines and soft colours were not what English theatre managers were used to nor, in Godwin's view, were they capable of appreciating it, and although Lawson approved of Moore's sketches, the management did not. It is unclear whether it was the actual lessee, Henry Labouchère, a wealthy journalist and, in 1867, a Liberal MP, who hoped to further the career of his mistress, the actress Henrietta Hodson, or the nominal lessee, the actor Alfred Wigan, whose name appeared on the prospectus and programmes, who insisted on bolder colours and traditional ornamentation; it might have been all three of them. Phipps was faced by an uncomfortable dilemma, he could champion Moore's design – it was the architect's responsibility to approve the proposed decorations – or he could lower his artistic ambitions and allow himself to be shackled by tradition. He compromised. Moore was allowed to paint his 30 ft. long 7 ft. high frieze of life-size Greek figures watching a play in delicate colours, while the management was allowed to satisfy their desire for large arabesques, that staple of theatre decoration, on box fronts and ceiling, painted by Green and King, and a profusion of glittering gold mouldings on the lower circles and in the proscenium arch. Godwin was deeply unimpressed, yet generous enough to praise the acoustics and sightlines.

On 24 October 1867, ten days after the opening night of Chute's theatre, the Queen's opened and Phipps was again called before the curtain to receive a rapturous applause for his efforts. Annoyingly for the management, the opening night's play, *The Double Marriage* by Charles Reade seems to have elicited less enthusiasm. It was based on a French novel by August Magnet, *White Lies*, but, as the Pall Mall Gazette noted:

'Its intricate plot and the process of its unravelment taxes the attention rather more severely than English audiences have been accustomed to. The Parisian playgoer endures with wonderful patience the deliberate evolvement of a tangled tale of sin and sorrow and mystery, although the whole evening may be occupied. But the British public is subject to some loss of temper if the dramatist's plot is not made tolerably plain to it at an early stage of the performance'.[38]

By this stage in his career, Phipps must have been well aware of the capriciousness of English theatre audiences, the nature of which varied not only between London and the provinces, but between every provincial town. As the rising tide of the theatrical free trade, which had spawned the opening of four new London theatres, including Queen's in the last year,[39] encouraged more property speculators to venture out into its choppy waters Phipps could look forward to more work. He already had another commission from Lawson, who was taking him to Paris to see the latest Parisian theatres, and a new office in London's West End at 9 Adam Street, Adelphi. Soon he would be able to leave Bath and move permanently to London with his family.

Endnotes

1. London Post Office Directory 1864. The Directories were usually compiled in the previous December.
2. BaRAS Report No. 2615/2012.
3. *Nottingham Review*, 29 September 1865, p. 8.
4. *Nottingham Review*, 29 September 1865, p. 8.
5. Nottingham Record Office, M8810, Ledger of Account for building Theatre Royal Nottingham 1864-7, p. 8.
6. Nottingham Record Office, M8810, Ledger of Account for building Theatre Royal Nottingham, 1864-7, p. 26.
7. *Nottingham Review,* 29 September 1865, p. 8.
8. *Builder*, 29 September 1865, p. 302.
9. Phipps was elected a Fellow on 12 February 1866.
10. *South Shields Gazette and Daily Telegraph*, 18 May 1866, p. 1.
11. *South Shields Gazette and Daily Telegraph*, 19 May 1866.
12. Information kindly supplied by Terry Sawyer.
13. *Era*, 1 July 1866, p. 13. *Builder,* 20 October 1866, p. 776.
14. *Builder*, 20 October 1866, p. 776.
15. *Builder*, 20 October 1866, p. 777.
16. K. Barker, *The Theatre Royal Bristol 1766-1966*, STR, 1974, pp. 155-6.
17. Builder, 9 March, 1867, p. 173.
18. Bristol Mercury, 19 October 1867, p. 6.
19. K.Barker, *Theatre Royal Bristol*, STR, 1974, p. 156, note 56.
20. *Bristol Mercury*, 23 February 1867, p. 7.
21. Ibid.
22. Watercolour by unknown artist of the New Theatre Royal auditorium, n.d. See H. Maguire, 'A View of the New Theatre Royal Bristol', *Theatre Notebook*, xlii, 1988, pp. 35-37.
23. *Building News*, 18 October 1867, p. 726.
24. *Builder*, 9 March 1867, p. 173.
25. *Bristol Mercury*, 19 October 1867, p. 6.
26. *Bristol Mercury*, 19 October 1867, p. 6.
27. G. Garlick, 'Neoclassicism and English Theatre Architecture', Ph. D Thesis, University of Exeter, 1996, pp. 41-43.
28. *Era*, 28 April 1867, p. 13.
29. C. Price, *The Professional Theatre in Wales*, University College, Swansea, 1984, p. 14. The theatre was demolished in 1898.

30 T.W.H. Leavitt, ed., *Australian Representative Men*, v.1 [unpaginated], Melbourne 1887. Information kindly supplied by Terry Sawyer.
31 *Era*, 19 May 1866, p. 11.
32 *Morning Post*, 4 October 1867, p. 3.
33 H. Morley, *The Journal of a London Playgoer*, London 1866, 1891. Reprinted, Leicester University Press, 1974, p. 18.
34 *Era*, 6 October 1867, p. 6.
35 *Building News*, 18 October 1867, p. 719.
36 *Morning Post*, 4 October 1867, p. 3.
37 *Building News*, 18 October 1867, p. 716.
38 Pall Mall Gazette, 28 October 1867, p. 8.
39 *Era*, 6 October 1867, p. 6.

4 NAVIGATING THE THEATRICAL FREE TRADE

The London Gaiety and Mecklenburgh Square

On the evening of the sixth of December eighteen sixty-seven Her Majesty's Theatre in London burnt to the ground. The cause of the fire was unclear; possibly a spontaneous combustion triggered by 'an oily rag and some lamp-black in a pile of shaving'.[1] Fortunately, there was no loss of life. With the embers barely cooled, Phipps, seeing an unexpected chance to design a monumental theatre on land owned by the Crown, wrote to the Lord Chamberlain on 9 December asking to be considered for the eventual rebuilding of the theatre:

– 'As you have kindly expressed your appreciation of my latest work [Queen's Theatre] ... might I ask the favour of your speaking for me in the matter of Her Majesty's should the appointment occur. There appear so many apparent interests in the property that I cannot see quite with whom the rebuilding will rest. My anxiety to be connected with this great national project must be my apology for thus troubling you.'[2]

Under the 1843 Theatres Act The Lord Chamberlain had been given authority to license theatres in 'the Cities of London and Westminster, the Borough of Finsbury and Marylebone, the Tower Hamlets, Lambeth and Southwark,' and in places where the sovereign sometimes resided such as Windsor. There was no time limit on the licences, but they usually had to be renewed annually. In addition he had the power to make 'rules' which theatre managers must follow or risk losing their licence. There were no strictures on the type of rules he could make; he could have laid down strict building and safety regulations, but the aristocratic holders of the position seem to have had little interest in such a drastic form of intervention.

The position of Lord Chamberlain was a political appointment and at this point the incumbent was Earl Bradford (1864-1868). The Office of the Lord Chamberlain was run by a senior civil servant, the Comptroller, who, at the time was Sir Spencer Ponsonby-Fane (1824-1915) the sixth son of the fourth Earl of Bessborough (a title in the Irish Peerage) who had taken over the post in 1857. Ponsonby remained in post until the end of the century exercising considerable influence over the British theatre as his masters, not always knowledgeable on theatrical matters, came and went according to the prevailing political wind.

Phipps's letter was a bold move for a provincial architect just venturing into the London theatre market and his apparent confusion over the 'interests in the property' suggests a lack of understanding of the speculative nature of metropolitan theatre building. A sketch plan and accompanying letter to one of the potential developers, such as the previous manager, Colonel James Mapleson, might have been more productive. The leaseholder, the earl of Dudley, later rebuilt Her Majesty's to plans by Charles Lee, but failed to find a tenant.

Phipps was still a novice when it came to the burgeoning theatrical free trade which had been made possible by the abolition of the patent theatres in the Theatres Act of 1843. It was no longer necessary for theatre owners to obtain an expensive royal patent in order to perform the drama in London or the provinces; anyone could apply to the Lord Chamberlain for a licence. The act did not spark a sudden rush of theatre building, but it encouraged the rise of the music hall.[3]

Lionel Lawson, however, had every intention of taking full advantage of the changing times and any disappointment Phipps might have felt at not getting the commission for Her Majesty's, was probably rapidly overtaken by Lawson's plans for a new theatre *cum* restaurant on a large corner site on the Strand, bordering Catherine Street, Exeter Street and Wellington Street. Lawson had gradually been buying up a string of properties in the area, including the old Strand Music Hall and his intention was to bring French taste and fashion to London.

To make sure that Phipps fully realised exactly what he had in mind, Lawson took his earnest provincial architect to Paris. Whether Phipps had had any close encounters with Parisian theatres, let alone restaurants, in the last four years, that is since he had admitted to ignorance of current Parisian theatre design during his Bristol lecture in 1863, is unclear but unlikely. Expanding his practice and being available to meet potential clients would have been his first priority, not a questionable study-trip to Paris to look at theatres leaving a wife and a growing family behind in Bath.

Since Lawson was as much in a hurry over the Gaiety as he had been over his Long-acre playhouse, the opening of the former was scheduled for December 1868, it would seem likely that the pair set off for Paris soon after the completion of the Queen's Theatre. If so, they would have been in time to catch the last days of the 1867 International Exhibition, which closed on 3 November. Even if they did not, the sweeping rebuilding of central Paris, launched by Napoleon III in 1853 and carried out by his 'Prefect of the Seine', Baron G. E. Haussmann – a ruthless and canny man with a penchant for vistas ending in monumental structures – would have provided enough new ideas to keep Phipps going for some time. The most impressive of these structures was, undoubtedly, the Paris Opera, designed by Charles Garnier, covering a site 564 ft. long, and 410 ft. wide, which was slowly rising from its unexpectedly watery foundations. Phipps must have marvelled at the conception, not least the size of the stage, the awe-inspiring height of the fly floors, and the multilayered depth below the stage floor. He was a technical man, and took careful note of the use of the iron framework embedded in a solid mass of cement concrete.[4] He discovered a similar construction method in the new Vaudeville Theatre (1866-69) by Auguste-Joseph Magne, which formed part of Napoleon's grand scheme of pulling down old theatres and replacing them with new ones erected on prominent corner sites where their façade formed an integral part of a residential and retail block. This was the authorities' way of recouping some of the cost, and, judging by Phipps's later work, he readily saw the merit in this concept of a multipurpose structure. An isolated site was the ideal for a theatre, but in the commercial reality of nineteenth-century society this, clearly, was not always possible, not even in Paris under a state-funded redevelopment programme. However, for a theatre architect wishing to humour a property developer, this was a workable proposition. The Vaudeville, situated on the corner of Boulevard des Capucines and Rue de la Chaussée D'Antin, had an elegantly curved, rusticated four-storey façade of three bays topped by a cupola, a design which Phipps carefully noted for future reference.

The new theatre that Phipps and Lawson took as their model for auditorium design for the Gaiety was, according to John Hollingshead, the Théâtre Lyrique at Place de Châtelet by G. Davioud.[5] Here it was the projecting balcony with small private boxes round the back instead of the

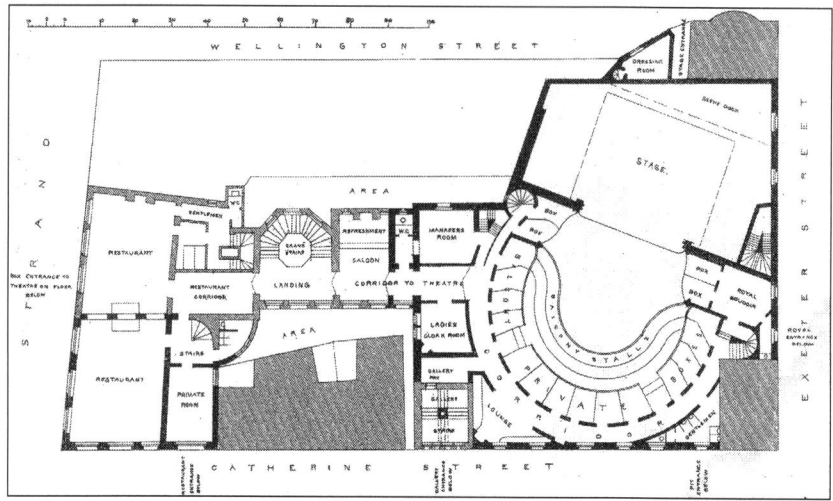

The Gaiety Theatre, London. Plan 1867. John Earl Collection.

old-fashioned dress circle that excited them. By a strange coincidence, Davioud, had been examining London theatres a year earlier on behalf of Haussmann who sent him to study the English low-price theatres and music halls, such as Finch Hill's and Paraire's Britannia in Hoxton, with a view to possibly introducing this type of theatre to Paris.[6] Davioud was unimpressed though at the same time he was slightly envious of the absence of regulations regarding 'he exact amount of space that constitutes a seat'. A space suitable for three seats in a Parisian theatre would be deemed sufficient for eight people standing in the Britannia. However, this generally accepted overcrowding coupled with a deplorable lack of adequate ventilation made for nauseous odours, particularly in the gallery, the unlit corridors were a safety hazard especially in event of panic, and as for the stinking urinals, these would have been banished to a public way by the Parisian police.

After his inspection of London theatres of all kinds, Davioud was forced to conclude that 'England is far from being the country of the arts and of comfort applied to masses of individuals' and that 'remuneration for capital invested is the chief aim of the constructor of theatres: art is scarcely taken into consideration'. It was a description that, in some ways fitted Lawson whose theatre investments were coolly based on the projected return.

The Gaiety Theatre, London. View of auditorium. John Earl Collection.

In this speculative world of English theatre design where the regulatory framework rested on a haphazard collection of hazy ideas on public safety to be interpreted at will by the Lord Chamberlain's Office in the case of theatres licensed by him, or by local magistrates, who often saw their role as upholders of the moral fabric rather than the structural framework, survival as a theatre architect required exceptional adroitness and adaptability. Technical competence and imaginative design was not enough; an ability to produce realistic estimates as well as to maintain budgetary control and stick to a given time-table were crucial aspects in this type of architecture.

On his return from Paris, Phipps put his discoveries to good use in the Gaiety design. He had clearly been much impressed by the latest French construction methods and all the tiers were built on an iron framework 'embedded in and filled between with a solid mass of cement concrete much on the principle adopted at the Grand Opera and the New Vaudeville Theatre in Paris', adding proudly: 'with the exception of the two Theatres at Paris ... "THE GAIETY" will be the only Theatre in Europe so constructed'.[7] His aim had been to create as fire-proof a theatre as possible and all passages, corridors and staircases were of stone or cement divided by brick walls. Even the proscenium columns were of solid stone.

Despite the fact that the theatre and restaurant complex were largely on an island site Phipps was not called upon to produce an elegant entrance façade as would have been the case in Paris. Lawson was not about to spend money on anything remotely reminiscent of Davioud's Palladio inspired frontages, or the New Vaudeville's discrete Baroque; that was an aspect of French theatre architecture that he was not interested in. As Hollingshead observed, a London theatre proprietor did not want a façade emulating a hotel or a bank, he wanted access to a chief thoroughfare and a 20 ft. wide entrance which was enough to satisfy the licensing authorities.[8] Thus, the old music hall entrance in the Strand was retained and renamed the Grand Entrance to Stalls and Boxes. The hall itself was, however, pulled down and replaced by elegant entrance lobbies on the ground floor where scented fountains played – the scent provided by the enterprising Mr Rimmel – with the café and restaurant above. The pit and gallery entrances were set well apart in the wide Catherine Street frontage, whereas the stage door was entered from Wellington Street while the royal entrance was discretely placed in Exeter Street. The latter also doubled as an emergency exit in case of panic; a stone staircase rose from the entrance all the way to the gallery floor 'with communication at every level'.[9]

This was true. However, the gallery stairs were set within a square stone tower where a narrow pay desk, at dress circle level, ensured that the ascent up the steps along the many right-angled turns proceeded in an orderly fashion. By the same token the rapidity of the descent at the end of the performance was held in check by the sharp angles and half landings. It seemed satisfactory on the drawing-board, but it was not a risk-free design. The possibility of scores of people, during a sudden exit in case of panic, rushing, stumbling and piling on top of each other among the sharp turns was very real, but not easy to remedy on the given site.

This solid structure was cleverly disguised by a lightness of touch in the auditorium design, reminiscent of Bath, but Phipps went further, creating an elegant gothic concoction within his circular plan with the front of the grand tier, as the dress circle was now described, "opening out by arms of a contrary flexure to the proscenium column".[10] He then turned the traditionally open dress circle into a French-style balcony with three rows of armchairs sealed off at the rear by a row of enclosed private boxes discreetly hidden behind artfully draped curtains. The latter added a certain *frisson* to the auditorium, a hint of improper assignations, unthinkable in a provincial theatre where the architecture was usually expected to underline the moral purpose of the drama. Thirty years earlier it had also been unacceptable in London; when the architect Samuel Beazley tried to introduce this French fashion in the Lyceum Theatre in 1834, it was considered too suggestive and was replaced by a standard dress circle.[11] When T. H. Wyatt tried, twenty years later, to present the Londoners with a balcony in the new Adelphi, he wisely left the boxes at the back open, and his design was much admired. By 1868, however, Lawson and Phipps judged the London upper- and middle-classes to be more in tune with their Parisian counterparts; correctly as it turned out.

There were five rows of armchairs in the stalls in front of a capacious pit, holding around 500. The *Pall Mall Gazette* was impressed:

'At the Gaiety the due status of the stalls is recognized and they are reached by commodious approaches almost on a level with the Strand while a tunnel under the pit enables the visitor to pass from one side of the house to the other without disturbing the audience who are already seated.'[12]

The upper circle, which was set back from the balcony, comprised four rows of seats with ample standing room behind. The front of the gallery formed a complete circle and could hold 600. The total capacity, including the 28 private boxes, was estimated at around 2000.[13]

Having eschewed plaster decorations in his previous theatres for acoustic and cleanliness reasons – they were dreadful dust traps – Phipps now resurrected this traditional mode of decoration and designed stylised roses for the subtly pointed arches in front of the gallery, and diamond-patterns for the upper tier fronts. The balcony, however, was finished with an iron railing in a Greek-style anthemion pattern exuding both security and elegance. These classical references do not appear to have impinged on the most arresting part of the decoration, the 30 ft. deep and 4 ft. 6 in. high frieze above the proscenium, designed and painted by H.S. Marks, showing a mediaeval court enthralled by the performance of a masque. Below, the act-drop depicting a villa on an Italian lake, painted by George Gordon, surrounded by in an elaborate frame, held its own against the clusters of thin columns forming the proscenium opening. The whole was an eclectic mix, with a lightness of touch and a hint of frivolity, perfectly attuned to the intended stage offerings. The invaluable Tasker had, yet again, not only acted as clerk of works but also designed and fitted up the stage machinery.

As so often with theatres, the construction process had not been entirely straightforward. The neighbouring *Morning Post* in Wellington Street threatened to take out an injunction against the builders for blocking out light and air. Phipps, Tasker and the contractors held a council of war and decided to take matters into their own hands: they would erect the offending block over a weekend, starting at six o'clock on Saturday morning and finishing at two o'clock on Sunday afternoon, during which time the newspaper office was closed. It was a Herculean task, but they succeeded and the ruse worked. The block was less offensive than the *Morning Post* had feared and no court action was taken.[14]

This forced pace of working was not sustainable in the long run and the journalist John Hollingshead, who had leased the theatre from Lawson after the plans had been decided but before the theatre was completed, feared Phipps had been grossly over-optimistic in agreeing to a completion date of 21 December 1868. He need not have feared; as usual Tasker delivered. Ten minutes before the doors opened to the public at half past six in the evening, the last of the workmen left the stage, carrying their tools and installed themselves in the 4 shilling-seats of the front row of the upper balcony. There was no shifting them, "they had built the (adjective) and they meant to see it opened".[15] Hollingshead wisely allowed them to remain and they, together with an enthusiastic and generally better attired audience, were treated to the new operetta *The Two Harlequins* with scenery '*A La Watteau*', a new comic drama *On the Cards*, adapted from the French, and a New Operatic Extravaganza by W. S. Gilbert, *Robert the Devil*. It was a witty and light-hearted programme, an escapist extravaganza in complete harmony with the auditorium design.

By the time Phipps was working on the Gaiety design he had moved his family to London to 26 Mecklenburgh Square. He was still listed under 48 Cornhill EC, in the 1867 London Post Office Directory but in the 1868 edition he appears under the Mecklenburgh Square address suggesting that he took up residence there towards the end of 1867 or beginning of 1868 after a brief sojourn at Adams Street in the Adelphi.[16] Lawson's patronage had given him the longed-for foot-hold in the competitive metropolitan market and the confidence, professionally and financially to take this audacious step. Interestingly, he is also listed in the Bath Directory for 1868/9 under 'Architects' as 'Phipps Charles J., F.S.A. & Hay J. Mountford, at 5 Paragon Buildings'. Phipps's pupil Arthur Garner later claimed to have joined the Mecklenburgh Square office in the summer of 1868,[17] and Phipps did not appear in any subsequent Bath Directories.

Finding the right place to live in London was not easy. The accommodation must be ample enough to provide the space for a growing architectural practice, not to mention a growing family. Ideally it should offer ready access to fresh air for the four children, which was difficult in the fog-ridden capital. Furthermore, it must be situated in the right social milieu for an upwardly mobile middle-class household.

Mecklenburgh Square, a garden square, just off Gray's Inn Road, laid out with trees and lawns and gravel paths next to the Foundling Hospital, answered to all requirements. The trees filtered the polluted air, and on the east side there was (and still is) a substantial terrace of four-storey houses with basements, built between 1810 and 1820, and thus large enough to accommodate Phipps's office as well as his wife and family and three servants: a cook, a maid and a governess.[18] The social setting was perfect, respectable, but not too grand. Their immediate neighbours were a barrister (at no. 27) and a publisher (no. 25), but there was also a sprinkling of medical men with families. Furthermore, the square was well placed for the West End where Phipps was hoping to establish his reputation as a leading theatre architect, but it was also close enough to Kings Cross and St Pancras railway stations for provincial theatre proprietors, looking for an accommodating architect, to call without great inconvenience, and for Phipps to catch the next train to secure a potential commission outside the capital.

The square's closeness to a new Anglo-Catholic church, St Alban

Mecklenburgh Square, London. Exterior view. Author's Collection.

the Martyr just off High Holborn, a beacon of architectural splendour designed by William Butterfield, might also have been an additional attraction, though its situation in the midst of filthy and dilapidated lodging houses, sweatshops, brothels and thieves' kitchens, was not. Mecklenburgh Square's official parish church, St Bartholomew's, lay at the more salubrious north end of Gray's Inn Road.

The London Vaudeville, the Dublin Gaiety and the Aberdeen Tivoli

After the frantic rush to complete the Gaiety Theatre, Phipps turned his attention to its adjoining restaurant while waiting for new theatre projects to materialise. However, nothing very startling appeared from London speculators, only the Vaudeville Theatre in the Strand, a cramped shadow of the Vaudeville in Paris, and the Hoxton Variety Theatre and then two promising provincial commissions came his way, one in Dublin, the other in Aberdeen.

The Gaiety Restaurant took longer than originally planned; not until October 1869 could the first guests take their seats on the first and second floor and choose from English, French and German cuisine to be savoured in either public or private dining rooms, all sumptuously decorated by George Gordon. For hungry spectators in the dress and upper circles the dining facilities were readily accessible through arched openings which linked the two buildings and also provided emergency exits in case of panic as the main staircase to the restaurant was entirely separate from the theatre.[19]

Despite the undoubted success of the Gaiety, 1869 did not end well for Phipps's professional reputation. At the New Theatre Royal in Bristol, on Boxing Night, the most popular theatre night of all being the official start of the pantomime season, nearly 2000 people were queuing for the pit and gallery along the 20 ft. wide

The Hoxton Variety Theatre, London. John Earl Collection.

sloping passage entered from Park Row and around the sharp turn which led to both doors on the left side.[20] As the doors opened the excited crowd surged forward, those in front who could not get through the doors fast enough, fell over and were trampled on by those behind. A desperate policeman, trying to stop the pushing from the back, shouted "Fire!" thereby creating total panic and people pushed in all directions. 18 people were crushed to death and many more injured. For Chute, whose advice and friendship had helped Phipps to carve out a career as a theatre architect, the loss of life was a terrible blow from which he never quite recovered. To Phipps the incident was a stark warning, which did not fully register.

By the time of the accident Phipps was working on his two London projects, the Vaudeville Theatre in the Strand (opened 16 April 1870) and the Variety Theatre in Hoxton (opened 13 March 1870) The latter was a minor affair next to a pub, but Phipps dignified the small theatre space with an Italianate façade, looking rather like an exercise from the drawing-board which he was determined to put to good use.

The Vaudeville, however, was more challenging. Phipps's client was another speculator, Wybrow Robertson, who had failed to make any profit from his billiards club at the back of nos. 403 and 404 in The Strand. He decided to use his constricted site for a theatre instead, possibly encouraged by his actress wife Mary Litton, but, as he had been unable to obtain possession of the buildings fronting the Strand, the existing facades had to be kept more or less intact. Thus, Phipps had to fit in the main entrance through an unobtrusive door opening onto a tight passage on the ground floor of no. 404.

Phipps yet again adapted his circular formula with curves of contrary flexure and produced a masterly example of how to squeeze the maximum number of spectators into a limited space on a tight budget without sacrificing the illusion of modernity and elegance. He turned the first circle into a "grand tier", with a balcony of three rows, behind which he placed the dress circle at a higher level.[21] He then combined the upper circle with the gallery, letting the former act as a decorous front to the rows of gallery seats that rose up behind it. Altogether he managed to make space, on paper at least, for nearly 1000 spectators. As usual George Gordon was responsible for the decoration which included the use of "rich colour on gold ground" on the balcony front, but unusually there is no mention of a clerk of works. Instead the "whole of the works in every department have been executed … under the personal direction of Mr. C.J. Phipps FSA." Interestingly, George Tasker had also moved to London at this point and was living in Clerkenwell,[22] but it seems that he was now working for Phipps as his quantity surveyor rather than as clerk of works,[23] perhaps he had had enough of the duties of the latter after his heroic exertions over the Gaiety.

On 21 April 1870, five days after the opening of the Vaudeville, Phipps found himself in Dublin Castle being cross-examined by the two highest law officers in Ireland, the Attorney General and the Solicitor General. The hearing was considering a proposal for a royal patent for a third theatre in Dublin and the suitability of the vacant site selected for its erection.[24]

The 1843 Theatres Act had not been imposed on Ireland where the old patent system still prevailed and Irish theatre managers were obliged to go through the irksome business of applying for a patent from the Lord Lieutenant before building a new theatre. Dublin already had two patent

The Vaudeville Theatre, London. View of auditorium 1879. John Earl Collection.

theatres, the handsome Theatre Royal designed by Samuel Beazley (1821) and the less handsome Queen's Royal Theatre (1841) and their respective managers saw no need for further competition, though with a population of just under 300.000, three theatres might not seem a great number. At least that was the argument of the new theatre's proposers, John and Michael Gunn, who ran a successful music business in the city, and who believed that Dubliners would welcome their own Gaiety Theatre based on the London model (though without the restaurant).

The Gunns, however, also faced stiff opposition from Irish nationalists, who objected on principle to a theatre based on a London model, designed by an English architect. Why was an Irish architect not chosen? Phipps, mindful of his need for new commissions, presented the court with his impressive list of finished theatres, a list that no other architect could equal, whether English or Irish. He did not buckle before the nationalist arguments, presented by the Home Rule Movement's founder Isaac Butt,

The Gaiety Theatre, Dublin. View of the auditorium. Coloured lithograph, n.d. John Earl Collection.

and the patent was eventually granted. However, raising money for the project turned out to be an even slower business and building did not begin until May 1871, by which time all concerned were more than keen to complete construction with all possible speed and teams of builders worked round the clock.

The Gunns, anxious to emphasise the seriousness of purpose behind their project despite the unserious name of their theatre, invited the city's political and business elite to a ceremonial laying of the first stone by the Lord Mayor on 1 July 1871.[25] By now hundreds of stones had already been laid, the walls were rising fast, and the pit floor had been completed. The latter was large enough to accommodate a marquee were a sumptuous luncheon for 200 guests was laid out, and once Phipps had read out a brief description of the theatre (to large applause) and the Lord Mayor, with the aid of Phipps, had placed a stone at the base of the proscenium (to further applause) the guests set down to eat. Phipps took his place at the top of the table with John Gunn, the Lord Mayor and ex-mayors and was the recipient of loud cheers at the end of the repast. To be *fêted* like this *before* a theatre had been completed was indeed a moment to savour and perhaps an expression of gratitude from his clients for Phipps's part in securing the patent.

Although the London Gaiety was the inspiration for the Dublin version, there were some differences. The pit was 58 ft. deep, as opposed to 53ft. in the London Gaiety, and it held 21 rows of seats, which included pit stalls at the front and accommodated a total of 700 spectators. The balcony, 7 rows deep and holding 200 armchairs, each 2 ft 6 in. wide, formed a semicircle of 28 ft. diameter 'opening out by curves of contrary flexure to a width of 37 ft. at the proscenium columns'. These were made of stone, as at the London Gaiety, and flanked the three tiers of private boxes.[26] At the back of the balcony were circular arches filled with plate-glass sash windows opening on to an enclosed corridor. The upper circle had 5 rows of seats for 210 persons with a corridor at the back separated from the seats 'by a partition high enough to lean on'. It would seem that Phipps had been asked to provide standing room wherever possible. The third tier was fronted by an amphitheatre with two rows behind which rose a steep gallery with nine rows, the whole accommodating around 700 people. According to Phipps's, invariably optimistic calculations, there would be space for around 2000 spectators.

Most of the auditorium décor was painted on the flat and with a hint of the Romanesque among the classical garlands. The centre of the circular-shaped ceiling was painted in turquoise and adorned with glittering stars and the supporting spandrels were 'filled in with illuminated scroll ornament on light ground'. In the panels above the proscenium boxes homage was paid to Irish culture in the form of scenes from Thomas Moore's *Irish Melodies* (1803). The proscenium opening was slimmer and taller than at the London Gaiety, being 28 ft. wide – anything wider would have made scene changing on the 54 ft. wide stage decidedly awkward – and, according to the *Builder*, 37 ft high.

The Gunn's were investing heavily in their new enterprise and Phipps was asked to provide an arresting façade along the 56 ft. wide King Street which would hold its own among the city's classical public buildings. He responded by turning to his Gothic Revival repertoire and produced a ground-floor arcade of lightly pointed arches carried on columns with foliated capitals, an inspired design which, reflected the interior decoration but also owed much to Ruskin's detailed analysis of Venetian Gothic architecture in *Stone's of Venice* (1851). Underneath the arcade were four distinct entrances and staircases to the different parts of the house though it seems the pit entrance might have been a little cramped.[27] On the opening night, 27 November 1871, the house was packed to capacity ready to enjoy Goldsmith's *She Stoops to Conquer* and, not least, the popular burlesque *La Belle Sauvage*. At the end of the performance, the Gunns and their architect 'were called before the curtain and loudly cheered'.[28]

The success in Dublin did not spawn any immediate theatre work in London. Phipps appears not to have entered the open competition for the underground Criterion theatre and restaurant in London in 1870 – maybe he had had enough of restaurants at that point – and the commission went to Thomas Verity (1837-1891). Nor did he pick up the alteration projects for the Old Vic (1871) or Astley's (1872) which both went to Jethro T. Robinson (1828/9-1878), a builder and property speculator from Hull who had teamed up with the circus promoter Charles Hengler in the 1860s and who was now trying to establish himself as a theatre architect in London. Robinson had had no formal architectural training, but his buccaneering spirit and theatrical contacts rapidly brought him commissions when he settled in the capital including the New Pavilion Theatre (1871) and the Alexandra Theatre (1873).

Phipps can hardly have welcomed Robinson's arrival, but in January 1872 some 'enterprising citizens' in Aberdeen came to his rescue. They were determined to replace their old Theatre Royal from 1795 with a playhouse 'more in conformity with the [city's] growing prosperity'.[29] The rising prosperity was not in doubt; in 1871 the population had reached over 76,000, the busy harbour had been extended by a new breakwater in concrete, the granite industry was flourishing and so was the ancient university, but the need to spend new-found wealth on a new theatre was less readily accepted. As the *Aberdeen Herald* noted:

'Aberdonians are not, generally speaking, a theatre-going people, yet those who do favour the drama are not by any means easily satisfied as to its exponents ... an actor who passes muster with the regular theatre-goers of Aberdeen need not fear appearing before an audience in any other city or town in the kingdom.'[30]

By the time Phipps arrived on the scene the promoters had already selected a site and secured the services of one the city's leading architects, James Matthews, so this would have to be a collaborative effort.[31] Matthews, 15 years older than Phipps, had a good record in local public buildings and his involvement would lend respectability to the proposal and quell any opposition from nationalists over the employment of an English architect for a Scottish theatre. Matthews knew little of theatre construction, but he understood the expectations of his fellow citizens and, no doubt, communicated them to Phipps. Fortunately, the two men discovered a common link, a past connection with Sir Gilbert Scott – Matthews had spent five years working in Scott's office[32] – and a mutual appreciation of the merits of the Gothic style.

The promoters' chosen site in Guild Street was not ideal in all respects. It had the virtues of being both central and endowed with a generously wide frontage of 74 ft., enough to squeeze in a couple of shops between the entrances and so keep the different classes of spectators from mingling unnecessarily while, at the same time, increasing the building's earning potential. On the other hand the site, which abutted Trinity Street at the back, was only 90 ft. deep, which was not quite enough for a modern auditorium intended to accommodate 1700 plus a stage commodious enough for a reasonable degree of scenic display. Though Expectations of scenic wonders might have been lower here than in London or Dublin, given the dilapidated state of the old Theatre Royal in Marischal Street, any improvement would be welcomed and thus the stage was allotted a modest depth of 29 ft. from the footlights.

As always, speed was of the essence. The promoters did not wish to lose momentum and formed a joint stock company which managed to raise £5000, enough to sign building contracts one of which was for fairly extensive concrete work with Messrs Drake and Son of London.[33] The end walls, as well as the side and party walls were to be constructed

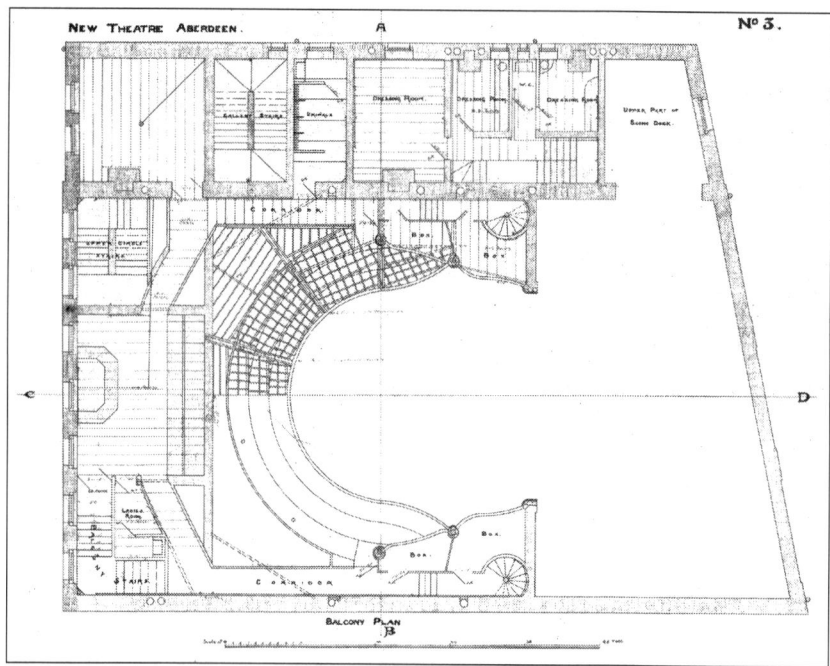

The Tivoli Theatre, Aberdeen. Balcony plan. 1872. © Aberdeen City Archives.

from poured concrete (eight parts gravel and sand and one part Portland cement) leaving some Aberdonians to question the weight-bearing capacities of this new material, but they were reassured, through the local press, that the balcony, boxes and gallery all rested on moulded iron columns supported by brick piers. The advantages of concrete was probably another issue where the two architects were of a similar mind, Phipps having used concrete in the London Gaiety and Matthews having seen the solidity of the new concrete breakwater in Aberdeen harbour.

Phipps, as before, successfully adapted his circular auditorium with its gracefully curved sides to fit the site: 'Mr Phipps having taken full advantage of his large experience in preparing the plans' as the *Aberdeen Herald* noted, suggesting that it was he and not Matthews who was responsible for the interior planning. Indeed, only an experienced theatre designer could have maximised the seating capacity in such a spatially economical manner using only two tiers. The first tier consisted of a low-level balcony, endowed with 120 of Phipps's 'patent chairs' spread over

The Tivoli Theatre, Aberdeen. Main frontage. Courtesy of Aberdeen Central Library.

three rows, behind which rose a deep upper circle (with space for 350).[34] The latter stretched back under a vertiginous gallery, intended to hold 700.

The pit allegedly could seat 550, but as the head height underneath the balcony front was only about 8 ft., it would seem there was pressure on the architects to keep costs down and not to raise the auditorium too high. The whole was decorated with gilt and bright colours, giving a 'gay and cheerful appearance' by George Gordon (a native of Aberdeen) who also painted the drop scene representing the 'silver strand' of Loch Katrine.[35] In the lunettes above the private boxes T. Phillips painted scenes form Walter Scott's poems, underlining the theatre's Scottish identity.

A combination of lack of space and scarcity of finance resulted in frugal circulation areas for the vast majority of the audience though the Guild Street frontage presented a lavish display of red and white granite further enlivened by red sandstone. In a city adorned by authoritative buildings mostly in clerical grey granite, Phipps and Matthews, in what might well have been a united spirit of innovation, created a positive riot of colour by adopting white granite and red sandstone for the arcading on all three floors in an elegant composition echoing John Ruskin's coloured illustration of the arched masonry of the 'Broletto of Como' in *Stone's of Venice*.[36] It was a façade which spoke of other worlds and hinted at delights inside while still retaining the utmost decorum.[37]

At the opening night on 19 December 1872 of the New Theatre and Opera House as it was officially called, the rich ornamental ironwork at the front of the balcony was much admired as were the cushioned and padded pit holding 530. There was seating for 1,650, but the total capacity including standing room, was estimated at 1,800. After a successful performance of the reliable middle-class crowd pleaser, *The Lady of Lyons* by Bulwer Lytton, there were calls for 'the architect Mr. Phipps and the energetic clerk of works Mr [William] Browne'.[38]

Aberdeen is a long way from London and the opening of a provincial Scottish theatre was of little interest to London speculators. Phipps's pupil Arthur Garner, perhaps finding the absence of theatre work uninspiring, gave up his pupilship 'by mutual consent'.[39] Around the same time, 1871, Phipps took on a more diligent pupil, Max Clarke (1851-1938), the only son of a Dublin medical doctor. Phipps and Clarke established a more fruitful working relationship and Clarke rose to become Phipps's office manager and remained with him until 1895.[40]

With a shortage of theatres on his books, Phipps had to look elsewhere for work and managed to secure commissions to rebuild the Star and Garter Hotel in Richmond (London) and to convert Crockford's Auction Hall in St. James's Street (London) into a comfortable gentlemen's club for an expanding Liberal Party.[41]

The most prominent feature of the Star and Garter Hotel was vast block masquerading as a French château by E. M. Barry (1864) which overshadowed the original eighteenth-century buildings. A large part of the latter had burnt down in 1870 and three years later the new owners, a limited company, decided to replace the ruins with a magnificent ballroom. Quite how Phipps acquired the commission is unclear, but his 80 ft. by 61 ft. ballroom overlooking a terrace beside the river Thames was truly spectacular with a 33 ft. high ceiling adorned with a counter-ceiling of ground glass from which hung a gas chandelier with 96 lights.[42] For those who wished to bask more closely in the reflections of the glittering ceiling Phipps installed a promenade in the form of an open loggia running around the room at height of 16 ft. with regular openings to tantalizing private dining rooms. It was the perfect setting for the capital's *nouveaux riches*.

The Liberal Party had more modest requirements. The number of liberal voters who wanted to join the original Liberal Club, the Reform Club had swelled after the extension of the franchise in 1868 and premises for an additional, junior club were deemed necessary. It was named the Devonshire Club after its first chairman the Duke of Devonshire. Here, Phipps adopted a restrained neoclassicism with Corinthian pilasters dividing panelled walls and with circular panels gracing the ceilings, a calm and soothing environment for frayed political nerves in need of a restorative brandy and cigars. It was a far cry from the exuberance of the Star and Garter.

It is possible that Phipps was a liberal supporter, but he might well have kept his politics to himself so as not to put off potential clients. In the absence of substantial projects he designed schools for the small towns of Lea and Pewsey in Wiltshire (1873) and entered a competition for a new opera house in Copenhagen, which, even if he did not win and he did not, made an impressive exhibit at the Royal Academy, the architectural profession's most exclusive shop window. The same year he also exhibited his planned alterations of the Crockford's Auction Hall and in 1874 a design for the proposed Emmanuel Church in Dulwich[43] together with the exterior of the Star and Garter Ballroom (he exhibited the interior in 1876).

In the meantime officialdom vandalised his Gaiety complex by insisting that the connections between the theatre and the restaurant be filled in with a two-foot brick wall to comply with the new Licensing Act of 1872.[44] The latter prohibited any 'internal communication between any licensed premises and any unlicensed premises which are used for public entertainment', though in this case Hollingshead also had a license to sell alcohol in the theatre bars. He raged against the decision, but to no avail, the authorities' fear of excessive consumption of liquor among the theatre audience outweighed any consideration for their safety and convenience, let alone the original architectural concept.

Phipps can hardly have been impressed but at the time he had other personal concerns. He was now the proud father of five children, another daughter Mary Rashleigh was born in 1873. The need for more regular and substantial commissions became even more urgent, but navigating the free trade in theatre building was not straightforward when anyone, it seemed, could call themselves a theatre architect.

Yet, as Phipps contemplated his future, he must have been aware that his circular auditorium formula, with its seductive curves of contrary flexure, was a design that brought a touch of much-needed modernity as well as comfort to the English playhouse. He knew too that theatre-going was growing in popularity across the country. London companies were touring again, taking advantage of the newly created vast rail network and thanks to the latter they could and did bring their scenery with them. And there were many provincial towns whose theatres needed upgrading to take advantage of this London-driven theatrical expansion, including the Nottingham Theatre Royal where he supervised a major renovation.

Then, in the summer of 1874, a group of drama-minded citizens in Worcester consulted Phipps about how best to reconstruct their old 18th-century Theatre Royal whose 'barnlike appearance harmonised with the poverty of all its internal features'.[45] They had £5000 to spend, raised through a joint stock company whose chairman, Captain Castle, was a keen amateur actor, and Phipps, after surveying the old theatre, recommended that it should be entirely reconstructed within the existing outer walls. In London, the large Philharmonic Hall in Islington by Finch Hill and Paraire also needed refurbishing. Phipps sent a short note to the architectural press regarding all three projects to remind the world that he was still in the business of theatre architecture.[46]

Endnotes

1. *Morning Post*, 14 December 1867, p. 3.
2. NA, LC 1/185/204.
3. J. Earl, *British Theatres and Music Halls*, Shire Publications 2005, pp. 14-15.
4. *Era*, 13 December 1868, p. 6.
5. J. Hollingshead, *Gaiety Chronicles*, London, 1898, p. 22.
6. *Builder*, 1 June, 1867, pp. 381-382.
7. *Era*, 13 December 1868, p. 6.
8. Hollingshead, p. 24.
9. *The Era*, 13 December 186, p. 6.
10. *Era*, 13 December 1868, p. 6.
11. G. Garlick, *To Serve the Purpose of the Drama*, STR 2003, p. 109.
12. *Pall Mall Gazette*, 19 December 1868, p. 10.
13. *Era*, 13 December 1868, p. 6.
14. Hollingshead, pp. 43-45.
15. Hollingshead, p. 53.
16. Directories were generally printed in the preceding December.
17. Information kindly supplied by Terry Sawyer.
18. London, St. Pancras, 1871 census.
19. Hollingshead, 1898, p. 100.
20. *Builder*, 1 January 1870, p. 17.
21. *Builder*, April 23 1870, p. 319.
22. Birth of a son in 1869 registered in 1871 census.
23. RIBA, LC17/5/3. Letter from Phipps to RIBA Council, dated 7 January 1879, in which he refers to Tasker as 'my Quantity Surveyor'.
24. *Irish Builder*, 1 May 1870, p. 99.
25. *The Era*, 9 July, 1871.
26. *Builder*, 2 December 1871, pp. 942-3.
27. *Irish Times*, 6 December 1872, p. 9
28. *Era*, 3 December 1871, p. 12.
29. *Aberdeen Herald*, 14 December 1872, p. 6.
30. *Aberdeen Herald*, 14 December 1872, p. 6.
31. *Aberdeen Journal*, 18 December 1872, p. 5.
32. *In Memoriam*, Aberdeen, 1898, p. 90
33. *Aberdeen Herald*, 14 December 1872, p. 6.

34 Phipps's chairs had made a regular appearance in his theatres from the start of his theatre career, but there is no record of a patent for them.
35 *Aberdeen Journal*, 18 December 1872, p. 5.
36 1851, Part 1, pl.V.
37 The cost was estimated at around £8000. *Aberdeen Herald*, 14 December 1872, p. 6.
38 *Aberdeen Journal*, 25 December 1872, p. 5 and *Era*, 29 December 1872, p. 7.
39 Garner became an actor and emigrated to Australia in 1873.
40 RIBA Biography file for Max Clarke.
41 *Builder*, 7 November, 1874, p. 922.
42 Richmond Borough Local History Notes.
43 Phipps did not gain the commission. The church was erected in 1877 to plans by E.C. Robins.
44 Hollingshead, *Gaiety Chronicles*, 1898, p. 233-9.
45 *Bercow's Worcester Journal*, 23 January 1875, p. 5.
46 *Building News*, 18 September 1874, p. 360.

5 FIGHTING SPIRIT 1875-77

The comparatively modest theatre projects, which Phipps thought prudent to announce in the *Building News*, looked more impressive in the press than they did in Phipps's accounts. RIBA architects calculated their 5% fee on the actual building costs, which for the Worcester Theatre Royal came to £2,836, leaving Phipps with a fee of £141 to which he added £57 in expenses for train fares, telegrams and postage.[1] His original estimate for building costs had been about £500 to £600 less, but Captain Castle excused this discrepancy by suggesting that 'the estimates had perhaps been somewhat hurriedly prepared'.[2] Given the dearth of theatre work in his office, it would not be surprising if Phipps had erred on the low side in his estimate in order to secure the commission. But Phipps gave value for money in 'his remarkable skill ... in utilising the space at his disposal to the greatest advantage' and managed to accommodate 1,500 persons, as opposed to the previous figure of 1,000, spread over private boxes, stalls, pit, balcony with upper circle behind and a gallery.[3] The stage was larger and the dressing rooms more comfortable. There were, however, only three entrances *cum* exits for the spectators all in the main frontage, one in the centre for the more expensive seats, one for the pit and one for the gallery. The latter, which held 14 rows of seats plus standing room, was 'reached by a winding staircase with the pay office conveniently placed a short distance up and [with] a strong barrier for preventing confusion'. Phipps's lauded ability to utilise every inch of space to the best economic advantage tended to come at a price: limited public safety.

This ambivalent attitude to public safety on the part of Phipps did not, it seems, duly concern his architectural colleagues on the RIBA Council who nominated him as a member of the Board in March 1875.[4] It was an honour to serve on the Institute's governing body and to Phipps it was also a confirmation that his forays into theatre architecture had been professionally worth while and not gone unnoticed by his peers. Not long after his election he was entrusted with alterations and repairs to Drury Lane, admittedly in conjunction with the Drury Lane architect Thomas Marsh Nelson, but the work gave Phipps a foothold with the theatre proprietors, and four years later, when Nelson retired, Phipps took over the post.

However, welcome as all this was, Phipps urgently needed something more substantial than a minor provincial theatre and a few London alterations to consolidate his position. He needed a grand design that would bring money and fame, something like London's projected National Opera House. The desirability of a new English National Opera House caught the public mood with a vengeance after the completion of the new Paris Opera in 1874 by Charles Garnier. Its magnificent splendour, which combined the ostentatious flamboyance of the baroque with the solid rigidity of neoclassicism to create an overwhelming symbol of France's superiority in all things cultural, far outshone E.M. Barry's handsome opera house (1857) in Covent Garden. It was an infuriating cultural challenge, which demanded a riposte.

Fortunately a suitable site was at hand, situated on the north side of the Thames, in an area overlooking the river which had been earmarked for development by the Metropolitan Board of Works. All that was needed was a strong-minded speculator able to raise the necessary finance. There was no question of a state subsidy waiting in the wings as in France; the British government had yet to fully grasp the theatre's potential as a symbol of national prestige with which to peacefully impress its continental neighbours, at least not to the extent of handing over taxpayer's money. The indefatigable and eternally optimistic impresario Colonel James Mapleson took on the role and raised £50,000. He spent £10,000 on the site, (where New Scotland Yard was later built) and announced an architectural competition. From Phipps's perspective, this was an opportunity not to be missed.

Phipps's competition drawings are now lost,[5] but it is not difficult to imagine him being equal to the task in the planning of the interior. His circular formula could readily have been adapted to incorporate the intended 3000 spectators and his ball-room design for the Star and Garter Hotel in Richmond could have served as a suitable template for saloons and circulation areas. The exterior might have proved more of a challenge; his Venetian mode might have been too delicate for the task and he had yet to master a daring and imaginative handling of the neoclassical idiom.

The coveted prize was won by Francis Fowler, whose theatre expertise seems to have been largely based his design for the Opera Comique in Holywell Street off the Strand in 1870, where he had daringly replaced the pit with stalls and put the pittites in a large amphitheatre.[6] Fowler, who was connected with the Metropolitan Board of Works, under whose auspices the sale of the site was being conducted, produced a design for a grandiose four-storey neoclassical pile with baroque overtones covering an area of 190 ft. by 200 ft. Unfortunately, Fowler did not take the soggy conditions of the ground into account and it soon transpired that 'in consequence of the bad substratum, a depth of 30 ft. will have to be attained before putting in concrete for the foundations'.[7] The building costs continued to escalate and an additional £55,000 was needed to complete Fowler's design. This proved too much for Mapleson's initial backers and work stopped in September 1876.[8] Whether Phipps had taken the water-logged substratum fully into account in his plans we shall probably never know.

Around this time Phipps took on another pupil, Ernest Woodrow (1860-1937), perhaps to help with the drawings for the Opera House, and perhaps also, because the premium, usually paid by architectural pupils, would be a useful boost to his finances. Woodrow was a year younger than Phipps's eldest son, Charles Eugen, who seems to have been working in the office at the time despite his chronic kidney condition which must have sapped his energy. By now, Max Clarke, who over the years developed a particular interest in fire safety, would have completed his articles and thus been able to supervise the younger assistants when Phipps was out of the office. Woodrow turned out to be a diligent student and, like Clarke, took a special interest in safety matters, an interest which might have been encouraged more by Clarke than Phipps, whose lack of concern for the cramped passages and exit routes at the Vaudeville, to which the Lord Chamberlain's Office tried to draw his attention during the mid-seventies, suggests a professional and personal unwillingness to involve himself too deeply in the nitty-gritty of public safety, at least at his client's expense.[9] Yet, Phipps must also have been an inspiring mentor; much later, in 1892, both Woodrow and Clarke held up his London designs as perfect examples of theatres specifically tailored to 'the particular and special business that the manager intends carrying on therein ...' based on a thorough understanding of the 'nightly working of the front of house as well as of the stage'.[10]

The disappointment over failing to win the opera house competition was soon mitigated by an unexpected fire at the Edinburgh Theatre Royal in Broughton Street in the autumn of 1875. Fortunately, there was no loss of life, and the proprietor Robert Wyndham smartly commissioned Phipps to design a new building. Edinburgh, with a population of nearly 200,000,[11] had four theatres at the time, none of them any longer attractive to the landed gentry or the large educated professional middle class, who had earlier constituted a reliable audience base. This unfortunate state of affairs was explained in the press as being due to the fact that 'Edinburgh theatres are all more or less defective in construction and uncomfortable in arrangement.'[12] Thus, Phipps's task was to entice the wealthier spectators back with proper construction and attention to comfort.

The Broughton Street site had been plagued by three fires in 23 years starting in 1853 when the Adelphi Theatre burned down. The playhouse was rebuilt and renamed the Queen's Theatre, later becoming the Theatre Royal, which, in turn, burned down in 1865. Once rebuilt, the second Theatre Royal on this site lasted a mere 10 years.[13] Given this startling number of conflagrations one might have expected fire prevention measures and public safety considerations to have been uppermost in the mind of Phipps and/or his clients, indeed to have been the guiding principles of the design. This appears not to have been the case, perhaps because Phipps was under pressure to increase the number of seats by 300 to a total of 2300.[14] The description in the *Builder* suggests a plainly decorated tightly packed auditorium of three tiers, the gallery, with one exit, extending back beyond the a circular flat ceiling, 'the outer edge of which ranges with the gallery front' and with a 39 ft high and 27 ft wide and plain proscenium opening.

The stage, equipped with seven traps, ten cuts and four bridges, sufficient machinery for a modicum of operatic spectacle, was 61 ft. wide between the walls and 59 ft. deep in the centre but a mere 36 ft. deep at the sides as Phipps had used the corners at the back to pack in dressing rooms and manager's offices on three floors. Above the scene dock, at the back of the stage, Phipps placed the painting workshop, relegating the property room to the equivalent space below the stage behind the stage machinery while the dancers and supers were crammed into the basement below the pit. The supers were regarded as the lowest of the low by Scottish theatre managers, they were expendable and easily replaceable and the accommodation, short of ventilation and a veritable death-trap in the event of fire, reflected this attitude.[15]

The building was another example of economical use of space but with little thought given to risk-assessment and the importance of a sufficient number of easily accessible escape routes before and behind the curtain. The decoration of the auditorium was equally economical, the gilt metal work fronting the dress circle being its most noticeable aspect. Like its predecessors on this site Phipps's theatre did not last long, having opened in January 1876 it was just over seven years, July 1884, before a fire took hold in the property room and spread with uncontrollable speed.[16]

Scotland soon provided another commission in the form a rebuilding of the eighteenth-century Theatre Royal in Dumfries which opened on 14 September 1876. It was built on the site of the old theatre incorporating additional ground at the front and the side. According to the *Era*, possibly quoting Phipps, the new theatre was 'somewhat in the shape of the Vaudeville, London and arranged in a similar way'.[17] It held twice as many spectators as before despite 'the auditorium being within the same enclosing walls as before'. This remarkable feat had been achieved 'by building the theatre downwards (as the roof is no higher than before) and thus a large pit is gained holding some 400-500 persons'.

One person who would have been unimpressed by the lack of exits in Phipps's Edinburgh and Worcester theatres, had he had occasion to visit them, was the Head of the London Fire Brigade, Captain Eyre Massey Shaw (1830-1908). Shaw had been appointed to reorganise the capital's fractured fire fighting services into a coherent and efficient force in 1861 and he had soon proved himself more than equal to the task.[18] Ten years into his post he had not only created Britain's best equipped and trained fire brigade, but he had also become a metropolitan celebrity, invited to balls, receptions and first nights, and according to the gossip magazine *Vanity Fair* was 'one of the most popular men in London'.[19]

Shaw was much preoccupied with fire prevention in theatres. He could not have helped but notice their shortcomings in this respect during his frequent visits to them, and in 1876 he published a book entitled *Fires in Theatres*. He had made a thorough study of the subject:

'I think I know every source of danger that exists, or can exist in such places, and I am strongly convinced that with proper construction, judicious management, and sound precautions, there would be no danger for the audiences and very little for the building, and this is my reason for writing on the subject'.[20]

While Shaw's basic tenet was perfectly sound, his direct line of attack on the rapidly expanding entertainment business was perhaps not the best way of winning friends and influencing theatre architects or managers. By calling for proper construction, judicious management and simple precautions he intimated that these factors were largely absent in the theatre industry and implied, possibly unwittingly, that the whole theatre industry was largely resting on a *laissez-faire* policy born of carelessness and greed. In this Shaw was largely correct, but it was not a situation that London theatre proprietors or their architects were willing to acknowledge; it would have been bad for business. John Hollingshead, who frequently liked to take on the role of spokesperson for the capital's theatre industry, dismissed Shaw's book outright:

'During the last fifty-three years ... not one member of the public has been burned ... the only deaths have been two – a manager and a dresser' despite the destruction by fire of 14 London theatres and nine provincial playhouses and that even after the Brooklyn fire (1876) not a single fire premium had been increased to the extent of twopence'.

It was, as he admitted, an impudent statement, but it was also an accurate reflection of the institutional complacency towards public safety that pervaded the theatre establishment, as well as the insurance industry, at the time.[21]

It is quite likely that Phipps shared Hollingshead's views to some extent. Architects rarely welcome advice from outsiders and none of Phipps's theatres had yet burnt down. His theatres were all properly constructed. He did not want his clients, past, present or future to think otherwise and he would not have appreciated Shaw's attempt to come between him and his patrons. Although he publicly agreed with many of Shaw's views, such as the need to keep all divisions of a theatre distinct 'as far as possible' in order to minimize the spread of fire with the importance of solid proscenium walls containing as few openings as possible and with the need for straight exit routes and stone staircases enclosed in brick walls,[22] he was a confirmed pragmatist and prepared to be flexible on safety matters in order to keep costs down and clients happy.

The Brooklyn Theatre fire in New York, which caused the death of around 300 spectators, might not have excited the British insurance industry but it moved the British government to widen the remit of the already sitting Select Committee on the Metropolitan Fire Brigade, chaired by Sir Henry Selwyn-Ibbetsen, then Under Secretary of State for the Home Office, to examine 'better means of preventing loss of life and property from fire in theatres and other places of public amusement'.[23] Phipps, who was as the country's most experienced theatre architect, was called to give evidence, in April 1877, and he made the most of this opportunity to voice his views on the essentials of theatre safety, on the workings of the Lord Chamberlain's Office and on the urgent need for a national inspectorate to oversee the construction of new theatres and improvements of older ones.

The Committee was much concerned with the basics of safety such as the number of exits, fire resisting materials and gauze covering for naked lights. As for exits, Phipps, rather peremptorily argued that the number of exits was less important than having straight ways to all exits 'which should be self-evident to the audience by notice or other means ... and no passages should be less than three feet wide'.[24] On fire-resisting materials, he expressed doubts about the use of iron girders because iron 'when heat was applied to it twisted into every variety of shape and pulled down the walls and partitions with it'[25] He also rejected the use of iron and brick posts for the stage floor, arguing that wooden posts could more easily be moved thus making the stage completely flexible in line with modern demands.[26] And yes, he had seen naked lights in the wings, but the permanent wing lights were always covered by gauze. Phipps did not see this as a serious fire hazard simply because: 'As a general rule the fires on stage take place in the top part of the building'.[27]

This was a statement of stunning naivety, but Phipps seems to have shared the complacent attitude of his clients that the fly men could always be relied upon to stop any fires in the gridiron from getting out of hand. Fortunately for all concerned they usually did.

On the thorny matter of theatre inspections, Phipps entirely agreed with the Marquess of Hertford, the then Lord Chamberlain, that he 'should be relieved from any duty in regard to the construction of theatres' and that duty 'should be placed in the hands of an entirely independent body'.[28] The inspectors should be appointed by the government, not a local authority, rather like the railway inspectorate that was appointed by the Board of Trade. Furthermore, these inspectors 'should be without private practice' and a theatre licence should only be issued once the independent inspectors had certified that the construction was satisfactory. He did not think that the Metropolitan Board of Works, whose chairman, Sir James Hogg MP, was a member of the Committee would be the right body for theatre inspections.[29] A separate department under the Home Office, run by qualified inspectors would be preferable.

In principle, Phipps was in favour of more frequent inspections but not by the Lord Chamberlain's Office.[30] To him, the present arrangement whereby some London theatres were initially licensed, usually for a year, by the Lord Chamberlain on the basis of the architect's plans, a site inspection and a final inspection on completion, and others by metropolitan magistrates, who might apply different standards, merely led to confusion. In theory, each application for the renewal of an annual licence should have triggered another inspection from the Lord Chamberlain's Office, but these tended to be of a rather perfunctory nature, concentrating on front of house areas, ingress and egress, cleanliness and order and good ventilation. As for the licensing of provincial theatres, the situation was even worse, in Phipps's eyes, as they were licensed by local magistrates guided by local by-laws and with little understanding of structural matters.

After a series of accidents, at the Princess's Theatre in 1863, when the dresses of the dancers caught fire from unprotected gas-jets in the wings, the Lord Chamberlain (Viscount Sydney) issued specific 'Regulations for the better Protection against Accidents by Fire at Theatres' in February 1864. The regulations required the fitting of metal guards on gas burners, the placing of wing lights four feet above the floor, the protection of foot lights, and, assuming the worst, a ready supply of wet blankets in the wings.[31] While they were an improvement on the exceedingly light-touch inspection-regime of before, these regulations had little bearing on the building's structure and could easily be flouted.

The absurdity of having some London theatres regulated by the Head of the Royal Household in the modern age of railways and steamships and the consequent superficial nature of these regulations coupled with the subjective interpretation of them by his consulting architects, clearly grated on Phipps, who strongly criticised what he saw as an inconsistent application of the regulations by the Lord Chamberlain's Office. Phipps did not mince his words alleging that the department had a tendency to panic and impose 'unjustifiably expensive alterations which caused a strain on managers.'[32]

There was, most probably, an element of personal grievance behind Phipps's attack. The current 'Architect and Surveyor to the Lord Chamberlain for the Metropolitan Theatres', who carried out the inspections and advised on alterations, happened to be Jethro T. Robinson, the builder from Hull turned theatre architect.

It is difficult to gauge how coveted, respected or effective this official post was. At the time of his appointment in 1876, Robinson was, undoubtedly, the country's most experienced builder of circuses, but he had only designed and built one theatre from scratch, the Alexandra Theatre (1873) in Park Road, close to Regent's Park, which had had a mixed reception in the press.[33] To Phipps, who by 1877 had fourteen theatres behind him of which eight were new builds, and who, was then working on three opera-houses simultaneously, to be told by an untrained architect what to do, must have been galling. Clearly, Phipps was the more competent of the two men, but Robinson, with his circus expertise, seems to have struck a chord with Hertford and Ponsonby, who were both devotees of equestrian entertainment and supporters of Hengler's enterprises.

Nevertheless, for Phipps, to openly assert that neither the Lord Chamberlain nor the Metropolitan Board of Works was competent to regulate theatre buildings, reveals a fighting spirit bordering on the reckless. But this was a calculated assault. Phipps was all too aware that many London theatre managers shared his views and furthermore that his life would be much simpler if consistent government-imposed safety standards were in place for all theatres across the country with their enforcement ensured by qualified inspectors. The design and planning process would be more straightforward, there would be no room for endless discussions over the hanging of doors and placing of exit routes with pontificating clients or their surveyors, there would be clarity and efficiency. Phipps, a man who had built his career on seizing opportunities, was determined to make the most of this summons to Parliament, he would make his mark in front of the political establishment; he had nothing to loose and all to gain. He was not against inspections, on the contrary, but he wanted inspectors appointed on merit not patronage. Phipps, the product of a rising meritocracy was fighting for his own professionalism to be recognised – he resented having the acceptance of his theatre designs dependent on the whims of the Lord Chamberlain's consulting architect or ignorant MBW inspectors, or, worst of all, self-opinionated magistrates and, he was all too aware that such a recognition could only come through a willingness by those in power to properly acknowledge the structural complexity and architectural worth of theatres.

The Committee did not rise to Phipps's attempt to bring theatre buildings under state control. To the sitting conservative government it probably seemed far too radical, even dangerous. Instead, its members recommended that the MBW should take charge of the public safety regulations of all London theatres: 'That no new theatre or large Music Hall should be finally licensed until certified that, in respect of position and structure, it satisfies all due requirements for the protection against danger from fire and that the Metropolitan Board should be the certifying authority.'[34] As for existing London theatres and halls, the MBW should have the power to call on proprietors to remedy structural defects that might be the cause of special danger and which 'could be remedied by a moderate expenditure' with an option for the proprietor to refer the whole matter to arbitration'.[35] The provincial theatres were left where they were, subject to the conceits of local worthies. It was a missed opportunity, which would come back to haunt another government ten years later.

While the recommendations appeared to relieve the Lord Chamberlain of his prerogative to license theatres and the architects' obligation to submit their plans to his office, the subsequent legislation, piloted through the Commons by Hogg and Ibbetsen in 1878, did not seek to revoke the powers given to him in the 1843 Theatres Act. There might well have been opposition in Parliament to such a move, possibly fuelled by a mistrust of the MBW's ability to carry out its theatrical obligations. Thus, Phipps was faced with the unappealing prospect of now having to submit two sets of plans for his subsequent London theatre commissions, one for the MBW and one for the Lord Chamberlain as well as navigating the tricky waters of provincial bye-laws. A case of out of the fire and into the frying pan!

Endnotes

1. Letter from Phipps to the Directors of the Theatre Royal Company Ltd, 10 May 1875. Worcester Record Office, BA4711, parcel roll, b.705:223.
2. Bercow's Worcester Journal, 12 December 1874, p. 5.
3. Bercow's Worcester Journal, 23 January 1875, p. 5.
4. RIBA, LC/12/6/7/. Letter from Phipps to Charles Eastlake accepting the proposed nomination, dated 16 March 1875.
5. D. Bassett, 'Striking But Ill-Starred: London's "Paris Opera" ', Country Life, Nov. 12, 1981, pp. 1700-03.
6. The Era 29 October 1870, cited in R. Mander and J. Mitchenson, The Lost Theatres of London, 1968, p. 289.
7. Builder, 12 June 1875, p. 528.
8. Architect, 22 Dec. 1883, p. 393. See also note .2.
9. National Archives, LC 1/276 161; LC 1/286 154, LC 1/ 358 71
10. Builder 26 March 1892, p. 242.
11. 196,979 in the 1871 census.
12. Unidentified press cutting dated 23 Nov. 1874. Edinburgh Local Studies, theatre press cuttings, v.1.YPN 2605 AIP.
13. The old Edinburgh Theatre Royal in Shakespeare Square was demolished in 1859 to make way for the General Post Office and the company transferred to the Adelphi.
14. Builder, 5 Feb. 1876, p. 127.
15. B. Bell, 'the Nineteenth Century' in A History of Scottish Theatre, ed. Bill Findlay, Edinburgh, 1998, pp. 165-66.
16. Builder, 5 July, 1884, p. 40.
17. Era, 17 September 1876, p. 7.
18. T. Rees, 'Who Was Captain Shaw?' in Edwin O. Sachs, Architect, Stagehand, Engineer and Fireman, ed. D. Wilmore, Theatresearch, 1998, pp. 95-112.
19. Vanity Fair, 'Men of the Day', Anon, No. 24, 1871.
20. E. .M. Shaw, Fires in Theatres, London 1876, p. 4.
21. Hollingshead, Gaiety Chronicles, pp. 424-25. Citing comments he made in connection with the hearings of the 1877 Select Committee on the Metropolitan Fire Brigade in 1877.
22. 1877 Select Committee on the Metropolitan Fire Brigade, paras. 1641, 1645, 1665.
23. HC Deb 8 March 1877, v.232, c1645.
24. 1877 Select Committee, paras. 1645,1665-6.
25. Era, 22 April 1877, p. 22.
26. 1877 Select Committee, para. 1660.

27 *Era*, 22 April 1877, p. 4.
28 *Era*, 22 April 1877, p. 4.
29 1877 Select Committee, para. 1603.
30 1877 Select Committee, para.1603.
31 T. Rees, Theatre *Lighting in the Age of Gas*, STR, 1978, pp. 160-63.
32 1877 Select Committee, paras. 1653-54.
33 See G. Garlick, 'Frank Matcham and the Legacy of Charles J. Phipps', *The Matcham Journal*, March 2016.
34 Report of 1877 Select Committee, p. 9.
35 Ibid, p. 10.

6 PERPETUUM MOBILE 1877 - MAY 1880

Three opera houses, two fires and Sadler's Wells

With three opera houses due to be completed by the end of the summer 1877, of which two were in Ireland, Phipps needed to delegate and he despatched his office manager Max Clarke to Cork, as clerk of works, to oversee the conversion of the Munster Hall into a theatre while he oversaw the opera houses in Londonderry and Leicester.

The Royal Opera House in Londonderry had been commissioned by the proprietor of the Belfast Theatre Royal, J.F. Warden. It was situated in Carlisle Road with a respectable frontage in red brick with three six-foot wide entrance doors. The centre door led to the balcony and upper circle, while the pit entrance was placed at the lower end of the façade and the gallery at the upper end.

The balcony and upper circle formed one tier, with space for 108 and 100 spectators respectively. The pit and gallery, allegedly, accommodated 700 person each and, miraculously: 'there is not a single seat which does not command a full and equally good view of the stage'.[1] It opened on 10 August 1877 with Bulwer-Lytton's ever popular *The Lady of Lyons* and with Warden expressing his indebtedness to Phipps.

Barely a month later, on 6 September 1877, the Leicester Royal Opera House in Silver Street opened its doors for a grand inaugural concert. Although sandwiched between existing buildings it was a large structure capable of accommodating 2,550 spectators. It had been commissioned by the Leicester Opera House and Music Hall Company whose ambitious directors aimed to cater for all tastes from opera to equestrian entertainment.

The owner's lofty aims were not immediately apparent from the three-storey, red-brick frontage in Silver Street. The seven-bay arcade on the ground floor, through which those aiming for balcony, upper circle or amphitheatre, entered, gave it a touch of gravitas, but, on the whole, the theatre had the air of a prosperous town house, with a nod in the direction of the currently fashionable Queen Anne Style.

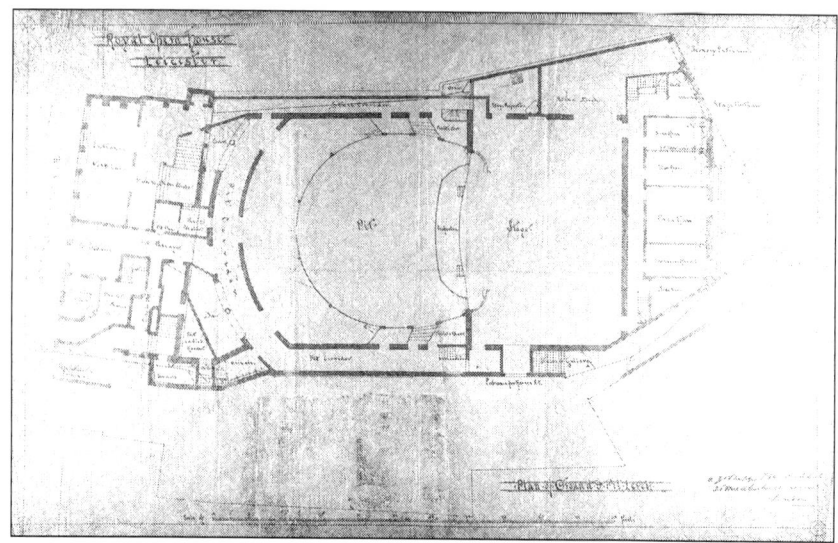

*The Royal Opera House, Leicester. Ground and Pit Plan signed by C.J. Phipps.
© Leicester Record Office.*

The interior was more ambitious. It featured an enormous pit holding 1,000 while the remaining spectators were spread over two tiers. The pit was designed to double as circus arena and ballroom and was placed on a hydraulically powered floor, which could be raised to make it level with the balcony. The latter was furnished with 150 arm chairs and behind these rose the upper circle with seats for 300. The upper tier was fronted by a single row of amphitheatre stalls for 100, which formed a social and visual bulwark for the extensive gallery behind, which, purportedly, held 1000 people. The gallery was entered from Cank Street at the back of the building, through a wide and long corridor 'which will hold 600 standing before opening'.[2] Judging by the plans, this figure was an unrealistic prediction.

Wisely, Phipps provided means for shrinking the auditorium for less popular entertainments by installing a screen that could be pulled across at the back of the dress circle, thus cutting off the upper circle, and another screen in the pit which shut off the last four rows at the back.

In Cork, Max Clarke was kept busy turning the Munster Hall, the largest hall in Ireland, into a proper theatre. It had been built in 1855 for concerts and lectures but now a limited company, led by the MP John G.

McCarthy, was hoping to have this long rectangular building transformed into a grand theatre *cum* opera house in the space of three months.

Prominently situated beside the river Lee, the hall terminated in an imposing rotunda, which Phipps turned into a splendid saloon 52 ft. in diameter and 35 ft. high.[3] The auditorium seated around 2,000 spread over a large pit, holding 1000, and two tiers similar to the Leicester Opera House. The lower tier accommodated 125 persons in a small dress circle, behind which was the upper circle with 200 chairs in five rows. At the back of the upper circle, separated only by a low division, was a lounge and promenade to which the circle spectators could withdraw if they felt the need to stretch their legs and converse during any *longeurs* in the performance. From there they could also meander towards the magnificent rotunda saloon.

The gallery was designed to hold 700. Thanks to an energetic local building contractor, urged on by Max Clarke, the New Cork Theatre Royal and Opera House opened, as planned, on 17 September 1877 with a spirited performance of the comedy *Our Boys* by Henry James Byron. The house was packed with 'every word being distinctly heard in all parts of the house'.[4]

After these hectic months, Phipps found himself unexpectedly bereft of further theatre commissions. But not for long. On 24 November 1877, another fire came to his aid. That it happened to be Phipps's own Theatre Royal in Worcester which burnt down leaving only the outer walls was, perhaps, slightly embarrassing, but no lives were lost as the fire took hold at seven in the morning, having, it seems, started underneath the stage. The local press was not surprised by the occurrence of the fire only by its ferocity: 'The old theatre was several times on fire, but a few buckets of water sufficed to prevent damage of any account being done.'[5]

Phipps, in dire need of a new theatre commission, immediately and 'voluntarily' set off for Worcester where he examined the ruins and discussed his findings privately with the company directors. Persistent and persuasive, he convinced them that the theatre could be rebuilt for the insurance sum of £3,000, 'as nearly the whole of the walls standing could be utilised'.[6]

The shareholders, called to a special meeting, were less easily swayed, insisting on proper plans and estimates, demanding fewer seats and better facilities for ingress and egress before they agreed to let the directors negotiate with Phipps. Thus, his second attempt at the Worcester Theatre Royal resulted in a far more serviceable building for the audience, with separate staircases for the dress circle and upper circle, a sloping dress circle so that the upper-circle spectators behind got a better view of the stage, a better slope to the pit and a redesigned gallery ceiling 'to give the occupants more facility for seeing the stage'.[7] Clearly, it was not merely the estimates for the first playhouse that had been hurriedly put together but also the plans. Phipps's second Worcester Theatre opened on 21 October 1878 with Shakespeare's *As You Like It*.

By the time Phipps was finally given the go-ahead in Worcester, he had agreed to the request of the RIBA Council to prepare plans 'for the reconstruction of the premises'.[8] It was, he admitted, 'a somewhat difficult problem' and, clearly mindful of the close scrutiny to which his plans would be subjected and not wishing to be out of pocket in case they did not live up to expectation, added: 'In the event of the proposed alterations not being carried out, any remuneration the Council may be pleased to award, I shall be happy to accept.'

The RIBA Council and its members had been deliberating for some time over how best to improve the cramped premises at 9 Conduit Street, a four-storey building in central London, owned by the Architectural Union Company. The place was a hotbed of architectural discussions in the capital, as it housed not only the RIBA but also its rival, the Architectural Association (founded in 1847). Phipps had been an enthusiastic supporter of the expansion plans from the beginning as well as an energetic collector of subscriptions for the improvement fund, factors which probably played a role in the Council's decision to ask Phipps to draw up plans and procure estimates: '… for the customary fee, as he was known to have had large experience in the planning out and altering of many places of public assembly.'[9].

The brief had much in common with some of Phipps's smaller theatre commissions: to improve lighting and ventilation in the Meeting Room on the first floor; replace the winding stairs to it; increase space in the library as well as in the tea and coffee room and in the lavatories; all at minimum expense and with minimum inconvenience to other tenants. He consulted his colleagues, and, possibly still under the influence of his latest opera house designs, boldly proposed that the RIBA should acquire the two floors above the old meeting room so that the latter could be converted into a generous-sized library, and a larger hall created on the second floor and rising through the third floor thus giving it a height of 24 ft. to balance the increased area, 45 ft. by 36 ft., which would provide seating for 250 as opposed to the 155 in the old room.

The decorative scheme, based on rectangular panels along the walls held in check by giant Corinthian columns the capitals of which were linked by graceful garlands, would not have been out of place in a dress circle foyer and echoed his Star and Garter designs. He thoughtfully provided lavatories both on this floor and on the mezzanine between the library and the hall accessed from the wide staircase with judiciously placed half-landings. It was an aspiring design that Phipps presented to his colleagues; these would be status-enhancing premises signalling the pivotal role professional architects occupied in modern society, they would lift the architectural profession way above the level of mere tradesmen, where some of their wealthier and/or 'tyrannical' clients still placed them.

Phipps had certainly fulfilled his brief, except for one crucial aspect: the request for minimum expense. His estimate of around £5000, including fittings and furniture, comparable to the cost of the Worcester Theatre, did not go down well with the membership, many of whom earned much less than Phipps, and not all of whom would have approved of the flighty theatrical garlands.

While praising Phipps's proposal, the council rejected it and set up a new Improvements Committee, which produced a more economical design in spring 1879 in which the old meeting room was retained but dignified (and better ventilated) by a coffered dome. The plans also included new stairs and new lavatories, while tea and coffee would be available in a small gallery hired for the purpose on meeting nights only. Phipps's grand design had simply proved too grand for his colleagues. In the end he accepted a fee of £100 for his labours while his quantity surveyor, G. R. Tasker agreed 'to accept the sum of £25 for his services'.[10]

Disappointing though this rejection must have been, another theatre fire had brought more work to the Phipps office. This time it was the Theatre Royal in Plymouth that was destroyed on 13 June 1878 leaving only the external walls and the fine neoclassical portico. When it first opened in 1813, its architect John Foulston, who had won the architectural competition promoted by Plymouth town council, had included not

The Theatre Royal, Plymouth., designed by John, 1810. Main Frontage Author's Collection.   Foulston

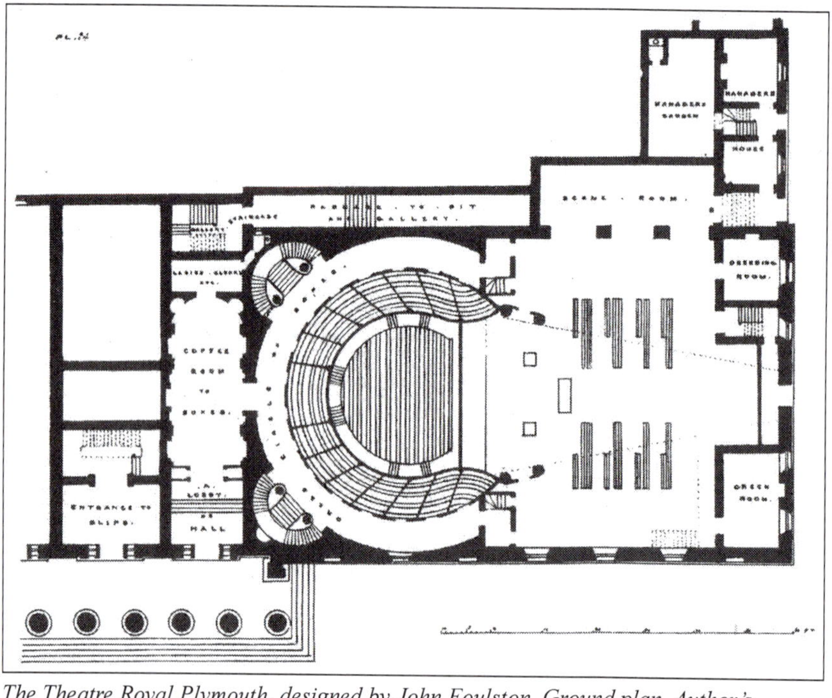

The Theatre Royal Plymouth, designed by John Foulston. Ground plan. Author's Collection.

only cast iron framing for the boxes and corridors in the circular shaped auditorium, but also a rolled iron roof, supported on iron girders, in order to make the theatre fire proof.[11] The iron framework and the iron roof collapsed in the heat of the fire. The girders survived but proved unusable, and the conflagration was a timely reminder of the fallibility of so-called fire-proof materials. As so often, the fire appeared to have started on stage, but fortunately after the performance had finished, so no lives were lost.

Phipps was swiftly recruited by the town council to rebuild their theatre. He did not spend time on an iron roof, but proposed a more traditional design based on wooden beams and best slate.[12] He also doubled the number of entrances and exits, separating dress circle occupants from the upper circle spectators and giving the pit and the gallery two means of egress each, though one of the pit exits opened into one of the gallery passages. He also carried forward the dress circle (equipped with Phipps's registered chairs) and lowered the pit, a design feature he would later repeat at the Haymarket Theatre Royal. He created a promenade at the back of the upper circle, which was divided from the seating by low boarding, for those who wanted to watch the performance standing up. In the pit, a quarter of the seating was dedicated to stalls, and in the gallery even those seated along the sides could now see the stage. The circle fronts and ceiling were decorated by fibrous plaster, the proscenium framed by Corinthian columns as before but now with a painted tympanum by William Harford.

Phipps also provided a larger stage, 60 ft. wide and 50 ft. deep with a stage-opening 28 ft. wide, and up-to date machinery and placed the dressing rooms in a separate building. Much of the new scenery, plus the backdrop, was painted by George Gordon.

The rebuilding had begun on 22 August and took four months and cost the corporation a total of £6,579, of which £5,784 was paid to the builder. Phipps's bill would thus have amounted to £289 plus expenses which would not have been negligible, as he spent two days a week in Plymouth supervising the work himself during the last six weeks.[13] The theatre opened on 24 December 1878 with a rehearsal of *Jack and the Beanstalk*.

The late autumn of 1878 was a hectic time, as he was consultant architect for the rebuilding of the Liverpool Rotunda and drawing up plans for a complete rebuild of the Sadler's Wells Theatre.

The Liverpool Rotunda, situated at the corner of Stanley Road and Scotland Street, was another commission triggered by yet another fire, in July 1877. The developer, Dennis Grannell, harboured grand plans for an entertainment centre that would include a theatre as well as a café, a tavern, billiard rooms, and American bowling alleys.[14] He engaged not only Phipps but also the architects of the original theatre, Messrs. E. Davies & Son[15] and as always with joint architectural ventures, it is difficult to establish who was responsible for what, but Phipps would clearly have advised on the theatre design and probably the exterior. The five-storey building, enlivened by alternating bands of dark and light brick, formed an imposing site with its two frontages seamlessly meeting in a handsome, curved corner on top of which rose a classical rotunda (inside of which was a camera obscura), a treatment which echoes the New Vaudeville in Paris. The theatre seated 700 in the pit stalls, 740 in the dress circle and around 350 in the amphitheatre and gallery, with standing room for 400.

In London, Sadler's Wells was waiting to be refurbished. Here, it was not a fire that prompted the commission, but its dilapidated state and an ambitious mother. The actor-manager Mrs S.F. Bateman had bought the lease of the theatre in August 1878 in order to promote the careers of her two daughters, Kate and Isabel. By November 1878 Phipps had completed the plans,[16] though building did not start until early January 1879.

Sadler's Wells was the first London theatre that Phipps's office tackled after the passing of the Metropolitan Management and Buildings Amendment Act, which gave the MBW responsibility for the structural management of theatres while still leaving the Lord Chamberlain to continue with his inspections and examinations of plans as he saw fit with the aid of his new consulting architect, Thomas Verity, who took over, after the sudden death of J.T. Robinson in 1878.

The MBW's chairman had been assiduous in piloting the Amendments Act through Parliament, but seems to have rather lost interest in theatres thereafter, perhaps because the Board was short of experts in this field who could be ordered to set up the appropriate procedure and regulations. It was not until 2 May 1879 that these were published, a situation which caused Phipps considerable difficulty.[17]

There was little in the regulations that Phipps, or theatre speculators, could really have objected to and those, such as Captain Shaw, who might have hoped for evidence of some startlingly radical thinking had to be content with 17 rules which partly re-affirmed the Fire Chief's recommendations, but which did not impose an undue burden of additional expense on managers and proprietors of theatres and music halls.

Briefly, Rules 1 and 2 demanded that for new theatres and music halls covering an area 'for the accommodation of the public' of 500 square feet and over, detailed plans, had to be deposited with the Board for approval before building could commence. The plans must include precise estimates of the number of people to be accommodated calculated on the basis of minimum of 1ft. 8 in. by 1ft. 6 in. per person in the gallery and a minimum of 2 ft. 4in. by 1 ft. 8 in. per person elsewhere in the auditorium. Rules 3 and 4 stipulated that all external walls had to be of brick and/or stone and as thick as the walls in the warehouse class of similar size – a case of the MBW taking its cue from the Board of Trade inspectors – and the proscenium wall must be of brick not less than 13 inches thick and carried 3 ft. above the roof and down to foundation level. There must be no openings in the proscenium wall except for one into the orchestra and one on each side of stage into the auditorium and these must be fitted with iron doors with no woodwork.

Staircases and floors of lobbies and passages had to be of (unspecified) fire resisting materials and every staircase used by the audience (not the performers!) had to be enclosed by brick walls. Stairs, passageways and corridors used by the audience, must not be less than 4ft. 6in. wide, and if they were intended to carry more than 400 persons they must have an additional width of 6 in. per 100 spectators (Rule 5). Doors and barriers were to open outwards (Rule 8) and no workshops or dressings room should be constructed over or underneath the auditorium (Rule 10) as Phipps had done at the Edinburgh Theatre Royal.

On the fraught question of the placing and number of exits, where Phipps had argued that straight, easily identifiable means of egress were more important than the actual number of exits, the MBW favoured greater numbers together with straight routes, though the wording borders on the cryptic:

> 'Where a portion of the audience is accommodated at a higher level than others, a separate means of exit of the width described above,

communicating directly with the street shall be provided from each floor or level'(Rule 7).

The rule appears to suggest that this separate exit should lead straight to the outside without straying into other passages or rooms, and that it applied both to theatres with circles and galleries rising in separate tiers on top of each other and to those which, like Phipps's Vaudeville, where the upper circle was placed directly behind the dress circle on a different level but on the same tier. The rider: 'At least one additional exit communicating with the different levels and opening directly into the street must be provided', while probably intended to strengthen the regulation, is nevertheless open to subjective interpretation.

Useful as these precautions were, as long as there was no requirement to include a fire- or smoke-resisting curtain – the feasibility of such measures was controversial territory which the MBW preferred not to enter – these regulations would do little to prevent a fire once started from spreading.

Before the MBW regulations had been published, Sadler's Wells had been gutted. Even part of the outer walls had been pulled down to allow for new approaches, which included a covered carriage-way facing St John's Terrace and a colonnade in Arlington Street together with staircases and improved entrances and exits to different parts of the theatre. Phipps, probably anxious to forestall any interference with his plans by the MBW once its Regulations were officially published, emphasised that the improvements had been made 'to meet the present requirements of the Lord Chamberlain, as well as the powers now possessed by the Metropolitan Board of Works ...'.[18]

By the end of March 1879, the stage portion, at the east end, had been rebuilt to encompass the old courtyard, the walls carried up to about 70 ft., to allow sufficient space for the operation of the latest machinery above the proscenium. In many ways, the finished theatre seems to have been a model of the MBW's safety regulations with wide stone staircases encased in brick walls, double doors all opening outwards and additional exits 'from the several parts of the house' with doors without locks but held on the inside by bolts 'which can be drawn by anyone'.[19] Hydrants connected to high pressure mains were placed in the family circle, at stage level and in the flies and there were two exits from the stage, one into the street and one into the stalls vestibule. Since the MBW had not yet got its theatre department up and running, the insistence on all these safety measures were probably largely due to Mrs Bateman wishing to protect both her daughters and her property from the ravages of fire.

Structural safety measures came at a price; the total cost added up to around £12,000, but when Sadler's Wells finally opened on 9 October 1879 with Isaac Pocock's adaptation of Walter Scott's *Rob Roy*, Mrs Bateman had a theatre of which she could be justly proud.

Phipps, meanwhile, was preoccupied with major alterations to the Royal Alexandra Theatre in Liverpool designed in 1866 by Edward Salomons (1828-1906). Originally named the Prince of Wales Theatre, the intention of the directors of the company behind the venture had been to erect, 'a handsome and luxurious playhouse worthy of the town', which in practice meant 'promoting' the pittites to the tier above the dress circle and filling the pit with stalls for' those who paid the most'.[20] This radical change had not gone down well in Liverpool and some of the stall space was returned to the pittites, except on opera nights.

Phipps's brief was to return the pit to its traditional status and make it larger. This he did by lowering the pit floor by 8 ft., making it level with Lime Street and, in the process, sacrificing the pit bar so that the pit could extend underneath the dress circle both a the back and at the sides. Thus he created seating for 800 as opposed to the previous 300.[21] He also increased the stage and the roof in what seems to have been a no frills income-generating exercise, where Mr William Browne acted as clerk of works. The Alexandra opened on 20 October 1879, only a couple of weeks after Sadler's Wells Theatre.

At the time of these two reconstructions Phipps, was mildly distracted first by complaint in April from the directors of the Worcester Theatre Company of an excess of £300. Phipps, ever ready with a counter-argument, insisted that he had only authorised £123 in extras and that anything above that was a matter for the builder. He also advised them not to go to arbitration[22] advice which they appear to have heeded. A few months later, Plymouth town council objected to the final bill of £7,060 for their Theatre Royal, which had overrun the original estimate by £481.[23] The Land Committee, which was responsible for the theatre, was unimpressed 'as they had obtained repeated assurance from Mr Phipps that there would be none'. The chairman of the committee 'distinctly remembered' being asked by Phipps, when the committee visited the theatre 'to sanction an extra for roofing a passage , but they refused to do so and Mr Phipps then said he would pay for the thing himself'. This seems to have been a heat-of-the-moment riposte by an irritated Phipps, who later, still peeved, patiently tried to explain the ins and outs of the construction process in a formal letter to the town council:

> 'I beg to disclaim having in any way giving orders involving extras. I was especially careful not to do so and the few matters I did order was at the time fully counterbalanced by omissions. Many works were done by orders of the clerk of the works and by Mr Newcombe [the lessee-manager] as being necessary for the building ... The plans and specifications have not been deviated from, but more work has been done than appears in the schedule of quantities, which must be paid for.'[24]

Just to make it absolutely clear that he would take no responsibility for the budget overrun, he further pointed out that:

> 'I have nothing to do with the quantities; they were prepared by an independent surveyor, who measured the works up afterwards and Clause 1 of the Contract is in error when it states the priced estimate to be signed by me. It is signed by the surveyor who took them out in the usual way'.

The town council paid the bill.

The Haymarket Theatre Royal

Phipps could afford to be high-handed. In August 1879, he was planning a comprehensive refurbishment of the Haymarket Theatre Royal for Squire Bancroft and his wife Marie Wilton, who were planning to take over the Haymarket Theatre Royal a month later. To Phipps, they were the ideal client: they had vision and money and were not afraid of modernity. Indeed, they shared Phipps's view that the traditional pit had run its course and should be replaced entirely by stalls. Until now none of Phipps's clients had dared to oust the pittites from the floor of the house, but the confident Bancrofts had no qualms about breaking a hallowed ancient theatrical tradition in the pursuit of greater profits, regarding the theatre, first and foremost, as 'a place of business' arguing that 'in a business sense [the manager] was entitled to the utmost profit he can contrive to secure'.[25]

The Theatre Royal, Haymarket, London, designed by John Nash. Author's Collection.

The Bancrofts had already proved their business acumen by turning the old dilapidated Queen's Theatre, known as the Dust Hole, situated just off Tottenham Street into a goldmine by ousting the lower-class, orange-eating audience with babes in arms, smartening up the premises, renaming the theatre The Prince of Wales – with due permission – and replacing the lurid melodramas with T.W. Robertson's drawing-room plays. By 1879 the couple had amassed more than enough money to move up the theatrical and social ladder to take over the Haymarket Theatre Royal and to transform it into London's most luxurious theatre, a home from home for the *nouveaux riches*, to whose ranks they themselves aspired.

Phipps's main problem was the restricted site. The theatre, which was situated on the east side of Haymarket Street between Little Suffolk Street and James Street, had begun life as the Little Theatre in the Haymarket in 1720. A hundred years later it was completely rebuilt by John Nash (1752-1835) on a rectangular and enclosed site (adjacent to the old playhouse) complete with its present magnificent hexastyle Corinthian portico. Architecturally elegant it was marred by a light-hearted U-shaped auditorium with poor sightlines and unreliable acoustics.

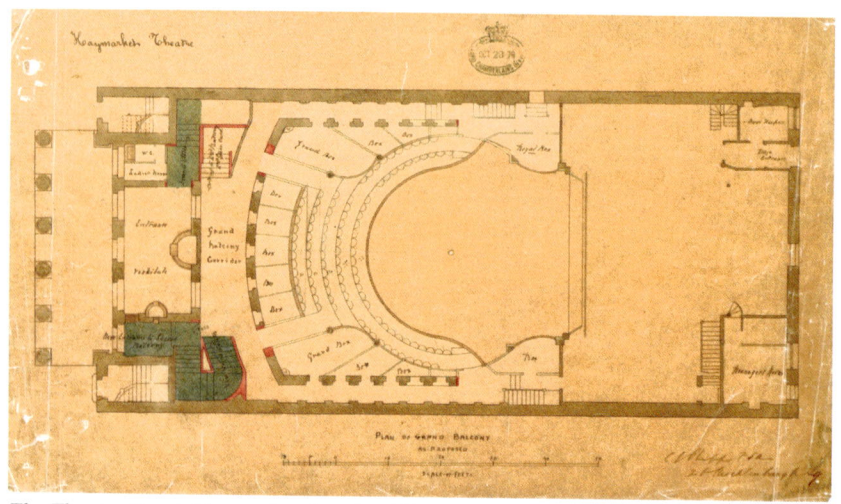

The Theatre Royal, Haymarket, London. Plan at Balcony Level, 1879 by C.J. Phipps. Coloured drawing. Crown Copyright, National Archives.

Despite its inconveniences it remained London's premier venue for legitimate comedy, 'that class of entertainment not suited to the galleries', as its actor-manager, J.B. Buckstone, observed in 1866, but popular with the pit and boxes.[26] The Bancrofts had every intention of continuing with a repertoire of comedy in which their acting skills were well honed and which, they believed, was probably the only form of drama a well-dined and tightly corseted upper-class audience could comfortably digest.

Phipps removed the old iron columns that had supported the tiers and installed cross beams and girders and raised the ceiling. He also lowered the pit floor and the stage by 2 feet,[27] and in this way he created more volume and a sensation of a lofty spaciousness in what had been a rather constrained auditorium. Yet, at the same time he was careful not to destroy the intimacy for which the theatre had always been justly famed, and to this end he repeated his Plymouth design and brought the balcony several feet closer to the stage. The stalls were placed in front of, the balcony, not underneath it, and this allowed Phipps to keep it low and to let its front, decorated with gilded acanthus leaves, chase an elegant bell-shaped curve, which turned abruptly inwards as it reached the ample proscenium boxes. At the back of the balcony, Phipps installed five private boxes plus a larger one on each side; the latter repeated in the upper two tiers and set between Corinthian columns.

The Theatre Royal, Haymarket, London. Composite view of interior, 1880. Author's Collection.

As the upper tiers were set well back from the front of the balcony, the occupants of the latter enjoyed a good view of the vaulted arches which supported the circular ceiling and which contained paintings of scenes from Shakespeare's plays. Shakespeare also appeared in the first circle front in the form of 13 recumbent characters including Hamlet, Ophelia, Malvolio, Touchstone, painted by J.D. Watson and F. Smith on gold ground.[28]

The arches, the paintings, the glittering balcony and the red upholstery created a fitting context for the theatre's *piece de résistance:* an entirely new proscenium design consisting of a four-sided gilded frame, 2 feet deep, the lower part of which formed the front of the stage and concealed the orchestra placed underneath it. At the top, it supported five vaulted arches, each lunette ornamented with a painting of one of the Muses and above these rose a large segmental tympanum with a painting depicting lines from Milton's *Comus,* acting as a reminder that this was a theatre for comedy with a serious purpose. Here the audience would be presented with a perfect illusion of moving and speaking pictures, reminiscent of the realism and moralism in William Powell-Frith's popular oil-paintings such as *The Road to Ruin* (1878) in which a penniless husband tries to write a play to keep the creditors at bay. It was a startlingly new concept.

Among this sophisticated elegance and pictorial illusion the socially mixed pittites would have formed a jarring note and they were consequently despatched to an amphitheatre in front of the gallery, euphemistically labelled the 'second circle' though it was in fact the third tier. From here they could admire the new picture-frame proscenium in its full glory without craning their necks, a small compensation for the loss of their customary close engagement with the actors. Much further back and higher up they were not best pleased and caused a mild riot on the opening night (31January 1880). The rioters were soon tamed and Phipps's interior did not suffer any serious damage. Suspecting there might be protests, Bancroft had issued a statement in *The Times* justifying the new seating arrangements on the basis of the prevailing economic climate:

> 'With the present expense of a first-class theatre it is impossible to give up the floor of the house, its most remunerative portion to low-priced seats ..., in order to make a sizeable profit.[29]

His undisguised commercial view was a sign of a clear shift in the theatre's role in society from once having been 'a powerful political engine, which could never be considered as private property'[30] to an engine for growth, a private business venture for anyone who had the means and determination to enter this competitive market. As the author and journalist T. H.S. Escott noted in 1879: 'The nineteenth century had become: the Age of Money ... Disguise it as we may, wealth is the governing form of our social system.'[31]

Appropriately enough, the theatre opened with Edward Bulwer-Lytton's *Money* (1840). The previous evening the Bancrofts presented Phipps with 'a very beautiful antique silver tankard, suitably inscribed, in remembrance of the occasion and in appreciation of the way the works were designed and brought to a satisfactory completion'.[32] They had good reason to be satisfied. Phipps had created a sparkling, glittering space, the architectural equivalent of champagne, the perfect environment for the *nouveaux riches*.

Torquay Theatre Royal (Royal Theatre & Opera House)

Considering the attention to detail demanded by the Haymarket, it is surprising that Phipps managed find the time to give Torquay, a burgeoning resort on the south Devon coast, its first proper theatre. Phipps had already provided a provisional plan for a new theatre in 1866, but the project fizzled out as there was still a majority among the local business and political class who saw the theatre as a road to ruin rather than a path to economic growth.[33] Since the town's economy was chiefly dependent on invalid tourism in the form of long-stay visitors in need of recuperation and amusement in a Mediterranean-type climate, this was a short-sighted decision and the 'theatre question' remained a focus for local debate until, in 1879, a wealthy local doctor and politician, W. D. Gillow, whose wife was an ardent theatre goer, decided that a theatre must be built. Tired of listening to endless laments from visiting invalids and their families concerning the lack of entertainment, 'the place was so dull – nothing to do in the evenings',[34] he persuasively argued that a proper theatre, 'would be a real boon and prevent many a sojourn being cut short in a fit of *ennui*'. Furthermore, 'it [a theatre] will of necessity circulate locally a very large sum of money in the year which would be of a general advantage'.

At the beginning of November 1879, Phipps visited Gillow in Torquay and assured him that he could transform the solidly built Assembly Rooms – also known as the Lyceum Theatre – in Abbey Road into a modern, first-class theatre. The large but fairly basic Assembly Rooms had been erected in 1863 by a wealthy Torquay coal merchant, but had proved unattractive even after it had been given a more theatre-like interior in 1871 by the local architect George S. Bridgman, possibly with the assistance of Frank Matcham.[35]

Gillow promptly bought the Assembly Rooms including an adjoining dwelling house, and formed a limited company to raise £8000,[36] while Phipps explained his design, including a plan and an 'interior view', in the company prospectus. The prospectus is now lost, but 'The Architect's Report' was published in the local newspaper though without the drawings.[37]

The peculiar topography of Torquay, where undulating hills chase each other down steep valleys beside the sea, leaving little room for flat ground, meant that the Assembly Rooms, in common with most

The Theatre Royal, Torquay. Main frontage. Author's Collection

of the town, had been built on a slope. It was an awkward, triangular-shaped, steeply sloping corner site with a narrow lane on one side and a dwelling house on the other. The main entrance lay in the respectable and chiefly residential Abbey Road at the top while the back of the building descended into Lower Union Lane where pubs and breweries lined the roadway. The two streets were connected by a fairly narrow, steep lane, with few strategic stone steps, sandwiched between the stone walls of the theatre and another building. The site was not ideal, but it was in the centre of town and easily accessible by all classes of spectators.

Phipps decided to keep not only the walls but also the roof – that way building could continue during wet weather – and, in order to obtain the requisite height for auditorium and stage, to dig down into the foundations and place the ground floor at a lower level. The auditorium and stage would run parallel with the Abbey Road, with the stage abutting the dwelling house which would be converted into dressing rooms, wardrobe and property room, thus extending the working stage area. As for the stage '[it] will be constructed with all the latest mechanical appliances, the peculiar slope of the site being well adapted for stowage of scenery outside the area of the working stage', according to Phipps.

The main frontage was in Abbey Road where three round-arched doorways, protected by a glazed awning, led to the stalls (holding 50), balcony stalls (holding 100) and upper circle (holding 120). Above the doors, Phipps constructed a wide loggia with two pairs of Ionic columns in the middle and an additional column at each end. The columns supported a plain entablature crowned by a modest triangular pediment behind which rose an impressive attic storey. It was an economical neoclassical facade, but not inelegant.[38]

The Abbey Road entrances opened into a semi-circular vestibule (with a box office), which led into a spacious foyer, 18 ft by 34 ft, 'lighted over and admirably adapted for the exhibition of pictures'.[39] From the saloon a wide doorway led directly 'into the corridor of the Theatre – the audience for the balcony and orchestra stalls turning to the left and for the rows behind the balcony to the right. No other part of the Theatre are entered from the saloon', Phipps assured his backers.

The pit, designed to accommodate 510 persons, would be entered from the Lower Union Lane and 'the amphitheatre and gallery by another doorway contiguous'. The amphitheatre consisted of the front row of the gallery with seats for 50. The gallery had space for 350, making the total number of spectators 1200. According to Phipps,

> 'The cost of the alterations, including builders work, special gas work, ornamental box fronts and plaster work, stage and machinery, armchairs, decorations, painting, gilding and upholstery, at about £2,500'.

This was rather a low estimate and the Local Board of Health, whose 'Roads Committee' had the responsibility of examining Phipps's plans complained about there being only one exit from the gallery and the fact that this one door opened inwards instead of outwards. Phipps, his mind on the Haymarket, dismissed this concern claiming that 'it was the practice now for doors to open inwards and for it to be arranged in such a manner that it could not be closed until the house was empty'.[40] This was a questionable assertion, bearing in mind the new regulations set out by the Metropolitan Board of Works which stated that all exit doors in London theatres must open outwards and that there should be two exits from every level. These had no direct bearing on provincial theatres, but they signalled a shift in official attitude towards safety, a shift which Phipps, it seems, had not yet absorbed. However, he agreed to broaden the 5 ft. wide gallery exit, and to make the doors open 'both ways', thereby side-stepping the issue of a second gallery exit, which, given the complexity of the site, would have been extremely difficult to incorporate. In the end, Phipps moved the gallery entrance half-way up the steeply sloping lane from Abbey Road to Lower Union Lane. The gallery door would thus have opened onto the back of the auditorium probably just below the first tier.[41]

Once the Haymarket was safely out of the way, Phipps regularly ' ran down on the Flying Dutchman' to inspect progress in Torquay,[42] travelling down once a week and spending the whole of the last week before the opening 'superintending the numerous matters of detail required in the completion'.[43] The interior, like its exterior, was discreetly elegant with the walls of the two-tiered auditorium, 'from the level of the pit floor to the gallery ceiling ... covered with a rich crimson paper with patterns in gold' and the oval ceiling painted in 'an elaborate design of Romanesque character'. The proscenium framing the 24 ft. wide stage opening was surmounted by an elliptical arch supported by Corinthian pilasters between which were two proscenium boxes on each side level with the two tiers.[44] As promised, the stage was fitted up with sliders, sinks and traps.

All this work had been accomplished in just over three months, a remarkable feat given the awkwardness of the site, and Phipps commented that 'in his large experience he had never had better contractors to deal with'.[45] This might have been an exaggeration, but it is a reminder of the extent to which architects depend not just on their clients but also on their builders for the success and failure of their designs.

Phipps attended the opening night, on 13 April 1880, when J.R. Planché's comedy *Who's Your Friend?* was performed. After the inaugural address, he took his bow in front of an enthusiastic audience before catching the train back to London to finalise his plans for the rebuilding of the Princess's Theatre in Oxford Street and to face the family tragedy that was slowly unfolding in Mecklenburgh Square.

Charles Eugene, Phipps's eldest son, now 18 years old, was losing his long and painful fight against the chronic kidney disease that had plagued him for 14 years. During the last 18 months his stoicism had been severely tested by a 'Suppuration of both kidneys',[46] a gruelling aggravation of his condition for which only palliative care, that is laudanum, was available. He died at home on 31 May 1880 in the presence of his father. For a brief moment the headlong rush from theatre to theatre stopped as the grieving parents buried their son at Highgate Cemetery.

Endnotes

1. *Architect*, v. 18, 18 Aug. 1877, p. 90. *Era*, 19 August 1877, p. 4.
2. *Leicester Chronicle*, 25 August 1877, p. 4.
3. *Builder* 29 Sept. 1877, p. 989.
4. *Era*, 23 September 1877, p. 7.
5. *Bercow's Worcester Journal*, 1 December 1877, p. 3.
6. *Bercow's Worcester Journal*, 9 February 1878, p. 5.
7. *Bercow's Worcester Journal*, 12 October 1878, p. 5.
8. RIBA, Library. Letters to Council, LC/ 16/5/1. Letter from Phipps to Charles Eastlake dated 4 February 1878.
9. RIBA, *Transactions*, p. 112.
10. RIBA, Library. Letters to Council, LC 16/17/5/3. Letter from Phipps to the President of the Council, dated 7 January, 1879.
11. F.I. Jenkins, 'John Foulston and the Public Buildings in Plymouth, Stonehouse and Devonport', *Journal of the Society of Architectural Historians,* (American), v. xxvii, pp. 124-35 (1968).
12. *Western Daily Mercury*, 9 December 1878, p. 2.
13. *The Era,* 5 January 1879.
14. *Builder,* 4 January 1879, p. 32.
15. *Liverpool Daily Post,* 11 Dec. 1878, p. 7.
16. NA, LC7/76.
17. 1892 Select Committee on Theatres, para. 2138.
18. *Builder,* 29 March 1879, p. 354.
19. *Building News* 17 Oct. 1879, p. 476.
20. *Builder*, 25 March 1871, p. 222.
21. *Builder,* 25 Oct. 1879, p. 1184.
22. *Bercow's Worcester Journal*, 12 April, 1879, p. 3.
23. *Builder,* 16 Aug. 1879, p. 924.
24. Letter from Phipps dated 31 July 1879. Cited in the *Builder*, 16 August 1879, p. 924.
25. F. Wedmore, *The Academy,* 7 Feb. 1880, cited in R. Jackson, ed., *Victorian Theatre*, London: A.& C. Black 1989, p. 62.
26. 1866 Select Committee, para. 3545.
27. *Builder* 23 Dec. 1879, p. 1438.
28. *Building News,* 6 Feb. 1880, p. 159.
29. 31 January 1880, p. 8.

30 Letter to *The Constitutional Review*, 11 October 1809, cited in M. Baer, *Theatre and Disorder in Late Georgian London*, Oxford, 1992, p. 77.
31 T H S Escott, *Club Cameos: Portraits of the Day*, London, n.d., p. 3.
32 *Building News*, 6 Feb. 1880, p. 159.
33 G. Garlick, 'Growing up on the English Riviera' in *Frank Matcham & Co.*, ed. D. Wilmore, Theatresearch, 2008, pp. 30, 37-38, 40.
34 *Torquay Directory*, 7 January 1880, p. 3.
35 G. Garlick, 'Growing up on the English Riviera' in *Frank Matcham & Co.*, ed. D. Wilmore, Theatreshire Books Ltd., 2008, pp. 40-43.
36 *Torquay Directory*, 22 Nov. 1879, p. 3.
37 *Torquay Directory*, 7 January 1880, p. 6, citing Phipps's prospectus.
38 Judging by a copy of an early program for the new Theatre Royal in E. N. Stevens and R. S. Casley's *The Theatre, Abbey Road, Torquay 1863-1933*,[1995], in the Local Studies Department of Torquay Central Library, the neoclassical façade was part of Phipps's original design.
39 Seat estimates from *Torquay Directory*, 7 Jan. 1880, p. 6, citing Phipps's Theatre Prospectus.
40 *Torquay Directory*, 7 January 1880, p. 3.
41 *South Devon Journal*, 14 April 1880, p. 5.
42 *Torquay Directory*, 25 Feb. 1880, p. 3.
43 *South Devon Journal*, 14 April, p. 5.
44 *South Devon Journal*, 14 April 1880, p. 5.
45 *South Devon Journal*, 14 April 1880, p. 5.
46 Death Certificate, Pancras, 1b/53.

7 ENMESHED IN RED TAPE
JUNE 1880 – DECEMBER 1881

There was no time to grieve the loss of the eldest son and heir. Trapped in a tight production line, Phipps had to marshal his thoughts and take command of his latest projects. In Glasgow, there was the Theatre Royal in Hope Street to supervise, an unexpected commission which had come Phipps's way after a ferocious fire in February. In London, the rebuilding of the old Princess's Theatre was about to start with an opening date set for early October and on his drawing-board were unfinished plans for a new Theatre Royal in Dublin and one in Sheffield. Waiting impatiently in the wings was Richard D'Oyly Carte, whose project for a new theatre in the Strand had ground to a halt after major disagreements with his original architect Walter Emden, and inside every London theatre hovered the spectre of the Metropolitan Board of Works, which, having boldly presented its safety regulation the previous year, had yet to work out how best to implement them. Theatre architects, proprietors and managers were thus still left in a procedural limbo two years after the MBW had officially taken responsibility, a situation which was in danger of upsetting Phipps's timetable as he, and his London clients, found themselves enmeshed in bundles of red tape.

The Glasgow Theatre Royal, situated at the head of Hope Street, had been erected in 1867 to designs by George Bell when it was known as the Royal Colosseum and Theatre Royal. Its auditorium held 3,000 dispersed over two galleries and a pit in a cavernous space that resembled 'an impenetrable vastness suffused with a feeling of gloom', reflecting, probably unintentionally, the dingy and smoky industrial metropolis itself.[1]. In 1869, when the old Theatre Royal in Dunlop Street had to make way for the railway, the Hope Street theatre was promoted to Theatre Royal. From Phipps's point of view the main problem was the theatre's situation in the centre of a complex of buildings which included a music hall and several shops. He also needed to replace the old hollow space with something more harmonious and light, but without reducing the audience capacity by more than a couple of

The Princess's Theatre, London. Composite view of interior, 1880. Author's Collection.

hundred. In a city with around 500,000 inhabitants, anything smaller simply would not do.

Phipps stuck to his tried and tested formula of three receding tiers with the graceful curve of the balcony tier almost, but not quite, embracing the stage thus preventing the vast pit, with seating for 1000, from looking like a tempestuous sea when full. The remainder of the total 2,758 persons were distributed over a dress circle holding 312 in Phipps's tip-up chairs, an upper circle for 300, and an amphitheatre for 366. Behind the amphitheatre rose a gallery of 16 benches.[2] The stage was a generous 72 ft. wide and the proscenium 36 ft. high and 31 ft. wide, the latter framed by pairs of fluted columns separated by proscenium boxes. With the addition of French Renaissance ornaments in light colours plus judicious gilding, the Glaswegians had, at last, acquired a Theatre Royal worthy of its name. The rebuilding took eight months, rather more than most of Phipps's theatres, but then this was an awkward site. The clerk of works was William Browne who was, probably the same 'energetic' William Browne who had been the clerk of works for the Aberdeen theatre in 1872. The theatre opened on 26 October 1880 with *As You Like It*.

That there were certain similarities between the Glasgow Theatre Royal and London's new Princess's Theatre, particularly in the decorative schemes, is hardly surprising given the pressure of work that Phipps and his staff were under. It is unclear exactly when Walter Gooch, the actor-manager of the Princess's, approached Phipps with a commission to rebuild the 40-year-old theatre; it might well have been before the fire in Glasgow. Gooch had had some remarkable popular successes with melodramas such as *Uncle Tom's Cabin* and, not least, *Drink,* Charles Reade's adaptation of Emile Zola's *L'Assommoir.* His decision to rebuild the Princess's was most likely driven partly by a desire to keep up with the Haymarket, partly by a realisation that the MBW might bear down on him as soon as they got their theatre department organised and demand better means of ingress and egress, and partly by his financial good luck. He had the money and was prepared to invest it in the building. He wanted a modern theatre with three receding circles within the existing walls, a larger stage and new dressing-rooms, plus a wholesale restructuring of the approaches to the theatre, all of which would necessitate a fourfold increase in the total area taken up by the building.[3]

Phipps produced detailed plans of the rebuilding for the MBW to which they seem not to have objected, perhaps, because at the time, the Board was tying itself in knots over Emden's plans for D'Oyly Carte's proposed new theatre. To avoid a similar situation Phipps went to great lengths to incorporate the MBW's new safety rules in order to 'lessen the risk of fire spreading in case such an event should ever occur,' by creating 'four distinct blocks: 1, The theatre proper including auditory, stage and scene-docks; 2, The approaches from Oxford-street, with saloons and staircases [for stalls, balcony and upper circle]; 3, The approaches from Winsley-street for pit and gallery; 4, The dressing-room block in Castle street'.[4] He also put in the obligatory nearly two feet thick solid brick wall between auditorium and stage and carried it above the roof. In his press release Phipps was at pains to point out 'a special feature [consisting] of a separate transfer staircase from the highest level of the gallery to the ground level of the pit' so that on crowded nights, which had indeed been many under Gooch's management, galleryites unable to find a seat could rush down to the back of the pit without disturbing the more refined spectators going up the main staircase. There were also escape stairs on the opposite side of the gallery leading into Oxford Street, indeed on every floor there were three distinct staircases.[5]

For the wealthier spectators there was no shortage of more sophisticated special features. The 17 ft. wide entrance in Oxford Street was one of them. Flanked by wide pilasters carrying a 'massive illumination supported by massive stone corbels and surmounted by a balustrade,' behind which lay a loggia framed by a tall triumphal arch in the Italian Renaissance manner. It was an arresting sight on the crowded street despite being jammed in between existing commercial buildings. Inside the tall vestibule, a 14 ft. staircase, divided by a brass rail in the centre, greeted visitors to the dress and upper circle. After the first flight, those destined for the dress circle moved effortlessly on through a lofty foyer ornamented with giant Corinthian pilasters and columns and decorated with etchings, plants and rippling fountains. From there it was but a short step for those in need of a cigar to the smoking-room and its open loggia from which the men about town could note the late arrivals to the theatre. This large circulation area was available not only to the balcony and stalls (140 and 100 spectators respectively) but also to the 400 upper circle visitors.[6]

Unlike the Bancrofts, Gooch was perfectly at ease with a socially mixed audience, which formed the basis for his financial success, and he had no intention of turfing out the pittites from their rightful place. On the contrary, he wanted a large pit holding between 800 and 1000, and Phipps ensured that its entrance from Winsley Street was on the level without a single step.

The decorative schemes for the Princess's and Glasgow Theatre Royal were almost identical. French Renaissance was again the theme, a light cream colour formed the background to the ceiling, crimson paper covered the walls while the private boxes were festooned with crimson curtains, which, when pulled back, revealed walls of green and gold. The Princess's opened a week later than planned on 6 November 1880, with H.A Jones's comedy *An Old Master* followed by *Hamlet* with Edgar Booth in the title role.

While the two theatres were taking shape during the summer months Phipps was rushing to complete his plans for a rebuilding of the Theatre Royal in Sheffield. The theatre in Tudor Street, erected in 1777[7] by the local business and professional community, was no longer fit for purpose in this sizeable manufacturing town despite numerous alterations over the years. The proprietors asked Phipps for advice, and somehow he found time to visit Sheffield in May 1880. He recommended a complete rebuilding as patching or repairing the structure 'would be a waste of money'.[8] Returning to London, Phipps quickly drew up the necessary plans and by early July a local building firm took on the contract. Speed was of the essence, and the architect infused a little more energy into the building operation ... than was originally intended'.

The exterior walls had been solidly built and were therefore retained, but the interior was transformed into a modern auditorium with a large pit (700-800) at ground level entered from the upper doorway in Tudor Street. It had a steeply sloping floor 'so that even for those who like to stand at the back a good view of everything on the stage can be obtained'. Ever mindful of safety factors these days, Phipps added that there were extra doors to Arundel Street plus three additional exits. The Tudor Street frontage also housed the entrance to the dress circle up a modest 6 ft. wide staircase to the comfort of 162 of Phipps's registered chairs, while the expected 300 spectators for the upper circle had a separate doorway and a staircase a mere 5 ft. wide. For the galleryites – the gallery held 12 rows – who entered from Arundel Street, Phipps emphasised that the 'pay box and barrier are constructed some way up the staircase so that on crowded nights or in wet weather a large number of persons can wait in the staircase until the pay place is opened'. It was a design feature that brought some control over the, often lively, queues for the gallery while keeping them dry as well as preventing anyone sneaking in without paying; on the other hand, in the event of a panic-driven exodus, the arrangement acted as a bottle-neck.

Phipps's energizing of the building workers paid off. The Sheffield Theatre Royal opened as planned on 1 November 1880 with a pantomime by Hanlon Lees, *Le Voyage en Suisse*.

Between supervisory visits to Glasgow, Sheffield and Oxford Street Phipps and his assistants were working on designs for a new Theatre Royal for Dublin at the behest of its proprietor Michael Gunn. An uncapped gas pipe had triggered a fearsome explosion before the start of the matinee on 9 February 1880, which sparked a furious fire that reduced Samuel Beazley's extensive neoclassical Theatre Royal (1821) to rubble in a few hours.[9] Gunn was determined to rebuild and 'almost immediately' instructed Phipps to 'design a Theatre which would be a worthy successor to the National Theatre of Ireland' on the same site.[10]

At last, a chance to make his mark with a truly grand public building! The office must have been buzzing with excitement, and, judging by the estimated audience number of 3,400 (of which 1300 in the gallery), Phipps's unsuccessful competition drawings for the English National Opera House were probably re-examined and possibly re-worked for Dublin. Phipps proposed a main entrance in Hawkins Street in the form of a carriage porch with five entrance doors, a first floor foyer 31 ft. long and 50 ft. wide and a stage 72 ft. wide by 65 ft. long and 65 ft. high to the gridiron. It was certainly grander than Beazley's, which had nearly bankrupted his client.

By the beginning of July, Phipps and his team had completed not only the drawings but also a 'large model of the interior of the theatre, exactly as it will appear, completely decorated', all of which were shown to 'a goodly company ... at Mr Gunn's offices in Beaufort Buildings'.[11] How often Phipps, or rather his team, prepared detailed models for his clients is difficult to determine; model-making was an invaluable exercise for his students, an excellent way of testing structural and spatial relationships, and it is quite likely that his office regularly produced models for the major theatres. Because of the Dublin theatre's size and cultural importance, Phipps might well have felt that a model would be an essential tool for determining the ideal scale of spatial relationships between circulation areas, audience space and stage, as once construction began there would be less chance for adjustment than there would be in a smaller theatre. Detailed architectural models are also seductive, more so than even delicately coloured drawings, and could be an effective means of persuading wavering speculators to put their money behind a new project. In this case, the meeting at Gunn's office must surely have been a fund-raising event in which the model would play a starring role; the project was too big for Gunn to fund himself.

Estimates for this rather grandiose project had, apparently, not been prepared in time for the meeting; this was unusual for Phipps, but, no doubt, he wanted to make sure he did not put them too high, which might put off potential investors, nor too low as Francis Fowler had done with the National Opera House and, more recently, the inexperienced Walter Emden with D'Oyly Carte's projected Savoy Theatre. Phipps, nevertheless, expressed the hope that tenders would be invited within a week. It is unclear whether tenders were ever invited, though a brief write-up by Phipps in the *Builder* four weeks later,[12] optimistically declared that the project could be completed by the autumn of 1881. The model was, however, not translated into bricks and mortar and Phipps had, yet again, been thwarted in his attempt to leave behind a truly grand theatre.

The Savoy Theatre

Phipps's disappointment, was, however, mitigated by Walter Emden's misfortune. Not long before the meeting in Gunn's office, Richard D'Oyly Carte had dismissed his architect and was now looking to Phipps to rescue his pet project, a purpose-built theatre for the Gilbert and Sullivan comic operas which had taken London society by storm for the last three years.

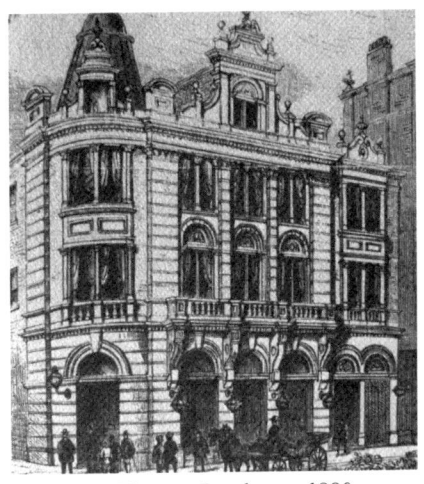

The Savoy Theatre, London, c. 1880. The Embankment frontage. Author's Collection.

Gilbert and Sullivan, after an abortive attempt at launching their light-hearted operas at the Gaiety in 1871 with *Thespis or the Gods Grown Old Together*, had formed the 'Comedy Opera Company' with D'Oyly Carte, and from 1877 their operas had notched up successful runs at the Opera Comique starting with *The Sorcerer*, followed by *H.M.S. Pinafore* (1878), *The Pirates of Penzance* (1880) and *Patience* (1881). In 1878 D'Oyly Carte took over what remained of the lease of the Opera Comique, but rather than invest more money in an inaccessible building on which the MBW might soon demand expensive alterations in the interest of safety, decided to erect his own theatre on a more accessible site between the Strand and the Embankment and early in 1880 commissioned Walter Emden to design the theatre for him.

At the time, Emden was an undischarged bankrupt; his transition from engineering into architecture, which had started so promisingly with alterations to the Globe ten years earlier, had not, so far, brought

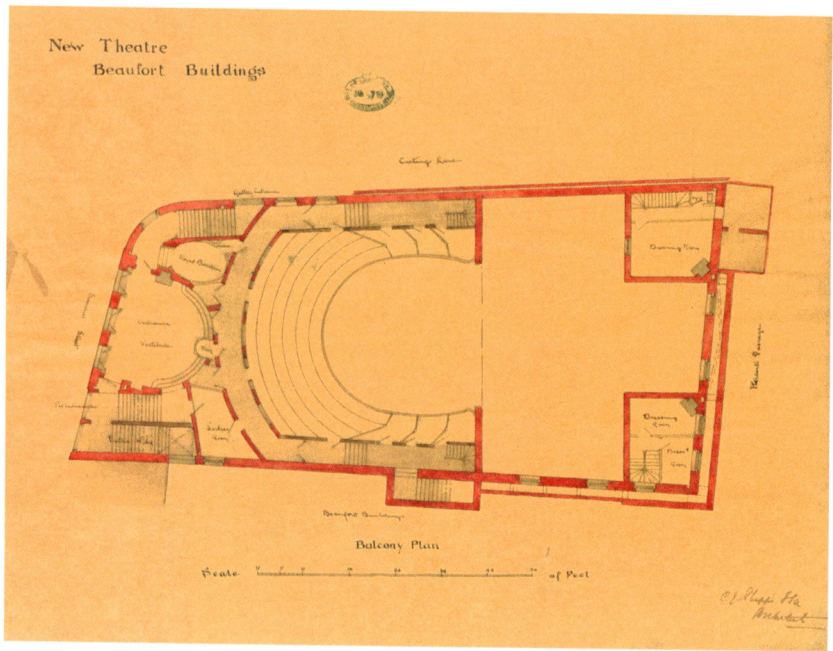

The Savoy Theatre, London. Plan at Balcony Level by C.J. Phipps, 1880. Coloured drawing. Crown Copyright, National Archives.

him financial security.¹³ The unpredictability of commissions, even bread-and-butter ones such as minor alterations to existing buildings, coupled with too many fickle clients who treated their architect's bills with the same contempt as those of their tailor, that is paying late if at all, made sudden financial collapse a very real possibility even for established architects. Carte knew Walter Emden's father, the theatre manager William S. Emden, and this might have been one reason why he had employed Emden. Carte also had very clear ideas on the kind of theatre he wanted, including the lighting, the detailed decoration of the auditorium and the precise colour scheme, and might have reasoned that an undischarged bankrupt architect would be more accommodating and easier to handle than someone like Phipps.

Carte, however, had failed to anticipate the interest the hitherto dormant MBW would take in his plans, which had the honour of becoming the first 'essayed under the Regulations made by the Metropolitan Board of Works … in respect of Theatres …' and the client and his architect

View of the auditorium of the Savoy Theatre, London, 1881. John Earl Collection.

soon found themselves enmeshed 'in the eccentricities of red tape'.[14] To begin with all went well. Carte had bought a freehold area of ground in Beaufort Buildings in the Strand, a steeply sloping, fairly narrow site, between the Strand and the Victoria Embankment in the precinct of the mediaeval Savoy Palace[15]. Before buying the plot, Carte had, through Emden, ascertained that the MBW 'would consent at once to open out a new street on the south side of this block, which street had been shown as open since 1875 on their plans issued to the public'. This was crucial to Carte as he wanted to place the main frontage on the Embankment side where the new street would form the carriage approach. The Board agreed providing Carte paid half the cost. The cheque was dispatched and the plans submitted to the Board's Buildings Act Committee only to be rejected on the grounds that the regulations had not been complied with. Emden, it seems, had not done his homework properly. Amended plans were submitted and approved by the MBW's 'professional advisers' who recommended acceptance. However, some Board members complained that the approaches were still inadequate and the plans were referred to its Works and General Purposes Committee.

While the Works Committee deliberated, the Strand District Board of Works rose up and lodged objections with both the MBW and the Lord Chamberlain to the erection of the theatre at all on the grounds that it would cause 'obstruction to traffic in the Strand'.[16] As Carte pointed out, it was difficult to see how a theatre with all its carriage entrances on the Embankment side could seriously obstruct the traffic flow in the Strand,[17] but the Strand District Board, perhaps not quite believing that the MBW would open up the promised new road from the Embankment, held fast to their opinion, thereby setting in motion further convoluted discussions by the MBW's Works Committee who referred the matter back to the Strand Board who in turn, sent the plans back to the MBW, who then referred the matter back yet again. And so it went on three times, a meaningless planning dispute worthy of a Gilbert and Sullivan opera. It is not surprising that Carte feared he would be driven to 'lunacy' before it was settled.

In June the matter was finally agreed, at which point Emden suddenly increased his original estimate of £12,000 to £18,000.[18] This was a steep increase and suggests some serious miscalculations along the way. Carte was furious. He fired Emden, who retaliated by applying for a High Court injunction to restrain Carte from using his plans and drawings for which he had not yet been paid.[19] Carte then rapidly approached Phipps, who would surely have suggested, indeed insisted – after all Carte was in a hole – that he would substitute his own plans for those of Emden. Thus, when the application for the injunction was heard in the Court of Chancery on Thursday 1 July 1880, the day before Phipps and Gunn were trying to raise funds for their Dublin project, Carte 'had already expressed his intention not to make use of them [Emden's plans]'. Indeed, Carte's counsel stated that his client 'should, in fact, be very glad not to do so,' before proceeding to add insult to injury by adding: 'Of course, if we do not use them we shall not pay for them', and arguing that 'the true object of the motion was to prevent the defendant employing another architect'.[20]

If Carte had hoped that by employing Phipps the MBW's planning application process would be speeded up, he was soon disappointed. Twelve years later Phipps was still haunted by the experience: 'I remember well the difficulty I had in getting the plans passed; not because there was anything in the plans unsatisfactory, but because they [the MBW] had not arranged their procedure.'[21]

His doubts concerning the MBW's competence and efficiency in matters of theatre planning, expressed to the 1877 Select Committee had, so far, proved well founded.

On 29 October 1880, four months after Carte had approached him, Phipps submitted his final plans for approval to the MBW. Two days later he stood on the stage of the Sheffield Theatre Royal receiving a rapturous ovation.[22] He was still at the peak of his profession, his experience as a theatre architect was unrivalled and it is perhaps not so surprising that he had little patience with red tape which involved his work being assessed by those who were, in his view, still stumbling around in the nursery of theatre design. That these unsteady beginners might, occasionally, have a valid point to make, was not a thought he was disposed to entertain.

Phipps also had to contend with Carte's requirements and his insistence on an 'Italian Renaissance' style, inside and out. Phipps seems to have been at ease with this, creating one of his finest frontages in Somerset Street – the street off the Embankment reached via Savoy Place and Savoy Hill – in the form of a three-storey façade of red brick enlivened by arches and friezes in Portland stone. The arches were resting on rather inelegant robust curved brackets which in turn supported a balustraded balcony, a treatment harking back to the Baroque but held in check by steadfast English brick. Maintaining social decorum, Phipps thoughtfully provided four separate entrances, one each for the stalls, dress circle, upper circle and pit. A pair of channelled giant pilasters discretely marked the royal entrance on a rounded corner at the angle of Somerset Street and Carting Lane while the gallery entrance was tucked away further up in Carting Lane along 'a rough and dimly lit approach', which did not find favour with the *Morning Post*.[23] Then, at the top of the building Phipps allowed the suppressed Baroque spirit to rise in a triumphant curvaceous pediment complete with urns and attendant segmental mini-pediments. It was a façade to lift the spirits, in the manner of Gilbert's and Sullivan's operas; a carefully controlled English exuberance.

The 'Italian Renaissance', – a loose term that covered a period from *c*.1450 to 1800 but which, in the case of the Savoy, seems to have referred to the classically tempered phase of 1700-1750 – also dominated the spatial and decorative treatment of the three-tiered auditorium even to the extent of the adoption of a simple horseshoe-shaped curve for the tier fronts rather than the circular shape with its pronounced contrary flexure favoured by Phipps in his earlier designs. He justified the horseshoe on the grounds of it 'being the best adapted for sight'.[24] Whether he had been persuaded in this by Carte and/or by the recent publicity for the perfections of the horseshoe-shaped La Scala auditorium, which had been the model for Francis Fowler's National Opera House, or because he felt the need to reinvent himself, or, more likely, a combination of all three, it was a useful shape for maximising seating capacity on a relatively narrow site.

A more prominent Baroque theatre feature was the broad arch in front of the almost square stage-opening, 30 ft. high by 32 ft. wide, and spanning the width of the private boxes, 'which, it is hoped, will assist the conveyance of sound'.[25] It was divided into panels filled with gilded Renaissance ornament and would have been quite at home in a Venetian 18th century opera house.[26] So would the three rows of opulent private boxes, with hangings of 'gold-coloured embossed satin'. Those level with the stalls were separated by blousy protruding brackets which supported the bulbous front of the middle boxes continuing the line of the dress circle and from which elegant slim columns rose up to carry the pilaster-clad front of the third level. Here another set of slim columns rose to support an entablature which ran right around the auditorium above the proscenium opening merging seamlessly into the gallery front, thus tying the audience space and proscenium together.

On the other hand, a more modern touch had been bestowed on the stage opening. There was no forestage; instead the stage opening was closed off by a slim ribbed and ornamented column at each end supporting straight ribs directly underneath the all-embracing entablature. The effect was that of a picture frame with the bottom piece missing, but given the attention-seeking decoration of the private boxes anything more elaborate would have overwhelmed the actors. The final touch, a segmental tympanum above the frieze filled with relief figures, cornucopias and arabesques on a gold ground entirely devoid of any didactic messages, reasserted the Baroque theme.

Underneath the fan-shaped ceiling, divided into geometric panels decorated with relief Renaissance ornament in tune with that on the box fronts, the tiers were arranged in the then standard London fashion. Thus, the dress circle, containing six rows of arm chairs for 160 people, reached out towards the stage but stopped just where the nine rows of stalls (seating 150) ended. Carte chose to keep the pit, but it was tucked away underneath the dress circle and held six rows with space for 250 and behind was 'a spacious open corridor for standing and promenading'.[27] One cannot help feeling that this, by now, standard provision, for the more restless souls among the spectators, must have been a distraction for the audience as well as an irritation for the actors, particularly during a coloratura aria or a tender scene between hero and heroine.

The upper circle was set back 9 ft. from the dress circle and seated the same number – 160 – but in five rows, and the amphitheatre *cum* gallery tier receded a further five feet with accommodation for up to 500 in eight rows. Carte was clearly aiming for a socially mixed audience, but one where the pittites and galleryites formed just over half the total number, thereby giving the wealthier spectators the illusion that they were the dominant force.

The stage, 'laid with all the latest improvement in mechanical contrivances', was 60 ft. wide, twice the width of the proscenium opening, and 52 ft. deep, with a clear height of 56 ft. above the stage floor 'for the working of the scenery' and a more modest sink below of 15 ft.[28] Behind the stage, in Herbert Passage, was a separate block for dressing-rooms and offices.

While Phipps was undoubtedly responsible for the detailed design Carte was determined to take credit for much of it: 'I think I may claim to have carried out some important improvements deserving special notice' he confidently asserted a few days before the opening. Arguing that the interiors of most theatres had 'been conceived with little if any artistic purpose and ... and executed in a more or less garish manner', his theatre, by adopting delicate plaster modelling in the manner of the Italian Renaissance throughout and avoiding any trace of the "Queen Anne" or "Early English" styles – as well as the influences of the currently fashionable aesthetic movement – so artfully lampooned in Gilbert and Sullivan's *Patience* – could now present 'a result which, I feel sure, will be appreciated by all persons of taste'.[29] He took responsibility for the colour scheme too, for the dominant application of white or pale yellow on the plaster moulds instead of the traditional gilding, which Carte dismissed as 'the Gingerbread School of Decorative Art'. Not that he was against gold, on the contrary, but as a background colour 'or in 'large masses', even going so far as to replace the traditional painted act-drop by a gold-coloured satin curtain. The latter would have made a startling contrast with the peacock-blue plush covering of the stalls and the blue stamped velvet on the balcony chairs in the strong light of the 'Swan' incandescent lamps.

The introduction of electric light was Carte's other innovation, and the decoration had clearly been designed with that in mind. The pale-coloured plaster ornaments would show up well in the steady bright light of the recently invented incandescent lamps; the white would hold its own and the gold ground would glisten. 'The Gingerbread School' and its accompanying garish manner had been useful in the days of flickering candles and unpredictable gas jets when all but the brightest of colours soon disappeared under a grey sooty film. Electricity would bring safety, better air quality and lower temperature for audience, actors and stage crew; it would also bring decorative freedom – not least for the scene painters. As the *Era* noted, scene painters, who had hitherto 'been compelled to make large allowances for the effect of the gaslight' would now be able to paint landscape scenes using the 'actual colour seen in daylight by the lover of nature'.[30] From now on, naturalism, whether desired or not, would invade the landscape sets.

Large steam engines placed in a separate building on a vacant plot next to the theatre drove a generator built by Siemens & Co, and Phipps proudly pointed out that 'this is the first instance of a public building being lighted permanently in all its departments by the electric light'.[31] However, 'the light of the future' was still an unpredictable source of illumination and a complete system of gas lighting, including a sun burner, had also been installed in case the generator stalled. Thus, on the opening night, 10 October 1881, the audience was initially greeted by a gas-lit auditorium and reassured by Carte, before the performance began that 'should the electric lights go out, the theatre would instantly be flooded with light from the great central sunburner'.[32] The stage, at all events, had to make do with the gas light as the generator could not cope with the whole theatre at this point.

Fortunately the incandescent lamps – invented by Joseph Swan in Newcastle 1875 and patented in 1878 – worked well when they were switched on in the auditorium just before the performance began, but they were either full on or full off. Engineers had yet to work out how to make the incandescent lamp mimic the flexibility of gas light, the great advantage of which was that it could be lowered and increased for dramatic effect during the performance. A reporter from the *Daily News* noted that the effect of the lamps on colour was slight 'only the gilding with which the ceiling is profusely decorated at once losing its lustre and becoming a yellow-white'. On the other hand, its effect on the ladies dresses and on the house in general was 'very striking'.[33]

The absence of the new technology on stage did not dampen the audience's enthusiasm on the opening night. The ever popular *Patience*, which already had 168 performances behind it, was performed under Sullivan's baton and was rapturously received and Carte and Phipps 'were called before the curtain' at the end.[34] Phipps had yet again risen to the challenges of a tyrannical client, but this time with the added difficulty of having to steer the project through the quadrille of red tape encircling the MBW and incorporating two parallel lighting systems. It was, by any standards, a remarkable achievement.

Not until 28 December, did electricity make its first appearance on the Savoy stage in yet another performance of *Patience*. A 'resistance' in the form of 'open spiral coils of iron wire', a poor conductor of electricity, had been interposed in the circuit thus allowing the lighting to be managed more like the old gas lights. The future of electric lighting in the theatre was, at last, assured, and with it came the demand for electric light in other public buildings as well as private dwellings. Electrical engineering suddenly became a promising career, and Phipps's second son, Alwyn Rashleigh Phipps (1865-1934) at that time working as 'Articled Clerk to Architect' and living in lodgings in Walthamstow,[35] would later seize the opportunities for a wealth-creating career that the new technology brought. (See Ch. 18) Whether he had worked on the Savoy with his father remains an open question, but it is quite possible that he had done so.

Belfast and Bristol

As the construction of the Savoy gathered momentum in the spring of 1881, Phipps proudly announced the completion of 'an important building at No 1 Portland Place opposite the Langham Hotel'.[36] It was a four-storey residential block with two complete ground floor residences (including basement) and a large flat on each of the upper floors.

A few months later, another theatre fire brought yet another commission.

This time it was the Belfast Theatre Royal, which burned to the ground. The next day, 8 June, the lessee, J.F. Warden telegraphed Phipps who responded with his customary speed and on 9 June was stepping carefully around the smouldering ruins planning a new theatre on the old site.[37]

Phipps had six months to complete the theatre from drawing to opening night in time for the lucrative Christmas audience. Belfast was a prosperous trade and manufacturing town and the Theatre Royal in Arthur Square had a loyal following, which Warden did not want to loose.

The new Belfast Theatre Royal was no larger than the old, but the perpendicular tiers had now been replaced by receding circles crowned by a circular ceiling. Freed from Carte's demands, he returned to his old circular shape gracing the first tier balcony with a front of contrary flexure. In the manner of the his Dublin Gaiety Theatre, the balcony was endowed with small private boxes on either side behind the second row of seats, while the back of the balcony was enclosed by a series of elliptical arches filled with plate-glass sash windows behind which was a corridor. The 'windows' could be opened when the theatre was crowded to allow standing spectators to enjoy the show, and closed when the balcony was less full to keep it 'warm and snug'.[38] Decoratively, Phipps adopted a lighter touch Italian Renaissance style than at the Savoy, with a colour scheme of cream, white and gold and a traditional proscenium (28 ft. wide by 31 ft. high) crowned by a segmental tympanum filled with a painting of Apollo and the Muses. Local class distinctions were observed in the entrance and exit arrangements in Arthur Square where balcony and upper circle spectators entered through the same centre doors, underneath a protective glass and iron canopy, only to be immediately separated by a barrier in the large vestibule each going their separate way. At the end of the performance, the upper circle visitors departed through a different exit further along the façade 'so that there would be no confusion or mingling of the audience to these two parts of the house'.

The Belfast Theatre Royal opened on 22 December 1881 with Bulwer-Lytton's *Money*. Both the play and the theatre were rapturously received, the more so when Warden assured the audience that 'no valuable improvement [had been] overlooked'.

Somehow Phipps also found time to refurbish the Bristol Theatre Royal during the autumn of 1881. The old playhouse had recently been taken over by the actor-manager Andrew Melville, who promptly commissioned Phipps and the city architect T. Pope to jointly bring the old Georgian theatre a little more up to date. The old forestage was cut back by 5 ft., but the proscenium doors were retained. Phipps's chairs replaced the old seats in the dress circle and the pit and gallery were furnished with new benches complete with backs. Above the more comfortable seating a new 9 ft. wide ventilator was installed, enclosed in gilt moulding and surrounded by a star-studded ceiling. There was nothing too radical, rather a gentle transformation in keeping with the Georgian spirit of the old playhouse.[39]

From Phipps's point of view, 1881 had served to consolidate his position as the country's foremost theatre architect, a surefooted professional who could navigate red tape, incorporate the latest advances in theatre lighting among a profusion of Italian Renaissance ornament, satisfy the finer point of provincial class distinction and treat a near perfect Georgian theatre with delicacy and respect.

Towards the end of the year Phipps was, however, brutally reminded of the fragility of theatre architecture and of his own position. On 8 December 1881, as the overture was playing to a packed audience at the Vienna Opera House (also known as the Ringtheater):

'The curtain was suddenly driven from the stage side by the force of something like an explosion and fell into the body of the theatre A dense volume of smoke followed and then great tongues of fire caught hold of the galleries, which were speedily in flames'.[40]

It was the dramatic start to an overwhelming conflagration in which several hundred people perished, mainly from the galleries. The theatre had an iron curtain which was not let down, allegedly because the men in charge had left their post.

This was Europe's second theatre disaster that year. In March a fire in Nice had caused the death of 150 people resulting in the French government hastily enacting new fire regulations for provincial theatres. All over the continent the authorities were issuing safety regulations and in London the Building Act Committee of the MBW requested the Superintending Architect to obtain translations of the new fire regulations from Vienna, Berlin and Hamburg.[41] The theatre critics of London's leading newspapers, now more than ever aware of the mortal danger they exposed themselves to on a nightly basis, joined in the clamour for more stringent safety measures demanding that 'a Government Official be held publicly responsible for the safety of theatres and places of amusement and [that he] be assisted by qualified inspectors'.[42] Clearly they were at one with Phipps on this question. The Home Secretary, Sir William Harcourt, not to be outdone, urged the MBW to investigate the state of London theatres, and the Board duly passed the baton to the capital's Chief Fire Officer, Captain Eyre Massey Shaw. The Lord Chamberlain, meanwhile, sent a longwinded circular to all London theatres requesting the managers to ensure that there are 'two separate and distinct systems of lighting for stage and auditory' so the latter would not be plunged into darkness in case of a fire on stage.[43]

Michael Gunn, anxious to reassure his Dublin audience of the Gaiety's building credentials asked Phipps to check 'the facilities of safe egress in case of panic'. Unsurprisingly Phipps found everything in good order and assured his patron that even on the most crowded nights the audience would be out in four minutes. 'The danger', Phipps innocuously remarked, 'is not from fire, but from a mad stampede'.[44] His comment suggests that he had not fully grasped the speed and ferocity with which the smoke and flames at the Ringtheater had engulfed the audience causing them to 'panic' in the darkness. The Vienna stampede had not been caused by mere hysteria as at his Park Row theatre in Bristol, but by a huge cauldron of fire preceded by plumes of dense, suffocating smoke.

Endnotes

1. *Glasgow Herald,* 27 October 1880, p. 4.
2. *Building News*, 22 October 1880, p. 485.
3. *Building News,* 29 October 1880, p. 513.
4. *Building News*, 29 October 1880, p. 513.
5. *Era,* 17 October 1880, p. 8.
6. *Era,* 17 October 1880, p .8.
7. Sheffield Archives: 'Wilson Deeds: Memorandum on proposal to adopt Mr Atkinson's plans for a new theatre'. Ref. 36 /12/1776.
8. *Sheffield and Rotherham Independent* 1 Nov. 1880, p. 3, citing Phipps's press release.
9. See G. Garlick, *The Theatre Designs and Plays of Samuel Beazley 1786-1851,* STR, 2003, pp. 43-51
10. *Era,* 4 July 1880, p. 7.
11. *Era,* 4 July 1880, p. 7.
12. 31 July 1880, p. 158.
13. *The Times*, 4 Nov. 1881, p. 4.
14. *The Times*, 22 May 1880, p. 2 and *Era,* 30 May 1880, p. 3.
15. *The Times*, 22 May 1880, p. 2. In 1864 a fire destroyed the buildings in the Savoy precinct leaving only the Chapel Royal from 1518.
16. Emden would later become a member of the Strand District Board and its Chairman.
17. *The Times*, 22 May 1880, p. 2.
18. *The Savoyard,* v .XX, no.2, Sept. 1981, pp. 4-6.
19. NA, LC1 370, no. 84, 1 July 1880.
20. *Era,* 4 July 1880, p. 7.
21. Report of the 1892 Select Committee on Theatres and Places of Public Entertainment. Para. 2138.
22. *Era,* 7 Nov. 1880, p. 9.
23. *Morning Post*, 10 October 1881, p .2.
24. *Building News* 23 Sept, 1881, p. 389.
25. *The Times,* 3 Oct 1881, p. 7.
26. For example San Benedetto, 1755. See M. Baur-Heinhold, *Theater des Barock*, Munich, 1966, pl. 255.
27. *Building News,* 23 September 1881, p. 389.
28. *Building News*, 23 September 1881, p. 389.

29   6 October 1881. Cited in R. Mander & J. Mitchenson, *The Theatres of London*, London: Rupert Hart-Davis, 1963, pp. 175-6
30   *Era,* 15 Oct.1881, p. 7.
31   *Building News*, 23 September 1881, p. 389.
32   *Daily News*, 11 October 1881, p. 6.
33   *Daily News* 11 October 1881, p. 6.
34   *Era*, 15 October 1881, p. 7.
35   1881 Census RG11 173/118/37.
36   *Building News*, 15 April 1881, p. 420.
37   *Era*, 17 Dec. 1881, p. 14.
38   *Era*, 17 Dec. 1881, p. 14.
39   See K. Barker, *Theatre Royal, Bristol, 1766-1866*, STR, 1974, pp. 167-9.
40   *Era*, 10 Dec. 1881, p. 5. Quoting a report sent by 'submarine telegraph'.
41   *Builder*, 31 Dec. 1881, p. 832.
42   *Builder*, 31 Dec. 1881, p. 832.
43   *Era*, 17 December 1881, p. 12.
44   *Builder*, 31 Dec. 1881, p. 832.

8 A MAN OF PROPERTY 1882 - 83

The 'Gentlemen Upstairs', Captain Shaw and Drury Lane

During the spring and summer of 1882, the MBW finally turned its collective mind towards theatres with an almost brutal decisiveness, thus causing Phipps much vexation yet also boosting his income. Thus, he had to defend the structure of his design for the London Gaiety while also examining Drury Lane in the hope of thwarting the Board's demands for major structural alterations through a clever compromise. Provincial clients in Hastings and Leamington Spa were simultaneously vying for his expertise and businessmen from Eastbourne were dangling the tantalising prospect of property ownership before his eyes (assuming he could raise the funds). This was an overflowing in-tray, a heady mixture challenging all Phipps's personal and professional talents, his legalistic mind as well as his planning expertise, his interest in new technology as well as his fundraising acumen – not to mention his interpersonal skills in dealing with demanding actor-managers and pernickety provincial magistrates.

Whether the MBW would have activated its 1879 Regulations quite so energetically at this time without the powerful impact of the Vienna Opera House disaster is a moot point. As it was, the combined effects of pressure from the Home Secretary together with withering comments in Parliament and in the national press, made its failure to establish a separate theatre department no longer tenable. The fact that the Board's 'gentlemen upstairs' as they were known by their employees, had become overwhelmed by its original remit to provide modern sewers, replace slums with artisan housing and construct new streets and embankments for the fast-growing capital was not a valid excuse, nor could they really hide behind the large debt mountain which they had recklessly amassed over the years by borrowing vast sums to buy up property in order to create new thoroughfares.[1] The latter probably explains why the three theatre surveyors finally recruited were only paid 'the ridiculously low salary of 3 guineas a week'.[2] Phipps's opposition to the Board taking on the theatre safety remit was soundly based; he knew that the structural responsibility for London's ever growing number of entertainment venues, numbering 57 theatres, 408 large music halls and 332 smaller ones in 1882, would be one Herculean task too many for an institution addicted to regulatory rigmarole.[3]

Phipps old friend and mentor E.W. Godwin, still despairing of English theatre design, wrote a strongly worded letter to the Chairman of the MBW, Sir James M'Garel Hogg, MP, listing what he regarded as the most glaring shortcomings on the safety front and, helpfully, offering suggestions on how to remedy them.[4] He utterly condemned the practice of erecting theatres to hold 2000 spectators on sites suitable for a building holding 800 – a habit with which Phipps was thoroughly familiar – the lack of clearly marked exit routes – a view publicly shared by Phipps, but one he did not always put into practice – the liberal use of wood and *carton pierre* in the auditorium, flapping 'sky borders' in the proximity of gas battens. He also condemned the practice of having the same gas meter for both the auditorium and the stage supply, which made it impossible to turn off the gas to the stage, where fires usually started, without plunging the whole building into darkness.

Instead, Godwin advocated the use of brick and terra cotta throughout the theatre wherever possible, including a terra cotta or iron framework for the seats, 'less useless decoration' (his old bugbear), a wrought iron screen instead of the traditional act drop, plus an iron curtain, and above all the adoption of electric light, without any additional gas laid on. He urged the Chairman to place regulations 'of this nature on the Statute-book and to be made retrospective ... not only for the welfare of the public but to the advantage of both owner and lessee'.

Clearly, Godwin felt that theatre speculators and their architects needed the rod of precise statutory regulation on their backs to take theatre safety seriously. This kind of official micromanagement is probably not what Phipps had had in mind when he advocated an inspection regime governed by the Home Office or the Board of Trade, he knew very well that such regulations would increase costs, large city centre sites were hard to find and therefore expensive, that an iron curtain would add another £500 and the installation of electric light, still in its experimental stages, was costly in space and equipment. The current boom in theatre building would retract and so would his income.

Phipps however, seems to have had a considerable interest in modern technology, possibly equal to that of his interest in antiquaries, and perhaps encouraged by his son Alwyn Rashleigh who saw his future in electrical engineering not in architecture. Ever the pragmatist Phipps would always do his utmost to oblige whenever his clients were willing and able to invest in the latest scientific inventions, just as he would continue to do his best to prevent his patrons from any 'needless' expenditure foisted on them by blinkered authorities.

Shaw began his inspection of London's theatres in January 1882 and completed his Report on the first seven of the 41 theatres on his list within five weeks with the aid of twenty-four of his most experienced officers.[5] The Report, covering Drury Lane, Covent Garden, the Gaiety, the Vaudeville, Opera Comique, the Strand and the Lyceum, all theatres popular with the upper- and middle-classes, was not an uplifting read. The Home Secretary, Sir William Harcourt, who had rashly promised to lay the Report before the House of Commons, decided, on reflection, that Shaw's sharp observations of the unhealthy structural state of some of London's leading theatres, which included the absence of brick-built proscenium walls and a shortage of gallery exits at both Drury Lane and Covent Garden, would be better kept out of the public eye. No need to cause unnecessary alarm, let alone searching questions in Parliament over the effectiveness of the 1878 Act or the indifference, so far, of the MBW towards its theatre responsibilities, a burden which its Chairman had been so eager to embrace four years earlier.

Harcourt's decision backfired. Rumours soon spread that the content was too alarming to be published. In the Commons Mr Dixon-Hartland MP, who took a keen interest in theatre regulation advocating changes that had much in common with Phipps's views, asked why the 1878 legislation had been practically neglected for so long? His parliamentary colleague, Mr Macfarlane, clearly no friend of the MBW, also wanted to know 'why the MBW had been lying upon its oars for four years?' Its chairman, M'Garel-Hogg, who combined his duties at the Board with those of an MP, vehemently protested that this was not the case and absolutely denied that he had, in an unguarded moment, privately admitted to Mr Dixon Hartland that 'the theatres in the Metropolis were in a dangerous state'.[6]

Outside Parliament, John Hollingshead, incensed by Shaw's criticisms of the Gaiety, of which he had been sent a copy, and not wishing a good story go to waste, published the report on his theatre together with a commentary by an equally furious Phipps, who took issue with Shaw's major criticisms.[7] As far as Phipps was concerned the wall between auditorium and stage, a crucial part of theatre structure which Shaw always pounced on, was actually carried through the roof except that it was carried through the stage roof to meet the higher auditorium roof. He also challenged Shaw's recommendation that the small ventilator over the back of the stage should be replaced by a larger ventilator with an opening of 1/10 of the roof area, so that any smoke and fire on the stage would seek to go back and up away from the auditorium instead of advancing towards the central ventilator above the auditorium thus suffocating the audience in the higher tiers before they could escape:

'The tendency would be exactly the reverse ... The cold air would blow down such an opening – and no one could act on the stage or sit in auditory with such a contrivance ... and the hanging scenery would be always swaying against the gas lights'.

He had a point. Theatre managers' addiction to swaying scenery and curtains, which, given the nature of stage machinery, were often placed close to the gas jets was the greatest of fire risks, and more often than not the cause of theatre conflagrations. Consequently any form of ventilation that encouraged flapping scenery to move unnecessarily on an already draughty stage, was undesirable. Phipps's solution, a compromise consisting of a smaller ventilator coupled with three sky lights, which, he contended, would quickly break in the case of fire, might, possibly, have been more likely to prevent a fire starting in the first place, while Shaw's recommendation might have precipitated a fire but, on the other hand, have given the galleryites a greater chance to escape once it had started. Their difference of opinion is an example of how difficult it was to produce clear regulations on theatre safety, which would actually achieve their purpose.

Phipps also objected to Shaw's criticism that 'the floors are chiefly constructed of wood' pointing out that 'the tiers rested entirely on an iron framework embedded in concrete' with floor boards on top and flatly refuted Shaw's point that scenery and costumes not belonging to the current performance was being 'dangerously' stored in the building; it was stored elsewhere, 'as there was no space and the lessee paid £300 a year for large workshops and magazines under Waterloo-bridge'. However, on one issue the three men were in complete agreement: the bricking up of the communicating doors between the theatre and the restaurant on the order of the Holborn magistrates had made the theatre less safe, but only the magistrates had the power to rectify the matter, a situation which Shaw seems not to have fully appreciated.

Smarting under what he clearly felt was unjust criticism of his professional standards, Phipps was more than ready to challenge the Board over its demands of a new proscenium wall and an additional gallery staircase at Drury Lane, at the cost of £1800, as estimated by the Board. This seemed to its new lessee, Arthur Harris, to be beyond 'moderate expenditure'. According to Phipps's evidence to the 1892 Select Committee on Theatres,[8] he tried to strike a deal with the head of the MBW's theatre section, the architect John Hebb, a man whose interests seemed to have focused mainly on obtaining free theatre tickets and advocating the preservation of historic churches threatened with restoration or demolition in Britain and Italy.[9] Phipps claimed he 'wanted to avoid the enormous expense of arbitration' and offered to rebuild the proscenium wall in brick 18 inches thick from the foundation to three feet above the roof, if the Board would withdraw the requirement for the extra staircase. Hebb declined as 'he had no power to say that he will agree to this or that' and the matter went to arbitration.

The parties met in front of the arbitrator Sir Henry Hunt, C.B. (appointed by the Home Secretary) in the middle of August. Apart from the obligatory QC on each side, the MBW was represented by two eminent architects, John Whichcord (1823-85), FSA and past president of the RIBA plus Henry Currey (1820-1900) architect to the Duke of Devonshire, with John Hebb and a London builder bringing up the rear. Neither Whichcord, architect of the magnificent Grand Hotel in Brighton and numerous self-important office blocks in central London, nor Currey, whose most noteworthy work was the revolutionary design for St Thomas's Hospital, knew anything about theatres, though Whichcord had written an *Essay on the Erection of Fire-Proof Houses and Flats* (published in 1855). By contrast, the Drury Lane proprietors put their faith entirely in Phipps's architectural expertise, supported by a surveyor from the Law Insurance Company and a representative of the leading London construction firm, Cubitts Builders.[10]

The combative QC for Drury Lane, Mr Littler, immediately went on the attack arguing that the theatre was quite safe as it was – Phipps's earlier offer to rebuild the proscenium wall had now, it seems, been withdrawn – and that it could be emptied in three minutes. To make it even safer the management offered to cover most of the wooden part of the theatre with a preparation invented by Mr Phipps and known as "coke breeze".' The parties and the arbitrator then departed for the Royal Aquarium to watch an experiment during which Phipps placed a side of wood coated in this preparation next 'to a large body of [burning] gas ... The gas was turned on for 15 minutes and the wood was left untouched by the fire'. Sadly, the reaction of those present at this experiment was not reported in the *Era*.

Back at the hearing, the Drury Lane QC 'complained that the Board had not called Captain Shaw ... a man who knew more about fires than any man alive'. He had, as the Board's QC, Mr White admitted, been deliberately kept back. This, Mr Littler asserted, was because 'they knew that a long examination of Captain Shaw would utterly destroy the claim they were making against the proprietors'. This was probably a correct supposition; Shaw was not schooled in the cut and thrust of court room argument, nor given to convoluted sentences or the minute dissection of the 'actual' meaning of words in a particular context. Phipps's analytical mind, on the other hand, was always on the alert for holes in the assertions of anyone who dared to question his professional competence and remarkably adept at circumnavigating any criticism from any quarter as he had clearly demonstrated in his counter-attack on Shaw over the Gaiety.

Shaw did, however, score one point in his absence. He had complained that at Drury Lane 'every possible hole and corner was converted into a gigantic storehouse and rubbish receptacle ... that constituted one of the greatest dangers'. Mr Littler conceded that there had been an 'enormous collection' of rubbish, 800 cart loads in fact, which had all been taken away. It seems unlikely that Phipps would not have been aware of this problem but presumably he felt that he was not legally, or indeed morally, responsible for the fire risk created by successive managements' fondness for squirreling away old scenery and props.

Sir John deferred his judgement until October, when he confirmed the need for a new proscenium wall and a new staircase from the upper gallery, which should link up with the existing stairs from the lower gallery leading to Russell Street rather than continue down along the Duke of Bedford's private staircase as the MBW had proposed.[11] The Duke's staircase was his private property as he was the freeholder and Phipps, his legal expertise to the fore, was not prepared to challenge the Duke's property rights in the interest of the galleryites, a point he had raised with Hebb when he failed to strike a deal with Board. Property rights were sacred, fire safety was not.

The Royal Strand Theatre, Hastings and Leamington Spa

Nevertheless, Phipps was prepared to recognise that sometimes both Shaw and the MBW got it right. Thus, he did not oppose the outright condemnation of the Royal Strand Theatre, 'one of the worst in London for its narrow entrances and exit' according to the *Building News*.[12] Its structural deficiencies were hardly a surprise, the building, fronting 168-9 The Strand, had originally begun life as a Panorama (1803) before being converted into a theatre in 1832. Despite its cramped passages, the public had flocked to enjoy the riotous burlesques that the Swanborough family of actor-managers had been staging there for the past 20 years, amassing a small fortune in the process. Consequently, they were now in a position to extend their theatre by acquiring additional land at the back as well as adjoining property fronting The Strand.

It was still a tight fit, but this was the kind of complex rebuilding which Phipps seemed to enjoy. The construction began in early July, 'long before' the theatre closed on 29 July,[13] while the plans for a new Leamington Spa Theatre Royal went through their final checks and the Gaiety Theatre in Hastings was rising fast.

After four months of hectic building, the Royal Strand Theatre opened at the end of November and Phipps's alterations were widely admired, in fact, rather more so than the opening programme where the advertised 'newness' of the plays, including a 'musical comedy' *Frolique,* turned out to be no more than an 'old friend with a new face'.[14] The playhouse, on the other hand had acquired much more than a new face:

> 'Even in the entrance [on the Strand side] the change had a pleasant influence on the audience ... wide, handsome approaches, well

lighted and beautifully decorated gave the visitors a luxurious sense of enjoyment which was realised to a still greater extent when they had taken their seats in the mellow old-gold-coloured stalls'.

By retaining only part of the side walls and some of the roof, Phipps had transformed the old auditorium into spacious circulation areas and the old stage into an elegant, horse-shoe shaped audience space and added an entirely new stage at the back 'so well planned that from all parts of the house the performances are distinctly visible'.[15] He kept the old divisions of the auditorium, however, placing six private boxes on either side of the gilded proscenium frame and found space for 107 seats in the stalls, behind which he had placed a 'spacious' pit. He also stuck to the original two tiers: a balcony 'divided into two prices but without any division' and featuring another 170 of his 'registered chairs'. Above was a gallery for 400.

The general ornamentation was Italian Renaissance with the box fronts in white and gold, a colour scheme repeated in the flat ceiling. In contrast the walls were papered in dark turquoise and peacock blue against claret-red curtains. In all he created an auditorium that exuded an atmosphere of luxurious comfort reminiscent of the Savoy, and raised audience expectations of a new and more sophisticated breed of performances than that which had hitherto graced the Strand's stage. A re-hash of old comedies spiced up with some fresh tunes would simply not do.

Phipps combined his supervision of the Strand Theatre with regular journeys south to Hastings 'a great resort for pulmonary invalids during the cold season of winter and spring' and north to the more vigorous Leamington Spa, which was 'regularly resorted to by lovers of the chase'. The latter, anxious to market itself as a fashionable watering place for Birmingham's jaded business community and the gentry, had sported a small theatre since 1813.[16] Hastings, on the other hand, had been careful to avoid such extravagance but here, as earlier in Torquay, complaints from the visiting invalids about the lack of stimulating entertainment had forced a change of heart among the town's elite. Both commissions were a joint enterprise with local architects – Messrs. Cross and Wells in Hastings and Messrs. Osborne and Reading (from Birmingham) at Leamington Spa – with Phipps supplying the theatrical know-how and, not least, his trusted London-based decorators, Messrs. G. Jackson and Son for the plaster work and Edward Bell for the general interior decoration. Both firms must, by now, have been so thoroughly familiar with Phipps design patterns and colour preferences that there would, perhaps not have been the need for detailed drawings at all times, an outline sketch would have been all they needed.

The extent to which Phipps was involved in other aspects of the design, such as the exterior, is difficult to say, but he might well have advised on the type of site that would be most suitable. In Hastings, the theatre was centrally placed on the corner of Queen's Road and Albert Road, yet, so as not to cause offense, discretely hidden in a four-storey Baroque-inspired office *cum* shopping complex, stretching 71 ft. along Queen's Road and 118 ft. on Albert Road, with a hint of Baroque flourish, reminiscent of the Savoy, above the main entrance in Queen Road.[17] It held around 1400 spectators dispersed over orchestra stalls, pit stalls, pit, dress circle, upper circle, amphitheatre, gallery and eight private boxes, altogether a complex gradation of seats intended to cater for the intricate social structure on which Hastings rested, possibly at the request of the local developer, George Gaze. The New Gaiety opened on 2 August 1882 with D'Oyly Carte's Company performing *H.M.S. Pinafore*, as Phipps was preparing for the Drury Lane appeal. He did not trumpet his Hastings involvement in the architectural press, suggesting that the exterior together with the shops and offices might have been mainly the work of the local superintending architects Messrs Cross and Wells.

In Leamington Spa, the theatre, situated in Holly Walk, did not have to masquerade as something else; its frontage presented a stout Italian Renaissance design with a rusticated ground floor harbouring seven entrance doors, above which rose another two floors, with Palladian windows flanking arcaded windows in the centre the whole finished off by an attic. A continental visitor would instantly have recognised the building for what it was: a temple to the theatrical arts. It held around 1200, with space for 500 in the pit behind two rows of stalls. There were two tiers, the upper one set well back from the dress circle with a small amphitheatre at the front protected by a high barrier from the steep gallery behind. The Italian Renaissance theme continued in the horse-shoe-shaped auditorium, decorated in cream and gold with an ellipse-shaped proscenium arch, the whole held together by a circular ceiling.[18] Here he employed another of his stalwart clerks of works, E. Nightingale, to supervise the construction. The theatre opened on 2 October 1882 with

The Theatre Royal, Leamington Spa. Main frontage. Courtesy of Leamington Spa History Group.

The Theatre Royal, Leamington Spa. View of Auditorium from stage. Courtesy of Leamington Spa History Group.

Sir Julius Benedict's opera *Lily of Kilarney*, with 'the staging quite up to the average'![19]

Eastbourne Theatre Royal

With the Hastings and Leamington Spa theatres out of the way, Phipps could devote himself to the pleasing expectation of, at last, emulating his father and becoming a man of property. No matter that the property in question had yet to be built, that it was destined to be situated in Eastbourne not London and that the ownership would have to be shared with other investors; in an age when property ownership conferred a social status of its own, this speculative opportunity could not be ignored.

The prospect of owning his own playhouse had unexpectedly been handed him by a group of businessmen from Eastbourne, who, in want of a permanent theatre but inexperienced in theatrical matters, had contacted Phipps for advice on how to proceed. Phipps, by nature a risk taker and an opportunist and with enough contacts among London theatre managers and proprietors to gather a sufficient number of investors, offered the town council a theatre '[which] he was willing both to design and build ... and to run at no expense to the citizens of the town'.[20] It was an offer the Eastbourne politicians could hardly refuse.

Aided by George Loveday, manager for J.L. Toole, the fundraising went well, but finding a suitable site proved more difficult. Much of Eastbourne was owned by the Duke of Devonshire, and Phipps enlisted his friend Henry Currey, the Duke's architect – the fact that they had been on opposite sides over the Drury Lane alterations was clearly no barrier – in order to procure a piece of land in Devonshire Park. The Duke was not interested, but Phipps, undeterred, found a new site, a villa with a large garden situated along the town's main thoroughfare, Seaside Road, not far from the railway station and 'purchased the land'.[21]

All too aware that small provincial theatres rarely paid their way, Phipps was anxious to incorporate not only shops but flats, the latter to be used by the manager and visiting players, or, if need be, rented out to visiting invalids. These additional functions of the three-storey building shaped the design of the main façade on Seaside Road with the ground floor entirely taken up by four, wide shop windows, interspersed with pilaster-framed doors, the centre one a little grander than the others. Phipps repeated the pilasters on the first floor consisting of 13 balustraded rectangular windows and again on the 11-bay wide second floor, thus giving the frontage an air of immutable respectability.

The town council's Building Committee, who scrutinised the plans in early December, was not so easily won over, however. They queried the lack of exits at the back in case of fire, and the surveyor pointed out that the incorporation of flats above the shops contravened, in his view, a local bye law.[22] At the height of his career, Phipps did not take kindly to this unexpected opposition from an upstart local surveyor and a small group of provincial councillors, whose town he was about to present with a proper theatre to be built and run at no cost to the rate payers. He did not have a high opinion of councillors nor of their bye-laws and, now, in his dual role as proprietor *cum* designer, his mind preoccupied with the complex planning of the much larger Edinburgh Lyceum as well as the Prince's Theatre and Hotel in London, he wanted the matter settled swiftly. On 23 December he travelled down to Eastbourne intent on striking a deal with the hapless surveyor. He would reduce the width of the building from 13 bays to 11, which would make it possible to add a back exit, and:

> 'At his [the surveyor's] suggestion in order to get the plans passed quickly I erased the above designations to the rooms [Bedrooms and Sitting Rooms] and substituted the word 'Offices' and on the second floor offices and chambers for Mr Phipps'.[23]

The ruse worked. On 6 January 1883, the town council passed the plans and building began in February. Interestingly Phipps opted to use the Leamington Spa contractor, John Fell, in conjunction with the clerk of works from the Hastings Gaiety, Mr Dillon, who would both have been familiar with Phipps's required building standards and presumably could be left to get one with the project without too much supervision on his part.

At the hearing for licence application before the Eastbourne magistrates on 16 July 1883, neither side was taking any chances. The town mustered a full bench of magistrates, who were presented with the newly engaged Scottish theatre manager Waldtern Pegg (sometime manager of the theatre in Paisley) backed up by the joint proprietors, Phipps and George Loveday and a self-assured London barrister, Mr Percy Gye, ready to sweep all before him.[24]

Gye's opening statement was calculated to reassure and impress:

'The theatre, which had cost between £8-9000 ... was not very large ... but sufficiently large for the town ... [and] had been constructed with every regard and in conformity with the rules and regulations laid down by the Lord Chamberlain and the Metropolitan Board of Works ... [so] there could be no question as to provision for safety'.

The MBW Regulations did not apply outside the capital nor, of course, did the Lord Chamberlain's Rules, but, it seems that Phipps, whatever his personal view of their efficacy, found them a useful accessory with which to quell any criticism of his own plans by provincial magistrates, whom, he could safely assume, were unlikely to know the exact nature of the London 'Regulations'. In this case Gye's assertion was a slight exaggeration. The MBW required immediate access to a public thoroughfare from all exits and although the Eastbourne theatre stood isolated 'in the centre of a large piece of ground,' only the frontage opened directly onto a public road.[25] The two additional pit exits on each side 'leading into open spaces' ended in the remnants of the original garden, from which there was but a short walk to a gate on either side opening onto Seaside Road. By this means Phipps had satisfied the building committee while keeping the four shops, with their elegantly glazed fronts, intact. As the son of a shopkeeper he was well aware that in small towns dependent on tourism, the shops formed the backbone of the local economy, not theatres. On the other hand, keeping all four shops and with no public roads bordering the sides, left Phipps with only three entrance doors in the Seaside Road frontage through which to entice the town's multilayered social divisions, the upper echelons of which preferred not to mingle with the lower ranks. With the pittites (estimated at 500) entering on the far right and the galleryites (estimated at 300) entering and exiting on the far left, the central door and vestibule had to cater not only for visitors to the stalls (50), private boxes (30) and balcony (180) in the normal way but also for those to the considerably cheaper upper circle (200). In a town where social distinctions mattered this might meet with some resistance, and Mr Gye was anxious to reassure the magistrates that there were two staircases leading from the vestibule, one on the right to the balcony and one on the left to the upper circle and so 'By this arrangement there would be no danger of a combination of people'. Propriety seemingly ensured, the licence was granted.

Unsurprisingly, the auditorium design owed much to that of Leamington Spa's Theatre Royal, in its horseshoe shape, its two tiers with the gallery squeezed into the roof behind the upper circle and its Italian Renaissance décor in ivory and gold. The opening performance on 2 August with J.L. Toole's company in *A Fool and His Money* was a great success. Phipps, together with his wife Honnor and son, Alwyn Rashleigh, hosted a celebration supper at the Albion Hotel 'where mutual congratulations were exchanged'.[26] Among the guests were Toole and Loveday, Mr and Mrs Gunn and Waldtern Pegg with his wife, the Scottish actress Jessie Villiers, destined to play leading parts both on and off stage. The choice of opening play turned out to be remarkably prescient as Phipps all too rapidly discovered that provincial theatre proprietors, unlike their metropolitan counterparts, trod a fragile path between the tripwires of middle class respectability, free-booting managers and local economic fluctuations.

Endnotes

1. *The Times*, 17 May, 1881, p. 5, quoting MBW's Annual Report for 1881.
2. *Era*, 18 March 1882, p. 4.
3. Figures from *Era*, 18 March 1882, p. 4.
4. *Era*, 28 January 1882, p. 4.
5. R. Cox, *Oh Captain Shaw!* London: Victor Green, 1984, p. 127.
6. *Hansard*, HC DEB, 16 February 1882, v. 266, cc 782-3.
7. *Era*, 20 May 1882, p. 15.
8. 1892 Select Committee, para. 2203.
9. Letters by John Hebb to the Royal Institute of British Architects 1870-90. RIBA Biography file.
10. *Era*, 19 August 1882, p. 6.
11. *Builder*, 14 October 1882, p. 506.
12. 17 November 1882, p. 599.
13. *Era*, 18 November 1882, p. 6.
14. *Era*, 25 November 1882, p. 6.
15. *Era*, 25 November 1882, p. 6
16. G. Garlick, *The Theatre Designs and Plays of Samuel Beazley*, STR 2003, p. 52.
17. *Hastings News*, 4 August 1882. According to M. Jones and J. Pick, *Mr Phipps's Theatre – The Sensational Story of Eastbourne's Royal Hippodrome*, Entertainment Technology Press, 2006, p. 32, the Hastings investors had asked Phipps to design a frontage 'which looked as little like a theatre as possible'.
18. *Building News*, 6 October 1882, p. 423.
19. *Era*, 7 October 1882, p. 14.
20. M. Jones and J. Pick, *Mr Phipps' Theatre* ETP, 2006, p 17.
21. Letter from Phipps to Eastbourne Town Council 14 July 1884. Cited in M. Jones and J. Pick, *Mr Phipps' Theatre,* ETP, 2006, p. 30.
22. Letter from Phipps to the Town Council, 14 July 1884, cited in Jones and Pick, *Mr Phipps Theatre* p. 66.
23. See note 22.
24. *Era*, 21 July 1883, p. 14.
25. M. Jones and J. Pick, *Mr Phipps' Theatre*, p. 32.
26. *Wrexham Advertiser*, 18 August 1882, p. 5.

9 THE MASTER BUILDER 1883 - 1885

The Edinburgh Lyceum

With his own property safely established, Phipps could devote himself wholeheartedly to the final stages of the construction of the Lyceum Theatre in Edinburgh for J.B. Howard and F.W. Wyndham. Howard and Wyndham were not content to merely to be the most successful joint lessees and managers of the Edinburgh Theatre Royal ever, but they were also imbued with a strong empire-building streak and they were now funding the construction of Britain's grandest and safest theatre in Scotland's capital. They were just the kind of clients with whom Phipps excelled, confident and forward-looking with a clear perception of their aims and objectives and not short of money.

With safety in mind they acquired a large central site on the corner of Grindlay Street and Cornwall Street, which had 'free space one all sides' thus enabling Phipps to duplicate all the entrances and exits as well as to design, what was probably the first consciously energy-saving theatre, by incorporating 'open lighting and ventilation' through the simple medium of large windows, an arrangement which would cut running costs by '£150 a year ... over similar buildings by the use of the sun instead of artificial lighting for all purposes except in the auditorium'.[1] Whether the Edinburgh sun would have provided sufficient light during the dark winter nights is debatable.

Proper ventilation was a perennial problem in theatres and opening windows in the corridors, including those backstage, would certainly help as would electric light. Electricity, however, was an expensive option, the main reason it took some time to catch on among theatre proprietors. Another was its unpredictability: the dangers of undetected exposed wiring short-circuiting the whole system was very real which is why many managers preferred gas with all its drawbacks of soot, foul air and overheating. At the Lyceum, as at the Savoy, gaslights were also installed, just in case the new technology failed.

The 95 ft. wide frontage in Grindlay Street gave Phipps ample opportunity to stamp his architectural authority on the building. He

stuck to the classical theme
which he had explored
in the Leamington Spa
Theatre Royal, perhaps
feeling that anything else
would be unthinkable in
a city whose appearance
was largely characterised
by restrained columns and
companionable pilasters
supporting polite pediments.
Thus, Phipps's slightly
portentous round-arched
arcade that framed the three
central doors for stalls and

The Royal Lyceum Theatre, Edinburgh. Main frontage. © Historic Environment Scotland (Scottish Colorfoto Collection).

dress circle patrons was perhaps unadventurous but it was in keeping with the Scottish classical tradition. The arcade formed a firm base for the first and second floors where the three middle bays, set between giant attached Corinthian columns and flanked by giant pilasters, formed an arresting centrepiece supervised by a triangular pediment. At night, the light from the three French windows in the large dress circle foyer on the first floor, 'furnished as a drawing room and lounge',[2] added a lighter touch against the giant Corinthian pilasters adorning the curved corner with Cornwall Street. Not everyone was impressed:

'It [the exterior] cannot be considered of much account as an addition to the architecture of the city, being a production of brick and compo [concrete] with the most commonplace detail of pilasters and pediment. It is, fortunately, not in a conspicuous, although in a suitable and convenient position.'[3]

There was plenty of brick and cement inside too. All the public staircases were, as Phipps pointed out to the magistrates at the licence hearing, 'entirely built of cement and enclosed in brick walls.'[4] The basement floor was also concreted 'so as to exclude damp', though the stage machinery, with all the latest improvements, was of wood while a 'substantial brick wall' separated the stage from the auditorium. In this case the wall needed to be exceptionally substantial in order it to take the weight of the first iron curtain in a British theatre. The proscenium

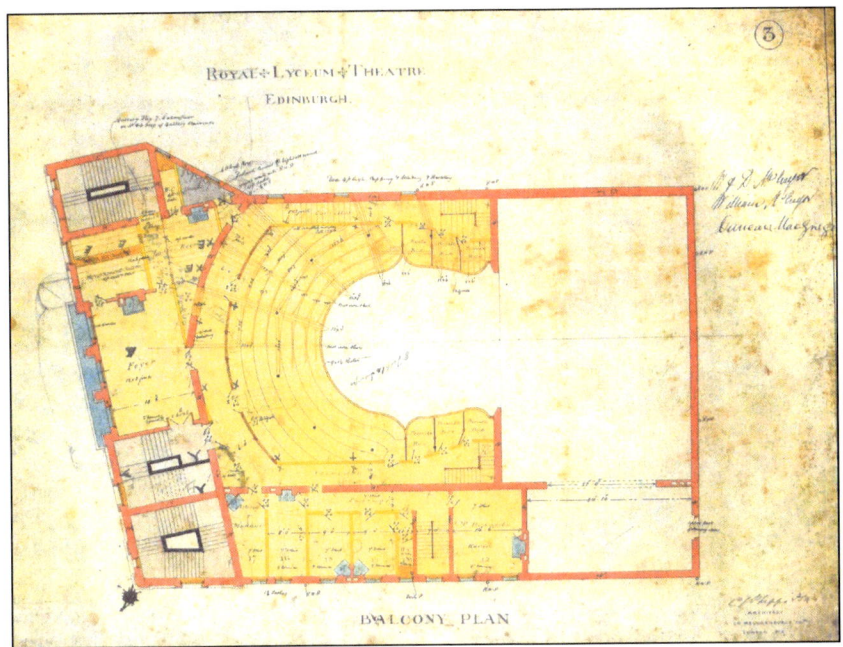

The Royal Lyceum Theatre, Edinburgh. Balcony Plan signed by C.J. Phipps. Coloured drawing. Courtesy of Edinburgh City Archives.

opening was 28 ft. square and rather like the Haymarket Theatre Royal 'given the character of a picture frame'.[5] The iron curtain was slightly wider, 30 ft. 6 in. to ensure it covered the stage opening completely, and 28 ft. 6in. high. It was a massive affair weighing, according to Phipps 'about 6 ¼ tons ... and constructed of two screens of wrought-iron plates 1/8 in. thick with an air space between them of 6 in.'[6] At the top it was 'framed and riveted to double wrought-iron girders secured to the heads of hydraulic rams, which are fitted with their cylinders on each side of the proscenium opening'. The water for working these rams came directly from the town mains, 'only' 84 gallons being needed to raise or lower the curtain in 50 seconds with the aid of a lever on stage pulled by the prompter. This particular iron curtain was a British invention by Alexander Clark, Gentleman, who in June 1882 and again in May 1883 had presented 'his fire-proof proscenium screen' to the Patent Office for provisional protection.[7] It was installed by Messrs Clark, Bunnett and Co. of London.

The stage was 78 ft. wide, including a scene dock, and 44 ft. long. The height of the gridiron was 60 ft. and the sink 20 ft., which was sufficient for whole scenes to be raised and lowered out of sight. There were 24 dressing rooms overlooking Cornwall Street and spread over four floors.

Howard and Wyndham seem to have had few illusions about the Edinburgh elite being sufficiently numerous or theatrically inclined to provide the major part of the audience. The total capacity was estimated at 2,400, twice that of Eastbourne, but the dress circle only held 209 of Phipps's chairs and the upper circle a mere 120 divided seats, behind which stretched a lower gallery for 500. Above this, on a gentle slope rose the upper gallery for around 1,000. Down below, a large pit, with 600 armed and upholstered seats was an attractive proposition for the middle class, buttressed from the immediate dangers of the stage by 121 orchestra stalls. The sight lines from the latter were unusually good as Phipps took care to lower the orchestra pit.

For this capacious auditorium Phipps adopted his newly favoured horseshoe curve for the tier fronts, but he added a touch of contrary flexure in the curve of the three private boxes. Above, a circular ceiling, its central space quite flat and decorated with 'tasteful' relief ornament in ivory – yet another variation on the adaptable Renaissance theme – surrounded by gilding and delicate colour, embraced the auditorium, while elegant coving linked its circumference to the picture-frame proscenium. The Renaissance style continued in the tier fronts and claret-coloured plush hangings in the private boxes coupled with a maroon curtain, which opened in the middle to reveal a monochrome act-drop representing a reproduction of Alma Tadema's 'Sappho and Alcamis' ensured a 'rich and chaste' appearance according to the *Era*.[8]

The opening night on 10 September 1883 was a triumph for all concerned. Howard and Wyndham had persuaded Henry Irving to bring Ellen Terry and the whole of the London Lyceum Company to present *Much Ado About Nothing* for the occasion and they issued invitations not only to the Edinburgh social elite but also to theatre managers around the country. Fortunately for Phipps, the iron curtain worked perfectly and Mr Howard led him onto the stage after the performance to take his customary bow.[9] A sumptuous commemoration supper followed at which Edinburgh lawyers and bankers were given an unrivalled opportunity to rub shoulders with Irving and Terry, the brightest stars of the theatrical establishment, and Phipps, together with his 18-year-old son Alwyn Rashleigh, could network among the profusion of theatre managers who were also present. He could allow himself this moment of glory; the Lyceum had cost around £17,000, the fee from which would give a hefty boost to his bank balance and his own, although more modest theatre in Eastbourne, seemed to be making a healthy economic and artistic start. The fact that Dixon-Hartland's Theatre Regulation Bill, which was designed to put all metropolitan and provincial theatres under the authority of the Home Secretary, had recently been thrown out by the House of Commons at its second reading,[10] was, no doubt, an irritation but probably not a surprise, and Phipps could comfort himself with the fact that there were at least a small number of politicians who took his views seriously.

The Prince's Theatre

Back in London there were two urgent projects waiting: the rebuilding of the Olympic theatre in Wych Street and the more lucrative construction of the Prince's Theatre and Hotel for the wealthy actor-manager Edgar Bruce. Phipps had the MBW to thank for both projects; their inspectors had demanded such a long list of improvement of Bruce's old theatre, the Prince of Wales in Tottenham Street, that he decided, possibly on Phipps's advice after two failed appeals, to find himself a better site for a new theatre.

As for the Olympic, it was just salvageable. It required a brick wall to divide the stage from the auditorium, complete reconstruction of the principal staircase, two new staircases for the gallery, additional exits and the removal of the pit and gallery refreshment bars as well as six rows of seats in the south-east angle of the gallery![11] It was work that was excellent training for his assistants, the kind of project that Ernest Woodrow could have handled with minor supervision and probably did. Two years later, by 1885 Woodrow was working for the MBW in the office of the Superintending Architect,[12] giving his new colleagues the benefit of a theatre expertise carefully honed under the watchful eye of their fiercest critic.

Phipps had first submitted plans for Bruce's new theatre to the MBW on 5 December 1882, while Bruce was still negotiating for yet more dilapidated property on what was a rather fragmented site fronting

*The Prince's Theatre, London. Composite views of interior, 1884.
John Earl Collection.*

Coventry Street (between Piccadilly and Leicester Square) and abutting Oxenden Street to the west, and Whitcombe Street on the east. As Bruce finalised more property deals, Phipps obligingly redrew the plans, submitting another set on 19 December and the final set on 16 January 1883.[13]

Bruce's choice of site suggests that he wanted his new theatre to rival his nearest competitors, the Haymarket, the Princess's and the Savoy by offering a luxuriously appointed playhouse which did not stint on safety nor on the latest developments in modern technology and comfort. Attached to the theatre would be a first-class 100-bed hotel fronting Coventry Street, complete with lift, a formal dining room, a grill room, a buffet and numerous private dining rooms overlooking Whitcombe Street, while the theatre would take up most of Oxenden Street. It was a huge undertaking and Phipps, clearly smitten by Scottish building industry's use of steam-cranes rather than external scaffolding, brought down the contractors he had used for the Edinburgh Lyceum, Messrs W. and D. McGregor, to carry out the work.[14] The *Building News* was impressed:

'The visitor to this part of London may have noticed the erection of a large block of buildings going on, without the usual cumbrous apparatus in the shape of external scaffolding. Two large steam cranes were erected at the corner on overhead scaffolds at a considerable elevation ... and with the aid of these the whole of the materials of the building were hoisted and adjusted.'[15]

There was plenty of heavy material to be hoisted; in the interest of fire safety all the floors, in the hotel as well as the theatre, were constructed of iron and concrete and overlaid with 'Burnettised' incombustible wooden blocks.[16] Then there was the iron curtain, measuring 36 ft. 6 in. by 26 ft. 6 in. and weighing about 7 ½ tons, the first to be fitted in a London theatre. Phipps, it seems, had spent much time researching the design of iron curtains 'from all parts of the world ... and inspected the iron curtain lately fixed at the Théâtre des Arts in Rouen.'[17] This curtain had, apparently, only 'one single plate' and took 2½ minutes to raise or lower as against Clark's which took 50 seconds.

Unsurprisingly, Phipps decided, in the end, to adopt the same version which he had used at the Edinburgh Lyceum, consisting of two screens of wrought-iron plates with a 6 in. air chamber in between and operated by a hydraulic system. The water was supplied from large tanks on the roof, which also provided the water for the hydraulic passenger lift in the hotel. Messrs Clark, Bunnett and Co. was again responsible for the iron curtain and its operating system and also for the lift which travelled 75 ft. For the latter Clark and Bunnett bored an 80 ft. deep well-hole and lined it with bricks all in the space of 10 days, a measure of the speed with which the building work was carried out.

There was no shortage of first-class hotels in the West End in the early 1880s, but not all were equipped with hydraulic passenger lifts and it seems likely that Phipps, with his interest in the latest technology persuaded Bruce that this would be an added attraction and therefore a worthwhile investment. The kitchens were situated on the top floor, above the bedrooms, through presumably the waiting staff did not benefit from the lift.

Although they were attached, the hotel and the theatre had little in common externally. The six-storey hotel block, attired in Portland stone in the French Renaissance style with pilasters, buxom brackets and varied fenestration, contrasted sharply with the theatre with its the red brick pilasters and dressings of Portland stone in the more sober Queen Anne style with echoes of the Savoy. By creating a curved entrance for the hotel on the corner of Coventry Street and Whitcombe Street and a grand theatre entrance at a corresponding circular corner of Coventry Street and Oxenden Street, Phipps brought the two disparate blocks together and ensured that the whole of the Coventry Street ground floor could be used for shops. The gallery, pit and upper circle entrances and exits were placed in Oxenden Street.

The grand theatre entrance, with echoes of the New Vaudeville in Paris, consisted of three round-arched doors, separated by voluptuous brackets. Once inside the circular vestibule, the visitors to the stalls, private boxes and balcony could admire the marble floor, and if they craned their necks, the vaulted and gilded ceiling decorated with figure-paintings before proceeding up the grand staircase to the balcony foyer, a sumptuous room, 18 ft. wide and 25 ft. long, in classical style. Alternatively, they might descend the stairs to the 8 rows of orchestra stalls. From the stalls there were but a few steps down to the basement where Phipps had placed not only a comfortable foyer (next to the wine-cellar) decorated in the 'Moorish' style but also a circular smoking-room, the latter directly underneath the entrance vestibule, and also in the 'Moorish' style, artfully enhanced by an abundance of ferns. The ferns were not merely decorative, they also acted as air-purifiers being one of the few species of plants that could survive in smog-ridden cities.

To further improve the air quality, Phipps introduced an early form of air-conditioning called 'the Aeolus Water Spray Method'. The ventilation of theatres had always been an intractable problem, they were either too stuffy or too draughty, and on the whole architects avoided placing circulation areas below street level. Phipps, however, appears to have been keen to harness the latest technological developments in finding new solutions to architectural conundrums when the money was available to do so. Exactly how this particular air purification system worked, is unclear, but assuming there is a clue in the name – Aeolus being the god of the winds – it might have been something similar to an air conditioning system patented in 1888 especially for theatres, whereby air was supplied to rooms by 'means of a cowl [on the roof], which may be assisted by a water spray'.[18] The air was led down an intake pipe at the bottom of which 'water is led away' and the air was then passed up another pipe to smaller distributing pipes. It was a sophisticated system of a type that would have appealed to Phipps as the pipes could allegedly be constructed inside or outside the building or built into the walls.

Beyond the stalls foyer and behind a very thick wall was the generator for the electric lighting – a Siemens SD dynamo machine driven by a 12 h-p. gas engine – which was used throughout most of the theatre, including, the corridors.[19] As before, Phipps also installed a complete gas lighting system and 'in some parts gas only will be used, in others the fittings are very ingeniously made for gas and electric light combined' according to the *Building News* in a statement, which reads as if its been taken straight from Phipps's press release. A saving in costs, but a dubious improvement in public safety.

In the auditorium, decorated in ivory white with liberally dispensed gilding, the incandescent electric lamps took centre stage. The fittings had been designed by Phipps, possibly assisted by his son Alwyn Rashleigh, and were, according to the *Building News* 'good in character and style, and accord well with the building, forming, indeed, its not least satisfactory feature'.[20] Four clusters, each with 30 of Swan's incandescent lamps hung from the circular ceiling and along the fronts of the balcony augmented by brackets 'with triplets of lights' along the front of the first circle.²¹ Only the gallery front was left without any adorning lamps, but then any such lights might have been overwhelmed by the ubiquitous sun burner in the centre of the ceiling. *The Times* was impressed:

> 'Brightness and refinement characterize the general scheme of the decorations, the upholstery being red orange plush, the walls Venetian red or Japanese bronze,... the whole being bathed in the soft light of electric lamps ... a model of snugness and elegance combined.'

It was, the paper concluded 'not so much a temple as a boudoir of the drama,' while still maintaining the 'time-honoured arrangement of pit and gallery'.²²

The theatre itself was not large, the horse-shoe shaped auditorium held around 1000, but it was surrounded by generous staircases and circulation areas for all parts of the house with separate entrances and exits for each section of the audience. Even 'the "gods" ... reach[ed] their domain by a staircase composed of successive breaks of four steps and a landing,' as the startled *Times* correspondent observed.²³

A boudoir with an iron curtain might seem a little incongruous, but the latter had been painted terra cotta to lessen its visual intrusion and would be used instead of the traditional green baize (there was a limit to the number of curtains a proscenium could satisfactorily cope with). The almost square proscenium opening, 30 ft. wide by 29 ft high, was topped by a tympanum with a painting by Mr Padgett. From the top of the tympanum the ceiling sloped upwards to the back of an unobtrusive gallery with only four rows of seats.

Phipps's architectural triumph was not, it seems, matched, by the opening performance. Bruce, in the role of Sir George Carlyon in *Honour Bound,* a one-act comedy by Sydney Grundy, which began the evening's entertainment, 'appeared weighed down by his new responsibilities and his acting [was] spiritless and tame'. The main piece, W.S. Gilbert's *The Palace of Truth*, fared rather better, but the real star appears to have been .the iron curtain, which, 'excited much comment and commendation'.²⁴

Trouble at Eastbourne

Phipps too, while basking in the glow of his solid reputation as the Master Builder of theatres, was beginning to get a whiff of the chill winds that were never far from a theatre proprietor's door. In Eastbourne receipts were falling when his manager, Waldtern Pegg, who had few contacts with the top London companies, the kind of performers that the Eastbourne middle class wanted to see, instead began serving up a string of run-of-the-mill provincial stock companies.[25] Determined to restore his fortunes, Pegg put all his energies and resources into the Christmas pantomime, *Jack the Giant Killer*, with Jessie Villiers as Jack. It ran successfully for a month, but this was not enough to sustain the theatre's fortunes. Nor did the success stop the gossiping about Pegg's private life. Jessie Villiers, it was rumoured, was not his wife but his mistress. The real Mrs Pegg was alive and well and living in Salford with the couple's three young children, having been abandoned by her husband in 1880 after five years of marriage.

After his departure, Pegg had sent his wife regular money, but when he met Jessie Villiers at the Paisley Theatre Royal in 1882 he stopped doing so and Mrs Elizabeth Pegg obtained a deed of separation under which Pegg was ordered to pay her 15 s. a week.[26] Pegg's solicitors then informed Elizabeth Pegg that her husband had acquired a mistress, masquerading as Mrs Pegg, and suggested that she sued for divorce. There would, they assured the real Mrs Pegg, be no opposition from her husband. Indeed, there was not, but Pegg must have realised that once a *decree nisi* had been granted to his wife, the whole sorry tale would be reported in the press – *The Times* was most assiduous in its reporting of divorce hearings – and Phipps and Loveday would send him packing.

To what extent Phipps and Loveday paid any attention, during the spring of 1884, to these unfavourable rumours regarding their theatre manager is impossible to say; they might have been more concerned over the Duke of Devonshire's sudden interest in building his own theatre in Devonshire Park. The theatre, aimed at 'fashionable company' and designed by the Duke's architect Henry Currey, would be a clear rival to their Theatre Royal.[27] This was not something Phipps and Loveday had bargained for, but there was little they could do except trust in Pegg's, none too obvious, managerial talents. Phipps certainly had his hands full; there was a commission for a new Theatre Royal in Northampton, a complete rebuild of the old Theatre Royal in Portsmouth, a new Grand Circus for Hengler and, perhaps the most appealing of all, the Savoy Turkish Baths awaiting his attention at the office.

Northampton and Portsmouth

The driving force behind a new Theatre Royal and Opera House in Northampton was a local newspaper editor, C.J. Franklin, who, had in mind a modest-sized theatre for this county town, with a population of around 70,000 in 1884 and home to a thriving boot and shoemaking industry. Indeed, the compact site, fronting Guildhall Road, only allowed for a constricted three-bay façade. Plain pilasters separated three arched doorways on the ground floor and three rectangular windows on the first floor, the whole topped by a pedimented attic. This minimalist façade in painted Ancaster stone caused some townspeople to wonder whether the theatre would be large enough to satisfy their needs, but they were reassured by the *Era*:

> 'Mr C.J. Phipps, the architect and the greatest living authority upon matters of this kind, has undertaken that the minimum capacity shall be 1500, while at high pressure, it will probably hold some 1,600 to 1,700, it is certainly unlikely that Northampton will require greater theatrical accommodation for many years to come.'[28]

One needs to remember that Phipps's estimated audience figures were, invariably over-optimistic and most probably based on an unrealistic perception of the degree of closeness or rather crush, that the pittites and galleryites were prepared to tolerate, while those in the balcony sat comfortably in his 'registered' chairs. Nevertheless, he did his utmost to live up to his promise, not least, by having planned a large pit 'covering the whole extent of the floor of the house' and 'furnished with benches with upholstered backs'. To keep noise levels from late arrivals down to a minimum, 'the floor [would be] paved with wood bricks'.[29]

As usual with smaller theatres, Phipps stuck to two tiers in his now favoured horse-shoe shape. Thus, the dress circle with the upper circle rising up behind formed the first tier, while a large gallery, fronted by a small amphitheatre, that reliable social stabiliser, formed the second tier ensuring maximum capacity with minimum social discommodity.

Into this smallish auditorium Phipps introduced the solid classical trappings normally reserved for larger theatres in the form of a tall and deep elliptical proscenium arch carried by pairs of Corinthian columns framing a single grand proscenium box on each side, while coved and decorated panels embraced the circular ceiling. Coupled with rococo-

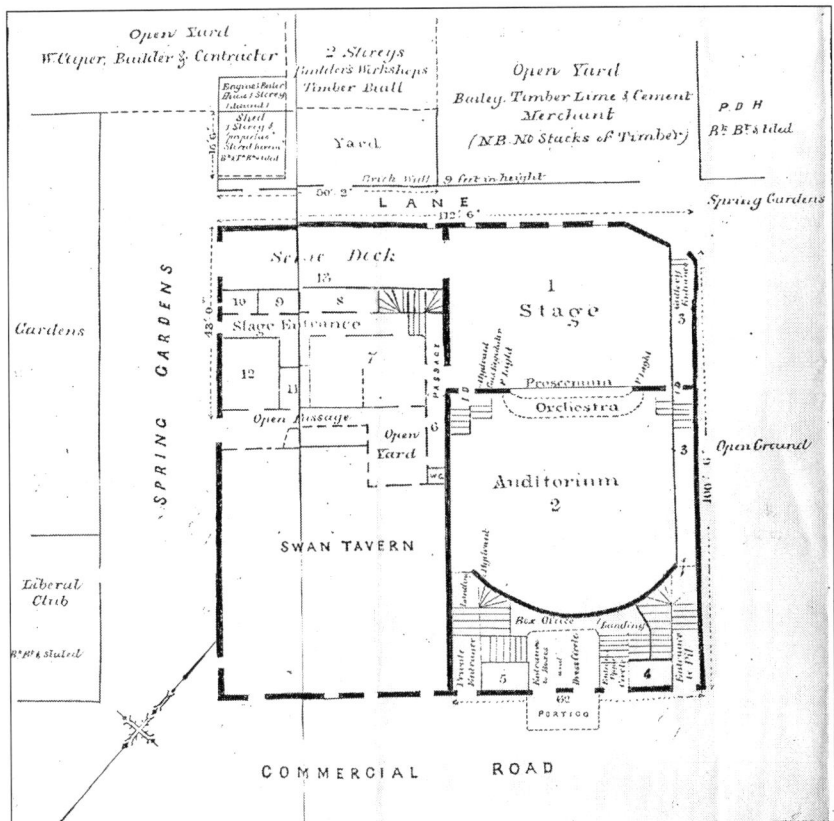

The Theatre Royal, Portsmouth, 1884. Ground plan from Deeds, n.d. Ref. 1297A (6). Reproduced by kind permission of Portsmouth Libraries & Archives Service, Portsmouth City Council. All rights reserved.

inspired decoration in gold and blue the interior was a design with echoes of the European 18th century court theatre, grand but compact, a gem, worthy of the 'the greatest living authority' on theatre architecture.

The Northampton Theatre Royal opened, as planned, on 5 May 1884 with *Twelfth Night*. After the performance, C.J. Franklin addressed the audience expressing his hope that 'the building was what they [the audience] wished and desired. He was sure their comfort had been studied most carefully by Mr Phipps and Mr Dorman [the clerk of works]'.[30] He then invited Phipps onto the stage and the latter 'was most heartily applauded'.

Whether the hearty applause was really deserved is debateable. The builder and Phipps between them appear to have underestimated the time necessary to complete the construction and extra men had to be drafted in during the last six weeks when work went on 'almost night and day'.[31] Under such circumstances short-cuts are almost bound to occur and it seems the orchestra pit had been made too small for the number of the required musicians and for the instruments to be properly heard. A new bar was also needed behind the pit 'in deference to the wishes of the magistrates. Furthermore:

'Close by will be a capital lavatory and offices, which will be open to the sky, and this will completely do away with the nuisance which was supposed to have previously existed ... [and] in the gallery a barrier has been opened and some stairs introduced.'[32]

Phipps appears not to have been involved in these alterations.

By the time the Northampton Theatre Royal opened, Phipps was busy redeveloping the old Theatre Royal in Portsmouth. The theatre had begun life in the early 1800s as a racquets court next to the Swan Tavern in Commercial Road before it was converted into a basic playhouse in 1856. By 1882, a local man, John Walter Boughton, had become the licensee and immediately ran into trouble with the local magistrates over the lack of exits.[33] Realising that only a new and larger theatre would satisfy the magistrates, he began buying up land around the playhouse over the years and then approached Phipps.

As usual time was of the essence and Phipps devised a plan whereby the new foundations could be dug and the new exterior walls could be erected around the old shell while the season was still in full swing. Thus, work began in the early spring of 1884. Not until May, when the season closed, were the builders able to pull down the old theatre within the shell of the new and start work on the interior structure and the roof.

Phipps gave the four-storey exterior fronting Commercial Road (now Guildhall Walk) a restrained neoclassical treatment with two giant Corinthian pilasters enclosing the three centre bays on the upper floors and adding another pilaster at each corner. Five round-arched doors took up the ground floor. A site plan describes the door next to the Swan Tavern as a 'Private entrance' while the door at the opposite end led to the pit. The three doors in the centre were designed exclusively for box and circle visitors, who were suitably protected against the weather by a projecting portico. The latter also formed the base for an eye-catching, first-floor, veranda-style smoking-room glazed with tall windows.[34]

The New Theatre Royal seems to have been well supplied with staircases:

> 'Each division of the house has a separate staircase, with an extra staircase on the opposite side to the main entrance for special use in case of need.'[35]

The stairs were, allegedly, 5 ft. 6 in. wide with handrails on both sides and all had square landings with no winding steps. Furthermore all the staircases were enclosed by brick walls and all doors opened outwards. Phipps and Broughton had clearly taken care to ensure that the magistrates should have nothing to complain about on safety grounds.

The building was large enough to allow for three tiers in the auditorium as opposed to the two in the old theatre. The dress circle projected towards the stage and held five rows of seats plus two private boxes at the back, echoing the Haymarket Theatre Royal. It seated around 200 in Phipps's tip-up chairs, which received much praise being 'roomy enough to allow fairly for the increasing amplitude of ladies' dresses'.[36] Whether he altered the original design of his armchairs over the years we do not know, but his wife and daughters might well have pointed out any shortcomings in the design as fashions changed.

The upper circle, which was set back a few feet, was furnished with cushioned seats and backs and the pit too was equipped with cushioned seats and back rails 'reminiscent of the new style of railway carriages' according to the *Hampshire Telegraph*. There were no cushions in the gallery, but it had an 'overflow staircase in case of panic'.

The proscenium opening was 30 ft. wide and 34 ft. high and surrounded by gilded frame which supported a segmental pediment with a painted lunette (by Ballard) with figures representing comedy and tragedy set into the tympanum. There were three proscenium boxes on each side level with the tiers with each box framed by its own coupled columns. The ceiling, proscenium and box parts were of ornamental fibrous plasterwork by Phipps's preferred plasterers, Messrs G. Jackson of London, who by now should have been thoroughly familiar with his 'Italian Renaissance style'. The fronts of the tiers were 'effectively gilded on a ground of cream colour',[37] forming a striking contrast with the two-toned terracotta coloured wallpaper. The gilding and painted decoration was, as usual, carried out by Edward Bell of London.

The auditorium was divided from the stage by a solid brick wall taken through the roof and 'much loftier than the house itself, according to the *Era*, which claimed, probably quoting Phipps, that the wall was 10 ft. deep and 60 ft. wide.[38] The stage 'was elaborately constructed with every mechanical contrivance of the latest pattern being fitted'. To the side of the stage, right behind the Swan Tavern, Phipps erected a separate block containing scene docks, dressing rooms, lime-light rooms and property store.

It would appear from the detailed description in the *Era* that Phipps had gone to some lengths to produce a theatre which complied, more or less, with MBW safety standards, a fact which he is keen to underline:

'The theatre has been built on the most approved principles, the rules and regulations of the Metropolitan board of Works having been strictly complied with in every particular'.

As we have seen, not least in relation to the Torquay Theatre Royal (1880), Phipps readily adopted a flexible interpretation of the MBW rules for theatres outside London. However, given the robust stance of the Portsmouth magistrates towards Boughton in the past, it would seem that they had adopted the MBW rules as their own and were intent on enforcing them.

Portsmouth Theatre Royal opened as planned on 4 August 1884 with a performance of Gilbert's and Sullivan's *Princess Ida*, watched by a distinguished audience, which included all that the city could muster in the way of civic and naval dignitaries. Both Boughton and Phipps were called for and loudly cheered.

More trouble at Eastbourne

Phipps was used to receiving ovations by now but his reception in Portsmouth probably felt all the sweeter after the unexpected animosity displayed by the magistrates and town council in Eastbourne when he had applied for renewal of his theatre licence some weeks earlier. They unexpectedly queried the legality of the original licence arguing that Phipps had infringed the infamous Bye Law 14 by including 'residential chambers' when, according to their surveyor, he had given an undertaking not to do so.[39] The reasoning behind this challenge seems a little obscure, but it is possible that the councillors felt that Waldtern Pegg's uninspired management coupled with the shocking rumours swirling around his persona might confer an aura of scandal over this the most respectable of seaside resorts. If the rumours were true, and the real Mrs Pegg was alive and well elsewhere, then Pegg and Jessie Villiers were openly living in sin in the theatre's residential chambers. Thus, by being seen to take a firm stand against the theatre's proprietor who, by providing the rooms that had facilitated this unsavoury state of affairs, the town council would, at least, publicly distance itself and its surveyor from the scandal and thus salvage the town's good name.

Phipps, of course, would have none of it. He demanded a meeting with the Building Committee to state his case, which was refused. Furious at the rebuff, he fired off an angry riposte to the Committee with a copy to the local paper,[40] in which he made it clear that he had never promised that the flats or chambers would be non-residential. Furthermore, the Building Committee, when they passed the plans, had made no objection to them in their final resolution, merely recommending that 'some back approach, should if possible, be provided as an additional exit in case of fire'. And as for the possibility, suggested by some council members, that they might take out an injunction against the proprietor for contravening the Bye Law, Phipps questioned whether this could be seen as appropriate use of ratepayers' money, adding, with the hubris of the 'greatest authority' on theatre architecture:

'I shall be most happy to meet any proceedings, having had the opinion of some of the best professional men in London that I have acted quite within the Bye Law in what I have done'.[41]

The Eastbourne politicians decided not to pursue the matter further. Indeed, there was no need, Pegg knew his time was up and less than three months later, in early October, Pegg and Jessie Villiers left Phipps's theatre to its fate taking the lease and licence with them.[42] They returned to the safety of Scotland where Pegg managed to secure the post of manager of the Inverness Theatre Royal.[43] Phipps and Loveday could do little except to advertise 'This magnificent' (alternatively) 'elegant theatre to let with immediate possession'.

There was, however, no rush of applicants who wanted to compete with the Duke of Devonshire's newly opened theatre in Devonshire Park and the Eastbourne Theatre Royal was left to linger.

Endnotes

1. *Building News*, 7 September 1883, p. 386.
2. *Era*, 1 September 1883, p. 4.
3. 21 July 1883, p .76. The façade had just been completed at that point.
4. *Era*, 1 September 1883, p. 4.
5. *Era*, 1 September 1883, p. 4.
6. *Builder*, 15 September 1883, p. 369.
7. T. Rees and D. Wilmore, *British Theatrical Patents*, STR 1996, pp. 51-2.
8. *Era*, 1 September 1883, p. 4.
9. *Era*, 15 September 1883, p. 7.
10. *Era*, 12 May 1883, p. 4.
11. *Era*, 4 August 1883, p. 4.
12. J. Earl, 'E.A.E. Woodrow: The nearly Invisible Man', in *Edwin O. Sachs – Architect, Stagehand, Engineer and Fireman,* ed. D. Wilmore, Theatresearch, 1998 p .43.
13. H. Maguire, 'C. J. Phipps (1835-1897) and Nineteenth-Century Theatre Architecture'. Unpublished Ph.D thesis, University of London, 1988, p. 146 and p. 150, n.37.
14. *Builder*, 24 November 1883, p. 684. Steam cranes had been used to construct the London docks in the early 1800s, but it seems they were not widely used in central London.
15. 11 January 1884, p. 42.
16. *Building News*, 11 January 1884, p. 43.
17. *Era*, 12 January 1884, p. 13.
18. Rees and Wilmore, 1996, p. 65. Pat. No. 5247.
19. *Building News*, 11 January 1884, p. 43.
20. 11 January 1884, p. 43.
21. *Era,* 12 January 1884, p. 13.
22. 19 January 1884, p. 8.
23. 19 January 1884, p. 8.
24. *Era*, 19 January 1884, p. 8.
25. M. Jones and J .Pick, *Mr Phipps' Theatre*, ETP, 2006, pp. 55-57.
26. *The Times*, 24 February 1885, p. 3.
27. Jones and Pick, pp. 58-9.
28. *Era*, 22 March 1884, p. 9.
29. *Era*, 22 March 1884, p. 9.
30. *Era*, 10 May 1885, p. 4.

31 *Era*, 22 March 1884, p. 9.
32 *Era*, 5 September 1885, p. 19.
33 *Era*, 7 October 1882, p. 4.
34 Photocopy of photograph of facade in 1897, courtesy of Donna Bish, Archivist at Portsmouth New Theatre Royal. The smoking-room was later extended by Matcham in 1900.
35 *Era*, 9 August 1884, p. 7. The report in the *Era* appears to be quoting Phipps's official description.
36 *Hampshire Telegraph*, 9 August 1884, p. 2.
37 *Era*, 9 August 1884, p. 7.
38 *Era*, 9 August 1884, p. 7.
39 See Jones and Pick, pp. 65-7.
40 *Eastbourne Gazette*, 19 July 1884, cited in Jones and Pick, pp. 65-67.
41 Cited in Jones and Pick, pp. 66-67.
42 Jones and Pick, p. 62.
43 Advert in *Era,* 1 November 1884, p. 1.

184 Charles John Phipps F.S.A - Architect to the Victorian Theatre

10 HUBRIS
JUNE 1884 - NOVEMBER 1886

Edinburgh Theatre Royal, Hengler's Grande Cirque and the Savoy Turkish Baths

With Portsmouth and Eastbourne taken care of, Phipps's was now able to devote his attention to his Edinburgh Theatre Royal in Broughton Street, which had followed the pattern set by its predecessors and succumbed to the flames on 30 June 1884. Fortunately for all concerned, not least Phipps's reputation, the fire was first noticed at midday when there were very few people in the building. It seems to have started in the property rooms, which Phipps had so carelessly placed behind the gallery, and spread with such ferocity that the fire brigade had to concentrate its efforts on saving the adjoining buildings rather than the theatre.[1] The interior was completely gutted but the outer walls held up and Phipps was asked to take charge of the rebuilding. Whether news of the fire triggered the opening of a champagne bottle in the office to drink prosperity to the

The Theatre Royal, Edinburgh on fire, 1884. John Earl Collection.

new building, an action that had allegedly become a regular tradition at 26 Mecklenburgh Square whenever news of a theatre fire reached a hubristic Phipps, who could look forward to receive the commission for its replacement, but it might well have done.[2]

'Due to the united and hearty co-operation of directors, architect and the contractors, Messrs. W. and D.M. McGregor', the rebuilding was completed in four months.[3] No doubt, the efforts of the clerk of works, William Browne, who had set the pace at Portsmouth, had also played an essential part.

Phipps saved time and his client's money by adhering largely to his old plans though with some important improvements, such as placing all workshops and stores, including the property rooms, outside the theatre and converting the space behind the gallery to a refreshment bar with improved access and exits. The gallery was given an additional exit opposite the original one,' but only to be used in case of emergency 'the door being secured by a light fastening that anyone could break'. The fear of anyone sneaking up to the gallery without paying was, clearly, still a major concern, overriding any safety issues.

The proscenium was modernised in tune with current fashion and the old arch was replaced by a richly gilded square frame above which rose a deep elliptical arch, resting on single pairs of Corinthian columns, and covering the proscenium boxes and orchestra pit. However, the installation of an iron curtain announced in the *Building News* on 26 December, 'was dispensed with',[4] presumably, in the end, deemed too expensive. As before, the theatre held around 2,300.

The new lessee, Cecil Berry, an experienced Glasgow manager, opened with Offenbach's operetta *The Rose of Auvergne* on 29 December 1884 to great acclaim. At the end, Cecil thanked Phipps for his tireless efforts and led him onto the stage to receive 'hearty cheers' from the audience. Phipps was well used to standing ovations, but they probably still gave him a thrill of a kind that no other building completion could match.

While keeping one eye on Edinburgh, Phipps was devoting his other eye, and probably more of his brainpower, to a more challenging construction in London, a new building for Hengler's *Grande Cirque* in Argyle Street. Already in 1882 the Metropolitan Board of Works had been so appalled by the structural defects in Jethro Robinson's building that it had asked the Lord Chamberlain, the Earl of Kenmare, to withhold his licence. The request was refused on the grounds that Hengler's was 'the best equestrian entertainment not only in London but ever known'.[5] In the summer of 1884, the MBW finally lost patience and resolutely closed the building on safety grounds. Hengler immediately re-negotiated his lease and consulted Phipps, who, apart from the Edinburgh project, was also overseeing alterations demanded by the MBW at the Princess's (completed 8 August), Sadler's Wells (completed 14 November) and the Variety at Hoxton (completed 31 October), as well as putting the finishing details to the plans for the Savoy Turkish Baths, readily accepted the new challenge.

Phipps had no experience of circus buildings, but, with his customary energy 'speedily prepared plans for a new equestrian temple' which rose on the old site in the space of just four months, ready for opening on 14 January 1885.[6] This was no mean feat considering the complex roof structure of which Phipps was justly proud judging by the detailed description of its anatomy which he provided for the *Era*. His circus roof was one of the largest roofs in London, a shallow dome constructed of iron trellis ribs and spanning 80 ft. The ribs were held together in the centre by a 6 ft. wide iron drum, which also acted as a ventilating shaft, the whole covered with slate and lined with fibrous plaster. Inside, Phipps created a perfect theatrical environment, suffused with an upper-class drawing-room atmosphere, in which Hengler's well-schooled horses and their patrons could each play their part. The circular ceiling, 46 ft. high from the centre of the ring, glowed with painted Italian ornament in gold and bright colours in the illumination from a sunlight consisting of eight chandeliers. The walls were painted red and crimson upholstery and curtains gave a warm feel to the seating arranged on a platform around the ring on the ground floor above which was the grand tier and a receding balcony tier. Permanent stables were placed at the back but linked to the grand-tier corridor so that seriously horse-minded spectators could inspect the performers at close quarters.

This frenzied activity on the theatre front was interspersed by a more relaxing project in the form of the Savoy Turkish Baths. The initiators of this addition to London's rapidly expanding Turkish bath scene was The Savoy Turkish Bath Company Limited formed at the end of 1883 with the object of raising £15,000 and acquiring 'the lease of the whole or of any part of the basement of Lancaster House, Savoy Street' for the purpose of constructing the finest Turkish baths in London.[7]

Among the directors was Michael Gunn, one of Phipps's closest friends, and it was presumably a recommendation from Gunn that secured the commission for Phipps, who seems to have delighted in the design process, possibly jointly with his office manager Max Clarke, who acted as clerk of works for this intricate structure. No wonder; this was an architectural escape, an opportunity to cast aside the formality of a rule-ridden classicism and indulge in 'Moorish' fantasies where the imagination had free play. Phipps lavished attention on every delicate detail to create a mesmerising stylistic unity among the interlocking spaces lit by electric light – the first Turkish baths to offer this healthy option – and provided the best heating and ventilation in the metropolis. There were marble walls and mosaic floors in the hot rooms, with temperatures that allegedly ranged from 120 degrees to 300 degrees Fahrenheit! After a strenuous session of hot air and cold plunge baths, clients could take refuge in the 'cooling room' covered with a richly patterned carpet with a small fountain in the centre surrounded by deep armchairs, a sofa and a chaise longue with strategically placed coffee tables and discrete alcoves with richly patterned curtains and simple beds, the whole lit by stained glass windows. It was a sensuous combination of luxury, comfort and supreme relaxation, a perfect retreat for an overworked architect and his friends. That Phipps frequented the baths seems likely, he was a social creature when he had the time and knew the value of networking. The fact that he acquired 50 shares in the Company in 1885 suggests that he believed (or hoped?) that this elegant cleansing institution had a secure future, and would provide him with a welcome escape from his labours as well as a useful dividend.

Exeter Theatre Royal, the London Lyceum and Dublin's Leinster Hall

The delights of the Savoy Turkish Baths were interrupted on 5 February 1885 by another provincial theatre fire. The Exeter Theatre Royal burnt to the ground, without loss of life, but the under-insured, absentee landlord was not disposed to rebuild it. In a city which had had a playhouse since 1737, life without one seemed unthinkable, and a theatre company was quickly formed, under the chairmanship of a leading local magistrate, William Horton Ellis, to raise the necessary funds to erect a new theatre.

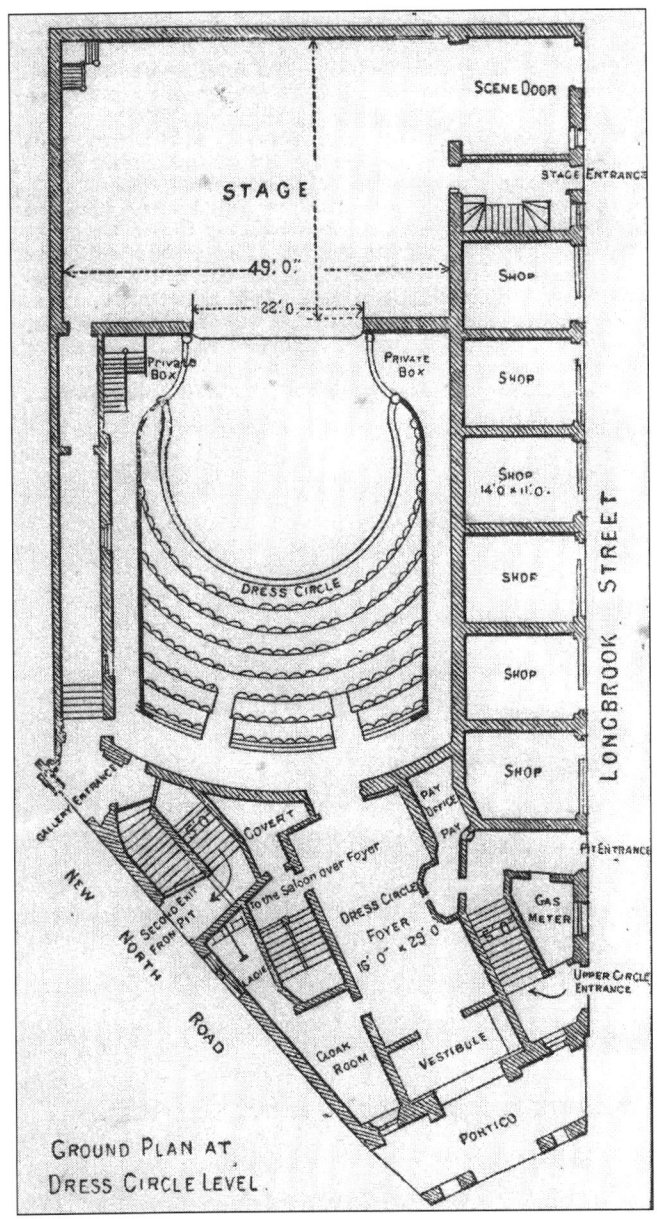

The Theatre Royal, Exeter. Ground plan, based on the architect's original plan, 1887. John Earl collection.

Ellis was determined to have the best theatre architect available and travelled to London to enlist Phipps for his cause. Thus Phipps, who never turned down a commission and was going down to Exeter anyway to assess the value of the old theatre on behalf the insurers, found himself by the middle of March 1885 walking round Exeter city centre examining suitable sites for the new theatre.

Perhaps overestimating the funds that the company would be able to raise in a recession-hit provincial city without the presence of any major industry – though his Bath and Eastbourne experiences ought to have imprinted on him the danger of trusting to local generosity in theatrical matters – Phipps chose a large isolated site (10,500sq. ft.) at the Junction of Longbrook Street and New North Road. It was a good, central site with space for placing workshops and store rooms in a separate block from the theatre itself, while leaving ample room for circulation areas and double exits from all sections of the auditorium and the stage, and, if need be, for shops.[8]

The Theatre Royal, Exeter, 1886. Main frontage. John Earl Collection.

After his initial visit, Phipps, used to thinking and working at a rapid pace, went back to London and drew up preliminary plans for the Longbrook site, which the directors of the theatre company had approved by the end of May 1885.[9] By this time they had also purchased Longbrook Street site for the alarming figure of £3000, which, in the context of a projected capital of £10,000 (in the form of 100 shares of £10 each), meant that any lavish expenditure on the theatre was out of the question. Their rash promise of 'at least 4 ½ % return', during a period of stagnation in the Exeter economy, was clearly designed to raise money quickly; however, their fellow Exonians were not convinced. The fundraising went slowly, and the directors, in dire need of cash, leased the back portion to the removal firm Pickfords, who erected warehouses and stabling on their new ground, thus scuppering any earlier grandiose plans that Phipps might have entertained. The directors also demanded the inclusion of six shops, a demand with which Phipps probably had considerable sympathy, after all he had insisted on four shops for his small theatre at Eastbourne, but any earlier notions on double exits now had to be re-worked at the same time as he was deeply engrossed in major alterations for Henry Irving at the London Lyceum.

The Lyceum commission was a project that Phipps probably regarded as more fitting for an experienced architect and FSA. Devising a new decorative scheme for the auditorium based on Raphael's frescoes in the Vatican Loggia, finding the right curve for the tier-fronts in order to the improve the sight lines, and bringing the stage up to modern standard for the nation's leading actor, would, surely have been more absorbing than another run-of-the-mill provincial playhouse.

The re-decorated and re-structured Lyceum re-opened on 5 September 1885 with *Olivia*, a comedy-drama by W. G. Wills based on an episode in Oliver Goldsmith's *The Vicar of Wakefield*, with Irving playing the Vicar. While the *Building News* enthused over Phipps's introduction of a decorative style that was 'pure Italian', that is based on Raphael's frescoes in the Vatican Loggia as well as the decorative schemes from the Massimi Palace and the Villa Madama in Rome using rich colouring on white ground surrounded by gold mouldings. For the *Era*, the brightly painted medallions of classical Greek authors in the ceiling surrounded by equally brightly painted friezes of young boys struck the wrong note:

> '... the colouring of the auditorium should be toned down and kept subordinate to the effect of the picture on the stage ... [it should] create a sense of reverent anticipation of high artistic effort'.[10]

The Exeter Theatre Royal, which had once, if only fleetingly, seemed like a promising provincial venture for the nation's most renowned theatre architect soon degenerated into a tedious exercise in paring down and cutting back in order to satisfy a parsimonious client. It had become an assignment suitable for an apprentice architect, and it would be surprising if Phipps had not handed over the plans to his assistants as he supervised the Lyceum alterations, only tweaking it a bit here and there when they got into difficulties.

On 11 July 1885, Phipps sent his plans, accompanied by a perfunctorily letter, to the city surveyor Donald Cameron urging him to 'bring them [the plans] before the Streets Committee on the 16th as we propose to start building operations almost immediately'. He also pointed out that the construction conformed to local bye laws, to the MBW regulations and to those of the Lord Chamberlain and reminded Cameron that he had constructed 'some 40 theatres, and I bring a somewhat large experience to bear on the subject.'[11] In other words, he was not prepared to countenance any criticism of an uninspired set of plans with two deep tiers and a large pit. The lower tier comprised the dress circle, while the upper tier held both the upper circle and, the gallery the latter ensconced behind a three-foot high barrier and consisting of a series of steps with no backs.[12] The gallery and the pit had only one exit – contrary to the MBW Regulations. Even the main entrance had been short-changed, adorned only by a small heavy-handed classical portico.

The whole design bore the hallmark of quick-fix solution, an adaptation of past glories including the circular-shaped dress circle front with a touch of contrary flexure coupled with a proscenium straight from the Northampton Theatre Royal.

Building did not start immediately. On 28 October 1885, Phipps was back in Exeter to explain his plans to Ellis and a small group of magistrates, in the hope, it appears, to secure a kind of 'pre-licence agreement' with the latter before the construction began. The magistrates queried the lack of second exits for the pit and gallery, and Phipps hastily found a solution to the pit, but ignored the second gallery door, which would have meant sacrificing at least one shop and the dressing-room above. He seemingly had neither the energy nor the inclination to fundamentally rethink his plans at the request of provincial magistrates and instead adopted the 'I-know-best' approach that had served him so well at Eastbourne.

There might also have been another reason behind Phipps's casual attitude to the Exeter theatre. He had a more complex, and economically more rewarding project on his mind. His long-standing friend Michael Gunn had commissioned a large concert hall for the old Theatre Royal site in Dublin, to be designed so that it could be converted into a theatre when Gunn had sorted out his patent problems. His failure to secure the patent and finding the requisite funds had stymied his original intention to rebuild the theatre according to Phipps's grand design after the fire in February 1880 (see Ch. 7). Fearing his ownership of the derelict site might be challenged when he no longer held the patent, the ever ambitious Gunn decided to stake his claim to it by erecting a large concert venue, to be named Leinster Hall, which he could later convert into a new Theatre Royal. Much hinged on this commission; Phipps must get everything right, from an imposing exterior, to comfortable seating, elegant circulation areas and, above all, excellent acoustics, while all the time bearing in mind its possible transformation into a theatre.

The site, on the corner of Hawkins Street and Poolbeg Street, was 200 ft. long and 84 ft. 6 in. wide. Phipps placed the principal entrance in Hawkins Street where he arranged five doorways in the centre of a rusticated ground floor covered by a glass canopy. The doors led into an outer vestibule followed by inner grander, central vestibule with staircases on either side leading to the first floor. The ground floor held seats for 1,500 in a floor space 102 ft. long and 64 ft. wide, while the first floor balcony had four rows of seats at the sides and back and held 600. There was also a second balcony, reached by a staircase from Poolbeg Street, seating 500.[13] The two upper floors had their own foyers and refreshment rooms, the one on the first floor lit by tall windows.

The space for the orchestra, situated where the stage would be, was 48 ft. 6 in. wide and 44 ft. deep with numerous rooms underneath for musicians, performers and chorus members. Planning ahead, Phipps thoughtfully raised the roof above the putative stage in anticipation of the gridiron and fly galleries to come.[14]

This was a unique project which could not just be left in the hands of the builder and the clerk of works; it required the regular presence of the supervising architect, apart from which the long-standing friendship between client and architect would have brought its own obligations.

It was Exeter's misfortune that the construction of its much anticipated Theatre Royal coincided with that of the much grander Leinster Hall and that their planned opening dates were within two weeks of each other. It was not that Phipps was unused to supervising two or even three building projects at the same time in different places – the extensive alterations to the Haymarket Theatre Royal, for example, had coincided with the building of the Torquay Theatre Royal in 1880, but there the travelling back and forth had been straightforward and quick. However, the triangular route from London to Dublin and back via Exeter was awkward and time-consuming, and the temptation to leave the builder, S. Bevan, and clerk of works, William Browne, to their own devices in Exeter must have been tempting.

William Browne is not an uncommon name and it has not been possible to establish whether the 'Exeter' William Browne was the same 'energetic clerk of works' who had been applauded by the audience at the opening of the New Theatre in Aberdeen in December 1872, and who acted in the same capacity at the Liverpool Rotunda in 1879, then at the Glasgow Theatre Royal in 1880, the Belfast Theatre Royal in 1881, the Portsmouth Theatre Royal in 1884 followed by the Edinburgh Theatre Royal also in 1884, but it would seem likely. Phipps tended to work with people he knew well particularly when he found himself obliged to divide his time unequally between his commissions, and, as in the case of Exeter, had to delegate the greater part of his supervisory duties to the clerk of works.

Construction on the Exeter theatre started before Christmas 1885 and proceeded at an unusually slow pace for a Phipps-designed theatre, but both he and the builder might have underestimated the difficulties of preparing sufficiently deep foundations on a multi-slope site during a wet winter. The obligatory 'Foundation Stone Ceremony' finally took place on 13 May 1886 – the stone was placed in the base of the entrance portico – and Phipps came down to supervise 'a ceremony hastened over in double-quick time'.[15] It poured with rain as William Ellis revealed to the Exeter dignitaries and the assembled public that S. Bevan's tender, which the Theatre Company had accepted, had been for £5,500, including six shops and furthermore that the total cost of the theatre would not exceed £6,500. The shops would 'bring in a good rental', though of, course, the main purpose 'was to give the town a Theatre'.

The brief ritual completed, those most closely involved with the Theatre withdrew to a sumptuous luncheon at the London Inn just across the road. Here, speeches interspersed with frequent toasts accompanied the eating. The mayor, R.R. M. Daw, ESQ was particularly fulsome in extolling the virtues of the new theatre and proudly announced: 'The plans passed under my observations as one of the Justices of Exeter and they afford the most ready means of exit in all directions'. While this statement did not quite amount to an official approval of the plans, it suggested that the magistrates had, at least, given them their tacit endorsement. William Ellis then proposed a toast to Phipps, praising the latter's long experience including the restoration of Irving's Lyceum before concluding:

'I am sorry not to have a local architect but building a Theatre is a special matter and it would be unwise and unsafe to trust the lives of the citizens in the hands of local architects – Oh, oh!'

Laughter ensued and Phipps stood up to reply:

'The proper time to congratulate the architect was when the building was finished. Up to the present time it has gone well with an admirable chairman, a good set of businessmen as a board of directors, an efficient man as contractor and a vigilant clerk of works.'

There appears to be no record of Phipps visiting Exeter again until he attended a site-meeting on 19 July 1886. By October, the theatre was still far from finished despite a certain amount of slipshod work and general cutting of corners as the plastering contractor George Steere noted with dismay:

'The sides of the Pit was to be plastered in fact we gave it one coat, but as there was such a hurry it was matched boarded in a few hours ... I have worked on many large buildings and some of the finest in England but never before saw so much wood take the place of what should have been iron.'[16]

Steer's comments cast doubt over both Bevan's lauded efficiency and William Browne's vigilance. Nevertheless, the new Theatre Royal opened, as planned, on 13 October 1886 with Sidney Herberte-Basing as lessee-manager. However catch-up building work continued for several months before Phipps was finally satisfied and gave Bevan his certificate of completion.

Herberte-Basing had initially advertised two singularly apt plays for the opening night: T.W. Robertson's *Breach of Promise* and A. W. Pinero's *The Magistrate,* but faced with what seems to have been total confusion on the opening night, he cancelled the second play.

George Steere, in his letter complaining about the overuse of wood, also recalled Phipps's reaction to the chaos that confronted him on the opening day:

'I was doing some work near the gallery entrance when Mr Phipps came to me and ordered me to stop it. I told him I was working under Mr Bevan's instructions. Then he said "Mr Bevan can go to ..." which I believe in Greek interpretation means Hades, and then he said "My will is law here", accordingly I stopped it.'

Indeed, Phipps's will was law on the building site and in that blistering moment he unexpectedly came face to face with the consequences of his cavalier attitude to the Exeter commission. In leaving William Browne to assert his authority over a builder all too prone to cutting corners in order to keep within his estimate as well as over an actor- manager with his own ideas on theatre design accumulated after years working in shoddy provincial playhouses, he had simply asked too much of his clerk of works. There was no other obvious explanation for the unfinished state of the building. He would have to assert his authority and do what he could to ensure that the opening night went smoothly. Just to make certain nothing untoward happened, Phipps offered to supervise the theatre's weakest point, the gallery stairs and pay box arrangements, where overexcited galleryites might cause bottlenecks.

As in all theatres the gallery stairs were designed to prevent any quick-footed person from entering the gallery without paying. Once through the street doors the galleryites faced a pair of double doors a few feet further on followed by a steep climb up fifteen winding steps of cement-concrete to the first landing where there was a door to the upper circle through which those galleryites, who had come early and gone up through the upper circle stairs passed through, while later arrivals waited in front of a 'stout door ... shutting off the gallery stairs,'[17] the so-called 'crush-door.' Once through that door, there was a flight of seven steps up to another landing, 10 ft. long and 5 ft. wide, where the pay box was situated. In order prevent a run on the pay box, a tall wooden post, 4 inches square, had been placed in front of the pay office, on one side of which there was room for one person to pass and on the other for two.[18]

The galleryites, having paid their money and received their metal tokens, were then free to race up a further 15 steps to the next landing and round another a sharp turn before mounting the last seven steps to the top of the gallery. Here, they were greeted by the check taker standing beside his box (2 ft. 6 in. high and 1 ft. 6 in. square), who collected their tokens and placed them in his box. Finally, the anxious spectators could enter the gallery right at the back, level with the top bench.

It was a tortuous route, but Phipps pronounced himself 'well satisfied with the way the gallery stairs had worked', according to Herberte-Basing.[19] Indeed, he could hardly have said otherwise without denigrating his own competence. As usual on the opening night of a Phipps theatre, the audience called for his appearance on stage at the end of the performance. As usual he obliged and with the Exonians enthusiastic applause ringing in his ears, trapping him securely in his own vanity, he was able to return to Dublin to supervise the last two weeks of the Leinster Hall construction.

The opening night of the Leinster Hall on 2 November 1886 was a great success. The inimitable Mme Patti thrilled the Dublin establishment with her beautiful voice to which the acoustics seem to have done justice, and the noble proportions of the building were much admired. At the post-performance supper in the large foyer, Michael Gunn, who had spent £25,000 on his hall,[20] was generous in his praise of both Phipps and the builder claiming 'he had had the good fortune of having a most able architect who designed the hall and a contractor who carried out the work in a most satisfactory manner'. The health of Phipps was then proposed by a Dr Shaw and Phipps, in his response 'spoke in commendation of the manner in which the contract had been carried out by the builder.' He also expressed his thanks to Mr Farrar, the clerk of works, who had been associated with him in the building of the hall'.[21]

Endnotes

1. *Builder*, 5 July 1884, p. 40.
2. *The Architect*, 28 May 1897, p. 343.
3. *Building News*, 26 December 1884, p. 105.
4. *Era*, 3 January 1885, p. 10.
5. *Morning Post*, 18 November 1882, p. 2; *Era*, 10 January 1885, p. 8.
6. *Era*, 1 January 1885, p. 8.
7. NA, BT31 3253/19102. I am indebted to Malcolm Shifrin, www.victorianturkishbath.org for the information on the Savoy Turkish Baths.
8. *Builder*, 4 April, 1885, p. 5.
9. *Exeter Evening Post*, 27 May 1885, p. 5.
10. *Building News*, 11 September 1885, pp. 427-28, *Era*, 12 September 1885, p. 14.
11. Inquest Evidence, p. 135. Box of Coroner's Papers, Exeter Theatre Fire 5 September 1887, Exeter City Archives Collection (ECA), Devon Heritage Centre.
12. *Report by Captain Eyre M. Shaw Concerning the Fire which occurred at the Theatre Royal, Exeter*, London 1888, para. 192.
13. *Era*, 6 November 1886, p. 15.
14. *Era*, 30 May 1891, p. 7.
15. *Daily Western Times*, 13 May 1886. Cutting from Box of Coroner's Papers, Exeter Theatre Fire 5 September 1887, ECA, Devon Heritage Centre.
16. Letter to the Editor of the *Devon Evening Express*, September 1887. Box of Coroner's Papers, Exeter Theatre Fire 5 September 1887. ECA, Devon Heritage Centre.
17. Captain Shaw's Report, para. 179.
18. *The Times*, 17 Sept. 1887, p. 7
19. Inquest Evidence, p. 170 Box of Coroner's Papers, ECA. Devon Heritage Centre.
20. *Era*, 30 May 1891, p. 7.
21. *Era*, 6 November 1886, p. 15. Farrar was also the machinist of the Dublin Gaiety.

11 BETRAYAL SEPTEMBER 1887

The Fire

On Monday 5 September 1887, the Exeter Theatre Royal presented *Romany Rye*, a sensation-drama by George Sims, in which 40, more or less evil characters attempt to outdo each other in villainy and skulduggery among 17 spectacular scene changes including a ship wreck, a struggling life-boat in stormy seas, hell-hole lodging houses and bustling seaports. It was an expensive production, beyond the means of a small provincial theatre, but help was at hand in the form of the Romany Rye Company, a touring company equipped with all the necessary actors and sets. The Exeter stage was just large enough to cope; even so every available space back stage was stacked with scenery and props, and the skills of the fly men and scene shifters were tested to their limits. It was usually a guaranteed crowd-puller, though on this warm and sultry Monday night the Exeter Theatre was only half full, with around 400 in the pit, including the pit stalls, 26 in the dress circle, a similar number in the upper circle and 192 in the gallery.

At twenty past ten in the evening, a dangling back cloth, placed nine inches behind the gas batten furthest from the stage opening, caught fire. This kind of incident was not uncommon and the usual procedure was to cut the ropes of the burning cloth and drop it onto the floor where the scene shifters would extinguish the flames with a fire hydrant and buckets of water. Unfortunately, the cloth (depicting a ship) was hung just too far out for the fly men to reach it, their path blocked by stacks of scenery, some already used, others waiting for the next scene change. In the cramped and hot conditions saturated with gas fumes, the flames from the 'ship cloth', unable to escape through the modest ventilation tower above the stage, were soon licking the scenery and ropes surrounding it and the fly men, in desperation, lowered the act drop. It was too late. The fire hydrant could not reach the burning cloths and less than two minutes later a burning flat fell against the act drop, the curtain bulged and smoke billowed into the auditorium, flames and sparks escaping through the sides. The smoke rose upwards, but in such quantities that

The Theatre Royal, Exeter on fire. 'The bulging of the curtain', 1887. John Earl Collection.

it soon overfilled the ventilator above the sunburner. Finding no escape, it sank down again like a dense, suffocating blanket and enveloped the gallery and its occupants in a fatal embrace.

The musicians stopped playing in mid-note, grabbed their instruments and scrambled through the two wooden doors below the stage into the

The Theatre Royal, Exeter. The fire as seen from the street, 1887. John Earl Collection.

smoke-filled mezzanine floor fumbling their way to the stairs that led up to the stage door and the safety of Longbrook Street. Simultaneously, the spectators in the stalls rose in unison made their way through the emergency exit door situated next to them, only hindered by a few agile pittites, who had scaled the barrier between the pit and the stalls desperate for the nearest door. Most of the pittites headed towards the pit entrance, but as the dense smoke-cloud sank further down, many lost their way and perished.

Because it was an unusually warm night, the dress circle attendant, Mrs Veal, had left the circle doors open to ventilate the auditorium. Seeing the sparks and flames shooting up towards the circle, she threw open the corridor doors and uncoiled the hose in the vestibule, while the dress-circle occupants moved swiftly through the foyer and vestibule onto the street. In the upper circle, a group of women rushing for the stairs on the New North Road side, collided with the upper circle attendant Mr

Harris, and pay box attendant James Coombes chatting in the corridor completely oblivious to the disaster unfolding around them. Coombes led the women down the stairs to the entrance floor, but those following behind missed the right turn on the landing, which led to the stairs for the vestibule, and found themselves in the saloon. They could not turn back, as the smoke was rapidly filling the corridors and the only way out was through the French windows onto the balcony to wait for a ladder.

As the curtain surged into the auditorium, the gallery audience rushed for the single exit at the back. A few tried scaling the barrier into the upper circle, but it seems that only one person, an agile telegraph boy, managed to escape that way.[1] Those who got through the door, promptly collided with the check box, which fell to the floor causing those behind to trip and fall. Unable to get up against the mounting crowd behind them, they quickly formed an additional block, soon large enough to fill the only exit. Those fortunate enough to make it past the check box ran into the post on the pay-box landing where a second block of trampled galleryites rapidly built up. Realising what was happening, the manageress of the upper circle bar opened the door between the upper circle corridor and the gallery staircase hoping to give those jammed on the pay-box landing another means of escape. It was a natural reaction in the circumstances, but the effect of the open door was the reverse of what she had intended. The draught pulled the smoke from the upper circle straight through the door into the gallery stair case, turning the latter into a flue and asphyxiating those trapped on the pay-box landing as well as those above or below. The gallery's single exit had been transformed from an escape route into a death trap.

The speed and intensity of the conflagration was beyond the capabilities of the local individual fire brigades, still the province of different insurance companies as the city council had not yet seen the need for a municipal force. Between them they had only one escape ladder, chained up outside the Guildhall. But for the decisive action of the landlord of the London Inn opposite the theatre, Robert Pople, who broke into a nearby builder's yards and brought out their ladders, the actors, who were trapped in their dressings rooms might not have been rescued, nor those clinging to the balcony and parapet outside the dress circle bar.

The scale and horror of the disaster did not become apparent until the morning when rescuers were finally able to enter the gallery staircase to

The Theatre Royal, Exeter. The auditorium after the fire, 1887. John Earl Collection.

find a seemingly never-ending tangle of burnt and asphyxiated bodies. In the evening a special public council meeting was convened by the Mayor, Alderman Burch to discuss the setting up of a relief fund. Captain Shaw, who happened to have arrived in Exeter on the day following the fire, on his way back from holiday in Spain, was invited to speak and he urged the setting up of a municipal fire service with all speed. The deputy chairman of the Theatre Company, the surgeon and city councillor Edward Domville, anxious to absolve the directors from any blame also spoke, declaring:

– 'They [the directors] thought they had done all that human skill could do to prevent such an accident ... and that for their own protection, they had chosen an Architect, who had special knowledge of the construction of such buildings and by whom the protection of the public would be adequately served.'[2]

In other words, the directors were not to blame for the disaster, but the advice from their chosen expert architect, however inconceivable the thought, might, after all, not have been entirely sound. It was a subtle and elegant betrayal of Phipps in tune with the general tenor of the first press reports, which, homing in on the high death toll on the gallery stairs, implied that the architect had much to answer for.

The Interview

Whether the proprietors telegraphed Phipps during the night of the fire is unclear and seems unlikely. Their public comments suggest that they were not, at that point, particularly anxious to secure his services for a rebuild, and, as far as is known, Phipps had no close friends in Exeter who might have informed him. Most probably news of the disaster reached him with the morning papers. Even the brief account in *The Times* (6 September) headed 'A Terrible Catastrophe' must have shaken him: 'There was but one gallery exit … the loss of life was appalling'. If he had opened the *Daily News*, the Liberal party's mouthpiece, he would have encountered a fuller description from their Exeter correspondent with his own name in the first paragraph: 'The Theatre was built to the latest improved design by Phipps' under the headline 'Supposed Loss of a Hundred Lives'. The *Morning Post* emphasised the panic in the gallery and the blocking of the one exit 'by a dense crowd of men and women wedged together, an almost immovable mass … burned to death despite the Fire Brigades heroic effort'.[3] The *Pall Mall* Gazette was even more damning:

'It [the theatre] seems to have been full of awkward

The Theatre Royal, Exeter. The third flight of the gallery stairs with pay box after the fire, 1887. John Earl Collection.

staircases and passages and cramped exits, which soon became blocked; and more deaths were due to such causes than to the fire itself. The gallery, which was crowded, had only one exit, which soon became blocked and the occupants of that part of the house were imprisoned in a furnace to be crushed, suffocated or burned to death.'[4]

It was not only the London press that carried reports of the horrors of the fire and the shortcomings of the building's design. Across the country provincial newspapers told the same story and no wonder; this was Britain's worst theatre fire. Every manager and theatre proprietor, inside and outside London, particularly those owning and working in a Phipps theatre, must have felt distinctly uncomfortable and likely to have made a mental note to steer clear of him in the future.

In Phipps's office the mood must have been very sombre indeed. This was not the kind of fire that called for the uncorking of champagne bottles. The professional reputation of the firm was at stake. The mere whiff of a suggestion that Phipps might have betrayed the trust of his client must be scotched at once. He could not let a fire at what had been a minor, but slightly troublesome provincial commission, ruin his reputation and livelihood let alone jeopardise his two current London theatre-contracts for the Lyric and the Shaftesbury Theatres. After the hectic pace of work during the first half of the 1880s the torrent of commissions had slowed to a quiet

'Bodies awaiting identification at the London Inn', 1887. John Earl Collection.

stream, with a major update for the Darlington Theatre at a cost of £4,500 completed in May 1887[5], while he had been snubbed over the, admittedly fairly minor, rebuild of his Northampton Opera House after a fire in the stage block in February 1887. That particular job had been handed to the local architect Charles Dorman who had acted as Phipps's assistant with the original building.[6] The public, though guarded, reference to 'faults' in the original design made by the popular Northampton manager I. Tarry, had also made a further, though slight, dent in his gold-plated reputation.[7] In Glasgow his position had already been challenged by the young and determined Frank Matcham who had designed the new Royalty Theatre in 1879, only to then rebuild Phipps's Philharmonic Theatre in London in 1882. Matcham was nearly twenty years his junior, but he was a sharp and aspiring young man and a potential usurper of Phipps's throne.

And there was his family to think of. The disaster at Exeter threatened to engulf his carefully nurtured reputation as a theatre specialist in ignominy and thus ending his career and bringing poverty and disgrace on his family. His eldest daughter, Ethel, had recently married a well-to do, young leather merchant, Edward England Pullman, from Chiswick, but he had two more daughters to find husbands for and he must not put their future at risk.[8] He must fight back with any means at his disposal; he had no other choice.

Fortunately for Phipps, the *Daily Telegraph* was more than willing to send a reporter for an in-depth interview on the day after the fire.[9] On home ground in his office, Phipps confidently opened the proceedings by declaring that 'any information on the construction of the theatre that I can give is at your disposal' before smartly trying to counteract any potentially awkward questions relating to the cause of the fire and the high death toll, by making it clear that as he had not yet been down to Exeter to inspect the remains and therefore 'deemed it inexpedient to pronounce any decided opinion as to the cause of the disastrous fire'. For a man given to decided opinions on any matter to do with theatre design this was a rash statement.

The journalist began innocently enough by asking when the theatre was built. Phipps seized the chance to spell out his credentials: 'In 1885 I was chosen as architect it being considered that my experience as architect of forty other theatres ... warranted my being able to superintend the erection the new theatre at Exeter'.

He then pulled out a roll of drawings from which he selected the ground plan of the Exeter theatre to demonstrate the peculiar site of the building: 'The theatre and the stage are built almost in a square ... and the large piece of land in front utilised as dress circle foyer, vestibule, staircase to gallery, second exit from pit, cloak room and portico.'

The interviewer then asked about the seating capacity. Phipps had his figures ready: 170 in the dress circle; 650 in the pit and stalls; 24 in the private boxes; 500 in the upper circle and gallery combined. Without it seems, showing his interviewer a plan of the design at the upper tier level, he quickly informed the reporter that this consisted of: 'A gallery, divided from the upper circle by a small barrier, three feet high, the front part holding 150, the back 350 ... [a barrier] over which anyone could easily climb.'

Whether he included himself in this reference to 'anyone', or indeed any members of the middle or upper classes is doubtful; the agile climbers he had in mind would have belonged to the humbler strata that usually occupied the gallery, labourers, shop assistants and servants, used to living in cramped conditions and running up and down steep and narrow stairs.

The reporter interjected a more pointed question: 'Now, with regard to the staircases, how were these situated?'

Phipps must have expected the question and planned his answer. It was only two years since he drew up the plans, too short a time to feign loss of memory over such details. After all, he had had quite a tussle with the magistrates over additional exit routes when he had showed them the plans before the building began. The second tier had been problematic from the start chiefly because of the row of six shops along Longbrook Street that his client wanted. Even Phipps, whose skill in manipulating tight spaces was legendary, had only found space for one gallery staircase and the magistrates had complained over the absence of a second exit for the galleryites They had insisted on a second exit from the pit too, but there he had managed to find a quick-fix solution by suggesting a new doorway and a short passage on the New North Road side beside the stalls, leading outside through a small enclosed courtyard (originally designed as a ventilation area) where he could erect concrete steps and a landing to connect with the single gallery exit. It was a convoluted arrangement, which would not have passed muster with the MBW, but it seemed to have satisfied the magistrates. Unfortunately, a second exit from the gallery was not so readily found. It would have to open into Longbrook Street, beside the pit entrance, and that would have meant losing a shop plus the dressing room above, alterations which required rather more thinking time and drawing effort than the few strokes with a pencil with which he had conjured up the second pit exit.

However, any such hazy memories were not for the *Telegraph* readers. He chose his words with the skill of a seasoned politician practised in the art of comprehensive evasion under the cloak of transparency:

'There was a separate staircase to each of the two divisions [the upper circle and the gallery] ... built entirely of concrete five feet wide and enclosed between brick walls, while the front portion of the gallery or upper circle had a corridor underneath communicating a both sides and at the back with the refreshment saloon, where there were four large casement windows opening on the portico'.

This appears to be an attempt on Phipps's part to upgrade the casement windows and their attendant portico to the status of emergency exit. In a pre-emptive strike he added: 'The staircase leading from it [the gallery] had no winding stairs and possessed a handrail on each side'.

His opponent, not entirely convinced, pressed on: 'Do you know of any awkward angles in the staircase?'

Phipps responded sharply: 'No I do not. In my opinion it was a very good staircase ... not a spiral one but square with several landings'.

He did not mention that the landings were made up several of tight right-angle turns, which could potentially become bottlenecks when overwhelmed by a rush of panic-stricken spectators. Instead, Phipps diverted attention away from his own potential failings to those of the galleryites: 'If they had jumped over the barrier, in all probability the loss of life would have been greatly lessened.'

The reporter, however, was reluctant to let go of the gallery stairs: 'Was the staircase quite clear?' he enquired, no doubt thinking of the pay box which several papers had mentioned as having caused an obstruction in the path of the running gallery audience. Phipps could not deny the presence of the pay box, but emphasised that the barriers should have been open and fastened to the walls.

The next question brought a change of tack: 'Is this the first theatre of your design that has burnt down?' Phipps became a little vague: 'No, two or three have been destroyed by fire.' He did not elaborate, leaving an opening for the inevitable follow-up on whether there had been any loss of life on these occasions? Phipps could not remember a single person being killed, but he did not mention that there had been no spectators present in the house during the earlier fires.

The interview moved on to the potential efficacy of iron curtains: 'If there had been an iron curtain at Exeter do you think it would have arrested the fire?' Phipps trod carefully: 'In all probability it would have saved the awful loss of life, but there is only one theatre in England ... in London provided with an iron curtain'.

He did not point out that this was in one of his theatres (the Prince's), nor that he had earlier installed a similar iron curtain at the Lyceum in Edinburgh, but moved quickly on to explain that: 'The expense of an iron curtain is, of course, very great and with the providing of this I have nothing to do, it rests with the management.'

This was a disingenuous statement on Phipps's part; the proprietors relied on his advice in this matter and for both the Lyceum and particularly the Prince's he had spent much time researching the latest developments in this field. Whether he had genuinely forgotten that the question of installing an iron curtain had been raised at the meeting in Exeter with the magistrates in October 1885, and that he had dismissed their idea out of hand, or merely chose not to remember this discussion, is a moot point.

Having divested himself of any blameworthiness over the lack of an iron curtain at Exeter, he decided to re-emphasise that only two of his 40-50 theatres had burnt down with no loss of life, before adding abruptly, and not to his own advantage: 'The greater part of the people killed at Exeter must have been suffocated in the rush downstairs from the gallery', thus bringing the interview back to fatal gallery stairs.

The journalist did not miss his cue: 'Which do you consider the most dangerous in a panic, going upstairs or going down?'

Phipps, perhaps because he had not fully comprehended that the gallery spectators at the front, in their rush up the steps to the exit at the back, had become wedged in a solid mass in the doorway, fell into the trap: 'It appears to me that a crowd has a much greater chance of getting away when proceeding upstairs ... Because, when proceeding down ... one is apt to stumble and fall, those behind only adding to the block, whereas the continual pushing up must clear the stairs by degrees'.

His adversary steamed on: 'How do you account for the rapidity with which the flames seem to have taken possession of the house?'

Momentarily Phipps became defensive: 'It is impossible for me to give any opinion', before suggesting that the actions of the stage crew and actors were largely to blame:

'Had the scene-dock door been closed, had the employees sought their exit by some other means, say the stage door, the curtain would have kept back the flames sufficiently long to enable the audience to quit the building'.

This was a desperate answer; he had no way of knowing whether his extravagant opinion had any basis in fact. Those reading the interview in the *Era* would have found a letter on the same page from the manager of the Romany Rye Company, Gilbert Elliott, refuting this allegation stating that 'the artists and others on the stage escaped through the stage door' and that ' the scene-dock door, which opened outwards, must have been burst open by the flames'.[10]

The reporter turned to the lighting of the playhouse: 'I suppose nothing but gas was used in this theatre?' Phipps felt himself on safer ground: 'No, and had the electric light been introduced this disaster would not have taken place', he added firmly.[1]

He did not reveal that Exeter had no electricity at the time – it was introduced in 1888 – nor that the cost of installing a generator in the basement as at the Prince's, would have been prohibitively expensive for his client. Seemingly at ease, Phipps launched into a description of the generous distribution of gaslights in the flies and their proximity to the scene-loft, filled with scenery: 'Almost as much as it would hold ... so there was plenty of material for the flames to feed upon once they had taken hold'.

This was another statement based on supposition, not a close inspection of the remains of the theatre, but he would have known that *Romany Rye* relied on a succession of rapid and breathtakingly complex scene changes for it popularity and that his opinion, therefore, would be hard to challenge.

A question concerning the placing of the dressing rooms followed, the answer to which gave Phipps an opportunity to accentuate his architectural skills: 'They were placed over a line of six shops, which ran outside the theatre in Longbrook Street ... and were separated from the shops by a fire-proof floor'. Furthermore they were reached by a separate staircase from any used in the theatre.

The interview was nearing its end and the reporter returned to the stage: 'With regard to the stage, now, what was the size of it?' Phipps's reply was prompt:'50 feet by 35 feet, ... really a very much larger stage than is usually to be found in provincial theatres of this size.' Determined, to the last, to put himself in the clear, if necessary by blaming others not present, Phipps added:

> 'The proscenium and the auditorium were quite distinct. As I have said before, if only an iron curtain had been in use, the flames would have been entirely shut off from the auditorium and been confined to the portion of the building where they broke out'.

Were the Exeter magistrates, who had been at the meeting with Phipps in 1885, to read this interview they might have been slightly surprised at Phipps's new-found missionary zeal regarding the efficacy of iron curtains, assuming they still had some recollection of that event. The chairman at the meeting, Horace P. Lloyd JP, certainly did, as Phipps would later discover.

For the time being Phipps could only hope that the interview would go some way towards stemming the torrent of criticism of his design that was flowing through the national press. The following day, even *The Times*, normally measured in it opinions, was blunt: 'The structure of the solitary staircase which formed the sole means of exit from the gallery will probably in no small degree explain the loss of life'.[12]

The Home Office

The morning after the fire the Secretary of State for the Home Department, Henry Matthews, was in a quandary. Before him lay a telegram from the Queen at Balmoral, who had earlier been telegraphed the dreadful news. Her Majesty is 'deeply shocked' and 'trusts enquiries will be made as to the cause', he read.[13] But what sort of enquiry? There would doubtless be further calls for such action in the press and from the House of Commons where he would have to make a statement that evening. There would be an inquest, of course, but might one of this magnitude be beyond the capabilities of a provincial coroner? The Government's Fire Inspector, Sir Charles Firth, was on his way to the scene, but he was no expert on theatres and his report was unlikely to pinpoint the cause of the fire or of the high death toll.

From the Home Secretary's perspective setting up an enquiry into a provincial theatre fire was not straightforward. He had no jurisdiction over provincial theatres nor was there any legal provision for a statutory court of enquiry into theatre accidents as there was for the railways and which had come into operation after the Tay Bridge Railway collapse in 1879 when 75 people were killed. That report, or rather two dissenting reports, had only recently landed on his desk and the whole wrangling procedure between the three technical experts involved had not been a good advertisement for examinations of this kind. Undecided he went to the House of Commons where the mood was sombre and the questions muted and predictable:

'Would steps be taken immediately to appoint Inspectors by and under the Home Office to inspect all places of amusement in the whole country?' And: 'Would an iron-screen now become a necessary fixture in all theatres?'

Matthews could only reply that such measures would require legislation adding, with uncharacteristic candour: 'The dreadful calamity at Exeter shows the necessity of legislation for Provincial theatres and the Government will give their attention to the subject'.[14]

The next day (Wednesday 7 September), Matthews received a letter from the Exeter coroner, Henry Hooper, informing him that he had decided to adjourn the inquest until the following Monday (11 September) to allow time for funerals to take place but also to give the Home Secretary time to arrange 'that some government official may be able to attend on behalf of the public'.[15] Matthews, himself a lawyer, discussed with his private secretary, G. Lushington, the possibility of sending a barrister to oversee the proceedings on behalf of the Home Office. Lushington duly wrote a 'Pressing' letter to Hooper asking if he would like the assistance of a barrister.[16]

There was a precedent for this; in 1883, after 197 children, aged between 7 and 11, died in a stampede from the gallery at Victoria Hall in Sunderland, the Home Office appointed Mr Hugh Shields, Q.C., to act as assessor for the Home Office at the inquest.[17] In this case, there had been no fire; the children had merely been to an afternoon performance of miscellaneous entertainment at the end of which they were invited onto the stage to receive a toy. There had been around 1000 children in the gallery, untroubled by much adult supervision, who naturally raced for the exit – there were two exits, but the second one was locked and had never been used – and the eager children soon fell over each other down the four flights of stairs with its sharp turns. The subsequent disaster was inevitable. In his Report, Shield blamed the loss of life largely on the inadequacy of the gallery exits.[18]

The following morning (8 September) Matthews received an unexpected letter from Captain Shaw, now back from Exeter at his headquarters at the Southwark Fire Brigade. Shaw offered 'to give any assistance to the Secretary of State which may be required', adding, temptingly, 'I will take all the trouble off your hands'.[19]

That Shaw should offer his assistance was hardly surprising, not least because he had already seen the burnt out-building for himself, but the offer to take 'all the trouble off the Home Secretary's hands suggests not only that he considered himself to be the best, but the only suitable person for the as yet unspecified task. Was the offer a straightforward act of genuine friendship? Possibly, but there is no clear evidence to suggest that the two men were particularly close. Was it, perhaps, a pre-emptive strike to prevent clever lawyers muscling in?

Shaw had much to gain professionally from acting as an official government representative at Exeter. It would allow him to make a thorough search of the ruins as well as to attend the inquest and possibly question the witnesses. He would be able to gather a mass of incontrovertible evidence, more than enough to back up his opinion on the inherent risk factors in English theatre design, to use as a battering ram with which to pressure reluctant theatre proprietors and architects to accept his recommendations instead of constantly challenging them. He might even convince the politicians of the need for more stringent regulation. Unhindered by eloquent lawyers, he could deliver a swift, straightforward report with clear recommendations and reaffirm his reputation as the country's most authoritative voice on matters of theatre safety. Professionally and personally, he would have much less to gain from a full public enquiry subsequent to the inquest. Such an enquiry, if given a sufficiently wide remit, would most likely get bogged down in a mire of rival opinions, rather like the MWB arbitration hearings, and worse, might stray into unhelpful territory such as the present state of fire precautions in London theatres over which he had not been able to exercise as much influence as he had hoped.

While Shaw's letter might have seemed like the answer to a prayer, Matthews did not immediately accept the offer. Instead the wavering Home Secretary wrote back asking Shaw whether he 'considered the rules laid down by the Metropolitan Board of Works on theatres adequate and if not what does he suggest?'[20] It was an interesting question which seems to imply that Matthews had considered the possibility that Phipps's design might be in some way to blame for the catastrophe. If Phipps really had followed the MBW rules, as he claimed, then clearly the rules were deficient, but if he had not, that was another matter altogether. As it happened, the MBW's days were numbered; it was about to be replaced by a new London County Council, and Shaw, perhaps for this reason, did not reply to the question. However, the same day (8 September) Matthews also despatched a note to the Hooper offering him a barrister to represent the people of Exeter.[21]

The following day, (Friday 9 September), Matthews received a telegram from Hooper asking 'for an independent experienced surveyor from a Government Department unconnected with the locality' to attend the inquest. Feelings were running high in Exeter and rumours of collusion between the Theatre Company, the architect and the magistrates were spreading among the shaken populace watching the seemingly never-ending stream of black hearses slowly winding their way through the streets. By then, it had become clear to Hooper that in this charged atmosphere, there was a desperate need for an objective assessment by a truly independent surveyor in order to enable both him and the jury to disentangle fact from opinion and to stem the incendiary rumour that the design and construction of the building had been chiefly responsible for the high death toll.

The request spurred Matthews into action. He would send Shaw. On the face of it the Fire Chief fitted Hooper's criteria perfectly. Indeed, there was no other obvious candidate who could boast of similar theatre surveying experience except Phipps. It probably did not occur to Matthews that Phipps's past public belittling of Shaw's safety recommendations in London might in any way influence the behaviour of these two men in the court room. On Sunday 10 September, Matthews wrote to Shaw requesting him to attend the inquest:

'... as a representative of the Home Office ... and to assist the Coroner in fully investigating the causes of the fire and of its rapid spread and fatal effects and to report ... whether this terrible disaster is to be ascribed to defects of construction, to negligence, to accident or to any combination of causes'.[22]

It was a remit that gave Shaw a slightly ambiguous role as assistant to the Coroner on the one hand and, on the other, as a one man enquiry team tasked with establishing the cause or causes that might have led to the this tragedy and to issue a full report thereon. Whether it actually gave him the right to question witnesses at the inquest or to seek to direct the proceedings is a moot point; he was representing the Home Office, but he was not a Queen's Counsel.

Shaw responded immediately: 'I will start for Exeter at once and I will do everything in my power to assist the Coroner and to carry out your instructions'. For this onerous task Shaw would receive a fee of 10 guineas a day plus travelling expenses.[23]

Before leaving, Shaw telegraphed the Devon Chief Constable to inform him that he had been appointed by the Home Secretary to act as 'Government Commissioner' at the inquest.[24]

Endnotes

1. 'Account of the destruction of the Exeter Theatre by fire on September 5th, 1887'/ compiled by F.S. Crouch, 1887, sxB/EXE/614.84/ACC, Local Studies Collection, Devon Heritage Centre. This is a 444 page Scrapbook of newspaper cuttings relating to the disaster.
2. F.S. Crouch, Scrapbook, p. 105. Cutting from *Exeter Evening Post*.
3. *Daily News*, 6 September 1887, p. 5, *Morning Post*, 6 September 1887, p. 5.
4. *Pall Mall Gazette*, 6 September 1887, p. 8.
5. *Northern Echo*, 30 May 1887, p. 3.
6. *Era*, 7 May 1887, p. 15.
7. *Era*, 19 February 1887, pp. 17-18.
8. The marriage took place in St Pancras Parish Church on 5 July 1887. Vol. 01B, page 125.
9. The interview was published in the *Daily Telegraph* on 7 September and later reprinted in other papers, including the *Era* (10 September, p. 15).
10. *Era*, 10 September 1887, p. 15.
11. Phipps's own home was, by this time, lit by electricity with the aid of an in-house gas engine maintained by his son Alwyn Rashleigh. *London Evening Standard*, 15 October, 1886.
13. NA, HO Memo on the Exeter Fire, B2074/4.
14. Hansard, HC Debate, 6 Sept. 1887, v. 320, cc. 1360-62.
15. NA, HO Memo, B2074/6.
16. Letter in Coroner's Paper's, Exeter Theatre Fire 5 September 1887. ECA, Devon Heritage Centre.
17. *Sheffield and Rotherham Independent*, 3 July, 1883, p. 2.
18. *Report of Hugh Shield Esq. Q.C. M.P., upon the Disaster at Sunderland on 16 June 1883*; Parliamentary Accounts and Papers 17, 1883, LIV, p. 3.
19. NA, HO Memo, B2074/9.
20. NA, HO Memo, B2074/10.
21. Letter in Coroner's Papers, ECA, Devon Heritage Centre.
22. Shaw's Report, printed 1888, p. A2.
23. NA, HO Memo, B2074/13 and 14.
24. Telegram in Coroner's Papers, ECA, Devon Heritage Centre.

12 THE INQUEST

The Coroner

The coroner, Henry W. Hooper (c.1818-1903), was an Exeter solicitor born and bred in the city and thoroughly familiar with its ways. On the afternoon of Tuesday 6 September Hooper empanelled a jury of 21 local men in the assembly room at Robert Pople's London Inn, where he normally conducted his inquests. Outside, the stable yard was filled with bodies, some intact, suffocated by the smoke and untouched by the flames, some only a heap of charred bones, guarded by policemen. Moving slowly in an orderly queue, distraught relatives and friends steeled themselves to try and identify family and friends, who had not been seen since they set off for the theatre, while Hooper issued burial orders. This grim business carried on through most of the following day until, late in the afternoon, at which point Hooper adjourned the inquest and led the jury across the square to inspect the remains of the theatre. Carefully picking their way through the burnt-out shell, the jurymen, determined to do all in their power to establish how such a disaster could have befallen their city, asked Hooper to issue an injunction preventing the theatre's owners from interfering with the building until after the inquest. It was a sensible request, which reflected the unease with which many Exonians regarded their political elite. As the *Western Times* (8 September) observed:

'[There is] a growing apprehension in the public mind that when the building of the Theatre was committed to a company of influential citizens too much was taken on Trust as to the security for the public safety ... and the proceedings of the composite characters of the directors must be fully investigated'.[1]

Hooper agreed, with the proviso that the city surveyor, Donald Cameron, could enter to shore up any walls in danger of imminent collapse and the rescue party could continue their search for corpses. He then adjourned the inquest a second time until Friday morning (9 September), when it would reconvene for the formal identification of any newly discovered bodies. The death toll, first announced in the press as around 100, had been mounting steadily through the days and Hooper's extant lists of the dead or missing eventually reached 180.[2] There may have been others who were never reported missing, and possibly some who took the opportunity to 'disappear' to start a new life elsewhere. The exact figure will never be known.

Immediately after the fire the magistrates sprang into action with unusual collective alacrity. On 6 September the magistrates' clerk, Isaac Pengelly, wrote to Hooper offering him the use of the Guildhall suggesting that its main hall would be a more fitting place for the occasion than the assembly room at the London Inn, where inquests wee traditionally held, and that it would allow greater public access.[3] This was a valid point.

The medieval hall, with its arched brace roof of darkened oak timbers and lit by a magnificent stained glass window, its walls covered with sumptuous Elizabethan oak panelling and with a sturdy oak gallery was, indeed, a more dignified setting with echoes of Westminster Hall, albeit on a more modest scale. Hooper, however, preferred his customary more informal territory. The jurymen, on the other hand, aware that the London Inn's initial role as a morgue, and its proximity to the burnt-out theatre had made it an emotionally charged space and thus, perhaps, less suitable for cool deliberation and questioning, persuaded Hooper to accept the offer. Any fears that Hooper might have harboured over witnesses or the jury being cowed by the medieval splendour of the Guildhall turned out to be groundless.

As for Phipps, desperate to attend the inquest, the medieval setting would most likely soothe his shattered nerves.

At 10 o'clock on Friday morning (9 September) a restless Phipps telegraphed Hooper: 'Sir, I am most anxious to give evidence. Will you kindly inform me when you will receive it so that I may be in attendance. Phipps. Architect.'[4]

Phipps seems to have feared that he might not be summoned and that he would thus be deprived of an opportunity to explain his design and defend his reputation on a public stage and later the same day wrote to Hooper confirming his telegraphic request.[5] The *Daily Telegraph* interview had failed to silence the growing chorus of critical voices in the London and provincial press condemning the single gallery exit and its convoluted construction. Indeed, the number of column inches devoted to the subject of theatre design and safety in general was overwhelming and Phipps must have felt the ground shifting under his feet. He needed to be heard.

Phipps need not have feared. Hooper, for his part, was determined to have as wide-ranging an enquiry as possible and had issued appeals for witnesses in the local press, on placards and through the town crier, who appears to have visited every street. A friend in Paignton, Gordon Campbell, provided him with brief summaries of inquest verdicts after mining accidents, railway disasters and gas works explosions, which, unhelpfully, revealed that the law was far from clear as to who bore the ultimate responsibility after major incidents where heavy loss of life was involved.[6] The Devon Chief Constable wrote and asked 'not to be called on Wednesday as he was busy that day', and the London engineer responsible for installing the hydrants wrote to point out that he 'had endeavoured to make known that the two Hydrants were inadequate, but could not obtain permission to install more'. Then there was the plastering contractor's letter (see Ch. 10) which the editor of the *Devon Evening Express* passed on to Hooper.

Hooper drew up lists of the order in which he intended to hear the witnesses, starting with those nearest the seat of the fire, i.e. 'People on Stage' followed by 'Orchestra', 'Pit Stall Attendants', Pit Stall Audience' and so on working his way through the auditorium up to the 'Gallery Audience', before taking 'Scientific evidence as to the construction of the theatre and licence and conditions and use of the building'.[7] To estimate an accurate time-table for such a hearing would have been impossible, and Phipps's and, indeed, the Chief Constable's request – the latter was not called – to be allocated a particular time seems rather presumptuous. Phipps, 'anxious to give evidence', travelled down to Exeter to attend the resumed inquest on Monday 12 September in the Guildhall accompanied by his lawyer, Mr Fladgate, one of London's leading solicitors and expert on all matters theatrical from the firm of Fladgate, Smith and Fladgate,

The Justices' Clerk, Horace Lloyd J.P. and the City Surveyor

By 10 o'clock in the morning of Monday 12 September the public gallery was filled to capacity with a stunned and quietly hostile crowd. The magistrates, seemingly anxious to exhibit a united and dignified public facade, took up their usual position on the dais opposite the gallery as if they were ready to question the witnesses themselves rather than be questioned. Indeed, the magistrates had opted not to be represented by legal counsel, a decision which would seem to suggest that they did not expect any awkward questions relating to the licensing of the theatre to arise, or that if such questions should occur, that they were under no obligation to answer them by virtue of their office.

Among other local dignitaries, who clearly expected to be called and arrived accompanied by lawyers were William H. Ellis, in his role as chairman of the Theatre Company rather than as a magistrate, assisted by his legal representative Mr Charles Roberts, and the Mayor A. Burch, accompanied by Mr Gidley who represented not only the Mayor but the citizens of Exeter. A further four lawyers completed the legal line-up, Mr E. Searle for some of the bereaved families, Messrs Friend and Beale who acted for the Romany Rye Company and Mr Sparkes for the manager of the Exeter Theatre Royal, Sidney Herberte-Basing.[8]

From Phipps's perspective Monday's hearing did not get off to a good start. Photographs of the burnt-out theatre, taken at Hooper's request by a local professional photographer, Owen Angel, were presented to the jury and Hooper outlined his intended order of witnesses, which suggested that Phipps might not be called upon for some time.[9] However, Hooper's grand plan immediately fell into disarray when it appeared that two key witnesses scheduled for that morning were missing. They were the stage manager of the Romany Rye company, Joseph, and the actor playing the chief villain, Fred Moulliott, who had been left in front of the back drop to amuse the audience while, unbeknown to him, a small fire in the flies transformed itself into an inferno. More fearful of losing their company's next engagement (at Portsmouth) than of disobliging the coroner, they had departed to borrow scenery and props for the following week. This was no easy task bearing in mind the quantities of complex sets needed for their production, but Hooper was unimpressed and the pair returned two days later.

Instead Hooper decided to begin, where he had originally intended to finish, with the licensing question and called Isaac Pengelly, the clerk to the justices. Pengelly's testimony, carefully worded and not straying outside the sparse notes in his minute book, revealed all too clearly, the vagueness of the 1843 Theatres Act in relation to the licensing of provincial theatres. There was scope for decisive intervention within the requirement to ensure 'decency and order', by robust and confident magistrates (as had lately been the case over exits at the Portsmouth Theatre Royal), if necessary with the aid of local bye-laws, but on the other hand, there was nothing in the Act that prevented a more laid-back approach by justices anxious, perhaps, not to offend local theatre proprietors. Thus, as theatre buildings became ever more complex constructions and therefore more difficult to grasp by laymen not well versed in interpreting building plans, the law, as it stood, was singularly unhelpful.

Hooper went straight to the heart of the matter: 'How did the justices satisfy themselves that the building was fit to be licensed? By inspecting the plans,' replied Pengelly. Hooper was not satisfied: 'Was it done by a professional man?' An obvious question, which immediately planted a doubt in everybody's mind as to the competence of the magistrates for such a task. 'By the justices', Pengelly retorted, adding, 'in the presence and with the assistance of the city surveyor Mr Cameron on 28 October 1885 and subsequently'. He omitted to mention that Phipps had also been present at this October meeting.[10] Indeed, the meagre minute entered by Pengelly in the Justices' Minute Book seems a remarkably sanitized version of the arguments:

> 'Application by Mr C.J. Phipps on behalf of the Exeter Theatre Company for the magistrates' approval of the proposed new building with reference to the licensing of it for stage plays. The plans were produced and explained, numerous apparent defects were discussed and Mr Phipps marked the improvements he would be prepared to effect and it being considered satisfactory, the magistrates intimated that if the theatre be erected precisely in accordance with the plans as amended there would be no objection to the granting of a licence.'[11]

Why Pengelly chose not to mention the discussion over the second exit is a mystery, unless he simply did not grasp its fundamental importance.

Surprisingly, the magistrates seem not to have taken much interest in the construction until almost a year later when the lessee, Sidney Herberte-Basing applied for a licence on 29 September 1886. This spurred them into action and on the following day they toured the building in the company of Cameron with Pengelly noting various changes that they wanted made including improvements in the sanitary arrangements.

The absence of a second gallery exit was not mentioned according to Pengelly.[12]

Step by step Pengelly disclosed, in as few words as possible, the nature of the subsequent inspections. The next one took place a week later, on 7 October 1886. This time Pengelly had notified Phipps of the date and time, but has also informed him that his presence was not necessary. Phipps, according to his later testimony, had responded by taking the first available train to Exeter, but by the time he arrived the magistrates were in the upper circle corridor more than half way through their inspection. They had pounced on him, wanting to know why there were no tanks and cisterns for the fire hydrants, as required by the MBW, at the same time dispatching Pengelly to fetch the Regulations. Phipps had pointed out that the hydrants were connected to the mains with one hydrant in the ground floor vestibule and the other, there were only two, on the prompt side of the stage. He was told to double the hose from 40 ft. to 80 ft.. According to Pengelly, the magistrates did not inspect the stage as the stage floor had not yet been laid (!) and did not venture up onto the fly galleries.[13] If they had done, they would have noticed the lack of a fire hydrant in the flies, which had actually been marked on the plan. They made a final inspection of sanitary arrangements on 12 October before Herberte-Basing was granted a temporary licence later that day.

When pressed by Hooper, Pengelly admitted that only one of the justices who finally granted the licence on 12 October1886 had actually been part of those who had inspected the building a few days earlier, on 7 October, when they 'had gone into every part of the house, including the gallery and the gallery stairs'. Pengelly could not say, however, if they had reported their findings to the magistrates who issued the licence, but he was quite clear on which alterations had been carried out and which ones had not been:

'All [the alterations] the justices had directed [on 28 October 1885] were carried out, but all their suggestions were not. One suggestion was of such a character that he [the architect] could not mark it on the plan without further consideration'.

According to Pengelly, the suggestion that had not been carried out was the additional exit for the gallery simply because 'the architect had satisfied the justices by pointing out that there was another means of escape over the three feet barrier, which divided it [the gallery] from the upper circle'. In reply to a question whether an iron curtain had been mentioned at this meeting, Pengelly squarely put the blame for its absence on Phipps: 'The architect said, in effect, that it would be practically of no use'.

Pengelly was followed by Horace C. Lloyd J.P., who had chaired that crucial meeting between Phipps and the magistrates on 28 October 1885. Lloyd presented a more detailed recollection of events than Pengelly, referring to the shortcomings in the plan and the magistrates' insistence on specific improvements. According to Lloyd, Phipps had 'attended on behalf of the Theatre Company ... and submitted plans with a view to obtain a licence'. There had been an 'animated' discussion over the number of exits: 'Exception was taken to inadequate exits from the pit ... from the stage generally ... to the mode in which doors opened and ... and to there being only one exit from the gallery'.

He was quite clear that there had been 'no approval of the plans at that meeting but an understanding that there would be no objection if the suggested alterations were made'. In a clear contradiction to Phipps's version in the *Daily Telegraph* interview on 7 September, and Pengelly's hazy memory, Lloyd added: 'One of those suggestions was for the provision of a second exit from the gallery. It was almost a *sine qua non*'.[14] He agreed that Phipps had raised objections to this suggestion on the grounds that 'a second gallery exit would require considerable structural reconstruction and that he needed time to consider. One of the justices suggested that an additional exit could be made into Longbrook Street'. Then Lloyd dropped a bombshell: 'The reply, and I am not prepared to say who made the reply, was that the rent of a shop was thereby lost'.[15] An audible gasp rose from the public gallery.

Assuming that Lloyd's memory was correct, one cannot help wondering who let slip this money-orientated response. It could have been any one of the magistrates with shares in the company; it could have been Pengelly, who did not even mention the discussion of the second exit in his minutes. It could conceivably have been Phipps, who understood the value of shops in theatres and who had already expressed his reluctance to fundamentally alter the plans, or possibly Ellis. The latter was, doubtless, under pressure from his fellow directors and shareholders to maximise income by all possible means. After all, the original prospectus had proposed a theatre with shops in order to attract investors. Both Ellis and Phipps would also have been mindful of the additional cost that a new gallery exit would bring. By the end of August 1885, the Theatre Company had only raised £322,[16] and Phipps must have been wondering whether his plans would ever get off the drawing board and into the hands of a builder. There was no incentive for him to spend more time and effort on this uncertain project, nor is Ellis likely to have been in a position to sanction further expense. Presumably the plans had been shown to and passed by his fellow directors, though there is no record of a meeting to this end. The company would have to borrow against capital to be raised in order to start building that year and its precarious financial situation might, partly, explain why Phipps, who was not averse to saving his clients money when necessary, was trying to wriggle out of incorporating a second gallery exit and circumnavigated the suggestion for the provision of an iron curtain.

Regarding the latter, Lloyd alleged that Phipps had argued that 'an iron curtain would obviate the necessity of increasing the modes of exit from the rear of the building as in the event of a fire in the body of the building, the iron curtain would give immediate relief to those engaged by the management'.

This appears to be a rather confused claim which laid Phipps open to a possible charge of professional incompetence and his lawyer swiftly intervened to ask whether any detailed minutes had been taken at this meeting. Lloyd had to admit that this had not been done, adding 'there ought to have been'.[17]

Phipps and Fladgate could allow themselves a quiet sigh of relief. Phipps would now be able to stick to the version of that fateful meeting, which he had given to the *Daily Telegraph,* secure in the knowledge that it could not be seriously challenged.

Lloyd was followed by the city surveyor, Donald Cameron, who held the original plans (now lost), in his hands. He revealed that the Streets Committee, set up under the Public Health Act of 1875, was primarily responsible for ensuring that all new buildings had an adequate water supply and a sufficient number of drains connected to the city's sewers, and that the committee had returned Phipps's first set of plans at the beginning of July purely because of unsatisfactory sanitary arrangements. Another sign of an over-hasty design process, perhaps.

Phipps did not quibble but amended the drawings as requested and returned them. At the second meeting the Streets Committee was unimpressed by the number of exits, and the absence of any estimate as to the number of spectators to be accommodated, which was unusual for Phipps. In the end, however, the committee concluded that it had no power to challenge these under the 1875 Public Health Act. It also persuaded itself that it was unable to enforce a local bye-law (no. 17), concerning adequate exits and entrances and ventilation in public buildings, as it did not, in their view, directly pertain to the 1875 Act. Exit routes for waste was a straightforward technical matter, but means of egress for unpredictable human beings were a different province altogether.

It is quite possible that someone on the Streets Committee communicated their concerns over exits and numbers privately to Ellis and that he in turn raised them with his fellow directors and with Phipps. Neither party wanted to lose momentum and Phipps might well have suggested a meeting with the magistrates to forestall any problems when it came to the official licence application. A meeting of this nature, assuming agreement was reached, would, in effect, transfer responsibility for the soundness of the design onto the magistrates. Phipps, who had little respect for local justices – whether this included Ellis is a moot point – had doubtlessly assured his client that he would be able to convince those attending this informal gathering of the merits of the plan as it stood. However, if Horace Lloyd is to be believed, the Exeter justices were not as easily won over as Phipps had maintained in his interview.

Cameron explained that he had inspected the construction site from time to time and had noticed, on one occasion, 'that a door was open on the first landing of the gallery stairs'. It was not on the plan but he had been told that it was for the management and would be locked:

'I did not then perceive the importance of the door and that persons escaping from the gallery might be met at that door by flames from the stage. It appeared that flames swept through this passage without it being on fire ... it acted as a flue.'[18]

By the end of Monday's hearing Hooper and Shaw must have been uncomfortably aware that this was far from a straightforward inquest. While the immediate cause of the fire would probably be possible to establish with some accuracy, the reasons why so many people had perished seemed to be rooted in a trail of false assumptions and incomplete information relating particularly to the licensing process. Disentangling evidence of this kind was a delicate matter and both Hopper and Shaw agreed that the justices' lack of a legal representative was an obstacle to any deeper probing on this vital subject. The following day, therefore, Hooper intimated to the Mayor that it might be desirable for the licensing magistrates to be legally represented.[19]

Cameron continued his testimony through most of Tuesday, when he revealed firstly, that no-one from the Streets Committee had actually visited the theatre during its

Captain E. M. Shaw. Author's Collection.

construction, secondly, that he had been under the impression that there would be an iron curtain and thirdly, that he had examined the theatre with the licensing magistrates on 7 October 1886 before the license was granted but merely in his capacity as 'custodian of the plans'.[20] As an employee of the City Council he could merely act on instructions, not on his own initiative. When he tried to show the justices that the alterations on the plans had been carried out he was told 'he was going beyond his province'.[21] During the visit with the magistrates he found that two openings from the orchestra pit to the area below stage did not have iron doors as they should have done. The question of a second gallery 'had not arisen at all'.

At the end of the day, Pengelly was recalled and disclosed that he had personally handed a copy of the MBW Regulations to the Secretary of the Theatre Company in July 1886, 'with the rules to be observed ticked in black ink'.[22] Whether Pengelly had discussed the marked rules with the magistrates or acted entirely on his own initiative is unclear. Equally, whether he had intended his marked copy solely for the directors of the Theatre Company as an *aide memoire*, or suggested they send it to Phipps to make him aware that the justices were cognizant of the MBW stipulations and would expect them to be adhered to even though they did not legally cover provincial theatres, remains an open question.

On the Wednesday morning (14 September), with the public gallery filled to capacity, the Mayor formally addressed the coroner regarding the desirability of the licensing magistrates being represented'.[23] He had had no time to speak to the justices but he could say that they wished:

'That this enquiry should be of the most thorough and searching character and would give the Coroner every assistance in their power ... and that by sending their clerk Mr Pengelly there to give evidence they were doing the best they could ... as [he] knew more of the whole proceedings than any of the magistrates seeing that the attendance at the various meetings on the subject was not always the same.'

As for the justices who actually signed the licence:

'He would say that they might have acted on the resolution come to by the magistrates on October 7. He mentioned this to show that the evidence of the magistrates might not be as important as the Court imagined.'

It was a curious statement, implying that the mayor felt quite at liberty to tell the Coroner's Court, that he knew better than the coroner what kind of evidence was important and should be pursued, and which was not. It bordered on the contemptuous and must have raised further suspicions in the mind of the jurors and the public over the nature of the magistrates' involvement from start to finish. Hooper and Shaw were unimpressed; to them the justices' evidence was of the utmost importance as Hooper made clear:

'It was a question of whether due care and caution were exercised before the licence was granted. Questions of importance were likely to arise on that point, and it would possibly shorten the inquiry if the magistrates were represented.'

His remark was not quite an accusation but it punctured the Mayor's assumption that the justices had no case to answer, and he agreed to consult his colleagues with all speed.

Much of the rest of the day was taken up by witnesses from the Romany Rye Company. Mr Graham, the stage manager for the company, who agreed that he was not disappointed by the stage construction or 'mechanical arrangements' in Exeter, on the other hand he did not express any admiration for them. He did not think the scene doors were opened after the fire broke out 'on account of the properties piled up against them'.

The scenic artist Charles Leigh was less complimentary about the stage, which he considered 'dangerous on account of the great heat and insufficient ventilation.' He also condemned the exit from the stage as being dangerous because it consisted of two doors, one a little way behind the other and as they opened in opposite directions they might jam in the form of a 'V' if opened together.

At the opening of Thursday's hearing the Mayor reported on his meeting with the justices 'which was largely attended'. They had reaffirmed their previous decision not to be represented by counsel on the grounds that 'the justices cannot recognise the Coroner's Court as the tribunal to say whether rightly or wrongly they exercised their discretion in granting the licence'.[24]

This collective expression of hubristic stubbornness did not impress either the jury or Hooper, but the latter, anxious to get ahead with the inquest, reluctantly accepted their decision. Clearly, the justices did not wish to reveal the extent of their confused procedure with regard the whole licensing business to their fellow Exonians let alone have it dissected in the national press. And then there was the question of personal loyalty to Ellis, whose dual role as magistrate and chairman of the Theatre Company left him open to accusations of a conflict of interest and undue influence over the granting of the licence. The reputation of their office was at stake.

Hooper briskly proceeded to call the limelights manager, who revealed that he had been summoned to a small fire in the fourth batten at 10.20 PM when the hose was already in action. He had been thrown by an explosion and escaped over the orchestra barrier where the piano was already burning. According to the musical director the act drop bulged out only one and a half minutes after it fell by which time 'below stage was like a furnace'.

The last witness that day was the money-taker for the gallery, James Coombes. On the fateful night the gallery was barely half full. He had sold 192 tickets, though 'the greatest number he had known in the gallery was 442'.

The Architect

The following day, Friday 16 September, further revelations regarding the inadequacy of the gallery exit emerged from the check taker John Howard, who, stationed at the top of the gallery stairs next to his wooden box, collected the metal tokens that the galleryites had received at the pay box in return for their money. Unlike the pay box, the check-box was not a permanent fixture, but the Howard claimed he had not been instructed by the management to remove it once everybody was in. As people began leaving the gallery, he went to his box to give them the checks (in case they wanted to return later on):

'They were forcing their way out' so fast that one person fell over. He was himself swept up by the rushing crowd and 'did not believe his feet touched a step until he reached the bottom'.[25]

Captain Shaw then rose to criticise the magistrates for refusing to answer questions, particularly as he wanted to establish whether, in their view, Phipps had followed the MBW Regulations. This was a question that the Home Secretary had specifically asked in his first response to Shaw's offer to investigate the fire, and to which Shaw had not replied. Now, when in a position to gather some useful evidence on which to base an answer to this pertinent question, he unexpectedly found himself thwarted by posse of provincial of magistrates who had taken refuge behind a vow of silence:

'I would like to express my deep regret that the authority which appeared to exist in the city for the protection of life in theatres has not thought fit to be represented.' Nevertheless: 'I now propose to place these regulations in the hands of witnesses and ask if [they] had been attended to.'[26]

In the absence of the magistrates Shaw had to make do with Pengelly and Cameron. The former merely repeated his earlier statements that Phipps had returned the MBW Regulations to him assuring him they would be observed, but he added that he thought that a similar assurance hade been given to the magistrates on their first visit to the theatre on 30 September 1886. The latter assertion elicited a swift response from Phipps's lawyer, who stated that his client had been in London on that day.

Cameron was more forthcoming. The proscenium walls were mainly 9 inches thick, not 13 inches as required by the MBW. The staircases and passages were not all of fire resisting material (Reg. 5) and passages from the dress circle to the stalls were only 3 ft. wide, not the required 4 ft. 6 in., and the same applied to the upper circle passages. The scene drop was not of fire-proof construction (Reg. 12). He also reaffirmed that he had accompanied the magistrates on their inspection immediately prior to granting the licence, but that the justices had not really checked the regulations against the building.[27]

Shaw had no further questions, but added pointedly: 'Had the magistrates, who were *prima facie* responsible been represented by counsel they might have gone further into details than was at present possible.'[28]

Judging by this comment, it would seem that Shaw, half way through the inquiry, far from keeping an open mind, had already decided where the real blame lay for the disaster: It was the justices' failure to identify the flaws in the plans that had been the primary cause of the scale of the disaster, rather than the architect's failure to produce a good design in the first place.

At last, Phipps was allowed to take the stand, but before he did, Shaw stood up to clarify Phipps's position:

'It must be quite understood that Mr Phipps was examined for the sake of his own personal reputation and to assist the jury and not for the purpose of shielding any authority not represented'.[29]

Why Shaw felt the need to introduce Phipps in this way is unclear. Was it merely an oblique assault on the magistrates? Or was he really trying to smooth his old adversary's path through an emotionally charged inquest?

Phipps had prepared himself well, even to the extent of bringing with him plans of a London theatre for which he had constructed staircases and passages in a similar way to those at Exeter and which was licensed by the Lord Chamberlain.[30] Phipps refused to name the theatre, but both the Vaudeville and Sadler's Wells would have fitted the bill. If Shaw had been so inclined, he could have challenged this dubious evidence as he and his assistants had examined the London theatres minutely on behalf of the MBW, but he was not skilled in circuitous arguments and could not risk Phipps or his advocate, getting the better of him in an undignified argument over what constituted acceptable safety standards in London. Shaw knew only too well that Phipps had never hesitated to challenge his safety recommendations in the past, and even his competence in that damning phrase 'Captain Shaw, not being a practical Surveyor ...', when he had challenged Shaw's 1882 Report on the parlous state of the Vaudeville Theatre in London.[31]

Bringing plans of a London theatre into the court room had been a gamble, but Shaw, anxious to keep the inquest short, did not rise to Phipps's challenge. With the magistrates having more or less ruled themselves out of the proceedings, Phipps could confidently assume that his own version of their mutual encounters was unlikely to be seriously questioned. Accordingly, and he launched into his prepared statement recounting how he had been approached by the Exeter Theatre Company in the early part of 1885, he had received 'verbal instructions to design a theatre', had duly prepared his plans and sent them to the City Surveyor in July 1885. Interestingly, he did not mention any discussion between himself and his client about the plans before he sent them to Cameron. Later in the summer Cameron had called on him in London and '[he] was given to understand that the Town Council, as the Urban Sanitary Authority, had passed the plans'.[32]

Phipps then claimed that he had suggested to his client 'that it would be more courteous to the magistrates to ask them to look at the plans before a brick was put in the ground' and a private meeting took place on 28 October 1885. For this he had prepared a copy of the plans, which he now held in his hand. The original plans and stalls exit and that 'the question of the gallery was discussed at great length'. He had pointed out that the gallery was one floor, which he proposed to divide by a low partition; the front part would be designated the upper circle and the back part would constitute the gallery before declaring:

'To each of these parts was a separate exit, which was in strict accordance with the rules of the Lord Chamberlain and I also said that the plans carried out all the essential points of the Board of Work rules.'[33]

Since the Lord Chamberlain's structural requirements tended to fluctuate from theatre to theatre and were not applicable outside London, Phipps was on pretty safe ground here, and he was careful to say that his plans merely carried out the *essential* points of the MBW rules, based, presumably, on his own judgment. He then claimed that the magistrates had said that 'they would be satisfied if the two alterations already suggested', that is those relating to the pit and stalls, were carried out, which was quite contrary to Horace Lloyd's claim.

As for the breaches of the MBW Regulations which Cameron had enumerated, Phipps justified his non-compliance with the rules on the grounds that he had built theatres in London with 9-inch instead of 13-inch thick proscenium walls and with passages and stairs no wider than those at Exeter with no objections raised by the authorities, claiming, in the same breath, that two doors under the stage 'was sometimes allowed'. Interestingly, no one in the court room, not even Shaw, felt moved to point out that this oversight by metropolitan authorities was no excuse for perpetrating bad building practice on unsuspecting provincial magistrates and audiences.

According to his statement, Phipps did not visit Exeter again after 28 October 1885 until 19 July 1886, a period of nearly 10 months, by which time 'the building had advanced a great deal'. Clearly he had forgotten the foundation-stone ceremony and the subsequent luncheon on 13 May 1885, which the justices and, in particular Ellis, presumably still remembered, but the latter refrained from challenging Phipps's memory.

Such a long absence from a building project by its architect is by any standards extraordinary even allowing for his preoccupation with Leinster Hall, and hardly commensurate with a Fellow of the RIBA. Even more surprising is Phipps's revelation that he only consulted his clerk of works, William Browne once over the arrangement of the gallery staircase.[34]

His statement completed, Phipps declared that 'he should be happy to answer any questions'. The jurors, clearly troubled by the design of the gallery stairs, did not hesitate: 'Do you consider that with the outlay of a couple of thousand pounds the place would have been rendered safer?'

– 'I do not', Phipps replied firmly.

This was a rash answer; clearly at odds with his categorical statement in the *Daily Telegraph* interview that an iron curtain would, doubtlessly, have saved lives.

– 'Did you assume that the audience could make their escape over the barrier in the stairs?'

– 'Certainly I did', declared Phipps. He paused: 'I did not reckon for the smoke'.

This was a remarkable admission of failure on his part. Whether he really was completely ignorant of the dangers of smoke inhalation or was aware but had simply forgotten to take this crucial issue into account, we will probably never know. Either way, 'not reckoning for the smoke' turned out to have been a serious error with dire consequences.

The jury then asked if Phipps had designed the post in the gallery stairs. Yes, he had in order 'to steady the stream going downstairs as well as regulating the entering stream'.[35]

The jurors, determined to plumb the depths of Phipps's thinking were not satisfied:

– 'Did you ever say that the rent of a shop would be lost by having a second exit into Longbrook Street?'

– 'I have never said anything of the sort,' he retorted.[36]

– 'Were the staircases in the gallery in accordance with your plan?'

– 'Yes, exactly so'.

– 'Have you ever recommended an iron curtain?'

– 'I have not.'

– 'You consider the theatre was protected against fire?'

– 'I consider it was a safe theatre'.

– 'Do you think an iron curtain would save the audience for any length of time?'

– 'That depends on the construction of the curtain.'

– 'Did you ever suggest a second exit from the gallery?'

– 'I did not; it was suggested to me by the magistrates'.[37]

Mr Searle, appearing for some of the victim's families, then did his best to pierce Phipps's hubris, by informing the court that the Plymouth Theatre Royal, designed by Phipps, had two gallery exits, 'one on each side, and one was entirely free from any sort of door until it got to the street, [while] the other passage went direct out into the street'. Turning to Phipps he bluntly asked: 'What is your object for constructing this theatre different from that one?

It was an obvious and fundamental question, one that anyone in Exeter, who knew both playhouses, and those of Phipps's architectural colleagues familiar with his best theatre designs, must have been asking themselves. It put Phipps on the spot, but he was saved by Hooper, who briskly intervened: 'This is going too far', and by his lawyer, Mr Fladgate's interjection: 'That is wide off the mark'.

Phipps did not attempt to answer the question, but if he had, he might have argued that a building is as good as its brief. For the Exeter theatre the brief seems to have been both vague and minimalist with no extant evidence of close involvement of the client through the planning and building process beyond the meeting in October 1885. By contrast, in Plymouth, the lessee and manager had clear and high expectations, as did the owner, Plymouth City Council, and Phipps rose to the occasion.

Searle pressed and asked about provision for escape from the flies. 'One door from the "flies" on the prompt side', Phipps replied, continuing:

> 'As a matter of fact, there was a window from which a person would have had to drop seven feet .It was not very often that there were two exits from the "flies" in a theatre. A ladder on one side was the usual'.

Mr Beale, acting for the Romany Rye Company, queried why the hydrant in the lower fly gallery had never been installed though it was marked on the plan. Phipps's reply was, by any standards, astonishing. He had never intended to have hydrant there and 'he did not know how it came to be shown on the plans at all!'.[38]

In response to a question by Mr Roberts, acting for the owners, Phipps claimed that 'it had never been intended from the outset that the Theatre should occupy more than the land it now stood on', but that the vendor had refused to sell unless the Theatre Company bought the whole site. Whether this was really the case is now impossible to verify, but one is left wondering why Phipps then chose a site that was larger than Ellis and his directors actually wanted.

As the day's proceeding drew to a close yet another Mr Glanville pointedly asked: 'In designing a theatre do you take into consideration panic and fire?' Phipps replied: 'Always thinking about it; hardly know how to prevent it'.

The answer has a slightly flippant ring to it, but Mr Glanville was not put off. Clearly of the view that the design of the Exeter gallery stairs had been more likely to increase panic than prevent it, succinctly summarized the complex structure of the gallery staircase, starting from the top with the seven steps down to a right-angle turn, followed by fifteen steps to the pay office and the barrier, before another complete turn round followed by seven steps to the door leading into the circle, and another turn followed by another fifteen further steps to the street door, before bluntly asking: 'As an expert do you think this is the right exit in case of fire?'

Phipps sidestepped the question: 'I think it was a very good staircase'.

Endnotes

1. 'Account of the destruction of the Exeter Theatre by fire on September 5th 1887', compiled by F.S. Crouch, 1887, p. 105. Local Studies Collection, Devon Heritage Centre.
2. Coroner's Papers, Exeter Fire 5 September 1887, ECA, Devon Heritage Centre.
3. Letter in Coroner's Papers, ECA, Devon Heritage Centre.
4. Coroner's Papers, ECA, Devon Heritage Centre.
5. Letter in Coroner's Papers, ECA, Devon Heritage Centre.
6. Coroner's Papers, ECA, Devon Heritage Centre.
7. Coroner's Papers, ECA, Devon Heritage Centre.
8. *Era*, 17 September 1887, p. 15.
9. Photos now in Coroner's Papers, ECA, Devon Heritage Centre.
10. Inquest evidence, p. 40. Coroner's papers, ECA, Devon Heritage Centre.
11. Justices' Minute Book 1885 .ECA, Devon Heritage Centre. Cited in D. Anderson, *The Exeter Theatre Fire*, ETP, 2002, p. 29.
12. Inquest evidence, p. 42, Coroner's Papers, ECA, Devon Heritage Centre.
13. Inquest evidence, p. 49, (Pengelly) and p. 137 (Phipps)
14. *Era*, 17 September 1887, p. 1.
15. F.S. Crouch, 'Account', 1887, p. 335.
16. D. Anderson, *The Exeter Theatre Fire*, ETP, 2002, p. 171, citing the company returns for 24 August 1885.
17. Inquest evidence, p. 54, Coroner's Papers, ECA Devon Heritage Centre.
18. *Era*, 17 September 1887, p. 15.
19. Coroner's Papers, ECA, Devon Heritage Centre.
20. *Era*, 17 September 1887, p. 15.
21. F.S. Crouch, 'Account', p. 336, Local Studies Collection, Devon Heritage Centre.
22. Inquest Evidence, pp. 97-98. Coroner's Papers, ECA, F.S. Crouch 'Account… p. 337, Local Studies Collection, Devon Heritage Centre.
23. *The Times*, 15 September 1887, p. 5
24. Letter read out in court by the Mayor. Coroner's Papers, ECA, Devon Heritage Centre.
25. John Howard, check taker. *The Times*, 17 September 1887, p. 7
26. Captain Shaw. *The Times*, 17 Sept. 1887, p. 7.
27. D. Cameron. *Exeter Evening Post*, 17 Sept. 1887, p. 7.
28. *The Times*, 17 Sept. 1887, p. 7.
29. Newspaper cutting, Coroner's Papers. ECA, Devon Heritage Centre.
30. *Exeter Evening Post*, 17 Sept. 1887, p. 7.

31 C. J. Phipps, *Observations on the report of Captain Shaw on the Vaudeville Theatre*, 5 May 1882, p. 2.
32 Verbatim report on the Inquest, *Exeter Evening Post*, 17 September, 1887, p. 7.
33 *Exeter Evening Post*, 17/9/1887, p. 7.
34 Answer to question by Mr Sparkes appearing for Herberte-Basing. *Exeter Evening Post*, 17/9/1887, p. 7
35 Inquest Evidence, p. 141, Coroner's Papers, ECA, Devon Heritage Centre.
36 *Era*, 24 Sept. 1887, p. 15.
37 *Exeter Evening Post*, 17 Sept. 1887, p. 7.
38 Inquest Evidence, p. 142, Coroner's Papers, ECA, Devon heritage Centre.

13 THE VERDICT

When the inquest resumed on Monday 19 September, Hooper, who was reaching the end of his list of witnesses, announced that once all the evidence that he wished to submit before the jury had been heard, he would adjourn the inquest for one day before summing up, during which he would be prepared to hear any fresh evidence that anyone might wish to offer.[1] One of the jurors suggested that the clerk of works should be called, but his request was immediately dismissed by Shaw as 'being quite unnecessary, the building having passed out of the hands of the contractors', adding, rather high-handedly, that: 'He was quite satisfied with the evidence before the Court'.

It is doubtful whether Shaw had the legal authority to obstruct the juror's request in this manner, but Hooper chose not to overrule Shaw, perhaps unsure of his own authority in relation to a Government Commissioner. As for the motivation behind Shaw's intervention, one is left wondering whether he had, by now, decided with whom the responsibility for the scale of the disaster lay and was therefore anxious to get back to London to write his report while his conclusions were still clear in his mind. Calling the clerk of works might prolong the proceedings considerably as his statements would most likely reveal more of Phipps's involvement (or lack of) in the construction process, thus giving rise to further questions by lawyers and jurors, and delay his report further. He had, after all, vowed to save the Home Secretary trouble, and to Shaw, the production of a speedy, straightforward report probably seemed the way to fulfil this promise.

Instead, the city surveyor, Douglas Cameron, was called yet again, this time to explain his own actions on the night of the fire. He had been summoned at 10.35 PM and when he reached the theatre he saw dresses and props being thrown from windows in Longbrook Street. Every window in New North Road was dark and the fire-escape was in position by the window opposite the gallery pay-box. The fire officer who went up could only see a heap of bodies on the stairs. Rescuers forced the exit door open and rushed in while the fire hose was directed into the gallery staircase to protect them while he mounted a ladder raised against a window above the porch. With the aid of a sailor who had followed him up, the two men managed to help several people to escape through the window. He estimated that the victims were at least 23 feet from any flame, yet their clothes were badly singed.

In a response to a question from Shaw, Cameron reiterated that he knew about the management door and an additional door from the dress circle passage into the gallery stairs. He also agreed that if these doors had not been there or had, at least, been closed the smoke could only have reached the gallery stairs from the pit, which would have taken longer.

While this was a vary valid point, it seems that the smoke had risen with remarkable speed to the top of the gallery to begin with and that, consequently it would have found its way down the gallery stairs as soon as the exit door was opened although more slowly.

The lessee and manager, Sidney Herberte-Basing was the next witness. With the aid of a loan from his aunt he had set himself up as an actor/manager and when he applied for the lease in January 1886, he already ran five different companies in the West Country from Falmouth to Weston-Super-Mare. This looked impressive on paper and the Exeter directors, who had only had one other applicant for the lease, accepted his offer.[2] He attended the laying of the Foundations stone on 12 May 1886, the excavations for the pit (12 feet under ground) and the cellars for the shops having taken longer than expected, and he returned during August and September to 'see how building progressed.'[3] Questioned on the means of exit, he praised the pit design which enabled 600 spectators to be evacuated in three minutes through the two exits. This might have been an exaggeration, but if it was correct, the pit's efficient means of egress was due to the magistrates' insistence on a second pit exit.

The speedy exit from the pit was not matched elsewhere. The clearing of the 151 spectators in the dress circle he estimated took around five minutes, but it took twice that long to evacuate the 95 people in the upper circle as there was no passage down the middle. In that context the estimated 8 minutes to clear the 400 people in the gallery, even without a passage down the middle, seems remarkable.[4]

When asked about the pay box arrangements on the gallery stairs, which Herberte-Basing must surely have discussed with Phipps, he maintained that he did not know when the post was placed there. This seems highly unlikely.

Regarding the siting of the check box, Herberte-Basing claimed 'it was there because it was necessary'. He did not deny that structural alterations had been made after the licence was granted without consulting the magistrates, but they had taken place before the clerk of works left, and he confidently asserted that 'everything had been passed as satisfactory' before Phipps finally issued his certificate of completion. And, yes there had been 'a trivial fire in the flies' once before, but he considered the Exeter Theatre Royal far safer than some theatres he had been in, which was probably true.

Herberte-Basing was followed by his deputy manager, Mr W.A. Buckstone, who had spent his last minutes in the building desperately running round trying to make sure that all the spectators got out. He had been behind the dress circle when he heard the cry 'Fire!' and had collided with three girls who had come through the iron pass door, the flames close behind them, into the side passage beside the private boxes. He banged the door shut and led the girls to safety.[5] He then rushed to the main foyer in the front to turn on the hose, which he left in charge of a policeman, raced around to the bottom of the gallery stairs and shouted up, but got no answer so assumed the gallery was cleared. Fearing that the 400 people in the pit might be stuck, he ran round there but found it empty with the stage 'all ablaze'. To make sure, he decided to check the pit refreshment room where he found half a dozen gentlemen calmly finishing their drinks with the barman relaxing in his shirtsleeves, all blissfully unaware of their perilous situation, and he 'shouted at them to get out'.[6]

Two more statements followed, one from a porter, who had helped to carry out bodies from the gallery stairs, prompting Hooper to comment that he deserved the thanks of his fellow citizens. Indeed, the recollection of the many spontaneous and selfless acts of heroism from ordinary people was a fitting note on which to end the hearing of witnesses.

No new witnesses approached the coroner during the Tuesday and on Wednesday morning at 11 o'clock Hooper delivered his summing up. The Guildhall was packed and among those present were a number of the magistrates, several directors of the theatre company, Herberte-Basing and Phipps.

Hooper began by stating that he thought the evidence showed very clearly that the fire had started above the stage and that 'some mistake appeared to have occurred in the shifting of the scenes'.[7] 'It was', he said, 'for the jury to say whether this mistake had anything to do with the fire', adding that, in his opinion, the difficulties in staging a new piece for the first time was an adequate explanation.

All the witnesses had agreed on the time and place of the outbreak of the fire and on the rapidity with which the flames spread. The question for the jury, however, would be: 'To consider whether the rapid spread of the flames was due to any carelessness or the absence of proper means for the extinction of fire'.

On this point the evidence had been contradictory, and Hooper reminded the jury of the evidence of Mr Sidney, the scenic artist, who did not know whether the hose on stage was in the charge of any particular person, if it had ever been used in a practice, and, furthermore, he had never seen a hydrant at gallery level. He had only seen a small hose 'like a garden hose' connected to a tap in the flies, while a newly employed flyman claimed to have seen neither a hose of any description nor any pails of water.

Hooper then dwelt at great length on the duty of the licensing magistrates and the powers vested in them for enforcing what they deemed necessary for the security of life. He must have been acutely aware, in common with most, if not all of the jurymen, that the social pressures on the magistrates to grant a licence would have been considerable. To have refused to license the theatre once the building was nearing completion, on the grounds that a second exit from the gallery had not been added, or for any other structural reason, would have caused a major scandal tarnishing Ellis's reputation and bringing the financial viability of the theatre company and their agreement with Herberte-Basing into question. The temptation for the magistrates to turn a blind eye during their ocular inspections of the theatre must have been overwhelming at times, and Hooper, mindful that justice must be seen to be done and that the jurors might still have doubts concerning their power of jurisdiction over the magistrates, added:

> 'Without attributing to the magistrates any disposition to evade their responsibility, I cannot agree with their contention that they are not amenable in the Coroner's Court for any negligence that might be proved against them.'

Having almost, but not quite, laid a charge of negligence against the justices,

Hooper proceeded to take a more lenient view of Phipps: 'I am satisfied with the evidence as to the gallery stairs being well constructed. The angles were calculated to relieve pressure to make the exit more secure.'

It is difficult to find any supporting evidence among the witness statements for this opinion, apart from Phipps's retort 'I think it is a very good staircase'. Given the cramped space that Phipps had allowed himself for the gallery stairs, he had, indeed, managed to produce a satisfactory design from the management point of view, if not for the end user, with sharp angles calculated to prevent any potential rush past the pay box up the stairs, angles, which, in turn, would also prevent too rapid an exit. It was probably no worse than many gallery exits in other provincial theatres. Nevertheless, for an architect, who claimed to be always thinking about panic, it was a poor design, the liberal use of fire resisting materials not withstanding. However, Hooper's apparent satisfaction with the construction of the gallery staircase went only so far as he continued:

'The questions for the jury are whether this single exit was sufficient and satisfactory means of egress for 400 people, whether or not loss of life was augmented by the obstructions placed there and by the door through which the smoke found its way so rapidly as to make the staircase impassable.'

Hooper then moved on to absolve the owners from any blame over the theatre's inadequate safety and fire prevention measures, asserting that they 'had done all in their power' on the question of responsibility for the security which the building afforded and the architect had given an assurance that the MBW regulations had been complied with. Quite how he had come to this conclusion is unclear, but he might have felt that it was not within his remit to grapple with the, often slippery, legal responsibilities, of property owners.

Turning to Phipps's statement that the reasons the MBW regulations had not been fully complied with in practice, was simply because they were not binding outside London, Hooper agreed that his was the case, before reminding the jury that Phipps had also claimed that the irregularities referred to at Exeter were acceptable in some London theatres, but he did not offer an opinion on the veracity of this part of Phipps's evidence. He then recalled Phipps's statements that he thought that the theatre was safe 'from a structural pint of view and that the means of escape from the gallery through the upper circle did away with the necessity for a second exit, adding:' It is for the jury ... to form their own opinion on these points'.

Finally, the coroner, perhaps surprisingly, exonerated the town council in their role as the urban sanitary authority from any blame, declaring that he thought 'they had done all that was required of them'.

Having thus singled out the justices and Phipps as the most likely people responsible for the scale of the disaster, he turned to the jury and asked them to consider two questions:

1. 'Did any act or any omission of duty on that part of any person or persons amount to culpable negligence?'

2. 'Was the loss of life immediately connected there with?'

Hooper's summing up had lasted around an hour, but the jury deliberated for nearly six hours before reaching a verdict. When the jurors finally returned to a tense and expectant court, their foreman George Seymour explained that there had been strong differences of opinion among the members with some, wanting to blame the architect alone for the disaster and others insisting that the magistrates were entirely responsible for the scale of the death toll. As the court held its collective breath Seymour read out the verdict:

'We find a verdict of accidental death, by unanimous vote of the jury, but, the jury make the following remarks as riders to their verdict'.

'1. We consider the Magistrates are much to blame, and deserve censure for not having completed their inspection of the theatre and satisfied themselves that all suggestions made by them had been carried out, especially the second exit from the gallery and that they allowed themselves to be misled by the architect in the matter of the exit from the gallery to the second circle. We consider also that it was unwise to grant a licence for a building in such an unfinished state. We regret the action of the Magistrates in declining as a body to recognise the authority of the Coroner's Court and their lack of courtesy to the Government Commissioner attending it.'

This was a stinging rebuke to the magistrates, pinpointing their mishandling of the whole licensing process from start to finish as well as questioning their competence and suitability for this onerous task. Apart from the justices, there would have been few present in the court room who disagreed with this condemnatory rider.

The jury then turned its fire on the town council:

'2. The jury regret that the Town Council's bye-laws do not allow their efficient control over public buildings especially as regards means of ingress and egress, and that their surveyor was not more fully instructed. We recommend a radical revision of such bye-laws without delay.'

Again the jurors could be confident that they were speaking for the majority of ordinary Exonians, who were unimpressed by the councillors' reluctance and/or inability to govern Exeter effectively. The failure of the council to establish a planning committee, backed up by more wide-ranging by-laws, and its endless prevarications over whether to set up a fully-equipped fire-fighting brigade or to content itself with a token single engine while relying on local insurance companies to provide their own at no cost to the council, had certainly contributed to the tragedy and underlined the city's poor governance.[8]

By now, Phipps must have wondered what the jury had in store for him and as the foreman read out the next two riders he had to steel himself to listen quietly to a public condemnation of his work and attitude, the like of which he had never been subjected to before:

'3. We deeply deplore that the architect having been engaged by the Directors as a specialist, should have produced a building with so many structural defects, especially in the place where so many of our fellow creatures fell at the second landing outside the pay office. We find that many persons lost their lives owing to the post erected there, and consider the post, the gateway below, and the pay office just above, with the door opening outwards, a very bad arrangement.'

Clearly the jury did not share Hooper's view that the gallery stairs had been well constructed. On the contrary, their blunt dressing-down of the London architect left no one in any doubt about the strength of their feelings.

But there was more; in their fourth and longest rider they turned to the question of the second gallery exit:

'4. The jury think that the architect failed in his duty in not providing a second exit from the gallery. They do not consider the way over the rail from the gallery into the second circle a legitimate exit in any case, and are surprised that Mr Phipps, a business man as well as an expert in theatre designing, should have suggested it in his evidence. The gallery staircase *per se* was not a ready exit from the gallery, and when the presence of the post is considered, which Mr Phipps admits was there on the opening night, they regard it as doubly dangerous.'

This was a blistering attack on Phipps's expertise, all the more wounding as he knew very well that the morning papers would carry the verdict in full and that it would, doubtless, be repeated in Saturday's *Era*. He could only hope that his frequently expressed opinion that the means of egress from the gallery were more than adequate, would carry more weight among theatre proprietors and managers than those of a provincial coroner's jury. The jury continued its assault:

'That Mr Phipps' explanation of the presence of a hydrant in the flies on the plan and not in fact was most unsatisfactory. The jury does not consider Mr Phipps is qualified to ignore the rule of the Metropolitan Board of Works as regards the erection of theatres, and they think that had he followed those rules as he alleged they would be, he would have acted wisely.'

Then, in a final reproof of Phipps's lack of forethought, they noted, with a tone of resigned sadness: 'Had the architect raised the roof of the auditorium several feet higher it could have carried up the smoke and allowed the gallery audience more time to escape.'

Having settled their score with Phipps, the jurors took the country's legislators to task:

'5. We consider that legislation bearing upon the inspection and remodelling of means of exit and stage working arrangements of all theatres, and the prevention of fires therein, should receive the earliest attention of Parliament.'

These were sentiments close to Phipps's heart as were those expressed in the following rider:

'6. The jury suggest that some effectual plan of excluding fire and smoke from the stage and other parts of the building be adopted by the fixing of a water screen or other apparatus.'

The jurors, riding high on their inspection theme and, perhaps, mindful that their fellow citizens would be looking for specific recommendations from them, went on to outline a more detailed inspection procedure, which might not have been altogether welcomed by the nation's Chief Constables:

'7. We consider that the Chief Constable should be empowered to make inspections at all times of all parts of the building without notice to the Directors or managers. That he makes such inspections at least once every month when the theatre is open, and thereupon transmits a report of his inspection to the Town Council, and states whether all fire hydrants, ventilation apparatus etc., are in perfect working order.'

And finally, in a desperate attempt to enforce complete transparency of the licensing process and prevent it becoming ensnared in a labyrinth of secrecy where different magistrates pursued their own agendas seemingly unaware of the findings of those who had preceded them:

'8. We suggest that before a Magistrates' licence is granted for any public building, such building shall be thrown open, (with all its approaches, entrances and exits) to the inspection under police supervision, of all householders of the Borough for a week after its final completion.'

This was not an altogether realistic proposition, but it served as sharp reminder to the Exeter magistrates that any trust they might previously have enjoyed among their fellow citizens had now entirely evaporated.

Phipps returned to London where the drawings for Mr Lancaster's Shaftesbury Theatre awaited him and where his Principal, Max Clarke had obtained a patent for an iron curtain,[9] paradoxically on the same day that his boss had been criticised for not providing one in Exeter. We do not know if Phipps had discussed the Exeter plans with Clarke, but as the office manager he must have been aware of the commission at the time.

For the next few days Phipps must have been uncomfortably aware that his future career as a theatre architect was no longer secure. The Exeter verdict appeared in full in Thursday morning's national and provincial papers as well as on the editorial page of Friday's (23 September) *Building News*, where Phipps's professional conduct, or rather lack of, was subject to some searing criticism:

'The rules laid down by the Metropolitan Board of Works as regards the erection of theatres are explicit enough, and though not binding in the provinces, we cannot see how they came to be so completely set aside even by an expert of Mr Phipps's standing ... A second gallery exit should, at all hazards, have been provided.'[10]

While stressing the need for urgent legislation to replace the licensing magistrates with competent officials, the journal was at pains to emphasise that, '... it is really the duty of architects of theatres, as of all other buildings, to take all reasonable precautions', before launching a final blast at Phipps:

> 'We write with reserve; but at present we cannot but think the censures of the jury on Mr Phipps are fully warranted by the facts. We should be glad to find any reasonable ground for a different conclusion.'

Continuing in the same withering tone, the journal reminded its readers that Phipps had written to the editor two weeks earlier complaining that 'he was "being abused by all the Press with no real knowledge of the matter" and that "when the proper time comes " he would supply us the plans of the structure at Exeter'. It is doubtful whether Phipps had actually envisaged that he would ever find himself in a situation when he might be called upon to honour this promise, but the *Building News* was not prepared to let him off the hook:

> 'The "proper time" has certainly come for any such justification as Mr Phipps may feel inclined to offer, but at present we certainly do not see how the two damaging points dwelt on by the jury – the insufficient exits to the gallery and the absence of the hydrant in the flies – are to be explained.'

There is no record of Phipps supplying the *Building News* with the Exeter plans.

The following morning the *Builder* brought scant comfort. Like its rival it supported the verdict as a just one, agreeing that the licensing magistrates must bear 'considerable responsibility' for not having made sure that the alterations they requested had all been carried out, but, the writer noted with a tone of sadness and regret:

> 'We fear it is impossible to deny that the main *onus* of the matter rests on the architect Mr Phipps, who, as a theatre-building specialist, ought to have been the person to be most urgent in insisting on every possible structural precaution being taken, whereas he appears to have adopted the opposite part of making light of the requirements and even promising things that were not delivered'.

The mere suggestion that Phipps, an architect at the height of his profession, could no longer be trusted to construct the building he had originally promised to deliver was a serious enough blow to his prestige and professional competence, but worse was to come:

'We wish we could defend the architect, but we can see no ground for doing so. He seems to have gone into the matter with as light a heart as if fatal disasters from the burning of theatres had never been heard of. We regret this on more than personal grounds, since it casts a discredit on the architectural profession which many ill-natured and illogical people will be eager to make the most of'.[11]

For Phipps, who had so eagerly sought, and succeeded, to be seen as a competent and trustworthy member of the Royal Institute of British Architects, to be accused of having brought disgrace on the whole of the architectural profession must have must have been extremely hurtful. The judgment of a provincial coroner's jury he could dismiss, but this was different. The architectural press had unceremoniously unmasked his carefully cultivated persona as a renowned theatre expert and revealed an incompetent blunderer who had failed to adopt recognised fire-safety measures and, worse, who had insisted that he had done nothing out of the ordinary, nothing blameworthy. By his inept handling of the Exeter design and his subsequent defensive demeanour he had opened the floodgates of public suspicion; how many more theatres were in a similar dangerous state? How many other public buildings were properly constructed? Were architects really as competent as they claimed? No wonder the architectural journals disowned him. He had rocked the very foundation of the profession.

Endnotes

1 *The Times*, 20 September 1887, p. 7.
2 Report of Bankruptcy hearing of Sidney Herberte-Basing. *Exeter Evening Post*, 10 May 1888.
3 *The Times*, 20 September 1887, p. 7.
4 Inquest evidence pp. 170-75, Coroner's Papers, ECA, Devon Heritage Centre.
5 Inquest evidence, pp. 186-87., Coroner's Papers, ECA, Devon Heritage Centre.
6 *The Times*, 20 September 1887, p. 7.
7 'Coroner's Summing Up and Directions to the Jury'. Coroner's Papers. ECA, Devon Heritage Centre. *The Times*, 22 September 1887, p. 5.
8 *Exeter Evening Post*, 17 September, 1887, p. 7.
9 T. Rees and D. Wilmore, *British Theatrical Patents, 1801-1900*, STR, 1996, pat. No. 12,817, p. 60.Clarke's patent was one of nine patents for fire proof curtains granted in the last four months of 1887.
10 *Building News*, 23 September 1887, p. 461.
11 *Builder*, 24 September 1887, p. 418.

14 THE REPORT

In contrast to Phipps, Shaw had little experience of provincial theatres and might not have realised that the rapid expansion of the provincial theatre during the previous twenty years had spawned a considerable number of new and rebuilt playhouses marred by careless design, pennypinching construction and meagre maintenance, any one of which might have succumbed to the same fate as the Exeter Theatre Royal. Unlike Phipps, he would not have come across the varying degrees of ignorance among provincial magistrates of their power in relation to theatre licensing, nor the readiness of many provincial managers to simply shrug their shoulders and carry on regardless when faced with hazardous theatres which the MBW would have attempted to close down in London. It seems that the Exeter Theatre Royal was the first provincial playhouse he had examined in detail. Unfortunately, he chose to do so 'on the principles and simple lines' which he and his colleagues had followed in their survey of London theatres in 1882,[1] a format entirely suitable for a survey of a working existing theatre, but not wide-ranging or deep enough to encompass the multiplicity of errors that had contributed to the Exeter tragedy. The result of this limited approach is a report – completed in only eight days after the close of the inquest – in which withering clarity is occasionally marred by unexpected U-turns into unsubstantiated conclusions.

The bulk of the report is devoted to a point by point analysis of numerous faults in the construction, though exactly how they had come about remained unclear as the drawings and plans did not contain clear specifications and had, anyway, not been fully adhered to. There had been alterations and additions in almost every part (para.10). This was not unusual, especially if the plans had been hastily conceived, as the lack of specifications suggests they had been in this case. The absence of detailed stipulations leaves many opportunities to cut corners to save money and in Exeter one gets the impression of construction on-the-hoof, where cheaper materials were substituted for more expensive ones, and decisions taken by the clerk of works, possibly beyond his competence, which ought to have been made by Phipps.

However, right from the start, Shaw seems to be at pains to avoid blaming Phipps directly, preferring instead to home in on the magistrates: 'The licensing authorities ordered that the theatre was to be constructed in accordance with the rules and regulations of the Metropolitan Board of Works in London'. (Para. 20).

His rather simplistic interpretation of who said what to whom and when seems to hinge on Pengelly's obtaining of a copy of the MBW Regulations in the summer of 1886, marking certain passages and sending the marked copy to the Theatre Company, who, in turn, apparently sent it on to Phipps. Whether this action on part of Pengelly actually constituted an order by the magistrates, given that he did not reveal whether he had been instructed to intervene in this way or was merely acting on his own initiative, is debatable.

Shaw, having established to his own satisfaction that the justices had made the MBW rules obligatory and instructed Phipps accordingly (para.22), then pinpoints the safety matters raised by the justices and which Phipps agreed to rectify, only to have to admit: 'On the insufficiency of the means of exit from the gallery ... the evidence does not clearly show that any actual order was given by them [the justices]' (para. 33).

Indeed it did not; we have only Horace Lloyd's recollection, unsupported by any minutes, that the magistrates had ordered that a second gallery exit must be installed. Shaw, however, apparently determined to hang the magistrates, resorts to the original prospectus, hastily composed by Phipps before the plans were drawn[2] and with which the magistrates had had no involvement, which stated that 'the upper floors would have each two distinct means of separate egress on opposite sides of the building'. He seems to have assumed that the aspirations expressed in the prospectus could be treated as some kind of contract which the authorities should have enforced.

Shaw accepted that the pay-box partition, the post and the gate on the gallery staircase 'were said not to have been erected at the time of the last inspection ...', but, as he observed, they were there on the opening night. (Para. 34).

It is possible that the carpenters were so behind with their work that they had not had time to complete the post and gate before the last inspection; it was clearly erected with ferocious speed once the magistrates had departed and neither Herberte-Basing not Phipps thought it necessary to inform the justices. The speed of its construction might have been the reason why Phipps offered to 'work the gallery' on the opening night in case some unforeseen structural or public order problem arose.

The Longbrook Street shops got short shrift from Shaw:

'Their frontage ... contributed in no small degree to this calamity. In addition to taking up the space on that side which should have been devoted to exits, the theatre was built over towards the New North Road side in order to obtain sufficient depth for the shops, thereby curtailing the space available for exits on that side also.'(Para. 43).

The inclusion of an unspecified number of shops had been announced in the prospectus, though why the directors seemingly insisted on six substantial shops on the truncated site is unclear. Phipps must have realised their presence would make impossible to provide double exits from all levels in the auditorium, but we do not know if he raised this with his client and got nowhere or whether he simply assured the directors that all would be well, confident that he could rise to the challenge.

In the following 112 paragraphs Shaw recorded with pitiless thoroughness the salient points and failures of the theatre's construction from roof to basement.

Thus, the iron pipe above the sunburner in the auditorium provided no means of escape from smoke, nor did the four-foot high ventilator over the stage because its louvre boards were turned downwards to prevent rain coming in (paras. 46-50).

The lowest floor, averaging a depth of 12 ft. below the main entrance appears, however, to have been well constructed with not an inch of wasted space. It was carried on brick piers and wood sleepers and comprised the pit, pit stalls, orchestra stalls, two private boxes and at the back, underneath the main vestibule, a refreshment saloon, cloak-room, lavatories, store room and meter room for the lighting of corridors and staircases (para. 96).

On the ground floor level Phipps had distributed the available space more generously, including a 37 ft. long and 16 ft. wide vestibule set askew to the theatre and with a wooden floor. There had, indeed, been a liberal use of wood instead of fire-resisting materials on this level including the dress circle corridors which had been squeezed into a width of 3 ft. 6.in against the MBW's requirement of 4 ft. 6 in. (paras.116-21).

According to Phipps's testimony the match boarding in the dress circle corridors was there 'to improve the sound'.[3]

The upper circle did have two exits, one down a straight line of concrete steps into Longbrook Street, but the other, leading to the New North Road side, followed such a labyrinthine pathway that it required a guide and it did not impress Shaw. It began with a passage at the back leading upwards to a short flight of stairs, which had a half turn on the right leading down another flight with yet a further sharp turn at the landing at the bottom which led into the vestibule. The first half turn was easily missed as the stairs actually continued straight up into the refreshment room, which had no other exit, and for panic-stricken spectators fleeing a fire the design it was more of trap than an escape route.

Shaw was equally contemptuous of the placing of the opening to the gallery stairs at the centre of the back row declaring that the reasons for so doing were 'doubtless ... that if the stairs had commenced at one corner of the gallery the absolute necessity of a second means of exit would have been too apparent to escape the notice of the authorities'. (Paras.193-4). Nor had he any time for the escape route over the barrier into the upper circle explaining with brutal clarity why the small number who had tried to scale the barrier perished:

'In doing so they brought their faces close up to where the ceiling of the auditorium ended, and they inhaled the strong blast of heated smoke at its fullest intensity ... which caused them to fall senseless into the upper circle, and seriously injuring its occupants. (Paras. 197-8).

As for the much criticised gallery stairs, Shaw, at first, seems to take a more lenient view: 'They were well constructed ... and the angles in it, though somewhat inconvenient in so steep a gradient, were not in themselves dangerous ... and designed to relieve the pressure of the crowd'. (Para. 223). For a relaxed crowd moving in orderly formation this would most likely be the case, but for a throng in a panic on a poorly lit staircase with many sharp angles – there were only three lamps one of which was obscured by the pay box – and without a continuing hand rail the risk of someone tripping over and being trampled on was very high.

However, while Shaw accepted the angles *per se* he did not expect them to be cluttered up with posts:

'There was a post at the angle above which the greatest number of bodies were found, and there can be no reasonable doubt that the position of that post and possibly the proximity of the fallen check box, combined with the darkness that prevailed, contributed to the loss of life'.(Para.225).

In other words, the fatal post was an important contributory factor to the high death toll, but it was not the sole or even main cause of the scale of the disaster:

'Even if the post had not been there, it is obvious that the means of exit from the gallery were altogether insufficient, and that there should have been on the opposite side another staircase of at least the same capacity'.

Thus, the lack of a second gallery exit was, to Shaw, an even more crucial factor in this disaster than the post.

He also condemned the connecting door between the upper circle and the gallery staircase, which had been added three weeks before the opening by Phipps 'at the request of management'[4] presumably Herberte-Basing. Innocently opened to give the fleeing galleryites an additional escape route, it had the opposite effect:

'The smoke, after filling the upper parts of the auditorium, near the great central light, worked down to that level, and drove through the open door, completely sealing the gallery stairs at that point against further exit'. (Para. 227).

At the end of his revelations of careless design and shoddy construction Shaw lets out a *crie de coeur:* 'It may be, as stated in evidence that there are elsewhere other theatres as bad as that of Exeter, but it may be confidently asserted that there can be very few worse'. (Para. 230).

Having presented a mass of evidence relating to faulty and inadequate design and construction, notably the absence of a second gallery exit, the placing of the only gallery exit at the centre back of the gallery, the post on the gallery stairs, the circuitous second exit from the upper gallery, and the inclusion of six shops, which appears to be weighted against the architect, Shaw retreats. Instead of accusing Phipps of professional failings, which had demonstrably contributed to the disaster, he returns to his original proposition that the only people responsible for this tragedy were the magistrates: 'Any one of these serious defects of construction should have prevented the licensing of the building as a theatre'. (Para. 209).

Shaw then seeks to explain how he has arrived at this conclusion by proclaiming that 'the theatre was completed to the satisfaction of the Theatre Company'. He does, however, admit that this assertion '... is only a presumption, but it is a very strong one as it is known that the company was in possession of the premises'. (Paras. 211-12). This question had not been raised at the inquest so we do not know if Phipps had fulfilled his contract with the company to the satisfaction of its directors and there is no suggestion on Shaw's part that he had asked them privately if this was the case. Indeed, the failure to question W.H. Ellis, the company chairman, who seems to have been present in court during most of the inquest, on this matter and on the inclusion of six shops, seems a curious omission on part of the coroner, but he might not fully have appreciated the level of influence of 'tyrannical clients' on the design of theatre projects. Shaw, on the other hand, ought to have been aware of this problem, but it was a complex issue with the potential for long-winded legal arguments, which might easily have strayed beyond both Shaw's and Hooper's capabilities and which would certainly have prolonged the inquest.

According to Shaw, once the company was in possession of the theatre 'the matter passed from the architect and the company became responsible', (para. 213), a statement, which, on the face of it, appears to absolve Phipps from responsibility for any professional mis-judgments committed before and during the construction. Presumably Shaw meant that the company had become *legally* responsible, which raises the question as to who was legally responsible during the construction period.

Continuing his straight-line reasoning, Shaw then argues that 'the company remained the responsible party' until the magistrates finally licensed the building when the state of the theatre and its safety became their province'. (Para. 214). Since the licence was only obtained just before the opening night, this deceptively definitive statement would seem to imply that the responsibility for ensuring that the required changes were made had rested with the company and not the magistrates. If Shaw really believed this to be the case, then the failure to call the directors at the inquest raises a question mark over Hooper's and Shaw's joint conduct of the proceedings.

Rather surprisingly, Shaw then claims that 'no evidence was offered of any subsequent acts of the occupiers, which could have contributed to the heavy loss of life' (para. 217), ignoring, what seems to have been a very last-minute installation of the post on the gallery stairs, before announcing with worrying certainty:

'It must therefore be taken as an absolute and undoubted fact that the building was constructed according to the wishes, and to a considerable extent, under the orders of the licensing authority.' (Para. 218).

Given the limited and contradictory statements given by the magistrate H.P. Lloyd, the Mayor, and, their clerk, Pengelly over which justices attended which inspection and whether they communicated their finding to each other, not to mention who actually ordered the passing round of a copy of the MBW Regulations to the owners and Phipps, it is difficult to see how these confusing pieces of evidence could be made to serve as an absolute fact.

Having made his views of the magistrates abundantly clear, Shaw moves on to deal briskly with the fire and its course, declaring: 'The fire arose in the flies through accident or neglect on the part of those employed and the heavy loss of life was caused by the bad construction of the theatre'. (Para 236).

This could be read as an indictment of Phipps, but this appears not have been Shaw's intention as he, in the following paragraphs launches an attack on the inquest jury's condemnation of the architect:

'The jury no doubt censured the licensing authority severely, but also apportioned some of the censure to the architect, and in doing so have laid the foundation of a precedent, which, if followed, might lead to endless difficulties.'

Shaw did not elaborate on the nature of these 'endless difficulties' but, judging by the next paragraph, he seems to have been anxious to forestall a further and wider inquiry into the Exeter disaster: ' In cases like this there can be but one responsible authority' and any attempt 'to fritter away responsibility can only end in confusion'. ((Paras. 238-9). Warming to his theme he proceeds to practically exonerate Phipps:

'If they admit the architect to a share of the responsibility why should they not also include the contractor, the clerk of works, the brick layers, the masons, the joiners ... even the labourers that dug the foundation?'

Shaw, it seems, had forgotten, or maybe he had not realised, that all the above worked under the architect and that he therefore carried the ultimate professional and moral responsibility for the building's soundness, something that the jury had fully appreciated.

Why Shaw was so determined not to attribute any responsibility to his old adversary is difficult to explain, but there were probably several reasons. The notion of a straight chain of command, essential in fire fighting was very probably second nature to him, but there might also have been a suspicion in Shaw's mind that openly castigating Phipps might lead to more trouble than it was worth. After all, Phipps had never hesitated to challenge Shaw's reports on the London theatres as he saw fit and with one of London's most prominent lawyers on his side the chances of him using the press to dispute Shaw's findings yet again were high. At worst, he might even take him to court for defamation of character. Shaw would have little to gain from such adversarial press coverage, which might diminish his own reputation and further embolden the capital's theatre proprietors and managers to continue to employ Phipps to challenge what they regarded, as excessive safety measures by the MBW. The co-operation of the managers and owners was essential for Shaw's mission to improve theatre safety in London and he would not want to risk their contempt.

In the end the jury's verdict, which recognised that the deaths had been caused by cumulative failures on the part of several individuals who had taken decision on the basis of false assumptions and incomplete information, came closer to the truth than Shaw's hastily compiled report despite its scrutiny of structural detail.

However, the main responsibility for the tragic consequences of the Exeter fire still rests with Phipps. The owners, by insisting on selling off a large part of the site and still insisting on incorporating six shops must take some responsibility, as must the council for inadequate bye laws and planning procedures, the 'management for insisting on the 'management door' and check box arrangement, and the magistrates for their bungling approach to the whole licensing process. But within this extraordinary muddle, Phipps, who was not slow to remind those involved of his own expertise, was the only one who understood, or ought to have understood, the full implications of his decisions over the inadequate ventilation in the roof above the stage and above the auditorium, the single gallery exit, the pay box and post arrangement, the lack of a hydrant in the flies, and the rejection of a an iron curtain. Yet, he chose to ignore these serious shortcomings in the plan. He ought to have known about the dangers of smoke inhalation, but for some reason he had, clearly, failed to grasp this crucial issue, which raises the question: how much of an expert was he on fire safety?

Why he decided to set aside the expertise he did have on planning and construction we will never know, but clearly the need to keep costs down was an important factor. Another was, no doubt, Phipps's tendency to skimp on space for gallery exits, common enough among theatre architects and supported by their clients on the grounds that if you pay less, you get less. And finally, there seems to have been a lingering sense of hubris, colouring his performance in the witness box, a feeling that as he was the most experienced theatre architect in the country, his decisions on ventilation matters and space saving solutions must, inevitably, be the right ones, even when they were wrong.

Endnotes

1 *Report by Captain Eyre M. Shaw, C.B. concerning the Fire which occurred at the Theatre Royal, Exeter on the 5th of September 1887*, London 1888, para. 9.
2 C.J. Phipps, Copy of Deposition, NA, B20704/17. See also Inquest Evidence, Coroner's Paper's, ECA, Devon Heritage Centre.
3 *Ibid.*
4 *Ibid.*

15 ATONEMENT

How deeply the Exeter experience penetrated Phipps's psyche is impossible to say. It is tempting to see his stalwart performance at the inquest as just that; a performance with Phipps playing the part of a misunderstood and falsely accused individual, attempting to steer a clear course through his commission while buffeted, in turn, by the huffing and puffing of his client, confused magistrates, an impecunious manager and an overstretched builder. It is, however, also possible, that this is how he really felt, that he was so convinced of his own rightness that he really did believe that the heavy loss of life was primarily the fault of others, even though he had conceded, under pressure, that he 'had not reckoned for the smoke'. On this last matter he was not alone in his confusion. The importance of a safety curtain had yet to be grasped not only by theatre proprietors and managers, who, generally, regarded such a cumbersome item as an unnecessary outlay, but by those who had the authority to insist on its inclusion, primarily the MBW, who could not decide which type to recommend, the Lord Chamberlain who, preferred managers to regulate themselves, and local magistrates, many of whom tended to follow London's lead in these matters.

There was no time to wait for London's lead this time. Provincial magistrates embraced theatre safety with new-found vigour as if desperate to atone for past omissions. In Nottingham, the magistrates, after inspecting Phipps's Theatre Royal several times, ordered the installation of fire proof doors in several places and a fire proof curtain and imposed a temporary limit of 300 in the gallery (less than half the original 650) until all their alterations had been completed.[1] In Colchester the justices ordered alterations to the exits at the Theatre Royal and referred the plans to an expert before they would grant a new licence.[2] In Manchester, under the leadership of the mayor, the magistrates drew up lists of suggested alterations themselves, to be sent to all theatre managers and granted only provisional licences for three months while their recommendations were carried out. They proposed that theatres should be licensed for a certain number of persons, as ships were, so that in case of any accidents due to overcrowding the proprietors and licence-holders would be liable, not the licensing authority. However they would first 'communicate with the Government in order to ascertain their authority'.[3] Clearly, it was not only the Exeter justices who were unsure of how much power they actually had in practice.

In Torquay the magistrates resolutely issued a summons to the lessee for failing to have the doors opening outwards and tied back during the performance. The defence blamed Phipps for having misrepresented the legal requirements for London theatres regarding doors having to open outwards. The Chairman of the Torquay Theatre Company suggested, rather desperately, that a second gallery exit opening onto the foyer roof (10 feet above the road) 'with a chained ladder to aid descent', could be added, but this was not pursued.[4] In Aberdeen, the public and the local press had been complaining for some time over the lack of exits at the Tivoli Theatre (1872), jointly designed by Phipps and local architect James Matthews, and with good reason as the only means of exit were the three narrow pay-door entrances in the main frontage. Now, however, after years of prevarication, the magistrates acted and appointed a committee consisting of the city architect, borough surveyor and an independent architect to examine the building. They were not impressed by the scant attention paid to fire safety by the two architects and called for a new fire-proof proscenium wall, an increased number of hydrants, a new fire-proof stairway to the dress circle as well as a new fire-proof stair to the gallery plus various improvements to existing exits.

Even the renowned manager of Drury Lane, Augustus Harris, who had just taken over the Grand Theatre in Glasgow, was only granted a one-month provisional licence because the single gallery staircase, for a gallery holding 900(!) was now deemed inadequate and an additional stairway had to be constructed. Until the latter was finished only 600 were allowed in the gallery.[5] In Croydon, the manager of the Theatre Royal proposed to replace the old, single, staircase to the gallery with one in iron, 3ft. 3in. wide 'in every part'. The magistrates examined the plans and felt it was too steep, but apparently not too narrow. It would seem, even in the context of this small sample, that Phipps's provision for the egress of the galleryites at Exeter was, by no means, the worst in the country.

What is clear is that Phipps had no intention of bowing his head in shame and retiring to a house in the country. He had a family to support and a social and professional position to maintain. He was not going to throw away his career, so carefully nurtured during 25 years and be remembered only for the Exeter fire and a joint commission with Frank Matcham for the Hanley Theatre Royal as his final design before disaster struck. The Hanley theatre was an enlargement of an older playhouse and included 'an entirely new auditorium' housing a vast pit 'with comfortable seats for 1,100, a circle for 200, an upper gallery for 250 and a gallery for 1000.[6] Why the lessee, James II Elphinstone, who commissioned the work, felt the need for two architects we do not know, but it is possible that Phipps acted as advisor. The work appears to have been completed in four months and Hanley's new Theatre Royal opened on 8 August 1887.

With the inquest, at last, behind him Phipps rushed to complete the plans for Lancaster's Shaftesbury Theatre, which he submitted to the MBW on the 30 September. The plans for the Lyric Theatre had already been approved by the Board on 29 July 1887. However, the aftermath of Exeter was still clouding Phipps's attempts to rehabilitate himself. At the beginning of October, he received an unexpected summons from a Mr Acland Davies of Crediton, who argued that Phipps had 'obtained a licence by fraudulent misrepresentation'.[7] Phipps's reaction would, surely have been to hand the whole matter over to Fladgate solicitors to sort out and it might well have been their investigations which discovered that the charge under which the summons was brought was not in fact covered by statute and the prosecution was dropped.

Nevertheless, the summons must have given Phipps some anxious moments, and then there was a further distraction in the form of reports in the London press on the lack of probity and transparency among the officials of the MBW. The handling of the sale of surplus land in Shaftesbury Avenue by the Superintending Architect's department featured prominently, and allegations of corruption and bribery were made in relation to the Board's assistant surveyor T.J. Robertson who, rather surprisingly, managed to maintain a coach with a liveried coachman on a salary of £450 a year.[8] The Board had already been pressed into conducting two internal and ineffective inquiries during the summer of 1887, during which the land speculator Statham Hobson's name had emerged in connection with Robertson. Phipps had acted as agent for Hobson in connection with the site on which the Lyric Theatre was to be built, and the whole business had been far from straightforward. And now, in mid-October, as Henry Leslie was in the last stages of trying to acquire the freehold of the last and crucial piece of the site, the Café L'Etoile on the corner of Shaftesbury Avenue and Great Windmill Street, there were calls from both Board members and the press for the appointment of a Royal Commission to disentangle the opaque dealings embedded among the Board's architects and valuers. The prospect must have triggered mixed feelings in Phipps, on the one hand he hadn't time for the Board as an institution, on the other hand, the last thing he needed now was to be exposed as an *aide de camps* of Hobson and drawn into an official enquiry.

Phipps had, over the years, managed to keep in the with Board rather more successfully than his rival Walter Emden, who, according to Edward Godwin, when asked to advise on the proposed plans for Terry's Theatre in the Strand by the developer Charles Wilmot, revealed that Emden 'was in a bad odour with the Board; and they would put obstacles in the way of passing his plans'.[9] Godwin had even suggested that Emden should associate himself with a member of the Board to get his plans for the Terry Theatre passed, but Emden had wisely refused. Phipps was less scrupulous; he had approached his old friend and colleague Francis Fowler, architect of the Opera Comique and the aborted National Opera House and, a long-standing member of the Board, when his ran into difficulties with the Theatres Sub-committee in 1884 over his designs for a rebuild of Hengler's Circus. Fowler's advice had proved invaluable and Phipps had expressed his gratitude in the form of a small 'voluntary present of £40'.[10]

In the circumstances it is, perhaps, not surprising that the alterations to the gallery at Sadler's Wells Theatre ordered in September by the Lord Chamberlain slipped his mind. In the Exeter aftermath The Lord Chamberlain's Office had discovered a new-found zeal for theatre inspections and on 29 October 1887 a stressed Phipps, suddenly remembering that he needed to do something about the gallery at Sadler's Wells, fired off a moderately apologetic letter to the Lord Chamberlain: 'I was, you may remember, present at your inspection in September but I cannot recollect what improvement of the gallery was suggested. If you let me know I will lay it before the proprietors.'[11] Three days later, Phipps, seemed to have found his notes: '... I find that there is a partition separating the gallery as at Exeter. I propose to remove that partition entirely so that the gallery then has two good and distinct exits into different streets'.[12]

The fact that neither the Lord Chamberlain nor the MWB had queried the absence of two 'good and distinct exits' from the Sadler's Wells gallery at the time of the theatre's rebuilding in 1879 (supervised by Max Clarke) and furthermore that they had both failed to insist on improvements until now, is a telling example of the inconsistent approach by both regulatory bodies towards theatre safety. Phipps had certainly not been bluffing at the Inquest when he maintained that the equivalent of his gallery design for the Exeter Theatre Royal had been passed, or rather ignored, by the London authorities.

Having cast his eyes over the theatres in the metropolis, the Lord Chamberlain remembered that he also had some influence over the provincial playhouses that operated under a royal patent[13] and wrote to the local managers of provincial patent theatres politely asking them to contact their local authorities with a view to having their buildings inspected. To ensure their compliance he also despatched a circular to the relevant town clerks informing them of his letter, thus giving town councils the opportunity to initiate the inspections if necessary.[14] The prospect of Phipps being further humiliated by an inspection report of his own theatre in Eastbourne, where the absence of a second exit from the pit, not to mention the gallery, might well have been seized upon by the town council. Propelled into a pre-emptive strike, Phipps and Loveday abruptly closed the Eastbourne Theatre Royal on 8 October 1887.[15] It remained closed for the next seven months.

In London, Terry's Theatre in the Strand designed by Walter Emden for the actor Edward Terry, was loaded with a multiplicity of exits and the latest safety features. When it opened on 17 October 1887, the specially written 'First Night Programme' devoted much space to explaining the fire proof curtain, the abundance of exits, the generous distribution of sprinklers, fire hydrants, fire proof paint, electric light and Messrs. Chubb's patent Panic Door Locks.[16] Between them Terry and Emden had raised the safety stakes for the West End theatre and Emden could now present himself to the public as the architect with real expertise on safety issues, far more up-to-date than Phipps.

Yet, by raising public awareness in this way of what could be done to make a theatre safe, Emden and Terry had also done Phipps a service;

from now on theatre speculators would find it more difficult to quibble over extra exits and expensive iron curtains. This more safety-conscious climate was to Phipps's advantage. He would and could prove his worth again; Emden might be an expert on safety, but so was he, when blessed with an enlightened client prepared to spend money. His new theatres in Shaftesbury Avenue would re-establish him as the nation's leading theatre architect; after all, he was still the master when it came to creating the perfect spatial connection between auditorium and stage.

This change in attitude away from a gung-ho spirit, which assumed any theatre fire could be checked by buckets of sand and water, towards the painful realisation that theatre fires were deadly monsters even in Britain also affected Parliament. The unthinkable had happened, and not in any old rickety playhouse, but in a theatre designed by the country's most renowned expert in the field. If a theatre, allegedly constructed according to current safety regulations, was unable to withstand the ravages of fire long enough to prevent a large proportion of the audience from a gruesome death, surely no theatre was now absolutely safe? Something must be done! There was a growing and uncomfortable acceptance that although Phipps had clearly failed in his professional duties at Exeter, the nation's legislators and theatre proprietors between them bore some responsibility too by having created a climate in which the economic twin pillars of entrepreneurial spirit and investment return had been allowed to take precedence over 'expensive' safety measures. A collective need for atonement, coupled with a sense of bewilderment over how best to avoid a similar catastrophe, seemed to grip the nation's legislature.

In the House of Commons, Members continued to press the Home Secretary for decisive action. Already, as the inquest began its formal hearing in Exeter, Sir Algernon Borthwick asked Matthews:

'Whether her Majesty's Government would this Session introduce a short measure conferring power on Her Majesty's Council to issue orders for the regulation and inspection of theatres and other places of amusement, such orders to be valid until a more comprehensive measure could be adopted by Parliament?'

It was a reasonable question given Matthews's statement the day after the fire on Tuesday 6 September that 'the dreadful calamity' had shown the need for legislation for provincial theatres. Barely a week later, the Home Secretary was less enthusiastic, pointing out that the remaining

Session was too short to undertake to pass even a brief Bill, but rather surprisingly, he offered to set up a theatre advice desk at the Home Office:

'Fully sensible of the great importance of the matter ... I think I can undertake ... that we will at the earliest opportunity, offer practical suggestions to any theatrical manager who chooses to avail himself of them for securing the safety of the public in the practical details of a theatre'.[17]

This seems to have been another rash promise without sound foundation The Home Office had no theatre advisors on its payroll, but it is, of course, possible that Matthews was, at this time, considering appointing a theatre expert to assist with the drafting of the new theatre regulations bill, which he had hinted at a week earlier.

His assurance did not dispel the Members' concerns over theatre safety. The following day, Matthews was forced to parry a question from Major Rasch, who enquired whether the Home Secretary 'would now order the publication of Captain Shaw's Report on London Theatres?'

The fact that Shaw's Report of 1882 had not yet been presented to Parliament despite numerous requests over the years from both Houses is an indication of the power that the chairman of the MBW and the Lord Chamberlain were able to exert over the government. From their point of view the Report rather torpedoed their public image as guardians of the public against the horrors of theatre fires, but one cannot help wondering whether a prompt publication of Shaw's findings might not have made Phipps think twice over his deeply flawed design for Exeter. An earlier publication would certainly have raised public awareness of the lamentable state of theatre safety in the English theatre. Such awareness might, in turn, have forced theatre proprietors, architects and magistrates across the nation to pay more attention to the inherent risk factors even, have put pressure on the government to strengthen the legislation for all theatres.

Matthews, heedful of the implications of making public Shaw's frank analysis, replied that the Report was confidential, but he would consult the Lord Chamberlain and the Board of Works 'as to whether it could be published with public advantage'.[18]

On 29 September he received Shaw's Report on the Exeter fire. As an experienced lawyer, familiar with the loose statuary regulations governing provincial theatres, Shaw's insistence on putting all the blame on the magistrates while, seemingly, exonerating everybody else involved must have disturbed him. This was a conclusion that could be challenged and was therefore not altogether helpful. On 5 October, Matthews ordered the Report to be printed,[19] before sending a copy to the Exeter magistrates to give them the right to reply. He did not lay Shaw's Exeter Report before Parliament at this stage, feeling, perhaps, that little would be gained by doing so. Nor did he present the legislators with the 1882 report; this was not a good time to reveal the Lord Chamberlain's past, almost criminally lax, inspection regime.

Shaw, having delivered his Exeter findings in record time, to his surprise ran into difficulties with the Treasury, who queried his claim for expenses for 16 days. Considering that Shaw had only attended the inquest for seven days the query is understandable, but then he could justifiably claim that he had spent another seven days writing his Report, making 14 days in all. Shaw was indignant and wrote to Matthews asking him to intercede on his behalf, adding, rather revealingly:

'I may tell you that but for me this Inquiry would have lasted some 40-50 days. All involved seemed bent on prolonging it. I would have served without payment. My only object was to save your Office trouble and I hope I have succeeded in doing this.'[20]

It is a depressing statement, which somehow manages to dismiss the Exeter catastrophe as a minor incident and at the same time almost belittle his own role as a Government Commissioner.

By the middle of November, a summary of Shaw's conclusions on the causes of the Exeter disaster suddenly appeared in the press, first in *The Times* (16 November), repeated in full in the *Era* (19 November) with a shorter version in *Lloyd's Weekly Newspaper* (20 November). *The Builder*, which had been less than supportive of Phipps after the Exeter Fire, confined itself to the briefest of summaries adding that while it accepted Shaw's view that

'the authorities who have licensed the theatre are from that moment the really responsible people this, of course, does not in any way preclude the moral responsibility of the architect in all such cases, as the designer of the theatre.'[21]

Quite who was behind the leak remains a mystery, but it might possibly have been Shaw, who, apparently had been informed that his report 'could not be published until "it is ordered by Parliament" ' by which time he [Captain Shaw] feared the whole thing will be forgotten.'[22]

The Exeter justices took some time to compose their response to Shaw's opinion, but when it came it, dated 30 November, it was rather more carefully argued than one might have expected from their unconvincing performance hitherto. They had done their homework and studied the opinion by N.M. Geary, QC, on the law relating to theatres, published in 1885.[23] They pointed out that in Acts 6th and 7th Vict. Cap. 68, under which the licence had been granted:

'There was no indication whatever that the Magistrates are to consider the structural condition of the building … and even if they were to do so, must be governed by the opinion of Experts and it is unreasonable to suppose that they are to be responsible for the Experts' mistakes and errors of judgment'.[24]

In an ideal world the Exeter magistrates ought to have had the confidence and experience to stand up to the bamboozling tactics so artfully thrust at them by Phipps, but it takes strong minds and clear heads to challenge the opinion of someone who is reputed to be the nation's undoubted expert in his field.

Stressing their point about the unsatisfactory wording of the statute, they further argued:

'The Magistrates cannot be held responsible for the defective state of the law with regard to the erection and supervision of Theatres in the provinces and they consider it deserving of attention that although this Act 6 and 7 Vict. cap. 68 applies to all theatres it was afterwards considered necessary in the Metropolis to supplement said Act by Statues 18 and 19 Vict. cap. 122 and again by 41 and 42 Vict. cap. 32.'

In other words, if the earlier legislation had been found wanting in respect of the London theatres it was equally wanting in respect of the provincial theatre and as far as the Exeter justices were concerned, the Acts brought in to supplement the regulation in the Metropolis, 'should be made compulsory in all Municipalities through the Sanitary Authority'.

This was a consideration that Shaw had disregarded in his Report, but it was not something a Home Secretary could brush aside. He sent the Justices' Reply to be printed and added it to the Report. When asked by his private secretary whether he should send Shaw a copy of the justices' response, Matthews, said: 'No. The law is defective'.[25] It seems he did not wish to inform Shaw that his conclusion was not really compatible with the law as it stood.

In the end, perhaps Shaw's most valuable service to the citizens of Exeter was his offer to form and train a full-time city fire brigade, an offer which the town council could hardly refuse. Here Shaw was in his element, recruiting and training volunteers and persuading the parsimonious council to invest in a 'Merryweather' steam fire engine pulled by two horses at a gallop and capable of shooting jets of water 130 ft high.[26]

In London the MBW passed Phipps's plans for the Shaftesbury Theatre on 18 November 1887 (after he had amended the gallery design two weeks earlier) and as building began he swiftly furnished the *Era* with details of its planned safety features.[27] The theatre would hold 1800 spectators and each division of the audience would be surrounded by a brick wall 'opening into a 6 ft wide corridor'. Furthermore, 'All the corridors, staircases and the framework of the tiers [would be] constructed of Portland cement concrete and iron.' However, lest anyone thought that this would be a utilitarian theatre entirely made of concrete, Phipps, who well understood the importance of audience comfort, reassured the paper's readers:

> 'The tiers will have wood floors fixed down tight into the cement concrete, it being quite as fire-resisting and much more comfortable to persons sitting than the cold concrete floors, however much they may be covered by with carpet or matting.'

The actors, however, had to make do with the cold concrete floors, and the same material would also be used for the mezzanine and the fly floors. Finally, there would be an iron curtain worked by hydraulic power.

Having signalled to the readers of the *Era* that he was at least as safety conscious as Walter Emden, Phipps devoted his energies to organising a deputation to the Home Office, on behalf of the nation's theatre proprietors and managers, to lobby against the MBW's plans to increase their powers over them 'by vesting themselves with absolute sovereignty' and to press for theatre regulation to be taken over by the Home Office.[28] Considering that the MBW and its powers were to be subsumed by the newly created London County Council in 1889, this determination on the part of the Board, in the last hours of its existence, to acquire yet more power seems a rather desperate move to little purpose, the more so as questions concerning past and present corrupt practices by its members and officials were now being raised openly in the press.[29]

In essence, as Phipps pointed out, the amendment was a simple one; it was intended to remove the clause in the 1878 Bill 'which requires structural alterations to be made for the better safety of the public, if such can be done at reasonable expense'.[30] It was a clause that had enabled Phipps to refer many of the Board's imposed repairs to an arbitration tribunal on behalf of his clients, though it is worth remembering that most of the MBW's requirements were carried out without fuss, even by Phipps.

Given the bewildered climate of atonement that seemed to have settled over London for the time being, it is, perhaps therefore not altogether surprising that the Board decided to seize the moment and push through a bill designed to give them absolute power to compel theatre managers to execute all its requests regardless of costs. However, the London theatre establishment, from which Phipps had not yet been cast out, was not prepared to let such a draconian regulation become law.

Endnotes

1 *Era*, 15 October 1887, p. 16.
2 *Era*, 15 October 1887, p. 16.
3 *Era*, 8 October 1887, p. 13.
4 E. Stevens and R. Casley, *The Theatre in Abbey Road, Torquay 1864-1924*, Chs. 19 and 18.
5 *Era*, 8 October 1887, p. 13
6 *Era* 13 August 1887, p. 15.
7 D. Anderson, *The Exeter Theatre Fire*, Entertainment Technology Press, 2002, p. 131.
8 *Pall Mall Gazette*, 16 July 1887, p. 1.
9 *The Times*, 27 June 1888, p. 5.
10 RIBA Letters to Council, RIBA Institutional Archives, British Architectural Library, Royal Institute of British Architects. C.J. Phipps, 26 October 1888, LC/28/4/19.
11 NA, LC1/489/240.
12 NA, LC1/489/241, 1 November 1887.
13 Provincial patents contained a provision that the theatre should be subject to the police regulations of the locality. NA, 61112/57. Letter from the Lord Chamberlain to Birmingham's Head Constable dated 20 November 1884.
14 NA, LC1/491/35, 28 September 1887.
15 *Era*, 15 October 1887, p. 17.
16 R. Mander and J. Mitchenson, *The Lost Theatres of London*, London Rupert Hart-Davis, 1968, pp. 509-10.
17 Hansard, HC Deb. 12 September 1887, v.321, c286.
18 Hansard, HC Deb. 13 September 1887, v.321, c482.
19 NA, B2074/17
20 NA, B2074/20. Letter dated 30 October 1887.
21 *Builder*, 19 November, 1887, p. 694.
22 *Pall Mall Gazette,* 1 December 1887, p. 4.
23 It was published by Messrs Stevens and Son of Chancery Lane.
24 NA, Home Office Memo on the Exeter Fire, B 2074/18c. Letter dated 30 November 1887.
25 NA, B2074/18c. Minute from 5 December 1887.
26 *Exeter Evening Post*, 18 September, 1887.
27 *Era*, 3 December 1887, p. 11. Amended gallery design dated 4 November. LMA, GLC/AR/BR/19/0449.

28 Letter from Phipps to the *Financial News*, 10 December 1887, p. 5.
29 *Era*, 15 October 1887, p. 16.
30 Letter from Phipps to the *Financial News*, 10 December 1887, p. 5.

16 THE SPECTRE OF CORRUPTION
DECEMBER 1887 – OCTOBER 1888

The Deputation

In the immediate aftermath of Exeter, Phipps not only redrew his plans for the Shaftesbury Avenue theatres, he also helped to organise a 200-strong deputation of metropolitan and provincial theatre and music hall proprietors and managers who were anxious to press the Home Secretary to support Mr Dixon-Hartland's Theatre Regulation Bill, which was then slowly working its way through Parliament. The Bill was a proposal to introduce a uniform system of theatre safety standards across the country to be administered by a government department – ideally the Home Office – an issue on which Phipps had campaigned for the last ten years.

The deputation, led by Mr Dixon-Hartland and made up of London's most senior theatre proprietors and managers, notably Augustus Harris, Squire Bancroft, John Hollingshead, Richard D'Oyly Carte and Herbert Beerbohm Tree, plus a large contingent of provincial managers, descended on Henry Matthews on 15 December 1887.[1] They submitted a Memorial to Matthews, in which they argued against the MBW Bill scheduled to be discussed in Parliament during the next session, and expressed their unanimous support for Dixon-Hartland's Bill.

It was a carefully orchestrated presentation in which the leading London managers each took their turn after Dixon-Hartland's opening speech. Squire Bancroft, as might be expected, held the stage for some time:

'We wish it to be distinctly understood, Sir, that we court inspection, and that we court inspection of the most rigid character, being quite prepared also to bear the cost ... We also desire that our responsibility to the public should be guarded by certificates of efficiency, but such certificates ... can only be of value when they are given by qualified people who are not only well paid but beyond reproach.'

As for the provincial theatre, he was equally clear:'[They] should be licensed by local authorities as now, but the efficacy of the building for the safety of the public should be in the hands of experts.'

Matthews, apparently struck by temporary amnesia regarding his promise in the House of Commons three months earlier, that his department would offer practical advice on theatre safety, was equally robust: 'You press the function on the Home Office, but the Home Secretary knows as little about theatres as a member of the Board of Works'. Bancroft, unimpressed, retorted: 'You could have regular inspectors. Theatre managers are willing to pay.'

The reason, according to Bancroft, that theatre managers were apparently willing to fund an inspection-scheme run by the Home Office was grounded in their deep mistrust in the ability of any elected body, from local authorities to the MBW, to oversee building inspections without meddling, with members having differing priorities and views on what constituted essential safety requirements, as, indeed, was the present situation and if necessary resorting to blackmail to get their way: 'There are theatres in the country which should never be allowed to exist', he declared dramatically and, unfortunately, correctly. Whether the public would be totally reassured by safety inspectors paid for by theatre managers is debatable. There might well have been scope for meddling under such an arrangement too.

John Hollingshead then waded in with figures to underline the scale of the theatre and music-hall industry and its importance to the national economy. Excluding Ireland, there were, he claimed, around 200 theatres, 160 music halls and an astonishing 950 halls of various descriptions including concert halls, galleries, church halls etc., distributed among 530 English towns, together 'representing £6,000,000 in money and employing 350,000 persons directly'. Consequently, nothing but a theatre bill dealing with the whole country would do.

Hollingshead was followed by Augustus Harris who took a swipe at the basic concept of English local government: 'We should like a law which would define under what regulations theatres should be open ... not that one set of men should make one regulation and another set another'.

– 'Is not that the spirit of local government?' Matthews ventured.

That, of course, was Harris's point. The much vaunted spirit of local government, that bastion of British democracy, had been unable to ensure a safe theatre in Exeter and in many other towns besides. Elected officials had been found wanting, and now the thought in the mind of all responsible theatre and music hall managers, was how best to prevent another disaster from occurring. If that meant trampling on the venerable ground of local democracy, so be it. They feared, probably rightly, that another tragedy on the Exeter scale might push their industry to the brink of extinction.

Phipps, whose experiences of local government in Bath had opened his eyes at the start of his career to the propensity of town council members and local officials to meddle in theatre planning, had never had much time for 'the spirit of local government'. He now stepped forward to briskly point out that the Memorial had been signed by managers in Glasgow, Newcastle-upon-Tyne, Manchester, Liverpool, Birmingham, Nottingham, Wigan, Leicester, Reading, York, Scarborough, Brighton, Torquay, Eastbourne, Cardiff, Southampton and Margate, many of whom were in the room. He then proceeded to remind his audience of his own prescient advocacy for the introduction of a national theatre-inspectorate at the hearings of the 1877 Committee on the Metropolitan Fire Brigade:[2]

'I remember well being severely cross-examined by the Chairman of the Metropolitan Board of Works, Sir James Hogg, as to the number of inspectors that would be required in the event of the Home Office taking this matter up; and I said I thought six or eight gentlemen would be sufficient for the inspection of provincial towns. That is my opinion still. There should be two or three principal inspector and the rest sub-inspectors. With this means of inspection, I think all provincial towns might be well inspected, not only to the structure of the buildings in the first place, but they might be constantly inspected'.

Determined not to give Matthews an opportunity to interrupt his flow, he switched to an unsparing attack on the attitude and working practices of the MBW:

'When the Metropolitan Board of Works had obtained their present powers the necessity of establishing a separate theatre department was pressed upon them by me. They would not hear of that at all; they relegated the whole question to a sub-committee. They considered that the matter was not of sufficient importance for the appointment of a special committee.'

After describing in detail the circuitous route that theatre plans travelled from the Board to the Building Committee to the Theatre Sub-committee to an MBW architect and back again via the two committees to the Board for final approval, he concluded bluntly:

'It has been most unpleasant and disagreeable during the last half-dozen years to have anything to do with the Metropolitan Board of Works. There is great delay in approving the plans.'

'Unpleasant' and 'disagreeable' are strong words and suggests a deeply felt contempt on Phipps's part of the Board and its clammy hand of corruption, a contempt which might, in part, explain, though not excuse, his cavalier attitude to the MBW regulations in connection with the Exeter Theatre Royal.

Matthews countered by suggesting that a government department, invested with control over theatres, might employ the same architect as the Board. Phipps saw no difficulty with this: 'We should not object to that, because you would have that gentleman under your control.' Matthews pressed on: 'Why should not a competent architect in Manchester superintend the Manchester theatres and a competent architect in Glasgow superintend the Glasgow theatres?' Phipps stood firm:

'All we want is that there should be uniformity of decision throughout the country. But gentlemen have so many views. The authorities at Liverpool are diametrically opposed to those at Manchester.'

Phipps knew better than most that this was indeed the case, and Matthews, perhaps swayed by the strength of feeling of the deputation, made another incautious promise of intent:

'I have it in my mind that some Bill on this subject would be necessary next year and everything that has fallen from you will have my fullest consideration in the preparation of the Bill'.

Having elicited a loose promise of later legislation in line with their Memorial, the leaders of the British theatre industry departed.

After the Christmas recess, both Houses of Parliament kept up the pressure on the Government to take action. The Exeter MP, Sir Stafford Northcote, asked pointedly if it was the Government's intention to 'introduce a Bill this Session to deal with the questions of access into and exit from theatres?' to which Matthews replied that the Government was now considering the question of greater safety in construction of theatres both in London and the Provinces and 'the expediency of introducing a Bill dealing with the subject'.[3]

The Commons was also seriously concerned with the alleged wrongdoings at the MBW and on 17 February 1888, Lord Randolph

Churchill successfully proposed that a Royal Commission of Inquiry should be set up to examine the workings of the MBW. In the House of Lords, meanwhile, the Earl of Stafford, addressing the Prime Minister, Lord Salisbury, 'ventured to hope' that Captain Shaw's Report of 1882 might now be presented to Parliament as he believed that the 'Report would be of much use for the future guidance of theatrical managers'. The chairman of the MBW Lord Magheramorne (formerly Sir James Hogg) disagreed as the defects pointed out by Shaw had been acted upon, apparently under Magheramorne's personal supervision: 'Many and many a weary day had been spent in going over theatres from top to bottom for the purpose of testing their safety.'

Considering that Magheramorne knew little of theatre safety it was hardly a reassuring statement. It was also, a probably unintended, disclosure of the lack of interest on his part in enforcing the Board's regulations. Given such a culture from the top, it is hardly surprising that officials and Board members adopted a flexible approach. The Prime Minister sided with MBW chairman and turned down the request on the grounds that the 1882 Report would produce a false impression of the present state of London theatres.[4]

The House of Lords, having failed to get its hands on Shaw's 1882 Report, tried another tack. On 21 February the Earl of Milltown rose to ask whether the Government would lay the Report by Captain Shaw 'relative to the calamitous fire in Exeter', on the Table? He hoped that 'this time it [his request] was neither too soon nor too late for he had striven to discover the *juste milieu* ... and that the Report could be produced without inconvenience or objection'. He had timed it well; the Exeter disaster was no longer news and his request was granted.[5]

At the end of March, Matthews had to admit that the government would not bring in its promised Theatres Bill.[6] No reason was given, but, very probably, the prospect of introducing a Bill standardising theatre safety regulations across the country, a concept that both torpedoed the spirit of local government and, implicitly the efficiency of MBW's and the Lord Chamberlain's inspection regimes, while also steering the Local Authorities Bill to its conclusion, seemed simply too daunting. The MBW, however, pressed ahead with its own Bill in April with no government support. The Bill's second reading was put off for six months, by which time the MBW would have been dismantled.[7]

The Royal Commission of Inquiry into the Metropolitan Board of Works

At the beginning of May the Royal Commission inquiring into the MBW began hearing evidence at Westminster. It was led by Lord Herschell, assisted by Mr H R Grenfell, a former governor of the Bank of England and Mr F.A. Bosanquet Q.C.. As reluctant witnesses paraded before him, Herschell adopted the manner of a patient but determined headmaster facing a line of misbehaving boys of weak intelligence, probing and cajoling in an effort to extract illuminating answers. Witnesses could be compelled to appear, but those who gave a full disclosure, in the eyes of the Commission, would be given a certificate, which would protect them from any later civil or criminal prosecution. This put Phipps in a dilemma. If called, he would need to reveal enough of his private dealings with Statham Hobson and Francis Fowler to satisfy the perspicacious lord, but not so much that it tarnished his reputation among the upright members of the RIBA Council.

It was Hobson, the one-time surveyor turned successful land-speculator, who dragged Phipps into the mire by casually mentioning that 'he had paid Mr Fowler, a member of the Board, £200, in connection with the Lyric Theatre in Shaftesbury Avenue of which Mr Phipps and Mr Fowler were the architects'.[8] At the next hearing, Hobson expanded his statement saying that the £200 had been paid to Fowler 'at the request of Mr Phipps'. However, 'he was in a little difficulty himself as to what the £200 had been paid for, but he believed that it was with regard to ancient lights'.[9] A baffled Herschell remarked that 'he could not understand why Hobson should not have paid Phipps the sum agreed and left him to pay Fowler what he pleased'.

Phipps was duly called to clarify matters, but he chose to merely confirm that the money had been paid 'as previously stated to Mr Fowler for his advice on ancient lights' and added that 'he had had no other monetary transactions with Mr Fowler'.[10] The latter was patently untrue, and either Phipps had truly forgotten about Fowler's assistance over the Hengler's Circus plans, which seems unlikely, or he was hoping that he would get away without disclosing his occasionally very close links with this particular member of the 'Inner Cabinet', a small select group who, according to a former deputy chairman of the Board, George Edwards, 'wished directly or indirectly to rule the proceedings'.[11]

Phipps, realising that his reticence might prove his undoing, three weeks later asked to appear before the Commission again 'to correct his earlier evidence'.

'Since the last meeting of the Commission, it has been brought to my knowledge by some memoranda that in 1884 I made him [Fowler] a present and I should like to relate the circumstances.'[12]

He then recounted of how, in June 1884, the MBW's Theatres Sub-committee had recommended that his plans for the rebuilding of Hengler's Circus on the old site should be rejected, on the grounds that the site was unsuitable, and how a distressed Hengler had come to him to ask what could be done before the final decision was taken by the committee. Phipps immediately went to the Board to see Fowler for advice on how to rescue the plans 'without the story getting into the press'.

Fowler advised him to write to the Clerk of the Board to ask for reconsideration of the matter and also to ask if he might be allowed to appear at the next meeting of the Theatres Sub-committee with a model to explain the details of the proposal more fully. Permission was granted and at the next meeting, at which Fowler was present, a long discussion ensued over the model and the conclusion was that, 'If we blocked up all the windows on the properties looking on to the Circus, then there would be no objection to the site as a site'. The plans were subsequently passed after which Phipps called on Fowler and gave him £40 saying, by way of explanation:' You have been very kind to me in this matter and I am very much obliged to you' According to Phipps, Fowler had not asked for any money and the transaction had been a 'voluntary present because he had served my client'.

It is difficult to see how Phipps could have avoided the 'voluntary present' trap. He was clearly grateful to Fowler over the Hengler Circus business, a commission he might well have lost without his assistance, but he must also have been acutely aware that if he did not show his gratitude in some tangible way, Fowler might have been disposed to block future applications on Phipps's part rather than support them. As the only theatre architect on the Theatres Sub-committee, his opinion carried much weight and without his tacit support Phipps might not have able to uphold his reputation among London theatre owners as someone who could be relied upon to get plans passed without endless wrangling. He later claimed, in a letter to the RIBA Council, that he had known Fowler for years and advised him on the latter's Opera Comique alterations in 1885 and over the building on the National Opera House site.[13]

The relationship between the two was clearly strong enough for Phipps to feel able to ask Fowler's advice when he ran into difficulties with negotiations on Statham Hobson's behalf in the summer of 1886, over a site in Shaftesbury Avenue. At the time, Phipps was fully occupied with the construction of Leinster Hall in Dublin and also had the Exeter Theatre Royal to attend to. Nevertheless, when Hobson called on him in July to ask him 'to treat for a client' in connection with a Shaftesbury Avenue site that he was hoping to acquire and then sell on to a property developer, Phipps accepted what looked like a potentially profitable challenge.

Hobson was not an ideal client. He had a reputation as someone who was quite relaxed about using people and money as he saw fit to advance his own fortune and Phipps must surely have been aware of these rumours. Hobson, however, offered, in addition to a fee, the prospect of a potential commission for Phipps to erect a building with an extensive frontage on Shaftesbury Avenue. As Phipps later explained to the RIBA Council:

'Before I could treat I had to prepare a complete set of plans, elevations and sections of a proposed Building for the site, which were afterwards put aside and for which I have received no payment except the fee from Hobson.'[14]

These speculative drawings were to act as a bait with which to attract the right buyer, who might, if suitably impressed, not only relieve Hobson of the site but also commission Phipps to act as his architect. What kind of building Phipps designed is not clear, but, given the circumstances, it is likely to have been a multi-purpose structure with a frontage suitable for any combination of hotel, offices, shops and possibly a theatre too, which could be, more or less, guaranteed to pass muster with the MBW. Thus, Phipps found himself not only acting as an agent for Hobson, but also soliciting on his own behalf.

Phipps later claimed that he was under the impression that the MBW had accepted Hobson's tender for a site backing on to Archer Street 'in writing on 8 July 1886',[15] but this claim is at variance with Francis Fowler's statement to the Inquiry that the tender had only been partially accepted in July, as it was subject to references. Hobson, however, apparently told the Board that he did not give references 'because he wanted to see if he could find a purchaser'.[16] It seems therefore that, whatever Phipps's claim, the Board's final acceptance of Hobson's tender depended, in practice, on Phipps being able to persuade a property speculator to develop the site in a manner acceptable to the Board.

By 29 July 1886, Phipps was in negotiations with a Captain C. J. F. Napier whose advisers complained that the site was dominated by houses in Archer Street 'with ancient lights' and that these houses would have to be purchased before they were prepared to proceed with the negotiations of the lease. The ancient right of householders to a certain amount of day-light in the houses was the bane of property developers and a legal minefield. The worldly Hobson must have realised that this would be a problem and decided to use Phipps to solve it. After two months of getting nowhere, Phipps, finding himself 'at my own risk compelled to secure three houses in Archer Street' turned to Fowler for advice on 27 September 1886. His use of the word 'compelled' suggests that Hobson was not prepared buy up these houses, presumably because he had not yet secured the tender.

To Phipps's relief, Fowler, however, knew exactly what to do; he identified the houses Phipps needed to buy the leases for, instructed him in how to deal with 'the rights of lights' of the other houses, making diagrams and specifying which householders Phipps must negotiate with and which ones he could safely ignore.[17] It was invaluable advice. Phipps managed to find a total of £5,100 with which to buy up the leases and freeholds of the three houses in Archer Street after which Hobson was able to offload the site to Captain Napier, who commissioned Phipps to design a theatre, the plans of which were sent to the MBW the following March and recommended for approval on 29 April 1887.[18]

It is understandable that Phipps felt that Fowler deserved to be paid for this excellent advice. He could have paid Fowler from his own fee, as Lord Herschell had suggested, but it would not be surprising if he had felt ill used by Hobson and that therefore the latter should pay. After all, Hobson was used to distributing large sums for sundry purposes and, in the circumstances, could not quibble over a payment for £200 in connection with 'ancient lights'. Furthermore, as long as Hobson wrote the cheque, no charge of bribery could be levelled directly at Phipps.

Now, as the unfortunate business began to unravel, Phipps, as he had done during the Exeter Inquest, protested his innocence, which, for a man of his experience of the world, and in particular of the MBW's working practices, was not entirely convincing:

> 'I was not aware that the tender was not actively completed, I considered it was some delay on the part of the Solicitors, but I was not consulted about it. It was the highest tender and much more than the Board has since got by public auction from adjoining plots'.[19]

As far as Phipps was concerned, the whole transaction had 'no reference to obtaining the site or to passing of plans ... and I say on my honour that it was not a "bribe" '.

At his first appearance before the Royal Commission, Phipps had omitted to mention that Fowler had asked him to return the cheque to Hobson in July 1887 at the time when the Board's chairman had begun a superficial investigation into Robertson's tendency to ask for 'voluntary presents' from prospective land and property developers in return for a smoothing of paths over property deals. However, when the cunning Hobson had revealed the transaction to Lord Herschell, Phipps had no choice but tell his side of the story:

> 'Mr Fowler sent for me and said. "I find that Mr Hobson's name is mixed up very considerably with Mr Robertson's in the inquiry made by the Board. You are aware that I have a cheque from him [Hobson] of £200 which ought not to have been paid to me, and I want to hand it back."

> 'I said, "I will take it, but I cannot cancel the transaction. Of course, the cheque paid to you appears in Mr Hobson's books. I will take it back and return it to Mr Hobson." 'This I did.'[20]

Fowler, when questioned later the same day, agreed that Phipps had given him a 'voluntary gift' of £40 though 'until I heard it here today I did not remember his doing it'.[21] Indeed, he could not recall how many 'voluntary gifts' he had received over the years as he did not keep detailed accounts. This was untrue; he later managed to find his account books for the benefit of the Inquiry.

As to his returning the £200 cheque to Hobson, he had 'acted on the impulse of the moment'. He suspected collusion between Robertson and Hobson and 'did not like the idea of having received £200 from Mr Hobson'. Lord Herschell, trying to establish precisely when Hobson's tender had been finally accepted, tentatively suggested: 'The tender had not been accepted in June but was accepted in September after you had been employed?' Fowler did not deny his conversation with Phipps: 'I had spoken to Mr Phipps'.

This brief reply did not cast Phipps in a good light and it is not surprising that the RIBA Council asked Phipps to explain himself. There were doubtless members on the Council who felt that Phipps had brought the profession into disgrace over his Exeter design and now felt that he was doing so again. Phipps was furious; his letter of reply reeks of indignation at the effrontery of his name being mentioned in connection with bribes: 'I am not aware the Evidence I gave before the Royal Commission on the Board of Works requires any Explanation,' he wrote on 1 August.[22] On 11 October 1888 he wrote again to the Undersecretaries of the RIBA, but now in a more emollient tone:

'Referring to your letter of 31 July last and my reply thereto I should be obliged if you will inform the Council that if they would like any information from me on any part in my Evidence, I shall be most happy to attend them and give them the fullest explanation.'[23]

The RIBA Council did demand a full explanation and on 25 October 1888 Phipps provided the details of the Hengler Circus business and the Hobson affair. He denied 'most emphatically' that the £200 had been a "bribe" and that he considered the voluntary present to Fowler of £40 'to have been a legitimate payment.[24]

While neither transaction was a 'bribe' in the sense of the money having been passed covertly to Fowler before he gave his advice, it is difficult to see how these opaque transactions of payment for services rendered, could be considered as anything other than a reward for privileged information from which Phipps would have benefitted financially and professionally.

Phipps vehemently denied any wrong-doing in his interactions with Fowler and in the context of what had been going on elsewhere in the MBW, his actions seem rather puny, but he seems to have felt that he had no choice but to adopt some of the 'unpleasant and disagreeable' practices that fuelled the MBW's progress through London. He had done his best to put an end to them by campaigning for the Board to be relieved of its responsibility for theatres. Now, a year after the Exeter fire, past errors of judgment, forced on him by the corrupt nature of the MBW, had come back to haunt him at the point when he was planning to re-launch his career with two new theatres in Shaftesbury Avenue and reclaim his reputation as the nation's most renowned and reliable theatre architect.

Endnotes

1. *Era*, 17 December 1887, p. 13. Henry Irving was in America on tour, but was 'in accord' with the deputation.
2. See Ch. 5.
3. Hansard, HC Deb., 16 February 1888, v. 322 c 543.
4. Hansard, HL Deb., 17 February 1888, v. 322, cc 692-5.
5. Hansard, HL Deb, 21 February 1888, v. 322, cc 985-6.
6. Hansard, HC Deb., 26 March 1888, v. 324 c 245.
7. Hansard HC Deb 17 April 1888, v. 324, cc 146-72.
8. *Lloyd's Weekly Newspaper*, 3 June 1888, p. 4.
9. *The Times*, 6 June 1888, p. 6.
10. *The Times*, 9 June 1888, p.7.
11. *Era*, 28 July 1888, p. 13.
12. *Era*, 7 July 1888, p. 14.
13. RIBA Letters to Council, RIBA Institutional Archives, British Architectural Library, Royal Institute of British Architects. Letter from C J Phipps to Council, dated 25 October 1888. LC/28/4/19.
14. RIBA, Letter from Phipps to Council, dated 25 October 1888. LC/28/4/19.
15. RIBA, Letter from Phipps to Council dated 25 October 1888. LC/28/4/19.
16. *Era*, 7 May 1887, p. 14. Report on the Royal Commission's Inquiry into the MBW.
17. RIBA, Letter to from Phipps to Council, dated 25 October 1888. LC/28/4/19.
18. *Era*, 7 May, 1887
19. RIBA, Letter from Phipps to Council, dated 25 October 1888. LC/28/4/19.
20. *The Times*, 30 June 1888, p. 15. Report on the Royal Commission's Inquiry into the MBW.
21. *Era*, 7 July 1888, p. 14.
22. RIBA, Letter from Phipps to Council, dated 1 August 1888. LC/28/3/2
23. RIBA, Letter from Phipps to Council dated 11 October 1888. LC 28/4/9.
24. RIBA, Letter from Phipps to Council dated 25 October 1888. LC 28/4/19.

17 THE RE-LAUNCH

While Phipps was preoccupied with saving his reputation in London, the Exeter Theatre Company was equally concerned with re-establishing its credentials with their fellow Exonians by transforming the charred, but still sound, outer walls of Phipps's building into a theatre that would be among the safest in Europe. In this they were unexpectedly aided by Henry Irving. The great actor, moved by the Exeter disaster, formulated his own principles for a 'safe theatre', on the basis of which the Manchester architect Alfred Darbyshire (1839-1908) drew up a preliminary plan which was published by the *Daily Telegraph* on 29 October 1887.[1] William Horton Ellis, who was still chairman of the theatre company, was much taken by the underlying absolute conditions for the plan, which Darbyshire later summarised as: 'Isolation: instant insulation between

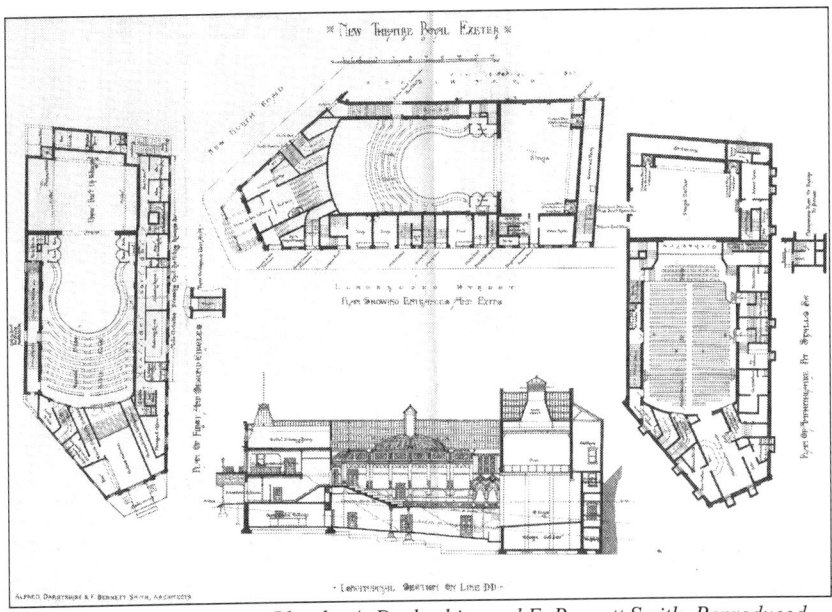

New Theatre Royal, Exeter. Plan by A. Darbyshire and E. Bennett Smith. Reproduced with the kind permission of the Devon Archives and Local Studies Service. ©Exeter City Council

stage and auditorium; no seat higher than the proscenium opening; two exits from every part; fire-proof roof of the stage [with] a large shaft with louvres; and [use of] fire-resisting materials.'[2]

There was nothing very new in these conditions, except for the insistence on keeping the seating below the proscenium arch, which in practice meant that there could only be a single tier above the pit and that the traditional gallery would have to go. This single tier or balcony would, as before, accommodate the dress circle at the front but with the upper circle situated behind on a slightly rising level thus giving the low balcony a much greater depth and correspondingly greater projection over the pit than normal. With such a design the back of the pit was liable to turn into an airless, dark hole, though within easy reach of the street. This undesirable space, Irving believed, could usefully serve as the 'gallery' with seats at no more than 6 pence, though the architect J.G. Buckle, in his stinging critique of the plan in the *Era*, doubted whether 'the gods' or anyone else would find this arrangement acceptable. He pointed out that in Phipps's Princess's Theatre in Oxford Street (1880) it was impossible to get a full view of the stage from the back of the pit because the balcony extended 30 ft over the ground floor, 'a distance not equalled in any other metropolitan theatre', adding icily: 'This theatre has probably had more uncomplimentary epithets bestowed upon it by lessees, actors and the public than any other London playhouse'.[3]

In Buckle's eyes, the great depth of the plan was an error; it placed too many spectators too far away from the stage to be able to hear and see the actors properly, it 'sacrificed comfort and dramatic adaptability [acoustics and sight lines] for relative safety' and was therefore unlikely to be popular with theatre-goers.

In Exeter, Ellis had no such qualms. He had convinced himself and around half of the company directors, that the Irving's and Darbyshire's design was the only plan that might persuade the townspeople back to the theatre, many of whom had openly vowed never to set foot in a playhouse again.[4] However, when Ellis commissioned Darbyshire to draw up preliminary plans for a new theatre on the old site utilising the surviving exterior walls, his fellow director, C. R. Ross, a merchant with architectural ambitions and a more monetarist mind-set, commissioned a local architect to draw up another set of plans, based on his own ideas which included several shops. Darbyshire's design had only three shops squeezed in between a multitude of exits and entrances on Longbrooke Street.[5]

At a meeting of the directors in June 1888, called to adopt Darbyshire's plans before presenting them to the shareholders to vote on, Ross insisted that his plans should also be presented: 'He could not see how clearing away the shops would add to public safety as the additional room would only provide for a larger dress-circle'.[6] This assertion ignited a fierce debate among the directors, with the 'pro more shops' faction gaining ground and the board split down the middle. Ellis still got his way; he used his casting vote to ensure that the shareholders would only be given the Darbyshire option.[7]

Whether Phipps, who still held one share in the Exeter Theatre Company, was sent a copy of the plan and, or cast a vote in favour or against, we do not know. Phipps was busy overseeing the construction of his two Shaftesbury Avenue theatres as well as rectifying his earlier design errors at Eastbourne. He added an extra exit from the orchestra stalls and two extra exits from the pit, but had to resort to building an outside concrete stairway to make a second exit from the gallery.[8] He also installed a 'metallic drop-scene as security against fire' in readiness for the re-opening on 21 May.[9]

The Shaftesbury Theatre

The Shaftesbury Theatre had been conceived as a vehicle for Lancaster's wife, the actress Ellen Wallis. She had acquired a great following in the provinces and had had some successful runs in London in Shakespearean roles. Originally Lancaster had commissioned James G. Buckle to design the theatre,[10] but for some reason Buckle fell out of favour and Phipps took over.[11]

The site, occupying 75 ft. north to Shaftesbury Avenue, 131 ft. east to Greek Street (later Newport Place), 130 ft. west to Nassau Street (now Gerrard Place) but a tight 66 ft. south to Gerrard Street, was almost an island site with ample scope for multiple exits opening directly into the street. Unfortunately, the site was not quite large enough to allow for a separate block for workshops and dressing rooms, sot Phipps had to squeeze in some of the dressing rooms in the basement and the rest right around the edge of the stage directly below the fly galleries and scene-painting gallery where the fire risk was particularly high. The risk would have been considerably less had the projected electric lighting been installed, but, this safety feature was temporarily dispensed with and instead gas was laid on throughout the building.[12] Phipps did, however, provide the higher-level dressing rooms with emergency exits in the form of casement windows, which opened onto iron balconies, which would offer the actors temporary safety while they waited to be rescued by the fire brigade. From the back of the stage there were a total of five exits into Gerrard Street.

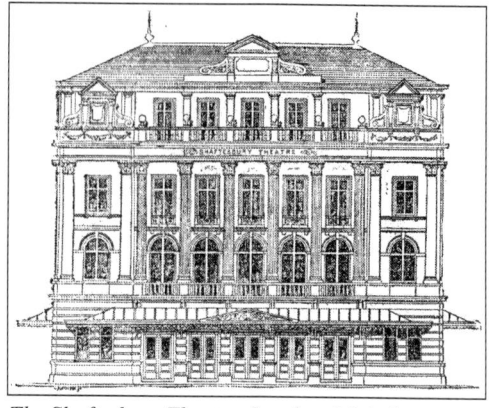

The Shaftesbury Theatre, London. Main frontage. Author's Collection.

Phipps's external iron balconies appear to have been new to London,[13] though Frank Matcham had earlier installed two iron 'alarm balconies' as an additional means of escape from the gallery in his Theatre Royal in Stockport (June 1888).[14] Both Phipps and Matcham might well have been influenced in their pioneering use of external fire escapes by the National Flemish Theatre (1886), designed by the Brussels-based architect Leon Baer, which featured such balconies along the sides of the building.[15] Indeed, Phipps, like Baer, erected further iron balconies along the sides 'of each tier for use in case of need'.[16]

While the iron balconies were an outwardly visible statement that the Shaftesbury was a theatre where safety was given the highest priority, the frontage on the Avenue signalled solidity and impeccable classical antecedents. A rusticated ground floor in Portland stone formed a reassuringly solid base for the upper three storeys in red brick. In the centre were five wide entrance doors, the middle three designed for the dress circle spectators and the other two for stalls patrons who entered a spacious and elegant rectangular lobby.

On the floors above rose giant Corinthian stone columns screening a loggia at upper circle level reached through casement windows from the generously proportioned refreshment room situated immediately behind. The loggia provided a pleasant promenade for jaded patrons and, crucially, another escape-route into the open air 'only 10 ft. from the ground', as Phipps was anxious to point out.[17] The columns carried a plain, solid-looking entablature from which rose the top floor graced by a balustraded balcony, which could be reached 'from the top platform of the gallery'.[18] It was a stately façade exuding trustworthiness and timelessness complete with handsome fire escapes.

Entrances to the upper circle, pit and gallery were placed both in Greek Street (later Newport Place) and Nassau Street (later Gerrard Place), making a total of six. The royal entrance was situated in Greek Street and Mr Lancaster's entrance in Nassau Street and both of these could be used in an emergency by the dress circle visitors. The total number of exits thus rose to 13 of which five were designated for the dress circle occupants.

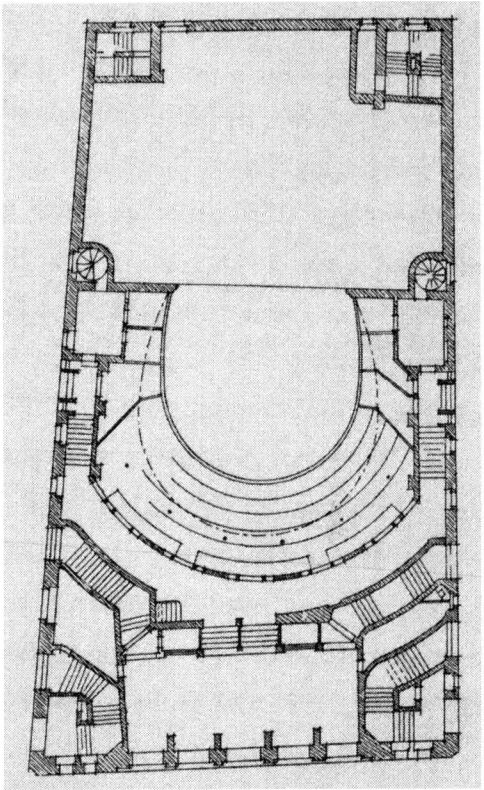

The Shaftesbury Theatre, London. Plan at Balcony level, 1887. John Earl Collection.

On 18 October, two days before the official opening, the Lancasters and Phipps opened the doors to a select gathering of London glitterati and members of the national press for a private inspection tour of the theatre. It seems to have been a carefully orchestrated preview where the champagne flowed freely judging by the sometimes gushing prose in which Phipps's work was described in the papers the following morning. The liberal *Daily News* was particularly fulsome describing the theatre as 'a conspicuous ornament to the new thoroughfare ... a fine square building in the Italian style' with the internal arrangements resembling both the Savoy and the Prince of Wales in its use of marble staircases and mosaic floors.[19] Impressed by the isolated site and the number of exits and ignoring the absence of electric light, it concluded: 'There is therefore reason to believe that the management only state a fact when they claim that it is one of the safest houses, if not the safest, in existence, in view of the risk of fire.'

The *Morning Post* admired the 6 ft. wide corridors surrounding the various tiers, the marble staircases leading from each side of the entrance hall to the stalls, and the fact that the dress circle was on level with the street 'which may be reached immediately'.[20] As for the pit, 'it was one of the most capacious and comfortable in London.

The Shaftesbury was not a huge theatre, it held around 1,800 spread over three tiers. Unusually for Phipps, he set the dress circle and the three private boxes on either side of the proscenium along an oval-shaped curve with no hint of contrary flexure. The dress circle held six rows of stalls, whereas the upper circle was a little shallower with five rows and on this level the circle and private box fronts formed more of a horseshoe.

The sides of the auditorium were dominated by the private boxes, of which there were seven at stalls level and three on each side level with the first and second tier. Festooned with brown plush hangings lined with salmon-coloured silk they formed a sophisticated prelude to the slim and gilded proscenium that surrounded the stage opening (30 ft. wide and 27 ft. high). The whole ensemble formed a fitting frame for William Telbin's act drop depicting Stratford-upon-Avon with a statue of Shakespeare and for the substantial green baize-covered iron curtain designed and patented by Phipps's office manager, Maximilian Clarke. The green baize covered a complex structure made of:

> 'A rectangular angle-iron or T-iron frame ... strengthened by horizontal, vertical and diagonal stays ... [which] form. a lattice work On either side of the lattice-work layers of slag wool, asbestos, or other mineral fibre, are secured by means of barbed wires, transverse bolts, staples, wire network or sheet metal'.[21]

The sides of the frame were fitted with angle-iron strips designed to slide in grooved bars built into the masonry of the stage opening, thus providing a very tight fit with no room for smoke to escape. The curtain was balanced by weights and could be raised and lowered either by means of a winch or 'vertical hydraulic rams'. Clarke also proposed that 'electric devices' (unspecified) might be used for releasing the curtain providing 'suitable brake devices' (also unspecified) were in place 'preventing too rapid a descent'. In the Shaftesbury, the iron curtain was worked by hydraulic power 'supplied from the mains of the Hydraulic Power Company, which run up in the subway underneath Shaftesbury Avenue'.[22]

To a large extent Phipps and Lancaster had fulfilled their promise to make this the safest of theatres, except in one crucial respect: lighting the theatre with gas.

Despite assuring the preview visitors that electric lighting was to be installed shortly 'all over the building', the general feeling in the press was one of disappointment over this failure. As the *Era* noted after its inspection: 'It seems a pity though, that the electric light is not be used from the beginning'.[23] One might have expected Phipps to have insisted on electric light being installed, especially after his strong advocacy of electricity in his interview after the Exeter fire. It is, however, possible, that Phipps simply could not find a suitably large space close to the theatre for the generators and accumulators with the building already taking up every inch of the island site.

The opening night (20 October 1888) with 'As You Like It' and featuring Ellen Wallis as Rosalind turned out to be something of a disappointment too. While the strong cast, including Miss Wallis, were praised for their individual characterisations, the overall pace of the production seemed a little slow for the London critics. Worse trouble was to come. On 17 November, when Bulwer-Lytton's *The Lady of Lyons* was due to begin, the iron curtain refused to rise. Max Clarke was sent for but was unable to shift the 'stubborn' curtain and the audience, having been entertained by the band, was politely asked to leave the theatre and 'take tickets for another evening'. Remarkably, as the *Era* observed, the spectators left 'without any expression of disapprobation'.[24] The problem was solved by the curtain's manufacturer, Messrs Clark, Bunnett & Co, who discovered that 'the valve of the curtain had become jammed through want of proper oiling and attention'.[25] Having been duly oiled by expert hands, the curtain went up and down 'to time' the following Monday accompanied by roars of laughter and applause.

The Lyric Club and the Lyric Theatre

It is unlikely that Phipps was duly concerned about the iron curtain problems; he had his hands full with the Lyric Theatre and its attendant chambers, flats and shops as well as with the conversion of the Prince's Hotel, in Coventry Street into the most elegant clubhouse in London.

The Lyric Club, founded in the mid-1880s as a musical and artistic club, reconstituted itself in 1888 with a new committee drawn from the aristocracy and the elite of the theatrical establishment, including Henry Irving, Squire Bancroft and Arthur Sullivan. The committee was 'determined not to be behind the times' among the rising welter of similar clubs offering smoking concerts and informal social gatherings,[26] and to this end they acquired the Prince's Hotel in Coventry Street and also St. Ann's, Barnes, a manor house by the Thames which was to be used as a summer clubhouse. Whether Phipps had anything to do with up-dating the Barnes property is unclear.

The Club described itself as 'a social and non-political club and 'one of the objects specified in the very first rule is to provide musical and dramatic entertainments periodically'.[27] The Exeter disaster notwithstanding, Phipps was the obvious choice as architect, having designed the original building, and having served Bancroft and Irving well in the past. And he did not disappoint; he created an 'exquisite little theatre with an elegant gallery at one end' on the ground floor, perfect for witty musical soirees, mini-operas or *tableaux vivants* 'of an amorous, but not too voluptuous nature'.[28] He also converted the first and second floor into a series of 'luxurious saloons for smoking and billiards', with a 45 ft. by 24 ft. dining room on the first floor, the walls of which were filled with panels of stamped leather, and re-fashioned 100 bedrooms, some of which seem to have been more like little apartments. He introduced the Moorish style into the smoking rooms and 'the entire club was fitted with the most elegant forms of electric lighting'.[29] The opening dinner on 18 November 1888, when the guests were serenaded by the band of the Grenadier Guards and surrounded by flowers and palm trees from the conservatories at Barnes, was a great success and the *Daily News* noted with approval that the many alterations had given 'Mr Phipps an opportunity of giving fresh proofs of his professional skills.'

The Shaftesbury Theatre and the Lyric Club did much to redeem Phipps's professional reputation among the metropolitan elite if not in among their provincial counterparts, but not quite enough. The Lyric Theatre, due to open a month later, would need to trump the Shaftesbury in every respect in order to restore his credentials. It was a delicate task; his involvement in the negotiations over the site, recently laid bare by the Public Inquiry into the MBW and the subsequent demand by the RIBA Council for a full explanation of his conduct, had made the Lyric a challenge of incalculable dimensions. Luckily for Phipps, the theatre-struck accountant, Henry J. Leslie, who replaced Captain Napier as Phipps's client, was a man with funds, high expectations and a shrewd understanding of the demands of London audiences.

The Lyric Theatre, London. Main frontage. Theatres Trust. Knight Brothers' British Mirror Series.

Quite when Leslie took over from Napier is unclear. Phipps's first plans for the Lyric, drawn up on behalf of Napier, had been passed by the MBW on 29 April 1887,[30] yet it seems that Leslie had leased the site from the end of September 1886.[31] This would suggest that Captain Napier was acting as a front man for Leslie, who, for reasons of his own, preferred not to reveal his hand at that stage. Leslie was then working for the lessee and manager of the Gaiety, George Edwardes and according to Hollingshead the two had mounted a new comic opera, *Dorothy*, at the Gaiety.[32] It was not a success and Edwardes sold his interest to Leslie who moved the production to the Prince of Wales, re-cast the title role and found himself with a gold mine. It ran for 817 consecutive performances at the Prince of Wales before Leslie was able to transfer it to the Lyric, which had been specially built for the purpose. From Leslie's perspective, English comic opera, which

The Lyric Theatre, 1888. View of the auditorium. Author's Collection.

appealed to all classes, was the future money spinner of the English theatre and he had, allegedly been planning for some time, to build a theatre, like the Savoy, exclusively devoted to such productions, but not to an exclusive audience. His theatre would offer attractive facilities for all, from a bar and refreshment rooms at gallery level to 'a dressing and bath room in the stalls lavatory for gentlemen desiring to dress at the theatre'.[33]

The site, which boasted a 150 ft. slanting frontage onto Shaftesbury Avenue was hemmed in by Great Windmill Street to the west, the narrow Rupert Street to the East and the troublesome Archer Street to the north. The four-storey façade, in red brick and Portland stone was much more low-key than Phipps's design for the Shaftesbury Theatre. No majestic columns here, instead rectangular windows, crowned by triangular pediments on the first and fourth floors, form a uniform line, the three bays at either end graced by a first floor shallow, balustraded balcony and topped by a two-bay recessed arcade underneath a high-pitched gable. The centre is identified by a broader gable, but the uninspired sparse deployment of Italian and Flemish Renaissance detail does little to lift the design beyond the ordinary multi-purpose pattern-book offerings. Presumably, Leslie did not think that investing in an arresting façade would bring a good return. He had his sights set on the interior.

The slanting frontage made the site almost triangular and Phipps had little choice but to place the auditorium and stage parallel with Archer Street in order to get sufficient room for the stage and rentable offices, the latter to be accessed from the Avenue, that Leslie insisted on including. There was thus no room to fit in a suitably grand entrance, with accompanying vestibule and foyer, in the centre of the building, as might have been expected with such an extensive façade; instead three doorways designed for the exclusive use of the 12 private boxes, orchestra and balcony stalls were placed at the upper end. Phipps did, however, fit in a single, large, circular doorway in the centre for the expensive-seat customers, with a small vestibule, useful perhaps, for any gentlemen in urgent need of the stalls bathroom before facing the ladies. Immediately to the left of the central doorway was the royal entrance and to the right, the upper circle doorway, followed by duplicate exits for the pit and gallery. Two-thirds of the seats were given over to the pit (300) and the gallery (700) though the audience to these vital parts had to manage with one corridor-shaped entrance each in Archer Street.

The Lyric's auditorium was slightly larger than the Shaftesbury's as Phipps's comparative figures show. Thus, the distance from the front of the first tier to the curtain in the Lyric was 38 ft., in the Shaftesbury 35 ft.; from the front of the upper circle 44 ft. in the Lyric and 40 ft. 8 in. the Shaftesbury while the gallery fronts were respectively 48 ft. and 44 ft. 6 in. away from the stage. The distance from the back of the pit to the curtain was very similar, 60 ft. at the Lyric and just over 58 ft. at the Shaftesbury.

The Lyric auditorium design was a mixture of the new and the traditional, the latter most evident in the proscenium. The width and height of the stage opening were the same at the Shaftesbury, 30 ft. by 27 ft., and although the actual stage opening at the Lyric was defined by a moulded alabaster picture frame, it was set into a traditional deep elliptical arch that rose gracefully above it complete with a profusely decorated tympanum. The arch was carried by pairs of gilded and fluted Corinthian columns made of scagliola,[34] between which were three superimposed private boxes. A further three private boxes, equally bedecked with hangings in gold and coral brocatelle, filled the sides of the balcony tier, which followed Phipps's favourite contrary flexure line. The balcony, placed at street level held eight rows for 163 spectators, while the upper circle with seven rows had room for 230. Below were seven rows of orchestra stalls seating 150, behind which was the pit with 13 rows, most of which were underneath the balcony.

In the stalls and pit the walls were lined with panelled walnut and sycamore with carved moulding 'specially designed and manufactured in Germany', with pale grey-blue and seats in blue velvet. The walls of the balcony, private boxes and upper circle were covered with gold-stamped leather-paper which must have made a glittering spectacle under the resplendent electrical chandelier. The electrolier, as it was called, 'was carried out from a suggestion of Mr Leslie's and represents an inverted bouquet of corn, barley and poppies in "prodigal confusion", (8ft. high and 6 ft. in diameter) a kind of rococo extravaganza with 150 lights.[35]

Both Phipps and Leslie seem to have been greatly impressed by the new all-electric Burg Theatre in Vienna, which opened in the early autumn of 1888[36], as not only were all the electrical fittings for the Lyric manufactured in Vienna but they were also installed under the direction of M. Emil Sechehaye, the Electrical Engineer of the Grand Opera and Hof-Burg theatres in Vienna'. There was no gas laid on, the whole theatre was lit entirely by electricity 'generated in adjacent premises belonging to the proprietor'. The premises in question were probably in the basement of the old Café L'Etoile (formerly Dr William Hunter's House) in Great Windmill Street, for which Leslie had managed to obtain the freehold in October 1887. This was an 18th-century four-storey townhouse, which Phipps linked-up with the stage and used for the dressing rooms.

There had clearly been no expense spared on the lighting of the house and the stage, and Leslie seems to have equally ready to fund a plethora of carefully calibrated decorative schemes for the circulation areas, on which Phipps gave a cautious free rein to his imagination giving each area its own personality. Thus, the vestibule, and the rectangular crush room beyond it, together with the passages outside the auditorium at ground level were all decorated in a florid 'Pompeian style', fashionable among the nouveaux riches and an appropriate setting for the elegantly dressed. In the basement, on the other hand, in line with the wood-panelling in the auditorium, the stalls foyer and smoking room were treated a more robust manner in the form of 'an imitation of Early Dutch interior'. The ceiling was supported by heavy beams with panels in pitch-pine and plaster decorations the walls sporting a high dado in copper bronze with the upper part being covered in very rich leather. A fire place with a heavy over mantel in stone framed by two old Dutch portraits completed this more masculine environment.[37] The ante room for the royal box was done up in the Robert Adam style.

Phipps reserved his most flamboyant scheme for the Grand Hall situated on the first floor at the back of upper circle corridor. It was 30 ft. long, 16 ft. wide and 18 ft. high and was intended to serve not only as a lounge and refreshment room in the intervals but also as small concert room. Here he deployed a turquoise-blue and green colour scheme in early French Renaissance style creating a geometrically ribbed ceiling and cornice, covering the walls with tapestries and panelled dados, installing leaded-glass windows with hangings of silk brocatelle and an oak parquet floor.

The Lyric did not have iron balconies but, like the Shaftesbury, it had an iron curtain worked by hydraulic power and installed by Messrs. Clark and Bunnett, though there is no mention of it being designed by Max Clarke. It had been painted by Mr. E.G. Banks to represent the Old Iron Gates leading to the Avenue of Chestnuts at Bushey Park.

The opening night (17 December 1888) with the popular 'Dorothy' was a great success, but despite Phipps's best efforts to rehabilitate himself as the nation's foremost theatre architect with one of London's most expensively fitted out theatre both before and behind the curtain – it cost £43,000 – the Lyric did not trigger any new major theatre commissions inside or outside the metropolis. Instead, Phipps had to make do with amending the plans for the Garrick Theatre and the Tivoli Music Hall by his rival Walter Emden, while outside London, the young Frank Matcham suddenly seemed to be the favoured theatre architect.[38]

The Garrick had been commissioned by W.S. Gilbert for the actor manager John Hare in early 1888, at the time when Phipps was busy with his two Shaftesbury Avenue theatres. Emden's plans for the Garrick were approved by the MBW on 6 June 1888 when the Board also agreed to issue a certificate on satisfactory completion of the building. However, Gilbert and Hare had a serious disagreement with Emden and asked Phipps to take over as the supervising architect.[39] Phipps amended Emden's drawings on 23 March 1889, adding glazing above the stage area and what seem to be structural reinforcements throughout the building.[40] About a week later Phipps applied to the London County Council's Theatre and Music Halls Committee for a certificate for the Garrick Theatre, though it was not originally his design.[41] At the time, the *Era* stated that the theatre had been erected 'mainly from the plans of Mr Emden with sundry alterations suggested and carried out by Mr C.J. Phipps',[42] while the *Morning Post* muddied the waters further by claiming the theatre had been built 'from the designs of Mr Emden and Mr C. J. Phipps'.[43] There is a certain similarity between Phipps's façade for the Shaftesbury Theatre and Emden's classical frontage for the Garrick, and the latter's semicircular vestibule at the Trafalgar Square corner seems to echo Phipps's treatment of the main entrance at the Lyric, suggesting that Emden owed more to Phipps than he might have cared to acknowledge.

The unfortunate incident with Max Clarke's iron curtain at the Shaftesbury Theatre apparently persuaded the Garrick's manager John Hare to leave out such an expensive safety measure: 'They do not always work well, as recent experience has proved', he observed, and instead there would be 'a couple of firemen on duty during the performance'.[44]

Phipps's involvement with the design and erection of the Tivoli Music Hall and Restaurant in the Strand, close to the Adelphi, is even more difficult to disentangle. Plans by Phipps in the London Metropolitan Archives dated 13 December 1888 were made from 'tracings received from Mr Emden'. However, this was nearly two months after the foundation stone for the Tivoli had been laid by H.J. Leslie on 18 October 1888, in his role as chairman of the newly formed The Tivoli Limited Company, which was financing the project. Was this another case of bringing in Phipps as supervising architect? It seems not. In the description of the Tivoli published in the *Builder*, this grandiose theatre and restaurant which finally opened on 24 May 1890, Walter Emden is credited with the design and there is no mention of Phipps.[45] The auditorium seems to have had remarkably poor sightlines, something that Phipps was rarely guilty of, and this factor alone suggests that Phipps had not been directly involved in the planning. Less than a year later the company went bankrupt, a new company was formed and Frank Matcham was commissioned to remodel the theatre into something more in line with audience expectations.

On 1 April 1889 the Local Government Act (51 & 52 Vict. cap 41) became law and the responsibility for provincial theatre safety was handed to the new local authorities. In London, a new authority, London County Council, came into operation slightly earlier, on 21 March 1889, which took over all the duties of the discontinued Metropolitan Board of Works, and many of its officers, including the superintending architect Thomas Blashill, who continued in this role at the LCC. Phipps's former assistant, E.A.E. Woodrow also joined the LCC. For Phipps, who distrusted local authorities in any shape or form, and who had had several encounters with Blashill over what would be acceptable as the right kind of bolt at the Shaftesbury Theatre,[46] these developments must have been frustrating, even disheartening. However, all was not yet lost. In the house of Commons, Dixon-Hartland persevered with his Theatre Bill to create a government-run national inspectorate of theatres based on Phipps's heartfelt and much ventilated proposal. The main objective of the Bill was to remove the control over London theatres and music halls from the new-born LCC, on the grounds that it was an elected body and therefore subject to policy changes, and instead hand the responsibility for enforcing public safety to a permanent government-run inspectorate for which theatre managers were willing to pay.[47] Dixon-Hartland, seemed, however to have a rather confused view over what actually constituted theatre safety and how it could be best achieved:'I do not care a straw as to the safety of the structures themselves; I leave that to the managers. What we ought to do is to see that the public can escape in the event of fire ... and guard against panic.'

The Home Secretary Henry Matthews, while admitting that there might be policy changes every three years at the LCC, resolutely dismissed the bill's proposal for a government-led inspectorate as unworkable in practice:

> 'Any Government Department which undertakes to control the management of theatres throughout the country will be undertaking a task which will be extremely difficult and expensive, and which is already perfectly well performed by local authorities'.

He had clearly not been convinced by Phipps's optimistic suggestion in December 1887 that half a dozen inspectors would suffice. At the time this estimate must have struck Matthews as a little naïve, if not hopelessly unrealistic, but perhaps Phipps was attempting to shield his clients, who had volunteered to fund the scheme, from unnecessary expense. For Matthews, equally determined to protect the government from needless expenditure, the simplest and cheapest solution was, undoubtedly, to pass the whole matter of theatre safety over to the new local authorities. He agreed, however, that the LCC probably had insufficient powers at present and he was happy to 'make the control of public buildings, in the interests of public safety, as complete and efficient as possible'.[48] Matthews won the House over and the second reading of the Theatre Bill was put off for another six months 'to give the Government time to bring in a Bill dealing thoroughly with the whole matter'. For Phipps, the chances of seeing his firmly held views on the management of theatre inspections ever becoming law were now very slim indeed.

In Exeter, a few months later, the rebuilt Theatre Royal, contained within Phipps's stout external walls, opened on 7 October 1889, on time, on budget and completely finished down to the last brushstroke. This remarkable achievement, as the *Exeter Evening Post* observed, 'was due in no small part to close co-operation between the Architect, the Builder and the Clerk of Works, William Axon, a cool-headed man who has left NO STONE UNTURNED'.[49] Darbyshire's auditorium with a horseshoe-shaped balcony presiding over an extensive lower level with stalls at the front, a pit in the middle and a 'gallery' or amphitheatre stowed underneath the balcony, was enthusiastically received, the acoustics proving excellent and the tight-fitting titancrete curtain reassuring the doubters. The much maligned Exeter Theatre Company had successfully re-launched itself.

Phipps had other concerns. He and his fellow investors were anxious to divest themselves entirely of their interest in the Eastbourne Theatre Royal, which had been a drain on everybody's resources for too long. Right from the beginning, Phipps had been unwise or unlucky or both in his choice of managers but, at last, he had persuaded a group of three of the provincial theatre's most experienced lessee-managers, Wallace Roberts, C. J. Archer and Fred Bartlett, not only to take over the lease but to buy out the present investors on the basis of an instalment plan.[50] The new triumvirate opened on 10 February 1890 with the pantomime *Blue Beard* and rapturous welcome, 'which promises well for the new management'.[51]

Relief over a solution to the Eastbourne problem must have been marred by absence of any major commissions. However, the sudden closure of Her Majesty's Theatre at the end of January 1890, due to bankruptcy, offered a glimmer of hope. The property speculator G.H. Todd-Heatly struck an agreement with the Crown, who owned the freehold, undertaking to rebuild the entire block, excluding the Royal Opera Arcade, by Christmas 1895. He had in mind a large hotel,[52] and at some point in 1890 commissioned Phipps to produce speculative plans and elevations for a hotel and shops to attract a leaseholder.[53]

Portrait of C. J. Phipps 1890, published in Building News. Author's Collection.

In April, Phipps's low profile received a minor boost when the *Building News* published a series of write-ups of 'Contemporary British Architects' complete with 'photo-lithographic illustrations'. The photograph of Phipps, taken by Mr Bassano of Bond Street, depicts him dressed in the latest fashion in a pose that is meant to exude authority and competence, but instead reveals a slightly slumped figure staring rather vacantly into space, a tired man not quite sure of his destiny.[54]

Endnotes

1. In Manchester, Darbyshire had carried out extensive alterations to the Prince's Theatre in 1869 and designed the Gaiety Theatre in 1884.
2. Alfred Darbyshire, *The Art of the Victorian Stage, 1907*; reissued B. Bloom, New York and London 1969, pp. 175-6.
3. *Era*, 12 November 1887, p. 8.
4. *Exeter Flying Post*, 7 October, 1889, p .3
5. Plans and longitudinal section of the New Theatre Royal Exeter by Alfred Darbyshire & F. Bennett Smith, Architects, printed on a single sheet among Coroner's Papers, Exeter Fire 5 September 1887, ECA, Devon Heritage Centre.
6. *Era*, 16 June 1888, p. 17. Report on meeting of the Directors of the Exeter Theatre Company.
7. The company terminated the lease with Pickfords and building on the enlarged site began in March 1889.
8. M. Jones and J. Pick, *Mr Phipps' Theatre*, Entertainment Technology Press, 2006, p. 82.
9. *Era*, 26 May 1888, p. 18.
10. *Era*, 4 June 1887, p. 14.
11. *Era*, 3 December 1887, p. 11.
12. *The Times*, 22 October 1888, p. 8.
13. *Era*, 20 October 1888, p. 8.
14. *Era*, 2 June 1888, p. 14.
15. *Era*, 17 September 1887, p. 13.
16. *Era*, 20 October 1888, p. 8.
17. *Era*, 3 December 1887, p. 3.
18. *Era*, 3 December 1887, p. 11.
19. *Daily News*, 19 October 1888, p. 3.
20. *Morning Post*, 19 October 1888, p. 5.
21. T. Rees and D. Wilmore, *British Theatrical Patents 1801-1900*, STR, 1996, p. 60, no. 12,817.
22. *Era*, 20 October 1888, p. 8.
23. *Era*, 20 October 1888, p. 8.
24. *Era*, 24 November 1888, p. 14.
25. Letter to *The Times*, 20 November 1888, p. 3
26. *Morning Post*, 29 May 1888, p. 5.
27. *Daily News*, 16 November 1888, p. 3.
28. *Era*, 19 December 1891, p. 7 and 25 June 1892, p. 10.

29 *Daily News*, 16 November 1888, p. 3. *Morning Post*, 19 November 1888, p. 2.
30 *Era*, 7 May, 1887, p. 14.
31 *Survey of London*, v. 31, pp. 74-5.
32 J. Hollingshead, *The Gaiety Chronicles*, London, 1898, p. 435.
33 *Builder* 22 December 1888, p. 454.
34 *Builder*, 29 December 1888, p. 478.
35 *Builder*, 29 December 1888, p. 478.
36 *Era*, 13 October 1888, p. 14. The Burg Theater was designed by Baron Hasenauer. See also *Builder*, 22 December 1888, p. 454.
37 *Builder*, 22 December 1888, pp. 453-54.
38 G. Garlick, 'Frank Matcham and the Legacy of C.J. Phipps', *The Matcham Journal*, v.3, April 2016.
39 H. Maguire, 'The Architect of the Garrick Theatre', *Theatre Notebook*, v. 42, no. 3, pp. 123-26.
40 LMA, GLC/AR/BR/07/0428.
41 *The Times*, 3 April 1889, p. 14.
42 *Era*, 27 April, 1889, p. 11.
43 *Morning Post*, 25 April 1889, p. 5.
44 *Morning Post*, 25 April 1889, p. 5.
45 *Builder*, 31 May, 1890, p. 398.
46 1892 Select Committee on Theatres, paras. 2162-2167.
47 Theatres (County of London Bill), Hansard, Deb. 8 May 1889, v. 335, cc. 1418-47.
48 Ibid. Cc. 1431-34.
49 *Exeter Evening Post*, 8 October 1889, p. 3.
50 M. Jones and J. Pick, *Mr Phipps' Theatre*, Entertainment Technology Press, 2006, pp. 101-102.
51 *Era*, 15 February 1890, p. 19.
52 *Era*, 2 May 1891, p. 7. The case of Leader v. Todd-Heatly.
53 Survey of London, v. 29, p. 245. NA, CRES 35/2073/14, 341, p. 14. Letter from Phipps to the Crown Commissioners regarding Her Majesty's Theatre and Carlton Hotel dated 29 October 1890.
54 *Building News*, 18 April 1890, pp. 546-8.

18 LONG SHADOWS
JUNE 1890 - DECEMBER 1893

Phipps's Shaftesbury Avenue theatres failed to elicit a steady flow of new work apart from Todd-Heatly's speculative proposition. The few commissions that came into Phipps's office in the early 1890 included only one new theatre, the Portsmouth Empire, the rest amounted to little more than a limited refurbishment of the Nottingham Theatre Royal, the remodelling of the Vaudeville in the Strand and the drawing up of plans for converting Leinster Hall into a theatre. It seemed as if theatre developers were not yet ready to re-associate themselves with the once renowned Phipps fearing, probably rightly, that his name no longer inspired confidence in potential investors or the public. He had not yet regained his reputation as the nation's foremost theatre architect and there were other men waiting to take his place. To the 55-year-old Phipps, intent on reclaiming his position and former work load, the rising popularity of Emden and Matcham among theatre developers was not a good omen.

The once much lauded Nottingham Theatre Royal was beginning to show its age and Phipps's brief was to, 'enhance the comfort of the audience'.[1] It is easy to forget, among the clamour for theatre safety that 'comfort' was, at least, as high on the Victorian audience's list of priorities as fire precautions. 'Comfort' was not just to do with comfortable seats and good sight lines, but included proper ventilation in the auditorium, welcoming vestibules, pleasant refreshment rooms and, not least, an adequate number of civilised cloakrooms.

At Nottingham, Phipps had to work within the given space, but by various subtle means he managed to create a vestibule on the ground floor for those arriving and leaving by carriage and to improve the ventilation in the auditorium by piercing the back wall of the upper circle and installing opening windows. He also conjured up more circulation space for the upper circle and pit by bringing the corridors behind these two sections into 'the body of the house to be used as promenades and lounges'. In the pit he replaced the 'ugly wooden barrier' between the orchestra and the stalls by light iron standards linked by a cord, and converted the pit seats to stalls. Even the gallery received more comfortable seats, and the tier fronts were repainted in cream and turquoise blue with the mouldings picked out in gold.

On 18 August 1890, as the work in Nottingham was nearing the end, Phipps sent his drawings, showing how the Leinster Hall could be converted into a large theatre, to Gunn.[2] Judging by Phipps's explanatory letter the splendid circulation areas would remain more or less intact and only the hall would need to be rebuilt. The two balconies would be replaced by three tiers 'in the usual theatre form', that is with a dress circle, seating 302, an upper circle for 480 and a gallery holding 600, while the extensive ground floor would be converted into a huge pit seating 700 and fronted by stalls for a mere 184 spectators. Thus, Phipps confidently expected to accommodate a total of 2,370 (exclusive of standing room), slightly more, as he pointed out than in the old Theatre Royal, and with more space given to each seat. He based this assertion on the basis of 'the complete surveys I made of the old Theatre Royal in the year of 1877 and from an examination of your [Gunn's] books'.

For this vast audience space Phipps proposed a proscenium opening 35 ft. wide (the same as Drury Lane) and a stage 63 ft. deep. There would be and iron curtain, three inches thick, the building would be lit by electric light and the dressing-rooms would be placed in a separate block and every section of the audience would have ready access to two exits. He had covered all possible safety aspects: 'In every respect I have made this scheme as perfect as it is possible to devise, not only for the comfort but for the safety of the public and those engaged on the stage'.

It could have been an impressive theatre, though not necessarily easy to fill, and Gunn did not pursue the project. In 1895 he sold Leinster Hall to a syndicate.

In July 1890, Phipps proudly notified the *Builder* that the Vaudeville Theatre in the Strand 'is about to be re-fronted, and altogether remodelled as regards its interior, under the direction of Mr C. J. Phipps'.[3] The lessee-manager, Thomas Thorne, had finally got possession of the two houses, nos. 403 and 404, which fronted the Strand and behind which the Vaudeville had originally been built. With the properties in his hand, Thorne was 'determined to bring his theatre

' "up-to-date" [both] inside and outside'.[4]

Phipps replaced the insignificant doorway through the ground floor of No. 404, which had constituted the main entrance since the theatre's construction in 1870, with a stylish façade containing a central archway, opening into an enlarged vestibule, and flanked by two side doors, one for the pit the other for the vestibule. The doorways were recessed, leaving a porch 6 ft wide 'closed to the thoroughfare by the patent [sliding] Bostock gates'. Above, Phipps placed a balcony fronted by an arcade of five arches, the whole forming an impressive loggia behind which lay the new grand foyer (26 ft. by 20 ft.). The upper storeys were reserved for offices for Thorne.

A new saloon was also built for the gallery and cloakrooms were inserted on every landing. In the auditorium, the seating capacity remained the same, but Phipps removed the private boxes at stalls level and instead installed more comfortable chairs, in peacock-blue plush, with improved passing room. He also took out the small rooms beside the amphitheatre, and crucially, the cove over the proscenium. With the cove gone he was able to create a new ceiling supported on groins springing from the outer walls and to crown the proscenium opening with a pediment, thus giving the auditorium 'a wonderful idea of enlarged space'.[5] This was a complex construction in tight spaces and the work was not finished until mid-January 1891 when the refurbishment met with much approval.

Phipps's superintendence of the Vaudeville was rudely interrupted by an invitation from the LCC's Theatres and Music Halls Committee to attend an inspection of the Gaiety Theatre on 19 November 1890. This inspection had been triggered by an earlier inspection by the LCC's superintending architect Thomas Blashill, who had discovered extensive use of match-boarding for the band room (situated below stage in the mezzanine) as well as in the property room (placed in the cellars) and in the scene painter's room (at upper circle level). Furthermore, many of the concrete doors were in a bad state 'full of holes and will not shut' and the gangway on the side of the pit and stalls was less than 3 feet in places. And then there was 'the presence of a lumber room above the auditorium ceiling'.[6]

At the time of the Gaiety's erection in 1868, combustible thin wooden walls of this nature would not have unduly worried the Lord Chamberlain's office, which, at that time, had the responsibility for ensuring plans complied with its vague notions of theatre safety. Nor, it seems, had the MBW insisted on the match-boarding being replaced by more solid walls in the early 1880s. However, after Exeter, Blashill and the chairman of the Theatres and Music Halls Committee, T.G. Fardell were determined to take action.

For Phipps, having to parry awkward questions from a critically minded committee led by an assertive Fardell and supported by Blashill plus two of his assistants, one of whom was Phipps's former pupil E. A. E. Woodrow, the experience must have been both embarrassing and tiresome, not to say humiliating. The minutes of the meeting reveal that the inspection team examined the structure in great detail including the roof. The latter, it seems, was constructed 'of unprotected timber the whole way', with the sunlight merely encased in sheet iron supported by wood and 'the whole place filled with rubbish and old stores' leaving room for only 12 buckets of water!⁷

There was much work to be done, but Phipps seems not to have kept copies of the relevant plans as the chairman, according to the minutes, informed Phipps that 'he must write and ask for permission to trace plans'. George Edwardes, who had taken over the Gaiety lease from Hollingshead in 1886, and spent money on redecorating the auditorium to designs by the architect W.H. Romaine-Walker (1854-1940) in the 'Indian Style', could do little but comply and over the next two years improvements were carried out under the watchful eye of Blashill's team who surveyed the Gaiety several times in 1891 and 1892.

Edwardes, however, had a greater building scheme in mind. He had acquired a site in Cranbourne Street, Leicester Square, where he proposed to erect a new theatre for the American actor Arthur Daly and his company. Daly had been visiting the London West-end on a regular basis with his popular company since 1884, but had now decided that it might be worth his while to have his own theatre in the metropolis. Edwardes, who was not short of money, offered to build the theatre and then to lease it to Daly. Given that Edwardes and Phipps knew each other well, Phipps might reasonably have hoped to have been offered the commission, but Edwardes bypassed him and instead asked the relatively unknown Spencer Chadwick to design the theatre. It must have been a personal as well as professional blow to Phipps, a blow that was not necessarily softened by being asked to advise Chadwick on the planning. By the end of October 1891, work had progressed sufficiently for the foundation stone to be laid and among a large number of theatrical luminaries who witnessed the ceremony were Phipps and his wife. The event was widely reported in the London press, the *Daily News* even announcing that the theatre 'was being built after the designs and plans of Mr C.J. Phipps',[8] while the *Era* and the *Morning Post*, noted that the plans and designs had been prepared by 'Mr Spencer Chadwick in consultation with Mr. C.J. Phipps, F.S.A.'.

The shadows of doubt which still lingered around Phipps might well have been one reason why he was abruptly sidelined over the Langham Place concert-hall project for which he and T.C. Knightley (District Surveyor for Hammersmith) had prepared joint plans in 1887, and which was finally to start building in 1891.[9] In February 1891, Knightley published a plan and detailed internal description of the hall in the *Builder*, presenting it entirely as his own work with no mention of any involvement from Phipps.[10] It appears that by this stage Phipps's original backer had pulled out from the project and Knightley had seized the chance to establish himself as the only architect of the hall. Short of finding another backer with more money and influence than Knightley's, there was nothing Phipps could do about the situation.

Phipps had to console himself with the Portsmouth Empire, the opening of which was scheduled for May 1891.[11] The theatre was situated on the Edinburgh Road next to the Central Hotel and presented a rather plain appearance in red brick dressed with Portland stone. Its most notable feature in this four-storey building was the first-floor balcony placed in the centre and set under a giant circular arch with a decorative frieze above.[12]

The construction work took considerably longer than intended and it was not until the end of September that the owners applied for a theatrical licence from the local magistrates. The justices were suspicious. The auditorium consisted of a large pit on a good incline with reclining seats made of ... 'Austrian bent wood with rests for the elbows', plus a balcony with a spacious promenade behind, and a gallery, the latter holding 300. There were, however, a rather large number of bars occupying the circulation areas together with an unusually high number of 'sumptuously furnished retiring rooms for the ladies'.[13] The whole set-up had the air of a music-hall in waiting and local music hall proprietors, who did not relish further competition, objected strongly. The justices sided with the objectors and the licence application was turned down. Not even Phipps's fervent declaration that 'every precaution against the possibility of panic had been taken', including an iron curtain to Max Clarke's design, managed to convince the magistrates that his client intended to keep to the drama and not stray into the raffish and carefree music hall preserve.[14]

Towards the end of 1891 Phipps made his will which he signed on 15 December 1891. It was witnessed by Peter Anderson, Architect, of 5 Thornhill Square, London and Henry Seton Morris, Architects Assistant, of 7 Theberton Street, West London, who were both working in Phipps's office at the time. The timing might have been prompted by his recurring heart problem. Sometime in 1888 he had been diagnosed with 'Mitral Disease of the Heart',[15] a chronic but progressive disease affecting the heart valves, not easily detected in its early stages and often caused by a genetic condition or rheumatic fever. This disease is more common in the young than in the old and it is possible that the serious 'fever' that forced Phipps to cut short his Grand Tour in 1857, had, indeed, been rheumatic fever.

Phipps appointed his wife, Honnor Phipps and her cousin, the solicitor Richard Eugen Sharps, of 20 Iverson Road, Brondesbury, Middlesex, to act as his executors. He directed that, other than household effects which he bequeathed to his wife absolutely, his property, real or personal, should be sold or called in and converted into a trust.[16] The trust was to be administered by the executors and the income from the trust was to be paid to his wife as long as she remained a widow. Thereafter the trust was to be divided into four equal shares between his children, Ethel, Alwyn, Ida and Mary, with the shares for his daughters 'to be for their separate use free from the control of their present or any future husband'. The will does not contain any details of his own investments at the time, but it specifies the kind of funds in which his trustees could invest. These included any public stocks or securities guaranteed by the United Kingdom Government or that of India or any other British Possession, railways stocks or any other securities having a fixed rate of interest and leasehold securities held for a term of at least sixty years. Investments in the theatre industry are not mentioned.

Phipps's income from fees and investment returns was still substantial enough to provide him and his family with a comfortable living at 26 Mecklenburgh Square. In the 1891 he employed three servants, a cook, a housemaid and a parlour maid.[17] At the time the census was taken the eldest daughter Ethel, who had become Mrs Edward Pullman in 1887, was living with her 'Leather Merchant' husband in Godalming, Surrey[18] and the youngest daughter, Mary Rashleigh, then 18 years old, was visiting the family of her future husband, Charles Henry Collier, the eldest son of a bank manager and estate agent also living in Godalming.[19] A year later, 21 April 1892, the couple were married at St Pancras Parish Church by the vicar of Godalming, at which point Charles Henry, who was described as a bank clerk in the 1891 census, claimed the status of 'Gentleman'.[20]

The second daughter Ida, now 25 years old, was still living at home as was her brother the 26-year-old Alwyn Rashleigh, described as an 'electrical engineer and employer'. He was then running a successful electrical engineering business in partnership with A.R. Dawson under the name of Rashleigh Phipps and Dawson which specialised in the 'artistic side of domestic illumination', that is in providing graceful and inventive lighting appliances suitable for wealthy drawing rooms and indeed theatre foyers and auditoria, with workshops in Stanhope Street, Euston Road and showrooms in Berners Street, W1.[21] In March 1892, the firm exhibited at the Electrical Exhibition at Crystal Palace, but in November the same year the partnership was dissolved, 'by mutual consent' and Rashleigh Phipps set up his own company under his own name.[22]

While Phipps must have been proud of his son's success, his own lack of the same must have rankled. However, in early 1892 Woodrow and Clarke made a concerted attempt to rehabilitate Phipps's reputation in the eyes of the architectural profession. The occasion was a lecture on 'Some Recent Developments in Theatre Planning' at a meeting of the Architectural Association on 18 March, in which first Woodrow, then Clarke, with the aid of drawings provided by Phipps for the occasion, singled out some of his London theatres for fulsome praise.[23]

Like his erstwhile tutor, Woodrow was quite clear that London theatres were, above all, commercial ventures and therefore: 'Theatres have to be built to pay'. He cited Phipps's remodelling of the Haymarket as the best example of a theatre designed to meet both the demands of the kind of expensively mounted performances that the Bancrofts specialised in and 'the class of people frequenting it'. On the other hand, filling the whole of the ground floor with expensive seats at theatres such as the Olympic or the Adelphi would be 'fatal'. Phipps's Lyric Theatre was to Woodrow a good example what could be done on an irregularly shaped plot and, interestingly, in view of the recent Gaiety inspection: 'A very clever arrangement of the auditorium is displayed by Mr Phipps in the planning of the Gaiety, on a site of most irregular formation, but with exits in four streets'.

Phipps's treatment of the sloping site of the Savoy was also singled out for praise as was the Shaftesbury for its 'simplicity in the plan and the uniformity of the two sides' where entrances on one side have a corresponding exit on the other.

Yet, Woodrow was also greatly impressed by Emden's Garrick Theatre, not only the planning but also the construction, particularly Emden's use of 'fire-proof' cantilevers, rather than visible iron columns, to support the tiers.

As the paper only covered London theatres with references to developments and regulations abroad, the Exeter Theatre Royal was not mentioned. Though, as Woodrow observed, when discussing the inevitable costs associated with safe theatre construction: 'A cheap theatre is sure to be a dangerous one'.

During the discussion that followed, Max Clarke, who was still working for Phipps, held the floor at some length, and in harmony with his boss, urged the LCC to provide clearly thought-through regulations for theatre buildings with all speed, pointing out, as an example, that the Shaftesbury Theatre, 'the first modern symmetrical theatre built in London', was ahead of the present regulations by providing '1ft. of exit per twenty-six persons' whereas the LCC only demanded 1 ft. of exit per eighty-eight persons.[24] He also took the opportunity to extol the virtues of his own iron-curtain design. He drew a comparison with a fire-proof curtain 'made of some material like twisted iron wire' which had been put up in Edinburgh some years ago, but which had been 'a complete failure', unlike his own which 'had been put up in London, Liverpool and two or three other places, before any regulations of the kind were made by the L.C.C.'.

Clarke's contribution was a carefully planned speech, possibly in consultation with Phipps, and towards the end he broached the subject of the Exeter design, which Woodrow had so deftly side-stepped.

'There was a small point in the planning of theatres which had not been sufficiently touched upon. Most people knew that at the Exeter Theatre fire a great many people were burnt to death, and those people were burnt because a man at the top of the gallery staircase had a wooden ticket box, which was knocked down, and the first person who left that part of the theatre tumbled over the fallen box. The box had no business to be there. The ticket man too had no business to have a chair at the top of the stairs; that should be absolutely prohibited.'[25]

How Clarke had arrived at this simplistic explanation of the cause of the high death toll – as we have seen the, wretched check box was but one cause of the many deaths, the absence of a second gallery exit and an iron curtain were the crucial factors – we will never know, but it was certainly a comforting notion from Phipps's perspective. This strategy of hiding a fundamentally flawed plan behind the check-taker's paraphernalia might have been an original idea of Clarke's, but it might also have emerged in discussion between the architect and his office manager as a useful damage-limitation response to the ferocious criticism of Phipps in the press. Both men would have been equally concerned to keep the reputation of the business from disappearing down a black hole. It might also, of course, be an indication that both Phipps and Clarke had convinced themselves beyond reasonable doubt that there had been nothing wrong with the plans; Phipps had, after all, been exonerated by the Chief of the Metropolitan Fire-Brigade.

The members of the LCC's Theatres and Music Halls Committee, increasingly aware of their onerous responsibility to keep London theatre audiences safe, pressed on with attempts to strengthen their powers over the theatres under their control, as Phipps had feared they might. They had already agreed with the Lord Chamberlain that the Council should take over his power of licensing theatres in certain districts, and that the Lord Chamberlain's Office should in future only concern itself with the censorship of plays and songs and not with structural safety. As a consequence, the LCC, now proposed that a new House of Commons Select Committee be set up to clarify LCC's powers over entertainment buildings while also taking the views of theatre proprietors into account. The government obliged and The House of Commons Select Committee on Theatres and Music Halls began its hearings on 28 March 1892 under the chairmanship of Mr Plunket, M.P., and First Commissioner of Works.

The Committee's remit was to investigate whether the current licensing laws, that is the 1843 Theatres Act and the rather older Music and Dancing Act 25th Geo. II cap. 36, were still able to uphold the distinction between the two forms of entertainment. The latter had been brought in to regulate singing and dancing entertainment in 18th-century assembly rooms before being pressed into service as a loose statuary framework for 19th-century music halls, but there was a growing and uneasy feeling among the authorities and theatre owners that the boundaries were becoming blurred to the disadvantage of the drama. Theatre managers felt threatened by the music-hall proprietors' attempts to turn once short sketches into something resembling plays, thus, potentially, taking away any theatre spectators who would prefer to smoke and drink while watching the drama unfold on stage. Smoking was exceedingly popular, not least among the expensive seat-customers, and Phipps took care to provide suitably dignified smoking-rooms for them, with a bar close by.

Music-hall proprietors, on the other hand, feared that theatre owners might start to apply for permission for smoking and/or drinking to be allowed during the performance, thus tempting their customers away. These burgeoning signs of a free trade turning into a free-for-all is exemplified by Phipps's Portsmouth Empire, a perfect example of a hybrid theatre-*cum*-music hall structure, which could switch its entertainment to whatever promised the greatest profit, and which prescient magistrates had stopped in its tracks.

Since the granting of theatre licences had become progressively more linked to the complex issues relating to the structural soundness of the building and provision for public safety, the question of how to protect the spectators from physical danger, as well as preserving their moral propriety, without jeopardising the economic value of the theatre business, was carefully examined. Hence, among the roll-call of leading metropolitan and provincial theatre managers and proprietors, Phipps and Emden, were invited to give their views on what constituted theatre safety and how best to enforce it.

Phipps appeared before the Committee twice: on Wednesday 27 April and again on Monday 2 May. Essentially, he raised the same points that he had first voiced at the 1877 Committee on the London Fire Brigade and subsequently to the Home Secretary, Henry Matthews, in 1887, that is the necessity of having a single government agency, preferably operating under the Home Office, to administer and inspect the structural safety of existing and new theatres and other entertainment buildings all over the country.[26] Though in one respect, Phipps's view had changed from 1877. At that time, the Lord Chamberlain was the chief theatre regulator in London and Phipps had complained of unnecessary interference from his department over, what seemed to him trivial matters. Now, however, he looked back on his many years' experience of working with the Lord Chamberlain's Office with pleasure:

'Everyone is very glad to do everything the Lord Chamberlain asks. I have heard him likened to the hand of iron in the glove of velvet He is very autocratic, but always treats you in a very polite way; but he will have what he wants done; and the action is very swift, because the Lord Chamberlain is not accustomed to what he asks for being put off.'[27]

Perhaps Phipps's apparent change of attitude towards the Lord Chamberlain's Office should be seen in the context of his recent ordeal over the Gaiety inspection. What had once seemed to Phipps as unnecessary meddling by the Head of the Queen's Household had now been overtaken by a more tortuous, but also more effective system from the point of view of theatre safety. Dealing with the Lord Chamberlain's Office had been, at times annoying, but it was straightforward, there was no rigmarole.

Phipps was no more impressed with the procedures of the Theatre Committee of the London County Council than he had been with those of the Metropolitan Board of Works. According to Phipps the LCC's Theatre Committee was equally unable to pass any plans, either for alterations to existing buildings or for entirely new theatres, without first referring them backwards and forwards for further reports and amendments, thus wasting his clients' time and money. He had nothing against their superintending architect, Thomas Blashill: 'Indeed, he is a very competent man ... [and] always scrupulously polite'.

The main problem, as Phipps saw it, was that Blashill had no power independent of the committee, unable even to make a decision over the type of bolts to be used on doors and barriers.[28] He was less impressed by Blashill's assistants, Woodrow excepted: '[He] was in my office for a considerable time and is competent to understand the plans and the various arrangements of theatres, and, in all probability, he has been, while with me, behind the scenes during the working'.[29]

Much of Phipps's evidence consists of rather tedious recollections, in minute detail, of his past skirmishes with the MBW and the LCC over bolts and dressing-room staircases, in order to press home his point that regulations decided by and enforced by an elected committee were, in practice, unworkable. At one point, when he was about to read the whole correspondence he had had with the MBW over the Haymarket Theatre in 1883, the alarmed chairman intervened: 'It is rather a long one; could you tell us the substance of it'?

Phipps was not pleased, and slipping into the haughty tone he often adopted when gainsaid, replied: 'I think I can tell you what it is in short if you wish, but I would like this correspondence on the Minutes.'

Mr Plunket was not so easily intimidated: 'If you hand it in, we can look at it ourselves and decide whether it is to appear in the minutes.'[30]

After Phipps's, seemingly never-ending tales of the woeful ignorance exhibited by the polite Mr Blashill over safety bolts, a topic on which Phipps clearly considered himself an expert, the Committee eventually, and almost by accident, arrived at the serious issue of danger from fire in theatres and how to avoid it. Phipps, suddenly, became short and brisk:

'The danger from fire, in my opinion, is simply up above the stage among the hanging scenery. ... [and] I consider that the electric light behind the scenes of a theatre is the greatest protection that the public can have'.[31]

From danger from fire there was but a short step to the Exeter disaster. The Committee, having been lectured by Phipps for nearly two days, now turned on him with pointed questions over the Exeter planning and its alleged lack of adherence to the MBW regulations. Phipps denied that his planning had been faulty and, rather indignantly, declared:

'I was never brought before the magistrate at all; ... and I never said that the theatre should be built in accordance with all the rules and regulations of the MBW; 'there were only three modifications of it; the corridor at the back of the dress circle was of wood, not stone, and that was not burnt'.[32]

He admitted that he had been censured by the jury, but that had been a verdict of panic, and, displaying a touch of panic himself, suddenly asserted: 'The 127 [sic] people who lost their lives did so on a staircase which Captain Shaw said was a particularly good staircase'.

He was adamant that the fire had not been caused in any way by the building, which, strictly speaking, was true, but he would not acknowledge that the fatal consequences of the fire had anything to do with him, on the contrary:

'During the construction several alterations were made without his knowledge ... in particular a second tier of flies, put up by the managers, where they stored 'combustible material and scenery from the old pantomime'.[33]

Whether Phipps only put in one tier of flies remains a moot point, as he never published his complete plans in the architectural press after the fire, as he had promised. However, assuming this was the case, it is still difficult to fathom why he believed that the best way to restore his professional reputation was to proclaim his ignorance of the, sometimes, careless building work at Exeter, when, he had been, to all intents and purposes, the supervising architect. While it might carry credence with some, it might raise question marks over his competence among more circumspect clients.

Having touted his ignorance as an excuse, he then, with breathtaking ease, paraded his personal expertise in theatre design as a good reason for discarding some of the MBW regulations as 'being of no importance', with regard to the Exeter plans, before triumphantly announcing that he had built five or six theatres since the Exeter fire. This was an exaggeration. He had built three: the Shaftesbury, the Lyric and the Portsmouth Empire. In the London theatres, he had followed the requirements of the MBW and the LCC and 'had in fact done a great deal more to make them fireproof'. That was certainly true; neither electric light nor an iron curtain was a requirement at the time; but then he had been working for ambitious clients with both vision and adequate funds.

The Committee produced its report by the end of June 1892.[34] Despite Phipps's best efforts, it did not recommend the setting up of a separate government office to implement an inspection programme of theatres nationwide, on the grounds that everything seemed to be working satisfactorily as it was both in the provinces and in Scotland and in Ireland, the only exception being the LCC. Here the Committee had taken some notice of Phipps's long-winded arguments over the procedural rigmarole that infected the LCC as much as it had done the MBW, and the report proposed that: 'Professional advisors should be given a free hand and an undivided responsibility in order to secure a uniform policy and procedure and avoid controversy'. Furthermore, the LCC: 'Should have a staff of fit and proper persons to act as inspectors of the safety of theatres and music halls'. In other words, not even the chairman of the LCC Theatres Committee should have the right to countermand his superintending architect as had happened on occasions over the question of which bolts could be used.

Phipps's complaints over the cost to the taxpayer of drawn-out arbitrations complete with expensive lawyers had also struck a chord with the 1892 Committee members who now recommended the appointment of: 'A standing arbiter attached to Her Majesty's Office of Works to deal with appeals when the LCC and theatre owners disagree over improvements'. At least, Phipps had won a partial victory.

By July 1892, the site of Her Majesty's Theatre was being cleared, ostensibly for 'another huge hotel and surrounding shops'.[35] Whether this re-development scheme was based on designs by Phipps is unclear but it seems likely. A plaintive letter in the *Era* argued that the proposed project was a terrible waste of a Crown-owned property in a prime West-end location, and that the site should, instead, be used for a public building, ideally for the benefit of the Royal Academy, which, according to the writer, badly needed re-housing in a purpose-built *Palais des Beaux Arts*.

In Bath a more concrete proposal beckoned. Its Theatre Royal was in need of modernisation and Phipps was asked to bring it up to London standards. He redecorated the auditorium in the current London fashion by papering the walls at the back of the tiers in a rich rose red wallpaper 'for the purpose of heightening the artistic effect, and accentuating the elegantly designed fronts of the three tiers,' the panels of which were painted in ivory white, pale blue and gold.[36] For the main vestibule he designed a mosaic floor and decorated the walls and ceiling with stencilling. He also replaced the old heavy entrance doors with 'handsome doors in teak polished a rich dark brown mahogany colour', again in line with the London trend. All doors were fitted with 'patent pneumatic springs' and the sanitary arrangements in cloak rooms and dressing rooms were brought up to date. Back stage the walls were distempered from top to bottom and the machinery overhauled. The total cost was £1,000.

New commissions were still thin on the ground, though there were more alterations with which to occupy the office. The Comedy Theatre in Panton Street (1881) originally designed by Thomas Verity, needed updating as neighbouring property became available and Phipps's drawings from 1893 show a new stage and adjoining dressing rooms on the additional site and an enlarged auditorium on the old site.[37] The office also busied itself with improvements to the back-stage area of Phipps's Strand Theatre (1882).[38]

Daly's theatre in Cranbourne Street finally opened on 27 June 1893. Whether Phipps had been in any way involved in supervising the building is unclear, but it would seem unlikely. In the absence of more concrete evidence, the extent of Phipps's contribution remains a matter for speculation, but he might possibly have advised on the design of the stage and its machinery and possibly on the cantilever construction. However, in the, generally favourable, press reports at the time of the opening Spencer Chadwick is given all the credit while Phipps's early involvement had evaporated in the long shadows that still surrounded his professional persona.

In November 1893, the Queen's Hall was finally completed and here there was, again, no mention of Phipps in the laudatory reviews of the building's design and acoustics. Phipps, aggrieved that his contribution had been ignored, wrote to the President of the RIBA, Mr Mac Vicar Anderson, staking his claim to partial authorship of the new hall. The President was not too sympathetic and while acknowledging Phipps's contribution concerning elevations and sections at the planning stage, finally pronounced that 'the design of the exterior and interior in other respects, as well as the successful completion of the hall, is due to Mr T. E. Knightley, under whose sole superintendence the building has been carried out'.[39]

On 18 October 1893, Rashleigh Phipps, secure in his own business, married Edith Constance Hill, and the couple set up home in Harrow.[40] Electrical engineering was clearly the new future. His father could only hope that Todd-Heatly's speculative venture on the site of the Her Majesty's Theatre would, at last, bring him a new major commission.

Endnotes

1. *Era*, 16 August 1890, p. 8.
2. *Era*, 30 May 1891, p. 7, citing letter from Phipps to Gunn.
3. *Builder*, 12 July 1890, p. 33.
4. *Era*, 10 January 1891, p. 11.
5. *Era*, 10 January 1891, p. 11.
6. Appendix to Report From the Select Committee on Theatres and Music Halls 1892, pp. 392-3
7. Report from 1892 Select Committee, p. 395.
8. *Daily News*, 31 October 1891, p. 3.
9. LMA, Theatre Plans, GLC/AR/BR/ 19 269.
10. *Builder*, 14 February 1891, pp. 128-9.
11. *Hampshire Telegraph*, 8 November 1890, p. 5.
12. Undated photo of the Portsmouth Empire in 'A History of Portsmouth Theatres' by H. Sargeant, FLA, in *The Portsmouth History Papers*, (Portsmouth City Council) No. 13, September 1971, p. 21. The Portsmouth Empire was demolished in 1958.
13. *Era*, 3 October 1891, p. 17.
14. *Era*, 3 October 1891, p. 17
15. GRO Death Certificate, 25 May 1897. District: Pancras, vol. 01B, p. 42.
16. Her Majesty's Court Service.
17. 1891 Census, St. Pancras, RG12, Piece: 123, Folio: 97, page 4.
18. 1891 Census, Guildford RG 12, Piece 561, Folio 122, page 53.
19. 1891 Census, Guildford RG 12, Piece 562, Folio 25, page.43.
20. GRO, Marriage Certificate, Yr. 1892, Qtr. June, District Pancras, vol.1B, page 168.
21. Historical Newspaper Archives, *The Colonies and India Newspaper*, 5 March 1892, p. 32.
22. *London Gazette*, 25 November 1892, p. 6938.
23. *Builder*, 26 March 1892, pp. 242-4.
24. *Builder*, 2 April 1892, p. 264.
25. *Builder*, 2 April 1892, p. 265.
26. 1892 Select Committee on Theatres and Music Halls, para. 2037.
27. 1892 Committee, para . 2152.
28. 1892 Committee, paras. 2192, 2162.
29. 1892 Committee, para. 2194.
30. 1892 Committee, paras. 2162-63.The correspondence was not included in the minutes.
31. 1892 Committee, para. 2195.

32 1892 Committee, paras. 2291-2, 2294.
33 *Era*, 7 May 1892, p. 8.
34 It was published in full in the *Era*, 25 June 1892, p. 15.
35 Letter in *Era* 30 July 1892, p. 10.
36 *Era*, 3 September 1892, p. 9.
37 LMA, Theatre plans, GLC/AR/BR/07/0 421.
38 LMA, Theatre Plans, GLC/AR/BR/07/005, 1893.
39 *Builder*, 30 December, 1893, p. 490.
40 GRO Marriage Certificate, Yr. 1896, Qtr. June, District Pancras, vol. 1B, page 188.

19 THINKING DIFFERENTLY 1894-95

At the beginning of 1894, the long shadows surrounding Phipps began to disperse. First there was an unexpected commission from Wolverhampton's political and business elite for a new theatre to replace their old Theatre Royal, which was followed by a request from the London land-valuer turned architect, Ernest Runtz, to advise on the remodelling of the old Pavilion Theatre in the East End. Then there was a more substantial commission to transform Hengler's Circus into an ice rink for the newly formed National Skating Palace Ltd. And in early 1895 a serious fire at the Theatre Royal in Glasgow brought in another major rebuilding project.

The rapidly expanding city of Wolverhampton, with a population of over 82,000 in 1891, owed its prosperity to a well developed manufacturing industry specialising in high standard iron and metalware. In 1893/4, an ambitious factory owner and leading local politician, Charles Tertius Mander argued that the old theatre, erected in 1845, and holding around 1600 spectators,[1] 'was not large enough to induce the best companies to visit the town'.[2] A man of action, he set up a new company to raise money for a larger theatre to be built on a prominent site in Lichfield Street, next to the newly erected Victoria Hotel. It seems the decision to build the new theatre was taken in early February by Mander, and less than five months later Phipps found himself attending the laying of the commemoration stone 'in glorious weather amid a pretty display of banners and bunting' in Lichfield Street and explaining 'by means of a number of plans and designs' what the new theatre would look like.[3] At the subsequent festive lunch in the Victoria Hotel, a Captain Hodson proposed a toast to 'The Architect and the Builder' and in his reply Phipps reassured the assembled company that,

'when he undertook a thing, he always did so with a determination to make it a success, and he fully believed that when the theatre was opened, it would be found, both on the score of convenience and safety equal to anything they had in London'.[4]

Mander and his fellow directors wanted a theatre that was large and comfortable enough 'to supply the dramatic wants of Wolverhampton and the neighbouring districts for years to come'.⁵ They saw no virtue in unnecessary competition and promptly bought up the old Theatre Royal, 'which would be devoted to other purposes'.⁶ They left the town's variety theatres, which they presumably regarded as less of a threat, to carry on.

Phipps took full advantage of the prominent rectangular site and designed a suitably imposing, but not ostentatious façade, dominated by a round-arched, first-floor loggia in the centre flanked by square pavilions with mansard roofs. The pavilions housed four shops and their position did not interfere unduly with the provision of double exits from every part of the auditorium, a provision which Phipps no longer dismissed as unnecessary.

On the ground floor, a line of solid square pillars separated the shops and the five entrance doors. Two of the entrances were designed for spectators to the pit stalls (holding 200) and the remainder for the dress-circle audience (holding 231 in Phipps registered chairs), who all had the pleasure of lingering in a 'handsome' vestibule, 23 ft. long and 21 ft.

The Grand Theatre, Wolverhampton. Main frontage, Lichfield Street.
From the Collections of Wolverhampton Archives and Local Studies.

wide, before proceeding to their seats. Those aiming for the amphitheatre and gallery entered, through separate doors, from the 8 ft. wide side passages which connected with Berry Street. Thus, 'all classes of the audience are kept apart' as Phipps explained.[7]

As at Exeter, Phipps stuck to two tiers, one for the dress circle and one for the upper circle or amphitheatre (seating 150) with the gallery behind (seating around 700). The two were separated by a division, but here, as Phipps is keen to stress, in his official description 'each division has two ways out to the staircases'. With a full gallery there would, surely, still have been a scramble at the end, but those who wanted avoid the crush could wait in the fresh air on the gallery balcony, which was placed discretely above the loggia and behind a chunky balustrade. The loggia was accessed through French windows from the expansive dress circle foyer, 15 ft. deep and 41 ft. wide. The total seating capacity was 2,151.

The size and shape of the site allowed Phipps to experiment with the design and make the dress circle wider and shallower than in his earlier

The Grand Theatre, Wolverhampton. View of proscenium with ornamented iron curtain. From the Collections of Wolverhampton Archives and Local Studies.

theatres, in fact, going so far as to make the width greater than the depth and still retain enough space at the sides for the entrances and exits and two gallery staircases. It may seem an insignificant measure now, but in practice this was a bold step as it altered the spatial relationship between auditorium and stage and thus subtly changed the way in which actors and spectators engaged with each other.

The Wolverhampton auditorium was 70 ft. wide, which meant that, in order to maintain good sightlines from the sides, the proscenium opening should be, at least, half that width, that is 35 ft.. The stage was slightly narrower at 65 ft. and, ideally, the stage opening should not be wider than half the width of the working stage, in order to keep the sweaty business of scene shifting out of sight of the audience. Phipps compromised; he made elegant, square-framed proscenium 35 ft. wide, but cut back the actual stage opening 'at the first entrance' to 30 ft., leaving those with seats nearest the stage with a limited view of the performers.

A single, slightly projecting, proscenium box at each side, framed by Corinthian columns, broke the dress circle curve and drew the eye to the flat circular ceiling decorated with radiating panels and supported by tall, coved panels on either side of the proscenium. The treatment was a skilful rerun of the much smaller ceiling in the Northampton Opera House, but it worked equally well in a larger setting and brought a similar sensation of an intimate space where performers and audience could easily reach out to each other. Delicately moulded decoration in fibrous plaster executed by Jackson and Sons of London, adorned the circle fronts and ceiling, and, as in the London theatres, white and gold dominated the colour scheme with claret-coloured embossed paper on the walls, 'with a lighter shade of plush for the curtains and other upholstery'. The decorative work was, as usual, carried out by Mr Bell of London.

Among the safety provision, the most impressive feature was, undoubtedly, the 'fire resisting curtain in one piece 4 in. thick, which will be taken up and down without any rolling and available to be lowered at any moment, and in the space of thirty seconds.'[8] In addition, the proscenium wall was carried up 18 ft. above the roof of the auditorium, but, interestingly, another crucial safety figure, electric lighting, was restricted to the fronts of the two circles, the back of the dress circle, the foyer and the vestibule.

The stage was 41 ft. 6 in. deep, with the gridiron placed 55 ft. up from the stage floor. It was, thus, big enough to cope with the larger touring companies, though they might have grumbled about the widely dispersed dressing rooms: two in the basement, two at stage level, four on the first floor and another four on the second floor. Something had to give in this clever design to fit in four shops as well as double exits for all classes.

Wolverhampton's Grand Theatre opened on 10 December 1894 with D'Oyly Carte's company performing *Utopia (Limited)*. As in the old days, Phipps was duly honoured by an enthusiastic audience at the end of the performance.[9] He could breathe a sigh of relief; he had re-asserted his credentials in the provinces.

While the Wolverhampton project clearly dominated his workload during 1894, Phipps also found time to draw up proposed alterations for the back-stage areas of the St James's Theatre in London,[10] to enter the competition for the Blackpool Winter Gardens Theatre, which he did not win, and to keep an eye on the alterations to the Pavilion Theatre in Whitechapel Road.

The driving force behind the redevelopment of the Pavilion was Ernest Runtz (1859-1913) who was chairman of the Pavilion Theatre Company Ltd.[11] He had originally trained as an auctioneer and valuer with Samuel Walker, and became his partner in 1883, but began training as an architect in 1889 at University College in London. The Pavilion venture appears to have been an attempt by Runtz to marry property speculation with the launch of his own career as a theatre architect, hoping, perhaps that his considerable experience of the former would make up for a lack of experience in the latter. The aim was to raise the tone of the house and encourage the upper classes to attend, but whether it was Runtz or his shareholders who called in Phipps to advise is unclear.

Two weeks after the opening of the Wolverhampton Grand, the Pavilion Theatre, now 'transformed and beautified' and sporting 'an entirely new façade of Doulton terracotta', was ready for action with *The Babes in Wood* pantomime. The new theatre seated around 2,700 in three tiers and plus a pit that provided long, leather-covered benches with backs 'and plenty of knee-room fauteuils'. All tastes were catered for and for those spectators who might prefer less intoxicating refreshments there were 'teetotal bars ... under the supervision of Messrs. J Lyons and Co.' in addition to the ordinary buffets.

Glasgow Theatre Royal and the National Skating Palace

In the early evening of Friday 1 March 1895, a group of cleaning ladies were sweeping the stage of the Glasgow Theatre Royal in readiness for the evening's performance, when a temperamental gas jet caught a nearby piece of scenery and set it alight. Within minutes the scenery was ablaze and the fire out of control. The fire brigade was called, but by the time they arrived the flames had engulfed the whole stage and even 'penetrated beneath the iron curtain'.[12] The cleaning ladies escaped, one with her dress on fire, but no lives were lost. However, because of the theatre's situation, hemmed in among more or less attached groups of buildings at the top of Hope Street, the firemen could not reach the seat of the fire from the street but had to 'take their hose up along the passages between the blocks and onto the roofs of the adjoining buildings' losing valuable time. After 30 minutes the roof fell in but the flames did not spread to the front entrance and after about four hours the fire was out.

The Glasgow Theatre Royal was then owned by Howard and Wyndham, who also owned the Royalty Theatre in Glasgow as well as the Lyceum and the Theatre Royal in Edinburgh. The two partners had recently formed a limited liability company, with a capital of £100,000, to run all four theatres, and they seem to have lost no time in commissioning Phipps to rebuild the smouldering embers.[13]

Phipps must have been acutely conscious of the fact that had this fire taken place during a performance, he would have been staring another catastrophe in the face, together with the total disintegration of his reputation as an eminent theatre architect. As it was, this unexpected fire gave him an opportunity for fresh thinking on the fire-safety problem, as here it was reported that the so-called iron curtain had let the flames slip through into the auditorium. Indeed the circumstances of the origin and rapid spread of the conflagration positively demanded a new design approach if he were to bolster his career and calm the public's fear of fire in theatres.

By 23 March 1895 Phipps had completed his drawings and both he and Max Clarke travelled up to Glasgow to explain the finer points. Phipps seems then to have dashed back to London, where he was finalising the plans for the conversion of Hengler's Circus in Regent

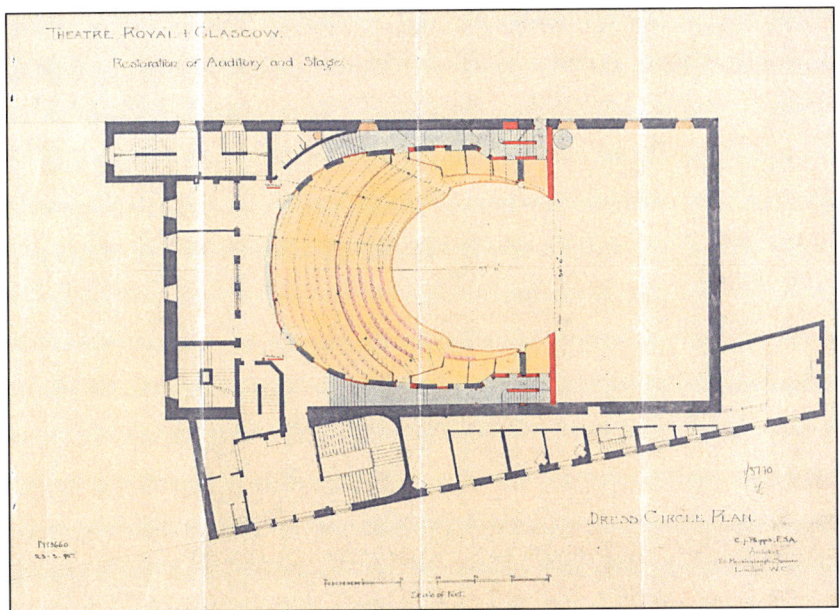

The Theatre Royal, Glasgow. Dress circle plan, 1895, by C.J. Phipps. Coloured drawing. © Glasgow City Archives Reference no. B4/12/1/3770.

Street into the National Skating Palace,[14] leaving Clarke to convince the Glasgow authorities of the virtues of the Theatre Royal plans. By 4 April, Clarke had reported back, and Phipps felt moved to reiterate some of the safety issues discussed with Mr J. Whyte, who seems to have been the City Surveyor, 'before the meeting of the Guild Court', which would have to pass the plans before the restoration could start.[15]

Whyte had stipulated that the galleries [sic] should be made of concrete, but Phipps objected on the grounds that:

'I do not think that any advantage to the public will be gained thereby; what I propose to do is, as shown on the plans, to have practically a double proscenium wall so that there shall be no contact between the roof of the auditorium and the roof over the stage'.

Furthermore there would be a tight-fitting fire-resisting curtain:

'The whole of the opening of the stage will be filled up by an iron [sic] resisting curtain 3" to 4" made of iron frame work covered on both sides with asbestos boards 3 eighths inch thick & filled in solid with silicate of cotton; this will be worked by hydraulic pressure & capable of being let down in 40 seconds'.[16]

Although Phipps does not say so, the design of the iron curtain, seems remarkably similar to Max Clarke's ideas, which he might well have developed further since patent application in 1887. Thus, the combination of the double proscenium wall with a tight-fitting iron curtain, while not preventing fires starting, would prevent them spreading beyond the stage:

'This is the greatest protection the public can have because supposing any accident should arise on the stage where it usually first occurs, all danger would be removed from the sight of the audience & a panic thereby avoided. In my opinion also the stage might be burnt down & the auditory saved entirely'.

Phipps also pointed out that the passages to the dressing rooms and the dressing room staircase would be of concrete, and that the gallery and upper circle stair would be covered with concrete at top [*sic*], 'and if possible, surrounding walls carried up through roof'. Interestingly, there seems to have been a slight disagreement between Clarke and Phipps concerning the width of the proscenium opening: ' I shall wish it to be an open question whether the proscenium opening shall be 35' 0" wide

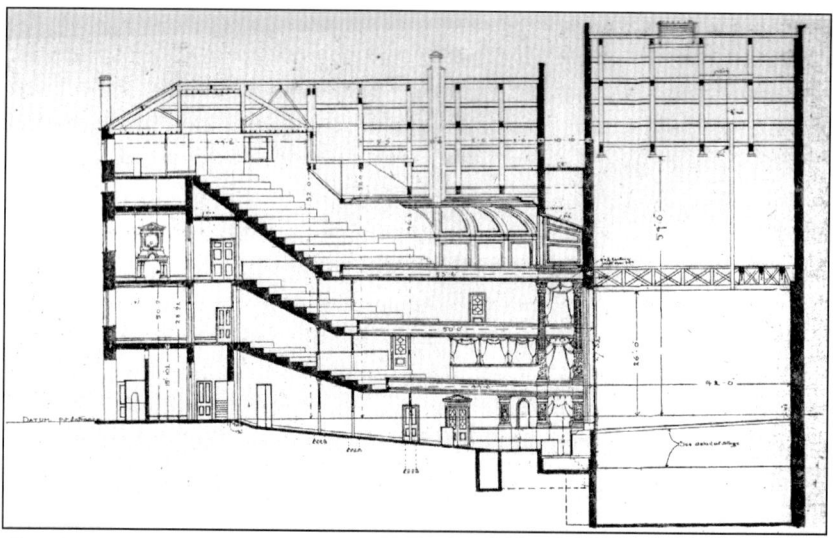

The Theatre Royal, Glasgow. Longitudinal section, 1895. Author's Collection.

as shown on plans or 31' 0" as figured by Mr Clarke. This is a question purely for the Management.'

On the plan at 'Ground Level' signed by Phipps and dated 25 March 1895, the proscenium opening is 35 ft. wide with a line across marking the 'Fire Curtain' annotated in what does not appear to be Phipps's hand: 'N.B. The opening of the proscenium to be 30' 0". 'The stage was 72 ft. wide, so Phipps's proscenium width was entirely appropriate, but it is possible that Clarke was concerned that the fire curtain of that width might be too heavy to work as quickly as promised.

A month later all formalities over the plans appear to have been settled and the reconstruction could begin. The present staircases would remain, but they were to be covered with concrete as Phipps had recommended.[17] The old horseshoe dress circle 'will have less of a sweep, being brought forward to the stage', the gallery would be reduced in size to allow for a refreshment saloon at the back, and an additional 300 seats would be squeezed into the pit.

With the opening date set for the beginning of September, speed, without any compromise on quality, was of the essence and remarkably Glasgow's re-built Theatre Royal opened on 9 September 1895 with H. Jones's play *The Masqueraders* performed by George Alexander's St. James's Company, as originally planned. The auditorium was found to be a vast improvement on Phipps's 1880 version. The acoustic properties were near perfect, which they had not been in the old house, and 'the draughts that were so disagreeably present in the latter' had been banished.[18] Clearly mindful of the complaints of draughts in the old theatre, Phipps claimed to have avoided this problem in the new auditorium by installing a new type of sunlight 'with two iron flues leading through the roof into the open air and so arranged that there was no possibility of a down-draught, but simply and up-cast'.[19] Flues from the gallery ceiling were also directed into the central flue and fresh air was brought in through 'proper channels', though he does not specify where these were placed. Central heating, in the form of hot water-pipes with radiators strategically placed in the corridors, added additional comfort. The boiler was placed in a separate building behind the stage. As Phipps crisply observed: 'It had been found necessary in practice at all theatres to have a means of warming'.

The improved acoustics were, almost certainly, due to some

fundamental changes to the auditorium space, including the lowering of the 'auditorium roof by 15 or 16 ft', the reduction of the depth of the stage from 52 ft. to 42 ft., and adding the surplus area to the pit floor. With seven rows of stalls at the front as before, there were now, allegedly, room, for around 1000 pittites sitting comfortably on cushioned seats.[20]

The first tier comprised the dress circle with 166 seats at the front and the family circle, with room for 158 behind a barrier. There were also three private boxes on either side behind the first row. As so often, the back wall of the circle was arranged in a series of arcades filled with glass, 'so that persons standing in the corridor may see the stage without going into the auditorium'. The second tier was entirely devoted to the upper circle and held 400. The gallery tier was, according to Phipps:

'A very spacious gallery, raised at the sides, and the curve of the front of the tier so designed that there is not a single seat in the gallery that has not a full and perfect view of the stage ... without the necessity of anyone standing up or leaning over'.[21]

The gallery held 800, making the total audience capacity close to 3,000, but despite this large capacity Phipps managed to create a surprisingly intimate atmosphere, not least through his treatment of the auditorium ceiling. At the back of the gallery was the refreshment saloon the ceiling of which carried over to the top rows of the gallery, making them, relatively, spacious before sloping downwards to connect with the main auditorium ceiling, which extended over the front rows, thus making the gallery a more inclusive part of the auditorium than in many other theatres. This inclusiveness was further reinforced by a series of groins springing from the sides of the gallery floor and extending to the flat circle in the centre. The groins, or rather coves, were not only a clever structural solution they were also likely to have been acoustically helpful. Fibrous plaster covered the ceiling, proscenium and box fronts – as usual executed by Messrs Jackson and Sons of London – while the colour scheme was, in tune with the fashion, confined to white and gold. By contrast the walls were papered in a rich terra cotta red with cherry-coloured plush hangings in the private boxes forming a voluptuous counterpoint to the gilded proscenium frame. The armchairs in the stalls, dress and family circle were covered in peacock blue and were supplied by C. Wadman's in Bath, who seem to have held the sole licence for the manufacture of Phipps's tip-up design.

The double proscenium wall was masked by three proscenium boxes on each side, flanked by solid Corinthian columns. The latter supported a segmental arch in the tympanum of which was a painting by Mr. Ballard of London representing Apollo and the Muses. A gilded straight sided frame enclosed the stage opening, the width of which was settled in Phipps's favour at 34 ft. with a height of 29 ft. The height of the gridiron was 59 ft.[22]

In his official description of the finished theatre, Phipps, put much emphasis on the novelty, safety and solidity of the construction, in particular on his double proscenium wall:

> 'One very important part of the construction ..., which has never before been attempted, is that there are two proscenium walls, 10 ft. apart, and following somewhat the lines of the pillars in the proscenium boxes; these walls are carried right up and the stage roof and the auditorium roof are thus entirely distinct and separated with a clear space of 10 ft. between them, there being also a fireproof roof formed immediately above the proscenium arch'.[23]

The fire-resisting curtain is also described in fine detail and as for the stage: 'It is constructed with every mechanical contrivance, and will be lighted entirely by electric light; gas is not laid on to any part.'

All these safety features, coupled with high-pressure mains hydrants on every floor, meant that Phipps's latest theatre was equipped with, what he described as:

'An immunity from danger which cannot be equalled', adding with cautious optimism, 'and it is hoped that this theatre may have a long life'.

Phipps was no stranger to hyperbole, but his second Theatre Royal in Glasgow was one of the safest theatres he had ever built. He had taken some time to get there, but here he had been working for two of the most enlightened clients in the business and together they had created what might be regarded as an exemplar of a fire-resisting theatre given the restriction of the site. Whether the Glasgow project was, in any way, a conscious or subconscious attempt on Phipps's part to finally redeem himself, at least partially, from past errors of judgment and downright negligence, we will never know, but assuming his Anglo-Catholic faith still held strong, the concept and prospect of redemption are likely to have entered his thoughts at some point.

At the close of the opening night's curtain-raiser, a comedietta [sic] called *Too Happy by Half,* Mr Wyndham made a brief speech in which he expressed his warmest thanks to Phipps and the builder Messrs Morrison and Mason of Glasgow, before leading Phipps onto the stage where he gratefully received the audience's enthusiastic applause.[24] As far as Glasgow was concerned, he had, indeed, redeemed himself.

With the Wolverhampton and Glasgow theatres Phipps had, at last, managed to reclaim some of his provincial territory in the face of the strong competition now offered by Frank Matcham. Between 1888 and 1895 Matcham had produced 22 new theatres and carried out alteration to another 20, mainly in the provinces, including Phipps's Prince's Theatre in Bristol. Theatre building was booming, and Matcham, like Phipps, had an innate understanding of how to create theatrical spaces that worked for both performers and spectators. He had also acquired a reputation for delivering his theatres on time. From Phipps's point of view, this was serious enough, but, in addition, Matcham offered something new: a glamorous, exuberant, playful decorative style with which to clothe his audience spaces, a style which taxed the skills of the fibrous-plaster craftsmen to their limits and conveyed an atmosphere of festive fun, gently held in check by a surreptitious symmetry. Phipps must have wondered how far he would have to go down this route, which by training and temperament did not come easily to him, in order to stay in the game.

At some point in 1895, possibly after the completion of the Glasgow Theatre Royal, Max Clarke left Phipps's office to set up his own practice at 4 Queen Square, Bloomsbury. The loss of his supportive and efficient office manager after all these years – he had joined as an articled pupil in 1872 – must have been a blow, though probably not unexpected; in some ways it is surprising that Clarke had remained so long before branching out on his own. He subsequently ran a successful general practice for many years and became a Fellow of the RIBA in 1904 and was often called upon to act as arbiter in compensation disputes. He died in 1938.[25]

Phipps had the National Skating Palace with which to occupy his thoughts. It was due to open at the beginning of January 1896 and required some careful attention to detail. According to the Morning Post, 'the whole building had been practically reconstructed and ... decorated in the most sumptuous manner'.[26] 'A splendid surface of ice covered the whole of the flooring of the old circus ring, the stables and the lower lines of seats, while the balconies had been turned into a restaurant, promenade and smoking gallery all with a good view of the skating. On the ground floor, Phipps had provided 'private dressing rooms, shower baths and skate lockers'. With music played by 'sparkling bands', plenty of attendants and expert skaters to teach novices how not to fall over, the scene was set for healthy and elegant entertainment.

In November 1895, as the ice rink was nearing completion, the developer of Her Majesty's site, Todd-Heatly's time was up and he had to admit defeat. He had failed to acquire the adjoining arcade and No. 2 Pall Mall and to find anyone prepared to lease either the projected theatre or the hotel within the stipulated five-year period and took refuge in bankruptcy. This was not good news for Phipps.

Endnotes

1. Drawing in Wolverhampton Archives, Dx-374, The Theatre Royal, Wolverhampton (1843-94). The architects were Messrs Meo and Ridley of London, who won the competition to design the theatre.
2. *Era*, 30 June 1894, p. 16.
3. *Era*, 30 June 1894, p. 16.
4. *Era*, 30 June 1894, p. 16.
5. *Era*, 8 December 1894, p. 11.
6. Once the Grand Theatre was up and running, the old Theatre Royal was pulled down, and the town council later built a new library on the site.
7. *Era*, 8 December 1894, p. 11. From Phipps's official description.
8. *Era*, 8 December 1894, p. 11.
9. *Era*, 2 December 1894, p. 7.
10. LMA, Theatre Plans GLC/AR/BR/07/0 446, dated 12 July 1894 and 27 July 1894.
11. *Era*, 23 June 1894, p. 7.
12. *Glasgow Herald*, 2 March 1895, p. 8.
13. *Glasgow Herald*, 2 March 1895, p. 8.
14. LMA Theatre Plans GLC/AT/BR/19/0 148. Basement, Circle and Gallery plans dated 28 March 1895.
15. Letter from Phipps to J. Whyte, Esq., 4 March 1895. CSG Archives, AGN601.
16. Ibid. The letter is typed and signed with a flourish by a confident Phipps, who had, by now, also acquired a telephone (tel.no. 7556), which was a relative rarity in the 1890s.
17. *Builder*, 4 May, 1895, p. 338.
18. *Era*, 14 September 1895, p. 14.
19. *Building News*, 13 September 1895, p. 391.
20. *Builder*, 14 September 1895, p. 191.
21. *Building News*, 13 September 1895, p. 391.
22. *Building News*, 13 September 1895, p. 391.
23. *Building News*, 13 September 1895, p. 391.
24. *Era*, 14 September 1895, p. 12.
25. RIBA. Biographical file of Maximilian Clarke (1851-1938).
26. *Morning Post*, 7 January 1896, p. 2.

20 RESOLUTION 1896 - 97

Between November 1895 and January 1896 Phipps's chances of proving his worth with a monumental building in the West-end looked very slim indeed. Todd-Heatly's departure had left the field open to other speculators waiting in the wings with plans at the ready. From Phipps's point of view, the most dangerous was the land speculator H.P. Okeden, who had commissioned Walter Emden to produce plans for an Imperial Opera House with surrounding shops for the site. Emden's drawings for a large, continental-style theatre with tight box-tiers set into a horseshoe-shaped auditorium seating 2,232 people – a clear attempt to rival Covent Garden[1] – were approved in January 1896, by the LCC Theatres Committee.[2] However, Okeden had not yet found a leaseholder prepared to take on Emden's grandiose theatre and Phipps's hope of a commission were now entirely dependent on the actions of Todd-Heatly's mortgagee.

Fortunately for Phipps the latter handed over the whole business to the Law Guarantee and Trust Society Ltd, who swiftly re-commissioned him to design a theatre and hotel and set about acquiring the adjoining building. Phipps's designs proved easier to market than Emden's and in February 1896 the Society clinched a deal with Herbert Beerbohm Tree to enter into a provisional contract for Phipps's theatre on the basis of preliminary plans which were submitted to the Crown Estates Office in the same month.[3]

Tree had been based with his company in the Haymarket Theatre since 1887 and was therefore thoroughly familiar with a Phipps's work. He had also tried out Phipps's new Theatre Royal in Glasgow – he followed George Alexander's company during the first season – and was now prepared to trust Phipps to deliver a theatre that would impress the whole of London. Tree was not short of money; his fondness for a grandiose acting style amid complex set-piece romantic scenery had brought in a small fortune during his years at the Haymarket, and having his own theatre in a prime West-end position would be a logical next step. It had, of course, to be a theatre that could stand up visually as well as structurally to his lavish productions and which would more than match the air of luxury and comfort that his audience had enjoyed at the Haymarket.

Tree did not, however, trust Phipps entirely when it came to the interior decoration. Like many of his *nouveaux riches* patrons, Tree was enthralled by the architect and interior designer William Henry Romaine-Walker (1854-1940) and asked him to act as his personal consulting architect.[4] Romaine-Walker had previously transformed the Gaiety auditorium into an 'Indian Style' experience, but his current speciality was a lush French classicism liberally endowed with rich ornamentation, suitable for the drawing rooms of the wealthy, though he could also do extreme Gothic when the need arose. Whether Phipps felt aggrieved over this arrangement we do not know, but he might not have worried too much as he could now concentrate on the spatial and structural problems and on designing a façade on a scale that had hitherto eluded him.

By 5 June 1896, Phipps had sent in 12 drawings for the LCC's approval.[5] The Theatre Committee, having noted that an earlier proposal for an Imperial Opera House had now been withdrawn, fast-tracked Phipps's plans and gave its approval on 16 June.[6] They could hardly have done otherwise; Queen Victoria had already given Tree her permission to call his new theatre 'Her Majesty's'.[7]

The extent to which Romaine-Walker or, indeed, Tree might have influenced the decorative aspects of the auditorium design in these drawings is difficult to determine. There is an uneasy relationship between the shell shaped proscenium, vaguely reminiscent of Phipps's first Vaudeville theatre, and the more neoclassical treatment of the proscenium boxes crowned by a triangular pediment. Another surprising touch is the larger than life-sized winged-figures crowding the spandrels of the upper-circle arcade which appear to be closely related to those occupying the auditorium in Daly's Theatre (1894). Whether both these elaborate features were Phipps's ideas or suggested by Romaine-Walker and/or Tree is unclear, but they were abandoned during the construction process and replaced by a sumptuous, yet restrained, classical design echoing the 18th-century opera house at Versailles.

Exactly a month after the LCC had passed the plans, the foundation stone of the theatre was laid and the contractor, Mr Lovatt of Wolverhampton (the builder of the Wolverhampton Grand Theatre) had 'undertaken to get the work finished by January 31 next.'[8] This was a rash promise for a building that was estimated to cost £55,000 even taking into account the assistance of George Tasker, who had steered Phipps's early theatres to their promised completion date. Tasker was now taking on the crucial role of quantity surveyor and measurer.

Phipps had given the theatre an 86 ft. wide frontage in the Haymarket increasing to 96 ft. at the Opera Arcade end. The entire depth of the building from east to west was 150 ft., making it isolated on three sides and taking up a third of the total site. According to the *Builder*, 'the architect had arranged that a wall of exceptional thickness shall separate the theatre from the hotel'.[9] The whole block would be built in Portland stone and inside the theatre several new features would be introduced, most notably a flat stage.[10] Thus, the plans that had just been passed were already changing. There would also be double proscenium wall as at Glasgow Theatre Royal and a fire-resisting curtain operated by hydraulic machinery.

The January finishing date came and went, but by the beginning of March 1897 Her Majesty's was at last nearing completion and the opening date was set for 28 April. To keep the interest of his potential spectators at fever pitch, Tree began publishing little snippets of tantalizing information in the *Era* under 'The Theatrical Gossip' column, beginning with the following startling announcement:

'Mr Tree hopes to introduce an arrangement by which the auditorium can be enlarged and reduced in size by shifting the stage and to adopt the American system of pumping volumes of iced air into the building on hot nights'.[11]

What Phipps thought of introducing such innovations six weeks before completion is probably unprintable.

By the beginning of April the scaffolding was coming down and as the heating had been 'in full play' since the last week in March 'there need be no fear of the presence of damp on the opening night'.[12]

The date of the first night, however, coincided with the LCC's Easter recess during which they would not be able to issue a certificate of completion, essential in order to obtain the performance licence from the Lord Chamberlain. This administrative problem was swiftly overcome by the Council dispatching its superintending architect Thomas Blashill to make a preliminary survey of the unfinished building on 31 March, on the basis of which the Theatre Committee would issue its certificate with the proviso that it was retained in the office and only actually handed to Tree after the building had been re-inspected and found to be 'satisfactorily completed'.[13]

*Her Majesty's Theatre, London. Composite view of exterior and interior.
Author's Collection.*

Blashill noted various deviations from the approved plans which he queried with Phipps, including the discarding of the shell-shaped proscenium for a semicircular arch in *Breche Violette* marble with ormolu ornamentation; the replacing of the proposed semi-circular line of the tier fronts with a shallower sweep; the raising of the gallery floor and of the floor in Tree's apartment above the gallery and, of course, the flat stage. Phipps, who must have been under intense pressure to get everything finished, dismissed Blashill's observations in a curt letter to the committee: 'I shall have to compare the set of drawing you have with the set of plans the place is built from, as I really do not know where these small alterations are'.[14]

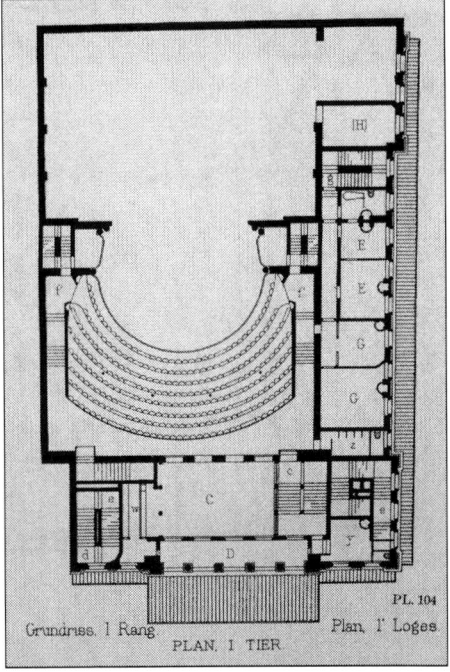

Her Majesty's Theatre, London. Plan at Balcony level. John Earl Collection.

At that point he had probably genuinely forgotten exactly when these changes had been introduced; like the flat stage, they are likely to have been decided on and incorporated in Phipps's working drawings at an early stage. Blashill did not object to the modifications and the sealed certificate was issued without any further ado.

On 24 April, Tree proudly showed his friends round his new theatre. There was still work to be done, but 'the contracts are peremptory and there is no doubt of their literal fulfilment in time for the 28th'. The application for seats had been overwhelming and the rehearsals of opening night's play, *The Seats of the Mighty*, as the *Era* observed: '... have made one thing clear – that the flat stage is infinitely preferable to the "raked" stage from every point of view, as even those very conservative gentry the scene-shifters admit'.[15]

The Times was quick to praise the exterior in Portland stone and red granite, the loggia 'and the cupola towering at the top':
'London is not rich in theatres of any architectural pretensions. Many have only a small frontage on the street, giving little promise of the decorative magnificence within. The new theatre, designed by Mr. C. J. Phipps, certainly does much to supply this deficiency.'[16]

Phipps had, indeed, taken full advantage of the scale and prominence of the site and, clearly intent on creating maximum visual impact, devised a uniform, monumental exterior for the theatre, and the proposed hotel, which was firmly anchored in French classicism with strong echoes of the Louvre. Two splendid square domes, set between elegant mansard roofs and topped by octagonal lanterns, closed each end of the six-storey block, in a building that oozes Parisian sophistication. Neither the theatre, which took up only about a third of the site at the north end, nor the hotel, could really have justified such grandiose architectural treatment on their own, but together they formed a magnificent monument to the capital's expanding high-class leisure industry.

The theatre's Haymarket frontage was nine bays wide with a projecting loggia formed by five giant Corinthian columns rising from a balustrade on the first floor. Below the balustrade, the centre part was taken up

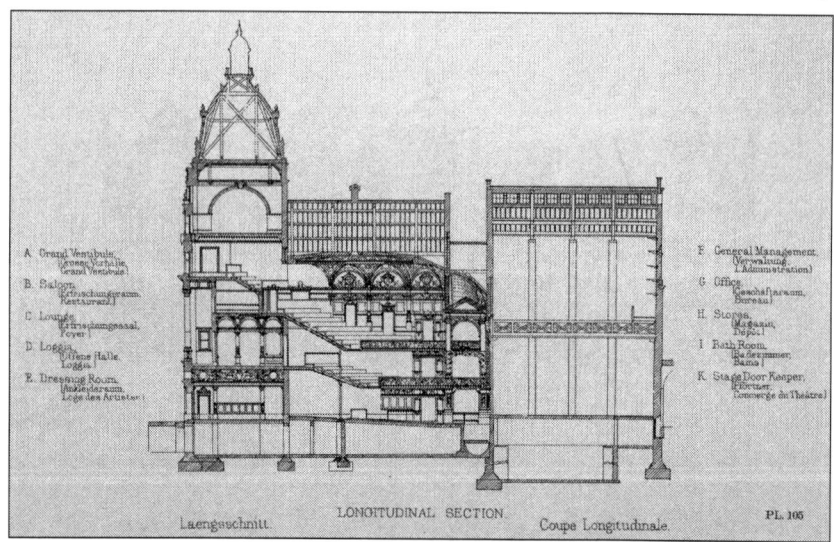

Her Majesty's Theatre, London. Longitudinal section, 1896. John Earl Collection.

by five entrance doors for the exclusive use of visitors to the stalls and dress and family circle, which lead into the main vestibule. The central doors were flanked by one door for pit spectators and another for those seeking the upper circle and gallery. All the entrances communicated directly with a central ticket office, a new feature born of Tree's wish to economise on box office-staff. The long Charles Street block was given over to additional exit doors with offices and dressing rooms above.

In his 'Technical Description', Phipps is at pains to emphasise that 'the theatre is arranged for an audience divided into five different classes',[17] thus reassuring the upper- and middle-class readers of the *Era* that, while he had introduced a central booking office and there were only two tiers in the auditorium, he had not forgotten the importance of upholding the expected level of social segregation in the circulation areas and the auditorium seating divisions.

The auditorium was 70 ft. wide, the same width as at the Grand Theatre in Wolverhampton, and the depth from the curtain line to the back of the pit was 61 ft.. Following standard practice, Phipps adopted a width of 35 ft. for the proscenium opening and, in tune with French 18th-century proscenium design, embellished the 29 ft. high opening with pairs of giant Corinthian columns on high bases, each pair flanking three single proscenium boxes, and supporting a deep elliptical arch ornamented with coffering. This imposing arrangement is more in line with Phipps's earlier proscenium designs at the Lyric and Glasgow Theatre Royal and might well have been his idea, rather than Romaine-Walker's. It was not only a clever way of masking the double proscenium walls, set 9 ft. apart, which separated the auditorium from the stage and were carried up above the roof, but it also allowed for a fan-shaped seating arrangement on the ground floor. Here orchestra stalls at the front were followed by pit stalls, which together took up eleven and a half rows of arm chairs while, the pit was considerably reduced, holding only six rows of pit benches with a total of 200 seats divided by arm rests and safely ensconced behind a partition.[18]

The two tiers were partly cantilevered and their shallow curves, which Blashill had noted as not corresponding to the original plan, were an improvement, allowing better sightlines and closer proximity to the stage for all the occupants. The first tier, which overhung the pit as well as several rows of the pit stalls, had a total of eight rows of chairs, which formed the dress circle, with a family circle set behind it. The second tier was the most complex, containing ten rows of armchairs divided into the upper circle (at the front) followed by the amphitheatre closed off by panelling. Together they held around 400 spectators. At the back of the amphi-theatre, Phipps slotted in a cross passage leading to the upper circle saloon. This device not only kept the amphitheatre and upper circle spectators ensconced in their own comfortable zone, but it also gave Phipps the opportunity to set the gallery, with five rows of benches, slightly higher up and on a steeper slope and to give the galleryites their own raised ceiling. A reassuring 6 ft. high panel in front of the gallery stymied any thoughts of accidental excursions into the upper circle whether triggered by panic or mischief. Technically, the gallery still formed part of the second tier, but in practice it was a separate entity with its own saloon bar behind. In total the theatre held 1,319 spectators, according to Phipps.[19]

The stage was the same width as the auditorium and 50 ft. deep from the curtain line to the back wall, and 60 ft. high from stage floor to gridiron. The height was certainly sufficient to allow extravagant back drops to be raised without rolling or folding them.

Mr Tree's New Theatre finally opened on 28 April 1897 with Gilbert Parker's drama in three acts *The Seats of the Mighty*. The play, an adaptation by Parker of his own novel, is a rather leaden piece set in France during the reign of Louis XV, with plenty of scope for elaborate set-piece scenery. The scenery would therefore be in complete harmony with the auditorium décor with its fluted and gilded columns and brown-speckled marble border that framed the proscenium, the massive gilt balustrade that separated the sunken orchestra from the stalls and with the round-arched blind arcade, supported by Corinthian marble pilasters with gilded capitals, which adorned the sides of the upper circle. From the centre of the domed ceiling hung a dazzling cut-glass and brass Louis Quatorze 'electrolier' and on the tier fronts blazed gilded reproductions of Fontainebleau-style candle brackets (with electric candles). It was a perfect setting for *The Seats of the Mighty*, and combined with Phipps's monumental facade, the whole structure offered a total theatrical experience for the majority of the spectators from the moment they approached the Haymarket façade and entered the elegant vestibule with the footmen in scarlet livery, ascended the rococo-inspired staircases and stepped into the sparkling auditorium bathed in electric light where cerise-coloured, velvet-covered chairs waited to embrace them. Once seated, they could admire the act drop, which depicted an enlarged version of a Gobelin tapestry originally designed by Coypel, featuring Dido receiving Aeneas and his companions while inhaling the 10,000 cubic ft. of fresh air pumped through the theatre every hour, courtesy of an exceptionally powerful fan in the basement.[20]

In all, Her Majesty's Theatre was a remarkable building grounded in imaginative planning and structural innovation, skilfully fused not only with the fashionable ornamentation of a re-imagined historical past, but also with the latest and safest in modern technology; it was Phipps at his best.

While Tree was the star of the opening night, the scenery appears to have impressed quite as much as his acting skills, particularly the surprise explosion in the last act 'when the Treasury Chamber is converted in an instant into a smoking ruin' and Tree's character is killed. The complex stage machinery had been devised by the machinist John White in the short space of four months and seems to have worked perfectly.[21]

At the end of the performance, Tree, appearing alone, thanked Phipps for the plans and Romaine-Walker for the decorations of the theatre. However, the two architects were not invited onto the stage; the evening was Tree's triumph. Phipps had to wait for the morning papers, which were full of praise for the wide two-tiered auditorium, the flat stage and the excellent acoustics. At last, he had retrieved his reputation as the nation's foremost theatre architect.

Phipps could now devote his efforts towards completing the Carlton Hotel's 250 bedrooms (all with private bathrooms), the Tivoli Theatre in Dover and the Passmore-Edwards Library in Southwark. At this point his career and professional standing seemed more assured than it had ever done since Exeter. He also had a young partner, his son-in-law Arthur Blomfield Jackson (1868-1951), to share the work load. Jackson had married Phipps's middle daughter Ida on 6 June 1896, and appears to have joined the firm at that time.[22]

On Saturday 22 May, Phipps travelled down to Dover to check progress on the Tivoli Theatre in Snargate Street due to open three weeks later (14 June 1897). It was a joint design by Phipps and Jackson and endowed with a ponderous façade with three bays flanking a central, round-arched loggia and an auditorium consisting of stalls, dress circle, pit and gallery and a single proscenium wall.[23] It was a 'bread-and-butter' commission, and Phipps could have sent Jackson, but chose to go himself, perhaps fearful that his partner might be less able to spot any short-cuts by the builder.

On his return to Mecklenburgh Square, Phipps felt unwell and went to bed, with the symptoms of a chill. However, this was no ordinary chill; it affected his long-standing kidney and heart problems and his condition worsened rapidly. In the circumstances there was little his physician could do. Two days after his visit to Dover, on Tuesday 25 May 1897, the 62-year-old architect died at his home of a fatal combination of 'Mitral Disease of the Heart, 9 Years, Oedema of Lungs and Nephritis, 2 days'.[24]

The burial service was held three days later at the Church of St Alban the Martyr in Holborn, after which Phipps was interred in Highgate Cemetery beside his son. Charles John Phipps, who, more than any other architect of his generation, had given the Victorian theatre building its own identity, and who had finally recaptured the architectural esteem he had once so carelessly lost, was suddenly gone.

Probate was granted to his widow, Honnor Phipps, on 14 August 1897.[25] The gross value of Phipps's personal estate amounted to £10,292.1s. 6d, a sizeable sum, which included £356. 10 s. in profits from the practice, while the rest seems to have been mainly from investments, as there was no leasehold of any value. Blomfield Jackson carried on the practice at Mecklenburgh Square until 1905. He was obliged to pay Honnor Phipps one third of the profits from the practice until April 1903.

To his annoyance Jackson was dismissed from the Carlton Hotel project and replaced by the architectural firm of Lewis Isaacs and Henry L. Lawrence, but he completed the other jointly designed commissions that Phipps left behind, including the Southwark Library, in a lavish Art Nouveau style, and, the less exciting roof repairs to the small parish church of All Saints in Rackenford, Devon (1897-1900). Later he totally re-furbished the St James's Theatre (1899-1900) in a manner that his deceased father-in-law would have approved of, but he chose to run a general practice rather than join what had now become a rather crowded field of British theatre architects.[26]

Endnotes

1. LMA, Theatre Plans GLC/AR/BR/ 2232.
2. *Era*, 25 January 1896, p. 19.
3. NA, LRRO 1/2513, Her Majesty's Theatre: approved drawings referred to in letter of 28 March 1896 to the Law, Guarantee and Trust Society Ltd, by C. J. Phipps.
4. *Builder*, 1 August 1896, p. 103.
5. LMA, Theatre Plans GLC/AR/BR/19/0431.
6. *Era*, 20 June 1896, p. 16. An additional, incomplete set of proposed plans are at Bristol University Drama Dept., Tree Collection.
7. *Era*, 13 June 1896, p. 15.
8. *Builder*, 1 August 1896, p. 103.
9. *Builder*, 1 August 1896, p. 103
10. The flat stage is already present on Phipps's signed, but undated, proposed plans now in the University of Bristol Theatre Collection.
11. *Era*, 13 March 1897, p. 13.
12. *Era*, 3 April 1897, p. 12 and 10 April 1897, p. 12.
13. *Era*, 17 April 1897, p. 9.
14. LMA, Theatre and Music Halls committee, LCC MIN/10, 829, March 31 and April 2, 1897.
15. *Era*, 24 April 1897, p. 12.
16. *The Times*, 26 April 1897, p. 13.
17. *Era*, 1 May 1897, p. 11.
18. *Builder*, 8 May 1897, p. 421.
19. *Builder*, 8 May 1897, p. 421.
20. *Era*, 1 May 1897, p. 13, and p. 11.
21. For details of the stage machinery see D. Wilmore, 'The Substage Equipment at Her Majesty's Theatre, London', *Theatre Notebook*, v. lii, no. 1, pp. 38-45.
22. GRO, Marriage Certificate, Yr.1896, Qtr. June, Distr. Pancras, v. 1B, p. 188. In the London Post Office Directory of 1895, Jackson is listed under Architects at 7 Bedford Row, WC.
23. *Era*, 8 May 1896, p. 18.
24. GRO, Death Certificate, Yr. 1897, Qtr. June, Distr. Pancras, v. 1B, p. 42.
25. Her Majesty's Court Service, Copy of Grant. The gross value equals the spending worth of around £590,000 in today's money according to the National Archives Currency Converter. Unfortunately, the minutes from the probate hearing at the National Archives, NA IR27, are badly burnt and barely legible.
26. *Builder*, 25 November, 1899, p. 496. *Era*, 13 January 1900, p. 10.

350 Charles John Phipps F.S.A - Architect to the Victorian Theatre

21 EPILOGUE

During the first half of the nineteenth century, British theatre proprietors and managers tended to see themselves not primarily as businessmen or women, but as custodians of the drama, as key-holders to a world of enlightened entertainment presented by actors in buildings of variable quality. Like any business enterprise it had to be financially viable in order to prosper, but there was a general acceptance that profits would fluctuate from season to season – theatre audiences were fickle beasts – and that great fortunes were unlikely to be made. Their tight profit margins rarely allowed for major refurbishments let alone new buildings, and they concentrated their efforts on finding the right performers for the right play in the hope that the spectators would not notice the uncomfortable seats and the draughts around their feet or stumble on the cramped staircases.

By the middle of the 19th century, the rising middle class, who formed a crucial group of (mostly) discerning spectators and who were enjoying more spacious and comfortable homes than they had ever done before, were no longer prepared to leave their fireside to visit a dirty and fume-ridden hall to watch a play, however well written and well acted. The theatre interiors were simply too depressing, steeped in an outmoded design nurtured by traditionalist managers. A new vision was desperately needed, together with a major injection of capital earmarked for the modernisation of fusty old theatres and the building of new ones both in London and the provinces, in order to bring back the audience.

Then, in 1862, a new vision of theatre design unexpectedly appeared from a church architect in-waiting, Charles John Phipps. A fire at the Bath Theatre Royal had galvanised him into formulating a more modernistic theatre plan, aided and abetted by the architect and theatre critic Edward Godwin and the theatre's manager James Chute. As a novice in this rather despised branch of architecture, Phipps was not steeped in the hand-me-down traditions of British theatre planning, but could approach the subject with fresh thinking. At Bath he showed what could be done even within a tight budget and old exterior walls and shrewd provincial businessmen with political clout took note and found their way to his office. In London, money and vision came from property speculators, enthused by the regeneration of large swathes of the city under the auspices of the Metropolitan Board of Works. The millionaire and part-owner of the *Daily Telegraph*, Lionel Lawson, led the way with the Queen's Theatre (1867) and, more spectacularly with the Gaiety in the Strand (1868-9). By then, Phipps was the most experienced theatre architect in the country and the natural choice for Lawson, who took it upon himself to educate Phipps in the latest developments in Parisian theatre design and upper-class restaurants. Phipps quickly learned that metropolitan audiences, to an even greater degree than their provincial counterparts, needed to be pampered and enraptured by the building itself as much as by the entertainment on stage.

John Hollingshead's shrewd management of the Gaiety, in which he acted as purveyor of a variety of theatrical fare served up in an enchanting and comfortable interior with ample facilities for socialising, clearly signalled the theatre's potential as a safe investment with a guaranteed return. Thus, the theatre building, with its modern accoutrements, became an essential marketing tool with which to hook past, present and future audiences. Other speculators, with or without any previous connection to the theatre, followed suit and as the free-trade culture took hold, proprietors and managers began to see themselves primarily as businessmen rather than mere keepers of the drama. As the actor-manager Squire Bancroft declaimed on the Haymarket stage, in an attempt to calm the displaced and disgruntled pittites on the night of the opening after Phipps's refurbishment in 1880: 'You ask me where's the pit? I am a businessman! ... I can't afford it! Has any money been taken in this theatre with the whole floor given over to the pit?'[1] His argument was grudgingly accepted and the performance was allowed to proceed.

The theatre's new role as a fashionable investment, together with a rapidly expanding rail network which made it possible for London and provincial theatre companies to tour the breadth and length of the country, fuelled the growth of theatre buildings on an unprecedented scale and Phipps was ready to capitalise on the opportunities that arose. He was a fast and decisive worker and brought invention, imagination and flair to English theatre design as well as an instinctive understanding of the absolute need to create a spatial relationship between auditorium and stage that allowed the actors to reach out to the spectators and the latter to feel drawn towards the action on stage. He understood that a theatre must work as a theatre first if it was to have any hope of becoming a successful investment vehicle, but that somehow this essential aim had to be balanced against the reality of high land values inside and outside London and the demands for opulence, comfort and respectability among the upper and middle classes whose support of the theatre was crucial for its financial and artistic viability. He was the perfect architect for the fast-growing theatre industry, though he had to suppress any desires to produce impressive exteriors that matched his interiors as only a very few of his clients saw their theatres as playing the subsidiary role of civic building and cultural landmark and were reluctant to invest in monumental façades.

Phipps's clients were generally looking for a quick turn-around from commission to drawing to finished building, and this fast and furious way of working seems to have suited his temperament. In a small office with no partner to share the load until the last few years of his life, it is no wonder that Phipps frequently repeated himself. He had no hesitation in taking an off-the peg design as long as it was from his own closet even when that design, as in the case of his first Vaudeville Theatre, had been less than perfect.

Phipps was a sound constructor and understood the practical needs of stage machinists and set designers and he was constantly looking for technical innovations in stage and auditorium lighting, fire prevention, heating and ventilation. However, he was less sure-footed when it came to finding workable solutions in the public safety realm. Predicting crowd behaviour in a panic was not his strong point and carefully planned safety measures were not really at the heart of his original design formula; instead he seems, sometimes, to have treated such matters as a troublesome afterthought. It is almost as if, on occasions, there was a touch of the buccaneer within him, a willingness to cast aside the irksome notion of social responsibility or, perhaps, more of an overwhelming desire to quickly finish off a tedious job. He delivered (mostly) on time, and sometimes on budget. It was this ambivalent attitude to theatre safety that corrupted his design for the Exeter Theatre Royal (1886).

By the middle of the 1880's, the theatre had become an investment vehicle on an industrial scale undreamt of in the mid-nineteenth century. Consequently, the proprietors and managers who petitioned the Home Secretary Henry Matthews in 1887 for a system of national inspection of theatre buildings did so because they regarded their theatres as part of a national industry which, like the railways, acted as a major contributor to the national economy and, for this reason, was entitled to ask for some government support in the form of a national inspection system.

Phipps, who had been one of the first to publicly advocate government regulation did so because he realized that this burgeoning industry, on which he was pinning his career, was fundamentally fragile. The theatre, in common with the expanding railway network, on which his career also relied, was utterly dependent on public confidence in its ability to deliver a worthwhile experience in a safe environment. There was no room for freebooters, unburdened by any sense of social responsibility, among managers or proprietors as Phipps knew to his cost, and he continued to advocate a national regulatory system staffed by experienced theatre architects for all theatres and music-halls to the end of his life. That he doggedly pursued this argument even immediately after the Exeter fire, when he was seen by many of his colleagues, though not by the whole of the industry, to have lost any professional and moral ground for doing so, is significant. Did he feel that a government appointed inspector might have saved many lives in Exeter by insisting on double exits from the gallery and an iron curtain? And did he believe that the lack of consistent and enforceable regulations outside London was entirely the fault of national politicians and that therefore they were to blame for the high death toll, while he had been left to follow a poor brief with contradictory demands?

Exeter nearly finished his career and one could argue that, maybe, it should have done. Phipps, however, was determined not to let this happen, hoping, it seems, that a consistent defensive attitude on his part would silence the critics and win over potential clients in sufficient numbers. Exeter would soon be forgotten. It did not work out like that.

Five years on, Exeter was still a live issue among parliamentarians, and Phipps was left in no doubt by the members of the 1892 Select Committee that they believed him partly responsible for the catastrophic loss of life. It was a wake-up call. For five years his career had been going nowhere. He would have to adopt a different approach; he would need to embrace theatre safety in all is aspects and, like Alfred Darbyshire, make it the basis of his design, but without sacrificing the inherent elegance of his spatial handling.

The commission from Wolverhampton came at the right point; Phipps had had time to mull over new ideas and was ready to design, what he later claimed to be, his favourite auditorium. The Glasgow fire brought another chance to develop new safety thinking. Recognising, at last, that the prevention of the spread of a fire on stage was as much the architect's responsibility as that of the stage crew, the management and the government, he designed the double proscenium wall, a structural feature that, in conjunction with an iron curtain, would save both lives and property. This was a measure that would, once and for all, announce to the world that C.J. Phipps, FSA, was the most skilful and safety conscious theatre architect around. After Glasgow he became the obvious choice for the redevelopment of Her Majesty's Theatre. Tree, or any other leading London theatre manager, would have had no good reason to turn him down in favour of Walter Emden.

To Phipps, Her Majesty's was the best opportunity he would ever get to reclaim his credentials as the country's most eminent theatre architect. He gave it his all and it was his masterpiece. The architect and engineer Edwin Sachs, in his magnum opus, *Modern Opera Houses and Theatres,* quibbled about the exterior, arguing that it did not adequately express the building's purpose as a theatre.[2] Sachs's criticism was a little misplaced; the exterior expressed the purpose of the building perfectly. The late Victorian West-end theatre was not primarily about serving the purpose of the drama, but a monument to commerce, to the flourishing leisure industry, to the wealth of a society whose inherent commercial instincts had made Britain the most prosperous country in the world and the ruler of much of it.

Phipps made an extraordinary contribution to British theatre architecture, lifting it out of its dependence on the Georgian playhouse design, while still retaining some of its elusive spirit of intimacy. He opened the door to modernity, incorporating the latest technology, both before and behind the curtain, creating performance spaces that enabled actors and spectators to engage with each other and, in the end, making the theatre safe for everyone and all this within the context of a hard-nosed, market-driven society. For this, he is justly remembered.

Yet, there will always be a shadow of doubt hanging over Phipps's reputation and as we admire the splendour of Her Majesty's, we should not forget those who died in the fire at the Exeter Theatre Royal nor Phipps's own public admission at the subsequent inquest: 'I did not reckon for the smoke'.

Endnotes
1 *Era*, 8 February, 1880, p. 5.
2 E. Sachs, *Modern Opera Houses and Theatres*, 3 vols., London, 1896-8, v.ii. p. 35.

APPENDIX I
THE STAGE AT THE THEATRE ROYAL, BATH IN 1863

'The wall dividing this part from the auditorium is of stone, 18 inches thick (the proscenium pillars and capitals being of freestone, moulded or carved, and left in its natural colour free from pain and any decoration, except occasional gilding). The opening is 28 feet and the height to the apex of the arch 30 feet. The stage entrance is on the left side facing the stage adjacent to the spacious magazine for scenery.

The stage staircases, two in number of Pennant stone, 3 feet 6 inches wide, lead respectively to actors' dressing-rooms and wardrobe on the O.P. side, and actresses' on the P. Side, also below to the mezzanine floor. On a level with the stage is the green-room proper. Close by the prompter are property, furniture and stage manager's rooms and three dressing-rooms for principal performers.

On the mezzanine floor, which is 8 feet high, are machinist's room, two store rooms, armoury, kitchen, musicians' room, large room for supernumeraries and numerous conveniences with doors at back, just below the level of a large yard belonging to the theatre. The whole of the mezzanine floor is boarded over on level with stage, and a pair of folding doors, 15 feet wide, opening into a yard and street at back so that scenery can be brought in and out with great facility. The beams supporting the fly floors are 22 feet from stage on underside, the fly floors being 2 feet higher, and are 10 feet wide. The floors are cradled down to 18 feet, which is the height of the wings and flats.

The painting-room occupies the whole of the end wall of the stage, the whole width as at Covent Garden; the beams being supported on trussed girders. The fly floors are partly supported by iron rod from the main tie-beams of roof. There are nine main tie-beams with framed principals and collars with four iron queen-posts dividing the strain upon the tie-beams into five equal parts. The purlins and rafters support a moderately flat roof, boarded and slated.

On the tops of the main beams over the stage are longitudinal pieces, which principally support the bridges and the machinery of the gas battens. The stage floor rises half-an-inch to the foot and is composed entirely of sliders; alternately two or three narrow cuts at the wings with wide ones at the entrances. They are all worked off by windlasses on the mezzanine floor. There are also the Corsican trap, four large traps in centre, and four smaller ones at sides in first and third entrances. A large bridge, 12 feet long by 4 feet wide, rises in the fifth entrance. The whole depth under the working part of the stage sinks to a depth of 16 feet, with a cement floor.

Fire plugs, always charged from the city mains, are taken inside the building, with hose, spanner and jet always attached.'

Extract from the *Builder*, 7 March 163, p. 165.

APPENDIX 2
THEATRE ROYAL HAYMARKET:

Official Description Published For Circulation Among The Audience On The Opening Night, Saturday 31 January 1880.
'The auditory is arranged in five divisions; all approached from the frontage in the Haymarket, and special attention has been paid to the various means of ingress and egress for the public. The stalls, balcony and private boxes are entered by three doorways under the portico opening into the vestibule, in which are the booking offices. A wide flight of stone steps leads from the left of this vestibule down to the stalls, and there is a corresponding staircase on the right side from the corridor of the balcony. This corridor is three steps above the vestibule, so that the balcony, which occupies the same position as the dress circle in the old theatre, is still kept on the same relative level with the street.

The first circle on [the] first floor is approached through a separate doorway under the portico by a wide flight of stone steps. The second circle is approached from the upper doorway outside the portico by a stone staircase. The gallery is approached by the lower doorway outside the portico, also by a stone staircase. The various staircases are entirely rebuilt, of easy ascent with level landings and without winding steps. The auditory still retains the distinguishing feature of the old theatre by having the balcony nearly level with the stage, but it has been advanced considerably nearer the proscenium, consequently lessening the centre area, which now only admits of the requisite number of stalls being placed in it. The two doorways to the stalls are adjoining the pillars of the proscenium boxes and are made features of the design. The first circle recedes so as to leave several rows of the balcony seats free and open. Behind the balcony are five private boxes and two large boxes at the sides. The second circle also recedes a little from the tier below, so that in every case the occupants of the first rows of seats have nothing between them and the main ceiling of the auditorium.

The scheme of the auditory is original and unlike any other theatre in the country. The proscenium, the arrangement of which was suggested by Mr. Bancroft, is a massive and elaborately gilded frame, complete on all sides, the lower part forming the front of the stage and concealing the orchestra, which is placed underneath. On either side of this frame are three tiers of proscenium boxes enclosed between columns and surmounted by Corinthian capitals. The same arrangement of columns is repeated at the angles of the square furthest removed from the proscenium, forming three boxes on either side of the three tiers. From these columns a series of vaulted arches support a circular ceiling and in the tympanum of each arch are figure subjects. The most important, over the proscenium (painted by F. Smith), exemplifies the following lines form Milton's *Comus*:

> *"Brightest Lady, look on me*
> *Thus, I sprinkle on your breast*
> *Drops, that from my fountain pure*
> *I have kept, of precious cure."*

On the frieze below is the motto: "Summa ars est celare artem". The four lunettes in the arches on either side are filled with the following subjects from Shakespeare's plays:

The Merchant of Venice, Act 3, Scene II, by J. D. Watson. "So may the outwards shows be least themselves, the world is still deceived with ornament."

Measure for Measure, Act 4, Scene I, by F. Smith. "Break off thy song and haste thee quick away."

As You Like It, Act 2, Scene I, by F. Smith.
"Poor deer, quoth he, thou mak'st a testament,
As wordlings do, giving thy sum of more
To that which had too much."

All's Well that Ends Well, Act 2, Scene I, by J.D. Watson.. "Here is my hand; the promises observ'd, thy will by my performance shall be serv'd."

Romeo and Juliet, Act 5, Scene III by, J. D. Watson."What's here? A cup clos'd in my true love's hand?"

A Midsummer Night's Dream, Act 3, Scene I, by F. Smith."Thou art as wise as thou art beautiful."

The Two Gentlemen of Verona, Act 2, Scene II, by J. D. Watson. "Why then we'll make exchange; here, take you this, and seal the bargain with a holy kiss."

Othello, Act 1, Scene III, by F. Smith. "Wherein I spoke of most disastrous chances; of moving accidents by flood and field."

In the five lunettes immediately over the proscenium are figures of the following muses: Terpsichore, Enterpe, Thalia, Erate, Melpomene, painted by T. Ballard.

The style adopted for the interior is Italian Renaissance. The general tone of the decoration is an ivory white, with all the mouldings and ornamentation gilded. The upholstery, seating and carpets being crimson and the walls of rose colour, the pattern specially designed, the curtains to the private boxes are of ivory coloured satin trimmed with gold fringe. The painted ornamentation upon the ceiling and round the lunettes is gold upon a delicate faun [sic] colour ground with grey sparingly used on the ceiling.

The front to the second circle has the panels filled with small allegorical figure-subjects by T. Ballard, on a gold ground, representing Dancing, Satire, Tragedy, Dressing, painting, going to the Play, Comedy, Coming from the Play, Poetry, Farce, Authorship. The panels of the first circle are filled with recumbent Shakespearian figures, seven painted by J. D. Watson, namely Touchstone, Caliban, Launce and his dog, Orlando, Cleopatra, Imogen, Hamlet; and six by F. Smith, namely, Timon, Malvolio, Ariel, Ophelia, Titania, Desdemona, all on gold ground. The front of the balcony is ornamented with acanthus leaf gilded.

The stalls and balcony are fitted with arm chairs and upholstered in crimson velvet. The curtains and carpets of velvet pile harmonise with the papers.

Below the entrance vestibule and balcony there is a foyer, from which on either side a wide corridor leads to the stalls. Adjoining the foyer is a refreshment saloon, painted and fitted up in the oriental manner. The floor of the entrance vestibule is of marble mosaic in an elaborate design, the centre formed by the Imperial crown, surrounded by the Rose, shamrock and Thistle, and the name of the Theatre in a border. In the vestibule the prevailing tone is olive green, with ornaments in gold and blue, and the panels in doors and fanlights are filled stained glass in gilded lead frames. On the levels of the first circle, second circle and gallery are refreshment-saloons and retiring-rooms for both ladies and gentlemen.

The auditory is lighted by one of Strode's sunlights. The new stage has been fitted with the usual machinery and this part of the building has been separated from the auditory by a solid cement concrete wall, taken from cellar to roof.'

Sourced from *The Morning Post*, 2 February 1880, p. 2.

The reporter's comments: 'The theatre, thus ingeniously designed and richly ornamented, has an air of almost palatial splendour. So does it glow and glitter with gold that it looks like a temple of Plutus; yet, effulgent as is the general effect, the treatment is so artistic as to ensure perfect harmony of tone'.

APPENDIX 3
LIST OF THEATRES DESIGNED OR ALTERED BY C.J. PHIPPS

DATE		
1863	Bath Theatre Royal.	Rebuild.
1865	Nottingham Theatre Royal.	New build.
1866	South Shields Theatre Royal.	New build with T.M. Clemence.
	Brighton Theatre Royal.	Extended.
1867	Swansea Theatre Royal.	Alterations.
1867	Queen's Theatre, London.	Rebuild.
1867	Bristol, Prince's Theatre.	New build.
1868	Gaiety Theatre, London.	New build.
1868	Variety Theatre, Hoxton, London.	New build.
1870	Vaudeville Theatre, London.	New build.
1871	Dublin, Gaiety Theatre.	New build.
1872	Aberdeen, Tivoli Theatre (Her Majesty's Opera House).	New build with J. Matthews.
1874	Philharmonic Theatre, London.	Conversion of The Philharmonic Hall.
1875	Worcester Theatre Royal.	Rebuild.
1876	Dumfries Theatre Royal.	Rebuild.
1876	Edinburgh Theatre Royal.	Rebuild.
1877	Derry Royal Opera House.	New build.
1877	Cork Theatre Royal and Opera House.	Rebuild of Munster Hall.
1877	Leicester Royal Opera House.	New build.
1878	Worcester Theatre Royal.	Rebuild.
1878	Liverpool New Rotunda.	Rebuild with E. Davis.
1878	Plymouth Theatre Royal.	Rebuild.
1879	Liverpool, Royal Alexandra.	Rebuild.
1879	Sadler's Wells Theatre.	Rebuild.
1880	Haymarket Theatre Royal, London	Rebuild. Façade retained

–1880	Glasgow Theatre Royal.	Rebuild.
1880	Princess Theatre, Oxford Street, London.	Rebuild.
1880	Sheffield Theatre Royal.	Rebuild.
1880	Torquay Theatre Royal.	Rebuild.
1881	Savoy Theatre, Beaufort Close, London.	New build.
1881	Belfast Theatre Royal.	Rebuild
1882	Strand Theatre, The Strand, London.	New build.
1882	Hastings, New Gaiety Theatre.	New build with Messrs Cross and Wells.
1882	Leamington Spa Theatre Royal.	New build with Messrs. Osborne and Reading.
–1883	Eastbourne Theatre Royal.	New build.
1883	Olympic Theatre, London.	Alterations.
–1883	Edinburgh Lyceum.	New build.
1883	Opéra Comique, London.	Alterations.
1883	Globe Theatre, London.	Alterations.
1884	Prince's Theatre (Prince of Wales), London.	New build.
1884	Hengler's Circus, Argyle Street, London.	Rebuild.
–1884	Northampton Royal Opera House.	New build.
–1884	Portsmouth Theatre Royal.	New build.
1884	Edinburgh Theatre Royal.	Rebuild.
1885	Lyceum, London.	Alterations.
1885	Gaiety Theatre, London.	Alterations.
1885	Opèra Comique, London.	Alterations.
1886	Exeter Theatre Royal.	New build.
1886	Dublin, Leinster Hall.	New build.
1887	Darlington Theatre Royal.	New build.
1887	Hanley Theatre Royal.	New build with. F. Matcham.
1888	Shaftesbury Theatre, London.	New Build.
–1888	Lyric Theatre, London.	New build.
1888	Royal Theatre, Torquay	Alterations

1889	Garrick Theatre, London.	Acted as supervising architect of Walter Emden's design.
1890	Nottingham Theatre Royal.	Alterations.
1891	Portsmouth Empire.	New build.
1891	Vaudeville Theatre, London.	Rebuild.
1892	Bath Theatre Royal.	Alterations.
1893	Daly's Theatre, London.	Consultant architect to Spencer Chadwick.
1893	Comedy Theatre, London.	Alterations.
1893	Strand Theatre, London.	Alterations.
-1894	Wolverhampton Grand Theatre.	New Build.
1894	Pavilion Theatre, London.	Consultant architect to E. Runtz.
1894	St James's Theatre.	Alterations.
1895	Glasgow Theatre Royal.	Rebuild.
1895	National Skating Palace, London.	Conversion of Hengler's Circus into ice rink.
1896	St. James's Theatre.	Alterations.
-1897	Her Majesty's Theatre, London.	New build.
1897	Dover, Tivoli.	New build.
1897	Kingston (London) New Theatre.	Consultant architect to C. Bourne.

APPENDIX 4
ARCHITECTURAL DRAWINGS EXHIBITED AT THE ROYAL WEST OF ENGLAND ACADEMY BY C. J. PHIPPS

1858 – Design for a Cemetery Chapel, Box.
– Design for Presbyterian Church, Bristol.
1863 – Competition design for a Mechanics' Institute, Leeds.
– Competition design for Corn Exchange, Newburn.
– Interior of Bath Theatre.
– Plans of Bath Theatre.
– Entrance to Bath Theatre.
– View of Greyhound Hotel, Bath.
– View of Cemetery Chapel, Pewsey, Wilts.
– Competition design for Town Hall, Tiverton.
1864 – 2nd Somerset Militia Stores, Bath.
– Proposed Schools at Pewsey, Wilts.
– Proposed Baths at Frome.
– Auction Offices and Sale Rooms, Broad Street, Bath.
– Shop Front, Bladud Buildings, Bath.
– Bank Chambers, Bath.
1865 – Buildings for the Stores and Staff of the 2nd Somerset Militia, erected at Bath.
– Second Premiated Design for Bath Theatre: Section of Auditory.

Source: Bath Central Library, Local Studies. File on C.J. Phipps.

APPENDIX 5
LIST OF ARCHITECTURAL DESIGNS EXHIBITED BY C. J. PHIPPS AT THE ROYAL ACADEMY

1863 – Theatre Royal Bath (no. 933).
1873 – Crockford's Auction Hall, St. James's, later the Devonshire Club (no. 1131).
 – The Opera House, Copenhagen (no. 1146).
1874 – View of the Terrace at the Star and Garter Hotel, Richmond (no. 1079).
 – Design for Emmanuel church, Dulwich (no. 1100).
1876 – Design of the Ballroom at the Star and Garter Hotel, Richmond (no. 978).
1897 – A View of Her Majesty's Theatre, London (no. 1760)

370 Charles John Phipps F.S.A - Architect to the Victorian Theatre

APPENDIX 6
NON-THEATRE WORK BY C.J. PHIPPS

Bandstand, Sydney Gardens, Bath, 1862.
Mortuary Chapel at Pewsey, Wiltshire, 1862
Somerset Militia Barracks, Bath, 1864.
Gaiety Restaurant, The Strand, London, 1869
New Pavilion at the Star and Garter Hotel, Richmond, Surrey, 1872.
The Devonshire Club, London, 1873.
Schools at Lea and Pewsey, Wiltshire, 1873.
Design for proposed Emmanuel Church, Dulwich, London, 1874. Church later built to designs by E.C. Robins, 1877.
St Giles Church, Lea, Wiltshire, 1878-80. Alterations.
Residential block at No. 1 Portland Place, London, 1881.
The Prince's Hotel, Coventry Street, London, 1884.
The Savoy Turkish Baths, Savoy Street, The Strand, London 1883-5
Chesterfield Gardens, Mayfair, London, c.1887. Alterations to the home of Mr and Mrs Fredrik Beer.
The Lyric Club, Coventry Street, London, 1888. Conversion of the Prince's Hotel into a clubhouse with a small concert hall/theatre.
Lyric Chambers and flats, Shaftesbury Avenue, London, 1888.
Star Life Assurance Society, 30 and 32 Moorgate Street, London. c. 1892.
Offices for the *Observer Newspaper*, 396 The Strand, London, n.d.
The Queen's Hall, Langham Place, London, 1891-93 with T.E. Knightley.
House of Assembly, Cape Town, 1894. Improvements to acoustics.
The Carlton Hotel, London, 1897.
St George the Martyr Library, Southwark, London, 1897-99, with A. B. Jackson.
All Saints Church, Rackenford, Devon, 1897-1900, with by A. B. Jackson.

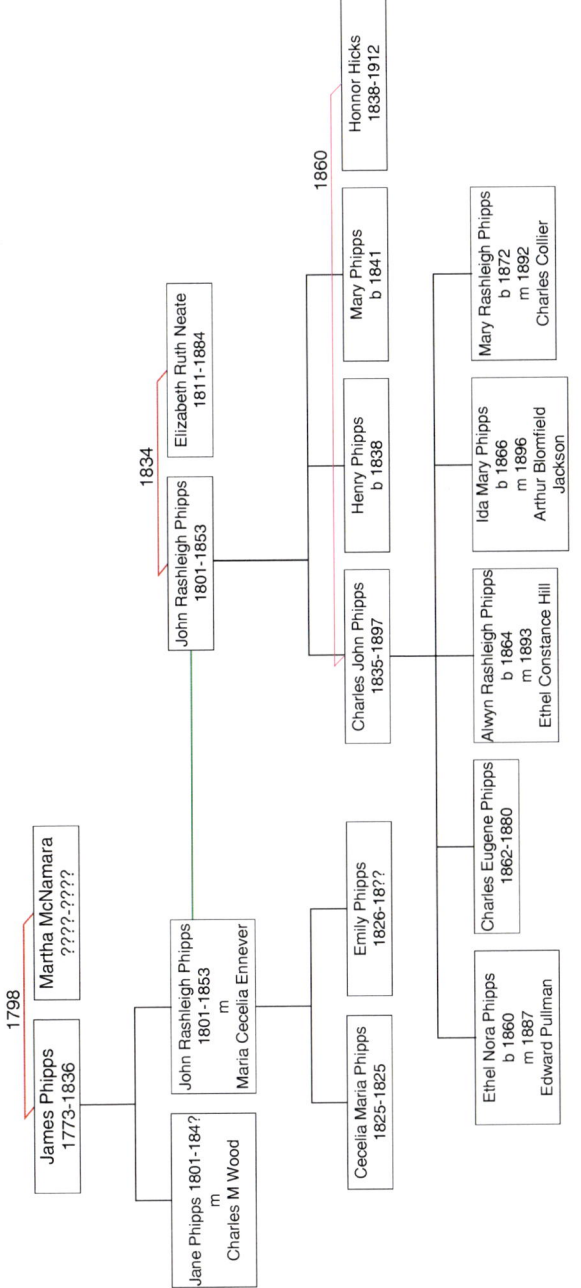

APPENDIX 8
THE LORD CHAMBERLAIN'S RULES AND REGULATIONS FOR THEATRES WITHIN HIS JURISDICTION

1. ALL doors and barriers to open outwards, or to be fixed back, during the time when the public are within the theatre.

2. All gangways, passages and staircases intended for the exit of the audience to be kept entirely free from chairs or any other obstructions, whether permanent or temporary.

3. An ample water supply, with hose and pipes, to be available to all parts of the house, where possible on the high-pressure main.

4. All fixed and ordinary gas-burners to be furnished with efficient guards. Movable and occasional lights to be, where possible, protected in the same manner, or put under charge of persons responsible for lighting, watching and extinguishing them. A separate and independent supply of light for the stage and auditory. No white-metal gas-pipes to be used in the building.

5. The footlights or floats to be protected by a wire guard. The first ground-line to be always without gas and unconnected with gas, whether at the wings or elsewhere. Sufficient space to be left between each ground-line, so as to lessen the risk from accident to all persons standing or moving among such lines.

6. The rows or lines of gas-burners at wings to commence four feet at least from the level of the stage.

7. Wet blankets or rugs, with filled buckets or water-pots, to be always kept in the wings, and attention to be directed to them by placards legibly printed or painted and fixed near them. As in Rule 4, some person to be responsible for keeping the blankets, buckets &c., ready for immediate use.

8. Hatchets, hooks or other means to cut down hanging scenery in case of fire, to be always in readiness.

9. The regulations as to fire to be always posted in some conspicuous

place, so that all persons belonging to the theatre may be acquainted with their contents. A report of any fire or alarm of fire, however slight, to be at once sent to the Lord Chamberlain's office.

10. Counter weights, where possible, to be carried to the walls of he building and cased in. The ropes attached to them to be constantly tested.

11. An annual inspection is made of all theatres. It is expected that all alterations suggested for the safety and convenience of the public will be carried out before the issue of t annual licence.

12. No structural alterations to be made in the theatre without the sanction of the Metropolitan Board of Works. Plans of such alterations to be sent to the Lord Chamberlain's office.

13. A copy of every new piece, or alterations of old pieces intended to be produced, to be forwarded for licence to the Examiner of Plays seven clear days before such intended production. No alteration of text when licensed for representation to be permitted without sanction.

14. Copies of all playbills to be sent to the Lord Chamberlain's office every Monday and whenever a change of performance is announced.

15. Notice of the change of title of a piece to be given to the Examiner of Plays.

16. The name and private address of the actual and responsible manager to be printed in legible type at the head of each bill.

17. Admission to be given at all times to authorised officers of the Lord Chamberlain's department and of the police.

18. No profanity or impropriety of language to be permitted on the stage.

19. No indecency of dress, dance or gesture to be permitted on the stage.

20. No offensive personalities or representations of living persons to be permitted on the stage, not anything calculated to produce riot or breach of the peace.

21. No exhibition of wild beasts or dangerous performances to be permitted on the stage. No women or children to be hung from the flies, nor fixed in positions from which they cannot release themselves.

22. No masquerade or public ball to be permitted in the theatre.

23. No encouragement to be given to improper characters to assemble or to ply their calling in the theatre.

24. Refreshments to be sold in the theatre only during the hours of performance, only to the audience and company engaged in the house, and only in positions which do not interfere with the convenience and safety of the audience.

25. No smoking to be permitted in the auditorium.

26. Theatre licences are granted for one year, from the 29th September. Licences are granted also for shorter periods, but all licences cease on the day above mentioned.

27. No public entertainment to be given in the theatre on the days excluded from the licence.

28. Applications for licences with the names and addresses of the actual and responsible manager and his two proposed sureties, who must be resident householders and ratepayers, must be forwards to the Lord Chamberlain's office seven clear days before the day for which the licence is required.

29. Theatre licences are granted, after consultation with the Metropolitan Board of Works, so far as the structural condition of the theatres concerned, only for buildings in which the above regulations can be carried out, and on the express condition that these and every other reasonable and practicable precaution against fire or the dangers arising therefrom are adopted.

30. The manager is held solely and entirely responsible for the carrying out of the above regulations, for the management of his theatre before and behind the curtain, and for the safety of the public and the members of his company.

31. All exits must be plainly indicated by placards and kept always available for the use of the audience.

32. The service of light for the auditorium and entrance passages must be separate from that for the stage.

LATHOM,
Lord Chamberlain.

The Earl of Lathom acted as Lord Chamberlain 1885-86, late 1886-92 and 1895-98.

The above version incorporates recommendations made in the *Report on Fires in Theatres*, 1877.

BIBLIOGRAPHY

A History of Scottish Theatre, edited by B. Finlay, Edinburgh: Polygon, 1998

Anderson, D., *The Exeter Theatre Fire.* Royston: Entertainment Technology Press, 2002.

Barker, K., *The Theatre Royal, Bristol 1766-1966.* London: Society for Theatre Research, 1974.

The Cambridge History of British Theatre, v.2 (1660-1895) edited by J Donohue. Cambridge University Press, 2004

Davis, T., *The Economics of the British stage, 1800-1914.* Cambridge University Press, 2000.

Earl, J. And Sell, M., *The Theatres Trust Guide to British Theatres 1750-1950.* London: A.C. Black, 2000.

Earl, J., *British Theatres and Music Halls.* Shire Publications, 2005.

Edwin O. Sachs, Architect, Stagehand, Engineer and Fireman, edited by David Wilmore, Theatresearch, 1998.

Garlick, G., *To Serve the Purpose of the Drama: The Theatre Designs and Plays of Samuel Beazley 1786-1851.* London: Society for Theatre Research, 2003.

Frank Matcham & Co, edited by D. Wilmore. Theatreshire Books Ltd., 2008.

Glasstone, V., *Victorian and Edwardian Theatres.* London: Thames and Hudson, 1975.

Howard, D., *London Theatres and Music Halls 1850-1950.* London: The Library Association, 1970.

Jackson, R. Ed., *Victorian Theatres.* London: A.&C. Black, 1989

Jones, M. and Pick, J., *Mr Phipps' Theatre – The Sensational Story of Eastbourne's Royal Hippodrome.* Cambridge: Entertainment Technology Press, 2006.

Leacroft, R., *The Development of the English Playhouse*. London: Methuen, 1983.

Mander R. and Mitchenson, J., *The Lost Theatres of London*. London: Rupert Hart-Davies, 1968.

Mander, R. and Mitchenson, J., *The Theatres of London*, 2nd.edition. London: Rupert Hart-Davis, 1963.

Penley, B.S., *The Bath Stage*. London: Lewis, 1892.

Rees, T., *Theatre Lighting in the Age of Gas*. London: Society for Theatre Research, 1978.

Rees, T. and Wilmore, D., *British Theatrical Patents 1801-1900*. London: Society for Theatre Research, 1996.

Rowell, G., *The Victorian Theatre*, 2nd edition. Cambridge University Press, 1978.

Sachs, E.O. and Woodrow, E.A.E., *Modern Opera Houses and Theatres*. 3 vols. London: Batsford, 1896-98.

Survey of London: Gen. Editor F.H.W. Sheppard, vols. 29, 30, London, 1960, vols. 31, 32, London 1963; vols. 33, 34, London 1966; vols. 35, 36, London 1970.

INDEX

A
Adelphi Theatre, Edinburgh 96
Air conditioning 173
Alexandra Theatre, London 84, 101

B
Bancroft, Marie 116
Bancroft, Squire 116, 118, 120, 132, 273, 274, 294, 313, 352, 359
Barry, E.M. 88, 94
Bateman, S.F. 112
Beale, Mr. 220, 234
Beazley, Samuel 75, 81, 133, 134, 147, 163
Bell, Edward 157, 180, 328
Berry, Cecil 186
Bevan, S. 194-196
Blashill 301, 310, 317, 318, 343, 345
Blashill, Thomas 301, 309, 317, 341
Boughton, John Walter 178, 180
Bristol Society of Architects 34, 35, 41, 48
Britannia Theatre 49, 72
Brooklyn Theatre 98
Browne, William 88, 115, 130, 186, 194-196, 232
Bruce, Edgar 169, 171-174
Buckle, J.G. 288, 289
Buckstone, J.B. 118
Buckstone, W.A. 239
Bunnett and Co 172
Bunnett and Co. of London 167
Bunnett & Co 293
Burch, A. 220

Burch, Al. 203

C
Cameron, Donald 192, 217, 221, 224- 226, 229, 231, 235
Carlton Hotel 305, 347, 348, 371
Chadwick, Spencer 310, 311, 321, 365
Chute, James Henry 24, 29, 30, 34-42, 46, 47, 56-59, 64, 79, 351
Clark, Alexander 167, 171, 172, 293
Clarke, Max 88, 92, 95, 105-, 188, 245, 248, 263, 292, 293, 299, 300, 312-315, 330-333, 336, 338
Clemence, T.H. 53, 54
Concrete 71, 74, 84-86, 95, 152, 166, 171, 196, 207, 208, 252, 268, 289, 309, 331-333, 361
Coombes, James 202, 228
Covent Garden Theatre 94, 151, 339, 357
Curry, Henry 153

D
Daly, Arthur 310, 321, 340, 365
Dance, George 21, 29, 31
Darbyshire, Alfred 287-289, 302, 304, 354
Darlington Theatre 206
Davioud, G. 71, 72, 74
Davis, Charles 30, 33, 34, 40, 53
Devilder, Mr 45
Devonshire Club 89, 369, 371
Dixon-Hartland, Frederick, M.P. 151, 169, 273, 301
D'Oyly Carte, Richard 129, 131-144, 157, 273, 329

Drury Lane Theatre 26, 93, 149, 151, 153, 154, 157, 159, 260, 308
Dublin 82
Dublin Gaiety 78

E
Ecclesiological Society 27, 36
E. Davies & Son 112
Edwardes, George 295, 310
Electricity 142, 143, 165, 210, 293, 298
Electric light 142, 143, 150, 165, 173, 188, 210, 263, 290, 292-294, 308, 318, 319, 328, 335, 347
Ellis, William Horton 188, 190, 192, 194, 195, 220, 223-225, 228, 232, 234, 240, 254, 287-289
Emden, Walter 129, 131, 134-138, 147, 262, 263, 264, 268, 299, 300, 307, 314, 316, 339, 355, 365
Escott, T.H.S. 120, 127
Exeter Guildhall 202, 218, 219, 239
Exeter Theatre Company 221, 231, 287, 289, 302, 304

F
Fardell, T.G. 310
Finch Hill and Paraire 39, 49, 50, 72, 90
Firth, Sir Charles 212
Fladgate, Mr. 219, 224, 233, 261
Foulston, John 109, 110, 126
Fowler, Francis 94, 95, 134, 140, 262, 278-283
Fuller, Thomas 24-26, 29

G
Gaiety Restaurant 78, 371

Gaiety Theatre, Dublin 11, 78, 81- 84
Gaiety Theatre, London 69, 71- 80, 83, 295
Garner, Arthur 55, 61, 77, 88
Garnier, Charles 71, 94
Garrick Theatre 299, 300, 305, 314, 365
Gas light 142, 143, 152, 173
Gidley, Mr 220
Gilbert, W.S. 76, 174, 299, 300
Gillow, W.D. 121
Godwin, Edward 34, 35, 37, 40- 42, 45-48, 54, 55, 63, 64, 150, 262, 351
Gooch, Walter 131, 132
Gordon, George 54, 59, 63, 76, 79, 80, 87, 111
Graham, Joseph 220, 227
Grande Cirque 185, 186
Green and King, London 45, 51, 55, 64
Gunn, John 81-84
Gunn, Michael 81, 82, 84, 133-135, 138, 146, 188, 192, 193, 197, 308, 322
Gwilt, Joseph 26

H
Harcourt, Sir William 146, 151
Harford, William 111
Harris, Augustus 260, 273, 274
Hebb, John 153, 155, 163
Hengler, Charles 84, 101, 175, 185-187, 262, 278, 279, 283, 325, 330, 364, 365
Herberte-Basing, Sidney 195, 197, 220-222, 236, 238-240, 248, 250, 253

Her Majesty's Theatre, London 11, 12, 47, 69, 70, 94, 303, 305, 320, 321, 337, 340-344, 347, 349, 355, 365, 369

Herschell, Lord 278, 281-283

Hobson, Statham 261, 262, 278, 280-283

Hodson, Henrietta 64

Hogg, Sir James 100, 102, 150, 151, 275, 277

Holiday, Henry 51, 59

Hollingshead, John 71, 74, 76, 89, 91, 92, 98, 103, 151, 273, 274, 295, 305, 310, 352

Home Office 12, 99, 100, 150, 211, 212, 215, 265, 268, 270, 273-275, 317

Hooper, Henry 212, 214, 217-222, 225-228, 233, 237-243, 254

Howard and Wyndham 165, 168, 330

Howard, John 228, 235

Hoxton Variety Theatre 78, 79

Hydraulic power 167, 172, 268, 293, 299, 332, 341

I

Iron balconies 290, 292, 299

Iron curtain 145, 150, 166-168, 171, 172, 174, 186, 209, 211, 223, 224, 226, 232, 233, 245, 257, 268, 292-294, 299, 300, 308, 312, 315, 319, 327, 330, 332, 354, 355

Irving, Henry 168, 191, 195, 285, 287, 288, 294

J

Jackson and Son 156, 328, 334

Jackson, Arthur Blomfield 48, 347, 348, 371, 373

K

Kean, Charles 41, 45, 46

Knightley, T.C. 311, 321, 371

L

Labouchère, Henry 64

Lambert, John 49-51

Lambert, William 49-52

Lancaster, John 245, 261, 289, 291, 293

Langham Place Concert Hall 311, 371

La Scala, Milan 140

Law Guarantee and Trust Society Ltd 339

Lawson, Lionel 60, 61, 64, 65, 70-77, 352

LCC's Theatres and Music Halls Committee 309, 315, 317, 320, 339

Leinster Hall, Dublin 188, 193, 197, 232, 280, 307, 308, 364

Leslie, Henry 262, 295, 297, 298, 300

Litton, Mary 80

Lloyd, Horace P. 211, 219, 223-225, 231, 250, 255, 266, 285

Local Government Act 301

London County Council (LCC) 214, 268, 300-302, 309, 314-320, 339, 340, 341, 349

Lord Chamberlain 69, 70, 73, 95, 99-102, 112, 114, 138, 146, 161, 186, 192, 230, 231, 259, 262, 263, 265, 266, 270, 277, 309, 315, 317, 341

Loveday, George 159, 160, 162, 175, 181, 263

Lyceum Theatre, London 75, 151, 168, 169, 188, 191, 192, 364

Lyric Club 294, 371

Lyric Theatre, London 11, 205, 261, 278, 294-297, 300, 314, 319, 364

M

Magheramorne, Lord (formerly Sir James Hogg) 277
Mander, Charles Tertius 325
Mapleson, Henry 70
Matcham, Frank 12, 104, 121, 127, 183, 206, 261, 290, 299, 301, 305, 307, 336, 364
Matthews, Henry. M.P. Home Secretary 211-215, 273-277, 301, 302, 317, 353
Matthews, James 85-87, 260, 264- 266, 268, 363
Melville, Andrew 144
Metropolitan Board of Works (MBW) 94, 95, 100-102, 112-114, 123, 129, 131, 135-139, 143, 145, 146, 149, 150, 151, 153, 155, 161, 163, 169, 180, 186, 187, 192, 208, 214, 222, 226, 229-231, 241, 244, 245, 249, 250, 251, 255, 256, 259, 261, 265, 268, 269, 273-285, 295, 299, 301, 310, 317-320, 352
Metropolitan Board of Works Regulations 112, 114, 123, 136, 149, 161, 192, 222, 226, 229, 231, 241, 250, 255, 276, 277, 318, 319
Metropolitan Management and Buildings Amendment Act 112
Moore, Albert 63, 64
Morley, Henry 61, 67

N

Nash, John 117
National Opera House 94, 134, 140, 262, 280
National Skating Palace 325, 330, 331, 336, 365
Nelson, Thomas Marsh 93, 94
New Gaiety Theatre, Hastings 157, 364

New Theatre Royal Bristol, later Prince's 58, 59, 66, 79
New Vaudeville Theatre, Paris 71, 74, 112, 172

O

Olympic Theatre, London 169, 314, 364
Opéra Comique, London 95, 135, 151, 262, 280, 364

P

Paris Opera 71, 94
Passmore-Edwards Library 347
Pavilion Theatre 84, 325, 329, 365
Pegg, Waldtern 160, 162, 175, 181
Pengelly, Isaac 218, 220- 223, 226, 227, 229, 235, 250, 255
Pewsey Mortuary Chapel 28-30, 367, 371
Philharmonic Theatre 206, 363
Phipps, Alwyn Rashleigh 143, 151, 162, 169, 173, 312, 313, 373
Phipps, Charles Eugene 28, 124, 373
Phipps, Elizabeth 19, 20, 22, 24, 373
Phipps, Ethel 206, 312, 313, 373
Phipps, Honnor 28, 162, 312, 348, 373
Phipps, Ida 49, 312, 313, 347, 373
Phipps, John Rashleigh 19, 21, 22, 24, 31, 373
Phipps, Mary Rashleigh 89, 313, 373
Phipps, William 19, 22-24, 31
Ponsonby, Sir Spencer 69, 70, 101
Pople, Robert 202, 217
Portland cement 86, 268
Portland Place, No 1 143, 371
Portsmouth Empire 307, 311, 316, 319, 322, 365

President of the RIBA 153, 321
Prince of Wales Theatre, London 117, 169, 292, 295, 364
Princess's Theatre, London 100, 124, 129, 130-132, 171, 187, 288, 364
Prince's Theatre and Hotel, London 160, 169
Public Health Act 1875: 224, 225

Q
Queen's Hall, London 321, 371
Queen's Theatre, London 61, 63, 69, 71, 96, 117, 352, 363

R
Rashleigh Phipps and Dawson 313
RIBA Council 91, 93, 108, 278, 280, 283, 295
Roberts, Charles 220, 234
Robertson, Wybrow 80
Robinson, Jethro T. 84, 101, 112, 186
Romaine-Walker, W.H. 310, 340, 345, 347
Rotunda, Liverpool 111, 112, 194, 363
Royal Academy 47, 63, 89, 320, 369
Royal Alexandra Theatre, Liverpool 115, 363
Royal Institute of British Architects (RIBA) 25, 27, 32, 48, 54, 56, 91-93, 103, 108, 126, 153, 163, 232, 247, 270, 278, 280, 283, 285, 295, 321, 336, 338
Royal Lyceum Theatre, Edinburgh 166, 167
Royal Opera House, Cork 105-107, 363
Royal Opera House, Leicester 105, 106, 363
Royal Opera House, Londonderry 105, 363

Royal Strand Theatre, London 155
Royal West of England Academy 47, 367
Runtz, Ernest 325, 329, 365
Ruskin, John 84, 88

S
Sadler's Wells Theatre 105, 111-115, 187, 230, 262, 263, 363
Salisbury, Lord 277
Salomons, Edward 115
Saunders, George 36
Savoy Theatre, London 134-139, 143, 144, 156, 157, 165, 171, 172, 175, 292, 296, 314, 364
Savoy Turkish Baths, London 185, 187, 188, 198, 371
Searle, E. 220, 233, 234
Select Committee on Theatres and Music Halls 1892: 126, 147, 153, 305, 315, 322, 354
Select Committee on the Metropolitan Fire Brigade 1877: 99, 103, 139
Selwyn-Ibbetsen, Sir Henry 99
Seymour, George 242
Shaftesbury Theatre 205, 245, 261, 268, 289-301, 314, 319, 364
Shaw, Eyre Massey 97, 98, 103, 113, 146, 149, 151-155, 163, 197, 198, 203, 213-216, 225, 226-232, 235, 237, 238, 249-258, 265, 266-268, 277, 319
Society of Antiquaries 28
Sparkes, Mr 220, 236
Star and Garter Hotel 88, 89, 94, 109, 369, 371
St James's Theatre, London 329, 348, 365
St. James's Theatre, London 365
St Martin's Hall, London 60

T

Tasker, George 52, 54, 56, 60, 63, 76, 80, 91, 109, 340, 341
Terry, Edward 263
Terry, Ellen 46, 168
Terry's Theatre, London 262, 263
Théâtre des Arts, Rouen 171
Théâtre Lyrique, Paris 71
Theatre Royal, Aberdeen (Tivoli Theatre) 11, 78, 84-87, 260, 363
Theatre Royal, Bath 11, 21, 29, 35, 38, 41, 43, 47-49, 320, 351, 357, 363, 365, 369
Theatre Royal, Belfast 105, 144, 194, 364
Theatre Royal, Brighton 55, 56, 363
Theatre Royal, Bristol 29, 57, 66, 79, 144, 148
Theatre Royal, Colchester 259
Theatre Royal, Cork 363
Theatre Royal, Croydon 260
Theatre Royal, Darlington 364
Theatre Royal, Dublin 81, 129, 133, 192, 193
Theatre Royal, Dumfries 97, 363
Theatre Royal, Eastbourne 159, 175, 181, 263, 302, 364
Theatre Royal, Edinburgh 96, 103, 113, 165, 185, 194, 330, 363, 364
Theatre Royal, Exeter 12, 188-195, 198-204, 220, 239, 249, 258, 263, 276, 280, 287, 302, 304, 314, 353, 355, 364
Theatre Royal, Glasgow 11, 12, 129, 130, 132, 194, 325, 330-336, 339, 341, 345, 364, 365
Theatre Royal, Hanley 261, 364
Theatre Royal Haymarket, London 111, 116,-119, 167, 179, 193, 359, 363
Theatre Royal, Inverness 181
Theatre Royal, Leamington Spa 155, 158, 162, 166, 364
Theatre Royal, Northampton 11, 175-178, 192
Theatre Royal, Nottingham 11, 49, 52-55, 66, 259, 307, 308, 363, 365
Theatre Royal, Paisley 175
Theatre Royal, Plymouth 109, 110, 115, 233, 363
Theatre Royal, Portsmouth 11, 175, 177-180, 183, 194, 221, 364
Theatre Royal, Sheffield 129, 132, 133, 139, 364
Theatre Royal, South Shields 52, 363
Theatre Royal, Stockport 290
Theatre Royal, Swansea 60, 363
Theatre Royal, Torquay 121, 122, 127, 180, 194, 364 (Royal Theatre & Opera House)
Theatre Royal, Wolverhampton 325, 326, 338
Theatre Royal, Worcester 90, 93, 107, 108, 363
Theatres Act 1843: 69, 70, 80, 102, 220, 316
Tivoli Music Hall and Restaurant, London 299, 300
Tivoli Theatre, Dover 347, 348, 365
Todd-Heatly, G.H. 303, 305, 307, 321, 337, 339
Tree, Herbert Beerbohm 273, 339, 340, 341, 343, 345-347, 349, 355

V

Vaudeville Theatre, Strand, London 11, 78-81, 95, 97, 114, 151, 230, 235, 307-309, 340, 353, 363, 365
Verity, Thomas 84, 112, 321
Victoria Hall, Sunderland 212

Vienna Opera House (Ringtheater) 145, 149
Villiers, Jessie 162, 175, 181

W

Wadman, C. 334
Wallis, Ellen 289, 293
Warden, J.F. 105, 144
Whyte, J. 331, 338
Wigan, Alfred 61, 64
Wilson, James 24-26, 28
Wood, John 20, 21
Woodrow, Ernest, A.E. 95, 169, 182, 301, 310, 313-317
Wyatt, B.D. 26
Wyatt, T. H. 39, 75
Wyndham, Frederick 165, 168, 330, 336
Wyndham, Robert 96

ENTERTAINMENT TECHNOLOGY PRESS

FREE SUBSCRIPTION SERVICE

Keeping Up To Date with

Charles John Phipps F.S.A.
Architect to the Victorian Theatre

Entertainment Technology titles are continually up-dated, and all major changes and additions are listed in date order in the relevant dedicated area of the publisher's website. Simply go to the front page of www.etnow.com and click on the BOOKS button. From there you can locate the title and be connected through to the latest information and services related to the publication.

The author of the title welcomes comments and suggestions about the book and can be contacted by email at:
gorel.garlick@btinternet.com

390 Charles John Phipps F.S.A – Architect to the Victorian Theatre

Titles Published by Entertainment Technology Press

50 Rigging Calls *Chris Higgs, Cristiano Giavedoni 246pp* **£16.95**
ISBN: 9781904031758
Chris Higgs, author of ETP's two leading titles on rigging, An Introduction to Rigging in the Entertainment Industry and Rigging for Entertainment: Regulations and Practice, has collected together 50 articles he has provided regularly for Lighting + Sound International magazine from 2005 to date. They provide a wealth of information for those practising the craft within the entertainment technology industry. The book is profusely illustrated with caricature drawings by Christiano Giavedoni, featuring the popular rigging expert Mario.

ABC of Theatre Jargon *Francis Reid 106pp* **£9.95** ISBN: 9781904031093
This glossary of theatrical terminology explains the common words and phrases that are used in normal conversation between actors, directors, designers, technicians and managers.

Aluminium Structures in the Entertainment Industry *Peter Hind 234pp* **£24.95**
ISBN: 9781904031062
Aluminium Structures in the Entertainment Industry aims to educate the reader in all aspects of the design and safe usage of temporary and permanent aluminium structures specific to the entertainment industry – such as roof structures, PA towers, temporary staging, etc.

autoCAD – A Handbook for Theatre Users *David Ripley 340pp* **£29.95**
ISBN: 9781904031741
From 'Setting Up' to 'Drawing in Three Dimensions' via 'Drawings Within Drawings', this compact and fully illustrated guide to AutoCAD covers everything from the basics to full colour rendering and remote 3D plotting. Third, completely revised edition, June 2014.

Automation in the Entertainment Industry – A User's Guide *Mark Ager and John Hastie 382pp* **£29.95** ISBN: 9781904031581
In the last 15 years, there has been a massive growth in the use of automation in entertainment, especially in theatres, and it is now recognised as its own discipline. However, it is still only used in around 5% of theatres worldwide. In the next 25 years, given current growth patterns, that figure will rise to 30%. This will mean that the majority of theatre personnel, including directors, designers, technical staff, actors and theatre management, will come into contact with automation for the first time at some point in their careers. This book is intended to provide insights and practical advice from those who use automation, to help the first-time user understand the issues and avoid the pitfalls in its implementation.

Basics – A Beginner's Guide to Lighting Design *Peter Coleman 92pp* **£9.95**
ISBN: 9781904031413
The fourth in the author's 'Basics' series, this title covers the subject area in four main sections: The Concept, Practical Matters, Related Issues and The Design Into Practice. In an area that is difficult to be definitive, there are several things that cross all the boundaries of all lighting design and it's these areas that the author seeks to help with.

Basics – A Beginner's Guide to Special Effects *Peter Coleman 82pp* **£9.95**
ISBN: 9781904031338
This title introduces newcomers to the world of special effects. It describes all types of special effects including pyrotechnic, smoke and lighting effects, projections, noise machines, etc. It places emphasis on the safe storage, handling and use of pyrotechnics.

Basics – A Beginner's Guide to Stage Lighting *Peter Coleman 86pp* **£9.95**
ISBN: 9781904031208
This title does what it says: it introduces newcomers to the world of stage lighting. It will not teach the reader the art of lighting design, but will teach beginners much about the 'nuts and bolts' of stage lighting.

Basics – A Beginner's Guide to Stage Sound *Peter Coleman 86pp* **£9.95**
ISBN: 9781904031277
This title does what it says: it introduces newcomers to the world of stage sound. It will not teach the reader the art of sound design, but will teach beginners much about the background to sound reproduction in a theatrical environment.

Basics: A Beginner's Guide to Stage Management *Peter Coleman 64pp* **£7.95**
ISBN: 9781904031475
The fifth in Peter Coleman's popular 'Basics' series, this title provides a practical insight into, and the definition of, the role of stage management. Further chapters describe Cueing or 'Calling' the Show (the Prompt Book), and the Hardware and Training for Stage Management. This is a book about people and systems, without which most of the technical equipment used by others in the performance workplace couldn't function.

Building Better Theaters *Michael Mell 180pp* **£16.95** ISBN: 9781904031406
A title within our Consultancy Series, this book describes the process of designing a theatre, from the initial decision to build through to opening night. Michael Mell's book provides a step-by-step guide to the design and construction of performing arts facilities. Chapters discuss: assembling your team, selecting an architect, different construction methods, the architectural design process, construction of the theatre, theatrical systems and equipment, the stage, backstage, the auditorium, ADA requirements and the lobby. Each chapter clearly describes what to expect and how to avoid surprises. It is a must-read for architects, planners, performing arts groups, educators and anyone who may be considering building or renovating a theatre.

Carry on Fading *Francis Reid 216pp* **£20.00** ISBN: 9781904031642
This is a record of five of the best years of the author's life. Years so good that the only downside is the pangs of guilt at enjoying such contentment in a world full of misery induced by greed, envy and imposed ideologies. Fortunately Francis' DNA is high on luck, optimism and blessing counting.

Case Studies in Crowd Management
Chris Kemp, Iain Hill, Mick Upton, Mark Hamilton 206pp **£16.95**
ISBN: 9781904031482
This important work has been compiled from a series of research projects carried out by the staff of the Centre for Crowd Management and Security Studies at Buckinghamshire Chilterns University College (now Bucks New University), and seminar work carried out in Berlin and Groningen with partner Youvope. It includes case studies, reports and a crowd management safety plan for a major outdoor rock concert, safe management of rock concerts utilising a triple barrier safety system and pan-European Health & Safety Issues.

Case Studies in Crowd Management, Security and Business Continuity
Chris Kemp, Patrick Smith 274pp **£24.95** ISBN: 9781904031635
The creation of good case studies to support work in progress and to give answers to those seeking guidance in their quest to come to terms with perennial questions is no easy task. The first Case Studies in Crowd Management book focused mainly on a series of festivals and events that had a number of issues which required solving. This book focuses on a series of events that had major issues that impacted on the every day delivery of the events researched.

Charles John Phipps F.S.A. Architect to the Victorian Theatre
Görel Garlick 402pp **£25.95** ISBN: 9781904031895
This book is the first in-depth biography of the leading Victorian theatre architect Charles Phipps. His designs dislodged the Victorian theatre from its dependence on the Georgian playhouse and ushered in a new modernity utilising the latest technology in lighting, stage machinery and building construction and his work was a major influence on younger architects, notably Frank Matcham. The book traces Phipps's colourful career and his, often fraught, relationships with clients, as well as his attitude to changing safety regulations and those who attempted to enforce them. The book also re-examines the Exeter Theatre fire and its aftermath, which reverberated throughout the country, and how Phipps managed to cling on to his career before returning with new ideas in his last years.

Close Protection – The Softer Skills *Geoffrey Padgham 132pp* **£11.95**
ISBN: 9781904031390
This is the first educational book in a new 'Security Series' for Entertainment Technology Press, and it coincides with the launch of the new 'Protective Security Management' Foundation Degree at Buckinghamshire Chilterns University College (now Bucks New University). The author is a former full-career Metropolitan Police Inspector from New Scotland Yard with 27 years' experience of close protection (CP). For 22 of those years he specialised in operations and senior management duties with the Royalty Protection Department at Buckingham Palace, followed by five years in the private security industry specialising in CP training design and delivery. His wealth of protection experience comes across throughout the text, which incorporates sound advice and exceptional practical guidance, subtly separating fact from fiction. This publication is an excellent form of reference material for experienced operatives, students and trainees.

A Comparative Study of Crowd Behaviour at Two Major Music Events
Chris Kemp, Iain Hill, Mick Upton 78pp £7.95 ISBN: 9781904031253
A compilation of the findings of reports made at two major live music concerts, and in particular crowd behaviour, which is followed from ingress to egress.

Control Freak *Wayne Howell* 270pp £28.95 ISBN: 9781904031550
Control Freak is the second book by Wayne Howell. It provides an in depth study of DMX512 and the new RDM (Remote Device Management) standards. The book is aimed at both users and developers and provides a wealth of real world information based on the author's twenty year experience of lighting control.

Copenhagen Opera House *Richard Brett and John Offord* 272pp £32.00
ISBN: 9781904031420
Completed in a little over three years, the Copenhagen Opera House opened with a royal gala performance on 15th January 2005. Built on a spacious brown-field site, the building is a landmark venue and this book provides the complete technical background story to an opera house set to become a benchmark for future design and planning. Sixteen chapters by relevant experts involved with the project cover everything from the planning of the auditorium and studio stage, the stage engineering, stage lighting and control and architectural lighting through to acoustic design and sound technology plus technical summaries.

Corporate Event Production – Effective, face-to-face, corporate communication or Reaching 'The guy at the back, with bad eyesight - who'd rather be in the bar'
David Clement 324pp £29.95 ISBN: 9781904031840
A real-world insight into a specific industry sector: Corporate Event Production – the business of face-to-face communication. What it actually feels like to work in live events. The subtitle of 'Reaching the guy at the back with bad eyesight – who'd rather be in the bar' encapsulates the producer's challenge of creating an equally memorable experience for all attendees.
Structured around the project timeline – from receipt of a brief, to creative response and pitching, through pre-production design and planning to creating and directing the show on the day – the book is full of industry anecdotes, over 160 reference images, useful tips and guidelines. The stage-by-stage process of designing an engaging and truly effective live event.

Cue 80 *Francis Reid* 310pp £17.95 ISBN: 9781904031659
Although Francis Reid's work in theatre has been visual rather than verbal, writing has provided crucial support. Putting words on paper has been the way in which he organised and clarified his thoughts. And in his self-confessed absence of drawing skills, writing has helped him find words to communicate his visual thinking in discussions with the rest of the creative team. As a by-product, this process of searching for the right words to help formulate and analyse ideas has resulted in half-a-century of articles in theatre journals. Cue 80 is an anthology of these articles and is released in celebration of Francis' 80th birthday.

The DMX 512-A Handbook – Design and Implementation of DMX Enabled Products and Networks   *James Eade 150pp*   **£13.95**   ISBN: 9781904031727
This guidebook was originally conceived as a guide to the new DMX512-A standard on behalf of the ESTA Controls Protocols Working Group (CPWG). It has subsequently been updated and is aimed at all levels of reader from technicians working with or servicing equipment in the field as well as manufacturers looking to build in DMX control to their lighting products. It also gives thorough guidance to consultants and designers looking to design DMX networks.

Electric Shadows: an Introduction to Video and Projection on Stage   *Nick Moran 234pp*   **£23.95**   ISBN: 9781904031734
Electric Shadows aims to guide the emerging video designer through the many simple and difficult technical and aesthetic choices and decisions he or she has to make in taking their design from outline idea through to realisation. The main body of the book takes the reader through the process of deciding what content will be projected onto what screen or screens to make the best overall production design. The book will help you make electric shadows that capture the attention of your audience, to help you tell your stories in just the way you want.

Electrical Safety for Live Events   *Marco van Beek 98pp*   **£16.95**   ISBN: 9781904031284
This title covers electrical safety regulations and good practise pertinent to the entertainment industries and includes some basic electrical theory as well as clarifying the "do's and don't's" of working with electricity.

Entertainment Electronics   *Anton Woodward 154pp*   **£15.95**   ISBN: 9781904031819
Electronic engineering in theatres has become quite prevalent in recent years, whether for lighting, sound, automation or props – so it has become an increasingly important skill for the theatre technician to possess. This book is intended to give the theatre technician a good grasp of the fundamental principles of electronics without getting too bogged down with maths so that many of the mysteries of electronics are revealed.

Entertainment in Production Volume 1: 1994-1999   *Rob Halliday 254pp*   **£24.95**   ISBN: 9781904031512
Entertainment in Production Volume 2: 2000-2006   *Rob Halliday 242poo*   £24.95   ISBN: 9781904031529
Rob Halliday has a dual career as a lighting designer/programmer and author and in these two volumes he provides the intriguing but comprehensive technical background stories behind the major musical productions and other notable projects spanning the period 1994 to 2005. Having been closely involved with the majority of the events described, the author is able to present a first-hand and all-encompassing portrayal of how many of the major shows across the past decade came into being. From *Oliver!* and *Miss Saigon* to *Mamma Mia!* and *Mary Poppins*, here the complete technical story unfolds. The books, which are profusely illustrated, are in large part an adapted selection of articles that first appeared in the magazine *Lighting&Sound International*.

Entertainment Technology Yearbook 2008 *John Offord 220pp £14.95*
ISBN: 9781904031543
The Entertainment Technology Yearbook 2008 covers the year 2007 and includes picture coverage of major industry exhibitions in Europe compiled from the pages of Entertainment Technology magazine and the etnow.com website, plus articles and pictures of production, equipment and project highlights of the year.

The Exeter Theatre Fire *David Anderson 202pp* **£24.95** ISBN: 9781904031130
This title is a fascinating insight into the events that led up to the disaster at the Theatre Royal, Exeter, on the night of September 5th 1887. The book details what went wrong, and the lessons that were learned from the event.

Fading into Retirement *Francis Reid 124pp* **£17.95** ISBN: 9781904031352
This is the final book in Francis Reid's fading trilogy which, with Fading Light and Carry on Fading, updates the Hearing the Light record of places visited, performances seen, and people met. Never say never, but the author uses the 'final' label because decreasing mobility means that his ability to travel is diminished to the point that his life is now contained within a very few square miles. His memories are triggered by over 600 CDs, half of them Handel and 100 or so DVDs supplemented by a rental subscription to LOVEFiLM.

Fading Light – A Year in Retirement *Francis Reid 136pp* **£14.95**
ISBN: 9781904031352
Francis Reid, the lighting industry's favourite author, describes a full year in retirement. "Old age is much more fun than I expected," he says. Fading Light describes visits and experiences to the author's favourite theatres and opera houses, places of relaxation and re-visits to scholarly institutions.

Focus on Lighting Technology *Richard Cadena 120pp* **£17.95** ISBN: 9781904031147
This concise work unravels the mechanics behind modern performance lighting and appeals to designers and technicians alike. Packed with clear, easy-to-read diagrams, the book provides excellent explanations behind the technology of performance lighting.

The Followspot Guide *Nick Mobsby 450pp* **£28.95** ISBN: 9781904031499
The first in ETP's Equipment Series, Nick Mobsby's Followspot Guide tells you everything you need to know about followspots, from their history through to maintenance and usage. Its pages include a technical specification of 193 followspots from historical to the latest versions from major manufacturers.

From Ancient Rome to Rock 'n' Roll – a Review of the UK Leisure Security Industry
Mick Upton 198pp **£14.95** ISBN: 9781904031505
From stewarding, close protection and crowd management through to his engagement as a senior consultant Mick Upton has been ever present in the events industry. A founder of ShowSec International in 1982 he was its chairman until 2000. The author has led the way on training within the sector. He set up the ShowSec Training Centre and has acted as

a consultant at the Bramshill Police College. He has been prominent in the development of courses at Buckinghamshire New University where he was awarded a Doctorate in 2005. Mick has received numerous industry awards. His book is a personal account of the development and professionalism of the sector across the past 50 years.

Gobos for Image Projection *Michael Hall and Julie Harper 176pp* **£25.95**
ISBN: 9781904031628
In this first published book dedicated totally to the gobo, the authors take the reader through from the history of projection to the development of the present day gobo. And there is broad practical advice and ample reference information to back it up. A feature of the work is the inclusion, interspersed throughout the text, of comment and personal experience in the use and application of gobos from over 25 leading lighting designers worldwide.

Health and Safety Aspects in the Live Music Industry *Chris Kemp, Iain Hill 300pp* **£30.00** ISBN: 9781904031222
This major work includes chapters on various safety aspects of live event production and is written by specialists in their particular areas of expertise.

Health and Safety in the Live Music and Event Technical Produciton Industry
Chris Hannam 74pp **£12.95** ISBN: 9781904031802
This book covers the real basics of health and safety in the live music and event production industry in a simple jargon free manner that can also be used as the perfect student course note accompaniment to the various safety passport schemes that now exist in our industry.

Health and Safety Management for Tour and Production Managers and
Self-Employment in the Live Music and Events Industry
Chris Hannam 136pp **£11.95** ISBN: 9781904031864
Two books in one: **Health and Safety Management for Tour and Production Managers** is designed to give simple, basic health and safety information to bands, artists, tour, stage and production managers, crew chiefs, heads of department, supervisors or line managers and has been designed as a follow on from *Health And Safety in the Live Music and Event Technical Production Industry*. It will also be of use to local crew companies, especially their crew chiefs and managers.
The second book is **Self-Employment in the Live Music and Events Industry**
A Guide for the Self-Employed and those who use the services of the Self-Employed

Health and Safety Management in the Live Music and Events Industry *Chris Hannam 480pp* **£25.95** ISBN: 9781904031307
This title covers the health and safety regulations and their application regarding all aspects of staging live entertainment events, and is an invaluable manual for production managers and event organisers.

Hearing the Light – 50 Years Backstage *Francis Reid 280pp* **£24.95**
ISBN: 9781904031185
This highly enjoyable memoir delves deeply into the theatricality of the industry. The author's almost fanatical interest in opera, his formative period as lighting designer at Glyndebourne and his experiences as a theatre administrator, writer and teacher make for a broad and unique background.

Introduction to Live Sound *Roland Higham 174pp* **£16.95**
ISBN: 9781904031796
This new title aims to provide working engineers and newcomers alike with a concise knowledge base that explains some of the theory and principles that they will encounter every day. It should provide for the student and newcomer to the field a valuable compendium of helpful knowledge.

An Introduction to Rigging in the Entertainment Industry *Chris Higgs 272pp* **£24.95**
ISBN: 9781904031123
This title is a practical guide to rigging techniques and practices and also thoroughly covers safety issues and discusses the implications of working within recommended guidelines and regulations. Second edition revised September 2008.

Let There be Light – Entertainment Lighting Software Pioneers in Conversation
Robert Bell 390pp **£32.00** ISBN: 9781904031246
Robert Bell interviews a distinguished group of software engineers working on entertainment lighting ideas and products.

Light and Colour Filters *Michael Hall and Eddie Ruffell 286pp* **£23.95**
ISBN: 9781904031598
Written by two acknowledged and respected experts in the field, this book is destined to become the standard reference work on the subject. The title chronicles the development and use of colour filters and also describes how colour is perceived and how filters function. Up-to-date reference tables will help the practitioner make better and more specific choices of colour.

Lighting for Roméo and Juliette *John Offord 172pp* **£26.95** ISBN: 9781904031161
John Offord describes the making of the Vienna State Opera production from the lighting designer's viewpoint – from the point where director Jürgen Flimm made his decision not to use scenery or sets and simply employ the expertise of lighting designer Patrick Woodroffe.

Lighting Systems for TV Studios *Nick Mobsby 570pp* **£45.00** ISBN: 9781904031000
Lighting Systems for TV Studios, now in its second edition, is the first book specifically written on the subject and has become the 'standard' resource work for studio planning and design covering the key elements of system design, luminaires, dimming, control, data networks and suspension systems as well as detailing the infrastructure items such as cyclorama, electrical and ventilation. TV lighting principles are explained and some history on TV broadcasting, camera technology and the equipment is provided to help set the scene!

The second edition includes applications for sine wave and distributed dimming, moving lights, Ethernet and new cool lamp technology.

Lighting Techniques for Theatre-in-the-Round *Jackie Staines 188pp* **£24.95**
ISBN: 9781904031017
Lighting Techniques for Theatre-in-the-Round is a unique reference source for those working on lighting design for theatre-in-the-round for the first time. It is the first title to be published specifically on the subject and it also provides some anecdotes and ideas for more challenging shows, and attempts to blow away some of the myths surrounding lighting in this format.

Lighting the Diamond Jubilee Concert *Durham Marenghi 102pp* **£19.95**
ISBN: 9781904031673
In this highly personal landmark document the show's lighting designer Durham Marenghi pays tribute to the team of industry experts who each played an important role in bringing the Diamond Jubilee Concert to fruition, both for television and live audiences. The book contains colour production photography throughout and describes the production processes and the thinking behind them. In his Foreword, BBC Executive Producer Guy Freeman states: "Working with the whole lighting team on such a special project was a real treat for me and a fantastic achievement for them, which the pages of this book give a remarkable insight into."

Lighting the Stage *Francis Reid 120pp* **£14.95** ISBN: 9781904031086
Lighting the Stage discusses the human relationships involved in lighting design – both between people, and between these people and technology. The book is written from a highly personal viewpoint and its 'thinking aloud' approach is one that Francis Reid has used in his writings over the past 30 years.

Miscellany of Lighting and Stagecraft *Michael Hall & Julie Harper 222pp* **£22.95**
ISBN: 9781904031680
This title will help schools, colleges, amateurs, technicians and all those interested in practical theatre and performance to understand, in an entertaining and informative way, the key backstage skills. Within its pages, numerous professionals share their own special knowledge and expertise, interspersed with diversions of historic interest and anecdotes from those practising at the front line of the industry. As a result, much of the advice and skills set out have not previously been set in print. The editors' intention with this book is to provide a Miscellany that is not ordered or categorised in strict fashion, but rather encourages the reader to flick through or dip into it, finding nuggets of information and anecdotes to entertain, inspire and engender curiosity – also to invite further research or exploration and generally encourage people to enter the industry and find out for themselves.

Mr Phipps' Theatre *Mark Jones, John Pick 172pp* £17.95 ISBN: 9781904031383
Mark Jones and John Pick describe "The Sensational Story of Eastbourne's Royal Hippodrome" – formerly Eastbourne Theatre Royal. An intriguing narrative, the book sets

the story against a unique social history of the town. Peter Longman, former director of The Theatres Trust, provides the Foreword.

Northen Lights *Michael Northen 256pp* **£17.95** ISBN: 9781904031666
Many books have been written by famous personalities in the theatre about their lives and work. However this is probably one of the first memoirs by someone who has spent his entire career behind scenes, and not in front of the footlights. As a lighting designer and as consultant to designers and directors, Michael Northen worked through an exciting period of fifty years of theatrical history from the late nineteen thirties in theatres in the UK and abroad, and on productions ranging from Shakespeare, opera and ballet to straight plays, pantomimes and cabaret. This is not a complicated technical text book, but is intended to give an insight into some of the 300 productions in which he had been involved and some of the directors, the designers and backstage staff he have worked with, viewed from a new angle.

Pages From Stages *Anthony Field 204pp* **£17.95** ISBN: 9781904031260
Anthony Field explores the changing style of theatres including interior design, exterior design, ticket and seat prices, and levels of service, while questioning whether the theatre still exists as a place of entertainment for regular theatre-goers.

People, Places, Performances *Remembered by Francis Reid 60pp* **£8.95**
ISBN: 9781904031765
In growing older, the Author has found that memories, rather than featuring the events, increasingly tend to focus on the people who caused them, the places where they happened and the performances that arose. So Francis Reid has used these categories in endeavouring to compile a brief history of the second half of the twentieth century.

Performing Arts Technical Training Handbook 2013/2014 *ed: John Offord 304pp*
£19.95 ISBN: 9781904031710
Published in association with the ABTT (Association of British Theatre Technicians), this important Handbook, now in its third edition, includes fully detailed and indexed entries describing courses on backstage crafts offered by over 100 universities and colleges across the UK. A completely new research project, with accompanying website, the title also includes articles with advice for those considering a career 'behind the scenes', together with contact information and descriptions of the major organisations involved with industry training – plus details of companies offering training within their own premises.

Practical Dimming *Nick Mobsby 364pp* **£22.95** ISBN: 97819040313444
This important and easy to read title covers the history of electrical and electronic dimming, how dimmers work, current dimmer types from around the world, planning of a dimming system, looking at new sine wave dimming technology and distributed dimming. Integration of dimming into different performance venues as well as the necessary supporting electrical systems are fully detailed. Significant levels of information are provided on the many

different forms and costs of potential solutions as well as how to plan specific solutions. Architectural dimming for the likes of hotels, museums and shopping centres is included. Practical Dimming is a companion book to Practical DMX and is designed for all involved in the use, operation and design of dimming systems.

Practical DMX   *Nick Mobsby   276pp*   **£16.95**   ISBN: 9781904031369
In this highly topical and important title the author details the principles of DMX, how to plan a network, how to choose equipment and cables, with data on products from around the world, and how to install DMX networks for shows and on a permanently installed basis. The easy style of the book and the helpful fault finding tips, together with a review of different DMX testing devices provide an ideal companion for all lighting technicians and system designers. An introduction to Ethernet and Canbus networks are provided as well as tips on analogue networks and protocol conversion. It also includes a chapter on Remote Device Management.

A Practical Guide to Health and Safety in the Entertainment Industry
Marco van Beek   120pp   **£14.95**   ISBN: 9781904031048
This book is designed to provide a practical approach to Health and Safety within the Live Entertainment and Event industry. It gives industry-pertinent examples, and seeks to break down the myths surrounding Health and Safety.

Production Management   *Joe Aveline   134pp*   **£17.95**   ISBN: 9781904031109
Joe Aveline's book is an in-depth guide to the role of the Production Manager, and includes real-life practical examples and 'Aveline's Fables' – anecdotes of his experiences with real messages behind them.

Rigging for Entertainment: Regulations and Practice   *Chris Higgs   156pp*   **£19.95**
ISBN: 9781904031215
Continuing where he left off with his highly successful An Introduction to Rigging in the Entertainment Industry, Chris Higgs' second title covers the regulations and use of equipment in greater detail.

Rock Solid Ethernet   *Wayne Howell   304pp*   **£23.95**   ISBN: 9781904031697
Now in its third completely revised and reset edition, Rock Solid Ethernet is aimed specifically at specifiers, installers and users of entertainment industry systems, and will give the reader a thorough grounding in all aspects of computer networks, whatever industry they may work in. The inclusion of historical and technical 'sidebars' make for an enjoyable as well as an informative read.

Sixty Years of Light Work   *Fred Bentham   450pp*   **£26.95**   ISBN: 9781904031079
This title is an autobiography of one of the great names behind the development of modern stage lighting equipment and techniques. It includes a complete facsimile of the famous Strand Electric Catalogue of May 1936 – a reference work in itself.

Sound for the Stage *Patrick Finelli 218pp* **£24.95** ISBN: 9781904031154
Patrick Finelli's thorough manual covering all aspects of live and recorded sound for performance is a complete training course for anyone interested in working in the field of stage sound, and is a must for any student of sound.

Stage Automation *Anton Woodward 128pp* **£12.95** ISBN: 9781904031567
The purpose of this book is to explain the stage automation techniques used in modern theatre to achieve some of the spectacular visual effects seen in recent years. The book is targeted at automation operators, production managers, theatre technicians, stage engineering machinery manufacturers and theatre engineering students. Topics are covered in sufficient detail to provide an insight into the thought processes that the stage automation engineer has to consider when designing a control system to control stage machinery in a modern theatre. The author has worked on many stage automation projects and developed the award-winning Impressario stage automation system.

Stage Lighting Design in Britain: The Emergence of the Lighting Designer, 1881-1950
Nigel Morgan 300pp **£17.95** ISBN: 9781904031345
This title sets out to ascertain the main course of events and the controlling factors that determined the emergence of the theatre lighting designer in Britain, starting with the introduction of incandescent electric light to the stage, and ending at the time of the first public lighting design credits around 1950. The book explores the practitioners, equipment, installations and techniques of lighting design.

Stage Lighting for Theatre Designers *Nigel Morgan 124pp* **£17.95**
ISBN: 9781904031192
This is an updated second edition of Nigel Morgan's popular book for students of theatre design – outlining all the techniques of stage lighting design.

Technical Marketing – Ideas for Engineers *David Brooks. 376pp* **£26.95**
ISBN: 9781904031857
When *Technical Marketing Techniques* was published in 2000, marketing was poised on the threshold of a new era. What advertising and design agencies then termed 'new media' was merely a glimpse of what was to follow as the Internet came to dominate and transform the way we did things. We coined the term Technical Marketing to describe a new way of operating for businesses and how they marketed their products and services on a global platform. 'Technical Marketing – Ideas for Engineers' retains a major opening section covering traditional marketing theory and then in the second section demonstrates how online and offline techniques can be integrated into an effective marketing communications plan. The final section of the book reviews the still evolving possibilities of digital marketing which is beginning to re write the rules of marketing.

Technical Standards for Places of Entertainment (2015) *ABTT 366pp A4* **£60.00**
ISBN: 9781904031833
Technical Standards for Places of Entertainment details the necessary physical standards required for entertainment venues. Known in the industry as the "Yellow Book" the latest completely revised edition was first published in June 2015.

Theatre Engineering and Stage Machinery *Toshiro Ogawa 344pp* **£30.00**
ISBN: 9781904031888
Theatre Engineering and Stage Machinery is a unique reference work covering every aspect of theatrical machinery and stage technology in global terms, and across the complete historical spectrum. Revised April 2016 to include addendum on ideal layouts for opera houses.

Theatre Lighting in the Age of Gas *Terence Rees 232pp* **£24.95**
ISBN: 9781904031178
Entertainment Technology Press has republished this valuable historic work previously produced by the Society for Theatre Research in 1978. Theatre Lighting in the Age of Gas investigates the technological and artistic achievements of theatre lighting engineers from the 1700s to the late Victorian period.

Theatre Space: A Rediscovery Reported *Francis Reid 238pp* **£19.95**
ISBN: 9781904031437
In the post-war world of the 1950s and 60s, the format of theatre space became a matter for a debate that aroused passions of an intensity unknown before or since. The proscenium arch was clearly identified as the enemy, accused of forming a barrier to disrupt the relations between the actor and audience. An uneasy fellow-traveller at the time, Francis Reid later recorded his impressions whilst enjoying performances or working in theatres old and new and this book is an important collection of his writings in various theatrical journals from 1969-2001 including his contribution to the Cambridge Guide to the Theatre in 1988. It reports some of the flavour of the period when theatre architecture was rediscovering its past in a search to establish its future.

The Theatres and Concert Halls of Fellner and Helmer *Michael Sell 246pp* **£23.95**
ISBN: 9781904031772
This is the first British study of the works of the prolific Fellner and Helmer Atelier which was active from 1871-1914 during which time they produced over 80 theatre designs and are second in quantity only to Frank Matcham, to whom reference is made.
This period is one of great change as a number of serious theatre fires which included Nice and Vienna had the effect of the introduction of safety legislation which affected theatre design. This study seeks to show how Fellner and Helmer and Frank Matcham dealt with this increasing safety legislation, in particular the way in which safety was built into their new three part theatres equipped with iron stages, safety curtains, electricity and appropriate access and egress and, in the Vienna practice, how this was achieved across 13 countries.

Theatres of Achievement *John Higgins 302pp* **£29.95** ISBN: 9781904031376
John Higgins affectionately describes the history of 40 distinguished UK theatres in a personal tribute, each uniquely illustrated by the author. Completing each profile is colour photography by Adrian Eggleston.

A Theatric Miscellany *Francis Reid 154pp* **£15.95** ISBN: 9781904031871
This book is about memories. Some of them are highlights of the author's life. Recall of other, more routine events, is triggered by discovery of a cache of sundry articles. A few make predictions that are still relevant but most guess the future wrongly. Either way, they make a small contribution to history.

Theatric Tourist *Francis Reid 220pp* **£19.95** ISBN: 9781904031468
Theatric Tourist is the delightful story of Francis Reid's visits across more than 50 years to theatres, theatre museums, performances and even movie theme parks. In his inimitable style, the author involves the reader within a personal experience of venues from the Legacy of Rome to theatres of the Renaissance and Eighteenth Century Baroque and the Gustavian Theatres of Stockholm. His performance experiences include Wagner in Beyreuth, the Pleasures of Tivoli and Wayang in Singapore. This is a 'must have' title for those who are as "incurably stagestruck" as the author.

Through the Viewfinder *Jeremy Hoare 276pp* **£21.95** ISBN:: 9781904031574
Do you want to be a top television cameraman? Well this is going to help!
Through the Viewfinder is aimed at media students wanting to be top professional television cameramen – but it will also be of interest to anyone who wants to know what goes on behind the cameras that bring so much into our homes.
The author takes his own opinionated look at how to operate a television camera based on 23 years' experience looking through many viewfinders for a major ITV network company. Based on interviews with people he has worked with, all leaders in the profession, the book is based on their views and opinions and is a highly revealing portrait of what happens behind the scenes in television production from a cameraman's point of view.

Vectorworks for Theatre *Steve Macluskie 232pp* **£23.95** ISBN: 9781904031826
An essential reference manual for anyone using Vectorworks in the Theatre Industry. This book covers everything from introducing the basic tools to creating 3D design concepts and using worksheets to calculate stock usage and lighting design paperwork. A highly visual style using hundreds of high resolution screen images makes this a very easy book to follow whether novice or experienced user.

Walt Disney Concert Hall – The Backstage Story *Patricia MacKay & Richard Pilbrow 250pp* **£28.95** ISBN: 9781904031239
Spanning the 16-year history of the design and construction of the Walt Disney Concert Hall, this book provides a fresh and detailed behind the scenes story of the design and technology from a variety of viewpoints. This is the first book to reveal the "process" of the design of a concert hall.

Yesterday's Lights – A Revolution Reported *Francis Reid 352pp* **£26.95**
ISBN: 9781904031321
Set to help new generations to be aware of where the art and science of theatre lighting is coming from – and stimulate a nostalgia trip for those who lived through the period, Francis Reid's latest book has over 350 pages dedicated to the task, covering the 'revolution' from

the fifties through to the present day. Although this is a highly personal account of the development of lighting design and technology and he admits that there are 'gaps', you'd be hard put to find anything of significance missing.

Go to www.etbooks.co.uk for full details of above titles and secure online ordering facilities. Most books also available for Kindle.